BIO-ORGANIC CHEMISTRY

Readings from

SCIENTIFIC AMERICAN

BIO-ORGANIC

CHEMISTRY

With introductions by

MELVIN CALVIN

and

MARGARET J. JORGENSON

UNIVERSITY OF CALIFORNIA, BERKELEY

W. H. FREEMAN AND COMPANY

SAN FRANCISCO AND LONDON

Each of the SCIENTIFIC AMERICAN articles in *Bio-organic Chemistry* is available as a separate Off-print at twenty cents. For a complete listing of approximately 600 articles now available as Off-prints, write to W. H. Freeman and Company, 660 Market Street, San Francisco, California 94104.

Printed in the United States of America.

Library of Congress Catalog Card Number: 68-16471

Preface

During the thirty-year period that organic chemists have been teaching introductory organic chemistry, both to chemistry students and to the much larger group of biology students and medical students, a great number of changes have taken place in the prevailing attitudes toward the subject matter and the students.

One of the most dominant changes has been the growth of our knowledge about the ways in which organic molecules interact with each other and with their environment to be transformed into new structures. Because of this growth, organic chemistry, which once was a catalog of responses, requiring a minimal understanding of theory, has now become a set of mechanistic principles into which the details of functional behavior may be fitted as specific examples. This transformation, although far from complete, has progressed enough that students of elementary organic chemistry are introduced initially to the structural and functional principles upon which the specific examples of functional organic chemistry, as it was once taught, are superimposed.

Another major development has been the increase in our knowledge of the ways in which the living organism functions in terms of the molecules of which it is structured, both the macromolecules and the small organic molecules which heretofore had been the principal subject matter of the area of organic chemistry known as natural product chemistry. This increased understanding of the molecular mechanisms of living organisms has increased the necessity for knowledge of organic chemistry in all its forms, both natural product chemistry and macromolecular (or polymer) chemistry. This, in turn, has led those of us who introduce the principles of organic chemistry to the general biology student to point out the relevance of these principles to his primary interests.

In a survey course of organic chemistry it is impossible to do justice to any bio-organic topics, because of the time limitation and the large number of fundamental organic principles that command priority. Limitations in space make it equally impossible to cover these topics adequately in any textbook of modest size. A set of authoritative, stimulating readings written at an introductory level could close the gap between the classically oriented elementary organic textbook and the detailed biochemical treatise. The readings we have selected for this volume, comprising thirty-two articles first published in *Scientific American*, constitute such a compromise. Our criteria for their inclusion here have been chemical emphasis, significance, novelty, and the level of presentation. In our classes it has been customary for us to digress briefly into many of the topics that are covered in these pages but are generally not found in text-books. The students have used the individual articles as a convenient point for further study. We have assigned the articles as supplementary reading to be reported on in a short paper or in a prepared answer to a question in the final examination.

The book has been organized into three sections. The first, *Macromolecular Architecture*, deals with the chemical and spatial description of giant biological molecules and their synthetic macromolecular models. The nine articles in it were written by eminent contributors in this area; more than half of these deal with research for which Nobel Prizes have been awarded. The spark of the original discovery, so often lost in the sketchy presentations of textbooks and monographs, is stimulatingly preserved in case histories of these studies.

Section II, *Biological Regulators*, treats organic molecules of smaller size that have the distinction of controlling and regulating the various functions of the living system. Our concern here is not so much with the biological function as with the chemical structure of the molecules that bear these properties.

The chemistry of a variety of compounds of prime concern to the natural products chemist, such as steroids, alkaloids, flavenoids, terpenes, and drugs, is included in this section. These compounds exemplify a large number of functional classes of organic molecules. In a systematic discussion of the various classes of organic compounds, a teacher can draw the student's attention to many of these naturally occurring representative members and their dramatic activity. Subjects that are reduced to dry chemical topics in most textbooks, such as the dramatic physiological effects of these compounds, are enlivened in these articles. Some of the topics in this section are highly esoteric, and discussions of these are not readily available elsewhere.

The last section, *Chemical Biodynamics*, includes those topics in biochemistry and molecular biology that depend heavily on a chemical kinetic interpretation. We have chosen articles in the field of chemical genetics, biosynthesis, photosynthesis, enzyme chemistry, chemical metabolism, and chemical evolution; it is from these fields that we select topics to highlight organic chemistry during the last week of the course. A presentation of one or more of these topics vividly demonstrates to the students the need to understand the fundamental principles of organic chemistry before he can fully comprehend the molecular bases of various biodynamic processes.

Because of the limitations of space, it was necessary to omit many other *Scientific American* articles relevant to the chemical areas represented in this selection. We will bring these to the attention of the student by listing their titles in the individual introductions that precede each section.

MELVIN CALVIN
MARGARET J. JORGENSON

January 1968

Contents

SECTION III: CHEMICAL BIODYNAMICS

NOTE ON CROSS-REFERENCES

Cross-references within the articles are of three kinds. A reference to an article included in this book is noted by the title of the article and the page on which it begins; a reference to an article that is available as an offprint but is not included here is noted by the article's title and offprint number; a reference to a SCIENTIFIC AMERICAN article that is not available as an offprint is noted by the title of the article and the month and year of its publication.

Macromolecular Architecture

I

Macromolecular Architecture

INTRODUCTION

The major structural materials of which living organisms are built belong to the group of biopolymers that includes proteins, nucleic acids, and polysaccharides. Yet these have heretofore been given only minor treatment in introductory textbooks of organic chemistry for biologists, and even for chemists, for that matter. We have, therefore, for this first section, selected a series of articles that deal with the intimate molecular architecture of two of these subgroups, proteins and nucleic acids. A suitable introduction to the third subgroup—the polysaccharides—is not yet available.

The first and last articles in this series are general discussions of polymer structure by two chemists, Herman Mark and Giulio Natta, who have contributed greatly to our knowledge of this structure. The general principles underlying the construction of organic polymers from simple units are discussed by Mark, and the ways in which synthetic polymers can be stereospecifically constructed in the laboratory are discussed by Natta. The effects that these organized structures have on some of the general properties of macromolecules are made clear in these two readings, and the simpler nonbiological polymers emerge as suitable macromolecular models for the study of the properties of complex biopolymers.

The authors of the second and third articles are more directly concerned with the physical chemistry of proteins and with the way in which the monomeric sequence of proteins is chemically determined. Paul Doty's article provides a basis for understanding the physical properties of proteins, and the article of Stein and Moore outlines the fundamental chemical methods that were developed (and have since been refined) to determine the sequence of the twenty or so amino acids in a protein chain, which may be of almost any length and involve hundreds of amino acid molecules. The discussion of the structure of insulin by Thompson includes a specific case history of the first determination of the sequence of amino acids in a true protein molecule. The determination of such sequences has reached so high a degree of refinement that approximately 200 of them are now known: 190 were listed in the 1966 *Atlas of Amino Acid Sequence in Proteins.*

The articles of Perutz and Phillips present the intimate three-dimensional architecture of the first protein molecules for which it has been determined and give some clues to what knowledge of this architecture enables us to understand. Zuckerkandl's article provides an introduction to a new kind of evolutionary study that must ultimately give us not only an understanding of the comparative chemistry of a class of protein molecules and of the factors that determine the specific functions of the molecules, but also a new insight into the infinite number of small stages and changes involved in the evolutionary history of living organisms.

The foregoing studies lead naturally into a discussion of the nucleic acids that control the structure of proteins, and the article of Francis Crick is a classic exposition of the fundamental principles of the mechanism of this control—of how the nucleic acid structure and sequence determine the protein sequence and structure. Holley's article on the sequence of bases in a simple nucleic acid (of something less than one hundred monomeric units) is the case history of the first determination of the structure of such a molecule: further work will undoubtedly lead to the synthetic creation of at least pieces of information-bearing nucleic acid molecules, and to their use in manipulating the development of organisms.

The following additional articles on synthetic and biological polymer chemistry have appeared in *Scientific American;* some of these are available in offprint form. F. O. Schmitt, *Giant Molecules in Cells and Tissues* (September 1957, offprint 35); R. D. Preston, *Cellulose* (September 1957): B. Wunderlich, *The Solid State of Polyethylene* (November 1964); P. J. W. Debye, *How Giant Molecules Are Measured* (September 1957); G. Natta, *How Giant Molecules Are Made* (September 1957); A. V. Tobolsky, *The Mechanical Properties of Polymers* (September 1967); B. Oster, *Polyethylene* (September 1957); H. F. Mark, *The Nature of Polymeric Materials* (September 1967); J. S. Fruton, *Proteins* (June 1950, offprint 10); L. Pauling, R. B. Corey, and R. Hayward, *The Structure of Protein Molecules* (July 1954, offprint 31); M. B. Hoagland, *Nucleic Acids and Proteins* (December 1959, offprint 68); J. C. Kendrew, *The Three-dimensional Structure of a Protein Molecule* (December 1961, offprint 121); A. Champagnot, *Protein from Petroleum* (October 1965, offprint 1020); C. H. Li, *The ACTH Molecule* (July 1963, offprint 160); F. H. Crick, *Nucleic Acids* (September 1956, offprint 54); R. L. Sinsheimer, *Single Stranded DNA* (July 1962, offprint 128) S. Spiegelman, *Hybrid Nucleic Acids* (May 1964, offprint 183); H. Fraenkel-Conrat, *Rebuilding a Virus* (June 1956, offprint 9).

MONOMERS are purified in these towers at the American Cyanamid Company's Fortier Plant near New Orleans, La. In this case the monomer is acrylonitrile made from acetylene and hydrocyanic acid gas. These latter substances are here obtained from natural gas.

1

Giant Molecules

HERMAN F. MARK

September 1957

Giant molecules—or high polymers, as the chemist calls them—have been feeding, clothing and housing man ever since he began to manipulate nature. Wood is a high polymer; so are meat, starch, cotton, wool and silk. They are among our oldest and most familiar materials, yet until this century they were a complete chemical mystery. As products of living things, they partake of the prejudice of nature for doing things in an elaborate way. The substances of life are made of the most complicated molecules we know. But their very complexity endows them with wonderfully versatile and powerful properties. The giant molecules therefore present a great challenge to chemists—not only to learn the secrets of their construction but also to devise new materials which nature has neglected to create. And within the past decade the chemistry of high polymers—living and nonliving—has made such rapid strides that it is today one of the most exciting fields in all science.

This development caps a century of remarkable advance in organic chemistry. Chemical understanding of living matter did not begin until 1828, when Friedrich Wöhler of Germany achieved the first test-tube synthesis of an organic substance—urea, a product of animal metabolism. His successors in the new science proceeded to work out the chemical structure and activity of a host of comparatively simple organic molecules: sugars, fats, fruit acids, soaps, alcohols, the coal and petroleum hydrocarbons, and so on. Over the past century many

thousands of scientists all over the world became absorbed in organic chemistry, developing ingenious techniques of investigation and constructing a clear theory of the behavior of the simpler organic substances, based on the behavior of the four-valent carbon atom. The theory made it possible to classify the properties of hundreds of thousands of substances, from the exhalations of gas wells to the pigments of flowers and the poisons of snakes. Organic chemistry gave birth to new synthetic products, such as dyes, perfumes, drugs, fuels, etc. Indeed, much of our present civilization—medical care, sanitation, printing, painting, photography, motor transportation, aviation—relies heavily on materials provided by "classical" organic chemistry.

All these substances were comparatively simple members of the organic family. Their bigger, more complicated relatives—proteins and the rest—got only

desultory attention from chemists, mainly because they were too difficult to deal with. The methods on which organic chemists relied for separation and analysis of organic substances—solution, melting, crystallization and the like—did not work with giant molecules. For example, cellulose, the chief component of wood, does not melt when heated; instead it hardens and decomposes. Nor can it be dissolved, except in chemicals which change it irreversibly to something different. The same is true of other organic high polymers, such as wool, silk, starch and rubber.

When chemists had the misfortune to produce large organic molecules accidentally during their experiments, they were generally crestfallen. The early literature of organic chemists is full of exasperated references to reactions which "resinified" and covered their glassware with waxy, gluey or sticky messes. These

THIS ARTICLE IS CONTINUED on page 10. On the next four pages is a chart listing the principal polymers made by man. At the left side of the chart are the structural formulas of monomers, the simple molecules which are strung together to form polymers. In the middle of the chart is a short section of the characteristic chain of each polymer. The complete chain is made up of hundreds or even thousands of monomeric units. Some of the chains are linked to other chains, as indicated in the formulas of the phenol formaldehyde and urea formaldehyde resins. The polymers in the chart are divided into two classes: addition polymers and condensation polymers. The basis of this division is given in the illustrations on pages 10 and 11. There are only nine atoms in the chart: carbon (C), hydrogen (H), oxygen (O), nitrogen (N), sulfur (S), chlorine (Cl), fluorine (F), silicon (Si) and sodium (Na). In most cases each atom is represented by its letter symbol. In some cases groups of atoms are abbreviated, for example, CH_3 and the benzene ring. The latter structure, containing six carbon atoms to which other atoms are attached, is represented by a hexagon. A single line between two atoms represents a single chemical bond; a double line, a double bond.

ADDITION POLYMERS

MONOMER	POLYMER	PRINCIPAL USES
ETHYLENE	POLYETHYLENE	1. FILMS 2. TUBING 3. MOLDED OBJECTS 4. ELECTRICAL INSULATION
VINYL CHLORIDE	POLYVINYL CHLORIDE	1. SHEETS 2. PHONOGRAPH RECORDS 3. COPOLYMER WITH VINYL ACETATE TO MAKE FLOOR COVERINGS, LATEX PAINTS, ETC.
ACRYLONITRILE	POLYACRYLONITRILE	1. FIBERS; E.G., ORLON, ACRILAN
VINYL ACETATE	POLYVINYL ACETATE	1. CHEWING GUM 2. ADHESIVES 3. TEXTILE COATINGS 4. TO MAKE POLYVINYL ALCOHOL (ON TREATMENT WITH ALKALI)
STYRENE	POLYSTYRENE	1. MOLDED OBJECTS 2. ELECTRICAL INSULATION 3. COPOLYMER WITH BUTADIENE TO MAKE BUNA-S AND GR-S RUBBER 4. TO MAKE ION-EXCHANGE RESINS (ON TREATMENT WITH SULFURIC ACID)
BUTADIENE	POLYBUTADIENE	1. BUNA RUBBER

Monomer	Polymer	Uses
ISOBUTYLENE H CH₃ \\ | C=C / | H CH₃	**POLYISOBUTYLENE** ...—CH₂—C(CH₃)₂—CH₂—C(CH₃)₂—...	1. COLD-FLOW RUBBER 2. COPOLYMER WITH SMALL AMOUNTS OF BUTADIENE TO MAKE BUTYL RUBBER

METHYL METHACRYLATE
 	
     CH₃
     |
 H₂C=C—C(=O)—O—CH₃
	POLYMETHYL METHACRYLATE
	
	 ...—CH₂—C(CH₃)(COOCH₃)—...
		1. TRANSPARENT SHEETS, RODS, TUBING; E.G., LUCITE, PLEXIGLAS
		 2. PLASTICS REINFORCED WITH GLASS FIBER

VINYLIDENE CHLORIDE H Cl \\ | C=C / | H Cl	**POLYVINYLIDENE CHLORIDE** ...—CH₂—CCl₂—CH₂—CCl₂—...	1. COPOLYMER WITH SMALL AMOUNTS OF POLYVINYL CHLORIDE TO MAKE FILMS; E.G., SARAN
CHLOROPRENE H Cl \\ | C=C / | H CH=CH₂	**POLYCHLOROPRENE** ...—CH₂—C(Cl)=CH—CH₂—...	1. OIL-RESISTANT RUBBER; E.G., NEOPRENE
TETRAFLUOROETHYLENE F F \\ / C=C / \\ F F	**POLYTETRAFLUOROETHYLENE** ...—CF₂—CF₂—CF₂—CF₂—...	1. CHEMICALLY RESISTANT FILMS, MOLDED OBJECTS, ELECTRICAL INSULATION; E.G., TEFLON
TRIFLUOROCHLOROETHYLENE F F \\ / C=C / \\ F Cl	**POLYTRIFLUOROCHLOROETHYLENE** ...—CF₂—CFCl—CF₂—CFCl—...	1. FILMS; E.G., KEL-F

CONDENSATION POLYMERS

MONOMERS	POLYMER	PRINCIPAL USES
ETHYLENE GLYCOL + TEREPHTHALIC ACID	POLYETHYLENE TEREPHTHALATE	1. FILMS; E.G., MYLAR 2. FIBERS; E.G., DACRON
GLYCEROL + PHTHALIC ANHYDRIDE	GLYPTAL RESIN	1. COATINGS 2. PLASTICIZERS FOR SHELLAC
ETHYLENE GLYCOL + MALEIC ANHYDRIDE	ALKYD RESIN	1. COATINGS
HEXAMETHYLENEDIAMINE + ADIPIC ACID	NYLON 66	1. FIBERS 2. MOLDED OBJECTS

Starting materials	Polymer	Uses
ETHYLENE DICHLORIDE + SODIUM POLYSULFIDE (Na_2S_4)	POLYSULFIDE RUBBER	1. CHEMICALLY-RESISTANT RUBBER; E.G., THIOKOL A, GR-P
DIMETHYLSILANEDIOL	SILICONE	1. TEMPERATURE-RESISTANT LUBRICANTS 2. TEMPERATURE-RESISTANT RUBBER 3. WATER-REPELLENT COATINGS
PHENOL + FORMALDEHYDE	PHENOL-FORMALDEHYDE RESIN	1. REINFORCED MOLDED OBJECTS; E.G., BAKELITE 2. VARNISHES 3. LACQUERS 4. ADHESIVES
UREA + FORMALDEHYDE	UREA-FORMALDEHYDE RESIN	1. MOLDED OBJECTS 2. TEXTILE COATINGS 3. ADHESIVES
ETHYLENE DIISOCYANATE + ETHYLENE GLYCOL	POLYURETHANE	1. FIBERS 2. RUBBER

unexpected products were always a disappointment to the chemist, seeking to purify a substance in nice crystalline form, and were an unalloyed nuisance to the bottle-washer who had to clean the glassware.

In short, up to about 30 or 40 years ago the big organic molecules offered little attraction to chemists. Classical organic chemistry was full of interesting and important problems. With so many green pastures around, why should a chemist invest his career in the risky and sticky business of investigating the macromolecules?

Nevertheless, in the 1920's the study of large molecules such as cellulose and rubber had already begun to look intriguing. In 1923 the writer of these lines (then 28 years old) confessed to his professor at Berlin, Wilhelm Schlenk, that he was strongly tempted to work in this new field. Schlenk, who had long been regarded as one of the most ingenious experimenters in organic chemistry, said: "If I were 20 years younger" (he was 55), "I might be very much attracted myself. Wait until you are 10 years older, and meanwhile demonstrate with 'classical' investigations that you are capable of tackling a problem of such proportions." It proved to be excellent advice.

Attempts to analyze the chemical composition of cellulose, rubber, starch and proteins had begun in the 1880's. Chemists had established that these substances, like all organic compounds, were composed mainly of carbon, hydrogen and oxygen; that cellulose was essentially a sugar compound; that starch was another carbohydrate; that natural rubber was basically a hydrocarbon; that

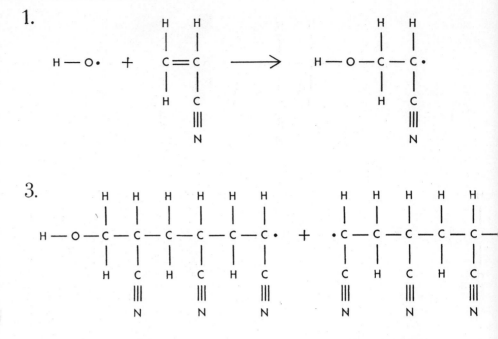

proteins contained considerable amounts of nitrogen and sometimes a little sulfur or phosphorus. The investigators soon decided that the main distinguishing feature of all these substances—what made their properties so different from other organic materials—must be the size of their molecules. The insolubility of the substances and their resistance to melting argued for large molecular size, because it had been found that ordinary organic compounds such as petroleum hydrocarbons became less and less soluble and acquired higher and higher melting points as they were combined into larger and larger molecules. The mechanical strength of cotton, wool

and silk also suggested that they were made of very large, strongly coherent molecules.

It was a logical deduction that each of the big molecules was made of certain building blocks—glucose in the cases of cellulose and starch, isoprene in the case of rubber and amino acids in the case of proteins. Chemists therefore began to call these compounds "poly" something: starch, for instance, was identified as a polysaccharide, meaning that it was composed of many sugar units. This is the basis of the present general terminology for the classes of compounds with which we are concerned: a monomer is a substance which can serve as a build-

ADDITION POLYMERIZATION is explained by example. A free radical (H-O) combines with a monomer (acrylonitrile) in such a way that the unsatisfied valence (*dot*) of the free

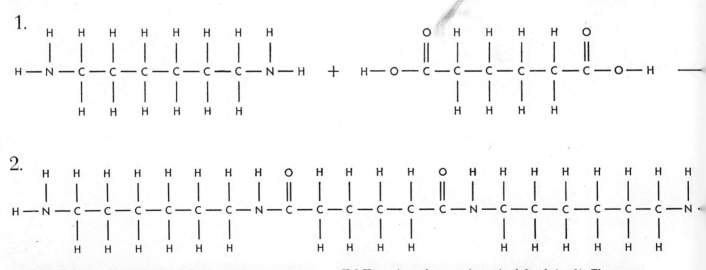

CONDENSATION POLYMERIZATION is a different process. Two molecules combine, usually with the elimination of water (H-O-H), to form the repeating unit of the chain (1). The repeating units then combine in the same manner (2). In this example

2.

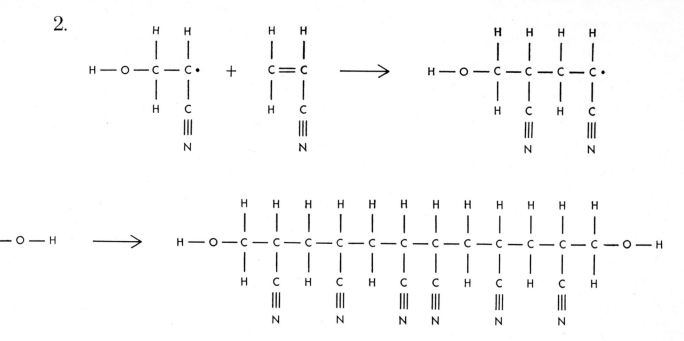

radical is transferred to the end of the monomer (1). The monomer now combines with another monomer (2). The process stops when two growing chains come together (3). In this case the free radical is obtained from the decomposition of hydrogen peroxide.

ing unit (*e.g.*, glucose); a polymer (from the Greek, meaning "many parts") is a combination of such units; a high polymer is a very large aggregation of units, *i.e.*, a compound of high molecular weight.

The spiritual father of high-polymer chemistry was Emil Fischer of Berlin, the great organic chemist of the late 19th and early 20th century. In his later years Fischer became fascinated by the mysterious chemistry of the organic macromolecules. Although loaded down with administrative duties for the German Academy of Sciences, Ministry of Education and National Research Council, he would retire to his private

laboratory early every morning to experiment with new compounds. Sitting on a stool and watching thoughtfully as faint precipitates appeared in his reaction flasks, or white powders reluctantly crystallized out of solution, he saw visions of the chemistry which was to come 20 years later. Fischer induced some of his ablest co-workers to study rubber, starch, polypeptides, cellulose and lignin (the other major component of wood). At about the same time the great organic chemist Richard Willstätter was beginning to synthesize polysaccharides and to discover new methods for isolating lignin and enzymes. These pioneers worked largely by intuition. Willstätter

was once asked, at a seminar where he reported a certain experiment, how he had happened to choose acetonitrile as the solvent, cobalt acetate as the catalyst and 75 degrees centigrade as the temperature. His answer was: "Just a thought, sir, just an idea."

Ignorance of the chemical structure of the high polymers did not, of course, debar their exploitation at the empirical level. Inventors discovered ways to convert cellulose into acetate fibers, films and coatings, into nitrated explosives and into many other useful products. Between 1870 and 1920 enterprising men (including Alfred Nobel) developed

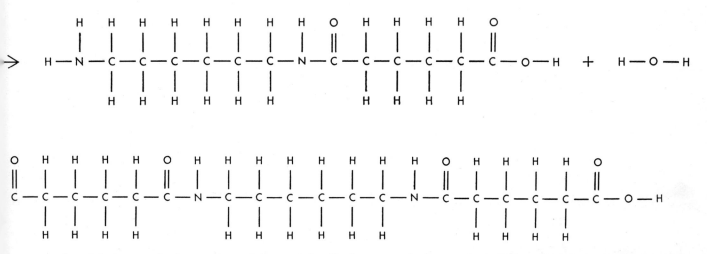

the original two molecules are those of hexamethylenediamine (*left*) and adipic acid (*right*). The polymer is nylon 66. The polymer in the example of addition polymerization is polyacrylonitrile. In both examples only a very short section of the chain is shown.

large industries based on cellulose derivatives. Meanwhile rubber also became a prominent article of commerce (and financial prosperity), thanks to Charles Goodyear's discovery, early in the 19th century, of the fact that heating it with sulfur (vulcanization) gave it useful properties. And proteins and starches likewise served as raw materials of other substantial manufacturing industries—leather, sizings, glues, adhesives, casein plastics and so on.

At the turn of the century there came an event which was to prove very significant in the development of high polymers. Leo H. Baekeland, a young Belgian chemist who had come to the U.S., took a deep interest in the sticky, resinous by-products which were such a bother to other chemists. He gave up a project on which he had been working and devoted himself to investigating the material that had fouled up his glassware. It was a gummy liquid, formed by a reaction between the common chemicals phenol and formaldehyde in solution in water. Baekeland found that by applying heat and pressure he could turn the liquid into a hard, transparent resin, which proved to be an excellent electrical insulator and to have good resistance to heat, moisture, chemicals and mechanical wear. So the synthetic plastics industry was born; other chemists went on to synthesize many other useful plastics of a similar (thermosetting) type, using formaldehyde with urea or aniline instead of phenol.

Thus by the second decade of this century factories all over the world were producing polymers in the forms of fibers, films, plastics, lacquers, coatings, adhesives and so on. Most of these were mere modifications of natural high polymers—conversions which transformed nature's substances (e.g., cellulose) into new materials of somewhat different properties. Baekeland's demonstration, on the other hand, paved the way for actual synthesis of polymers from simple materials. But all this was empirical; the basic principles governing the structure and behavior of polymers were still unknown. Chemists knew something about the "how" but not the "why."

It became increasingly important to know the why, in order to improve the products, to standarize the manufacturing processes and to reduce costs. Whenever, in such cases, the chemists of the factories tried to find out how they should best handle their systems and why they behaved as they did, they were disappointed by the lack of fundamental knowledge about polymers. Their academic colleagues in the universities had to confess that the exploration of large molecules was still in a state of infancy.

Soon after World War I a number of far-seeing leaders in science and industry recognized that a systematic exploration of polymer chemistry would pay large returns, industrially and in basic knowledge. Several of the leading organic chemists in the U.S. abandoned their successful careers in industry to gamble on full-time basic study of large molecules. Their studies were richly rewarded. One of the most fertile investigations was the memorable work of Wallace H. Carothers in the laboratories of E. I. du Pont de Nemours & Company. Supported by the vast resources of that organization and by a large group of brilliant collaborators, he developed a systematic knowledge of the chemistry of polymerization and synthesized many hundreds of polymers. This campaign produced, among other things, nylon and the synthetic rubber neoprene. While the scientific world was fascinated by the wealth and clarity of the fundamental results of the research, the du Pont Company drew great satisfaction and profit from its practical applicability. Rarely in the history of chemistry has basic research paid off so rapidly and so handsomely.

These events of the 1920's and 1930's encouraged many academic scientists and industrial researchers to turn to the large molecules. After having been a stepchild for many years, polymer chemistry became fashionable. Under the leadership of Hermann Staudinger in Germany, Thé Svedberg in Sweden and Kurt H. Meyer and Carl S. Marvel in the U.S., it moved rapidly ahead on a broad front—in experiments and in theory. Polymerization processes were developed and refined, their mechanisms explored, their products meticulously described (after having synthesized a new molecule one is naturally curious to know exactly what he has made). Very precise methods of describing the properties and behavior of polymers were developed, based on measurements of osmotic pressure, diffusion, sedimentation, light-scattering and viscosity.

Chemists could now discern a general pattern in the formation of giant molecules. Basically the high polymers were built by the linking of monomers end to end in chains, sometimes several thousand units long. But the chains then grouped themselves in two distinctly different ways. They either (1) coiled up to form a ball-shaped molecule (like a mass of intertwined spaghetti), or (2) lined up in straight, more or less rigid bundles (like wires in a cable). In general the coiled polymers had the characteristics of a rubber, while the straight-bundle type formed fibers or rigid plastics. The chemical character of the

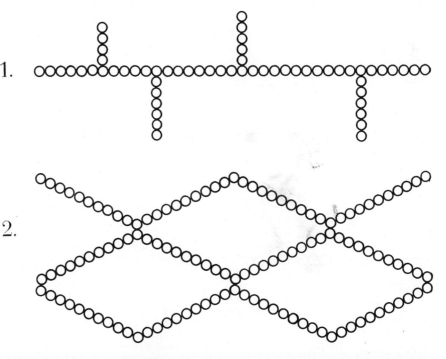

POLYMER CHAINS CAN GROW by branching (1) or can be connected by cross-linking (2). The balls in this drawing and the one on the opposite page are not atoms but monomers.

chains determined whether they would coil up at random or align themselves in bundles: if the chains were relatively rigid and contained chemically attracting groups along their length, they would attach themselves to one another side by side in bundles.

As the principles governing the properties of polymers began to shape up in the minds of the investigators, an exciting new prospect emerged. It was a matter of great intellectual satisfaction to be able to reduce the behavior of these substances to orderly laws and predict it with mathematical precision. But no less stirring was the new creative power made possible by this knowledge. The technological progress of mankind has been largely a history of putting available materials to use. It is a considerable step forward to invent the materials themselves on order. And this is the stage we have now reached in polymer chemistry. Starting from a need for some material of specified properties, we are in a position to create a new material tailored to fill that need.

As the building stones for this enterprise we now have some 40 readily available organic monomers, largely derived from coal and oil. These 40 building units can produce an almost limitless number of combinations. Already they have given us scores of important new man-made materials: all the synthetic fibers, rubbers and plastics. The production of these monomers in the U.S. now amounts to about $2 billion a year.

Polymer chemists in the U.S. and abroad are engaged in a vast effort to develop processes which will facilitate the creation of new products and reduce the cost of the present ones. They are exploring various polymerization methods, catalysts, continuous processes, and conditions which will control reactions such as very high pressures, high and low temperatures, irradiation. Knowledge of the principles underlying the chemical properties is sufficiently advanced so that the chemists can introduce into a giant molecule a monomer which will endow it with a high melting point or great resistance to solvents or high tensile strength or some other desired quality.

The products made so far can be considered only a foretaste of more spectacular ones to come. There are several frontiers inviting exploration. For example, the largest high polymers now in production have molecular weights in the neighborhood of 200,000. There is reason to believe that larger molecules would be much stronger. Consequently several industrial laboratories are looking into the possibilities for producing "super high polymers" with molecular weights in the millions. Another active frontier is the investigation of ways to raise the resistance of polymers to heat. The plastics, fibers, rubbers and coatings now made break down at temperatures of 600 degrees Fahrenheit or less. But the prospects for making high polymers which will be able to withstand substantially higher temperatures look promising: they may be based on certain highly stable organic molecules such as diphenyl oxide or diphenylmethylene, with additions of resistant elements such as fluorine, boron or silicon.

Looking much farther into the future, we can even see possibilities for synthesizing biological molecules—not to create life but to furnish aids to or substitutes for living tissues. Already we have a synthetic polymer which can serve some of the functions of blood serum. Although our chemical laboratories do not begin to approach the orderliness or perfection with which a living organism builds its high polymers, we can take hope from the fact that we have a vastly larger number of monomers at our disposal than any living system has, and therefore can make an even greater variety of products.

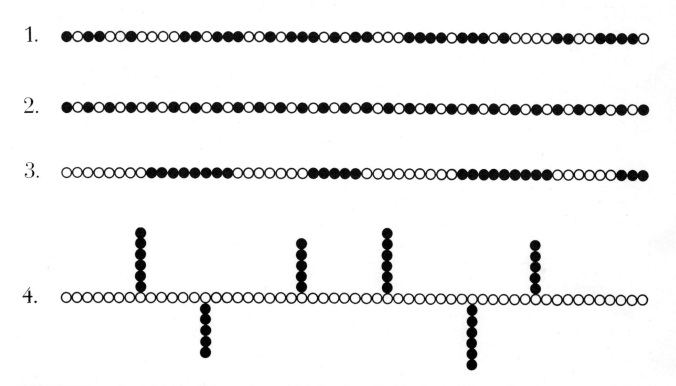

COPOLYMERS are polymer chains in which more than one kind of monomeric unit occurs. Here one kind of monomer is represented by a white ball; the other, by a black. The form of such copolymers may be random (1), alternating (2), "block" (3) or "graft" (4).

2

Proteins

PAUL DOTY

September 1957

Thousands of different proteins go into the make-up of a living cell. They perform thousands of different acts in the exact sequence that causes the cell to live. How the proteins manage this exquisitely subtle and enormously involved process will defy our understanding for a long time to come. But in recent years we have begun to make a closer acquaintance with proteins themselves. We know they are giant molecules of great size, complexity and diversity. Each appears to be designed with high specificity for its particular task. We are encouraged by all that we are learning to seek the explanation of the function of proteins in a clearer picture of their structure. For much of this new understanding we are indebted to our experience with the considerably simpler giant molecules synthesized by man. High-polymer chemistry is now coming forward with answers to some of the pressing questions of biology.

Proteins, like synthetic high polymers, are chains of repeating units. The units are peptide groups, made up of the monomers called amino acids [see diagram below]. There are more than 20 different amino acids. Each has a distinguishing cluster of atoms as a side group [see next two pages], but all amino acids have a certain identical group. The link-

ing of these groups forms the repeating peptide units in a "polypeptide" chain. Proteins are polypeptides of elaborate and very specific construction. Each kind of protein has a unique number and sequence of side groups which give it a particular size and chemical identity. Proteins seem to have a further distinction that sets them apart from other high polymers. The long chain of each protein is apparently folded in a unique configuration which it seems to maintain so long as it evidences biological activity.

We do not yet have a complete picture of the structure of any single protein. The entire sequence of amino acids has been worked out for insulin [see "The Insulin Molecule," by E. O. P. Thompson, on page 34 of this collection]; the determination of several more is nearing completion. But to locate each group and each atom in the configuration set up by the folded chain is intrinsically a more difficult task; it has resisted the Herculean labors of a generation of X-ray crystallographers and their collaborators. In the early 1930s W. T. Astbury of the University of Leeds succeeded in demonstrating that two X-ray diffraction patterns, which he called alpha and beta, were consistently associated with certain fibers, and he identified a third with collagen, the pro-

tein of skin, tendons and other structural tissues of the body. The beta pattern, found in the fibroin of silk, was soon shown to arise from bundles of nearly straight polypeptide chains held tightly to one another by hydrogen bonds. Nylon and some other synthetic fibers give a similar diffraction pattern. The alpha pattern resisted decoding until 1951, when Linus Pauling and R. B. Corey of the California Institute of Technology advanced the notion, since confirmed by further X-ray diffraction studies, that it is created by the twisting of the chain into a helix. Because it is set up so naturally by the hydrogen bonds available in the backbone of a polypeptide chain [see top diagram on page 18], the alpha helix was deduced to be a major structural element in the configuration of most proteins. More recently, in 1954, the Indian X-ray crystallographer G. N. Ramachandran showed that the collagen pattern comes from three polypeptide helixes twisted around one another. The resolution of these master plans was theoretically and esthetically gratifying, especially since the nucleic acids, the substance of genetic chemistry, were concurrently shown to have the structure of a double helix. For all their apparent general validity, however, the master plans did not give us the complete configuration in three dimensions

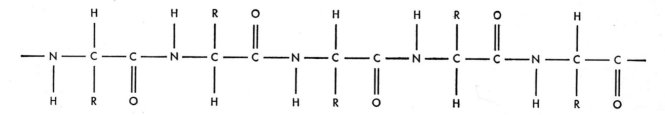

POLYPEPTIDE CHAIN is a repeating structure made up of identical peptide groups (CCONHC). The chain is formed by amino acids, each of which contributes an identical group to the backbone plus a distinguishing radical (R) as a side group.

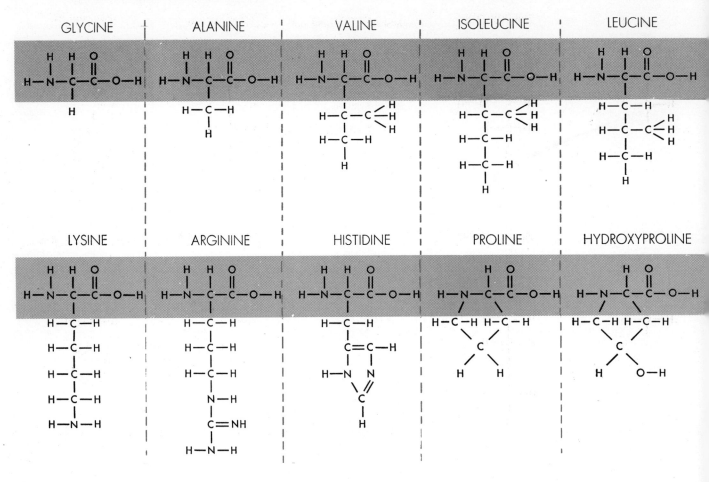

AMINO ACIDS, the 20 commonest of which are shown in this chart, have identical atomic groups (*in colored bands*) which react to form polypeptide chains. They are distinguished by their unique side groups. In forming a chain, the amino group (NH_2) of one

of any single protein.

The X-ray diffraction work left a number of other questions up in the air. Since the alpha helix had been observed only in a few fibers, there was no solid experimental evidence for its existence elsewhere. There was even a suspicion that it could occur only in fibers, where it provides an economical way to pack polypeptides together in crystalline structures. Many proteins, especially chemically active ones such as the enzymes and antibodies, are globular, not linear like those involved in fibers and structural tissues. In the watery solutions which are the natural habitat of most proteins, it could be argued, the affinity of water molecules for hydrogen bonds would disrupt the alpha helix and reduce the chain to a random coil. These doubts and suppositions have prompted investigations by our group at Harvard University in collaboration with E. R. Blout of the Children's Cancer Research Foundation in Boston.

In these investigations we have employed synthetic polypeptides as laboratory models for the more complex and sensitive proteins. When Blout and coworkers had learned to polymerize them to sufficient length—100 to 1,000 amino acid units—we proceeded to observe their behavior in solution.

Almost at once we made the gratifying discovery that our synthetic polypeptides could keep their helical coils wound up in solutions. Moreover, we found that we could unwind the helix of some polypeptides by adjusting the acidity of our solutions. Finally, to complete the picture, we discovered that we could reverse the process and make the polypeptides wind up again from random coils into helixes.

The transition from the helix to the random coil occurs within a narrow range as the acidity is reduced; the hydrogen bonds, being equivalent, tend to let go all at once. It is not unlike the melting of an ice crystal, which takes place in a narrow temperature range. The reason is the same, for the ice crystal is held together by hydrogen bonds. To complete the analogy, the transition from the helix to the random coil can also be induced by heat. This is a true melting process, for the helix is a one-dimensional crystal which freezes the otherwise flexible chain into a rodlet.

From these experiments we conclude that polypeptides in solution have two natural configurations and make a reversible transition from one to the other, depending upon conditions. Polypeptides in the solid state appear to prefer the alpha helix, though this is subject to the presence of solvents, especially water. When the helix breaks down here, the transition is to the beta configuration, the hydrogen bonds now linking adjacent chains. Recently Blout and Henri Lenormant have found that fibers of polylysine can be made to undergo the alpha-beta transition reversibly by mere alteration of humidity. It is tempting to speculate that a reversible alpha-beta transition may underlie the process of muscle contraction and other types of

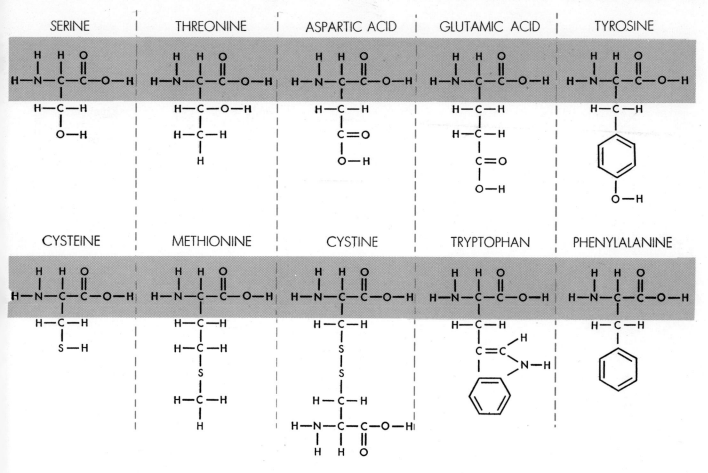

molecule reacts with the hydroxyl group (OH) of another. This reaction splits one of the amino hydrogens off with the hydroxyl group to form a molecule of water. The nitrogen of the first group then forms the peptide bond with the carbon of the second.

movement in living things.

Having learned to handle the polypeptides in solution we turned our attention to proteins. Two questions had to be answered first: Could we find the alpha helix in proteins in solution, and could we induce it to make the reversible transition to the random coil and back again? If the answer was yes in each case, then we could go on to a third and more interesting question: Could we show experimentally that biological activity depends upon configuration? On this question, our biologically neutral synthetic polypeptides could give no hint.

For the detection of the alpha helix in proteins the techniques which had worked so well on polypeptides were impotent. The polypeptides were either all helix or all random coil and the rodlets of the first could easily be distinguished from the globular forms of the second by use of the light-scattering technique. But we did not expect to find that any of the proteins we were going to investigate were 100 per cent helical in configuration. The helix is invariably disrupted by the presence of one of two types of amino acid units. Proline lacks the hydrogen atom that forms the crucial hydrogen bond; the side groups form a distorting linkage to the chain instead. Cystine is really a double unit, and forms more or less distorting cross-links between chains. These units play an important part in the intricate coiling and folding of the polypeptide chains in globular proteins. But even in globular proteins, we thought, some lengths of the chains might prove to be helical. There was nothing, however, in the over-all shape of a globular protein to tell us whether it had more or less helix in its structure or none at all. We had to find a way to look inside the protein.

One possible way to do this was suggested by the fact that intact, biologically active proteins and denatured proteins give different readings when observed for an effect called optical rotation. In general, the molecules that exhibit this effect are asymmetrical in atomic structure. The side groups give rise to such asymmetry in amino acids and polypeptide chains; they may be attached in either a "left-handed" or a "right-handed" manner. Optical rotation provides a way to distinguish one from the other. When a solution of amino acids is interposed in a beam of polarized light, it will rotate the plane of polarization either to the right or to the left [see diagrams at top of page 20]. Though amino acids may exist in both forms, only left-handed units, thanks to some accident in the chemical phase of evolution, are found in proteins. We used only the left-handed forms, of course, in the synthesis of our polypeptide chains.

Now what about the change in optical rotation that occurs when a protein is denatured? We knew that native protein rotates the plane of the light 30 to 60 degrees to the left, denatured protein 100 degrees or more to the left. If there was some helical structure in the protein, we surmised, this shift in rotation might be induced by the disappearance of the helical structure in the denaturation process. There was reason to believe that the helix, which has to be either left-handed or right-handed, would have optical activity. Further, although it appeared possible for the helix to be wound either way, there were grounds for assuming that nature had chosen to make all of its helixes one way or the other. If it had not, the left-handed and right-handed helixes would mutually cancel out their respective optical rotations. The change in the optical rotation of proteins with denaturation would then have some other explanation entirely, and we would have to invent another way to look for helixes.

To test our surmise we measured the optical rotation of the synthetic poly-peptides. In the random coil state the polypeptides made an excellent fit with the denatured proteins, rotating the light 100 degrees to the left. The rotations in both cases clearly arose from the same cause: the asymmetry of the amino acid units. In the alpha helix configuration the polypeptides showed almost no rotation or none at all. It was evident that the presence of the alpha helix caused a

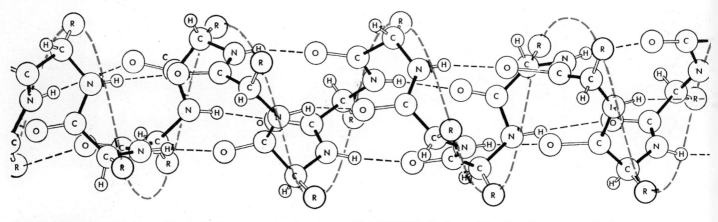

ALPHA HELIX gives a polypeptide chain a linear structure shown here in three-dimensional perspective. The atoms in the repeating unit (CCONHC) lie in a plane; the change in angle between one unit and the next occurs at the carbon to which the side group

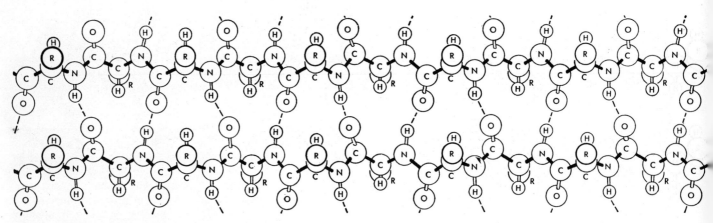

BETA CONFIGURATION ties two or more polypeptide chains to one another in crystalline structures. Here the hydrogen bonds do not contribute to the internal organization of the chain, as in the alpha helix, but link the hydrogen atoms of one chain to the oxygen

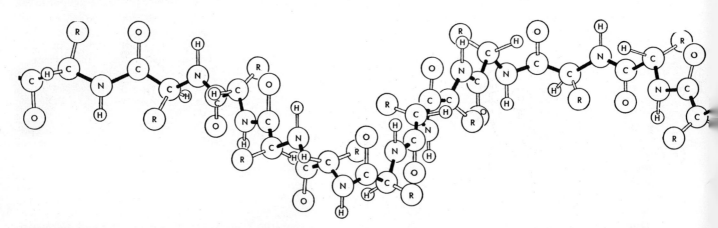

RANDOM CHAIN is the configuration assumed by the polypeptide molecule in solution, when hydrogen bonds are not formed. The flat configuration of the repeating unit remains, but the chain rotates about the carbon atoms to which the side groups are at-

counter-rotation to the right which nearly canceled out the leftward rotation of the amino acid units. The native proteins also had shown evidence of such counter-rotation to the right. The alpha configuration did not completely cancel the leftward rotation of the amino acid units, but this was consistent with the expectation that the protein structures would be helical only in part. The experiment thus strongly indicated the presence of the alpha helix in the structure of globular proteins in solution. It also, incidentally, seemed to settle the question of nature's choice of symmetry in the alpha helix: it must be right-handed.

When so much hangs on the findings of one set of experiments, it is well to double check them by observations of another kind. We are indebted to William Moffitt, a theoretical chemist at Harvard, for conceiving of the experiment that provided the necessary confirmation. It is based upon another aspect of the optical rotation effect. For a given substance, rotation varies with the wavelength of the light; the rotations of most substances vary in the same way. Moffitt predicted that the presence of

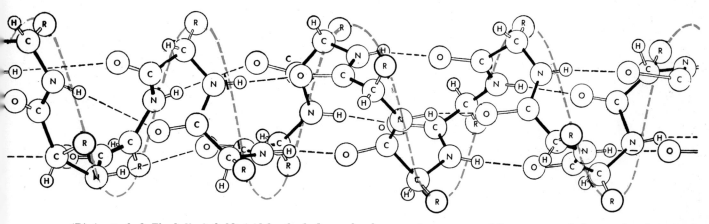

(R) is attached. The helix is held rigid by the hydrogen bond (*broken black lines*) between the hydrogen attached to the nitrogen in one group and the oxygen attached to a carbon three groups along the chain. The colored line traces the turns of the helix.

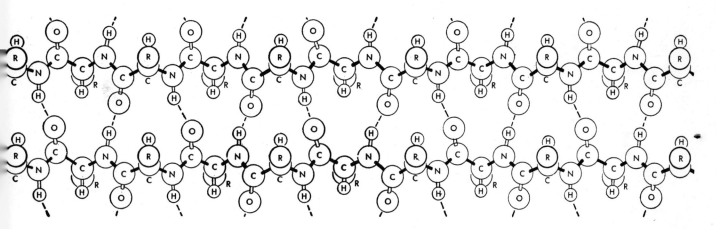

atoms in the adjoining chain. The beta configuration is found in silk and a few other fibers. It is also thought that polypeptide chains in muscle and other contractile fibers may make reversible transitions from alpha helix to beta configuration when in action.

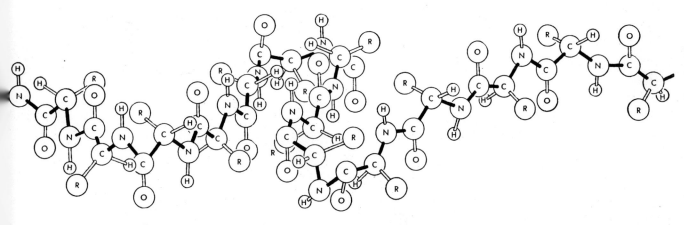

tached. The random chain may be formed from an alpha helix when hydrogen bonds are disrupted in solution. A polypeptide chain may make a reversible transition from alpha helix to random chain, depending upon the acid-base balance of the solution.

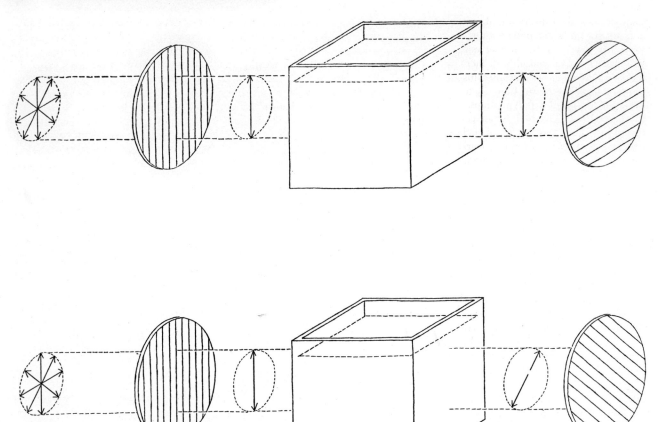

OPTICAL ROTATION is induced in a beam of polarized light by molecules having certain types of structural asymmetry. At top a beam of light is polarized in the vertical plane and transmitted unchanged through a neutral solution. At bottom asymmetrical molecules in the solution cause the beam to rotate from the vertical plane. The degree of rotation may be determined by turning the second polarizing filter (*right*) to the point at which it cuts off the beam. The alpha helix in a molecule causes such rotation.

the alpha helix in a substance would cause its rotation to vary in a different way. His prediction was sustained by observation: randomly coiled polypeptides showed a normal variation while the helical showed abnormal. Denatured and native proteins showed the same contrast. With the two sets of experiments in such good agreement, we could conclude with confidence that the alpha

helix has a significant place in the structure of globular proteins. Those amino acid units that are not involved in helical configurations are weakly bonded to each other or to water molecules, probably in a unique but not regular or periodic fashion. Like synthetic high-polymers, proteins are partly crystalline and partly amorphous in structure.

The optical rotation experiments also

provided a scale for estimating the helical content of protein. The measurements indicate that, in neutral solutions, the helical structure applies to 15 per cent of the amino acid units in ribonuclease, 50 per cent of the units in serum albumin and 85 per cent in tropomyosin. With the addition of denaturing agents to the solution, the helical content in each case can be reduced to zero. In

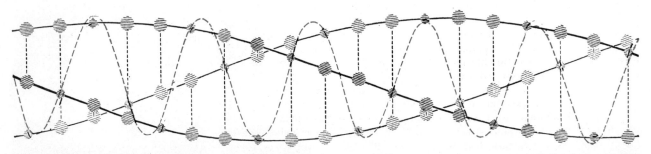

COLLAGEN MOLECULE is a triple helix. The colored broken line indicates hydrogen bonds between glycine units. The black broken lines indicate hydrogen bonds which link hydroxyproline units and give greater stability to collagens in which they are found.

some proteins the transition is abrupt, as it is in the synthetic polypeptides. On the other hand, by the use of certain solvents we have been able to increase the helical content of some proteins—in the case of ribonuclease from 15 to 70 per cent. As in the polypeptides, the transition from helix to random coil is reversible. The percentage of helical structure in proteins is thus clearly a variable. In their natural environment, it appears, the percentage at any given time represents the equilibrium between the inherent stability of the helix and the tendency of water to break it down.

In a number of enzymes we have been able to show that biological activity falls off and increases with helical content. Denaturation is now clearly identified with breakdown of configuration, certainly insofar as it involves the integrity of the alpha helix. This is not surprising. It is known that catalysts in general must have rigid geometrical configurations. The catalytic activity of an enzyme may well require that its structure meet similar specifications. If this is so, the rigidity that the alpha helix imposes on the otherwise flexible polypeptide chain must play a decisive part in establishing the biological activity of an enzyme. It seems also that adjustability of the stiffness of structure in larger or smaller regions of the polypeptide chain may modify the activity of proteins in response to their environment. Among other things, it could account for the versatility of the gamma globulins; without any apparent change in their amino acid make-up, they are able somehow to adapt themselves as antibodies to a succession of different infectious agents.

The next step toward a complete anatomy of the protein molecule is to determine which amino acid units are in the helical and which in the nonhelical regions. Beyond that we shall want to know which units are near one another as the result of folding and cross-linking, and a myriad of other details which will supply the hues and colorings appropriate to a portrait of an entity as intricate as protein. Many such details will undoubtedly be supplied by experiments that relate change in structure to change in function, like those described here.

In the course of our experiments with proteins in solution we have also looked into the triple-strand structure of collagen. That structure had not yet been resolved when we began our work, so we did not know how well it was designed for the function it serves in structural tissues. Collagen makes up one third of the proteins in the body and 5 per cent of its total weight; it occurs as tiny fibers or fibrils with bonds that repeat at intervals of about 700 Angstroms. It had been known for a long time that these fibrils could be dissolved in mild solvents such as acetic acid and then reconstituted, by simple precipitation, into their original form with their bandings restored. This remarkable capacity naturally suggested that the behavior of collagen in solution was a subject worth exploring.

Starting from the groundwork of other investigators, Helga Boedtker and I were able to demonstrate that the collagen molecule is an extremely long and thin rodlet, the most asymmetric molecule yet isolated. A lead pencil of comparable proportions would be a yard long. When a solution of collagen is just slightly warmed, these rodlets are irreversibly broken down. The solution will gel, but the product is gelatin, as is well known to French chefs and commercial producers of gelatin. The reason the dissolution cannot be reversed was made clear when we found that the molecules in the warmed-up solution had a weight about one third that of collagen. It appeared that the big molecule of collagen had broken down into three polypeptide chains.

At about the same time Ramachandran proposed the three-strand helix as the collagen structure. Not long afterward F. H. C. Crick and Alexander Rich at the University of Cambridge and Pauline M. Cowan and her collaborators at King's College, London, worked out the structure in detail. It consists of three polypeptide chains, each incorporating three different amino acid units—proline, hydroxyproline and glycine. The key to the design is the occurrence of glycine, the smallest amino acid unit, at every third position on each chain. This makes it possible for the bulky proline or hydroxyproline groups to fit into the links of the triple strand, two of these nesting in each link with the smaller glycine unit [see diagram on page 20].

One question, however, was left open in the original model. Hydroxyproline has surplus hydrogen bonds, which, the model showed, might be employed to reinforce the molecule itself or to tie it more firmly to neighboring molecules in a fibril. Independent evidence seemed to favor the second possibility. Collagen in the skin is irreversibly broken down in a first degree burn, for example, at a temperature of about 145 degrees Fahrenheit. This is about 60 degrees higher than the dissolution temperature of the collagen molecule in solution. The obvious inference was that hydroxyproline lends its additional bonding power to the tissue structure. Moreover, tissues with a high hydroxyproline content withstand higher temperatures than those with lower; the skin of codfish, with a low hydroxyproline content, shrivels up at about 100 degrees. Tomio Nishihara in

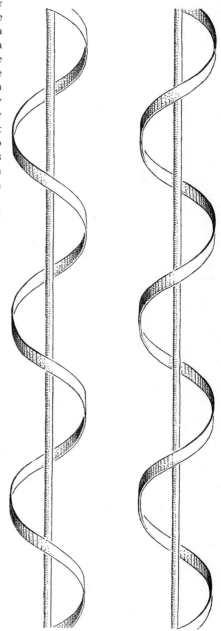

ASYMMETRY of a helix is either left-handed (*left*) or right-handed. Helix in proteins appears to be exclusively right-handed.

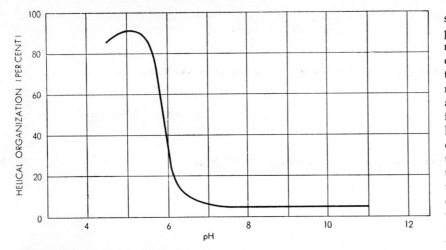

ALPHA HELIX BREAKDOWN is induced in solutions of some polypeptides when the pH (acidity or alkalinity) reaches a critical value at which hydrogen bonds are disrupted.

our laboratory has compared the breakdown temperatures of collagen molecules and tissues from various species and found that the tissue temperature is uniformly about 60 degrees higher. Thus we must conclude that the extra stability conferred by hydroxyproline goes directly to the molecule and not to the fibril.

The structure of collagen demonstrates three levels in the adaptation of polypeptide chains to fit the requirements of function. First there are the chains as found in gelatin, with their three amino acids lined up in just the right sequence. These randomly coiled and quite soluble molecules are transformed into relatively insoluble, girderlike building units when united into sets of three by hydrogen bonds. The subtly fashioned collagen molecules are still too fragile to withstand body temperatures. When arranged side by side, however, they form a crystalline structure which resists comparatively high temperatures and has fiber-like qualities with the vast range of strengths and textures required in the different types of tissues that are made of collagen.

The story of collagen, like that of other proteins, is still far from complete. But it now seems that it will rank among the first proteins whose molecular structure has been clearly discerned and related in detail to the functions it serves.

3

The Chemical Structure of Proteins

WILLIAM H. STEIN AND STANFORD MOORE

February 1961

Six years ago, after a decade of pioneering research, Frederick Sanger and his colleagues at the University of Cambridge were able to write the first structural formula of a protein—the hormone insulin. They had discovered the precise order in which the atoms are strung together in the long chains that make up the insulin molecule. With this truly epochal achievement, for which Sanger received a Nobel prize in 1958, there opened a new chapter in protein chemistry.

Some idea of the significance of this chapter for chemistry and biology can be gained from the realization that proteins comprise more than half the solid substance in the tissues of man and other mammals. Proteins are important mechanical elements and perform countless essential catalytic and protective functions. Only when the structures of large numbers of proteins have been worked out will biochemists be in a position to answer many of the fundamental questions they have long been asking. The goal is still far off, but there has been much progress in this challenging field.

Before embarking on a summary of some of the recent developments, it is well to point out that the chemical approach does not provide a complete solution to the problem of protein structure. The order of links in the chain is not the whole story. Each chain is coiled and folded in a three-dimensional pattern, no less important than the atom-by-atom sequence in determining its biological activity. Chemical methods can provide only a partial insight into this three-dimensional, or "tertiary," structure. In the past few years the spatial problem has begun to yield to X-ray analysis. The present article, however, is primarily concerned with the chemical rather than the physical line of attack.

Proteins are very large, they are com-plex and they are fragile. The molecule of insulin, one of the smallest proteins, contains 777 atoms. Some protein molecules are thought to be 50 times bigger, although even the size of the largest ones is not definitely settled. Fortunately most of them are constructed on the same general plan. The links, or building blocks, in the molecular chains are amino acids. In their uncombined form each of these substances consists of an amino group (NH_2) and a carboxyl group ($COOH$), both attached to the same carbon atom. Also attached to this carbon are a hydrogen atom and one of 24 different "side groups." When the amino acids link together in a protein molecule, they join end to end, the carboxyl group of one combining with the amino group of the next to form a "peptide bond" ($-CO-NH-$) and a molecule of water (HOH). Since each component has lost a molecule of water, it is called an amino acid "residue." Under the action of acids, alkalis or certain enzymes, peptide chains break apart, the $-NH-$ groups regaining a hydrogen atom and the $-CO-$ groups a hydroxyl group (OH). Thus each residue regains a molecule of water and the peptide bonds are said to have been hydrolyzed.

Among the amino acids the one called cystine is unique. Its molecule is a sort of Siamese twin containing two $-NH_2$ and two $-COOH$ groups, with identical halves of the molecule joined by a disulfide bond ($-S-S-$). One cystine molecule can therefore enter into two separate peptide chains, cross-linking them by means of the disulfide bond. Cystine can also cause a single chain to fold back on itself.

The Insulin Molecule

Much of the chemistry of proteins had been laboriously uncovered in many years of research before Sanger took up the study of insulin. His success rested largely on two advances in technique. One was the development of paper chromatography by the British chemists A. J. P. Martin and R. L. M. Synge. By means of this elegant method tiny samples of complex mixtures can be fractionated on a piece of filter paper and their components identified [see "Chromatography," by William H. Stein and Stanford Moore, which is available as Offprint #81]. The second key to the problem was Sanger's discovery of a way to label the amino group at the end of a peptide chain. He found that a dinitrophenyl (DNP) group could be attached to free amino groups to form a yellow compound. Even when the peptide is fragmented into separate amino acids, the DNP group remains attached to the residue at the end of the chain, thus making it possible to identify this residue.

The details of Sanger's analysis have already been described in this magazine by one of his co-workers ["The Insulin Molecule," by E. O. P. Thompson, page 34]. Here we shall review their work very briefly. With the help of the DNP method they first established that the insulin molecule consists of two chains. These chains are held together by the $-S-S-$ bonds of cystine residues. By treating the hormone with a mild oxidizing agent the experimenters were able to open the disulfide bonds and thus separate the two intact chains. One proved to contain 21 amino acids; the other, 30. They then proceeded to cleave each chain into smaller pieces by treating it with acid, which hydrolyzes peptide bonds more or less at random. The fragments were separated by chromatography and by other means, labeled at their amino ends by the DNP method, broken down further, separated again, relabeled and so on. In this way the order of amino acids in a large number of small pieces was established. By shattering the chain many times and noting overlapping sequences in the various fragments the Cambridge group at last deduced the complete succession of amino acid residues in each part of the molecule.

After the completion of this Herculean task an almost equal effort was required simply to determine the pairing of the half-cystine residues. One chain was found to contain four half-residues of cystine and the other chain two. To find out which ones were paired it was necessary to break the molecule into smaller fragments containing different pairs of half-cystine residues with their disulfide bonds intact. In the process, however, the cystine halves tended to trade part-

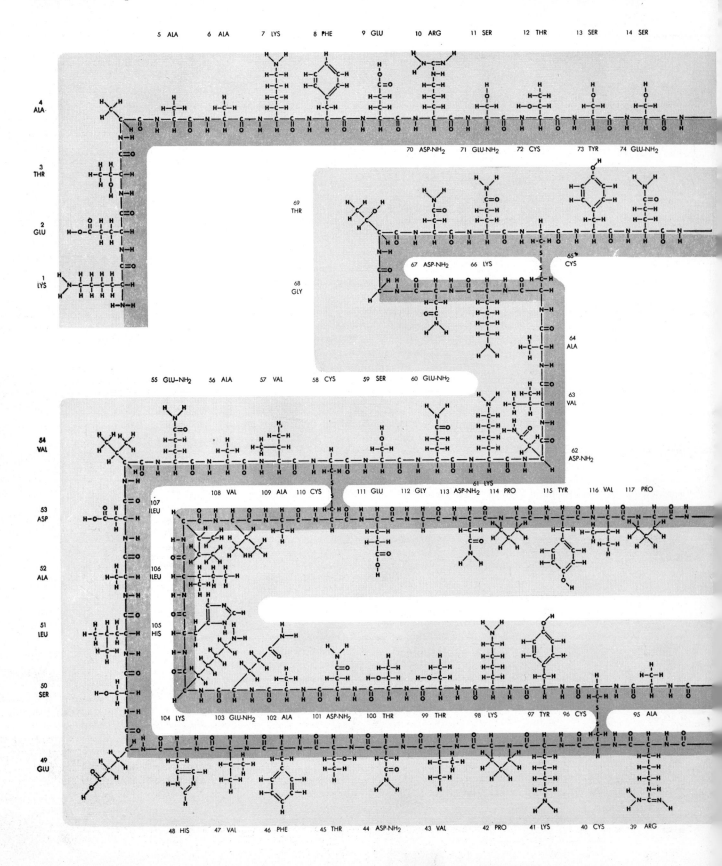

ners and produce spurious pairings. Finally a way around the difficulty was worked out, and the disulfide bonds were unequivocally pinned down.

Once Sanger had shown that the problem was solvable a number of workers began to attack the structure of larger proteins. In the six years that have passed two more molecules have been completely delineated and others are on the way. Last year the analysis of the structure of ribonuclease, an enzyme that digests ribonucleic acid, was completed in the authors' laboratory. Ribo-

nuclease contains 124 amino acid residues. As this article was in preparation Gerhard Schramm and his associates in Germany and Heinz L. Fraenkel-Conrat, Wendell M. Stanley and their colleagues at the University of California announced that they had finished working out the structure of the 158-amino-acid-residue protein in tobacco mosaic virus.

At first sight it might seem that any protein should yield to a massive effort along the lines used so successfully with insulin. As Sanger and others realized, however, it is not so simple as that—if simple is the word for 10 years of unremitting work. Problems multiply rapidly with increasing molecular size, and an approach that was difficult and time-consuming in the case of insulin can become fruitless and interminable.

One aid to further progress has been the development of more precise methods for identifying and measuring small quantities of amino acids. Several years ago the authors undertook to apply column chromatography for this purpose. Instead of filter paper we use a five-foot

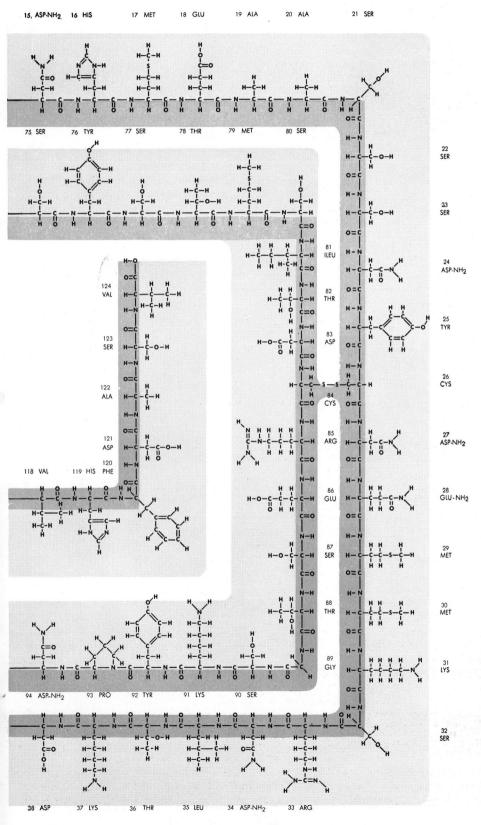

ALA	ALANINE
ARG	ARGININE
ASP	ASPARTIC ACID
ASP-NH₂	ASPARAGINE
CYS	CYSTINE
GLU	GLUTAMIC ACID
GLU-NH₂	GLUTAMINE
GLY	GLYCINE
HIS	HISTIDINE
ILEU	ISOLEUCINE
LEU	LEUCINE
LYS	LYSINE
MET	METHIONINE
PHE	PHENYLALANINE
PRO	PROLINE
SER	SERINE
THR	THREONINE
TYR	TYROSINE
VAL	VALINE

MOLECULE OF RIBONUCLEASE, an enzyme that digests the cellular substance ribonucleic acid (RNA), is diagramed in two dimensions on these two pages. In this structural formula are 1,876 atoms: 587 of carbon (C), 909 of hydrogen (H), 197 of oxygen (O), 171 of nitrogen (N) and 12 of sulfur (S). The backbone of the chain of amino acid residues is in the darker shaded area; the side chains characteristic of the various amino acids are in the lighter shaded area. The amino acid residues are numbered from 1 to 124, beginning at the amino end of the chain. Abbreviations for amino acids appearing in the diagram are indicated above.

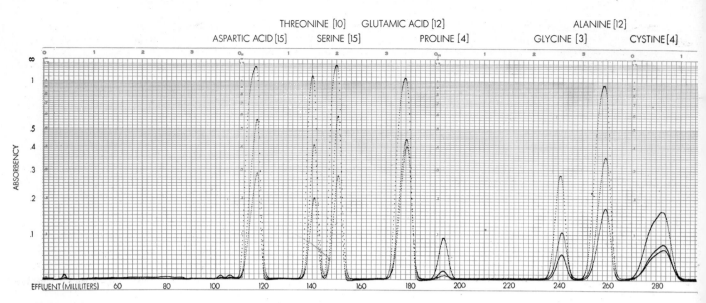

THREONINE [10]   GLUTAMIC ACID [12]   ALANINE [12]

ASPARTIC ACID [15]   SERINE [15]   PROLINE [4]   GLYCINE [3]   CYSTINE [4]

AMINO ACID ANALYSIS is recorded as a series of peaks by an automatic analyzer. The trace reproduced here was obtained in the analysis of a hydrolyzed sample of ribonuclease. The names of the amino acids that were found appear above their corresponding peaks. The number of residues of each in the ribonuclease molecule, determined by the intensity of blue color formed with a special reagent, is shown in brackets. (Proline gives proportionately less color than the other amino acids.) Histidine, lysine, arginine

column of an ion-exchange resin. One or two milligrams of an amino acid mixture placed at the top of the column are washed down through the column by solutions of varying acidity. Depending on their relative affinity for the solutions and for the resin, the individual amino acids move down the column at different rates. By proper choice of salt solutions, acidity and temperature, it is possible to adjust the rates of travel so that the separate amino acids emerge from the bottom of the column at predetermined and well-spaced intervals. To detect the colorless amino acids we heat them with ninhydrin, a reagent that yields a blue color. The intensity of the color is proportional to the amount of amino acid.

In the final version of the device, developed in collaboration with D. H.

AMINO ACID ANALYZER is photographed in the authors' laboratory at the Rockefeller Institute. Vertical tubes in center are ion-exchange columns. Photometer unit is enclosed in case at top left; recorder is at bottom left. Next to it on the bench is heating bath.

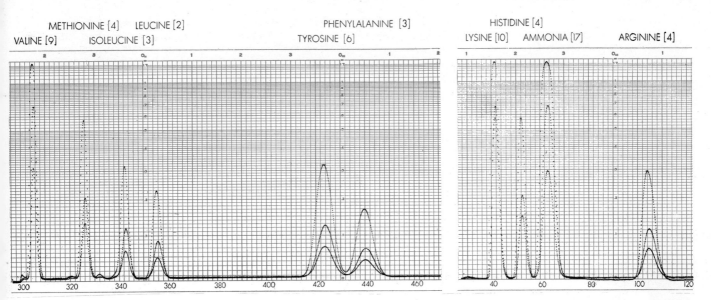

METHIONINE [4]   LEUCINE [2]   PHENYLALANINE [3]   HISTIDINE [4]
VALINE [9]   ISOLEUCINE [3]   TYROSINE [6]   LYSINE [10]   AMMONIA [17]   ARGININE [4]

and ammonia are determined with a separate ion-exchange column and recorded separately (*right*). The ammonia is released by the hydrolysis of residues of asparagine and glutamine in the intact ribonuclease molecule. In the process these substances are con-verted to aspartic acid and glutamic acid respectively. Horizontal scale measures milliliters of solution to have passed through the columns; vertical scale, color intensity. Different curves show absorbencies at different wave lengths and depths of solution.

Spackman, the amino acid analysis is accomplished automatically. The outflow from the column is continuously mixed with ninhydrin, sent through a heating bath and then analyzed by a photometer attached to a recorder. As it flows out of the bath and into the photometer the solution is alternately colorless (when it contains no amino acid) and blue (when an amino acid is present). A continuous plot of the intensity of the blue color shows a series of peaks, each corresponding to a particular amino acid, the area under the peak indicating the amount of that amino acid in the sample. With the automatic amino acid analyzer one operator, working part time, can carry out a complete quantitative analysis of the amino acids from a hydrolyzed protein in 24 hours. The device played an essential role in the work on ribonuclease.

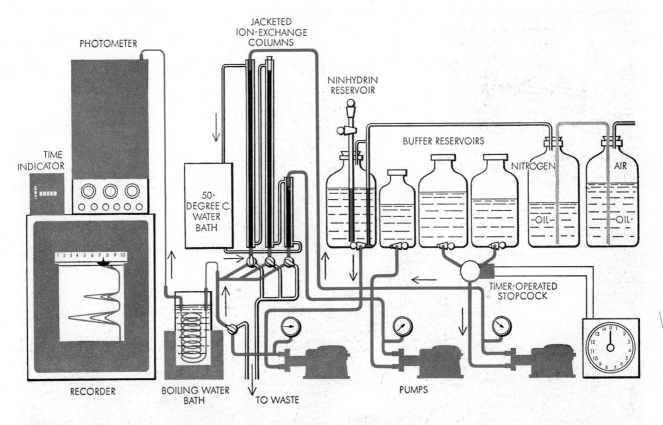

AUTOMATIC ANALYZER for amino acids is diagramed schematically. The two pumps at lower right drive salt solutions through ion-exchange columns. The third pump delivers color reagent (ninhydrin) to a stream emerging from bottom of column. The mixture passes through boiling water bath, where blue color is developed. Intensity of the color is measured by the photometer.

We chose ribonuclease for study for several reasons. The protein, first isolated from beef pancreas in 1920, was available in relatively pure form, having been crystallized by Moses Kunitz of the Rockefeller Institute in 1940. It was known to be a rather small protein, with a molecular weight of about 14,000. (The molecular weight of insulin is 5,733.) Moreover, the manner in which ribonuclease breaks down the ribonucleic acid (RNA) molecule had been worked out in several laboratories. As a result there was a chance of correlating its structure, once that was established, with its biochemical function.

As a first step in the program C. H. W. Hirs, together with the authors, further purified crystalline ribonuclease with the aid of ion-exchange resins. When a hydrolyzed sample was analyzed, it proved to contain a total of 124 amino acid residues of 17 different kinds, plus a quantity of ammonia [see illustration on pages 26 and 27]. The presence of ammonia in-

dicated that some of the aspartic acid and glutamic acid that showed up in the analysis came not from residues of these amino acids in the protein molecule but from the related amino acids, asparagine and glutamine. When the last two are hydrolyzed, they are converted to aspartic and glutamic acids and ammonia. Thus the intact ribonuclease molecule contains 19 different kinds of amino acid residue.

There were four residues of cystine and therefore four disulfide bonds. At about that time Christian B. Anfinsen of the National Heart Institute demonstrated, by the DNP method, that ribonuclease consists of a single peptide chain. Therefore the disulfide bonds must cause the folding together of sections of the same chain.

After opening up the disulfide bonds by oxidation, Hirs proceeded to break the 124-link chain into smaller pieces. Here Sanger's method of random hydrolysis with acid did not seem promising. It

probably would produce so many small fragments that they would be almost impossible to separate. And even if they were isolated and their structure determined, it seemed unlikely that the sequence of amino acids in the complete chain could be deduced from these small bits and pieces. For a more selective method of dissection we turned to the protein-splitting enzymes. A number of these had been purified and their mode of attack on peptide chains elucidated at the Rockefeller Institute by Max Bergmann and Joseph S. Fruton and their colleagues. The most specific is trypsin, which cleaves only bonds involving the carboxyl groups of the amino acids arginine and lysine. Others, such as chymotrypsin and pepsin, also confine their activity to certain bonds, though not so selectively as does trypsin.

Since there are 10 lysine and four arginine residues in ribonuclease, Hirs first treated the protein with trypsin. The products were separated from one an-

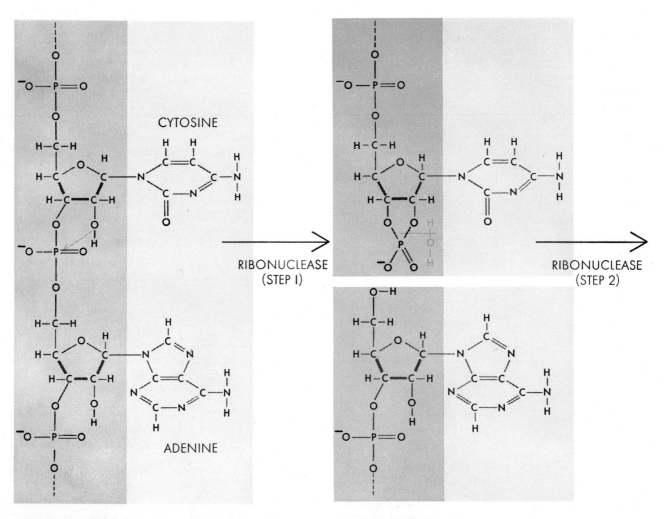

SPLITTING OF RIBONUCLEIC ACID molecule by ribonuclease takes place in two steps. Backbone of the molecule, of which a segment is shown in dark shaded area, is attacked at the phosphorus atom following cytosine (or uracil) but not adenine (or guanine). In the first step the bond between phosphorus and the oxygen atom below it opens, splitting the molecule, a different oxygen uniting

other by the use of columns of ion-exchange resins, and each was then analyzed for amino acids. All told, 13 peptide fragments were isolated, ranging from peptides with only two amino acid residues to some containing more than 20. Among them they accounted for all of the 124 amino acid residues of ribonuclease. To obtain additional fragments Hirs and J. L. Bailey also split the molecule at other points with chymotrypsin and with pepsin.

The amino acid composition of all the fragments was determined, and the residue at the amino end identified in some of them. With this knowledge it was possible, in a sort of crossword-puzzle fashion, to derive a partial structural formula that showed the order in which the various peptides produced by the different enzymatic cleavages must have been arranged in the parent molecule.

The next step was to determine the sequence of amino acid residues within the fragments. One extremely valuable

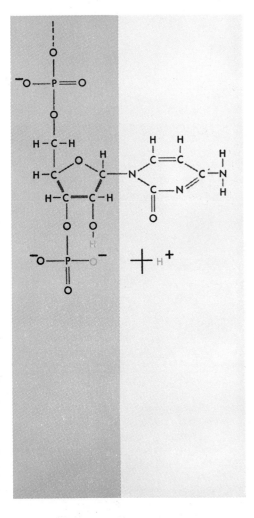

with the phosphorus (*dashed arrow*). In second step another phosphorus-oxygen bond is cleaved with addition of water (H·O·H).

tool, developed by Pehr Edman in Sweden, was a reaction that can clip off one amino acid unit at a time from the amino end of a peptide sequence. There was also a pair of enzymes that can do the same sort of job in some cases, one at the amino and the other at the carboxyl end. Using these and other means, Hirs analyzed 24 peptides completely and examined parts of many more. Each step of each manipulation was monitored on the amino acid analyzer.

After five years of work the complete sequence of the ribonuclease chain was finally established [*see illustration on pages 24 and 25*]. Spackman then undertook to determine the arrangement of the four disulfide bonds. As in the case of insulin, the problem turned out to be difficult. Two of the bonds were particularly fragile. Only after a long study did Spackman find out how to break ribonuclease into peptides that contained cystine residues with their disulfide bonds intact. Once this had been accomplished the crosslinks could be located and the complete formula written down.

Here we must emphasize that, while the complete formula is certainly correct in most respects, it must still be considered a working hypothesis. Although a great deal of quantitative data supports it, and although Anfinsen's laboratory has derived about a quarter of it independently, we still cannot be completely certain of the results. Degradative experiments, in which molecules are broken down, do not offer final proof for an organic chemical structure; the last word comes when a postulated structure is synthesized and then shown to have all the same properties as the natural product. In spite of the substantial advances of the past few years in the synthesis of complex peptides, it will probably be some time before a molecule of the size of ribonuclease is put together. Until then we must be on the lookout for surprises, because it is entirely possible that ribonuclease contains chemical linkages that are not revealed by the degradative techniques we employed. (For example, unusual linkages have already been found in peptide antibiotics by Lyman C. Craig and his associates at the Rockefeller Institute.)

In any case, our formula has one important deficiency: it is two-dimensional. As we have mentioned, the biological activity of a protein molecule usually depends not only on the sequence of its amino acids but also on how the peptide chain is coiled. Ribonuclease is no exception: it is inactivated by disruption of its three-dimensional structure. Of course, the order of amino acids in any

peptide chain must influence its spatial arrangement. Certain sequences are known to preclude certain kinds of folding. To what extent a given sequence may require a given kind of folding is not yet clear.

Although much structural information can be obtained through chemical techniques, they can go only part of the way with a molecule as big as that of a protein. For many years X-ray crystallography has been applied to the problem, recently with striking success. A description of this work must await a separate article. Here we shall merely mention that in a series of brilliant investigations British groups headed by J. C. Kendrew and Max F. Perutz have worked out, respectively, the complete spatial arrangement of the peptide chains in the oxygen-carrying proteins myoglobin and hemoglobin. The sequences of amino acids in these molecules have not yet been determined, although they doubtless will be soon. Indeed, it may prove possible to discover the order by X-ray methods alone, which would provide a valuable check on the methods of organic chemistry. When the sequences are found, it will be possible to place each amino acid residue in its proper position on the models of the coiled chains derived from X-ray studies. At that exciting moment the first true picture of a protein will have been drawn. Unfortunately the methods used by Kendrew and Perutz have not yet been successful with insulin or ribonuclease. Sooner or later, however, the difficulties will be resolved and we shall have the complete portraits of these molecules as well.

Active Sites of Enzymes

In the meantime the techniques of organic chemistry are throwing considerable light on one aspect of the relation between the structure of proteins and their function. That is the question of the "active site" of enzymes. Being proteins, enzymes are all large molecules. Often their substrates—the substances they act on—are very much smaller. For example, ribonuclease splits not only ribonucleic acid but also the comparatively small molecule cyclic cytidylic acid [*see illustration on page 31*]. In such a case only a small portion of the enzyme molecule can be in contact with the substrate when the two are joined together, as they are during the reaction catalyzed by the enzyme. This portion is known as the active site. The concept of an active site does not imply that the rest of the enzyme has no function. Sometimes part of the molecule is dispensable; sometimes it is not. The whole molecule may perhaps be something like a precision lathe, where a ton or more of machinery is required to bring a few ounces of metal in the cutting tool to bear accurately on the work. Similarly, the bulk of the enzyme molecule may be required to bring the active site into proper contact with the substrate. The problem facing the chemist is to discover which amino acid residues make up the active site and just what biological function the rest of the molecule performs.

Now that the structure of an enzyme —ribonuclease—is known, one can hope to find its active site and see how that section is related to the rest of the molecule. Workers in a number of laboratories are engaged in the effort and are making good progress. Before considering their results, it is appropriate to look at some of the earlier work on the active sites of enzymes.

A particularly illuminating series of investigations began in a most unlikely fashion with the study of nerve gases. Developed by the Germans during World War II but happily never used, these substances are phosphate esters of various organic alcohols. (An ester is the compound formed by the reaction of an acid and an alcohol.) They are extremely toxic, rapidly causing death by respiratory paralysis when they are inhaled or even absorbed through the skin. Studies of their physiological action showed that they inactivate choline esterase, an enzyme that breaks down acetylcholine in the body. This last substance plays an essential part in regulating the transmission of nerve impulses. When allowed to accumulate in excessive amounts, it deranges the nervous system, destroying its control over the breathing apparatus.

As soon as the relationship between nerve gas intoxication and choline esterase was established, several laboratories set out to discover the nature of the reaction between the two substances. It was quickly discovered that one molecule of nerve gas combined with one molecule of choline esterase to give an inactive product. The next question was: What part of the large protein molecule is involved? This could not be answered directly because the choline esterase molecule is too large to be studied in detail by the methods available. Besides, it has not been isolated in sufficient amounts. Irwin B. Wilson and David Nachmansohn of the Columbia University College of Physicians and Surgeons approached the problem from the other side; they determined how the reaction

between the enzyme and the nerve gas or other inhibitors was influenced by the exact chemical structure of the much smaller organic phosphate molecules. They could then deduce many properties of the enzyme surface. As a result of these investigations a compound was devised that could displace the nerve gas from its combination with choline esterase and so reactivate the enzyme.

Then came an important observation. A. K. Balls and E. F. Jansen of Purdue University found that an organic phosphate called DFP (for diisopropylphosphorofluoridate) also inhibits the enzyme chymotrypsin. This protein was available in large quantities and it had already been extensively studied. On examination of the reaction with DFP, Balls and Jansen found that again one molecule of phosphate combined with one enzyme molecule. Subsequently the point of attachment was identified as a specific serine residue in the enzyme molecule.

There must be something special about this particular serine residue: DFP does not react with the free amino acid serine. No more than one molecule of DFP combines with each molecule of chymotrypsin in spite of the fact that the enzyme has 25 serine residues. And any treatment that destroys the enzymatic activity of chymotrypsin, even temporarily, also destroys its ability to react with DFP. Concluding from this evidence that the reactive serine is part of the active site of the enzyme, several groups of chemists have investigated the sequence of amino acids around it. They labeled the serine with DFP containing radioactive phosphorus and then broke down the inactivated chymotrypsin with other enzymes. From the mixture of fragments a peptide containing the labeled serine was isolated. The serine residue proved to be flanked by an aspartic acid residue on one side and a glycine residue on the other.

Meanwhile several other enzymes had been found to be sensitive to DFP. In all of them the inactivation proved to involve a reaction with a single serine residue. Analysis disclosed that in two of the enzymes the serine had the same neighbors as in chymotrypsin. In two others the sequence proved to be glutamic acid followed by serine and alanine. The two arrangements are in fact much alike because glutamic acid and aspartic acid are closely related chemically, as are glycine and alanine.

Finding the same type of sequence in so many enzymes strikingly confirms a major tenet of biochemistry: a similarity

in function must reflect a similarity in structure. But this cannot be the whole story. Although the enzymes are alike in some respects, they are not identical. They do not all catalyze exactly the same reactions and so their active sites must differ in some ways. Of course the sequence aspartic acid, serine and glycine is not by itself biochemically active, nor are the larger peptide fragments that contain it. The serine in them does not react with DFP. Additional residues are required, but which ones, and how they are oriented in space with respect to the active serine, is still largely unknown.

There is persuasive evidence that the active site of these enzymes also includes a histidine residue. Yet in two of the enzyme molecules quite a number of residues on each side of the crucial trio have been identified, and histidine is not among them. If histidine does form part of the active site and is near the active serine, it must be brought there by a folding of the chain. Although still hypothetical, the idea that the amino acid units in an active site are brought into juxtaposition from different sections of a peptide chain by three-dimensional coiling is attractive. Among other things, this hypothesis explains why disrupting only the three-dimensional structure of an enzyme leads to loss of activity. The picture will become much clearer when the complete structures of the DFP-sensitive enzymes are worked out.

Ribonuclease is not sensitive to DFP, but it too can be inactivated by a specific chemical reaction involving a particular amino acid residue. The inactivating agent is either iodoacetic acid or bromoacetic acid, and it combines with a histidine residue. Two investigators in England, E. A. Barnard and W. D. Stein, have obtained evidence that the histidine residue concerned is the one at position 119, six residues from the carboxyl end of the ribonuclease chain. Neither reagent reacts with any of the other three histidines in the molecule. Unfolding the chain or otherwise destroying the activity of ribonuclease prevents the reaction with this residue. Thus the histidine residue at position 119 seems almost surely a part of the active site of ribonuclease. Other studies implicate the aspartic acid at position 121 (removing it together with the last three residues inactivates the molecule, whereas splitting off the last three alone does not) and perhaps also the lysine at position 41.

Some remarkable experiments by F. M. Richards at Yale University have provided much information about the relationship between the activity of the enzyme and its over-all structure. Using a bacterial enzyme called subtilisin, Richards succeeded in splitting the ribonuclease molecule at a single point—the bond between the alanine at position 20 and the serine at position 21. Although the peptide link had been broken, the two fragments did not separate from each other nor did the combination lose enzymatic activity. Treatment with mild acid, however, separated the altered ribonuclease into two parts, one a peptide of 20 residues, the other a large fragment of 104 residues. Neither fragment by itself exhibited activity. But when dissolved together in a neutral solution they recombined instantly, and enzymatic activity was regained. The peptide bond did not re-form under these gentle conditions. Instead the two fragments were held together by so-called

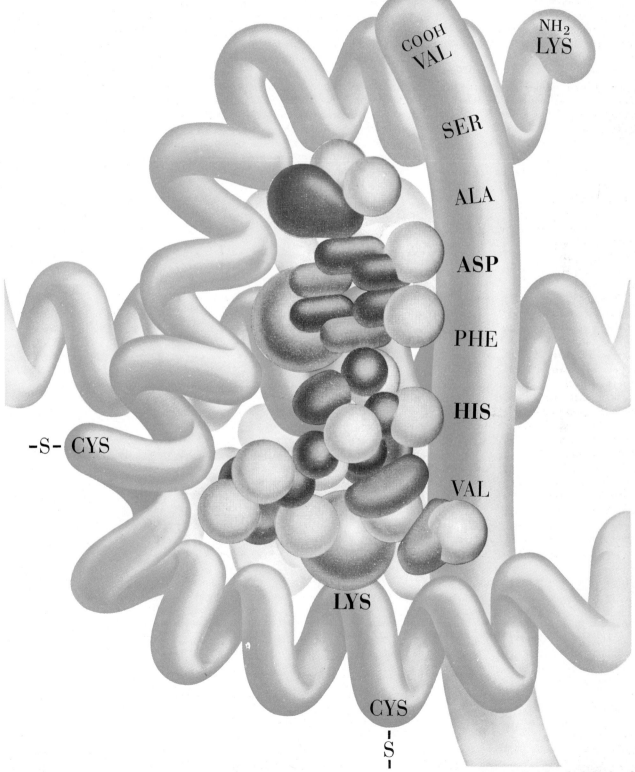

ACTIVE SITE of ribonuclease is represented in this strictly hypothetical conception. A small molecule on which the enzyme acts is shown in gray, nested in a form-fitting cavity on the enzyme surface. Peptide chain, some of which is believed to be helical and some not, is shown in color. Some of the amino acid residues thought to form part of the active site are shown in bold type.

secondary forces, probably analogous to those that unite enzymes and their substrates. The simplest explanation, though not the only one, for these results is that activity depends on the juxtaposition of one or more amino acid residues from among the first 20 with one or more in the rest of the molecule.

This brief account of the research on active sites by no means exhausts the work being done on ribonuclease, nor does it exhaust the list of enzymes under investigation. To mention another, the protein-digesting enzyme papain (found in the papaya) has been studied for years at the University of Utah School of Medicine by Emil L. Smith and his colleagues. They have gone far toward determining its structure and have, in addition, made the striking observation that more than 100 amino acid residues of the 185 in the native enzyme can be whittled away without abolishing its activity. The structures of trypsin and chymotrypsin are also being energetically studied, particularly by Hans Neurath and his associates at the University of Washington.

As structural chemistry advances, answers to a number of other fascinating biological problems begin to appear. One can study the differences among analogous protein molecules produced by different species. Sanger is the pioneer in this field, with his studies of the structure of the insulin produced by the cow, the pig and the sheep. Also of great interest are the differences in protein molecules produced by members of the same species under the influence of genetic mutation. In this area a good deal has already been learned about abnormal hemoglobins, and much more will be known when the complete structure of the hemoglobin molecule has been worked out.

Finally, the recent elucidation of the complete amino acid sequence in the protein of tobacco mosaic virus opens the way to a deeper understanding of the natural synthesis of proteins. The virus consists of protein and ribonucleic acid. According to present theory, the protein is synthesized by infected tobacco-plant cells under the direction of the viral nucleic acid. Now it may be possible to follow this process in detail.

The next few years of research on proteins should be exciting ones, both for chemists and biologists.

4

The Insulin Molecule

E. O. P. THOMPSON

May 1955

Proteins, the keystone of life, are the most complex substances known to man, and their chemistry is one of the great challenges in modern science. For more than a century chemists and biochemists have labored to try to learn their composition and solve their labyrinthine structure [see "Proteins," by Joseph S. Fruton, which is available as Offprint #10]. In the history of protein chemistry the year 1954 will go down as a landmark, for last year a group of investigators finally succeeded in achieving the first complete description of the structure of a protein molecule. The protein is insulin, the pancreatic hormone which governs sugar metabolism in the body.

Having learned the architecture of the insulin molecule, biochemists can now go on to attempt to synthesize it and to investigate the secret of the chemical activity of this vital hormone, so important in the treatment of diabetes. Furthermore, the success with insulin has paved the way toward unraveling the structure of other proteins with the same techniques, and work on some of them has already begun.

The insulin achievement was due largely to the efforts of the English biochemist Frederick Sanger and a small group of workers at Cambridge University. Sanger had spent 10 years of intensive study on this single molecule. When he commenced his investigation of protein structure in 1944, he chose insulin for several reasons. Firstly, it was one of the very few proteins available in reasonably pure form. Secondly, chemists had worked out a good estimate of its atomic composition (its relative numbers of carbon, hydrogen, nitrogen, oxygen and sulfur atoms). Thirdly, it appeared that the key to insulin's activity as a hormone lay in its

structure, for it contained no special components that might explain its specific behavior.

Insulin is one of the smallest proteins. Yet its formula is sufficiently formidable. The molecule of beef insulin (from cattle) is made up of 777 atoms, in the proportions 254 carbon, 377 hydrogen, 65 nitrogen, 75 oxygen and 6 sulfur. Certain general features of the organization of a protein molecule have been known for a long time, thanks to the pioneering work of the German chemist Emil Fischer and others. The atoms form building units called amino acids, which in turn are strung together in long chains to compose the molecule. Of the 24 amino acids, 17 are present in insulin. The total number of amino acid units in the molecule is 51.

Sanger's task was not only to discover the over-all chain configuration of the insulin molecule but also to learn the sequence of all the amino acids in the chains. The sequence is crucial: a change in the order of amino acids

changes the nature of the protein. The number of possible arrangements of the amino acids of course is almost infinite. One can get some notion of the complexity of the protein puzzle by remembering that the entire English language is derived from just 26 letters (two more than the number of amino acids) combined in various numbers and sequences.

Sanger followed the time-honored method used by chemists to investigate large molecules: namely, breaking them down into fragments and then attempting to put the pieces of the puzzle together. A complete breakdown into the amino acid units themselves makes it possible to identify and measure these components. But this gives no clue to how the units are combined and arranged. To investigate the structure a protein chemist shatters the molecule less violently and then examines these larger fragments, consisting of combinations of two, three or more amino acids. The procedure is somewhat like dropping a pile of plates on the floor. The

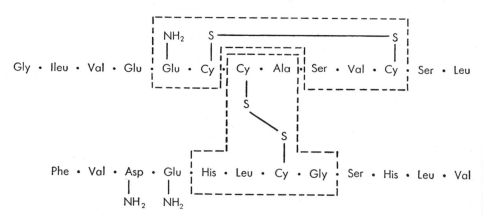

COMPLETE MOLECULE of insulin is depicted in this structural formula. Each amino acid in the molecule is represented by an abbreviation rather than its complete atomic structure. The key to these abbreviations is in the chart on page 37. The molecule consists

first plate may break into 10 pieces; the second plate may also give 10 pieces but with fractures at different places; the next plate may break into only eight fragments, and so on. Since the sample of protein contains billions of molecules, the experiment amounts to dropping billions of plates. The chemist then pores through this awesome debris for recognizable pieces and other pieces that overlap the breaks to show how the broken sections may be combined.

An amino acid consists of an amino group (NH_3^+), a carboxyl group (COO^-) and a side chain attached to a carbon atom. All amino acids have the amino and carboxyl groups and differ only in their side chains. In a protein molecule they are linked by combination of the carboxyl group of one unit with the amino group of the next. In the process of combination two hydrogen atoms and an oxygen atom drop out in the form of a water molecule and the link becomes CO–NH. This linkage is called the peptide bond. Because of loss of the water molecule, the units linked in the chain are called amino acid "residues." A group of linked amino acids is known as a peptide: two units form a dipeptide, three a tripeptide and so on.

When a peptide or protein is hydrolyzed—treated chemically so that the elements of water are introduced at the peptide bonds—it breaks down into amino acids. The treatment consists in heating the peptide with acids or alkalis. To break every peptide bond and reduce a protein to its amino acids it must be heated for 24 hours or more. Less prolonged or drastic treatment, known as partial hydrolysis, yields a mixture of amino acids, peptides and some unbroken protein molecules. This is the plate-breaking process by which the detailed structure of a protein is investigated.

One of the key inventions that enabled Sanger to solve the jigsaw puzzle was a method of labeling the end amino acid in a peptide. Consider a protein fragment, a peptide, which is composed of three amino acids. On hydrolysis it is found to consist of amino acids A, B and C. The question is: What was their sequence in the peptide? The first member of the three-part chain must have had a free (uncombined) amino (NH_3) group. Sanger succeeded in finding a chemical marker which could be attached to this end of the chain and would stay attached to the amino group after the peptide was hydrolyzed. The labeling material is known as DNP (for dinitrophenyl group). It gives the amino acid to which it is attached a distinctive yellow color. The analysis of the tripeptide sequence proceeds as follows. The tripeptide is treated with the labeling material and is then broken down into its three amino acids. The amino acid which occupied the end position, say B, is now identified by its yellow color. The process is repeated with a second sample of the tripeptide, but this time it is only partly hydrolyzed, so that two amino acids remain as a dipeptide derivative colored yellow. If B is partnered with, say, A in this fragment, one knows that the sequence must be BA, and the order in the original tripeptide therefore was BAC.

Another tool that played an indispensable part in the solution of the insulin jigsaw puzzle was the partition chromatography method for separating amino acids and peptides, invented by the British chemists A. J. P. Martin and R. L. M. Synge [see "Chromatography," by William H. Stein and Stanford Moore; this is available as Offprint #81]. Obviously Sanger's method of analysis required separation and identification of extremely small amounts of material. With paper chromatography, which isolates peptides or amino acids in spots on a piece of filter paper, it is possible to analyze a mixture of as little as a millionth of a gram of material with considerable accuracy in a matter of days. As many as 40 different peptides can be separated on a single sheet.

With the knowledge that the insulin molecule was made up of 51 amino acid units, Sanger began his attack on its structure by investigating whether the units were strung in a single long chain or formed more than one chain. Among the components of insulin were three molecules of the amino acid cystine. The cystine molecule is unusual in that it has an amino and a carboxyl group at each end [see its formula in table on page 37]. Since such a molecule could cross-link chains, its presence in insulin suggested that the protein might consist of more than one chain. Sanger succeeded in proving that there were indeed two chains, which he was able to separate intact by splitting the sulfur links in the cystine molecule. Using the DNP labeling technique, he also showed that one chain began with the amino acid glycine and the other with phenylalanine.

Sanger proceeded to break each chain into fragments and study the pieces —especially overlaps which would permit him to build up a sequence. Concentrating on the beginning of the glycine chain, Sanger labeled the glycine with DNP and examined the peptide fragments produced by partial hydrolysis. In the debris of the broken glycine chains he found these sequences attached to the labeled glycine molecules: glycine-isoleucine; glycine-isoleucine-

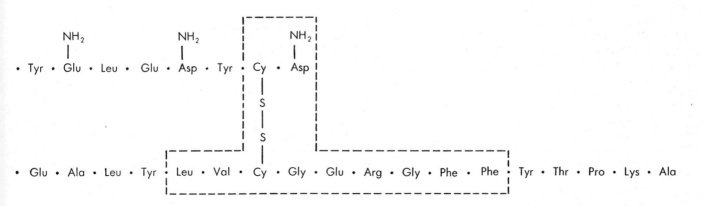

of 51 amino acid units in two chains. One chain (top) has 21 amino acid units; it is called the glycyl chain because it begins with glycine (Gly). The other chain (bottom) has 30 amino acid units; it is called the phenylalanyl chain because it begins with phenylalanine (Phe). The chains are joined by sulfur atoms (S-S). The dotted lines indicate the fragments which located the bridges.

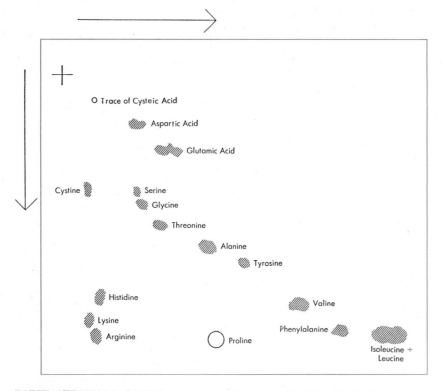

PAPER CHROMATOGRAPHY separates the 17 amino acids of insulin. In the chromatogram represented by this diagram insulin was broken down by hydrolysis and a sample of the mixture placed at the upper left on the sheet of paper. The sheet was hung from a trough filled with solvent which carried each amino acid a characteristic distance down the paper. The sheet was then turned 90 degrees and the process repeated. The amino acids, with the exception of proline, appear as purple spots when sprayed with ninhydrin.

still left several gaps in the chain. Sanger and Tuppy now resorted to another method to find the missing links. They split the phenylalanine chain with enzymes instead of by acid hydrolysis. The enzyme splitting process yields longer fragments, and it leaves intact certain bonds that are sensitive to breakage by acid treatment. Thus the investigators obtained long chain fragments which bridged the gaps and revealed the missing links.

After about a year of intensive work Sanger and Tuppy were able to assemble the pieces and describe the structure of insulin's phenylalanine chain. Sanger then turned to the glycine chain and spent another year working out its structure, with the assistance of the author of this article. The glycine chain is shorter (21 amino acids) but it provided fewer clues: there were fewer key pieces that occurred only once, and two amino acids (glutamic acid and cystine) cropped up in so many of the fragments that it was difficult to place them unequivocally in the sequence.

One detail that remained to be decided before the structure could be completed was the actual composition of two amino acids in the chain. Certain amino acids may occur in two forms: e.g., glutamic acid and glutamine. Glutamic acid has two carboxyl (COO^-) groups, whereas glutamine has an amide ($CONH_2$) group in the place of one of the carboxyls [see opposite page]. The difference gives them completely different properties in the protein. Similarly there are aspartic acid and asparagine. Now acid hydrolysis changes glutamine to glutamic acid and asparagine to aspartic acid. Consequently after acid hydrolysis of a protein one cannot tell which form these amino acids had in the original chain. The question was resolved by indirect investigations, one of which involved comparing the products obtained when the same peptide was broken down by acid hydrolysis and by enzymes which do not destroy the amide groups.

By the end of 1952 the two chains were completely assembled. There remained only the problem of determining how the two chains were linked together to form the insulin molecule. But this was easier said than done. As so often happens, what looked simple in theory had complications in practice.

The bridges between the chains, as we have noted, must be cystine, because this amino acid has symmetrical bonds at both ends. The fact that insulin

valine; glycine-isoleucine-valine–glutamic acid; glycine-isoleucine-valine–glutamic acid–glutamic acid. Thus it was evident that the first five amino acids in the glycine chain were glycine, isoleucine, valine and two glutamic acids. Similar experiments on the phenylalanine chain established the first four amino acids in that sequence: phenylalanine, valine, aspartic acid and glutamic acid.

Sanger and a colleague, Hans Tuppy, then undertook the immense task of analyzing the structure of the entire phenylalanine chain. It meant breaking down the chain by partial hydrolysis, separating and identifying the many fragments and then attempting to put the pieces of the puzzle together in proper order. The chain, made up of 30 amino acids, was by far the most complex polypeptide on which such an analysis had ever been attempted.

The bewildering mixture of products from partial breakdown of the chain—amino acids, dipeptides, tripeptides, tetrapeptides and so on—was much too complicated to be sorted out solely by chromatography. Sanger and Tuppy first employed other separation methods (electrophoresis and adsorption on

charcoal and ion-exchange resins) which divided the peptide fragments into groups. Then they analyzed these simpler mixtures by paper chromatography. They succeeded in isolating from the fractured chain 22 dipeptides, 14 tripeptides and 12 longer fragments [see chart on pages 38 and 39]. Although these were obtained only in microscopic amounts, they were identified by special techniques and the sequences of their amino acids were determined.

These were the jigsaw pieces that had to be reassembled. Just as in a jigsaw puzzle there are key pieces around which the picture grows, so in this case there were some key pieces as starting points. For instance, the chain was known to contain just one aspartic acid. Six peptides with this amino acid were found in the debris from partial breakdown of the chain [see chart]. The aspartic acid was attached to from one to four other amino acids in these pieces. Their sequences showed that in the original make-up of the chain the order must have been phenylalanine-valine–aspartic acid–glutamic acid–histidine.

Other sequences were pieced together in a similar way until five long sections of the chain were reconstructed. But this

FORMULA	NAME	ABBREVIATION	PHENYLALANYL	GLYCYL
$CH_2(NH_3^+) \cdot COO^-$	Glycine	Gly	3	1
$CH_3-CH(NH_3 \cdot COO^-$	Alanine	Ala	2	1
$CH_2OH-CH(NH_3^+) \cdot COO^-$	Serine	Ser	1	2
$CH_3 \cdot CHOH-CH(NH_3^+) \cdot COO^-$	Threonine	Thr	1	0
$\begin{array}{c}CH_3 \\ \searrow CH-CH(NH_3^+) \cdot COO^- \\ CH_3\end{array}$	Valine	Val	3	2
$\begin{array}{c}CH_3 \\ \searrow CH \cdot CH_2-CH(NH_3^+) \cdot COO^- \\ CH_3\end{array}$	Leucine	Leu	4	2
$\begin{array}{c}CH_3 \cdot CH_2 \\ \searrow CH-CH(NH_3^+) \cdot COO^- \\ CH_3\end{array}$	Isoleucine	Ileu	0	1
$\begin{array}{c}CH_2-CH_2 \\ | \qquad | \\ CH_2 \quad CH-COO^- \\ \searrow NH^+ \end{array}$	Proline	Pro	1	0
$\begin{array}{c}CH=CH \\ CH \qquad\quad C \cdot CH_2-CH(NH_3^+) \cdot COO^- \\ CH-CH\end{array}$	Phenylalanine	Phe	3	0
$\begin{array}{c}CH=CH \\ HO-C \qquad\quad C \cdot CH_2-CH(NH_3^+) \cdot COO^- \\ CH-CH\end{array}$	Tyrosine	Tyr	2	2
$NH_2CO \cdot CH_2-CH(NH_3^+) \cdot COO^-$	Asparagine	Asp (NH$_2$)	1	2
$COOH \cdot CH_2 \cdot CH_2-CH(NH_3^+) \cdot COO^-$	Glutamic Acid	Glu	2	2
$NH_2 \cdot CO \cdot CH_2 \cdot CH_2-CH(NH_3^+) \cdot COO^-$	Glutamine	Glu (NH$_2$)	1	2
$\begin{array}{c}NH_2-C-NH \cdot CH_2 \cdot CH_2 \cdot CH_2-CH(NH_3^+) \cdot COO^- \\ || \\ NH\end{array}$	Arginine	Arg	1	0
$\begin{array}{c}CH=C \cdot CH_2-CH(NH_3^+) \cdot COO^- \\ | \qquad | \\ NH \quad N \\ \searrow\!\!\diagup \\ CH\end{array}$	Histidine	His	2	0
$CH_2NH_2 \cdot CH_2 \cdot CH_2 \cdot CH_2-CH(NH_3^+) \cdot COO^-$	Lysine	Lys	1	0
$\begin{array}{c}COO^- \qquad\qquad\qquad\qquad COO^- \\ \searrow CH-CH_2-S-S-CH_2-CH\diagup \\ NH_3^+ \qquad\qquad\qquad\qquad NH_3^+\end{array}$	Cystine	CyS | CyS	2	4
			30	21

AMINO ACIDS of insulin are listed in this chart. Their chemical formulas are at the left. The dots in the formulas represent chemical bonds other than those suggested by the atoms adjacent to each other. The number of amino acid units of each kind found in the phenylalanyl chain are listed in the fourth column of the chart. The fifth column comprises a similar listing for the glycyl chain.

	Phe	Val	Asp	Glu	His	Leu	CySO₃H	Gly	Ser	His	Leu	Val	Glu	Ala	Leu	Tyr
PEPTIDES FROM ACID HYDROLYZATES	Phe •	Val		Glu •	His		CySO₃H •	Gly		His •	Leu		Glu •	Ala		
		Val •	Asp		His •	Leu					Leu •	Val		Ala •	Leu	
			Asp •	Glu		Leu •	CySO₃H		Ser •	His		Val •	Glu			
	Phe •	Val •	Asp			Leu •	CySO₃H •	Gly				Val •	Glu •	Ala		Tyr
				Glu •	His •	Leu			Ser •	His •	Leu					
		Val •	Asp •	Glu							Leu •	Val •	Glu			
					His •	Leu •	CySO₃H							Ala •	Leu •	Tyr
	Phe •	Val •	Asp •	Glu					Ser •	His •	Leu •	Val				Tyr
					His •	Leu •	CySO₃H •	Gly			Leu •	Val •	Glu •	Ala		
	Phe •	Val •	Asp •	Glu •	His				Ser •	His •	Leu •	Val •	Glu			
				Glu •	His •	Leu •	CySO₃H			His •	Leu •	Val •	Glu			
									Ser •	His •	Leu •	Val •	Glu •	Ala		
SEQUENCES DEDUCED FROM THE ABOVE PEPTIDES	Phe •	Val •	Asp •	Glu •	His •	Leu •	CySO₃H •	Gly								Tyr
									Ser •	His •	Leu •	Val •	Glu •	Ala		
PEPTIDES FROM PEPSIN HYDROLYZATE	Phe •	Val •	Asp •	Glu •	His •	Leu •	CySO₃H •	Gly •	Ser •	His •	Leu					
			NH₂	NH₂												
												Val •	Glu •	Ala •	Leu	
					His •	Leu •	CySO₃H •	Gly •	Ser •	His •	Leu					
PEPTIDES FROM CHYMOTRYPSIN HYDROLYZATE	Phe •	Val •	Asp •	Glu •	His •	Leu •	CySO₃H •	Gly •	Ser •	His •	Leu •	Val •	Glu •	Ala •	Leu •	Tyr
			NH₂	NH₂												
PEPTIDES FROM TRYPSIN HYDROLYZATE																
STRUCTURE OF PHENYLALANYL CHAIN OF OXIDIZED INSULIN	Phe •	Val •	Asp •	Glu •	His •	Leu •	CySO₃H •	Gly •	Ser •	His •	Leu •	Val •	Glu •	Ala •	Leu •	Tyr
			NH₂	NH₂												

Asp and Glu positions carry NH_2 groups.

STRUCTURE OF GLYCYL CHAIN OF OXIDIZED INSULIN

Gly • Ileu • Val • Glu • Glu • CySO₃H • CySO₃H • Ala • Ser • Val • CySO₃H • Ser • Leu • Tyr •

(with NH_2 below the second Glu)

SEQUENCE OF AMINO ACIDS in the phenylalanyl chain was deduced from fragments of the chain. The entire sequence is at the bottom above the dotted line. Each fragment is indicated by a horizontal sequence of amino acids joined by dots. The fragments are arranged so that each of their amino acids is in the vertical column above the corresponding amino acid in the entire chain.

THOMPSON · THE INSULIN MOLECULE   39

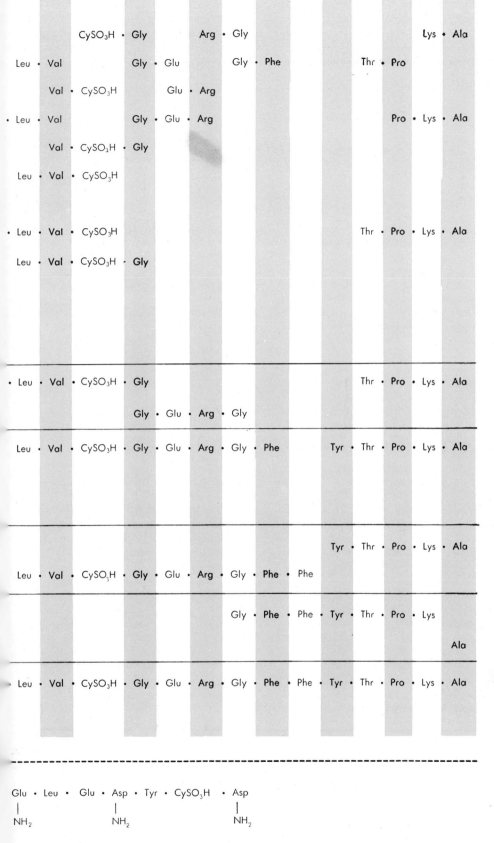

The shorter fragments (*group at the top*) were obtained by hydrolyzing insulin with acid. The longer fragments (*groups third, fourth and fifth from the top*) were obtained with enzymes. The same method was used to deduce the sequence in the glycyl chain (*bottom*).

contains three cystine units suggested that there might be three bridges, or cross-links, between the chains. It appeared that it should be a simple matter to locate the positions of the bridges by a partial breakdown of the insulin molecule which gave cystine-containing fragments with sections of the two chains still attached to the "bridge" ends.

When Sanger began this analysis, he was puzzled to find that the cystine-containing peptides in his broken-down mixtures showed no significant pattern whatever. Cystine was joined with other amino acids in many different combinations and arrangements, as if the chains were cross-linked in every conceivable way. Sanger soon discovered the explanation: during acid hydrolysis of the insulin molecule, cystine's sulfur bonds opened and all sorts of rearrangements took place within the peptides. Sanger and his associate A. P. Ryle then made a systematic study of these reactions and succeeded in finding chemical inhibitors to prevent them.

By complex analyses which employed both acid hydrolysis and enzyme breakdown, Sanger and his co-workers L. F. Smith and Ruth Kitai eventually fitted the bridges into their proper places and obtained a complete picture of the structure of insulin [*see diagram at bottom of pages 34 and 35*]. So for the first time the biochemist is able to look at the amino-acid arrangement in a protein molecule. The achievement seems astounding to those who were working in the field 10 years ago.

To learn how insulin's structure determines its activity as a hormone is still a long, hard road. It will be difficult to synthesize the molecule, but once that has been accomplished, it will be possible to test the effect of changes in the structure on the substance's physiological behavior. Evidently slight variations do not affect it much, for Sanger has shown that the insulins from pigs, sheep and steers, all equally potent, differ slightly in structure.

The methods that proved so successful with insulin, plus some newer ones, are already being applied to study larger proteins. Among the improvements are promising new techniques for splitting off the amino acids from a peptide chain one at a time—clearly a more efficient procedure than random hydrolysis. The rate of progress undoubtedly will be speeded up as more biochemists turn their attention to the intriguing problem of relating the structure of proteins to their physiological functions.

5

The Hemoglobin Molecule

M. F. PERUTZ

November 1964

In 1937, a year after I entered the University of Cambridge as a graduate student, I chose the X-ray analysis of hemoglobin, the oxygen-bearing protein of the blood, as the subject of my research. Fortunately the examiners of my doctoral thesis did not insist on a determination of the structure, otherwise I should have had to remain a graduate student for 23 years. In fact, the complete solution of the problem, down to the location of each atom in this giant molecule, is still outstanding, but the structure has now been mapped in enough detail to reveal the intricate three-dimensional folding of each of its four component chains of amino acid units, and the positions of the four pigment groups that carry the oxygen-combining sites.

The folding of the four chains in hemoglobin turns out to be closely similar to that of the single chain of myoglobin, an oxygen-bearing protein in muscle whose structure has been elucidated in atomic detail by my colleague John C. Kendrew and his collaborators. Correlation of the structure of the two proteins allows us to specify quite accurately, by purely physical methods, where each amino acid unit in hemoglobin lies with respect to the twists and turns of its chains.

Physical methods alone, however, do not yet permit us to decide which of the 20 different kinds of amino acid units occupies any particular site. This knowledge has been supplied by chemical analysis; workers in the U.S. and in Germany have determined the sequence of the 140-odd amino acid units along each of the hemoglobin chains. The combined results of the two different methods of approach now provide an accurate picture of many facets of the hemoglobin molecule.

In its behavior hemoglobin does not resemble an oxygen tank so much as a molecular lung. Two of its four chains shift back and forth, so that the gap between them becomes narrower when oxygen molecules are bound to the hemoglobin, and wider when the oxygen is released. Evidence that the chemical activities of hemoglobin and other proteins are accompanied by structural changes had been discovered before, but this is the first time that the nature of such a change has been directly demonstrated. Hemoglobin's change of shape makes me think of it as a breathing molecule, but paradoxically it expands, not when oxygen is taken up but when it is released.

When I began my postgraduate work in 1936 I was influenced by three inspiring teachers. Sir Frederick Gowland Hopkins, who had received a Nobel prize in 1929 for discovering the growth-stimulating effect of vitamins, drew our attention to the central role played by enzymes in catalyzing chemical reactions in the living cell. The few enzymes isolated at that time had all proved to be proteins. David Keilin, the discoverer of several of the enzymes that catalyze the processes of respiration, told us how the chemical affinities and catalytic properties of iron atoms were altered when the iron combined with different proteins. J. D. Bernal, the X-ray crystallographer, was my research supervisor. He and Dorothy Crowfoot Hodgkin had taken the first X-ray diffraction pictures of crystals of protein a year or two before I arrived, and they had discovered that protein molecules, in spite of their large size, have highly ordered structures. The wealth of sharp X-ray diffraction spots produced by a single crystal of an enzyme such as pepsin could be explained only if every one, or almost every one, of the 5,000 atoms in the pepsin molecule occupied a definite position that was repeated in every one of the myriad of pepsin molecules packed in the crystal. The notion is commonplace now, but it caused a sensation at a time when proteins were still widely regarded as "colloids" of indefinite structure.

In the late 1930's the importance of the nucleic acids had yet to be discovered; according to everything I had learned the "secret of life" appeared to be concealed in the structure of proteins. Of all the methods available in chemistry and physics, X-ray crystallography seemed to offer the only chance, albeit an extremely remote one, of determining that structure.

The number of crystalline proteins then available was probably not more than a dozen, and hemoglobin was an obvious candidate for study because of its supreme physiological importance, its ample supply and the ease with which it could be crystallized. All the same, when I chose the X-ray analysis of hemoglobin as the subject of my Ph.D. thesis, my fellow students regarded me with a pitying smile. The most complex organic substance whose structure had yet been determined by X-ray analysis was the molecule of the dye phthalocyanin, which contains 58 atoms. How could I hope to locate the thousands of atoms in the molecule of hemoglobin?

The Function of Hemoglobin

Hemoglobin is the main component of the red blood cells, which carry oxygen from the lungs through the arteries to the tissues and help to carry carbon dioxide through the veins back to the lungs. A single red blood cell contains about 280 million molecules of hemoglobin. Each molecule has 64,500 times the weight of a hydrogen atom and is made up of about 10,000 atoms of hydrogen, carbon, nitrogen, oxygen and sulfur, plus four atoms of iron, which are more important than all the rest. Each iron atom lies at the center of the group of atoms that form the pigment called heme, which gives blood its red color and its ability to combine with oxygen. Each heme group is enfolded in one of the four chains of amino acid units that collectively constitute the protein part of the molecule, which is called globin. The four chains of globin consist of two identical pairs. The members of one pair are known as alpha chains and those of the other as beta chains. Together the four chains contain a total of 574 amino acid units.

In the absence of an oxygen carrier a liter of arterial blood at body temperature could dissolve and transport no more than three milliliters of oxygen. The presence of hemoglobin increases this quantity 70 times. Without hemoglobin large animals could not get enough oxygen to exist. Similarly, hemoglobin is responsible for carrying more than 90 percent of the carbon dioxide transported by venous blood.

Each of the four atoms of iron in the hemoglobin molecule can take up one molecule (two atoms) of oxygen. The reaction is reversible in the sense that oxygen is taken up where it is plentiful, as in the lungs, and released where it is scarce, as in the tissues. The reaction is accompanied by a change in color: hemoglobin containing oxygen, known as oxyhemoglobin, makes arterial blood look scarlet; reduced, or oxygen-free, hemoglobin makes venous blood look purple. The term "reduced" for the oxygen-free form is really a misnomer because "reduced" means to the chemist that electrons have been added to an atom or a group of atoms. Actually, as James B. Conant of Harvard University demonstrated in 1923, the iron atoms in both reduced hemoglobin and oxyhemoglobin are in the same electronic condition: the divalent, or ferrous, state. They become oxidized to the trivalent, or ferric, state if hemoglobin is treated with a ferricyanide or removed from the red cells and exposed to the air for a considerable time; oxidation also occurs in certain blood diseases. Under these conditions hemoglobin turns brown and is known as methemoglobin, or ferrihemoglobin.

Ferrous iron acquires its capacity for binding molecular oxygen only through its combination with heme and globin. Heme alone will not bind oxygen, but the specific chemical environment of the globin makes the combina-

HEMOGLOBIN MOLECULE, as deduced from X-ray diffraction studies, is shown from above (*top*) and side (*bottom*). The drawings follow the representation scheme used in three-dimensional models built by the author and his co-workers. The irregular blocks represent electron-density patterns at various levels in the hemoglobin molecule. The molecule is built up from four subunits: two identical alpha chains (*light blocks*) and two identical beta chains (*dark blocks*). The letter "N" in the top view identifies the amino ends of the two alpha chains; the letter "C" identifies the carboxyl ends. Each chain enfolds a heme group (*colored disk*), the iron-containing structure that binds oxygen to the molecule.

X-RAY DIFFRACTION PATTERN was made from a single crystal of hemoglobin that was rotated during the photographic exposure. Electrons grouped around the centers of the atoms in the crystal scatter the incident X rays, producing a symmetrical array of spots. Spots that are equidistant from the center and opposite each other have the same density.

ing. To preserve this order during X-ray analysis crystals are mounted wet in small glass capillaries. A single crystal is then illuminated by a narrow beam of X rays that are essentially all of one wavelength. If the crystal is kept stationary, a photographic film placed behind it will often exhibit a pattern of spots lying on ellipses, but if the crystal is rotated in certain ways, the spots can be made to appear at the corners of a regular lattice that is related to the arrangement of the molecules in the crystal [see illustration at left]. Moreover, each spot has a characteristic intensity that is determined in part by the arrangement of atoms inside the molecules. The reason for the different intensities is best explained in the words of W. L. Bragg, who founded X-ray analysis in 1913—the year after Max von Laue had discovered that X rays are diffracted by crystals—and who later succeeded Lord Rutherford as Cavendish Professor of Physics at Cambridge:

"It is well known that the form of the lines ruled on a [diffraction] grating has an influence on the relative intensity of the spectra which it yields. Some spectra may be enhanced, or reduced, in intensity as compared with others. Indeed, gratings are sometimes ruled in such a way that most of the energy is thrown into those spectra which it is most desirable to examine. The form of the line on the grating does not influence the positions of the spectra, which depend on the number of lines to the centimetre, but the individual lines scatter more light in some directions than others, and this enhances the spectra which lie in those directions.

"The structure of the group of atoms which composes the unit of the crystal grating influences the strength of the various reflexions in exactly the same way. The rays are diffracted by the electrons grouped around the centre of each atom. In some directions the atoms conspire to give a strong scattered beam, in others their effects almost annul each other by interference. The exact arrangement of the atoms is to be deduced by comparing the strength of the reflexions from different faces and in different orders."

Thus there should be a way of reversing the process of diffraction, of proceeding backward from the diffraction pattern to an image of the arrangement of atoms in the crystal. Such an image can actually be produced, somewhat laboriously, as follows. It will be noted that spots on opposite sides of the center of an X-ray picture have the same

tion possible. In association with other proteins, such as those of the enzymes peroxidase and catalase, the same heme group can exhibit quite different chemical characteristics.

The function of the globin, however, goes further. It enables the four iron atoms within each molecule to interact in a physiologically advantageous manner. The combination of any three of the iron atoms with oxygen accelerates the combination with oxygen of the fourth; similarly, the release of oxygen by three of the iron atoms makes the fourth cast off its oxygen faster. By tending to make each hemoglobin molecule carry either four molecules of oxygen or none, this interaction ensures efficient oxygen transport.

I have mentioned that hemoglobin also plays an important part in bearing carbon dioxide from the tissues back to the lungs. This gas is not borne by the iron atoms, and only part of it is bound directly to the globin; most of it is taken up by the red cells and the noncellular fluid of the blood in the form of bicarbonate. The transport of bicarbonate is facilitated by the disappearance of

an acid group from hemoglobin for each molecule of oxygen discharged. The reappearance of the acid group when oxygen is taken up again in the lungs sets in motion a series of chemical reactions that leads to the discharge of carbon dioxide. Conversely, the presence of bicarbonate and lactic acid in the tissues accelerates the liberation of oxygen.

Breathing seems so simple, yet it appears as if this elementary manifestation of life owes its existence to the interplay of many kinds of atoms in a giant molecule of vast complexity. Elucidating the structure of the molecule should tell us not only what the molecule looks like but also how it works.

The Principles of X-Ray Analysis

The X-ray study of proteins is sometimes regarded as an abstruse subject comprehensible only to specialists, but the basic ideas underlying our work are so simple that some physicists find them boring. Crystals of hemoglobin and other proteins contain much water and, like living tissues, they tend to lose their regularly ordered structure on dry-

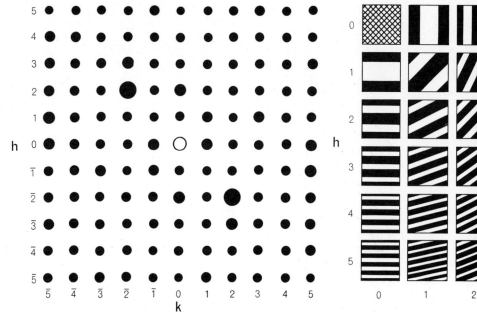

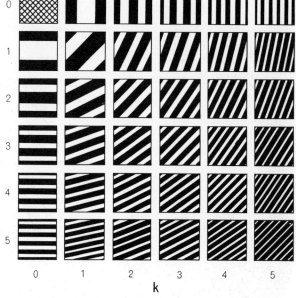

INTERPRETATION OF X-RAY IMAGE can be done with a special optical device to generate a set of diffraction fringes (*right*) from the spots in an X-ray image (*left*). Each pair of symmetrically related spots produces a unique set of fringes. Thus the spots in-

dexed $2,\bar{2}$ and $\bar{2},2$ yield the fringes indexed 2,2. A two-dimensional image of the atomic structure of a crystal can be generated by printing each set of fringes on the same sheet of photographic paper. But the phase problem (*below*) must be solved first.

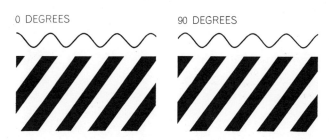

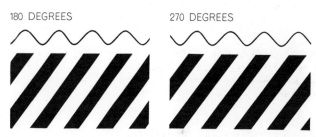

0 DEGREES   90 DEGREES   180 DEGREES   270 DEGREES

PHASE PROBLEM arises because the spots in an X-ray image do not indicate how the fringes are related in phase to an arbitrarily chosen common origin. Here four identical sets of fringes are

related by different phases to the point of origin at the top left corner. The phase marks the distance of the wave crest from the origin, measured in degrees. One wavelength is 360 degrees.

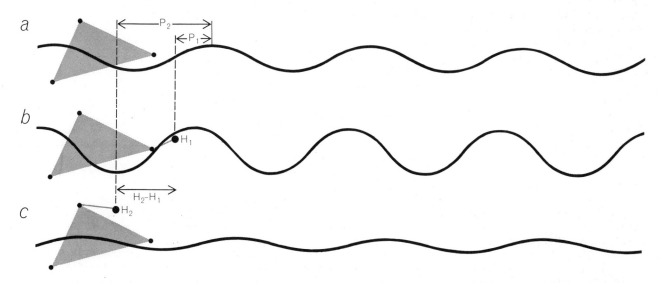

HEAVY-ATOM REPLACEMENT METHOD provides information about phases by changing the intensities of the X-ray diffraction pattern. In *a* a highly oversimplified protein (a triangle of three atoms) scatters a sinusoidal wave that represents the amplitude and phase of a single set of fringes. In *b* and *c*, after heavy atoms H_1

and H_2 are attached to the protein in different positions, the wave is changed in amplitude and phase. The heavy atoms can serve as points of common origin for measuring the magnitude of the phases (P_1 and P_2) of waves scattered by the unaltered protein. The distance between H_1 and H_2 must be accurately known.

degree of intensity. With the aid of a simple optical device each symmetrically related pair of spots can be made to generate a set of diffraction fringes, with an amplitude proportional to the square root of the intensity of the spots. The device, which was invented by Bragg and later developed by H. Lipson and C. A. Taylor at the Manchester College of Science and Technology, consists of a point source of monochromatic light, a pair of plane-convex lenses

and a microscope. The pair of spots in the diffraction pattern is represented by a pair of holes in a black mask that is placed between the two lenses. If the point source is placed at the focus of one of the lenses, the waves of parallel light emerging from the two holes will interfere with one another at the focus of the second lens, and their interference pattern, or diffraction pattern, can be observed or photographed through the microscope.

Imagine that each pair of symmetrically related spots in the X-ray picture is in turn represented by a pair of holes in a mask, and that its diffraction fringes are photographed. Each set of fringes will then be at right angles to the line joining the two holes, and the distance between the fringes will be inversely proportional to the distance between the holes. If the spots are numbered from the center along two mutually perpendicular lines by the indices h and k, the relation between any pair of spots and its corresponding set of fringes would be as shown in the top illustration on the preceding page.

The Phase Problem

An image of the atomic structure of the crystal can be generated by printing each set of fringes in turn on the same sheet of photographic paper, or by superposing all the fringes and making a print of the light transmitted through them. At this point, however, a fatal complication arises. In order to obtain the right image one would have to place each set of fringes correctly with respect to some arbitrarily chosen common origin [*see middle illustration on preceding page*]. At this origin the amplitude of any particular set of fringes may show a crest or trough or some intermediate value. The distance of the wave crest from the origin is called the phase. It is almost true to say that by superposing sets of fringes of given amplitude one can generate an infinite number of different images, depending on the choice of phase for each set of fringes. By itself the X-ray picture tells us only about the amplitudes and nothing about the phases of the fringes to be generated by each pair of spots, which means that half the information needed for the production of the image is missing.

The missing information makes the diffraction pattern of a crystal like a hieroglyphic without a key. Having spent years hopefully measuring the intensities of several thousand spots in the diffraction pattern of hemoglobin, I found myself in the tantalizing position of an explorer with a collection of tablets engraved in an unknown script. For some time Bragg and I tried to develop methods for deciphering the phases, but with only limited success. The solution finally came in 1953, when I discovered that a method that had been developed by crystallographers for solving the phase problem in simpler structures could also be applied to proteins.

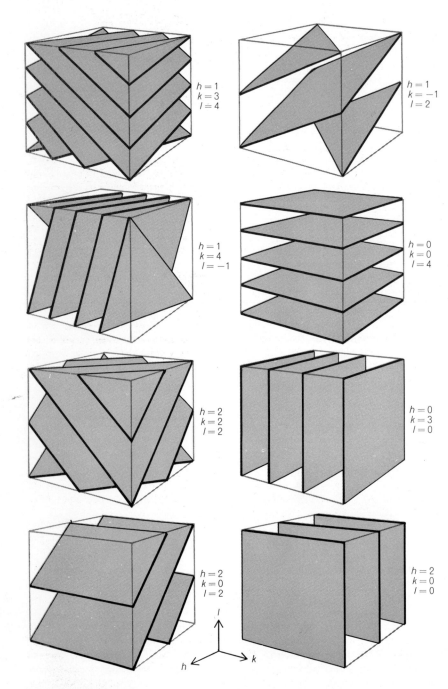

THREE-DIMENSIONAL FRINGES are needed to build up an image of protein molecules. For this purpose many different X-ray diffraction images are prepared and symmetrically related pairs of spots are indexed in three dimensions: h, k and l and $\bar{h}$, $\bar{k}$ and $\bar{l}$. Each pair of spots yields a three-dimensional fringe like those shown here. Fringes from thousands of spots must be superposed in proper phase to build up an image of the molecule.

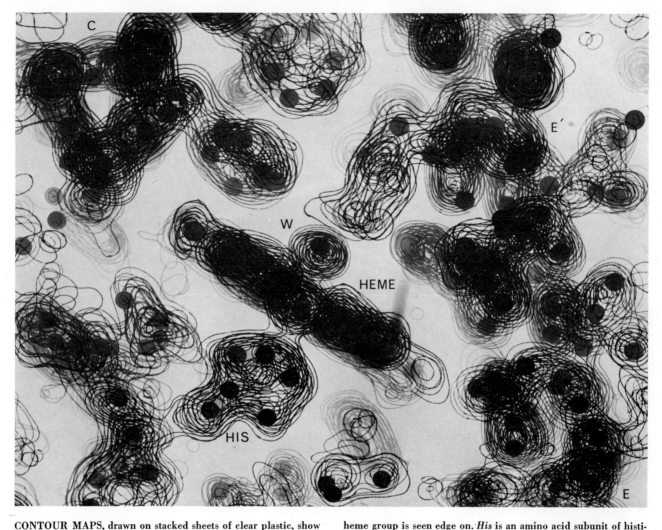

CONTOUR MAPS, drawn on stacked sheets of clear plastic, show a portion of the myoglobin molecule as revealed by superposition of three-dimensional fringe patterns. The maps were made by John C. Kendrew and his associates at the University of Cambridge. Myoglobin is very similar to the beta chain of hemoglobin. The heme group is seen edge on. *His* is an amino acid subunit of histidine that is attached to the iron atom of the heme group. *W* is a water molecule linked to the iron atom. The region between *E* and *E'* represents amino acid subunits arranged in an alpha helix. *C* is an alpha helix seen end on. The black dots mark atomic positions.

In this method the molecule of the compound under study is modified slightly by attaching heavy atoms such as those of mercury to definite positions in its structure. The presence of a heavy atom produces marked changes in the intensities of the diffraction pattern, and this makes it possible to gather information about the phases. From the difference in amplitude in the absence or presence of a heavy atom, the distance of the wave crest from the heavy atom can be determined for each set of fringes. Thus with the heavy atom serving as a common origin the magnitude of the phase can be measured. The bottom illustration on page 43 shows how the phase of a single set of fringes, represented by a sinusoidal wave that is supposedly scattered by the oversimplified protein molecule, can be measured from the increase in amplitude produced by the heavy atom H_1.

Unfortunately this still leaves an am-biguity of sign; the experiment does not tell us whether the phase is to be measured from the heavy atom in the forward or the backward direction. If n is the number of diffracted spots, an ambiguity of sign in each set of fringes would lead to 2^n alternative images of the structure. The Dutch crystallographer J. M. Bijvoet had pointed out some years earlier in another context that the ambiguity could be resolved by examining the diffraction pattern from a second heavy-atom compound.

The bottom illustration on page 43 shows that the heavy atom H_2, which is attached to the protein in a position different from that of H_1, diminishes the amplitude of the wave scattered by the protein. The degree of attenuation allows us to measure the distance of the wave crest from H_2. It can now be seen that the wave crest must be in front of H_1; otherwise its distance from H_1 could not be reconciled with its distance from H_2. The final answer depends on knowing the length and direction of the line joining H_2 to H_1. These quantities are best calculated by a method that does not easily lend itself to exposition in nonmathematical language. It was devised by my colleague Michael G. Rossmann.

The heavy-atom method can be applied to hemoglobin by attaching mercury atoms to the sulfur atoms of the amino acid cysteine. The method works, however, only if this attachment leaves the structure of the hemoglobin molecules and their arrangement in the crystal unaltered. When I first tried it, I was not at all sure that these stringent demands would be fulfilled, and as I developed my first X-ray photograph of mercury hemoglobin my mood alternated between sanguine hopes of immediate success and desperate forebodings of all the possible causes of failure. When the diffraction spots ap-

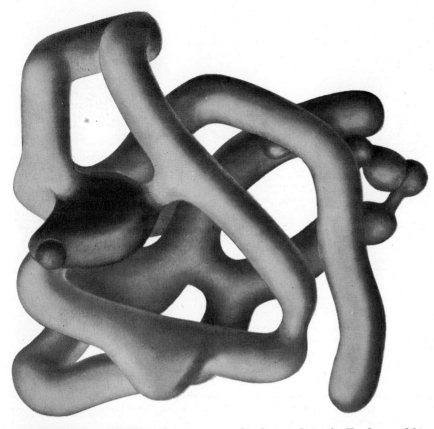

MYOGLOBIN MOLECULE, as first reconstructed at low resolution by Kendrew and his co-workers in 1957, had this rather repulsive visceral appearance. The sausage-like knot marks the path of the amino acid chain of the molecule. The dark disklike shape (here placed at an incorrect angle) is the heme group. A more detailed and more correct view of myoglobin, as seen from the other side, appears at bottom right on the opposite page.

compounds of the protein, each with heavy atoms attached to different positions in the molecule. Then the results have to be corrected by various geometric factors before they are finally used to build up an image through the superposition of tens of thousands of fringes. In the final calculation tens of millions of numbers may have to be added or subtracted. Such a task would have been quite impossible before the advent of high-speed computers, and we have been fortunate in that the development of computers has kept pace with the expanding needs of our X-ray analyses.

While I battled with technical difficulties of various sorts, my colleague John Kendrew successfully applied the heavy-atom method to myoglobin, a protein closely related to hemoglobin [see "The Three-dimensional Structure of a Protein Molecule," by John C. Kendrew; this is available as Offprint #121]. Myoglobin is simpler than hemoglobin because it consists of only one chain of amino acid units and one heme group, which binds a single molecule of oxygen. The complex interaction phenomena involved in hemoglobin's dual function as a carrier of oxygen and of carbon dioxide do not occur in myoglobin, which acts simply as an oxygen store.

Together with Howard M. Dintzis and G. Bodo, Kendrew was brilliantly successful in managing to prepare as many as five different crystalline heavy-atom compounds of myoglobin, which meant that the phases of the diffraction spots could be established very accurately. He also pioneered the use of high-speed computers in X-ray analysis. In 1957 he and his colleagues obtained the first three-dimensional representation of myoglobin [see illustration on this page].

It was a triumph, and yet it brought a tinge of disappointment. Could the search for ultimate truth really have revealed so hideous and visceral-looking an object? Was the nugget of gold a lump of lead? Fortunately, like many other things in nature, myoglobin gains in beauty the closer you look at it. As Kendrew and his colleagues increased the resolution of their X-ray analysis in the years that followed, some of the intrinsic reasons for the molecule's strange shape began to reveal themselves. This shape was found to be not a freak but a fundamental pattern of nature, probably common to myoglobins and hemoglobins throughout the vertebrate kingdom.

In the summer of 1959, nearly 22 years after I had taken the first X-ray

peared in exactly the same position as in the mercury-free protein but with slightly altered intensities, just as I had hoped, I rushed off to Bragg's room in jubilant excitement, expecting that the structure of hemoglobin and of many other proteins would soon be determined. Bragg shared my excitement, and luckily neither of us anticipated the formidable technical difficulties that were to hold us up for another five years.

Resolution of the Image

Having solved the phase problem, at least in principle, we were confronted with the task of building up a structural image from our X-ray data. In simpler structures atomic positions can often be found from representations of the structure projected on two mutually perpendicular planes, but in proteins a three-dimensional image is essential. This can be attained by making use of the three-dimensional nature of the diffraction pattern. The X-ray diffraction pattern on page 42 can be regarded as a section through a sphere that is filled with layer after layer of diffraction

spots. Each pair of spots can be made to generate a set of three-dimensional fringes like the ones shown on page 6. When their phases have been measured, they can be superposed by calculation to build up a three-dimensional image of the protein. The final image is represented by a series of sections through the molecule, rather like a set of microtome sections through a piece of tissue, only on a scale 1,000 times smaller [see illustration on preceding page].

The resolution of the image is roughly equal to the shortest wavelength of the fringes used in building it up. This means that the resolution increases with the number of diffracted spots included in the calculation. If the image is built up from part of the diffraction pattern only, the resolution is impaired.

In the X-ray diffraction patterns of protein crystals the number of spots runs into tens of thousands. In order to determine the phase of each spot accurately, its intensity (or blackness) must be measured accurately several times over: in the diffraction pattern from a crystal of the pure protein and in the patterns from crystals of several

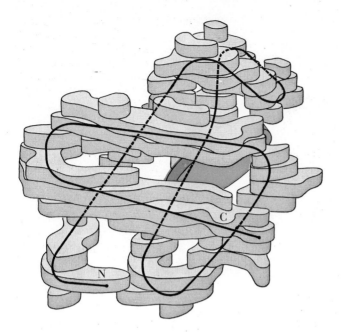

HEMOGLOBIN CHAINS, alpha at left and beta at right, are re-drawn from models built by the author and his colleagues. The superposed lines show the course of the central chain. A heme group (*color*) is partly visible, tucked in the back of each model.

pictures of hemoglobin, its structure emerged at last. Michael Rossmann, Ann F. Cullis, Hilary Muirhead, Tony C. T. North and I were able to prepare a three-dimensional electron-density map of hemoglobin at a resolution of 5.5 angstrom units, about the same as that obtained for the first structure of myoglobin two years earlier. This resolution is sufficient to reveal the shape of the chain forming the backbone of a protein molecule but not to show the position of individual amino acids.

As soon as the numbers printed by the computer had been plotted on contour maps we realized that each of the four chains of hemoglobin had a shape closely resembling that of the single chain of myoglobin. The beta chain and myoglobin look like identical twins, and the alpha chains differ from them merely by a shortcut across one small loop [*see illustration below*].

Kendrew's myoglobin had been extracted from the muscle of the sperm whale; the hemoglobin we used came from the blood of horses. More recent observations indicate that the myoglobins of the seal and the horse, and the hemoglobins of man and cattle, all have the same structure. It seems as though the apparently haphazard and irregular folding of the chain is a pattern specifically devised for holding a heme group in place and for enabling it to carry oxygen.

What is it that makes the chain take up this strange configuration? The extension of Kendrew's analysis to a high-

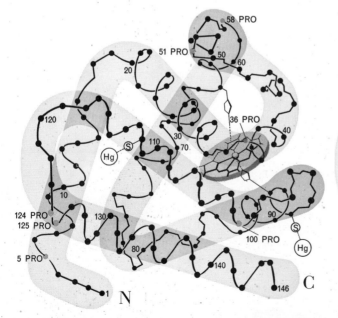

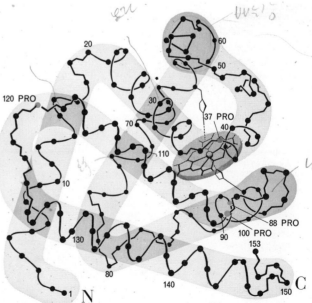

BETA CHAIN AND MYOGLOBIN appear at left and right. Every 10th amino acid subunit is marked, as are proline subunits (*color*), which often coincide with turns in the chain. Balls marked "Hg" show where mercury atoms can be attached to sulfur atoms (*S*).

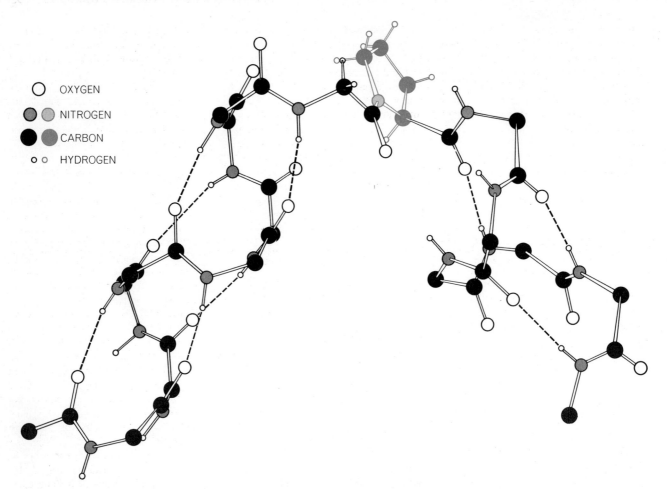

OXYGEN

NITROGEN

CARBON

HYDROGEN

CORNER IN HEMOGLOBIN MOLECULE occurs where a subunit of the amino acid proline (*color*) falls between two helical regions in the beta chain. The chain is shown bare; all hydrogen atoms and amino acid side branches, except for proline, are removed.

er resolution shows that the chain of myoglobin consists of a succession of helical segments interrupted by corners and irregular regions. The helical segments have the geometry of the alpha helix predicted in 1951 by Linus Pauling and Robert B. Corey of the California Institute of Technology. The heme group lies embedded in a fold of the chain, so that only its two acid groups protrude at the surface and are in contact with the surrounding water. Its iron atom is linked to a nitrogen atom of the amino acid histidine.

I have recently built models of the alpha and beta chains of hemoglobin and found that they follow an atomic pattern very similar to that of myoglobin. If two protein chains look the same, one would expect them to have much the same composition. In the language of protein chemistry this implies that in the myoglobins and hemoglobins of all vertebrates the 20 different kinds of amino acid should be present in about the same proportion and arranged in similar sequence.

Enough chemical analyses have been done by now to test whether or not this is true. Starting at the Rockefeller Institute and continuing in our laboratory, Allen B. Edmundson has determined the sequence of amino acid units in the molecule of sperm-whale myoglobin. The sequences of the alpha and beta chains of adult human hemoglobin have been analyzed independently by Gerhardt Braunitzer and his colleagues at the Max Planck Institute for Biochemistry in Munich, and by William H. Konigsberg, Robert J. Hill and their associates at the Rockefeller Institute. Fetal hemoglobin, a variant of the human adult form, contains a chain known as gamma, which is closely related to the beta chain. Its complete sequence has been analyzed by Walter A. Schroeder and his colleagues at the California Institute of Technology. The sequences of several other species of hemoglobin and that of human myoglobin have been partially elucidated.

The sequence of amino acid units in proteins is genetically determined, and changes arise as a result of mutation. Sickle-cell anemia, for instance, is an inherited disease due to a mutation in one of the hemoglobin genes. The mutation causes the replacement of a single amino acid unit in each of the beta chains. (The glutamic acid unit normally present at position No. 6 is replaced by a valine unit.) On the molecular scale evolution is thought to involve a succession of such mutations, altering the structure of protein molecules one amino acid unit at a time. Consequently when the hemoglobins of different species are compared, we should expect the sequences in man and apes, which are close together on the evolutionary scale, to be very similar, and those of mammals and fishes, say, to differ more widely. Broadly speaking, this is what is found. What was quite unexpected was the degree of chemical diversity ·among the amino acid sequences of proteins of similar three-dimensional structure and closely related function. Comparison of the known hemoglobin and myoglobin sequences shows only 15 positions—no more than one in 10—where the same amino acid unit is present in all species. In all the other positions one or more replacements have occurred in the course of evolution.

What mechanism makes these diverse

chains fold up in exactly the same way? Does a template force them to take up this configuration, like a mold that forces a car body into shape? Apart from the topological improbability of such a template, all the genetic and physicochemical evidence speaks against it, suggesting instead that the chain folds up spontaneously to assume one specific structure as the most stable of all possible alternatives.

Possible Folding Mechanisms

What is it, then, that makes one particular configuration more stable than all others? The only generalization to emerge so far, mainly from the work of Kendrew, Herman C. Watson and myself, concerns the distribution of the so-called polar and nonpolar amino acid units between the surface and the interior of the molecule.

Some of the amino acids, such as glutamic acid and lysine, have side groups of atoms with positive or negative electric charge, which strongly attract the surrounding water. Amino acid side groups such as glutamine or tyrosine, although electrically neutral as a whole, contain atoms of nitrogen or oxygen in which positive and negative charges are sufficiently separated to form dipoles; these also attract water, but not so strongly as the charged groups do. The attraction is due to a separation of charges in the water molecule itself, making it dipolar. By attaching themselves to electrically charged groups, or to other dipolar groups, the water molecules minimize the strength of the electric fields surrounding these groups and stabilize the entire structure by lowering the quantity known as free energy.

The side groups of amino acids such as leucine and phenylalanine, on the other hand, consist only of carbon and hydrogen atoms. Being electrically neutral and only very weakly dipolar, these groups repel water as wax does. The reason for the repulsion is strange and intriguing. Such hydrocarbon groups, as they are called, tend to disturb the haphazard arrangement of the liquid water molecules around them, making it ordered as it is in ice. The increase in order makes the system less stable; in physical terms it leads to a reduction of the quantity known as entropy, which is the measure of the disorder in a system. Thus it is the water molecules' anarchic distaste for the orderly regimentation imposed on them by the hydrocarbon side groups that forces these side groups to turn away from water and to stick to one another.

Our models have taught us that most electrically charged or dipolar side groups lie at the surface of the protein molecule, in contact with water. Nonpolar side groups, in general, are either confined to the interior of the molecule or so wedged into crevices on its surface as to have the least contact with water. In the language of physics, the distribution of side groups is of the kind leading to the lowest free energy and the highest entropy of the protein molecules and the water around them. (There is a reduction of entropy due to the orderly folding of the protein chain itself, which makes the system less stable, but this is balanced, at moderate temperatures, by the stabilizing contributions of the other effects just described.) It is too early to say whether these are the only generalizations to be made about the forces that stabilize one particular configuration of the protein chain in preference to all others.

At least one amino acid is known to be a misfit in an alpha helix, forcing the chain to turn a corner wherever the unit occurs. This is proline [see illustration on opposite page]. There is, however, only one corner in all the hemoglobins and myoglobins where a proline is always found in the same position: position No. 36 in the beta chain and No. 37 in the myoglobin chain [see bottom illustration on page 47]. At other corners the appearance of prolines is haphazard and changes from species to species. Elkan R. Blout of the Harvard Medical School finds that certain amino acids such as valine or threonine, if present in large numbers, inhibit the formation of alpha helices, but these do not seem to have a decisive influence in myoglobin and hemoglobin.

Since it is easier to determine the sequence of amino acid units in proteins than to unravel their three-dimensional structure by X rays, it would be useful to be able to predict the structure from the sequence. In principle enough is probably known about the forces between atoms and about the way they tend to arrange themselves to make such predictions feasible. In practice the enormous number of different ways in which a long chain can be twisted still makes the problem one of baffling complexity.

Assembling the Four Chains

If hemoglobin consisted of four identical chains, a crystallographer would expect them to lie at the corners of a regular tetrahedron. In such an arrangement each chain can be brought into congruence with any of its three neighbors by a rotation of 180 degrees about one of three mutually perpendicular

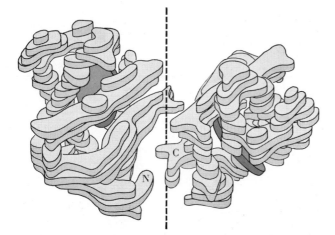

FOUR CHAINS OF HEMOGLOBIN are arranged in symmetrical fashion. Two alpha chains (left) and two beta chains (right) face each other across an axis of symmetry (broken vertical lines). In the assembled molecule the two alpha chains are inverted over the two beta chains and nested down between them. When arranged in this manner, the four chains lie at the corners of a tetrahedron.

axes of symmetry. Since the alpha and beta chains are chemically different, such perfect symmetry is unattainable, but the actual arrangement comes very close to it. As a first step in the assembly of the molecule two alpha chains are placed near a twofold symmetry axis, so that a rotation of 180 degrees brings one chain into congruence with its partner [see illustration on preceding page].

Next the same is done with the two beta chains. One pair, say the alpha chains, is then inverted and placed over the top of the other pair so that the four chains lie at the corners of a tetrahedron. A true twofold symmetry axis now passes vertically through the molecule, and "pseudo-axes" in two directions perpendicular to the first relate the alpha to the beta chains. Thus the arrangement is tetrahedral, but because of the chemical differences between the alpha and beta chains the tetrahedron is not quite regular.

The result is an almost spherical molecule whose exact dimensions are $64 \times 55 \times 50$ angstrom units. It is astonishing to find that four objects as irregular as the alpha and beta chains can fit together so neatly. On formal grounds one would expect a hole to pass through the center of the molecule because chains of amino acid units, being asymmetrical, cannot cross any symmetry axis. Such a hole is in fact found [see top illustration on page 41].

The most unexpected feature of the oxyhemoglobin molecule is the way the four heme groups are arranged. On the basis of their chemical interaction one would have expected them to lie close together. Instead each heme group lies in a separate pocket on the surface of the molecule, apparently unaware of the existence of its partners. Seen at the present resolution, therefore, the structure fails to explain one of the most important physiological properties of hemoglobin.

In 1937 Felix Haurowitz, then at the German University of Prague, discov-

ered an important clue to the molecular explanation of hemoglobin's physiological action. He put a suspension of needle-shaped oxyhemoglobin crystals away in the refrigerator. When he took the suspension out some weeks later, the oxygen had been used up by bacterial infection and the scarlet needles had been replaced by hexagonal plates of purple reduced hemoglobin. While Haurowitz observed the crystals under the microscope, oxygen penetrated between the slide and the cover slip, causing the purple plates to dissolve and the scarlet needles of hemoglobin to re-form. This transformation convinced Haurowitz that the reaction of hemoglobin with oxygen must be accompanied by a change in the structure of the hemoglobin molecule. In myoglobin, on the other hand, no evidence for such a change has been detected.

Haurowitz' observation and the enigma posed by the structure of oxyhemoglobin caused me to persuade a graduate student, Hilary Muirhead, to attempt an X-ray analysis at low resolution of the reduced form. For technical reasons human rather than horse hemoglobin was used at first, but we have now found that the reduced hemoglobins of man and the horse have very similar structures, so that the species does not matter here.

Unlike me, Miss Muirhead succeeded in solving the structure of her protein in time for her Ph.D. thesis. When we examined her first electron-density maps, we looked for two kinds of structural change: alterations in the folding of the individual chains and displacements of the chains with respect to each other. We could detect no changes in folding large enough to be sure that they were not due to experimental error. We did discover, however, that a striking displacement of the beta chains had taken place. The gap between them had widened and they had been shifted sideways, increasing the distance between their respective iron atoms from 33.4 to 40.3 angstrom units [see illustration on page 51]. The arrangement of the two alpha chains had remained unaltered, as far as we could judge, and the distance between the iron atoms in the beta chains and their nearest neighbors in the alpha chains had also remained the same. It looked as though the two beta chains had slid apart, losing contact with each other and somewhat changing their points of contact with the alpha chains.

F. J. W. Roughton and others at the University of Cambridge suggest that the change to the oxygenated form of

RESIDUE NUMBER	HEMOGLOBIN			MYOGLOBIN
	ALPHA	BETA	GAMMA	
81	MET	LEU	LEU	HIS
82	PRO	LYS	LYS	GLU
83	ASN	GLY	GLY	ALA
84	ALA	THR	THR	GLU
85	LEU	PHE	PHE	LEU
86	SER	ALA	ALA	LYS
87	ALA	THR	GLN	PRO
88	LEU	LEU	LEU	LEU
89	SER	SER	SER	ALA
90	ASP	GLU	GLU	GLN
91	LEU	LEU	LEU	SER
92	HIS	HIS	HIS	HIS
93	ALA	CYS	CYS	ALA
94	HIS	ASP	ASN	THR
95	LYS	LYS	LYS	LYS
96	LEU	LEU	LEU	HIS
97	ARG	HIS	HIS	LYS
98	VAL	VAL	VAL	ILEU
99	ASP	ASP	ASP	PRO
100	PRO	PRO	PRO	ILEU
101	VAL	GLU	GLU	LYS
102	ASP	ASN	ASN	TYR

ALA	ALANINE	GLY	GLYCINE
ARG	ARGININE	HIS	HISTIDINE
ASN	ASPARAGINE	ILEU	ISOLEUCINE
ASP	ASPARTIC ACID	LEU	LEUCINE
CYS	CYSTEINE	LYS	LYSINE
GLN	GLUTAMINE	MET	METHIONINE
GLU	GLUTAMIC ACID	PHE	PHENYLALANINE

PRO	PROLINE
SER	SERINE
THR	THREONINE
TYR	TYROSINE
VAL	VALINE

AMINO ACID SEQUENCES are shown for corresponding stretches of the alpha and beta chains of hemoglobin from human adults, the gamma chain that replaces the beta chain in fetal human hemoglobin and sperm-whale myoglobin. Colored bars show where the same amino acid units are found either in all four chains or in the first three. Site numbers for the alpha chain and myoglobin are adjusted slightly because they contain a different number of amino acid subunits overall than do the beta and gamma chains. Over their full length of more than 140 subunits the four chains have only 20 amino acid subunits in common.

hemoglobin takes place after three of the four iron atoms have combined with oxygen. When the change has occurred, the rate of combination of the fourth iron atom with oxygen is speeded up several hundred times. Nothing is known as yet about the atomic mechanism that sets off the displacement of the beta chains, but there is one interesting observation that allows us at least to be sure that the interaction of the iron atoms and the change of structure do not take place unless alpha and beta chains are both present.

Certain anemia patients suffer from a shortage of alpha chains; the beta chains, robbed of their usual partners, group themselves into independent assemblages of four chains. These are known as hemoglobin *H* and resemble normal hemoglobin in many of their properties. Reinhold Benesch and Ruth E. Benesch of the Columbia University College of Physicians and Surgeons have discovered, however, that the four iron atoms in hemoglobin *H* do not interact, which led them to predict that the combination of hemoglobin *H* with oxygen should not be accompanied by a change of structure. Using crystals grown by Helen M. Ranney of the Albert Einstein College of Medicine, Lelio Mazzarella and I verified this prediction. Oxygenated and reduced hemoglobin *H* both resemble normal human reduced hemoglobin in the arrangement of the four chains.

The rearrangement of the beta chains must be set in motion by a series of atomic displacements starting at or near the iron atoms when they combine with oxygen. Our X-ray analysis has not yet reached the resolution needed to discern these, and it seems that a deeper understanding of this intriguing phenomenon may have to wait until we succeed in working out the structures of reduced hemoglobin and oxyhemoglobin at atomic resolution.

Allosteric Enzymes

There are many analogies between the chemical activities of hemoglobin and those of enzymes catalyzing chemical reactions in living cells. These analogies lead one to expect that some enzymes may undergo changes of structure on coming into contact with the substances whose reactions they catalyze. One can imagine that the active sites of these enzymes are moving mechanisms rather than static surfaces magically endowed with catalytic properties.

Indirect and tentative evidence suggests that changes of structure involv-

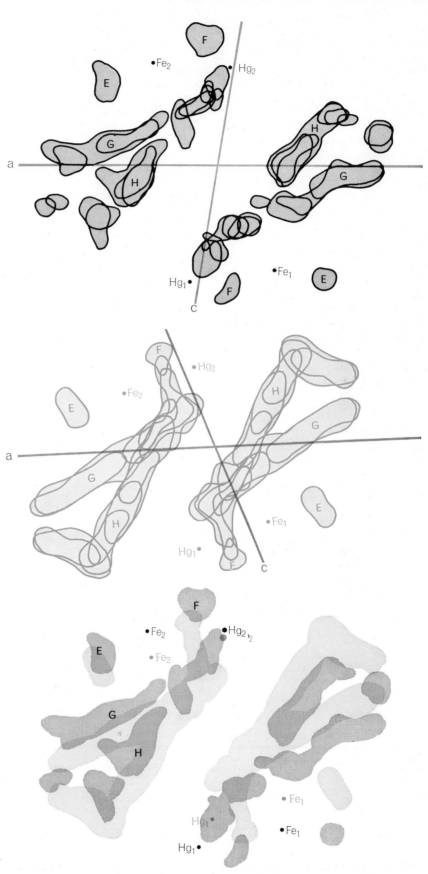

MOVEMENT OF HEMOGLOBIN CHAINS was discovered by comparing portions of the two beta chains in "reduced" (oxygen-free) human hemoglobin (*top*) with the same portions of horse hemoglobin containing oxygen (*middle*). The bottom illustration shows the outlines of the top and middle pictures superposed so that the mercury atoms (Hg_2) and helical regions (E, F, G, H) of the two chains at left coincide. The iron atoms (Fe_2) do not quite match. The chains at right are now seen to be shifted with respect to each other.

ing a rearrangement of subunits like that of the alpha and beta chains of hemoglobin do indeed occur and that they may form the basis of a control mechanism known as feedback inhibition. This is a piece of jargon that biochemistry has borrowed from electrical engineering, meaning nothing more complicated than that you stop being hungry when you have had enough to eat.

Constituents of living matter such as amino acids are built up from simpler substances in a series of small steps, each step being catalyzed by an enzyme that exists specifically for that purpose. Thus a whole series of different enzymes may be needed to make one amino acid. Such a series of enzymes appears to have built-in devices for ensuring the right balance of supply and demand. For example, in the colon bacillus the amino acid isoleucine is made from the amino acid threonine in several steps. The first enzyme in the series has an affinity for threonine: it catalyzes the removal of an amino group from it. H. Edwin Umbarger of the Long Island Biological Association in Cold Spring Harbor, N.Y., discovered that the action of the enzyme is inhibited by isoleucine, the end product of the last enzyme in the series. Jean-Pierre Changeux of the Pasteur Institute later showed that isoleucine acts not, as one might have expected, by blocking the site on the enzyme molecule that would otherwise combine with threonine but probably by combining with a different site on the molecule.

The two sites on the molecule must therefore interact, and Jacques Monod, Changeux and François Jacob have suggested that this is brought about by a rearrangement of subunits similar to that which accompanies the reaction of hemoglobin with oxygen. The enzyme is thought to exist in two alternative structural states: a reactive one when the supply of isoleucine has run out and an unreactive one when the supply exceeds demand. The discoverers have coined the name "allosteric" for enzymes of this kind.

The molecules of the enzymes suspected of having allosteric properties are all large ones, as one would expect them to be if they are made up of several subunits. This makes their X-ray analysis difficult. It may not be too hard to find out, however, whether or not a change of structure occurs, even if it takes a long time to unravel it in detail. In the meantime hemoglobin will serve as a useful model for the behavior of more complex enzyme systems.

6

The Evolution of Hemoglobin

EMILE ZUCKERKANDL

May 1965

Every living thing carries within itself a richly detailed record of its antecedents from the beginning of life on earth. This record is preserved in coded form in the giant molecules of deoxyribonucleic acid (DNA) that constitute the organism's genome, or total stock of genetic information. The genetic record is also expressed more tangibly in the protein molecules that endow the organism with its form and function.

These two kinds of molecule—DNA and protein—are living documents of evolutionary history. Although chemically very different, they have in common a fundamental characteristic: they are both made up of a one-dimensional succession of slightly differing subunits, like differently colored beads on a string. Each colored bead occupies a place specifically assigned to it unless the heritable changes called mutations either change the color of a bead or displace, eliminate or add a bead (or several beads) at a time. In addition the protein molecules are folded in a specific way that enables them to carry out their specific functions.

To examine these molecular documents of evolutionary history a new discipline has emerged: chemical paleogenetics. It sets itself the ambitious goal of reconstructing, insofar as possible, how evolution proceeds at the molecular level. The new discipline is still in its infancy because almost nothing is yet known about the linear sequence of subunits that embody the code for a single gene in a molecule of DNA. Viruses, the smallest structures containing the blueprints for their own replication, possess from a few to several hundred genes. Each gene, in turn, consists of a string of several hundred code "letters." It has not been possible to

isolate a single gene from any organism for chemical analysis.

It has been possible, however, to study and determine the chemical structure of a number of individual polypeptide chains that embody the coded information contained in individual genes. The term "polypeptide" refers to the principal chain of a protein molecule; it describes a sequence of amino acid molecules that are held together by peptide bonds. Such bonds are formed when two amino acid molecules link up with the release of a molecule of water; when they are linked in this way, the amino acids are called residues.

Because three code letters in DNA are required to make a "word" specifying one amino acid molecule, there is a certain compression of information between the gene and the polypeptide chain it encodes. A "structural" gene containing 600 code letters is required to specify a polypeptide containing 200 amino acid residues. The reason for the three-to-one ratio is that there are 20 kinds of amino acid and only four kinds of DNA code letters, embodied in subunits called bases, to identify them; a minimum of three code letters, or bases, is needed to specify each amino acid. (In fact, three code units can specify 64 different items, and there is evidence that more than one DNA triplet exists for some of the amino acids.)

Enough is now known about the amino acid sequence of certain polypeptides to enable the chemical paleontologist to test the validity of three basic postulates. The first asserts that polypeptide chains in present-day organisms have arisen by evolutionary divergence from similar polypeptide chains that existed in the past. The present and past chains would be similar in that many of their amino acid residues match; such

chains are said to be homologous. The second postulate is that a gene existing at some past epoch can occasionally be duplicated so that it appears at two or more sites in the genome of descendent organisms. Thus a contemporary organism can have two or more homologous genes represented by two or more homologous polypeptide chains, which have mutated independently and are therefore no longer identical in structure. The third postulate holds that the mutational events that are most commonly retained through natural selection are those that lead to the replacement of a single amino acid residue in a polypeptide chain.

In addition to these three postulates I would like to suggest a fourth that is much more controversial: Contemporary organisms that look much like ancient ancestral organisms probably contain a majority of polypeptide chains that resemble quite closely those of the ancient organisms. In other words, certain animals said to be "living fossils," such as the cockroach, the horseshoe crab, the shark and, among mammals, the lemur, probably manufacture a great many polypeptide molecules that differ only slightly from those manufactured by their ancestors millions of years ago. This postulate is controversial because it is often said that evolution has been just as long for organisms that appear to have changed little as for those that have changed much; consequently it is held that the biochemistry of living fossils is probably very different from that of their remote ancestors. My own view is that it is unlikely that selective forces would favor the stability of morphological characteristics without at the same time favoring the stability of biochemical characteristics, which are more fundamental.

As an example of the application of chemical paleogenetics I shall describe how evolutionary changes are reflected in the molecular structure of hemoglobin, the oxygen-carrying protein of the blood. Hemoglobin is the most complex protein whose detailed molecular composition and structure are known in man, in his near relatives among the primates and in his more distant relatives such as horses and cattle. The composition and structure of hemoglobin molecules in more primitive organisms such as fishes are rapidly being worked out.

Hemoglobin is a particularly good subject for chemical paleogenetics because it is produced in several slightly variant forms even within an individual organism, and the study of these variants suggests how their components may have descended from a common ancestral form. A molecule of hemoglobin is composed of four large subunits, each a polypeptide chain. Each

FAMILY RESEMBLANCES are exhibited by the polypeptide chains found in several kinds of hemoglobin and by the polypeptide chain of sperm whale myoglobin. Hemoglobin is the oxygen-carrying molecule of the blood; myoglobin stores oxygen in muscle. Polypeptides are molecular chains whose links are amino acid units, usually called residues. The hemoglobin chains comprise either 141 or 146 residues; the myoglobin chain, 153. Each molecule of hemoglobin contains two subunits of a polypeptide chain called alpha (α) and two of a chain called beta (β). In human adults about 2 percent of the hemoglobin molecules contain delta (δ) chains in place of beta chains. Two other chains, gamma (γ) and epsilon (ε, *not shown*), are manufactured during fetal life and can also serve in place of the β-chain. The illustration enables one to compare the four principal chains (α, β, γ, δ) found in human hemoglobin with the β-chains found in the hemoglobin molecules of gorillas, pigs and horses. The δ-, γ- and α-chains are ranked below the human β-chain in order of increasing number of differences. The gorilla β-chain differs from the human β-chain at only one site. The pig β-chain appears to differ at about 17 sites (based on the known differences), and the horse β-chain at 26 sites. The number of differences indicates roughly how far these animals are separated from man on the phylogenetic tree. Relatively few sites have been completely resistant to evolutionary change. Only 11 of the sites (*colored circles*) have the same residues in all known hemoglobin and myoglobin chains, and only 15 more sites (*colored triangles*) have the same residues in all known chains of hemoglobin. Among the four principal chains of normal human hemoglobin the same residues are found at 49 sites. The β-, δ- and γ-chains, which are closely related, have 103 sites in common. The three-dimensional conformation of all these chains is illustrated at the top of page 57.

chain enfolds an iron-containing "heme" group that can pick up an atom of oxygen as hemoglobin passes through the lungs and release it in tissues where oxygen is needed.

The principal kind of hemoglobin found in the human adult is composed of two alpha chains and two beta chains, and it is believed that they too have a common ancestry. The alpha chain comprises 141 amino acid residues; the beta chain, 146. Although the two chains are quite similar in their three-dimensional conformation, they differ considerably in composition. When the two chains are placed side by side, there are 77 sites where the residues in the two chains are different and only 64 sites where the residues are the same. Both the similarities and the differences are of interest to the chemical paleontologist.

The reader may wonder at this point how one can assume that the alpha and beta chains of human hemoglobin have a common ancestry if they are now more different than they are alike. The answer is that it seems most improbable that two different and unrelated polypeptide chains could evolve in such a way as to have the same function, the same conformation and a substantial number of identical amino acid residues at corresponding molecular sites. Consequently the chemical paleontologist interprets their marked difference in amino acid sequence as evidence that a long time has elapsed since they diverged from a common ancestor.

ALA	ALANINE	LEU	LEUCINE
ARG	ARGININE	LYS	LYSINE
ASN	ASPARAGINE	MET	METHIONINE
ASP	ASPARTIC ACID	PHE	PHENYLALANINE
CYS	CYSTEINE	PRO	PROLINE
GLN	GLUTAMINE	SER	SERINE
GLU	GLUTAMIC ACID	THR	THREONINE
GLY	GLYCINE	TRY	TRYPTOPHAN
HIS	HISTIDINE	TYR	TYROSINE
ILEU	ISOLEUCINE	VAL	VALINE

RESIDUE THE SAME IN ALL CHAINS SHOWN
RESIDUE THE SAME IN ALL KNOWN HEMOGLOBIN AND MYOGLOBIN CHAINS
RESIDUE THE SAME IN ALL HEMOGLOBIN CHAINS SHOWN
RESIDUE THE SAME IN ALL KNOWN HEMOGLOBIN CHAINS
RESIDUE THE SAME IN FOUR MAIN HUMAN HEMOGLOBIN CHAINS
RESIDUE THE SAME AS THAT IN HUMAN BETA CHAIN
RESIDUE DIFFERENT FROM THAT IN HUMAN BETA CHAIN
RESIDUE NOT DETERMINED
(SOME RESIDUE ASSIGNMENTS ARE TENTATIVE)

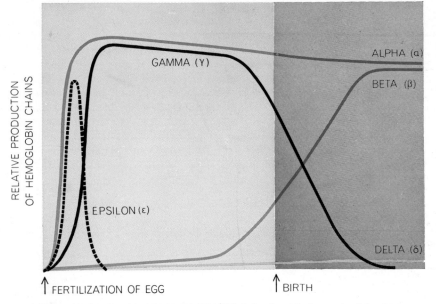

OUTPUT OF HUMAN HEMOGLOBIN CHAINS shifts abruptly during fetal development. Throughout life two of the four subunits in normal hemoglobin are α-chains. These chains pair first with epsilon (ε) chains, then with γ-chains. Just before birth β-chains begin to replace γ-chains. Simultaneously δ-chains appear and also pair with some α-chains.

The argument for a common ancestry is strengthened by the fact that in the hemoglobins of man the beta chain is sometimes replaced by chains with still other amino acid sequences known as gamma, delta and epsilon chains. The epsilon chain is manufactured only for a brief period early in fetal life. The gamma chain replaces the beta chain during most of embryonic development and disappears almost entirely shortly after birth. Throughout adult life a small fraction of the hemoglobin in circulation contains delta chains rather than beta chains [see the illustration on this page.]. The beta, gamma and delta chains are all 146 units long and closely resemble one another in amino acid sequence. There are only 39 differences in amino acid residues between the beta and the gamma chains and only 10 between the beta and the delta chains. The sequence of the human epsilon chain has not yet been established.

One other oxygen-carrying protein molecule figures in this discussion of hemoglobin evolution: the protein known as myoglobin, which does not circulate in the blood but acts as an oxygen repository in muscle. Myoglobin is a single polypeptide chain of 153 amino acid residues that has nearly the same three-dimensional configuration as the various hemoglobin chains. In fact, the unraveling of the three-dimensional structure of sperm whale myoglobin in 1958 by John C. Kendrew and his colleagues at the University of Cambridge marked the first complete determination

of the structure of any protein molecule. Two years later Kendrew's colleague M. F. Perutz announced the three-dimensional conformation of the alpha and beta chains of horse hemoglobin; their topological similarity to myoglobin was immediately apparent [see "The Three-dimensional Structure of a Protein Molecule," by John C. Kendrew, which is available as Offprint #121, and "The Hemoglobin Molecule," by M. F. Perutz, for which see page 40 of this volume].

In amino acid sequence whale myoglobin and the alpha and beta chains of human hemoglobin are far apart. The sequence for human myoglobin is only now being determined, and it is apparent that it will be much closer to the sequence of whale myoglobin than to that of any of the human hemoglobin chains. Whale myoglobin and the alpha chain of human hemoglobin have the same residues at 37 sites; whale myoglobin and the human beta chain are alike at 35 sites. Again the chemical paleontologist regards it as probable that myoglobin and the various hemoglobin chains have descended from a remote common ancestor and are therefore homologous.

Although I have been speaking loosely of the evolution and descent of polypeptide chains, the reader should keep in mind that the molecular mutations underlying the evolutionary process take place not in polypeptide molecules but in the structural genes of

DNA that carry the blueprint for each polypeptide chain. The effect of a single mutation of the most common kind is to change a single base in a structural gene, with the result that one triplet code word is changed into a different code word. Unless the new code word happens, to specify the same amino acid as the old code word (which is sometimes the case) the altered gene will specify a polypeptide chain in which one of the amino acid residues is replaced by a different one. The effect of such a substitution is usually harmful to the organism, but from time to time a one-unit alteration in a polypeptide chain will increase the organism's chances of survival in a particular environment and the organism will transmit its altered gene to its progeny. This is the basic mechanism of natural selection.

As I have mentioned, there are also types of mutation that produce deletions or additions in a polypeptide chain. And there are the still more complex genetic events in which it is believed a structural gene is duplicated. One of the duplicates may later be shifted to a different location so that copies appear at two or more places in the genome. Such gene duplication, followed by independent mutation, would seem to account for the various homologues of hemoglobin found in all vertebrates.

Duplicate genes may have several values for an organism. For example, they may provide the organism with twice as much of a given polypeptide chain as it had before the duplication. They may also have subtler and more important values. It may be that the gamma chain found in fetal hemoglobin is particularly adapted to the needs of prenatal existence whereas the beta chain that replaces the gamma chain soon after birth is more suitable for life outside the womb. The precise value to the organism of having these two kinds of hemoglobin chain available at different stages of development remains to be discovered. It is somewhat puzzling that adult humans who have a certain genetically controlled abnormality go through life with gamma chains rather than beta chains in a significant fraction of their hemoglobin and show no ill effects.

Even without detailed knowledge of the role of duplicate genes it is clear that they are valuable both for the evolution of species and for the development of the individual organism. For purposes of evolution they provide two (or more) copies of genetic material that

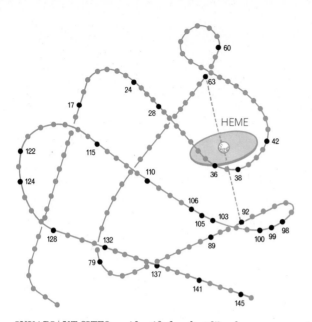

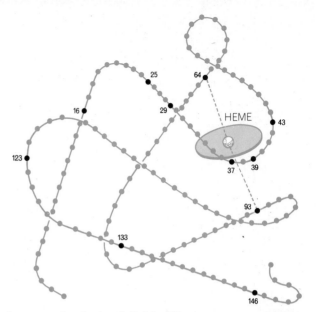

INVARIANT SITES are identified on knotlike shapes representing the three-dimensional structure of the polypeptide chains of hemoglobin and myoglobin. The 26 numbered sites at left are occupied by the same residues in all known hemoglobin chains. Eleven of

these same sites (*assigned slightly different numbers at right*) are occupied by the same residues in all known chains of hemoglobin and myoglobin. Presumably the invariant sites are important in establishing the structure and function of these polypeptides.

are free to evolve separately. Thus a duplicate gene may be transformed so completely that it gives rise to a new type of polypeptide chain with a function entirely different from that of its ancestor. In the life history of an individual organism the existence of duplicate genes at different sites in the genome enables the organism to obtain a supply of an essential polypeptide without activation of the whole genome. In this way gene duplication makes possible a more complex pattern of gene activation and inactivation during an organism's development.

It is not always easy to decide when two polypeptide chains are homologous and when they are not. As long as one is dealing with rather similar chains that serve the same function—as in the case of the various hemoglobin chains—there is a strong *prima facie* case for homology. As the amino acid sequences of more and more polypeptides are deciphered, however, one can expect ambiguities to arise.

One potential source of ambiguity arises in the identification of "corresponding" molecular sites. Such sites are often made to correspond by shifting parts of one chain with respect to the homologous chain [*see illustration below*]. The shifts are justified on the grounds that deletions or additions of one to several residues in a row have occurred during the evolution of certain polypeptide chains. A shift is considered successful when it maximizes the number of identities between the segments of two chains. The argument, therefore, is somewhat circular in that the shifts are justified by the presumed deletions (or additions) and the deletions (or additions) by the shifts. The argument that breaks the circle is that by invoking a small number of shifts, homologous polypeptide chains can be brought to display remarkable coincidences, whereas nonhomologous chains cannot be. There remains, however, the problem of placing the concept of homology on an objective basis. An effort is being made to do this with

the help of a computer analysis of real and hypothetical polypeptide chains.

Now that the reader has this background I can provide a more detailed statement of the aims and methods of chemical paleogenetics. Fundamentally it attempts to discover the probable amino acid sequence of ancestral polypeptide chains and also the probable base sequence in the genes that controlled them. It is concerned with the fate of the descendent line of each gene. It inquires whether gene duplication has occurred and, if so, when it occurred; it asks what became of the duplicate genes, how they may have been shifted to various parts of the genome and how they have mutated. Finally it is concerned with the factors that regulate the rate and timing of the synthesis of the various polypeptide chains.

Present evidence suggests (although exceptions are known) that the number of differences between homologous polypeptide chains of a certain type found in different animals is roughly

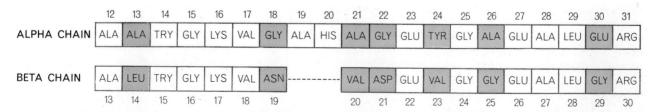

	12	13	14	15	16	17	18	19	20	21	22	23	24	25	26	27	28	29	30	31
ALPHA CHAIN	ALA	ALA	TRY	GLY	LYS	VAL	GLY	ALA	HIS	ALA	GLY	GLU	TYR	GLY	ALA	GLU	ALA	LEU	GLU	ARG
BETA CHAIN	ALA	LEU	TRY	GLY	LYS	VAL	ASN	----------	VAL	ASP	GLU	VAL	GLY	GLY	GLU	ALA	LEU	GLY	ARG	
	13	14	15	16	17	18	19		20	21	22	23	24	25	26	27	28	29	30	

CORRESPONDING REGIONS of the α- and β-chains of human hemoglobin show how a short deletion must be inferred in the β-chain to produce a good match at corresponding sites. An earlier

one-unit deletion in the α-chain explains why α-site 12 corresponds to β-site 13. By postulating the two-unit deletion shown here the two chains can be made to have the same residues at 11 sites.

proportional to the relatedness of these animals as established by standard methods of phylogenetic classification. Indeed, the readily observable differences among living things must be to a significant extent the expression of differences in their enzymes—the proteins that catalyze the chemical reactions of life—and therefore of differences in the amino acid sequences of the polypeptide chains that form the enzymes. It is probable that observable differences also reflect differences in the regulation of rate and timing of the synthesis of polypeptide chains rather than differences in the amino acid sequence of these chains.

On the other hand, a difference in sequence may express itself primarily as a difference in rate and timing. It is quite probable that regulatory enzymes play an important role, and less obvious regulatory mechanisms may also exist. It has been suggested, for example, that differences in rate and timing may be attributable to certain sequences of bases in DNA that never find expression in a polypeptide chain. It seems in the last analysis, however, that the differences between organisms, if the environment is kept constant, boil down to differences in molecular sequences. These differences may reside in base sequences in genes, which are then expressed in amino acid sequences in polypeptide chains; they may reside in other base sequences that are not so expressed; finally they may reside in the sequential order in which genes are distributed within the genome.

Although chemical paleogenetics will ultimately have taxonomic value in providing a fundamental way of measuring the distance between living things on the evolutionary scale, this is not its prime objective. A major value of analyzing evolutionary changes at the molecular level will be to provide a deeper understanding of natural selection in relation to different types of mutation.

Let me proceed, then, to apply the methods of chemical paleogenetics to the myoglobin-hemoglobin family of polypeptide chains. The top illustration at the right shows the number of differences in amino acid sequence between four animal-hemoglobin alpha and beta chains and the corresponding human chains. For purposes of rough computation let us assume that the alpha and beta chains evolve at the same rate and pool the number of differences they exhibit. The reason for doing this is to

ANIMAL	NUMBER OF DIFFERENCES		MEAN NUMBER OF DIFFERENCES, ALL CHAINS	ESTIMATED TIME SINCE COMMON ANCESTOR
	ALPHA CHAIN	BETA CHAIN		
HORSE	17	26		
PIG	∼ 18	∼ 17	∼ 22	80 MILLION YEARS
CATTLE	∼ 27			
RABBIT	∼ 27			

COMPARISON OF HEMOGLOBIN CHAINS offers a way to estimate the number of years required to produce an evolutionarily effective change at one site. The values given here for the number of differences represent a comparison with the α- and β-chains of human hemoglobin. The mean of 22 differences between any pair of human and animal chains implies an average of 11 mutations per chain, or about one change per seven million years.

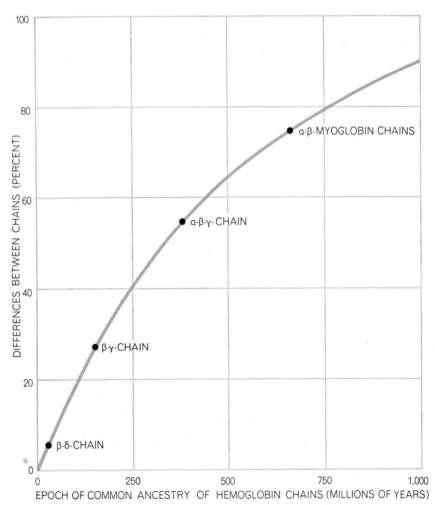

AGE OF ANCESTRAL HEMOGLOBIN-MYOGLOBIN CHAINS is plotted on a curve computed by Linus Pauling. Except for myoglobin the chains represented are those of humans. Where only a few differences are observed it is assumed that about seven million years are needed to establish an effective mutation. But where chains show large differences today it can be assumed that more than one mutation occurred at a given site in the course of evolution. For example, the α-chain and β-chain each differ from the myoglobin chain at about 110 sites. Thus the ancestral α-β-myoglobin chain appears on the curve where the vertical axis reads 75 percent (110/146 is about 3/4). This point corresponds to a period about 650 million years ago rather than the 385 million years that would be obtained if 55 mutations per gene line (110 ÷ 2) were simply multiplied by seven million.

establish a mean value for the number of apparent amino acid substitutions that have occurred in the alpha and beta chains of the four animal species (horse, pig, cattle and rabbit) since the time when the four species and man had a common ancestor. The mean difference is 22 apparent changes in the two chains, or an average of 11 changes per chain. If the common ancestor of man and the four other animals lived about 80 million years ago, as is thought to be the case, the average time required to establish a successful amino acid substitution in any species is about seven million years. Until more chains have been analyzed, however, 10 million years per substitution is a good order-of-magnitude figure.

Such a figure can now be used for a different purpose: to estimate very roughly the time elapsed since the four principal types of chain in human hemoglobin had a common ancestor. In making such a calculation one must employ statistical principles to allow for the following fact. The greater the number of differences in sequence be-

tween two homologous chains, the greater the chances that at some molecular sites more than one amino acid substitution will have been retained temporarily by evolution since the time of the common ancestor. An appropriate calculation was recently performed by Linus Pauling, with the result shown in the bottom illustration on the preceding page. The curve in the illustration allows one to read off the probable time of existence of the common molecular ancestor of various polypeptide chains as a function of the percentage of differences in amino acid sequence between the chains.

The two chains that are most nearly alike—the beta and delta chains—differ at only 10 sites and presumably were the most recent to arise by duplication of a common genetic ancestor. To exhibit 10 differences each gene line would have to undergo only five changes, which implies an elapsed time of roughly 35 million years on Pauling's chart. The beta and gamma chains are different at 37 sites and thus seem to have arisen by gene duplication about

150 million years ago. The beta and alpha chains are different at 76 sites and therefore their common ancestor goes back some 380 million years. If the calculation is valid as a rough approximation, the common genetic ancestor of the hemoglobin chains now circulating in the human bloodstream dates back to the Devonian period and to the appearance of the first amphibians.

The curve also indicates very roughly how long it has been since the chains of hemoglobin and myoglobin may have arisen as the result of duplication of a common ancestral gene. The differences in amino acid sequence between hemoglobin chains and myoglobin are so numerous that their common molecular ancestor may date back about 650 million years to the end of the Precambrian era, long before the appearance of the vertebrates. This suggests, in turn, that it may be possible to find in living invertebrates a distant relative of the vertebrate hemoglobins and myoglobins.

Let me turn now from discussing the overall differences between homologous polypeptide chains to the question of how one might construct a molecular "phylogenetic tree." Such a tree would show an evolutionary line of descent for an entire family of polypeptide molecules. One can also construct individual trees for individual molecular sites. Later this site-by-site information can be synthesized to obtain probable residue sequences for complete ancestral chains.

If the amino acid residue is the same in two homologous chains at a given molecular site, there is a certain probability that the same residue was also present in the common ancestor of the two chains. There is also a chance, of course, that the ancestral residue was different and that the identity observed in the two homologous existing chains was produced by molecular convergence or simply by coincidence. Traditional paleontology reveals many examples of convergences at the level of large-scale morphology. In chemical paleogenetics molecular convergence or coincidence is particularly troublesome because the path from difference to similarity runs directly counter to that needed to trace a molecular phylogenetic tree. About all one can say at this stage in the development of the new discipline is that convergence or coincidence do not seem to occur often enough to vitiate the effort of constructing such trees.

The illustration at the left shows

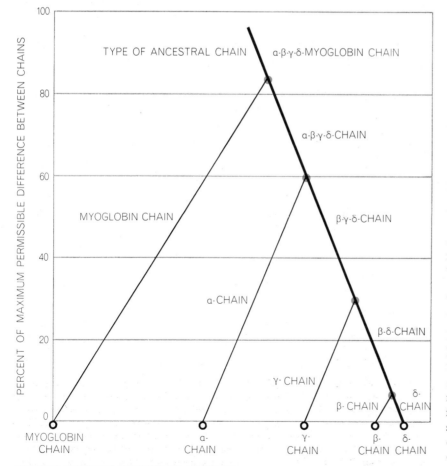

HEMOGLOBIN-MYOGLOBIN RELATIONSHIP is traced back through evolution, based on the number of differences in the various chains. The four colored dots indicate where ancestral genes were presumably duplicated, giving rise each time to a new gene line.

schematically, in the form of an inverted tree, the probable evolutionary relationships for the known chains of human hemoglobin and myoglobin. The tree also represents the relationships of any given molecular site in these chains. The epsilon chain has been omitted because too little is known about it. The vertical axis is not an absolute time scale but shows how chain differences rate on a scale in which the maximum permissible difference is 100 percent. Some of the branching points in the tree are assumed to coincide with a gene duplication. Following such duplication the resulting independent genes (and their polypeptide chains) evolve separately. The most ancient duplication presumably separated the myoglobin gene from the gene that ultimately gave rise, by repeated duplications, to the alpha, beta, gamma and delta genes of hemoglobin. Additional gene duplications will surely have to be postulated along various lines.

The next molecular phylogenetic tree [*see top illustration at right*] attempts to reconstruct the evolutionary changes at one particular site (site No. 4 in the human alpha chain) that led to the amino acid residues now observed at that site in various animal species, including man. As the genetic code is being worked out, it is becoming possible to distinguish amino acid substitutions that may have occurred in one step from those requiring two or more steps. It is a principle of chemical paleogenetics that in postulating a possible ancestral amino acid residue one should prefer the residue that can be reached by invoking the fewest number of mutations in the genetic message. In the tree just referred to the residue of the amino acid alanine has been selected as the residue at site No. 4 in the ancestral polypeptide chain from which the 17 present-day hemoglobin chains are descended. This selection may seem odd; among the 17 chains eight have proline in the No. 4 position and only four have alanine. (The remaining five chains have glycine, glutamic acid or serine in the No. 4 position.) The explanation is that if proline is assumed to be in the No. 4 position in the most remote ancestral chain, one has to postulate nine or 10 evolutionarily effective amino acid substitutions in the various descendent chains to reach the residues actually observed in the 17 present-day chains, but if alanine is selected as the ancestral residue, only eight effective substitutions are needed.

The choice of alanine becomes more impressive when it is shown that no

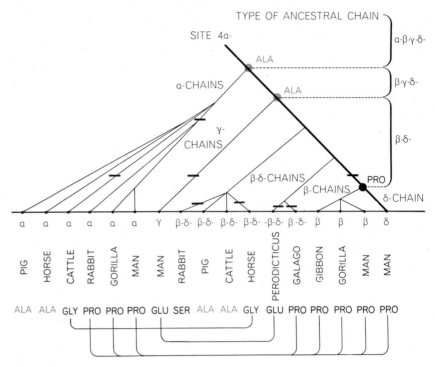

ANCESTRAL RESIDUE can be traced by trying to establish the simplest lines of descent for residues now found at a particular site in polypeptide chains of hemoglobin. The residues shown across the bottom occupy site No. 4 in the human α-chain. (*Perodicticus* and *Galago* are small monkeys commonly known as the potto and the bush baby.) Alanine (*ala*) is selected as the probable residue in the earliest ancestral chain because it provides a line of descent requiring fewer mutations than any other that might be selected: eight. They are represented by short horizontal bars. The lines at the bottom identify convergences or coincidences: identical residues that presumably resulted from independent mutations.

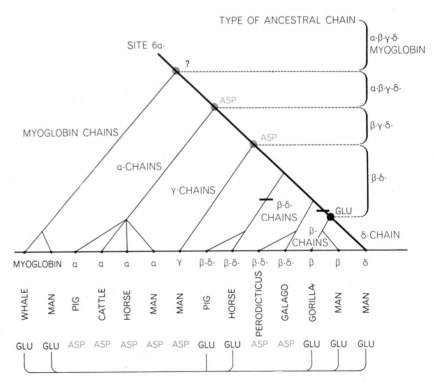

AMBIGUOUS ANCESTRAL RELATIONSHIP is encountered when the present-day residues at a particular site are those of two amino acids that frequently replace each other, such as glutamic acid (*glu*) and aspartic acid (*asp*). The sites compared are No. 6 in the α-chain of human hemoglobin. Note that myoglobin has been included in this evolutionary tree.

	1	2	3	4	5	6	7	8	9	10
BETA-GAMMA-DELTA ANCESTRAL CHAIN	(VAL)	HIS	LEU	(THR) (SER)	ALA	GLU	ASP	LYS	?	THR
PRESENT HUMAN CHAINS — BETA	VAL	HIS	LEU	THR	PRO	GLU	GLU	LYS	SER	ALA
DELTA	VAL	HIS	LEU	THR	PRO	GLU	GLU	LYS	THR	ALA
GAMMA	GLY	HIS	PHE	THR	GLU	GLU	ASP	LYS	ALA	THR

RECONSTRUCTION OF ANCESTRAL CHAIN represents a synthesis of evolutionary trees for individual sites as illustrated on the preceding page. This chart shows the first 10 sites in the ancestral β-γ-δ-chain and the corresponding region in its three present-day descendants. Residues in the δ-, γ- and ancestral chains that differ from those in the contemporary β-chain are shown in color. Gray indicates uncertain or unknown residues.

more than one amino acid substitution is needed in any single line of descent to explain the residues currently observed. If proline is made the ancestral choice, double substitutions—the ones least likely to occur—must be postulated in three of the lines of descent. The choice of any other amino acid for the ancestral position would necessitate many more substitutions. Alanine is therefore adopted as the most probable ancestral residue—a conclusion that is not likely to need revision unless the genetic code is revised with regard to proline. In this particular example molecular coincidence is represented in some of the chains that now contain proline, glutamic acid and glycine.

The problem of identifying a probable ancestral residue is often difficult. At a site where there are frequent interchanges between residues that seem to be more or less functionally equivalent, any conclusion about ancestry becomes doubtful. This is demonstrated at site No. 6, as numbered in the human alpha chain, where there is a frequent interchange between aspartic acid and glutamic acid [see bottom illustration on preceding page].

The information from a series of molecular phylogenetic trees can finally be synthesized to produce a complete sequence of residues representing the composition of an ancestral polypeptide chain. The illustration above shows such a postulated sequence for the first 10 sites of the polypeptide chain that is presumed to be the ancestor of the beta, gamma and delta chains now present in human hemoglobin.

In order to establish by chemical paleogenetics the evolutionary relationship between two different organisms it should not be necessary to know the sequential composition of thousands or even hundreds of homologous polypeptide chains. To require such knowledge would be discouraging indeed. It can reasonably be predicted, however, that a comparison of relatively few chains—perhaps a few dozen—should yield a large fraction of the maximum amount of information that polypeptide chains can provide. The reason is that even relatively few chains should yield a good statistical sample of the evolutionary behavior of many chains.

Chemical paleogenetics offers many new possibilities. For example, after one has reconstructed a number of ancestral polypeptides for some ancient organism one should be able to make various deductions about some of its physiological functions. One might be able to decide, for instance, whether it could live successfully in an atmosphere composed as we know it today or whether it was designed for a different atmosphere.

From similar polypeptide reconstructions it may be possible to make informed guesses about organisms, such as soft-bodied animals, that have left no fossil record. In this way the state of living matter in past evolutionary times can be pieced together, at least in part, without the help of fossil remains. But one of the main attractions of chemical paleogenetics is the possibility of deriving strictly from molecular sequences a phylogenetic tree that is entirely independent of phylogenetic evidence gathered by traditional methods. If this can be accomplished, one can compare the two kinds of phylogenetic tree—the molecular and the traditional—and see if they tell the same story of evolution. If they do, chemical paleogenetics will have provided a powerful and independent confirmation of the already well-documented theory of evolution.

7

The Three-dimensional Structure of an Enzyme Molecule

DAVID C. PHILLIPS

November 1966

One day in 1922 Alexander Fleming was suffering from a cold. This is not unusual in London, but Fleming was a most unusual man and he took advantage of the cold in a characteristic way. He allowed a few drops of his nasal mucus to fall on a culture of bacteria he was working with and then put the plate to one side to see what would happen. Imagine his excitement when he discovered some time later that the bacteria near the mucus had dissolved away. For a while he thought his ambition of finding a universal antibiotic had been realized. In a burst of activity he quickly established that the antibacterial action of the mucus was due to the presence in it of an enzyme; he called this substance lysozyme because of its capacity to lyse, or dissolve, the bacterial cells. Lysozyme was soon discovered in many tissues and secretions of the human body, in plants and most plentifully of all in the white of egg. Unfortunately Fleming found that it is not effective against the most harmful bacteria. He had to wait seven years before a strangely similar experiment revealed the existence of a genuinely effective antibiotic: penicillin.

Nevertheless, Fleming's lysozyme has proved a more valuable discovery than he can have expected when its properties were first established. With it, for example, bacterial anatomists have been able to study many details of bacterial structure [see "Fleming's Lysozyme," by Robert F. Acker and S. E. Hartsell; SCIENTIFIC AMERICAN, June, 1960]. It has now turned out that lysozyme is the first enzyme whose three-dimensional structure has been

determined and whose properties are understood in atomic detail. Among these properties is the way in which the enzyme combines with the substance on which it acts—a complex sugar in the wall of the bacterial cell.

Like all enzymes, lysozyme is a protein. Its chemical makeup has been established by Pierre Jollès and his colleagues at the University of Paris and by Robert E. Canfield of the Columbia University College of Physicians and Surgeons. They have found that each molecule of lysozyme obtained from egg white consists of a single polypeptide chain of 129 amino acid subunits of 20 different kinds. A peptide bond is formed when two amino acids are joined following the removal of a molecule of water. It is customary to call the portion of the amino acid in-

corporated into a polypeptide chain a residue, and each residue has its own characteristic side chain. The 129-residue lysozyme molecule is cross-linked in four places by disulfide bridges formed by the combination of sulfur-containing side chains in different parts of the molecule [see illustration on opposite page].

The properties of the molecule cannot be understood from its chemical constitution alone; they depend most critically on what parts of the molecule are brought close together in the folded three-dimensional structure. Some form of microscope is needed to examine the structure of the molecule. Fortunately one is effectively provided by the techniques of X-ray crystal-structure analysis pioneered by Sir Lawrence Bragg and his father Sir William Bragg.

ALA	ALANINE	GLY	GLYCINE	PRO	PROLINE
ARG	ARGININE	HIS	HISTIDINE	SER	SERINE
ASN	ASPARAGINE	ILEU	ISOLEUCINE	THR	THREONINE
ASP	ASPARTIC ACID	LEU	LEUCINE	TRY	TRYPTOPHAN
CYS	CYSTEINE	LYS	LYSINE	TYR	TYROSINE
GLN	GLUTAMINE	MET	METHIONINE	VAL	VALINE
GLU	GLUTAMIC ACID	PHE	PHENYLALANINE		

TWO-DIMENSIONAL MODEL of the lysozyme molecule is shown on the opposite page. Lysozyme is a protein containing 129 amino acid subunits, commonly called residues (see key to abbreviations above). These residues form a polypeptide chain that is cross-linked at four places by disulfide (–S–S–) bonds. The amino acid sequence of lysozyme was determined independently by Pierre Jollès and his co-workers at the University of Paris and by Robert E. Canfield of the Columbia University College of Physicians and Surgeons. The three-dimensional structure of the lysozyme molecule has now been established with the help of X-ray crystallography by the author and his colleagues at the Royal Institution in London. A painting of the molecule's three-dimensional structure appears on pages 64 and 65. The function of lysozyme is to split a particular long-chain molecule, a complex sugar, found in the outer membrane of many living cells. Molecules that are acted on by enzymes are known as substrates. The substrate of lysozyme fits into a cleft, or pocket, formed by the three-dimensional structure of the lysozyme molecule. In the two-dimensional model on the opposite page the amino acid residues that line the pocket are shown in dark green.

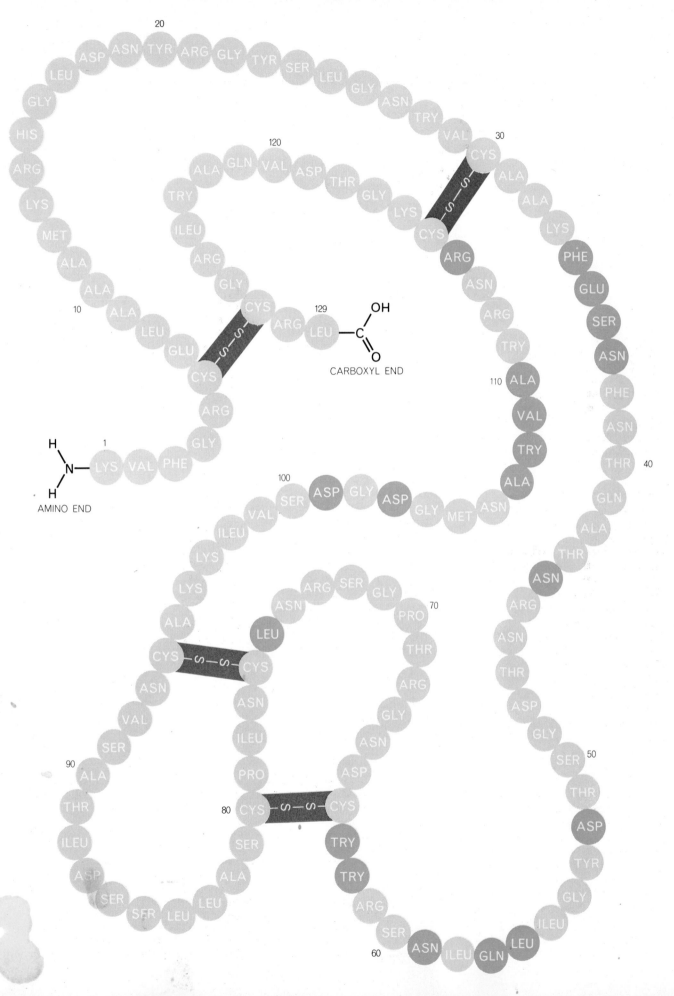

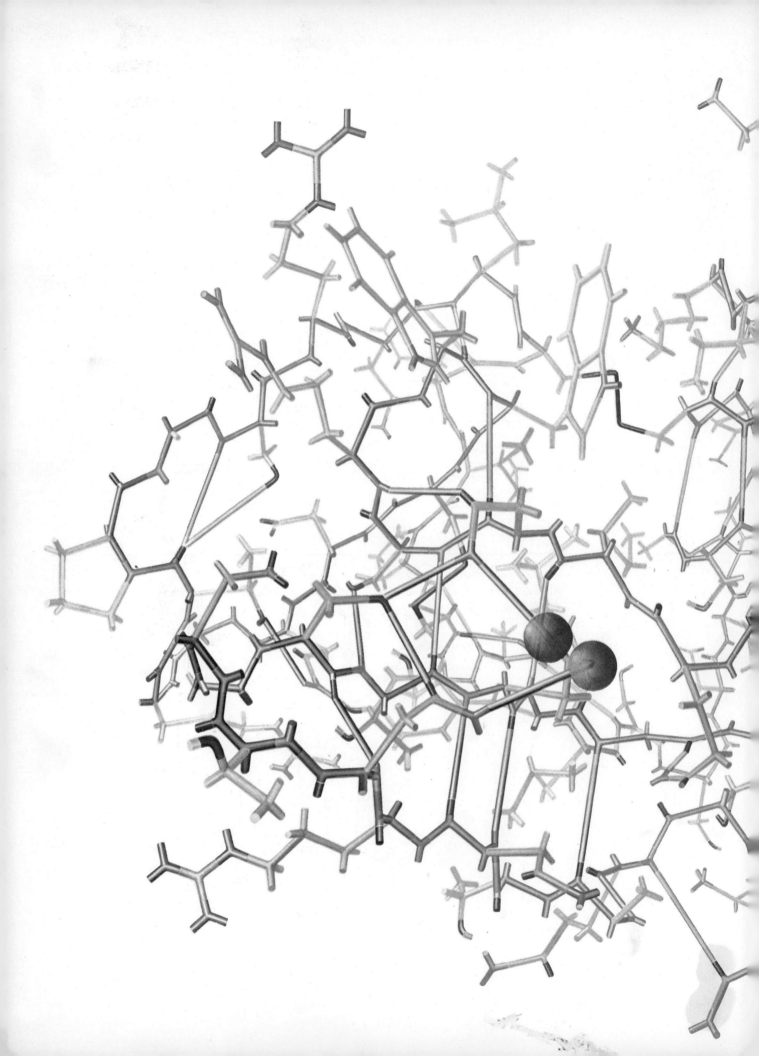

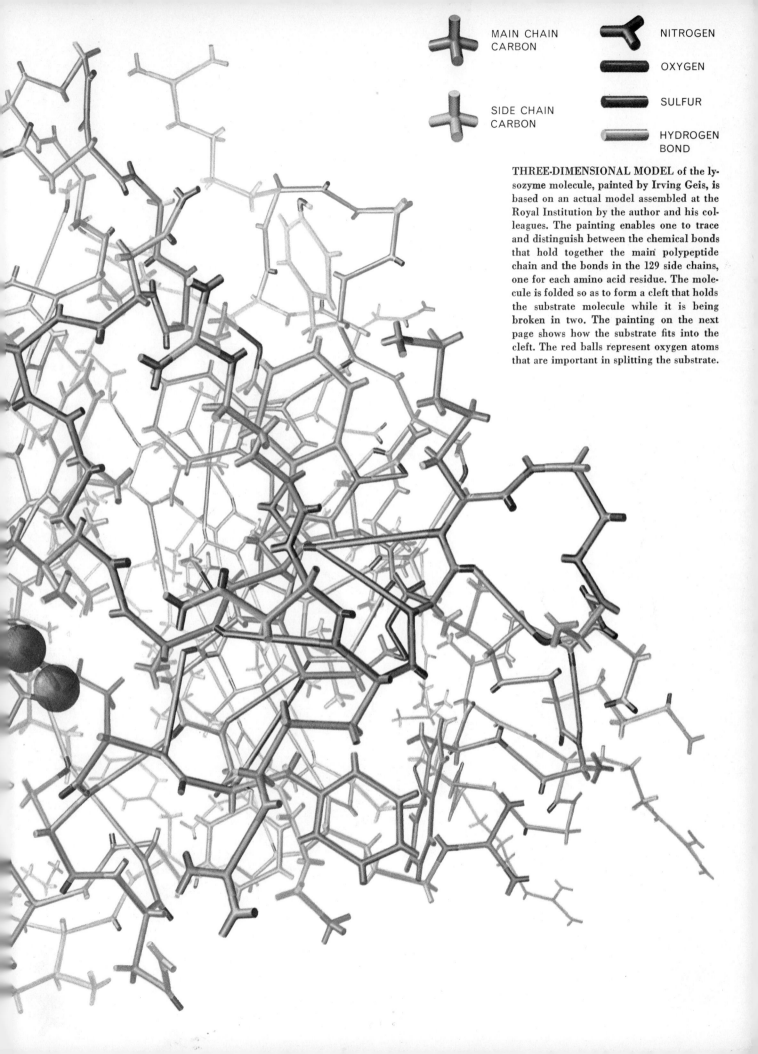

MAIN CHAIN
CARBON

SIDE CHAIN
CARBON

NITROGEN

OXYGEN

SULFUR

HYDROGEN
BOND

THREE-DIMENSIONAL MODEL of the lysozyme molecule, painted by Irving Geis, is based on an actual model assembled at the Royal Institution by the author and his colleagues. The painting enables one to trace and distinguish between the chemical bonds that hold together the main polypeptide chain and the bonds in the 129 side chains, one for each amino acid residue. The molecule is folded so as to form a cleft that holds the substrate molecule while it is being broken in two. The painting on the next page shows how the substrate fits into the cleft. The red balls represent oxygen atoms that are important in splitting the substrate.

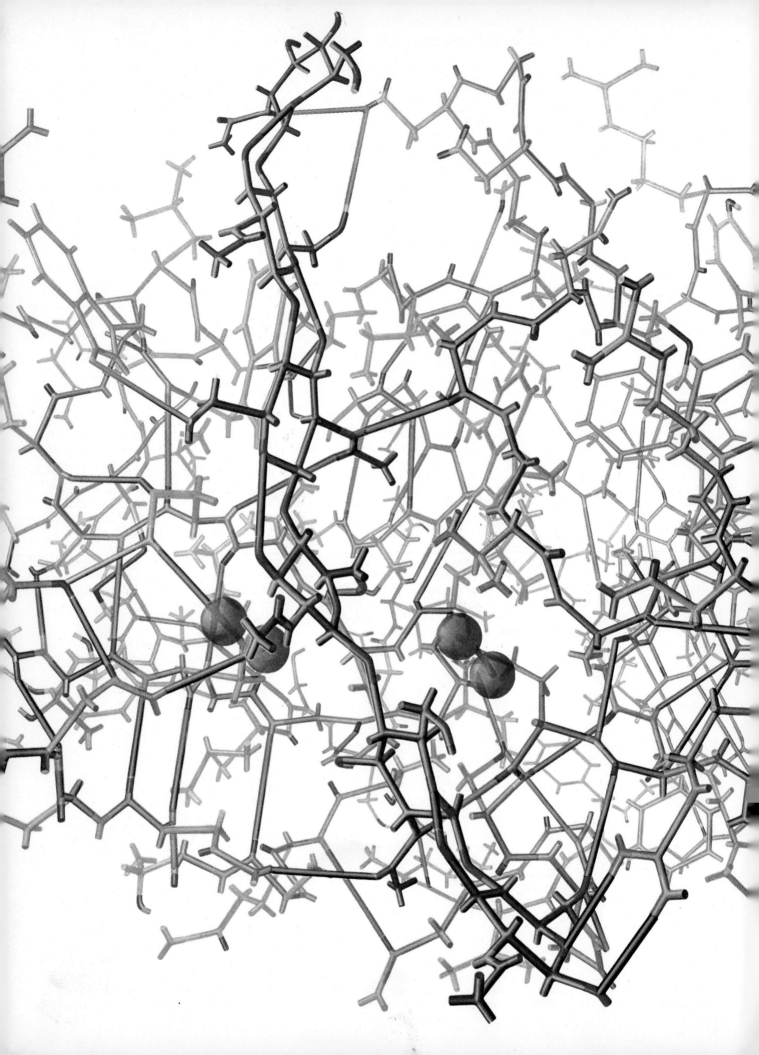

The difficulties of examining molecules in atomic detail arise, of course, from the fact that molecules are very small. Within a molecule each atom is usually separated from its neighbor by about 1.5 angstrom units (1.5×10^{-8} centimeter). The lysozyme molecule, which contains some 1,950 atoms, is about 40 angstroms in its largest dimension. The first problem is to find a microscope in which the atoms can be resolved from one another, or seen separately.

The resolving power of a microscope depends fundamentally on the wavelength of the radiation it employs. In general no two objects can be seen separately if they are closer together than about half this wavelength. The shortest wavelength transmitted by optical microscopes (those working in the ultraviolet end of the spectrum) is about 2,000 times longer than the distance between atoms. In order to "see" atoms one must use radiation with a much shorter wavelength: X rays, which have a wavelength closely comparable to interatomic distances. The employment of X rays, however, creates other difficulties: no satisfactory way has yet been found to make lenses or mirrors that will focus them into an image. The problem, then, is the apparently impossible one of designing an X-ray microscope without lenses or mirrors.

Consideration of the diffraction theory of microscope optics, as developed by Ernst Abbe in the latter part of the 19th century, shows that the problem can be solved. Abbe taught us that the formation of an image in the microscope can be regarded as a two-stage process. First, the object under examination scatters the light or other radiation falling on it in all directions, forming a diffraction pattern. This pattern arises because the light waves scattered from different parts of the object combine so as to produce a wave of large or small amplitude in any direction

according to whether the waves are in or out of phase—in or out of step—with one another. (This effect is seen most easily in light waves scattered by a regularly repeating structure, such as a diffraction grating made of lines scribed at regular intervals on a glass plate.) In the second stage of image formation, according to Abbe, the objective lens of the microscope collects the diffracted waves and recombines them to form an image of the object. Most important, the nature of the image depends critically on how much of the diffraction pattern is used in its formation.

X-Ray Structure Analysis

In essence X-ray structure analysis makes use of a microscope in which the two stages of image formation have been separated. Since the X rays cannot be focused to form an image directly, the diffraction pattern is recorded and the image is obtained from it by calculation. Historically the method was not developed on the basis of this reasoning, but this way of regarding it (which was first suggested by Lawrence Bragg) brings out its essential features and also introduces the main difficulty of applying it. In recording the intensities of the diffracted waves, instead of focusing them to form an image, some crucial information is lost, namely the phase relations among the various diffracted waves. Without this information the image cannot be formed, and some means of recovering it has to be found. This is the well-known phase problem of X-ray crystallography. It is on the solution of the problem that the utility of the method depends.

The term "X-ray crystallography" reminds us that in practice the method was developed (and is still applied) in the study of single crystals. Crystals suitable for study may contain some

10^{15} identical molecules in a regular array; in effect the molecules in such a crystal diffract the X radiation as though they were a single giant molecule. The crystal acts as a three-dimensional diffraction grating, so that the waves scattered by them are confined to a number of discrete directions. In order to obtain a three-dimensional image of the structure the intensity of the X rays scattered in these different directions must be measured, the phase problem must be solved somehow and the measurements must be combined by a computer.

The recent successes of this method in the study of protein structures have depended a great deal on the development of electronic computers capable of performing the calculations. They are due most of all, however, to the discovery in 1953, by M. F. Perutz of the Medical Research Council Laboratory of Molecular Biology in Cambridge, that the method of "isomorphous replacement" can be used to solve the phase problem in the study of protein crystals. The method depends on the preparation and study of a series of protein crystals into which additional heavy atoms, such as atoms of uranium, have been introduced without otherwise affecting the crystal structure. The first successes of this method were in the study of sperm-whale myoglobin by John C. Kendrew of the Medical Research Council Laboratory and in Perutz' own study of horse hemoglobin. For their work the two men received the Nobel prize for chemistry in 1962 [see "The Three-dimensional Structure of a Protein Molecule," by John C. Kendrew, which is available as Offprint #121, and "The Hemoglobin Molecule," by M. F. Perutz, which begins on page 40 of this volume].

Because the X rays are scattered by the electrons within the molecules, the image calculated from the diffraction pattern reveals the distribution of electrons within the crystal. The electron density is usually calculated at a regular array of points, and the image is made visible by drawing contour lines through points of equal electron density. If these contour maps are drawn on clear plastic sheets, one can obtain a three-dimensional image by assembling the maps one above the other in a stack. The amount of detail that can be seen in such an image depends on the resolving power of the effective microscope, on its "aperture," or the diffraction pattern that has been included in the formation of the if the waves diffracted through ciently high angles are included

MODEL OF SUBSTRATE shows how it fits into the cleft in the lysozyme molecule. All the carbon atoms in the substrate are shown in purple. The portion of the substrate in intimate contact with the underlying enzyme is a polysaccharide chain consisting of six ringlike structures, each a residue of an amino-sugar molecule. The substrate in the model is made up of six identical residues of the amino sugar called N-acetylglucosamine (NAG). In the actual substrate every other residue is an amino sugar known as N-acetylmuramic acid (NAM). The illustration is based on X-ray studies of the way the enzyme is bound to a trisaccharide made of three NAG units, which fills the top of the cleft; the arrangement of NAG units the bottom of the cleft was worked out with the aid of three-dimensional models. strate is held to the enzyme by a complex network of hydrogen bonds. In this making each straight section of chain represents a bond between atoms selves lie at the intersections and elbows of the structure. Except for resenting oxygen atoms that are active in splitting the polysaccha is made to represent the electron shells of atoms because they w

(corresponding to a large aperture), the atoms appear as individual peaks in the image map. At lower resolution groups of unresolved atoms appear with characteristic shapes by which they can be recognized.

The three-dimensional structure of lysozyme crystallized from the white of hen's egg has been determined in atomic detail with the X-ray method by our group at the Royal Institution in Lon-don. This is the laboratory in which Humphry Davy and Michael Faraday made their fundamental discoveries during the 19th century, and in which the X-ray method of structure analysis was developed between the two world wars by the brilliant group of workers led by William Bragg, including J. D. Bernal, Kathleen Lonsdale, W. T. Astbury, J. M. Robertson and many others. Our work on lysozyme was begun in 1960 when Roberto J. Poljak, a visiting worker from Argentina, demonstrated that suitable crystals containing heavy atoms could be prepared. Since then C. C. F. Blake, A. C. T. North, V. R. Sarma, Ruth Fenn, D. F. Koenig, Louise N. Johnson and G. A. Mair have played important roles in the work.

In 1962 a low-resolution image of the structure was obtained that revealed the general shape of the molecule and

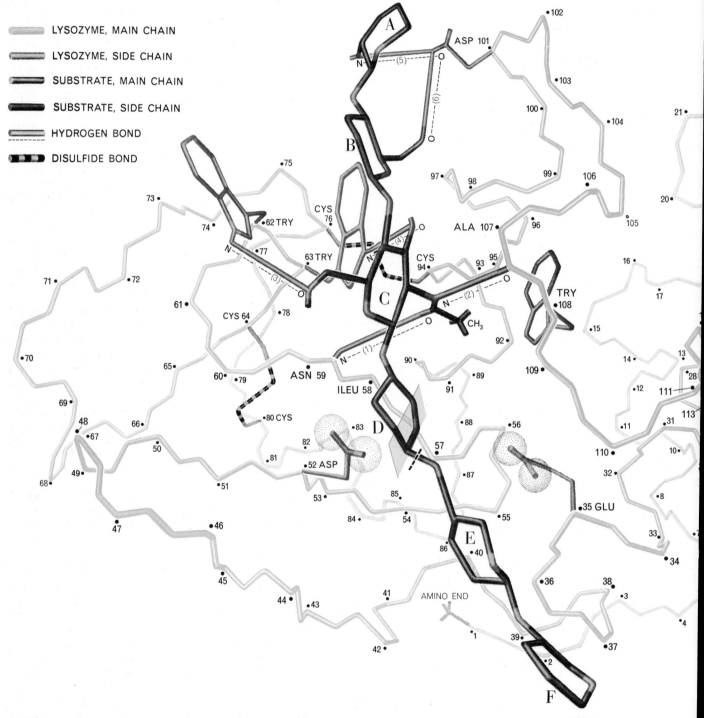

MAP OF LYSOZYME AND SUBSTRATE depicts in color the central chain of each molecule. Side chains have been omitted except for those that produce the four disulfide bonds clipping the lysozyme molecule together and those that supply the terminal connections for hydrogen bonds holding the substrate to the lysozyme. The top three rings of the substrate (A, B, C) are held to the underlying enzyme by six principal hydrogen bonds, which are identified by number to key with the description in the text. The lyso-

showed that the arrangement of the polypeptide chain is even more complex than it is in myoglobin. This low-resolution image was calculated from the amplitudes of about 400 diffraction maxima measured from native protein crystals and from crystals containing each of three different heavy atoms. In 1965, after the development of more efficient methods of measurement and computation, an image was calculated on the basis of nearly 10,000 diffraction maxima, which resolved features separated by two angstroms. Apart from showing a few well-separated chloride ions, which are present because the lysozyme is crystallized from a solution containing sodium chloride, the two-angstrom image still does not show individual atoms as separate maxima in the electron-density map. The level of resolution is high enough, however, for many of the groups of atoms to be clearly recognizable.

The Lysozyme Molecule

The main polypeptide chain appears as a continuous ribbon of electron density running through the image with regularly spaced promontories on it that are characteristic of the carbonyl groups (CO) that mark each peptide bond. In some regions the chain is folded in ways that are familiar from theoretical studies of polypeptide configurations and from the structure analyses of myoglobin and fibrous proteins such as the keratin of hair. The amino acid residues in lysozyme have now been designated by number; the residues numbered 5 through 15, 24 through 34 and 88 through 96 form three lengths of "alpha helix," the conformation that was proposed by Linus Pauling and Robert B. Corey in 1951 and that was found by Kendrew and his colleagues to be the most common arrangement of the chain in myoglobin. The helixes in lysozyme, however, appear to be somewhat distorted from the "classical" form, in which four atoms (carbon, oxygen, nitrogen and hydrogen) of each peptide group lie in a plane that is parallel to the axis of the alpha helix. In the lysozyme molecule the peptide groups in the helical sections tend to be rotated slightly in such a way that their CO groups point outward from the helix axes and their imino groups (NH) inward.

The amount of rotation varies, being slight in the helix formed by residues 5 through 15 and considerable in the one formed by residues 24 through 34. The effect of the rotation is that each NH group does not point directly at the CO group four residues back along the chain but points instead between the CO groups of the residues three and four back. When the NH group points directly at the CO group four residues back, as it does in the classical alpha helix, it forms with the CO group a hydrogen bond (the weak chemical bond in which a hydrogen atom acts as a bridge). In the lysozyme helixes the hydrogen bond is formed somewhere between two CO groups, giving rise to a structure intermediate between that of an alpha helix and that of a more symmetrical helix with a three-fold symmetry axis that was discussed by Lawrence Bragg, Kendrew and Perutz in 1950. There is a further short length of helix (residues 80 through 85) in which the hydrogen-bonding arrangement is quite close to that in the three-fold helix, and also an isolated turn (residues 119 through 122) of three-fold helix. Furthermore, the peptide at the far end of helix 5 through 15 is in the conformation of the three-fold helix, and the hydrogen bond from its NH group is made to the CO three residues back rather than four.

Partly because of these irregularities in the structure of lysozyme, the proportion of its polypeptide chain in the alpha-helix conformation is difficult to calculate in a meaningful way for comparison with the estimates obtained by other methods, but it is clearly less than half the proportion observed in myoglobin, in which helical regions make up about 75 percent of the chain. The lysozyme molecule does include, however, an example of another regular conformation predicted by Pauling and Corey. This is the "antiparallel pleated sheet," which is believed to be the basic structure of the fibrous protein silk and in which, as the name suggests, two lengths of polypeptide chain run parallel to each other in opposite directions. This structure again is stabilized by hydrogen bonds between the NH and CO groups of the main chain. Residues 41 through 45 and 50 through 54 in the lysozyme molecule form such a structure, with the connecting residues 46 through 49 folded into a hairpin bend between the two lengths of comparatively extended chain. The remainder of the polypeptide chain is folded in irregular ways that have no simple short description.

Even though the level of resolution achieved in our present image was not enough to resolve individual atoms, many of the side chains characteristic of the amino acid residues were readily identifiable from their general shape. The four disulfide bridges, for example, are marked by short rods of high electron density corresponding to the two relatively dense sulfur atoms within them. The six tryptophan residues also were easily recognized by the extended electron density produced by the large double-ring structures in their

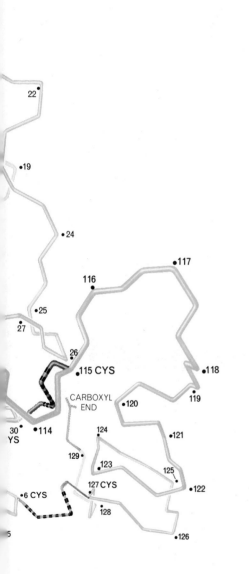

zyme molecule fulfills its function when it cleaves the substrate between the *D* and the *E* ring. Note the distortion of the *D* ring, which pushes four of its atoms into a plane.

FIRST 56 RESIDUES in lysozyme molecule contain a higher proportion of symmetrically organized regions than does all the rest of the molecule. Residues 5 through 15 and 24 through 34 (*right*) form two regions in which hydrogen bonds (*gray*) hold the residues in a helical configuration close to that of the "classical" alpha helix. Residues 41 through 45 and 50 through 54 (*left*) fold back against each other to form a "pleated sheet," also held together by hydrogen bonds. In addition the hydrogen bond between residues 1 and 40 ties the first 40 residues into a compact structure that may have been folded in this way before the molecule was fully synthesized (*see illustration at the bottom of these two pages*).

side chains. Many of the other residues also were easily identifiable, but it was nevertheless most important for the rapid and reliable interpretation of the image that the results of the chemical analysis were already available. With their help more than 95 percent of the atoms in the molecule were readily identified and located within about .25 angstrom.

Further efforts at improving the accuracy with which the atoms have been located is in progress, but an almost complete description of the lysozyme molecule now exists [*see illustration on pages 64 and 65*]. By studying it and the

results of some further experiments we can begin to suggest answers to two important questions: How does a molecule such as this one attain its observed conformation? How does it function as an enzyme, or biological catalyst?

Inspection of the lysozyme molecule immediately suggests two generalizations about its conformation that agree well with those arrived at earlier in the study of myoglobin. It is obvious that certain residues with acidic and basic side chains that ionize, or dissociate, on contact with water are all on the surface of the molecule more or less readily accessible to the surrounding

liquid. Such "polar" side chains are hydrophilic—attracted to water; they are found in aspartic acid and glutamic acid residues and in lysine, arginine and histidine residues, which have basic side groups. On the other hand, most of the markedly nonpolar and hydrophobic side chains (for example those found in leucine and isoleucine residues) are shielded from the surrounding liquid by more polar parts of the molecule. In fact, as was predicted by Sir Eric Rideal (who was at one time director of the Royal Institution) and Irving Langmuir, lysozyme, like myoglobin, is quite well described as an oil drop with a polar coat. Here it is important to note that the environment of each molecule in the crystalline state is not significantly different from its natural environment in the living cell. The crystals themselves include a large proportion (some 35 percent by weight) of mostly watery liquid of crystallization. The effect of the surrounding liquid on the protein conformation thus is likely to be much the same in the crystals as it is in solution.

It appears, then, that the observed conformation is preferred because in it the hydrophobic side chains are kept out of contact with the surrounding liquid whereas the polar side chains are generally exposed to it. In this way the system consisting of the protein and the solvent attains a minimum free energy, partly because of the large number of favorable interactions of like groups within the protein molecule and between it and the surrounding liquid, and partly because of the relatively high disorder of the water molecules that are in contact only with other polar groups of atoms.

Guided by these generalizations, many workers are now interested in the possibility of predicting the conforma-

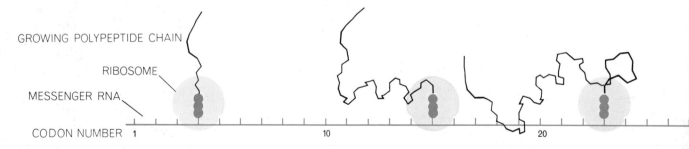

FOLDING OF PROTEIN MOLECULE may take place as the growing polypeptide chain is being synthesized by the intracellular particles called ribosomes. The genetic message specifying the amino acid sequence of each protein is coded in "messenger" ribonucleic acid (RNA). It is believed several ribosomes travel simultaneously along this long-chain molecule, reading the message as they go.

tion of a protein molecule from its chemical formula alone [see "Molecular Model-building by Computer," by Cyrus Levinthal; available as Offprint #1043]. The task of exploring all possible conformations in the search for the one of lowest free energy seems likely, however, to remain beyond the power of any imaginable computer. On a conservative estimate it would be necessary to consider some 10^{129} different conformations for the lysozyme molecule in any general search for the one with minimum free energy. Since this number is far greater than the number of particles in the observable universe, it is clear that simplifying assumptions will have to be made if calculations of this kind are to succeed.

The Folding of Lysozyme

For some time Peter Dunnill and I have been trying to develop a model of protein-folding that promises to make practicable calculations of the minimum energy conformation and that is, at the same time, qualitatively consistent with the observed structure of myoglobin and lysozyme. This model makes use of our present knowledge of the way in which proteins are synthesized in the living cell. For example, it is well known, from experiments by Howard M. Dintzis and by Christian B. Anfinsen and Robert Canfield, that protein molecules are synthesized from the terminal amino end of their polypeptide chain. The nature of the synthetic mechanism, which involves the intracellular particles called ribosomes working in collaboration with two forms of ribonucleic acid ("messenger" RNA and "transfer" RNA), is increasingly well understood in principle, although the detailed environment of the growing protein chain remains unknown. Nevertheless,

it seems a reasonable assumption that, as the synthesis proceeds, the amino end of the chain becomes separated by an increasing distance from the point of attachment to the ribosome, and that the folding of the protein chain to its native conformation begins at this end even before the synthesis is complete. According to our present ideas, parts of the polypeptide chain, particularly those near the terminal amino end, may fold into stable conformations that can still be recognized in the finished molecule and that act as "internal templates," or centers, around which the rest of the chain is folded [see illustration at bottom of these two pages]. It may therefore be useful to look for the stable conformations of parts of the polypeptide chain and to avoid studying all the possible conformations of the whole molecule.

Inspection of the lysozyme molecule provides qualitative support for these ideas [see top illustration on opposite page]. The first 40 residues from the terminal amino end form a compact structure (residues 1 and 40 are linked by a hydrogen bond) with a hydrophobic interior and a relatively hydrophilic surface that seems likely to have been folded in this way, or in a simply related way, before the molecule was fully synthesized. It may also be important to observe that this part of the molecule includes more alpha helix than the remainder does.

These first 40 residues include a mixture of hydrophobic and hydrophilic side chains, but the next 14 residues in the sequence are all hydrophilic; it is interesting, and possibly significant, that these are the residues in the antiparallel pleated sheet, which lies out of contact with the globular submolecule formed by the earlier residues. In the light of our model of protein fold-

ing the obvious speculation is that there is no incentive to fold these hydrophilic residues in contact with the first part of the chain until the hydrophobic residues 55 (isoleucine) and 56 (leucine) have to be shielded from contact with the surrounding liquid. It seems reasonable to suppose that at this stage residues 41 through 54 fold back on themselves, forming the pleated-sheet structure and burying the hydrophobic side chains in the initial hydrophobic pocket.

Similar considerations appear to govern the folding of the rest of the molecule. In brief, residues 57 through 86 are folded in contact with the pleated-sheet structure so that at this stage of the process—if indeed it follows this course—the folded chain forms a structure with two wings lying at an angle to each other. Residues 86 through 96 form a length of alpha helix, one side of which is predominantly hydrophobic, because of an appropriate alternation of polar and nonpolar residues in that part of the sequence. This helix lies in the gap between the two wings formed by the earlier residues, with its hydrophobic side buried within the molecule. The gap between the two wings is not completely filled by the helix, however; it is transformed into a deep cleft running up one side of the molecule. As we shall see, this cleft forms the active site of the enzyme. The remaining residues are folded around the globular unit formed by the terminal amino end of the polypeptide chain.

This model of protein-folding can be tested in a number of ways, for example by studying the conformation of the first 40 residues in isolation both di-

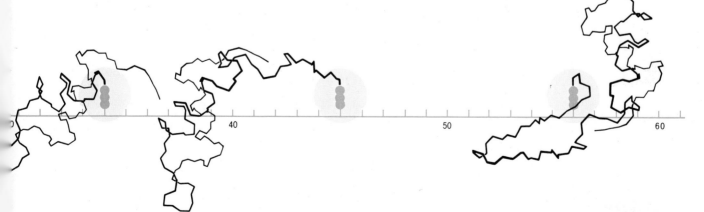

Presumably the messenger RNA for lysozyme contains 129 "codons," one for each amino acid. Amino acids are delivered to the site of synthesis by molecules of "transfer" RNA (dark color). The illustration shows how the lysozyme chain would lengthen as a ribosome travels along the messenger RNA molecule. Here, hypothetically, the polypeptide is shown folding directly into its final shape.

rectly (after removal of the rest of the molecule) and by computation. Ultimately, of course, the model will be regarded as satisfactory only if it helps us to predict how other protein molecules are folded from a knowledge of their chemical structure alone.

The Activity of Lysozyme

In order to understand how lysozyme brings about the dissolution of bacteria we must consider the structure of the bacterial cell wall in some detail. Through the pioneer and independent studies of Karl Meyer and E. B. Chain, followed up by M. R. J. Salton of the University of Manchester and many others, the structures of bacterial cell walls and the effect of lysozyme on them are now quite well known. The important part of the cell wall, as far as lysozyme is concerned, is made up of glucose-like amino-sugar molecules linked together into long polysaccharide chains, which are themselves cross-connected by short lengths of polypeptide chain. This part of each cell wall probably forms one enormous molecule—a "bag-shaped macromolecule," as W. Weidel and H. Pelzer have called it.

The amino-sugar molecules concerned in these polysaccharide structures are of two kinds; each contains an acetamido (–NH · CO · CH$_3$) side group, but one of them contains an additional major group, a lactyl side chain [see illustration below]. One of these amino sugars is known as N-acetylglucosamine (NAG) and the other as N-acetylmuramic acid (NAM). They occur alternately in the

polysaccharide chains, being connected by bridges that include an oxygen atom (glycosidic linkages) between carbon atoms 1 and 4 of consecutive sugar rings; this is the same linkage that joins glucose residues in cellulose. The polypeptide chains that cross-connect these polysaccharides are attached to the NAM residues through the lactyl side chain attached to carbon atom 3 in each NAM ring.

Lysozyme has been shown to break the linkages in which carbon 1 in NAM is linked to carbon 4 in NAG but not the other linkages. It has also been shown to break down chitin, another common natural polysaccharide that is found in lobster shell and that contains only NAG.

Ever since the work of Svante Arrhenius of Sweden in the late 19th century enzymes have been thought to work by forming intermediate compounds with their substrates: the substances whose chemical reactions they catalyze. A proper theory of the enzyme-substrate complex, which underlies all present thinking about enzyme activity, was clearly propounded by Leonor Michaelis and Maude Menton in a remarkable paper published in 1913. The idea, in its simplest form, is that an enzyme molecule provides a site on its surface to which its substrate molecule can bind in a quite precise way. Reactive groups of atoms in the enzyme then promote the required chemical reaction in the substrate. Our immediate objective, therefore, was to find the structure of a reactive complex between lysozyme and its polysaccha-

ride substrate, in the hope that we would then be able to recognize the active groups of atoms in the enzyme and understand how they function.

Our studies began with the observation by Martin Wenzel and his colleagues at the Free University of Berlin that the enzyme is prevented from functioning by the presence of NAG itself. This small molecule acts as a competitive inhibitor of the enzyme's activity and, since it is a part of the large substrate molecule normally acted on by the enzyme, it seems likely to do this by binding to the enzyme in the way that part of the substrate does. It prevents the enzyme from working by preventing the substrate from binding to the enzyme. Other simple amino-sugar molecules, including the trisa charide made of three NAG units, behave in the same way. We therefore decided to study the binding of these sugar molecules to the lysozyme molecules in our crystals in the hope of learning something about the structure of the enzyme-substrate complex itself.

My colleague Louise Johnson soon found that crystals containing the sugar molecules bound to lysozyme can be prepared very simply by adding the sugar to the solution from which the lysozyme crystals have been grown and in which they are kept suspended. The small molecules diffuse into the protein crystals along the channels filled with water that run through the crystals. Fortunately the resulting change in the crystal structure can be studied quite simply. A useful image of the electron-density changes can be calculated from

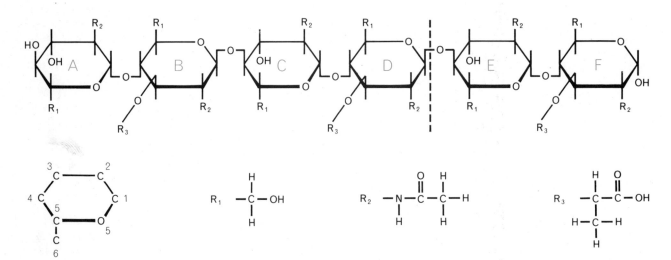

POLYSACCHARIDE MOLECULE found in the walls of certain bacterial cells is the substrate broken by the lysozyme molecule. The polysaccharide consists of alternating residues of two kinds of amino sugar: N-acetylglucosamine (NAG) and N-acetylmuramic acid (NAM). In the length of polysaccharide chain shown here A, C and E are NAG residues; B, D and F are NAM residues. The inset at left shows the numbering scheme for identifying the principal atoms in each sugar ring. Six rings of the polysaccharide fit into the cleft of the lysozyme molecule, which effects a cleavage between rings D and E (see illustration on pages 68 and 69).

measurements of the changes in amplitude of the diffracted waves, on the assumption that their phase relations have not changed from those determined for the pure protein crystals. The image shows the difference in electron density between crystals that contain the added sugar molecules and those that do not.

In this way the binding to lysozyme of eight different amino sugars was studied at low resolution (that is, through the measurement of changes in the amplitude of 400 diffracted waves). The results showed that the sugars bind to lysozyme at a number of different places in the cleft of the enzyme. The investigation was hurried on to higher resolution in an attempt to discover the exact nature of the binding. Happily these studies at two-angstrom resolution (which required the measurement of 10,000 diffracted waves) have now shown in detail how the trisaccharide made of three NAG units is bound to the enzyme.

The trisaccharide fills the top half of the cleft and is bound to the enzyme by a number of interactions, which can be followed with the help of the illustration on pages 68 and 69. In this illustration six important hydrogen bonds, to be described presently, are identified by number. The most critical of these interactions appear to involve the acetamido group of sugar residue C [*third from top*], whose carbon atom 1 is not linked to another sugar residue. There are hydrogen bonds from the CO group of this side chain to the main-chain NH group of amino acid residue 59 in the enzyme molecule [*bond No. 1*] and from its NH group to the main-chain CO group of residue 107 (alanine) in the enzyme molecule [*bond No. 2*]. Its terminal CH_3 group makes contact with the side chain of residue 108 (tryptophan). Hydrogen bonds [*No. 3 and No. 4*] are also formed between two oxygen atoms adjacent to carbon atoms 6 and 3 of sugar residue C and the side chains of residues 62 and 63 (both tryptophan) respectively. Another hydrogen bond [*No. 5*] is formed between the acetamido side chain of sugar residue A and residue 101 (aspartic acid) in the enzyme molecule. From residue 101 there is a hydrogen bond [*No. 6*] to the oxygen adjacent to carbon atom 6 of sugar residue B. These polar interactions are supplemented by a large number of nonpolar interactions that are more difficult to summarize briefly. Among the more important nonpolar interactions, however, are those between sugar residue B and the ring system of residue

62; these deserve special mention because they are affected by a small change in the conformation of the enzyme molecule that occurs when the trisaccharide is bound to it. The electron-density map showing the change in electron density when tri-NAG is bound in the protein crystal reveals clearly that parts of the enzyme molecule have moved with respect to one another. These changes in conformation are largely restricted to the part of the enzyme structure to the left of the cleft, which appears to tilt more or less as a whole in such a way as to close the cleft slightly. As a result the side chain of residue 62 moves about .75 angstrom toward the position of sugar residue B. Such changes in enzyme conformation have been discussed for some time, notably by Daniel E. Koshland, Jr., of the University of California at Berkeley, whose "induced fit" theory of the enzyme-substrate interaction is supported in some degree by this observation in lysozyme.

The Enzyme-Substrate Complex

At this stage in the investigation excitement grew high. Could we tell how the enzyme works? I believe we can. Unfortunately, however, we cannot see this dynamic process in our X-ray images. We have to work out what must happen from our static pictures. First of all it is clear that the complex formed by tri-NAG and the enzyme is not the enzyme-substrate complex involved in catalysis because it is stable. At low concentrations tri-NAG is known to behave as an inhibitor rather than as a substrate that is broken down; clearly we have been looking at the way in which it binds as an inhibitor. It is noticeable, however, that tri-NAG fills only half of the cleft. The possibility emerges that more sugar residues, filling the remainder of the cleft, are required for the formation of a reactive enzyme-substrate complex. The assumption here is that the observed binding of tri-NAG as an inhibitor involves interactions with the enzyme molecule that also play a part in the formation of the functioning enzyme-substrate complex.

Accordingly we have built a model that shows that another three sugar residues can be added to the tri-NAG in such a way that there are satisfactory interactions of the atoms in the proposed substrate and the enzyme. There is only one difficulty: carbon atom 6 and its adjacent oxygen atom in sugar residue D make uncomfortably close contacts

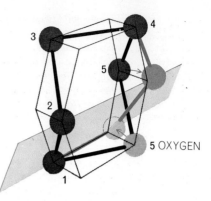

"CHAIR" CONFIGURATION (*gray*) is that normally assumed by the rings of amino sugar in the polysaccharide substrate. When bound against the lysozyme, however, the D ring is distorted (*color*) so that carbon atoms 1, 2 and 5 and oxygen atom 5 lie in a plane. The distortion evidently assists in breaking the substrate below the D ring.

with atoms in the enzyme molecule, unless this sugar residue is distorted a little out of its most stable "chair" conformation into a conformation in which carbon atoms 1, 2 and 5 and oxygen atom 5 all lie in a plane [*see illustration above*]. Otherwise satisfactory interactions immediately suggest themselves, and the model falls into place.

At this point it seemed reasonable to assume that the model shows the structure of the functioning complex between the enzyme and a hexasaccharide. The next problem was to decide which of the five glycosidic linkages would be broken under the influence of the enzyme. Fortunately evidence was at hand to suggest the answer. As we have seen, the cell-wall polysaccharide includes alternate sugar residues of two kinds, NAG and NAM, and the bond broken is between NAM and NAG. It was therefore important to decide which of the six sugar residues in our model could be NAM, which is the same as NAG except for the lactyl side chain appended to carbon atom 3. The answer was clear-cut. Sugar residue C cannot be NAM because there is no room for this additional group of atoms. Therefore the bond broken must be between sugar residues B and C or D and E. We already knew that the glycosidic linkage between residues B and C is stable when tri-NAG is bound. The conclusion was inescapable: the linkage that must be broken is the one between sugar residues D and E.

Now it was possible to search for the origin of the catalytic activity in the neighborhood of this linkage. Our task was made easier by the fact that John A.

Rupley of the University of Arizona had shown that the chemical bond broken under the influence of lysozyme is the one between carbon atom 1 and oxygen in the glycosidic link rather than the link between oxygen and carbon atom 4. The most reactive-looking group of atoms in the vicinity of this bond are the side chains of residue 52 (aspartic acid) and residue 35 (glutamic acid).

One of the oxygen atoms of residue 52 is about three angstroms from carbon atom 1 of sugar residue D as well as from the ring oxygen atom 5 of that residue. Residue 35, on the other hand, is about three angstroms from the oxygen in the glycosidic linkage. Furthermore, these two amino acid residues have markedly different environments. Residue 52 has a number of polar neighbors and appears to be involved in a network of hydrogen bonds linking it with residues 46 and 59 (both asparagine) and, through them, with residue 50 (serine). In this environment residue 52 seems likely to give up a terminal hydrogen atom and thus be negatively charged under most conditions, even when it is in a markedly acid solution, whereas residue 35, situated in a nonpolar environment, is likely to retain its terminal hydrogen atom.

A little reflection suggests that the concerted influence of these two amino

acid residues, together with a contribution from the distortion to sugar residue D that has already been mentioned, is enough to explain the catalytic activity of lysozyme. The events leading to the rupture of a bacterial cell wall probably take the following course [see illustration on this page].

First, a lysozyme molecule attaches itself to the bacterial cell wall by interacting with six exposed amino-sugar residues. In the process sugar residue D is somewhat distorted from its usual conformation.

Second, residue 35 transfers its terminal hydrogen atom in the form of a hydrogen ion to the glycosidic oxygen, thus bringing about cleavage of the bond between that oxygen and carbon atom 1 of sugar residue D. This creates a positively charged carbonium ion (C^+) where the oxygen has been severed from carbon atom 1.

Third, this carbonium ion is stabilized by its interaction with the negatively charged aspartic acid side chain of residue 52 until it can combine with a hydroxyl ion (OH^-) that happens to diffuse into position from the surrounding water, thereby completing the reaction. The lysozyme molecule then falls away, leaving behind a punctured bacterial cell wall.

It is not clear from this description that the distortion of sugar residue D plays any part in the reaction, but in fact it probably does so for a very interesting reason. R. H. Lemieux and G. Huber of the National Research Council of Canada showed in 1955 that when a sugar molecule such as NAG incorporates a carbonium ion at the carbon-1 position, it tends to take up the same conformation that is forced on ring D by its interaction with the enzyme molecule. This seems to be an example, therefore, of activation of the substrate by distortion, which has long been a favorite idea of enzymologists. The binding of the substrate to the enzyme itself favors the formation of the carbonium ion in ring D that seems to play an important part in the reaction.

It will be clear from this account that although lysozyme has not been seen in action, we have succeeded in building up a detailed picture of how it may work. There is already a great deal of chemical evidence in agreement with this picture, and as the result of all the work now in progress we can be sure that the activity of Fleming's lysozyme will soon be fully understood. Best of all, it is clear that methods now exist for uncovering the secrets of enzyme action.

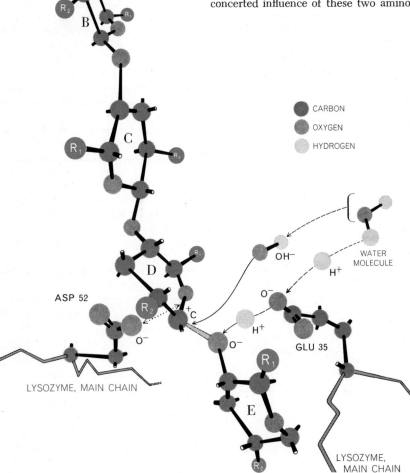

CARBON
OXYGEN
HYDROGEN

ASP 52

LYSOZYME, MAIN CHAIN

OH⁻

WATER MOLECULE

H⁺

GLU 35

LYSOZYME, MAIN CHAIN

SPLITTING OF SUBSTRATE BY LYSOZYME is believed to involve the proximity and activity of two side chains, residue 35 (glutamic acid) and residue 52 (aspartic acid). It is proposed that a hydrogen ion (H⁺) becomes detached from the OH group of residue 35 and attaches itself to the oxygen atom that joins rings D and E, thus breaking the bond between the two rings. This leaves carbon atom 1 of the D ring with a positive charge, in which form it is known as a carbonium ion. It is stabilized in this condition by the negatively charged side chain of residue 52. The surrounding water supplies an OH⁻ ion to combine with the carbonium ion and an H⁺ ion to replace the one lost by residue 35. The two parts of the substrate then fall away, leaving the enzyme free to cleave another polysaccharide chain.

8

The Structure of the Hereditary Material

F. H. C. CRICK

October 1954

Viewed under a microscope, the process of mitosis, by which one cell divides and becomes two, is one of the most fascinating spectacles in the whole of biology. No one who watches the event unfold in speeded-up motion pictures can fail to be excited and awed. As a demonstration of the powers of dynamic organization possessed by living matter, the act of division is impressive enough, but even more stirring is the appearance of two identical sets of chromosomes where only one existed before. Here lies biology's greatest challenge: How are these fundamental bodies duplicated? Unhappily the copying process is beyond the resolving power of microscopes, but much is being learned about it in other ways.

One approach is the study of the nature and behavior of whole living cells; another is the investigation of substances extracted from them. This article will discuss only the second approach, but both are indispensable if we are ever to solve the problem; indeed some of the most exciting results are being obtained by what might loosely be described as a combination of the two methods.

Chromosomes consist mainly of three kinds of chemical: protein, desoxyribonucleic acid (DNA) and ribonucleic acid (RNA). (Since RNA is only a minor component, we shall not consider it in detail here.) The nucleic acids and the proteins have several features in common. They are all giant molecules, and each type has the general structure of a main backbone with side groups attached. The proteins have about 20 different kinds of side groups; the nucleic acids usually only four (and of a different type). The smallness of these

numbers itself is striking, for there is no obvious chemical reason why many more types of side groups should not occur. Another interesting feature is that no protein or nucleic acid occurs in more than one optical form; there is never an optical isomer, or mirror-image molecule. This shows that the shape of the molecules must be important.

These generalizations (with minor exceptions) hold over the entire range of living organisms, from viruses and bacteria to plants and animals. The impression is inescapable that we are dealing with a very basic aspect of living matter, and one having far more simplicity than we would have dared to hope. It encourages us to look for simple explanations for the formation of these giant molecules.

The most important role of proteins is that of the enzymes—the machine tools of the living cell. An enzyme is specific, often highly specific, for the reaction which it catalyzes. Moreover, chemical and X-ray studies suggest that the structure of each enzyme is itself rigidly determined. The side groups of a given enzyme are probably arranged in a fixed order along the polypeptide backbone. If we could discover how a cell produces the appropriate enzymes, in particular how it assembles the side groups of each enzyme in the correct order, we should have gone a long way toward explaining the simpler forms of life in terms of physics and chemistry.

We believe that this order is controlled by the chromosomes. In recent years suspicion has been growing that the key to the specificity of the chromosomes lies not in their protein but in their DNA. DNA is found in all chromosomes

—and only in the chromosomes (with minor exceptions). The amount of DNA per chromosome set is in many cases a fixed quantity for a given species. The sperm, having half the chromosomes of the normal cell, has about half the amount of DNA, and tetraploid cells in the liver, having twice the normal chromosome complement, seem to have twice the amount of DNA. This constancy of the amount of DNA is what one might expect if it is truly the material that determines the hereditary pattern.

Then there is suggestive evidence in two cases that DNA alone, free of protein, may be able to carry genetic information. The first of these is the discovery that the "transforming principles" of bacteria, which can produce an inherited change when added to the cell, appear to consist only of DNA. The second is the fact that during the infection of a bacterium by a bacteriophage the DNA of the phage penetrates into the bacterial cell while most of the protein, perhaps all of it, is left outside.

The Chemical Formula

DNA can be extracted from cells by mild chemical methods, and much experimental work has been carried out to discover its chemical nature. This work has been conspicuously successful. It is now known that DNA consists of a very long chain made up of alternate sugar and phosphate groups [see diagram on the next two pages]. The sugar is always the same sugar, known as desoxyribose. And it is always joined onto the phosphate in the same way, so that the long chain is perfectly regular, repeating the same phosphate-sugar sequence over and over again.

But while the phosphate-sugar chain is perfectly regular, the molecule as a whole is not, because each sugar has a "base" attached to it and the base is not always the same. Four different types of base are commonly found: two of them are purines, called adenine and guanine, and two are pyrimidines, known as thymine and cytosine. So far as is known the order in which they follow one another along the chain is irregular, and probably varies from one piece of DNA to another. In fact, we suspect that the order of the bases is what confers specificity on a given DNA. Because the sequence of the bases is not known, one can only say that the *general* formula for DNA is established. Nevertheless this formula should be reckoned one of the major achievements of biochemistry, and it is the foundation for all the ideas described in the rest of this article.

At one time it was thought that the four bases occurred in equal amounts, but in recent years this idea has been shown to be incorrect. E. Chargaff and his colleagues at Columbia University, A. E. Mirsky and his group at the Rockefeller Institute for Medical Research and G. R. Wyatt of Canada have accurately measured the amounts of the bases in many instances and have shown that the relative amounts appear to be fixed for any given species, irrespective of the individual or the organ from which the DNA was taken. The proportions usually differ for DNA from different species, but species related to one another may not differ very much.

Although we know from the chemical formula of DNA that it is a chain, this does not in itself tell us the shape of the molecule, for the chain, having many single bonds around which it may rotate, might coil up in all sorts of shapes. However, we know from physical-chemical measurements and electron-microscope pictures that the molecule usually is long, thin and fairly straight, rather like a stiff bit of cord. It is only about 20 Angstroms thick (one Angstrom = one 100-millionth of a centimeter). This is very small indeed, in fact not much more than a dozen atoms thick. The length of the DNA seems to depend somewhat on the method of preparation. A good sample may reach a length of 30,000 Angstroms, so that the structure is more than 1,000 times as long as it is thick. The length inside the cell may be much greater than this, because there is always the chance that the extraction process may break it up somewhat.

Pictures of the Molecule

None of these methods tells us anything about the detailed arrangement in space of the atoms inside the molecule. For this it is necessary to use X-ray diffraction. The average distance between bonded atoms in an organic molecule is about 1½ Angstroms; between unbonded atoms, three to four Angstroms. X-rays have a small enough wavelength (1½ Angstroms) to resolve the atoms, but unfortunately an X-ray diffraction photograph is not a picture in the ordinary sense of the word. We cannot focus X-rays as we can ordinary light; hence a picture can be obtained only by roundabout methods. Moreover, it can show clearly only the periodic, or regularly repeated, parts of the structure.

With patience and skill several English workers have obtained good diffraction pictures of DNA extracted from cells and drawn into long fibers. The first studies, even before details emerged, produced two surprises. First, they revealed that the DNA structure could take two forms. In relatively low humidity, when the water content of the fibers was about 40 per cent, the DNA molecules gave a crystalline pattern, showing that they were aligned regularly in all three dimensions. When the humidity was raised and the fibers took up more water, they increased in length by about 30 per cent and the pattern

tended to become "paracrystalline," which means that the molecules were packed side by side in a less regular manner, as if the long molecules could slide over one another somewhat. The second surprising result was that DNA from different species appeared to give identical X-ray patterns, despite the fact that the amounts of the four bases present varied. This was particularly odd because of the existence of the crystalline form just mentioned. How could the structure appear so regular when the bases varied? It seemed that the broad arrangement of the molecule must be independent of the exact sequence of the bases, and it was therefore thought that the bases play no part in holding the structure together. As we shall see, this turned out to be wrong.

The early X-ray pictures showed a third intriguing fact: namely, that the repeats in the crystallographic pattern came at much longer intervals than the chemical repeat units in the molecule. The distance from one phosphate to the next cannot be more than about seven Angstroms, yet the crystallographic repeat came at intervals of 28 Angstroms in the crystalline form and 34 Angstroms in the paracrystalline form; that is, the chemical unit repeated several times before the structure repeated crystallographically.

J. D. Watson and I, working in the Medical Research Council Unit in the Cavendish Laboratory at Cambridge,

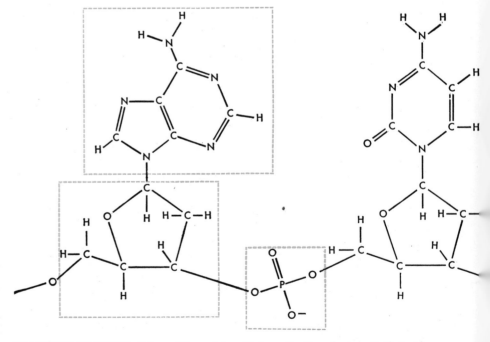

FRAGMENT OF CHAIN of desoxyribonucleic acid shows the three basic units that make up the molecule. Repeated over and over in a long chain, they make it 1,000 times as long

were convinced that we could get somewhere near the DNA structure by building scale models based on the X-ray patterns obtained by M. H. F. Wilkins, Rosalind Franklin and their co-workers at Kings' College, London. A great deal is known about the exact distances between bonded atoms in molecules, about the angles between the bonds and about the size of atoms—the so-called van der Waals' distance between adjacent non-bonded atoms. This information is easy to embody in scale models. The problem is rather like a three-dimensional jig saw puzzle with curious pieces joined together by rotatable joints (single bonds between atoms).

The Helix

To get anywhere at all we had to make some assumptions. The most important one had to do with the fact that the crystallographic repeat did not coincide with the repetition of chemical units in the chain but came at much longer intervals. A possible explanation was that all the links in the chain were the same but the X-rays were seeing every tenth link, say, from the same angle and the others from different angles. What sort of chain might produce this pattern? The answer was easy: the chain might be coiled in a helix. (A helix is often loosely called a spiral; the distinction is that a helix winds not around a cone but around a cylinder, as

a winding staircase usually does.) The distance between crystallographic repeats would then correspond to the distance in the chain between one turn of the helix and the next.

We had some difficulty at first because we ignored the bases and tried to work only with the phosphate-sugar backbone. Eventually we realized that we had to take the bases into account, and this led us quickly to a structure which we now believe to be correct in its broad outlines.

This particular model contains a pair of DNA chains wound around a common axis. The two chains are linked together by their bases. A base on one chain is joined by very weak bonds to a base at the same level on the other chain, and all the bases are paired off in this way right along the structure. In the diagram opposite, the two ribbons represent the phosphate-sugar chains, and the pairs of bases holding them together are symbolized as horizontal rods. Paradoxically, in order to make the structure as symmetrical as possible we had to have the two chains run in opposite directions; that is, the sequence of the atoms goes one way in one chain and the opposite way in the other. Thus the figure looks exactly the same whichever end is turned up.

Now we found that we could not arrange the bases any way we pleased; the four bases would fit into the structure only in certain pairs. In any pair

there must always be one big one (purine) and one little one (pyrimidine). A pair of pyrimidines is too short to bridge the gap between the two chains, and a pair of purines is too big to fit into the space.

At this point we made an additional assumption. The bases can theoretically exist in a number of forms depending upon where the hydrogen atoms are attached. We assumed that for each base one form was much more probable than all the others. The hydrogen atoms can be thought of as little knobs attached to the bases, and the way the bases fit together depends crucially upon where these knobs are. With this assumption the only possible pairs that will fit in are: adenine with thymine and guanine with cytosine.

The way these pairs are formed is shown in the diagrams on page 80. The dotted lines show the hydrogen bonds, which hold the two bases of a pair together. They are very weak bonds; their energy is not many times greater than the energy of thermal vibration at room temperature. (Hydrogen bonds are the main forces holding different water molecules together, and it is because of them that water is a liquid at room temperatures and not a gas.)

Adenine must always be paired with thymine, and guanine with cytosine; it is impossible to fit the bases together in any other combination in our model. (This pairing is likely to be so funda-

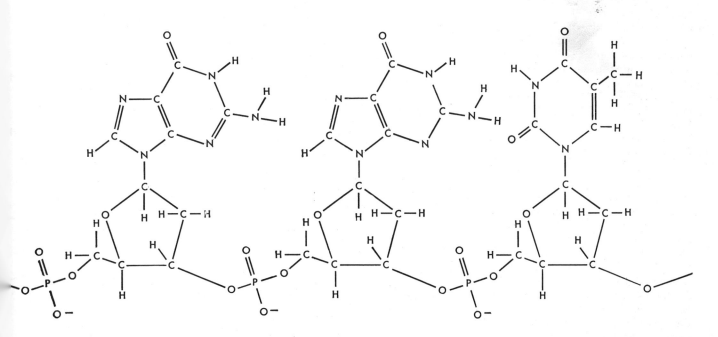

as it is thick. The backbone is made up of pentose sugar molecules (marked by the middle colored square), linked by phosphate groups (bottom square). The bases (top square), adenine, cytosine, guanine and thymine protrude off each sugar in irregular order.

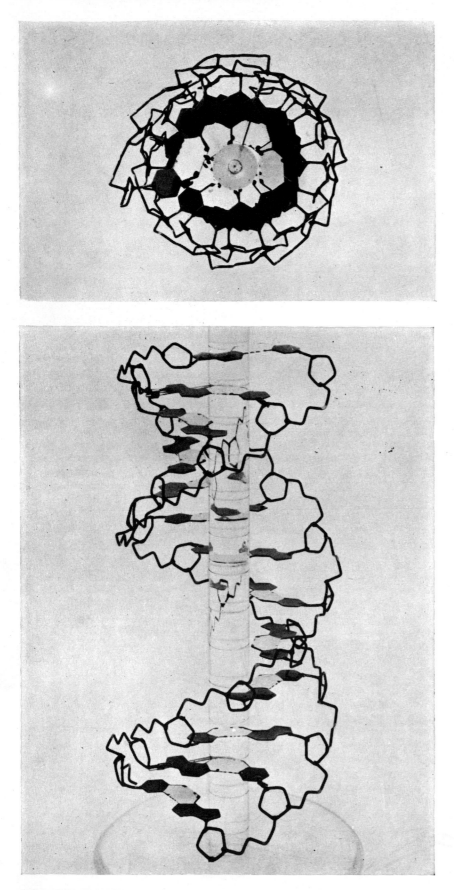

STRUCTURAL MODEL shows a pair of DNA chains wound as a helix about the fiber axis. The pentose sugars can be plainly seen. From every one on each chain protrudes a base, linked to an opposing one at the same level by a hydrogen bond. These base-to-base links act as horizontal supports, holding the chains together. Upper photograph is a top view.

mental for biology that I cannot help wondering whether some day an enthusiastic scientist will christen his newborn twins Adenine and Thymine!) The model places no restriction, however, on the sequence of pairs along the structure. Any specified pair can follow any other. This is because a pair of bases is flat, and since in this model they are stacked roughly like a pile of coins, it does not matter which pair goes above which.

It is important to realize that the specific pairing of the bases is the direct result of the assumption that both phosphate-sugar chains are helical. This regularity implies that the distance from a sugar group on one chain to that on the other at the same level is always the same, no matter where one is along the chain. It follows that the bases linked to the sugars always have the same amount of space in which to fit. It is the regularity of the phosphate-sugar chains, therefore, that is at the root of the specific pairing.

The Picture Clears

At the moment of writing, detailed interpretation of the X-ray photographs by Wilkins' group at Kings' College has not been completed, and until this has been done no structure can be considered proved. Nevertheless there are certain features of the model which are so strongly supported by the experimental evidence that it is very likely they will be embodied in the final correct structure. For instance, measurements of the density and water content of the DNA fibers, taken with evidence showing that the fibers can be extended in length, strongly suggest that there are two chains in the structural unit of DNA. Again, recent X-ray pictures have shown clearly a most striking general pattern which we can now recognize as the characteristic signature of a helical structure. In particular there are a large number of places where the diffracted intensity is zero or very small, and these occur exactly where one expects from a helix of this sort. Another feature one would expect is that the X-ray intensities should approach cylindrical symmetry, and it is now known that they do this. Recently Wilkins and his co-workers have given a brilliant analysis of the details of the X-ray pattern of the crystalline form, and have shown that they are consistent with a structure of this type, though in the crystalline form the bases are tilted away from the fiber axis instead of perpendicular, as in our model. Our construction was based on

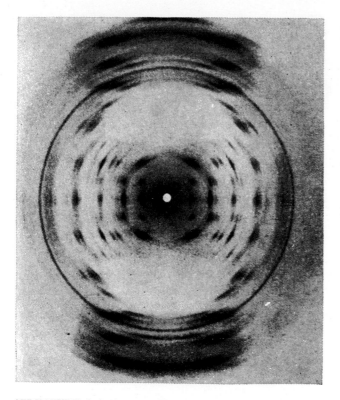

STRUCTURE A is the crystalline form of DNA found at relatively low humidity. This X-ray photograph is by H. R. Wilson.

STRUCTURE B is the paracrystalline form of DNA. The molecules are less regularly arranged. Picture is by R. E. Franklin.

the paracrystalline form.

Many of the physical and chemical properties of DNA can now be understood in terms of this model. For example, the comparative stiffness of the structure explains rather naturally why DNA keeps a long, fiber-like shape in solution. The hydrogen bonds of the bases account for the behavior of DNA in response to changes in pH. Most striking of all is the fact that in every kind of DNA so far examined—and over 40 have been analyzed—the amount of adenine is about equal to the amount of thymine and the guanine equal to the cytosine, while the cross-ratios (between, say, adenine and guanine) can vary considerably from species to species. This re-

markable fact, first pointed out by Chargaff, is exactly what one would expect according to our model, which requires that every adenine be paired with a thymine and every guanine with a cytosine.

It may legitimately be asked whether the artificially prepared fibers of extracted DNA, on which our model is based, are really representative of intact DNA in the cell. There is every indication that they are. It is difficult to see how the very characteristic features of the model could be produced as artefacts by the extraction process. Moreover, Wilkins has shown that intact biological material, such as sperm heads and bacteriophage, gives X-ray patterns very

similar to those of the extracted fibers.

The present position, therefore, is that in all likelihood this statement about DNA can safely be made: its structure consists of two helical chains wound around a common axis and held together by hydrogen bonds between specific pairs of bases.

The Mold

Now the exciting thing about a model of this type is that it immediately suggests how the DNA might produce an exact copy of itself. The model consists of two parts, each of which is the complement of the other. Thus either chain may act as a sort of mold on which a complementary chain can be synthe-

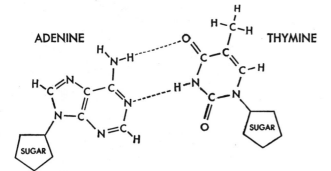

ONE LINKAGE of base to base across the pair of DNA chains is between adenine and thymine. For the structure proposed, the link of a large base with a small one is required to fit chains together.

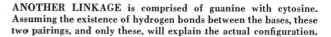

ANOTHER LINKAGE is comprised of guanine with cytosine. Assuming the existence of hydrogen bonds between the bases, these two pairings, and only these, will explain the actual configuration.

sized. The two chains of a DNA, let us say, unwind and separate. Each begins to build a new complement onto itself. When the process is completed, there are two pairs of chains where we had only one. Moreover, because of the specific pairing of the bases the sequence of the pairs of bases will have been duplicated exactly; in other words, the mold has not only assembled the building blocks but has put them together in just the right order.

Let us imagine that we have a single helical chain of DNA, and that floating around it inside the cell is a supply of precursors of the four sorts of building blocks needed to make a new chain. Unfortunately we do not know the makeup of these precursor units; they may be, but probably are not, nucleotides, consisting of one phosphate, one sugar and one base. In any case, from time to time a loose unit will attach itself by its base to one of the bases of the single DNA chain. Another loose unit may attach itself to an adjoining base on the chain. Now if one or both of the two newly attached units is not the correct mate for the one it has joined on the chain, the two newcomers will be unable to link together, because they are not the right distance apart. One or both will soon drift away, to be replaced by other units. When, however, two adjacent newcomers are the correct partners for their opposite numbers on the chain, they will be in just the right position to be linked together and begin to form a new chain. Thus only the unit with the proper base will gain a permanent hold at any given position, and eventually the right partners will fill in the vacancies all along the forming chain. While this is going on, the other single chain of the original pair also will be forming a new chain complementary to itself.

At the moment this idea must be regarded simply as a working hypothesis. Not only is there little direct evidence for it, but there are a number of obvious difficulties. For example, certain organisms contain small amounts of a fifth base, 5-methyl cytosine. So far as the model is concerned, 5-methyl cytosine fits just as well as cytosine and it may turn out that it does not matter to the organism which is used, but this has yet to be shown.

A more fundamental difficulty is to explain how the two chains of DNA are unwound in the first place. There would have to be a lot of untwisting, for the total length of all the DNA in a single chromosome is something like four centimeters (400 million Angstroms). This

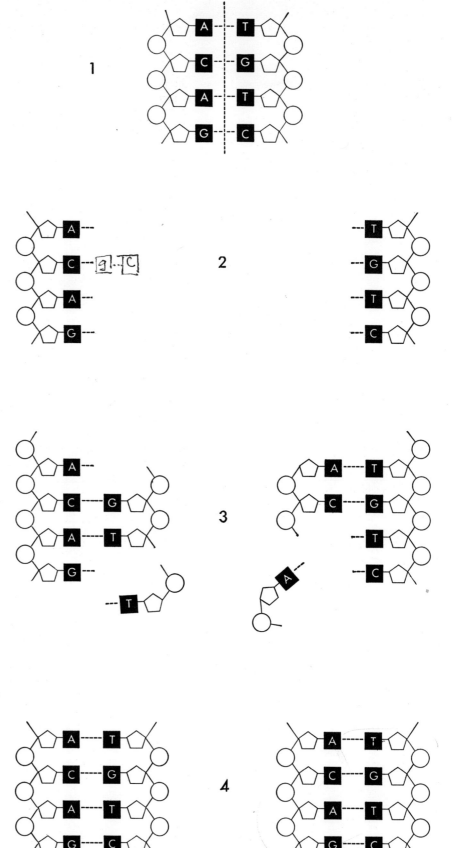

REPLICATION mechanism by which DNA might duplicate itself is shown in diagram. A helix of two DNA chains unwinds and separates (1). Two complementary chains of DNA (2) within the cell begin to attach DNA precursor units floating loosely (3). When the proper bases are joined, two new helixes will build up (4). Letters represent the bases.

means that there must be more than 10 million turns in all, though the DNA may not be all in one piece.

The duplicating process can be made to appear more plausible by assuming that the synthesis of the two new chains begins as soon as the two original chains start to unwind, so that only a short stretch of the chain is ever really single. In fact, we may postulate that it is the growth of the two new chains that unwinds the original pair. This is likely in terms of energy because, for every hydrogen bond that has to be broken, two new ones will be forming. Moreover, plausibility is added to the idea by the fact that the paired chain forms a rather stiff structure, so that the growing chain would tend to unwind the old pair.

The difficulty of untwisting the two chains is a topological one, and is due to the fact that they are intertwined. There would be no difficulty in "unwinding" a single helical chain, because there are so many single bonds in the chain about which rotation is possible. If in the twin structure one chain should break, the other one could easily spin around. This might relieve accumulated strain, and then the two ends of the broken chain, still being in close proximity, might be joined together again. There is even some evidence suggesting that in the process of extraction the chains of DNA may be broken in quite a number of places and that the structure nevertheless holds together by means of the hydrogen bonding, because there is never a break in both chains at the same level. Nevertheless, in spite of these tentative suggestions, the difficulty of untwisting remains a formidable one.

There remains the fundamental puzzle as to how DNA exerts its hereditary influence. A genetic material must carry out two jobs: duplicate itself and control the development of the rest of the cell in a specific way. We have seen how it might do the first of these, but the structure gives no obvious clue concerning how it may carry out the second. We suspect that the sequence of the bases acts as a kind of genetic code. Such an arrangement can carry an enormous amount of information. If we imagine that the pairs of bases correspond to the dots and dashes of the Morse code, there is enough DNA in a single cell of the human body to encode about 1,000 large textbooks. What we want to know, however, is just how this is done in terms of atoms and molecules. In particular, what precisely is it a code for? As we have seen, the three key components of living matter—protein, RNA and DNA—are probably all based on the same general plan. Their backbones are regular, and the variety comes from the sequence of the side groups. It is therefore very natural to suggest that the sequence of the bases of the DNA is in some way a code for the sequence of the amino acids in the polypeptide chains of the proteins which the cell must produce. The physicist George Gamow has recently suggested in a rather abstract way how this information might be transmitted, but there are some difficulties with the actual scheme he has proposed, and so far he has not shown how the idea can be translated into precise molecular configurations.

What then, one may reasonably ask, are the virtues of the proposed model, if any? The prime virtue is that the con-figuration suggested is not vague but can be described in terms acceptable to a chemist. The pairing of the bases can be described rather exactly. The precise positions of the atoms of the backbone is less certain, but they can be fixed within limits, and detailed studies of the X-ray data, now in progress at Kings' College, may narrow these limits considerably. Then the structure brings together two striking pieces of evidence which at first sight seem to be unrelated—the analytical data, showing the one-to-one ratios for adenine-thymine and guanine-cytosine, and the helical nature of the X-ray pattern. These can now be seen to be two facets of the same thing. Finally, is it not perhaps a remarkable coincidence, to say the least, to find in this key material a structure of exactly the type one would need to carry out a specific replication process; namely, one showing both variety and complementarity?

The model is also attractive in its simplicity. While it is obvious that whole chromosomes have a fairly complicated structure, it is not unreasonable to hope that the molecular basis underlying them may be rather simple. If this is so, it may not prove too difficult to devise experiments to unravel it. It would, of course, help enormously if biochemists could discover the immediate precursors of DNA. If we knew the monomers from which nature makes DNA, RNA and protein, we might be able to carry out very spectacular experiments in the test tube. Be that as it may, we now have for the first time a well-defined model for DNA and for a possible replication process, and this in itself should make it easier to devise crucial experiments.

9

The Nucleotide Sequence of a Nucleic Acid

ROBERT W. HOLLEY

February 1966

Two major classes of chainlike molecules underlie the functioning of living organisms: the nucleic acids and the proteins. The former include deoxyribonucleic acid (DNA), which embodies the hereditary message of each organism, and ribonucleic acid (RNA), which helps to translate that message into the thousands of different proteins that activate the living cell. In the past dozen years biochemists have established the complete sequence of amino acid subunits in a number of different proteins. Much less is known about the nucleic acids.

Part of the reason for the slow progress with nucleic acids was the unavailability of pure material for analysis. Another factor was the large size of most nucleic acid molecules, which often contain thousands or even millions of nucleotide subunits. Several years ago, however, a family of small molecules was discovered among the ribonucleic

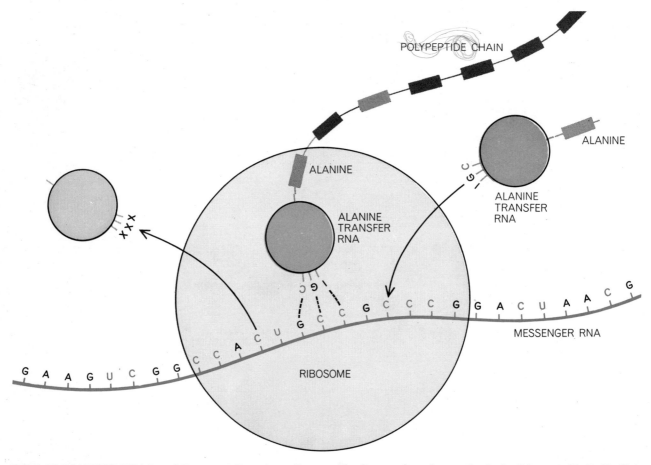

ROLE OF TRANSFER RNA is to deliver a specific amino acid to the site where "messenger" RNA and a ribosome (which also contains RNA) collaborate in the synthesis of a protein. As it is being synthesized a protein chain is usually described as a polypeptide. Each amino acid in the polypeptide chain is specified by a triplet code, or codon, in the molecular chain of messenger RNA.

The diagram shows how an "anticodon" (presumably I—G—C) in alanine transfer RNA may form a temporary bond with the codon for alanine (G—C—C) in the messenger RNA. While so bonded the transfer RNA also holds the polypeptide chain. Each transfer RNA is succeeded by another one, carrying its own amino acid, until the complete message in the messenger RNA has been "read."

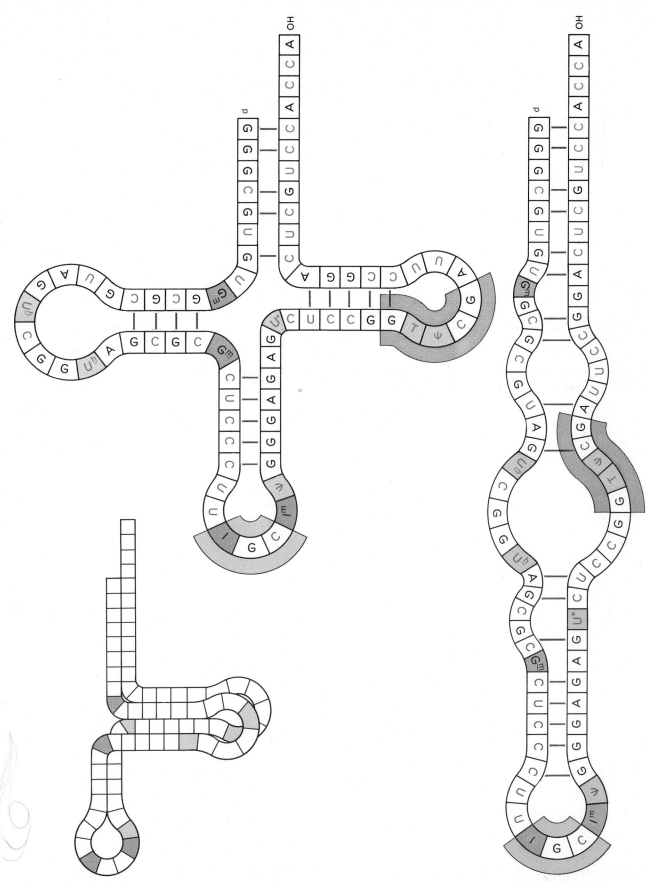

HYPOTHETICAL MODELS of alanine transfer ribonucleic acid (RNA) show three of the many ways in which the molecule's linear chain might be folded. The various letters represent nucleotide subunits; their chemical structure is given at the top of the next two pages. In these models it is assumed that certain nucleotides, such as C—G and A—U, will pair off and tend to form short double-strand regions. Such "base-pairing" is a characteristic feature of nucleic acids. The arrangement at the lower left shows how two of the large "leaves" of the "clover leaf" model may be folded to-gether. The triplet I—G—C is the presumed anticodon shown in the illustration on the opposite page. The region containing the sequence G—T—Ψ—C—G may be common to all transfer RNA's.

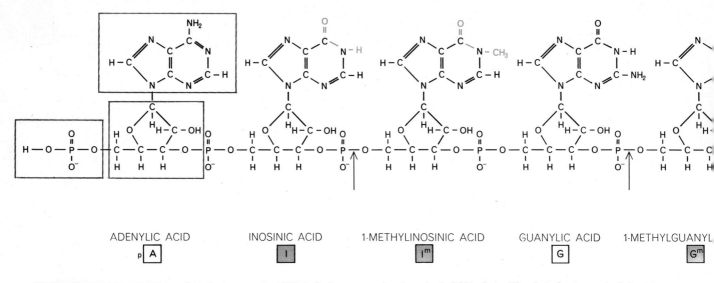

ADENYLIC ACID
p|A|

INOSINIC ACID
|I|

1-METHYLINOSINIC ACID
|Iᵐ|

GUANYLIC ACID
|G|

1-METHYLGUANYL
|Gᵐ|

NUCLEOTIDE SUBUNITS found in alanine transfer RNA include the four commonly present in RNA (A, G, C, U), plus seven others that are variations of the standard structures. Ten of these 11 different nucleotide subunits are assembled above as if they were linked together in a single RNA chain. The chain begins at the left with a phosphate group (*outlined by a small rectangle*) and is followed by a ribose sugar group (*large rectangle*); the two groups alternate to form the backbone of the chain. The chain ends at the right with

acids. My associates and I at the U.S. Plant, Soil and Nutrition Laboratory and Cornell University set ourselves the task of establishing the nucleotide sequence of one of these smaller RNA molecules—a molecule containing fewer than 100 nucleotide subunits. This work culminated recently in the first determination of the complete nucleotide sequence of a nucleic acid.

The object of our study belongs to a family of 20-odd molecules known as transfer RNA's. Each is capable of recognizing one of the 20 different amino acids and of transferring it to the site where it can be incorporated into a growing polypeptide chain. When such a chain assumes its final configuration, sometimes joining with other chains, it is called a protein.

At each step in the process of protein

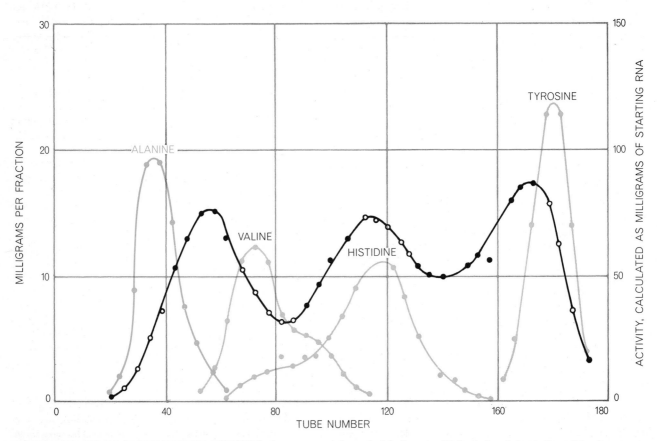

COUNTERCURRENT DISTRIBUTION PATTERN shows two steps in the separation of alanine transfer RNA, as carried out in the author's laboratory. After the first step the RNA content in various collection tubes, measured by ultraviolet absorption, follows the black curve. Biological activity, indicated by the amount of a given amino acid incorporated into polypeptide chains, follows the colored curves. Pure transfer RNA's of four types can be obtained by reprocessing the tubes designated by open circles.

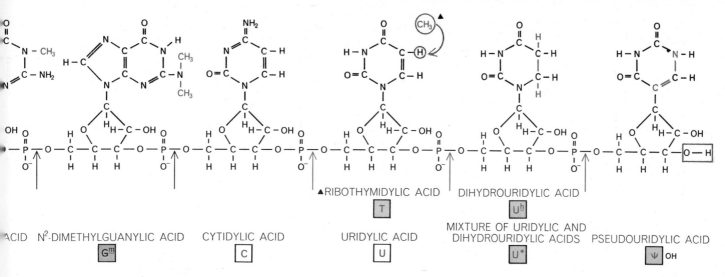

a hydroxyl (OH) group. Each nucleotide subunit consists of a phosphate group, a ribose sugar group and a base. The base portion in the nucleotide at the far left, adenylic acid, is outlined by a large rectangle. In the succeeding bases the atomic variations are shown in color. The base structures without color are those commonly found in RNA. Black arrows show where RNA chains can be cleaved by the enzyme takadiastase ribonuclease T1. Colored arrows show where RNA chains can be cleaved by pancreatic ribonuclease.

synthesis a crucial role is played by the structure of the various RNA's. "Messenger" RNA transcribes the genetic message for each protein from its original storage site in DNA. Another kind of RNA—ribosomal RNA—forms part of the structure of the ribosome, which acts as a jig for holding the messenger RNA while the message is transcribed into a polypeptide chain [see illustration on page 82]. In view of the various roles played by RNA in protein synthesis, the structure of RNA molecules is of considerable interest and significance.

The particular nucleic acid we chose for study is known as alanine transfer RNA—the RNA that transports the amino acid alanine. It was isolated from commercial baker's yeast by methods I shall describe later. Preliminary analyses indicated that the alanine transfer RNA molecule consisted of a single chain of approximately 80 nucleotide subunits. Each nucleotide, in turn, consists of a ribose sugar, a phosphate group and a distinctive appendage termed a nitrogen base. The ribose sugars and phosphate groups link together to form the backbone of the molecule, from which the various bases protrude [see illustration at top of these two pages].

The problem of structural analysis is fundamentally one of identifying each base and determining its place in the sequence. In practice each base is usually isolated in combination with a unit of ribose sugar and a unit of phosphate, which together form a nucleotide. Formally the problem is analogous to determining the sequence of letters in a sentence.

It would be convenient if there were a way to snip off the nucleotides one by one, starting at a known end of the chain and identifying each nucleotide as it appeared. Unfortunately procedures of this kind have such a small yield at each step that their use is limited. The alternative is to break the chain at particular chemical sites with the help of enzymes. This gives rise to small fragments whose nucleotide composition is amenable to analysis. If the chain can be broken up in various ways with different enzymes, one can determine how the fragments overlap and ultimately piece together the entire sequence.

One can visualize how this might work by imagining that the preceding sentence has been written out several times, in a continuous line, on different strips of paper. Imagine that each strip has been cut in a different way. In one case, for example, the first three words "If the chain" and the next three words "can be broken" might appear on separate strips of paper. In another case one might find that "chain" and "can" were together on a single strip. One would immediately conclude that the group of three words ending with "chain" and the group beginning with "can" form a continuous sequence of six words. The concept is simple; putting it into execution takes a little time.

For cleaving the RNA chain we used two principal enzymes: pancreatic ribonuclease and an enzyme called takadiastase ribonuclease T1, which was discovered by the Japanese workers K. Sato-Asano and F. Egami. The first enzyme cleaves the RNA chain immediately to the right of pyrimidine nucleotides, as the molecular structure is conventionally written. Pyrimidine nucleotides are those nucleotides whose bases contain the six-member pyrimidine ring, consisting of four atoms of carbon and two atoms of nitrogen. The two pyrimidines commonly found in RNA are cytosine and uracil. Pancreatic ribonuclease therefore produces fragments that terminate in pyrimidine nucleotides such as cytidylic acid (C) or uridylic acid (U).

The second enzyme, ribonuclease T1, was employed separately to cleave the RNA chain specifically to the right of nucleotides containing a structure of the purine type, such as guanylic acid (G). This provided a set of short fragments distinctively different from those produced by the pancreatic enzyme.

The individual short fragments were isolated by passing them through a thin glass column packed with diethylaminoethyl cellulose—an adaptation of a chromatographic method devised by R. V. Tomlinson and G. M. Tener of the University of British Columbia. In general the short fragments migrate through the column more rapidly than the long fragments, but there are exceptions [see illustration on next page]. The conditions most favorable for this separation were developed in our laboratories by Mark Marquisee and Jean Apgar.

The nucleotides in each fragment were released by hydrolyzing the fragment with an alkali. The individual nucleotides could then be identified by paper chromatography, paper electrophoresis and spectrophotometric analysis. This procedure was sufficient to establish the sequence of each of the dinucleotides, because the right-hand member of the pair was determined by the particular enzyme that had been used to produce the fragment. To establish the sequence of nucleotides in larger fragments, however, required special techniques.

Methods particularly helpful in the separation and identification of the fragments had been previously described by Vernon M. Ingram of the Massachusetts Institute of Technology, M. Las-

kowski, Sr., of the Marquette University School of Medicine, K. K. Reddi of Rockefeller University, G. W. Rushizky and Herbert A. Sober of the National Institutes of Health, the Swiss worker M. Staehelin and Tener.

For certain of the largest fragments, methods described in the scientific literature were inadequate and we had to develop new stratagems. One of these involved the use of an enzyme (a phosphodiesterase) obtained from snake venom. This enzyme removes nucleotides one by one from a fragment, leaving a mixture of smaller fragments of all possible intermediate lengths. The mixture can then be separated into fractions of homogeneous length by passing it through a column of diethylaminoethyl cellulose [see illustration on opposite page]. A simple method is available for determining the terminal nucleotide at the right end of each fraction of homogeneous length. With this knowledge, and knowing the length of each fragment, one can establish the sequence of nucleotides in the original large fragment.

A summary of all the nucleotide sequences found in the fragments of transfer RNA produced by pancreatic ribonuclease is shown in Table 1 on page 88. Determination of the structure of the fragments was primarily the work of James T. Madison and Ada Zamir, who were postdoctoral fellows in my laboratory. George A. Everett of the Plant, Soil and Nutrition Laboratory helped us in the identification of the nucleotides.

Much effort was spent in determining the structure of the largest fragments and in identifying unusual nucleotides not heretofore observed in RNA molecules. Two of the most difficult to identify were 1-methylinosinic acid and 5,6-dihydrouridylic acid. (In the illustrations these are symbolized respectively by I^m and U^h.)

Because a free 5'-phosphate group (p) is found at one end of the RNA molecule (the left end as the structure is conventionally written) and a free 3'-hydroxyl group (OH) is found at the other end, it is easy to pick out from Table 1 and Table 2 the two sequences that form the left and right ends of the alanine transfer RNA molecule. The left end has the structure pG—G—G—C— and the right end the structure U—C—C—A—C—COH. (It is known, however, that the active molecule ends in C—C—AOH.)

The presence of unusual nucleotides

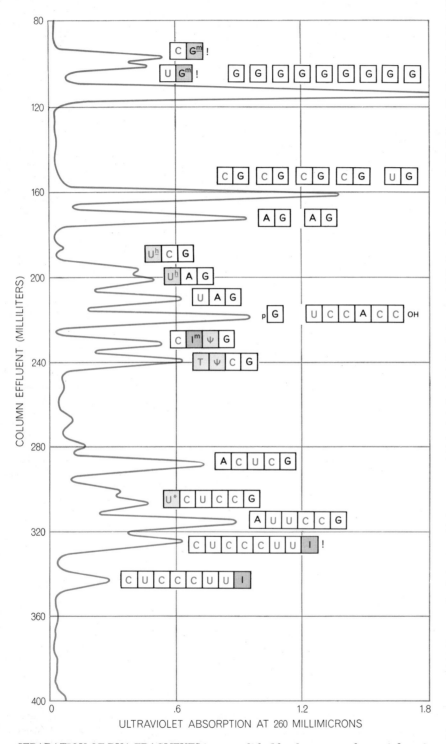

SEPARATION OF RNA FRAGMENTS is accomplished by chromatography carried out in a long glass column packed with diethylaminoethyl cellulose. The curve shows the separation achieved when the column input is a digest of alanine transfer RNA produced by takadiastase ribonuclease T1, an enzyme that cleaves the RNA into 29 fragments. The exclamation point indicates fragments whose terminal phosphate has a cyclical configuration. Such fragments travel faster than similar fragments that end in a noncyclical phosphate.

and unique short sequences made it clear that certain of the fragments found in Table 1 overlapped fragments found in Table 2. For example, there is only one inosinic acid nucleotide (I) in the molecule, and this appears in the sequence I–G–C– in Table 1 and in the sequence C–U–C–C–C–U–U–I– in Table 2. These two sequences must therefore overlap to produce the overall sequence C–U–C–C–C–U–U–I–G–C–. The information in Table 1 and Table 2 was combined in this way to draw up Table 3, which accounts for all 77 nucleotides in 16 sequences [*see illustration on page 89*].

With the knowledge that two of the 16 sequences were at the two ends, the structural problem became one of determining the positions of the intermediate 14 sequences. This was accomplished by isolating still larger fragments of the RNA.

In a crucial experiment John Robert Penswick, a graduate student at Cornell, found that a very brief treatment of the RNA with ribonuclease T1 at 0 degrees centigrade in the presence of magnesium ions splits the molecule at one position. The two halves of the molecule could be separated by chromatography. Analyses of the halves established that the sequences listed in the first column of Table 3 are in the left half of the molecule and that those in the second column are in the right half.

Using a somewhat more vigorous but still limited treatment of the RNA with ribonuclease T1, we then obtained and analyzed a number of additional large fragments. This work was done in collaboration with Jean Apgar and Everett. To determine the structure of a large fragment, the fragment was degraded completely with ribonuclease T1, which yielded two or more of the fragments previously identified in Table 2. These known sequences could be put together, with the help of various clues, to obtain the complete sequence of the large fragment. The process is similar to putting together a jigsaw puzzle [*see illustrations on pages 90 and 91*].

As an example of the approach that was used, the logical argument is given in detail for Fragment A. When Fragment A was completely degraded by ribonuclease T1, we obtained seven small fragments: three G–'s, C–G–, U–G–,U–G^m– and pG–. (G^m is used in the illustrations to represent 1-methylguanylic acid, another of the unusual nucleotides in alanine transfer RNA.) The presence of pG– shows that Frag-

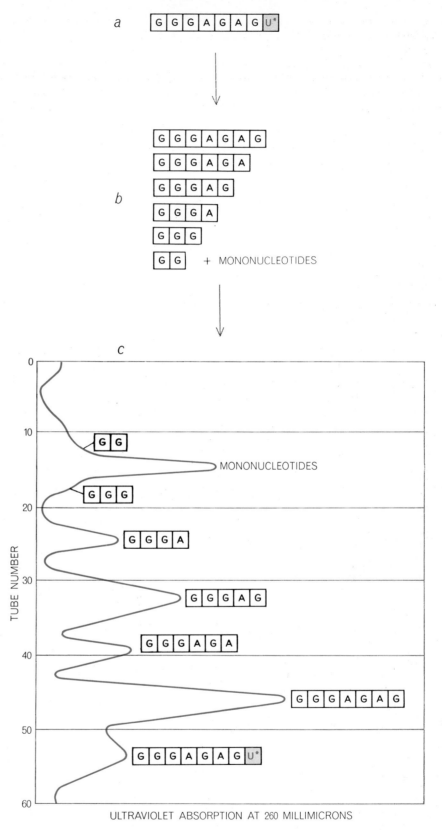

NEW DEGRADATION METHOD was developed in the author's laboratory to determine the sequence of nucleotides in fragments five to eight subunits in length. The example above begins with a fragment of eight subunits from which the terminal phosphate has been removed (*a*). When the fragment is treated with phosphodiesterase found in snake venom, the result is a mixture containing fragments from one to eight subunits in length (*b*). These are separated by chromatography (*c*). When the material from each peak is hydrolyzed, the last nucleoside (a nucleotide minus its phosphate) at the right end of the fragment is released and can be identified. Thus each nucleotide in the original fragment can be determined.

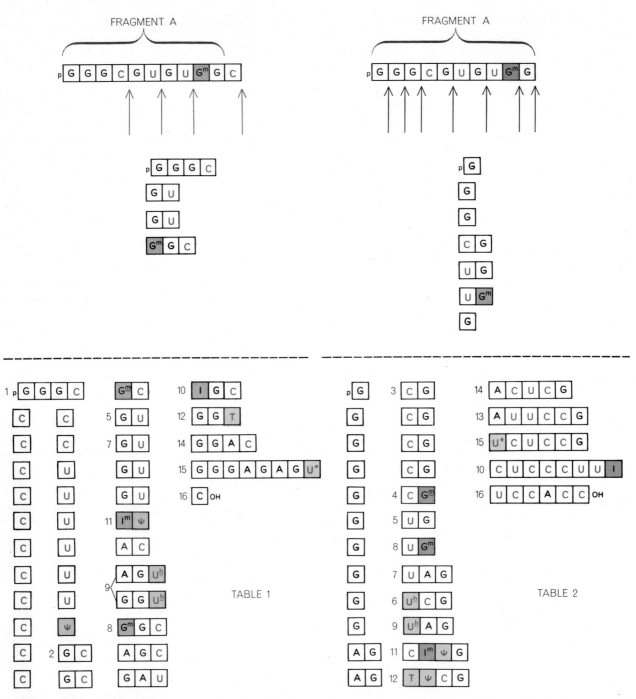

ACTION OF TWO DIFFERENT ENZYMES is reflected in these two tables. Table 1 shows the fragments produced when alanine transfer RNA is completely digested by pancreatic ribonuclease, which cleaves the molecule to the right of nucleotides containing bases with pyrimidine structures (C, U, U^h, ψ and T). The diagram at top left shows how pancreatic ribonuclease would cleave the first 11 nucleotides of alanine transfer RNA. The diagram at top right shows how the same region would be digested by takadiastase ribonuclease T1. Table 2 contains the fragments produced by this enzyme; they all end in nucleotides whose bases contain purine structures ($G, G^m, G^{\underline{m}}$ and I). The numbers indicate which ones appear in the consolidated list in Table 3 on the opposite page.

ment *A* is from the left end of the molecule. Since it is already known from Table 3 that the left terminal sequence is pG–G–G–C–, the positions of two of the three G–'s and C–G– are known; the terminal five nucleotides must be pG–G–G–C–G–.

The positions of the remaining G–, U–G– and U–G^m– are established by the following information. Table 3 shows that the U–G^m– is present in the sequence U–G^m–G–C–. Since there is only one C in Fragment *A*, and its position is already known, Fragment *A* must terminate before the C of the U–G^m–G–C– sequence. Therefore the U–G– must be to the left of the U–G^m–, and the structure of Fragment *A* can be represented as pG–G–G–C–G–...U–G–...U–G^m–, with one G– remaining to be placed. If the G– is placed to the left or the right of the U–G– in this structure, it would create a G–G–U– sequence. If such a sequence existed in the molecule, it would have appeared as a fragment when the molecule was treated with pancreatic ribonuclease; Table 1 shows that it did not do so. Therefore the remaining G– must be to the right of the G^m–, and the sequence of Fragment *A* is pG—G—G—C—G—U—G—U—G^m—G—.

Using the same procedure, the entire structure of alanine transfer RNA was worked out. The complete nucleotide sequence of alanine transfer RNA is shown at the top of the next two pages.

The work on the structure of this molecule took us seven years from start to finish. Most of the time was consumed in developing procedures for the isolation of a single species of transfer RNA from the 20 or so different transfer RNA's present in the living cell. We finally selected a fractionation technique known as countercurrent distribution, developed in the 1940's by Lyman C. Craig of the Rockefeller Institute.

This method exploits the fact that similar molecules of different structure will exhibit slightly different solubilities if they are allowed to partition, or distribute themselves, between two nonmiscible liquids. The countercurrent technique can be mechanized so that the mixture of molecules is partitioned hundreds or thousands of times, while the nonmiscible solvents flow past each other in a countercurrent pattern. The solvent system we adopted was composed of formamide, isopropyl alcohol and a phosphate buffer, a modification of a system first described by Robert C. Warner and Paya Vaimberg of New York University. To make the method applicable for fractionating transfer RNA's required four years of work in collaboration with Jean Apgar, B. P. Doctor and Susan H. Merrill of the Plant, Soil and Nutrition Laboratory. Repeated countercurrent extractions of the transfer RNA mixture gave three of the RNA's in a reasonably homogeneous state: the RNA's that transfer the amino acids alanine, tyrosine and valine [*see bottom illustration on page 84*].

The starting material for the countercurrent distributions was crude transfer RNA extracted from yeast cells using phenol as a solvent. In the course of the structural work we used about 200 grams (slightly less than half a pound) of mixed transfer RNA's isolated from 300 pounds of yeast. The total amount of purified alanine transfer RNA we had to work with over a three-year period was one gram. This represented a practical compromise between the difficulty of scaling up the fractionation procedures and scaling down the techniques for structural analysis.

Once we knew the complete sequence, we could turn to general questions about the structure of transfer RNA's. Each transfer RNA presumably embodies a sequence of three subunits (an "anticodon") that forms a temporary bond with a complementary sequence of three subunits (the "codon") in messenger RNA. Each codon triplet identifies a specific amino acid [see "The Genetic Code: II," by Marshall W. Nirenberg, which is included in this volume, page 270].

An important question, therefore, is which of the triplets in alanine transfer RNA might serve as the anticodon for the alanine codon in messenger RNA. There is reason to believe the anticodon is the sequence I—G—C, which is found in the middle of the RNA molecule. The codon corresponding to I—G—C could be the triplet G—C—C or perhaps G—C—U, both of which act as code words for alanine in messenger RNA. As shown in the illustration on page 2, the I—G—C in the alanine transfer RNA is upside down when it makes contact with the corresponding codon in messenger RNA. Therefore when alanine transfer RNA is delivering its amino acid cargo and is temporarily held by hydrogen bonds to messenger RNA, the I would pair with C (or U) in the messenger, G would pair with C, and C would pair with G.

We do not know the three-dimensional structure of the RNA. Presumably there is a specific form that interacts with the messenger RNA and ribosomes. The illustration on page 3 shows three hypothetical structures for alanine transfer RNA that take account of the propensity of certain bases to pair with other bases. Thus adenine pairs with uracil and cytosine with guanine. In the three hypothetical structures the I—G—C sequence is at an exposed position and could pair with messenger RNA.

The small diagram on page 3 indicates a possible three-dimensional folding of the RNA. Studies with atomic models suggest that single-strand regions of the structure are highly flexible. Thus in the "three-leaf-clover" configuration it is possible to fold one side leaf on top of the other, or any of the leaves back over the stem of the molecule.

One would also like to know whether or not the unusual nucleotides are concentrated in some particular region of the molecule. A glance at the sequence shows that they are scattered throughout the structure; in the three-leaf-clo-

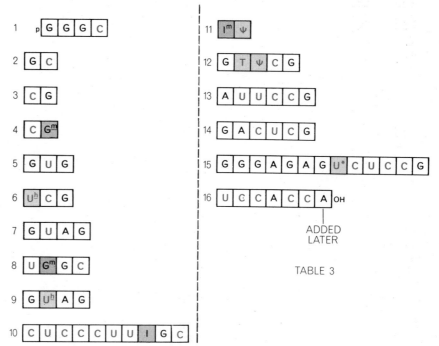

CONSOLIDATED LIST OF SEQUENCES accounts for all 77 nucleotides in alanine transfer RNA. The consolidated list is formed by selecting the largest fragments in Table 1 and Table 2 (*opposite page*) and by piecing together fragments that obviously overlap. Thus Fragment 15 has been formed by joining two smaller fragments, keyed by the number 15, in Table 1 and Table 2 on the opposite page. Since the entire molecule contains only one U*, the two fragments must overlap at that point. The origin of the other fragments in Table 3 can be traced in similar fashion. A separate experiment in which the molecule was cut into two parts helped to establish that the 10 fragments listed in the first column are in the left half of the molecule and that the six fragments in the second column are in the right half.

COMPLETE MOLECULE of alanine transfer RNA contains 77 nucleotides in the order shown. The final sequence required a care-

ful piecing together of many bits of information (*see illustration at bottom of these two pages*). The task was facilitated by degrada-

ver model, however, the unusual nucleotides are seen to be concentrated around the loops and bends.

Another question concerns the presence in the transfer RNA's of binding sites, that is, sites that may interact specifically with ribosomes and with

the enzymes involved in protein synthesis. We now know from the work of Zamir and Marquisee that a particular sequence containing pseudouridylic acid (Ψ), the sequence G–T–Ψ–C–G, is found not only in the alanine transfer RNA but also in the transfer RNA's for

tyrosine and valine. Other studies suggest that it may be present in all the transfer RNA's. One would expect such common sites to serve a common function; binding the transfer RNA's to the ribosome might be one of them.

Work that is being done in many

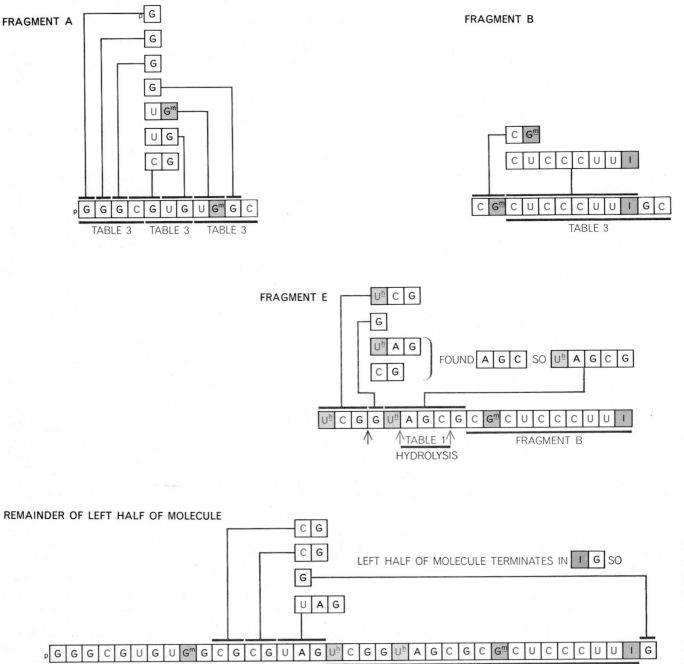

FRAGMENT C   FRAGMENT D

FRAGMENT F   FRAGMENT G

tion experiments that cleaved this molecule into several large fragments (*A, B, C, D, E, F, G*), and by the crucial discovery that the molecule could be divided almost precisely into two halves. The division point is marked by the "gutter" between these two pages.

laboratories around the world indicates that alanine transfer RNA is only the first of many nucleic acids for which the nucleotide sequences will be known. In the near future it should be possible to identify those structural features that are common to various transfer RNA's, and this should help greatly in defining the interactions of transfer RNA's with messenger RNA, ribosomes and enzymes involved in protein synthesis. Further in the future will be the description of the nucleotide sequences of the nucleic acids—both DNA and RNA— that embody the genetic messages of the viruses that infect bacteria, plants and animals. Much further in the future lies the decoding of the genetic messages of higher organisms, including man. The work described in this article is a step toward that distant goal.

FRAGMENT C

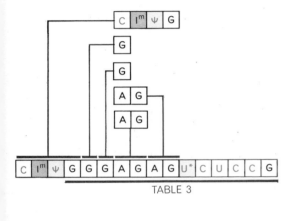

TABLE 3

FRAGMENT D

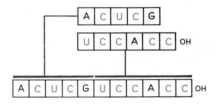

FRAGMENT F

FRAGMENT G

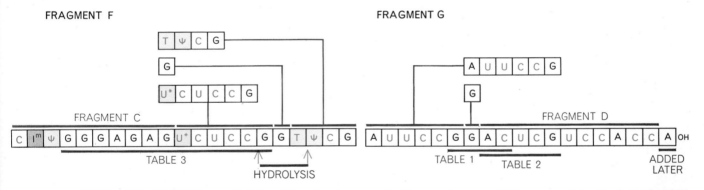

ASSEMBLY OF FRAGMENTS resembled the solving of a jigsaw puzzle. The arguments that established the sequence of nucleotides in Fragment *A* are described in the text. Fragment *B* contains two subfragments. The larger is evidently Fragment 10 in Table 3, which ends in G—C—. This means that the C—G^m— fragment must go to the left. Fragment *E* contains Fragment *B* plus four smaller fragments. It can be shown that *E* ends with I—, therefore the four small pieces are again to the left. A pancreatic digest yielded A—G—C—, thus serving to connect U^h—A—G— and C—G—. A partial digestion with ribonuclease T1 removed U^h—C—G—, showing it to be at the far left. The remaining G— must follow immediately or a pancreatic digest would have yielded a G—G—C— sequence, which it did not. Analyses of Fragments *A* and *E* accounted for everything in the left half of the molecule except for four small pieces. The left half of the molecule was shown to terminate in I—G—, thus the remaining three pieces are between *A* and *E*. Table 1 shows that one U^h is preceded by A—G—, therefore U—

A—G— must be next to *E*. The two remaining C—G—'s must then fall to the left of U—A—G—. Fragment *C* contains five pieces. Table 3 (Fragment 15) shows that the two A—G—'s are next to U* and that the two G—'s are to the left of them. It is also clear that C—I^m—Ψ—G— cannot follow U*, therefore it must be to the left. Fragment *D* contains two pieces; the OH group on one of them shows it to be to the right. Fragment *F* contains Fragment *C* plus three extra pieces. These must all lie to the right since hydrolysis with pancreatic ribonuclease gave G—G—T— and not G—T—, thus establishing that the single G— falls as shown. Fragment *G* gave *D* plus two pieces, which must both lie to the left (because of the terminal C_OH). Table 1 shows a G—G—A—C— sequence, which must overlap the A—C— in A—C—U—C—G— and the G— at the right end of the A—U—U—C—C—G—. Fragments *F* and *G* can join in only one way to form the right half of the molecule. The molecule is completed by the addition of a final A_OH, which is missing as the alanine transfer RNA is separated from baker's yeast.

10

Precisely Constructed Polymers

GIULIO NATTA

August 1961

It is often said in the chemical industry that 10 years are required to carry a new product from the test tube to tank-car production. Seven years have now passed since our laboratory in the Politecnico di Milano discovered "stereospecific" catalytic processes for creating "stereoregular" polymers from simple asymmetric hydrocarbon molecules such as those of propylene. The term "stereospecific" signifies that the catalysts are able to link the simple structural units of the polymer—the asymmetric monomers —into precisely ordered three-dimensional structures rather than into structures assembled more or less at random. The precise ordering of structure yields polymers with new and useful physical properties. The new stereoregular polypropylene polymers produced by our methods, and by similar methods successfully developed by others, have been in large-scale production in the U.S. since early this year, following the completion last year of three major plants. The polymers have been commercially available in Italy since 1957. Only last year our laboratory was successful in carrying stereospecific polymerization methods another step forward, suggesting that still-new varieties of stereoregular polymers may achieve practical importance before too many years have passed.

Our recent work has led to the synthesis of polymers that, when placed in solution, have the property of rotating the plane of polarization of a beam of plane-polarized light. They are said, therefore, to be optically active. It was Louis Pasteur who discovered, about 1850, that tartaric acid comes in two isomeric forms, one able to rotate polarized light to the right, the other able to rotate it to the left. A mixture of the two forms in equal amounts is called a racemic mixture. Since Pasteur's time it has been shown that compounds with optical activity are widely used in nature as the monomers of the polymeric constituents of living matter, for example proteins, cellulose and starch. To display optical activity an organic molecule must contain at least one asymmetric carbon atom, meaning a carbon linked to a different kind of atom (or group of atoms) through each of its four valence bonds [*see illustration below*]. For reasons difficult to explain (and perhaps not yet fully explained) the electron

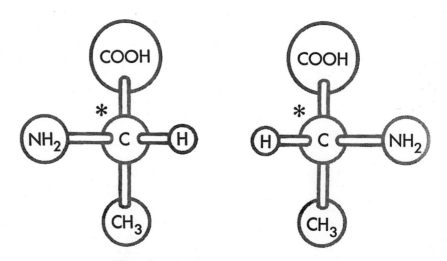

OPTICAL ISOMERS OF ALANINE, one of the 20-odd amino acids that link up to form proteins, illustrate what is meant by an "asymmetric" carbon atom. The central carbon is asymmetric because it has attached to each of its four chemical bonds a different kind of atom or group of atoms. When in solution one configuration, called L(−)-alanine (*left*), rotates plane-polarized light to the left; its mirror image, D(+)-alanine (*right*), rotates polarized light to the right. Natural proteins are all built from L(−)-amino acids.

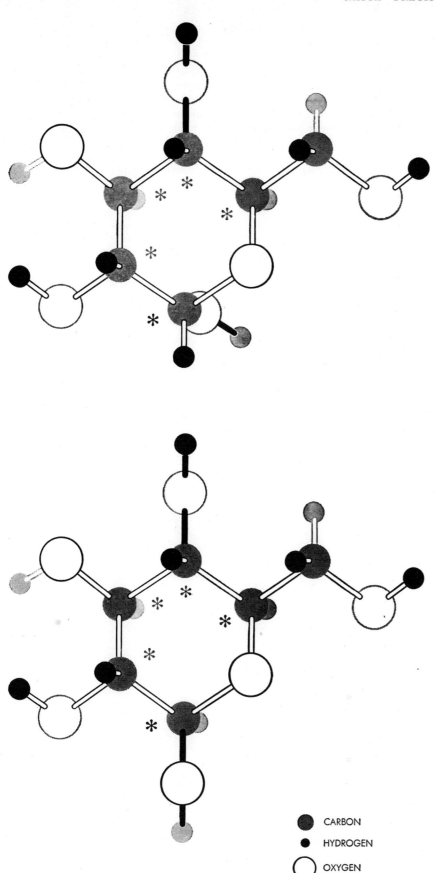

CARBON

HYDROGEN

OXYGEN

OPTICAL ISOMERS OF GLUCOPYRANOSE, a natural sugar, each contain five asymmetric carbon atoms (*starred*). Plants make chiefly *alpha*-D(+)-glucopyranose (*top*) and *beta*-D(+)-glucopyranose (*bottom*), which differ only at one carbon (*dark star*). The former polymerizes to form starch, latter to form cellulose (*see illustrations on opposite page*).

cloud around an asymmetric atom—which need not be carbon—causes polarized light to rotate.

A compound containing one asymmetric carbon atom can exist in two isomeric forms, called enantiomers; one is the mirror image of the other, as the right hand is of the left. An optically active compound is assigned to the dextro (D) or levo (L) series according to the position of its asymmetric carbon atom (or atoms) with respect to that in certain reference compounds. This classification is independent of the way the compound in question actually rotates polarized light. If the rotation is to the right, the compound is labeled (+); if to the left, (−).

For more than a century chemists have sought methods of synthesizing one particular isomer in preference to its optical twin. Ordinary methods of synthesis produce all possible optical isomers in equal abundance. One way to obtain an excess of a particular isomer is to employ optically active starting materials. Chemists have made only negligible progress, however, in achieving an "absolute asymmetric synthesis"—one that employs unselected starting materials. The idea that irradiation of the reactants with polarized light might favor one isomeric product over another has been tested without success.

No one has been able to explain why all natural proteins should be built up from L-series amino acids. Presumably the exactly equivalent D series would do just as well. A giant molecule containing a random mixture of L and D types, however, would lack the distinctive physical properties of normal proteins. It is the ordered repetition of molecules sharing a common symmetry that endows a giant molecule with crystalline properties. By "crystalline" is meant the ability of a molecule to pack together with others in orderly array. Crystallinity endows a polymer with strength and rigidity. In contrast, a polymer lacking an ordered structure is generally amorphous.

Although two enantiomers may have almost identical physical properties, the polymers formed from them may differ greatly. A remarkable example of this is found in starch and cellulose, which are made from two D-series sugars that differ in only one isomeric detail. Starch is a chainlike polymer made from *alpha*-D(+)-glucose; cellulose is a comparable chain made from *beta*-D(+)-glucose [*see illustrations at left and on opposite page*]. The slight differences between the two sugars give rise to different types of chain and thus to profound differences in their polymers: starch can be digested by man and animals, cellulose cannot. It is apparent, therefore, that the ability to synthesize giant molecules from optically active organic compounds—and also to decompose them—is an important characteristic of living organisms.

One would like to know if life on other planets shows the same stereoisomeric preferences as life on earth. It is generally assumed that the preference of earth life for L-amino acids and D-sugars is a simple accident, tracing back, perhaps, to an accident of catalysis when life first began. If only accident is involved, there would seem to be a good chance that life elsewhere is built around amino acids and sugars having optical activities different from those preferred on earth. If space explorers ever discover plants or animals on another planet, it will be of some importance to learn the precise steric configuration of these organisms. An extraterrestrial plant that appeared to be edible

would be totally unassimilable if it contained D-amino acids and L-glucose.

Our own efforts at asymmetric synthesis of polymers are a direct outgrowth of the work that led in 1954 to stereoregular polypropylene. It will be recalled that in 1954 polyethylene was already well known as the plastic material used in "squeeze" bottles. Ethylene (C_2H_4) is the simplest hydrocarbon containing a double chemical bond. When it polymerizes, the double bond breaks and provides two free connecting links to join with two other molecules of ethylene—one on each side—in which bonds have similarly been broken. In this fashion thousands of ethylene units can link up to form a long chain, which packs together well with other similar chains. The result is a crystalline polymer that is both strong and flexible but has a rather low melting point.

The propylene monomer (C_3H_6) is an ethylene molecule in which one hydrogen atom has been replaced by a methyl

group (CH_3). Unlike the molecule of ethylene, the propylene molecule is structurally asymmetric. Consequently if propylene is allowed to polymerize, the resulting polymer can take various steric configurations. If the polymerization is "undirected," the methyl groups will fall at random along the chain, now on one side, now on the other. Such chains do not pack well together and the result is a rubbery, amorphous polymer of relatively low strength. We called this structure "atactic," meaning without order. We found that certain catalysts would direct the polymerization so that the methyl groups would all fall on one side of the chain or would alternate regularly from side to side; in both cases the resulting polymers are crystalline. The former chains we called "isotactic"; the latter, "syndiotactic" [*see illustrations on pages 95 and 98*].

Isotactic polypropylene, because of its special structure, has a high melting point and yields a polymer of high crystallinity that is harder, tougher and

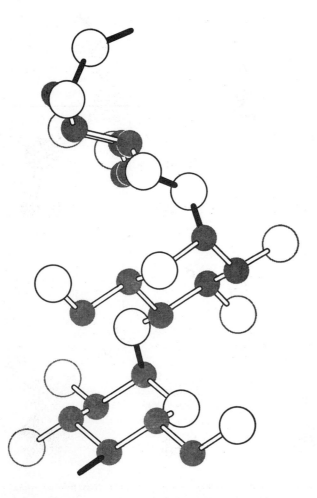
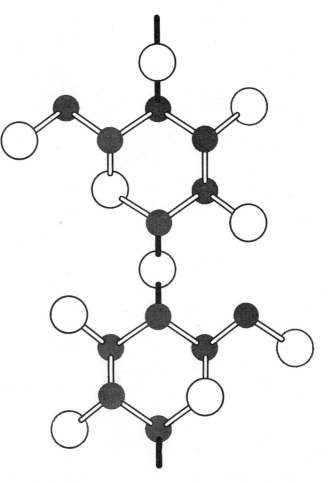

STARCH AND CELLULOSE (*left and right*) are giant molecules formed from *alpha*-D(+)-glucopyranose and *beta*-D(+)-glucopyranose respectively. In this illustration hydrogen atoms, shown in the monomers on the opposite page, have been omitted for clarity. Although the monomers have nearly identical physical properties, the giant molecules created from each are quite different.

more heat-resistant than polyethylene. As a textile fiber it is as strong as nylon and 30 per cent lighter in weight. It can also be produced in the form of a thin transparent film, as clear as cellophane and stronger if its polymer units are oriented by stretching. Extruded into pipes or molded into complex shapes, it can compete with metals in many applications.

If ethylene is doubly substituted so that one hydrogen atom on each carbon is replaced with a different group of atoms, yielding a molecule with the type formula CHR:CHR', stereospecific polymerization gives rise, as shown in the illustration on the opposite page, to three ordered configurations: threo-di-isotactic (R and R' on the same side of the chain), erythro-di-isotactic (R and R' on opposite sides) and di-syndiotactic (R and R' alternating regularly from one side to the other). Polymers of each of these configurations, made in our laboratory,

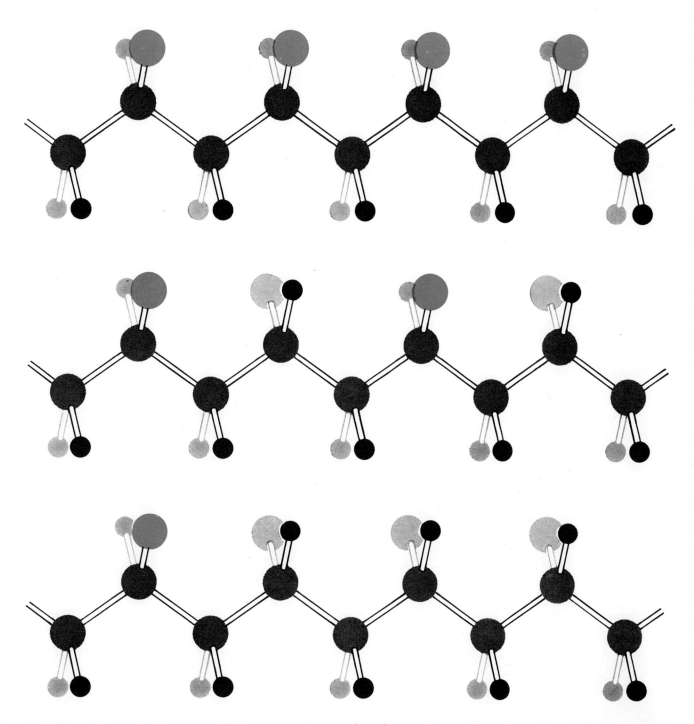

ORDERED AND DISORDERED POLYMERS can be produced when so-called vinylic (CH₂:CHR) monomeric units link up in head-to-tail succession. "R" (*colored ball*) may represent any group of atoms; thus if R is CH₃, the vinyl monomer is propylene and the polymer is polypropylene. The main chain of carbon atoms has been drawn as if flattened in a plane. (*Three-dimensional views appear on page 98.*) When R groups are all on one side of the chain (*top*), the polymer is called "isotactic." When R groups alternate from side to side (*middle*), the polymer is "syndiotactic." When R groups are disposed at random (*bottom*), the polymer is "atactic."

show a number of interesting properties. Their commercial value remains to be determined.

These various stereoregular polymers represented a small but definite step toward asymmetric synthesis in that each giant molecule is formed by long sequences of monomeric units having the same steric configuration. However, the giant molecules forming a crude vinyl isotactic polymer, such as isotactic polypropylene, do not display optical activity, primarily because inner compensations cancel out whatever slight optical activity might arise. It is true that in such polymers each carbon attached to a side group is asymmetric, but the asymmetry is very slight because it is due almost solely to difference in length and in configuration of the two portions of chain linked to two of its bonds. As we shall see, appreciable optical activity will occur in a polymer only when the asymmetry arises from strong nonuni-

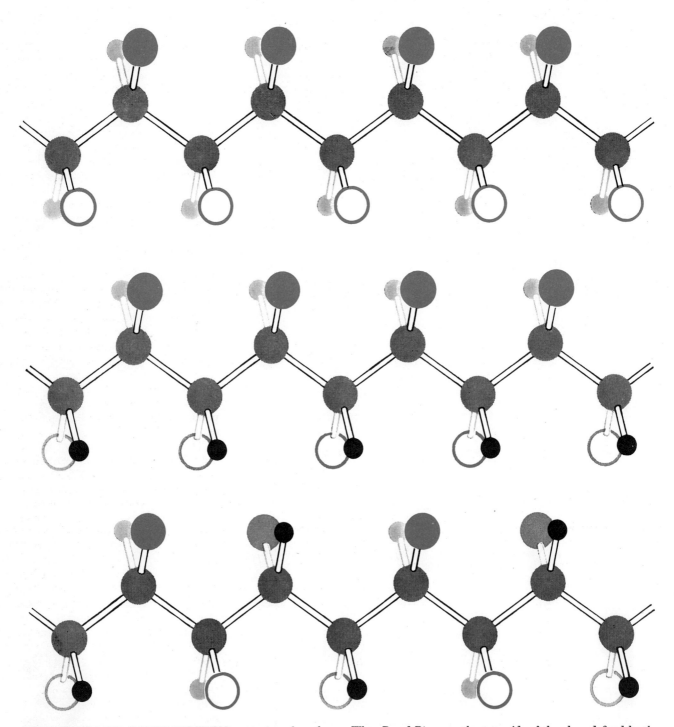

MORE INTRICATE STEREO-ORDERING can arise when the vinyl monomer contains a different R group on each carbon, yielding a molecule of the form CHR:CHR'. New spatial arrangements are possible because the first carbon carries a hydrogen atom plus an R group, instead of two hydrogens, which are indistinguishable. When R and R' are on the same side of the plane defined by the carbon chain (*top*), the polymer is threo-di-isotactic. When all the R groups are on one side and all the R' groups on the other side (*middle*), the polymer is erythro-di-isotactic. When R and R' alternate from side to side (*bottom*), the polymer is di-syndiotactic.

formities of atomic configuration in the immediate vicinity of each of many carbon atoms.

So far we have not mentioned a common and important type of isomerism that is due simply to variations in three-dimensional structure and which is therefore called geometric isomerism. Geometric isomers arise in organic compounds that contain a double bond between two carbon atoms. When connected by a double bond, two carbon atoms are no longer free to rotate around a common axis, as they are when they are joined by a single bond. As a result it is possible to create isomers of different spatial geometry, depending on whether or not distinctive substituents attached to the two carbons are locked on the same side of the molecule, giving rise to the "cis" isomer, or on opposite sides, yielding the "trans" isomer.

In nature two well-known polymers, identical in chemical composition, are distinguished by their cis and trans geometric isomerism. Cis-1,4-polyisoprene is natural rubber, whereas trans-1,4-polyisoprene is gutta-percha [see top illustration on page 99]. The properties of the two substances are very different. Rubber, when vulcanized, is strong and elastic. Gutta-percha, vulcanized, becomes hard and tough rather than strong. It is often used as a covering for golf balls.

Early efforts to synthesize natural rubber failed because the monomer, isoprene (C_5H_8), would not link up in the required stereoregular form. In 1954, with new principles of stereospecific polymerization, a true synthetic rubber was synthesized in the U.S. and a true gutta-percha was created in our Milan laboratories. The polyisoprene synthetic rubber is now being produced commercially by at least two U.S. firms.

Our laboratory was the first to show that an excellent synthetic rubber is also produced by cis-1,4-polybutadiene. Cheaper than isoprene, butadiene (C_4H_6) has a single hydrogen atom where isoprene has a methyl group. Butadiene was commercially manufactured on a large scale in the U.S. during World War II as the principal ingredient in butadiene synthetic rubbers, which have been made in large volume ever since. The new stereoregular polymers of butadiene show elastic and dynamic properties quite similar to those of natural rubber and are far superior to those of the old butadiene synthetics, which have a nonuniform chemical composition and a disordered three-dimensional structure.

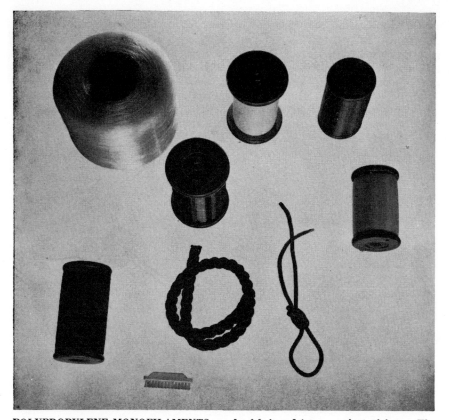

POLYPROPYLENE MONOFILAMENTS can be fabricated into a variety of forms. The strength of the polymer derives from its stereoregularity and high crystallinity. "Crystallinity" means that long-chain molecules of the polymer lie side by side in orderly fashion.

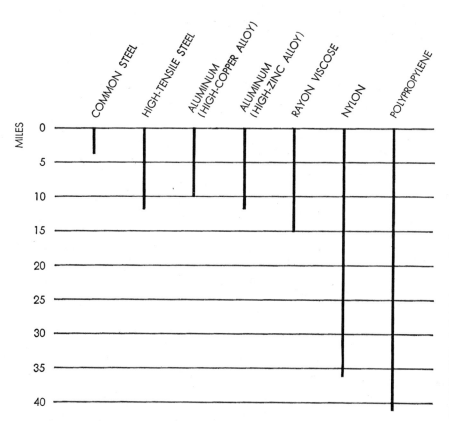

SELF-SUPPORTING LENGTHS OF VARIOUS FILAMENTS reflect, in a single value, a material's weight as well as its strength. The value is independent of diameter. Aluminum, although weaker than steel, can support as many miles of its own length. Polypropylene is almost as strong as nylon and 30 per cent lighter, hence its superiority by this measure.

We have been able to produce synthetic rubbers containing more than 98 per cent of *cis*-1,4-polybutadiene, which even exceeds the steric purity of 97 to 98 per cent of *cis* units found in natural rubber. Automobile tires made from these high-purity polybutadienes compare very favorably with tires of natural rubber in durability, riding qualities and low heat build-up when operating at high speeds.

Out of this work with butadiene and related diolefins (molecules with two sets of double bonds) have come polymers demonstrating optical as well as geometric isomerism. Our approach to achieving optical isomerism has been to create polymers from derivatives of diolefins, such as butadiene, in which at least one hydrogen atom in each molecule has been replaced with more complex atomic substituents. When monomers of this sort are polymerized in a stereospecific way, the repetition of complex configurations produces strong local asymmetries in a large fraction of the carbon atoms. Each single giant molecule, if it could be extracted from the polymer and examined alone, should show optical activity. As normally produced, however, the polymer mix will contain equal numbers of isomeric molecules of opposite optical activity.

Our goal, therefore, was to find conditions that would favor the polymeriza-

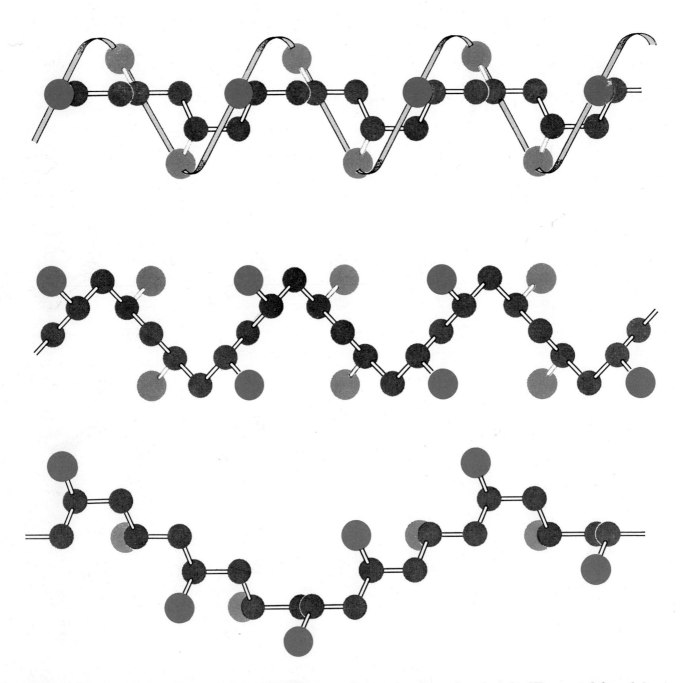

THREE-DIMENSIONAL VIEWS OF POLYPROPYLENE correspond to the simplified views on page 95, except here hydrogen atoms are omitted. Colored balls represent methyl groups (CH₃).

In isotactic polypropylene (*top*) the CH₃ groups define a helix (*gray ribbon*). In syndiotactic polypropylene (*middle*) structure is also regular. Atactic polypropylene (*bottom*) is nonregular in form.

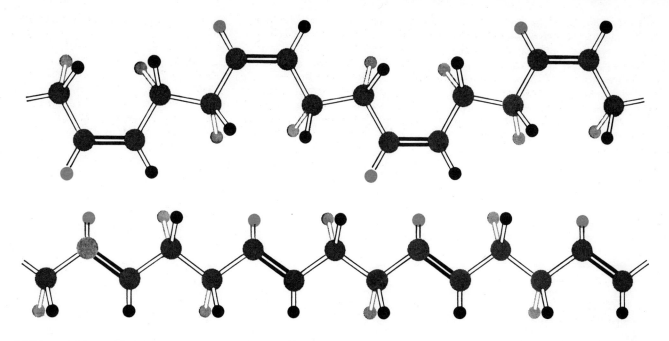

RUBBER AND GUTTA-PERCHA (*top and bottom*) are geometric isomers built up from units of the same monomer, isoprene (C_5H_8). Rubber is *cis*-1,4-polyisoprene. The "*cis*" means that a methyl group (*color*) and a neighboring hydrogen (*black*) are on the same side of each pair of carbon atoms joined by a double bond. The "1,4" means that the four-carbon chain of the monomer is linked into the polymer through its first and fourth carbons. Gutta-percha is *trans*-1,4-polyisoprene, indicating that methyl groups and adjacent hydrogens lie across from each other. If the methyl groups in rubber are replaced by hydrogen atoms, the resulting polymer is *cis*-1,4-polybutadiene, a new and commercially promising synthetic with properties very similar to those of *cis*-1,4-polyisoprene.

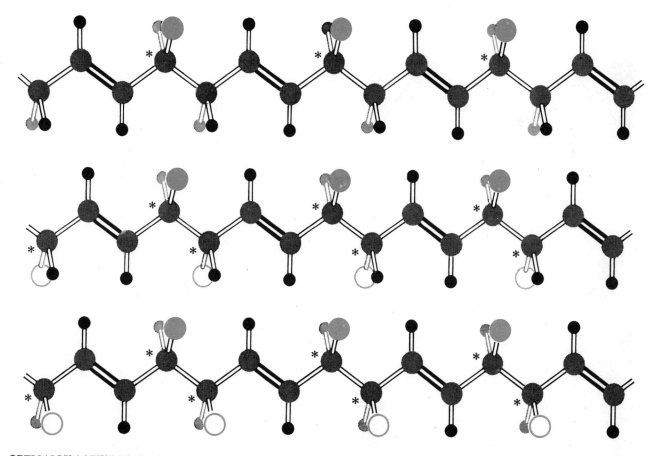

OPTICALLY ACTIVE POLYMERS can be created from butadiene monomers containing substituents (*color*) for hydrogen either on the first carbon atom or on the first and fourth in the four-carbon chain of the monomer. The polymer of singly substituted butadiene (*top*) is of the *trans*-1,4-isotactic type. Polymers of doubly substituted butadiene can show erythro-di-isotactic succession (*middle*) or threo-di-isotactic succession (*bottom*). The asymmetric carbons are starred; each polymer can exist in the form of its mirror image.

tion of only one of the two optically active forms. The first successful asymmetric synthesis of this kind was achieved last year at the Politecnico di Milano with esters of sorbic acid.

Sorbic acid itself can be regarded as a butadiene molecule that has been lengthened by a methyl (CH_3) group at one end and by a carboxyl (COOH) group at the other. Stereospecific polymerization of certain sorbic acid esters yields crystalline polymers having a "polytactic" structure: each monomer has three different sites of stereoisomerism—one of geometric type and two of optical type—which repeat regularly throughout the polymer.

In polymerizations carried out with a catalyst (butyllithium) that does not have in itself centers of optical asymmetry, there is nothing to establish at the outset a preference for one steric configuration over another. The result is a polymeric substance in which half the molecules have one configuration and half have another. Both molecules, however, are of the erythro-di-isotactic type [see bottom illustration on the preceding page].

When a catalyst (isoamyllithium) that has a center of optical asymmetry was selected, the resulting molecules were preponderantly of one optical configuration. This was the first asymmetric synthesis of a giant molecule starting from a monomer that was not itself optically active. It is true, however, that the optically active macromolecules contain an optically active end group derived from the catalyst, which is partially consumed during the polymerization.

Subsequently we achieved asymmetric synthesis without consumption of pre-existing optically active reagents. The catalyst for this polymerization was a so-called organometallic compound that was bound to an optically active organic base. Although the base does not take part in the chemical reaction, it provides the steric guidance for the synthesis. (The catalyst is of ionic nature, meaning that the giant molecule grows outward from the catalyst like a growing hair. Oriented monomeric units are fed in at the base of the "hair" with the formation of an ionic bond that joins the end of the hair to the catalyst.)

This is not yet an "absolute" asymmetric synthesis inasmuch as some optical activity is required in the catalyst. The synthesis may suggest, nevertheless, a simplified model of the way nature carries out at least some stereospecific syntheses of optical isomers.

ARTICLES OF MOLDED POLYPROPYLENE yield tough parts and fittings coming into industrial use. In addition to strength the polymer has good heat and chemical resistance.

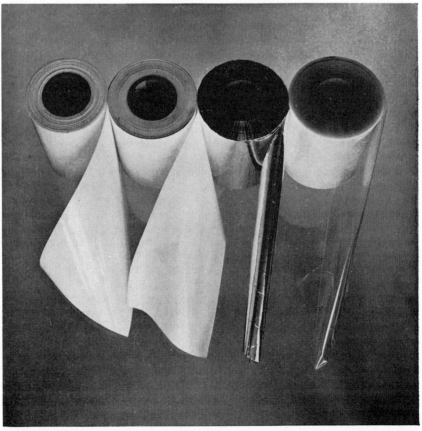

POLYPROPYLENE FILM resembles polyethylene but is stronger. The articles shown on this page and on page 97 are fabricated from polypropylene made by Montecatini of Italy.

SECTION

II

Biological Regulators

II

Biological Regulators

INTRODUCTION

In this section we are concerned with the molecular structure of the relatively small molecules that play a primary part in the regulation of the behavior of organisms through their effect on the activities of the giant molecules, or biopolymers, whose structures were discussed in Section I. In a sense, study of such molecules constitutes a special subdivision of the classical area of organic chemistry—a subdivision that we call the chemistry of organic natural products—but those considered here are specifically the ones whose regulatory action on the behavior of living organisms is beginning to be understood.

The first two selections, by Collier and by Steward, on factors which regulate the control of growth of plant cells, are followed by two articles on the small molecules that control the behavior of insects—both the molecules of attractants, which are small, volatile compounds used to convey information between insects, and those that affect development and metamorphosis. Next is an article on the flowering pigments, whose regulatory function is yet to be explicitly recognized. This is followed by a discussion of the structural features of molecules that affect the olfactory nerve cells of the higher animals. A classical discussion of the structure of steroids and of the relation of that structure to some of their physiological functions by one of the earlier workers in this field, Louis Fieser, is followed by a discussion of alkaloids, whose medicinal functions in the regulation of nervous activity have long been known.

The last four articles in this section have to do with the structure of both synthetic and natural pharmaceutical materials whose regulatory action on both humans and higher animals are obvious, even though the detailed mechanisms by which many of them achieve their effect are still not known to us: for example, the mechanisms of action even of aspirin, not to speak of the hallucinogenic drugs, remain still to be elucidated. Study of their structure and of the relationship between structure and activity can provide the outlines of a map which will guide the future investigator in his search for their modes of action.

A number of other articles dealing with the regulatory function of organic molecules have been published in *Scientific American*; some are are available in offprint form. S. Frank, *Carotenoids* (January 1956); S. Zuckerman, *Hormones* (March 1957); E. H. Davidson, *Hormones and Genes* (June 1965, offprint 1013); H. E. Himcorich, *The New Psychiatric Drugs* (October 1955, offprint 446); L. Z. Freedman, *Truth Drugs* (March 1960, offprint 497); R. O. Roblin, Jr., *The Imitative Drugs* (April 1960); L. J. Roth and R. W. Monthei, *Radioactive Tuberculosis Drugs* (November 1956); J. Schubert, *Chelation In*

Medicine (May 1966); A. H. Rose, *New Penicillins* (March 1961); F. B. Salisbury, *Plant Growth Substances* (April 1956, offprint 110); P. K. Stumpf, *ATP* (April 1953, offprint 41); J. D. Woodward, *Biotin* (June 1961); M. D. Kamen, *A Universal Molecule of Living Matter* (August 1958); A. J. Haagen-Smit, *Smell and Taste* (March 1952, offprint 404); A. E. Fisher, *Chemical Stimulation of the Brain* (June 1964, offprint 485); F. A. Fuhrman, *Tetrodotoxin* (August 1967); C. M. Williams, *Third-generation Pesticides* (July 1967, offprint 1078); P. R. Ehrlich and P. H. Raven, *Butterflies and Plants* (June 1967, offprint 1076).

11

Kinins

H. O. J. COLLIER

August 1962

It has been known for half a century that the smooth functioning of the body depends in large measure on hormones, the "chemical messengers" secreted by particular glands and transported to their site of action in the bloodstream. More recently physiologists have discovered that various substances with hormone-like properties are in effect manufactured on the spot, from the blood or other fluids, precisely when and where they are needed. These active substances, made without the aid of special glands, have been called local hormones. Because local hormones are released near their sites of action and are usually destroyed rapidly, their physiological roles have been hard to establish. In the past few years, however, good progress has been made in defining the activity and nature of a number of these elusive hormones. Among them is the group of substances called kinins.

Kinins can be regarded as miniature proteins. Ordinary proteins are giant molecules built up of hundreds or thousands of amino acid subunits, of which there are 20-odd varieties. The properties of a protein depend on the number and kind of amino acids it contains, on the order in which they are linked together and on the cross links between them. Proteins containing fewer than 100 or so amino acid units are commonly called polypeptides, or simply peptides. The kinins are peptides, but because the study of kinins is so new there is no general agreement as yet on the number and kind of amino acid units that characterize a kinin. Until more kinins have been thoroughly investigated the outline of the group will probably remain vague. The core of the group is nonetheless already formed by several well-defined peptides with similar biological properties. These are kinins that were first obtained from the plasma of mammalian blood and from mammalian urine. Later, surprisingly, similar substances were found in the venom of wasps. Study of a few of these substances provides most of what is so far known of the genesis, nature and action of kinins. The knowledge growing around this core should lead to the definition of a group of highly active peptides and to an explanation of their role in the working of the body.

Kinins were discovered as biologically active products of blood many years before their chemistry was known. They were revealed by an experimental technique familiar in physiology. A segment of intestine, cut from an animal's body immediately after death, is suspended in a warm, oxygenated solution resembling blood in salinity and alkalinity. The segment is suspended from a lever; this transmits the movements of the intestine to a stylus that rests on a revolving drum covered with a sheet of smoked paper. As the intestine contracts and relaxes, the stylus draws a curved trace on the paper. A number of biologically active substances will make the intestine contract or relax. These responses are exquisitely sensitive and their amplitude varies directly according to the dose of active substance applied.

In 1937, using this technique, E. Werle, W. Götze and A. Keppler, then at the Düsseldorf Academy of Medicine, first demonstrated that such a thing as a kinin existed. When they treated a segment of guinea pig colon with human blood serum or an extract of salivary gland, nothing happened. But if the two fluids were mixed and applied immediately, the tissue contracted sharply [see illustration, page 110]. If the mixture was left standing for a few minutes, it lost its activity. The German workers concluded that an enzyme in salivary gland released from some component in blood a highly active but unstable substance. Eleven years later, in 1948, Werle named the substance kallidin. (The generic term "kinin" came later.)

The enzyme in salivary gland that released kallidin from blood was kallikrein, a protein that had been studied in Germany even before the discovery of kallidin. Kallikreins had been extracted from pancreas, urine, the wall of the gut and other sites, and were known by their ability to lower blood pressure when injected into the veins of an animal. This effect, it is now believed, is due to the release of kallidin within the body.

We owe to Werle and his group not only the first demonstration of a kinin but also the concept of how it is released in the blood. Normally no kallidin can be detected in the bloodstream of man or other animals. But the release mechanism can be set off by a variety of physical or chemical changes, such as acidification, dilution with salt solution, addition of acetone or papain (an enzyme derived from the papaya plant) or by allowing the blood to come in contact with glass. Some, if not all, of these treatments activate the kallikrein, which is normally present in blood in an inactive form. The kallikrein in turn chops off molecules of kallidin as peptide fragments of one of the large plasma proteins (alpha-two globulin). These events take place in plasma or serum obtained from blood, and they can also be set off in the body by injecting kallikrein or one of the agents that activate it [see illustration, page 109].

When a mechanism exists in the body for release of a highly active substance, a second substance is usually provided to destroy or inactivate the first. Such inactivating agents are enzymes that are often given names with the suffix "-ase." For example, blood and tissues contain potent esterases that quickly destroy acetylcholine, a substance that stimulates the contraction of a muscle when liberated from a certain kind of nerve ending. It is not surpris-

ing, therefore, that blood contains inactivators of kallikrein and enzymes—carboxypeptidases—that destroy kallidin. For this reason stored plasma or serum does not contain much free kinin.

There is a striking similarity between the release of kallidin and the deposition of fibrin, which is the main event in blood clotting. In both cases there exists a natural mechanism that is set in motion by abnormal conditions. The end products of each come from the action of enzymes (kallikrein and thrombin)

on globulins normally present in plasma. Both of these end products may later be destroyed by other enzymes present or released in blood—kallidin by carboxypeptidase and fibrin by plasmin (sometimes called fibrinolysin).

The mechanism that releases kallidin and that which forms fibrin not only seem modeled on a similar pattern but also share some of the same cogwheels. One of these is the Hageman factor, named after the patient in whom its lack was first observed. In the absence

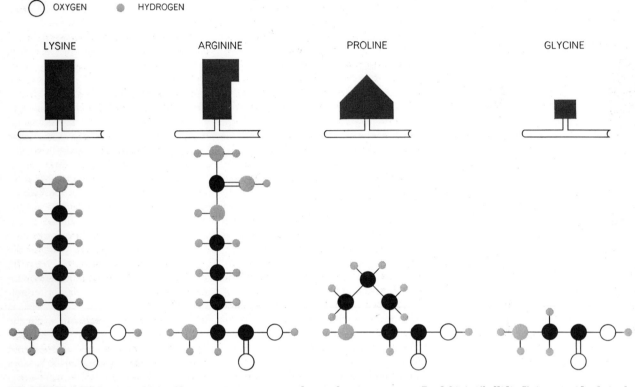

SIX AMINO ACIDS, of 20-odd found in proteins, appear as subunits in the two kinins whose structure has been established within the past two years. Bradykinin (kallidin I) is a peptide chain that is created from the linkage of nine amino acids, as shown below.

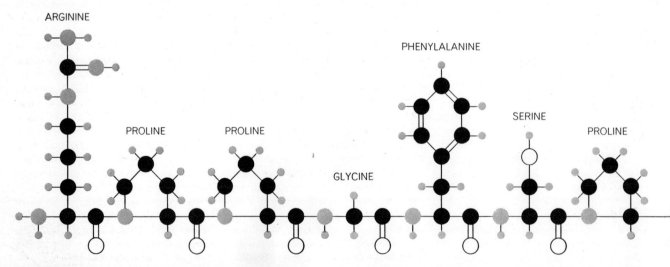

BRADYKININ (KALLIDIN I) is a peptide that appears in the bloodstream as a "local hormone." Related peptides are also found free in the venom of certain wasps. A peptide linkage is formed between two amino acids when the hydroxyl (OH) group of one acid links up with a hydrogen (H) atom in the amino group (NH_2) of a second acid to form water. The water splits away, allow-

of the Hageman factor, blood brought into contact with glass fails to clot at a normal rate and also fails to yield kinin. Both clotting and kinin release can be brought about by adding the Hageman factor from normal blood. The part this factor plays in both processes underlines their likeness and shows how complex is the system of activators and inhibitors that make it likely that clots and kinin will form when a blood vessel is broken.

Probably because of World War II,

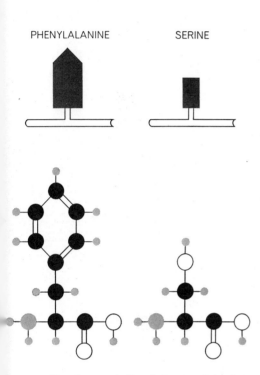

PHENYLALANINE   SERINE

Proteins are similar chains containing hundreds or thousands of amino acid subunits.

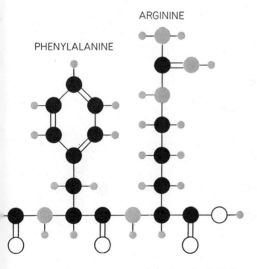

PHENYLALANINE

ARGININE

ing the two amino acids to be joined. Kallidin II and other kinin and kinin-like structures are illustrated on the next page.

the first studies on kinins passed almost unnoticed outside Germany. Then in 1949 M. Rocha e Silva, W. T. Beraldo and G. Rosenfeld of the University of São Paulo published an unexpected observation. They were studying the effects of the venom of the South American snake *Bothrops jararaca* on the dog. They noticed that the venom released from dog's blood a substance that was highly active on pieces of intestine isolated from the guinea pig. At first they suspected that the venom had triggered the release of histamine, a substance frequently produced when tissues are irritated and undergo an allergic reaction. They found, however, that the effect of the substance was not abolished by antihistamines and that the response took about seven times as long to reach a peak as did the response to histamine [*see top illustration on page 111*]. They called the new substance bradykinin from the Greek words *bradys*, meaning "slow," and *kinein*, meaning "to move." The relation between bradykinin and kallidin was not to be clarified until 1961.

The São Paulo group showed that bradykinin could be liberated by the action of the digestive enzyme trypsin on plasma globulin; this meant that bradykinin could be made from raw materials available in bulk. Bradykinin was therefore the first of the kinins to be prepared pure, to have its chemical structure worked out and to be synthesized from the amino acids that compose it, but this is getting ahead of the story.

Globulins that yield kinins exist not only in blood but also in other fluids of the body, such as lymph, ascites (an abnormal accumulation of fluid in the abdomen), amniotic fluid (which surrounds the fetus in the uterus) and colostrum (the first milk after childbirth). Little is known as yet about the kinins that can be liberated from these fluids. They are a mine in which investigators may still strike rich deposits.

The discovery of kallidin and bradykinin showed that salivary glands and snake venom both contain enzymes that can release kinins from blood. Since the poison glands of snakes are modified salivary glands, this is understandable. More surprising is the fact that the venom of some insects contains free, active kinins.

In 1954 R. Jaques and M. Schachter, then at the National Institute for Medical Research in London, found the first venom kinin in the common wasp (*Vespa vulgaris*). The London workers removed the sting apparatus from hun-

dreds of wasps to get enough material to show the main properties of the new substance. Schachter's group coined the word "kinin" by chopping "brady" from "bradykinin," which the wasp substance most closely resembled. Although Schachter and his colleagues have been unable to find a kinin in bee venom, they have just detected another kinin in the venom of the European hornet (*Vespa crabro*). In due course other species of the genus *Vespa* will no doubt yield kinins, and probably kinins will eventually be found in the venom of other genera and even of other orders.

If wasp venom is kept for some time, the kinin disappears, but it stays active if the venom is first heated. This suggests that venom contains an enzyme that can destroy kinin. The kinins of the wasp and the hornet are highly concentrated in the fluid that these insects inject into their victims. Also contained in the fluid are other interesting substances: histamine and serotonin in the wasp fluid, and both these substances plus acetylcholine in the hornet fluid. The three substances, the molecules of which are smaller than those of the peptides, are also local hormones that occur naturally in the mammalian body. There they act on nerves, muscles and blood vessels, in some ways just as the kinins do.

The inactivation of kinins by enzymes such as chymotrypsin shows that kinin activity depends on a molecular structure containing peptide links. By means of such links the basic amino (NH_2) group of one amino acid joins the acidic carboxyl (COOH) group of another to make a larger molecule. This linkage scheme is common to both peptide molecules, which contain relatively few amino acids, and proteins, which contain hundreds. It is not difficult to show that kallidin and bradykinin are peptides and that they are smaller, for example, than the several varieties of insulin, each of which consists of 48 amino acid units. Two forms of the pituitary hormone corticotrophin have 39 amino acid units. Two other pituitary hormones, oxytocin and vasopressin, contain eight amino acid units and are comparable in size to the kinins.

Because living tissue can sometimes detect a single change in the type or even order of the amino acids in a peptide, the exact structure of each kinin is important and also bears on the ultimate definition of the group. Before the structure can be determined, the peptide must be completely purified. In 1959

D. F. Elliott, G. P. Lewis and E. W. Horton of the National Institute for Medical Research in London prepared pure bradykinin. Following the method of Rocha e Silva, they obtained their starting material by reacting crystalline trypsin with globulin from ox blood. After analyzing the pure compound, Elliott and his co-workers proposed, in April, 1960, that bradykinin consists of eight amino acid units in the following sequence: arginine-proline-proline-glycine-phenylalanine-serine-phenylalanine-arginine.

Within two months three independent teams of industrial scientists had synthesized this octapeptide and found it inactive. R. A. Boissonnas of the Swiss firm Sandoz Ltd. discussed this with

Elliott. Boissonnas's group then began to make other peptides of related structure, while Elliott's group reviewed its own work, looking for errors. Boissonnas and his co-workers found that when one of the prolines of the inactive octapeptide was put in another position, the new compound had weak bradykinin-like activity. They then made a nine-amino-acid peptide with prolines present in both positions; this had all the activity of pure bradykinin. More or less simultaneously Elliott's group found that they had missed a third molecule of proline in reaching their proposed structure. They called the inactive octapeptide "boguskinin" and assigned to bradykinin the structure of the nonapeptide that Boissonnas had synthesized.

Meanwhile the chemical structure of the original kinin, kallidin, was still unknown, but it resembled bradykinin so closely in biological activity that many workers thought it must be the same substance. A year ago J. V. Pierce and M. E. Webster of the National Institutes of Health in the U.S. reported that they had obtained two different kallidins from human plasma treated with human urinary kallikrein. Their analysis showed that kallidin I was identical with bradykinin, whereas kallidin II was a 10-amino-acid peptide in which the amino acid lysine was attached to the arginine in position 1 of bradykinin. Soon afterward Ernest D. Nicolaides, Horace A. DeWald and Duncan A. McCarthy, Jr., of Parke, Davis & Co. synthesized this

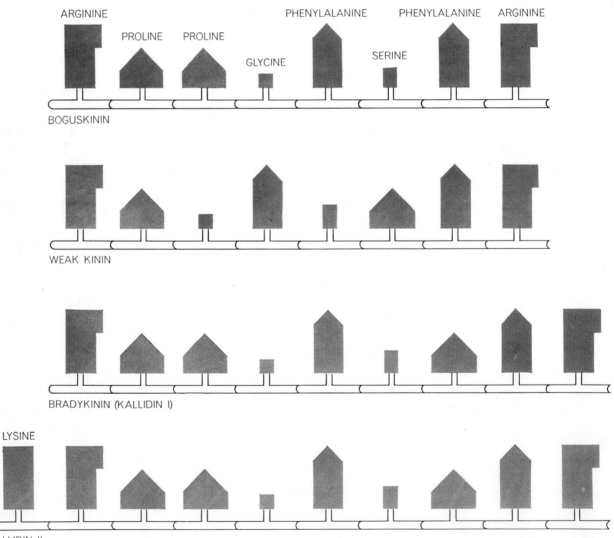

SIGNIFICANCE OF STRUCTURE emerges from a comparison of four peptides closely resembling one another. The octapeptide at top was the first structure proposed for bradykinin. When it proved inactive, it was named "boguskinin." Moving one of the pro-line units to the right, between serine and phenylalanine, gave a peptide with weak kinin activity. Addition of a third proline, to replace the one moved, produced bradykinin, or kallidin I. Addition of lysine to left end of the chain produced kallidin II.

decapeptide, which showed high kinin activity.

These adventures in peptide synthesis show not only the problems and surprises in this field of work but also the apparent capriciousness of living tissues in discriminating between chemical structures. Whereas the loss of a proline in position 7 inactivates bradykinin, the addition of a lysine to position 1 hardly affects its potency. Switching a proline from the position on the left of glycine to that on the right of serine makes a weak kinin from the inactive octapeptide [see illustration on opposite page].

The discovery that bradykinin, first detected as a product of the action of foreign enzymes on globulin, is released naturally in human plasma as one form of kallidin throws the terminology of plasma kinins into some confusion. While the difficulty stays unresolved, the term "kinin," qualified by site of release, provides a useful description.

Let us return, then, to the biological activity of the kinins. As we have seen, their profound effect on isolated pieces of intestine led to their discovery. The muscles that show such sensitivity belong to the category of smooth muscle. This type of muscle provides the motive power not only of the intestines but also of most of the other tubular systems of the body: the blood vessels (except capillaries), the air passages of the lungs and the ducts that carry the reproductive cells, urine and digestive juices. Isolated pieces of smooth muscle associated with such tubes usually respond sensitively to kinins, some by contraction, some by relaxation.

When injected into the bloodstream of man or animals, kinins also have powerful effects on the smooth muscles as they exist in the body. For example, in some species they affect the smooth muscles in the walls of the bronchioles of the lung. In the guinea pig less than one microgram (a millionth of a gram) of bradykinin, injected into a vein, will make the bronchioles constrict and so increase resistance to the flow of air into and out of the lungs. Injection of histamine, serotonin or acetylcholine has a similar effect, but the response to kinin develops more slowly [see second illustration from top on page 111].

In all mammals tested, kinins from blood and venom relax the muscles of the blood vessel walls, causing more blood to flow to the area involved and blood pressure to fall. In a recent experiment at the National Institute for Medical Research one microgram of

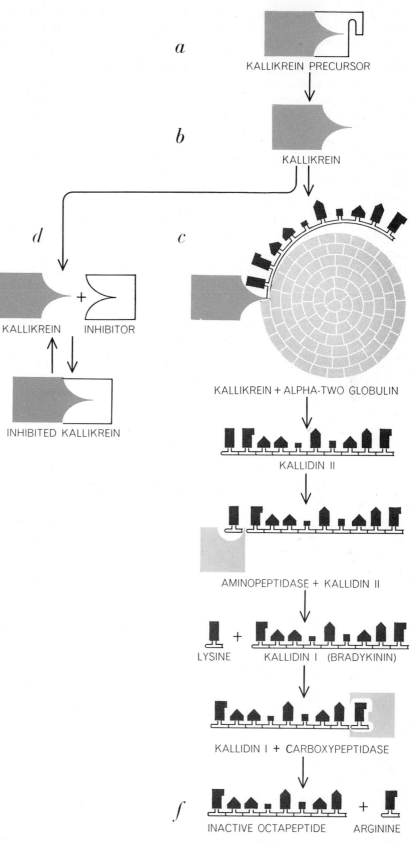

KININ RELEASE AND INHIBITION can occur rapidly in the blood in response to local requirements. Release of kallidin II is a two-step process. Blood contains a protein (a) that is a precursor of kallikrein. When kallikrein is released or activated (b), it chops a short peptide fragment, kallidin II, from one of the large globular proteins, alpha-two globulin (c). The blood also contains an inhibitor for kallikrein (d). Another enzyme, aminopeptidase, can remove lysine from kallidin II, producing kallidin I (e). Finally, kallidin I can be inactivated by carboxypeptidase, an enzyme that removes arginine (f).

pure bradykinin was injected into an artery in the arm of a healthy volunteer. For a short period after the injection blood flowed through the forearm more than six times faster than before.

Kinins can also dilate the capillaries to the point where they become leaky. This can be shown by injecting a dye such as Pontamine blue into a vein of a guinea pig. Normally the dye circulates in the blood without passing out into the tissues, but if a kinin is injected into the skin, a blue patch quickly appears because the capillaries become permeable to the dye. Such an increase in the leakiness of capillary walls is the direct cause of wealing in response to injury. A like effect is seen after the injection of histamine, but kinins are more potent.

Another characteristic of kinins is that they cause pain in human skin. C. A. Keele and his colleagues at Middlesex Hospital in London first showed this by a handy method. A small cantharidin plaster is left on the surface of the skin overnight and raises a blister. The loose skin over the blister is cut away and substances to be tested for their ability to cause pain are applied in dilute solution to the raw surface underneath. The subject presses on a rubber bulb with a force corresponding to the intensity of

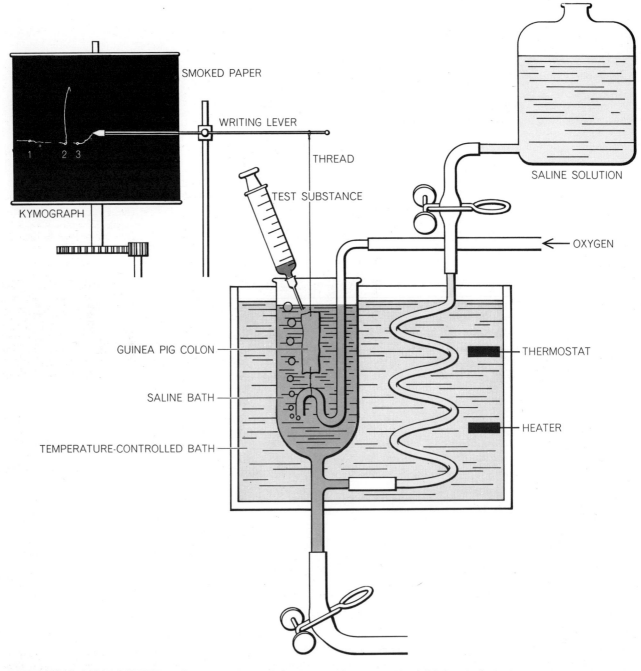

SMOKED PAPER

WRITING LEVER

THREAD

TEST SUBSTANCE

KYMOGRAPH

SALINE SOLUTION

OXYGEN

GUINEA PIG COLON

THERMOSTAT

SALINE BATH

HEATER

TEMPERATURE-CONTROLLED BATH

BIOLOGICAL ASSAY METHOD is the type used in 1937 by the discoverers of kallidin: E. Werle, W. Götze and A. Keppler of the Düsseldorf Academy of Medicine. They observed the reaction of a section of guinea pig colon suspended in a saline bath. Movement of the colon was recorded by a kymograph. When an extract of salivary gland was added to the bath, there was no response (*trace 1*). When the gland extract was mixed with human serum, the colon segment contracted sharply (*2*). When the mixture was left standing six minutes, the response was slight (*3*), showing that the active substance, later named kallidin, was being inactivated.

pain felt, and this pressure is transmitted to a pen writing on moving paper. By this method the Middlesex workers showed that blood plasma and fluids exuding into inflamed or injured tissues can yield a pain-producing substance. This is probably kallidin. They also found that weak solutions of acetylcholine, of serotonin and of several peptides, including bradykinin, cause pain. Needless to say, wasp kinin is also a potent pain provoker.

Most of the biological actions of kinins parallel those of histamine. But tests with pure bradykinin show that, molecule for molecule, it is a much more potent substance. The table on the next page lists a number of biological preparations together with the dose of bradykinin needed to evoke a response. One can see that for a sensitive tissue such as rat uterus, bradykinin is effective at a concentration of .1 nanogram (one-tenth of a billionth of a gram) per milliliter of solution.

So far kinins have shown one characteristic interaction with drugs. Aspirin, phenylbutazone, amidopyrine and phenazone, which belong to the group of agents variously described as analgesic-antipyretic, antirheumatic and anti-inflammatory, potently suppress the constriction of bronchioles that bradykinin evokes in guinea pigs. This action is selective, since the same drugs do not affect the constriction due to histamine, serotonin or acetylcholine [*see bottom illustration at right*]. Such studies are providing a clue to the mode of action of aspirin, which has so long remained a mystery. When we first observed this drug antagonism in the pharmacological laboratory of Parke, Davis & Co. in England, we thought it might explain in a simple way both what kinin does in the body and how these anti-inflammatory drugs act. Unfortunately our hopes of a simple explanation have been disappointed, because the drugs did not selectively antagonize other actions of kinins in experimental animals or in isolated organs.

What research has revealed so far about kinins can be summarized in a paragraph. Applied at appropriate sites, these peptides cause pain, wealing, dilation of blood vessels and movement of smooth muscle. Within the body they are released as local hormones, where needed, when kallikrein circulating in the bloodstream is activated locally by the appropriate enzyme. Kinins can also enter the body in the venom injected by certain insects. Mechanisms that inacti-

1 STANDARD BRADYKININ
2 TEST BRADYKININ
3 HISTAMINE

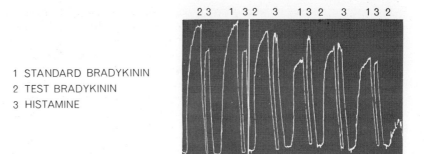

EFFECT OF BRADYKININ on isolated guinea pig intestine is compared with faster acting histamine. This kymograph trace was made by M. Rocha e Silva, W. T. Beraldo and G. Rosenfeld of the University of São Paulo, who discovered bradykinin in 1948. They found that the substance was released from dog's blood by the venom of a certain snake.

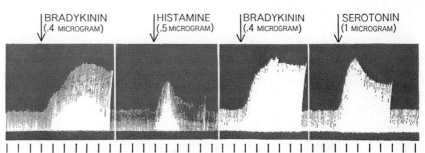

CONSTRICTION OF BRONCHIOLES in the lungs of a guinea pig is evoked by bradykinin, histamine and serotonin, administered intravenously. The constriction is measured by resistance of lungs to inflation, shown by height of trace. Experiment was performed by J. A. Holgate, M. Schachter, P. G. Shorley and the author at Parke, Davis & Co. in London.

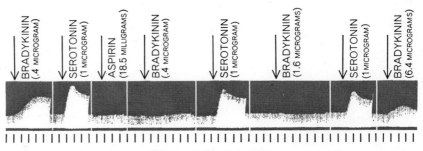

RECORDS OF PAIN were made by a volunteer who pressed a series of switches indicating the intensity of pain produced by acetylcholine and wasp kinin, applied to an exposed blister base on his forearm. The first two test solutions contained one milligram per milliliter of active substance. The last two were only one-tenth as concentrated. Study was conducted by D. J. Holdstock, A. P. Mathias and Schachter at University College London.

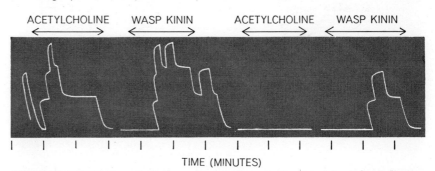

EFFECTIVENESS OF ASPIRIN in suppressing the action of bradykinin and serotonin is determined by measuring resistance of guinea pig lungs to inflation. First two traces show normal rise in resistance after intravenous injection of the two substances. Aspirin is then injected intraperitoneally. Four minutes later bradykinin is again injected, followed by two injections of serotonin and two more larger doses of bradykinin. Aspirin suppresses action of bradykinin but not of serotonin. The study was made by the author and associates.

vate kinins exist in the blood and elsewhere. Kinins resemble some other physiological substances in action or in mechanism of release. For example, they are like histamine in many of their effects on living tissue; kallidin resembles fibrin in how it is produced and destroyed. Finally, anti-inflammatory drugs specifically antagonize kinins in their bronchiole-constricting action in guinea pigs.

Obviously there is much to be learned about the full role of the kinins as they come and go in blood and tissue fluids. Nonetheless, two minor parts played by these peptides can be discerned, and several reasonable suggestions have been made as to their major roles.

One minor part is that played by the kinins in wasp venom. Here they keep company with other pain substances, all of which are amply enough concentrated to hurt when injected into skin. Wasps and hornets display warning coloration, which may be expected to protect them, provided the warning is occasionally reinforced by a sharp pain. Although the individual insect that inflicts this pain may perish, most members of the species are thereby more likely to escape molestation.

More complicated is the possible role of kallikrein and kallidin in the mammalian body. So far only one part that they play has been elucidated. This is in the rare disease hereditary angioedema. People with this disease are subject to localized swellings in skin, muscle, larynx or digestive tract, which are transitory but liable to recur. These swellings are caused by fluid passing from the blood into the tissues, usually at places where pressure has been applied or a blow has been received. If the larynx is involved, there is danger that the passage of air will be blocked.

In 1960 N. S. Landerman, E. L. Becker and H. E. Ratcliffe of Walter Reed Army Hospital showed that the serum of a patient with this disease increased the permeability of blood capillaries more than normal serum did, when each was diluted in order to activate kallikrein and then was injected into the patient's own skin. They attributed this effect to an unknown factor in the patient's serum, which they and M. E. Webster have recently identified as the inherited lack of a natural kallikrein inhibitor. In short, hereditary angioedema results from an inborn defect in the mechanism of kallidin release.

Apart from these two instances, the roles of the kinins remain uncertain. Some biologists have suggested that release of kallidin provides a way of increasing blood supply to parts of the body that need it, such as muscles or glands that are working hard or regions in which circulation is blocked. Another suggestion is that kallidin is released in allergic states such as asthma and urticaria, in which it contributes to some of the symptoms. A third hypothesis, which the work on angioedema makes particularly plausible, is that kallidin plays a part in the blistering or swelling of skin that commonly follows burns, blows or infections by microbes. The swelling arises from an increase in the leakiness of capillary blood vessels. This probably helps to combat injury by allowing protective antibodies (which are large molecules) and white cells (which are many times larger) to pass from the blood into the affected tissue.

Kallidin has the actions needed to fulfill these roles, and the mechanism for its release exists. The probability that it actually takes part is increased by the recent demonstration that kallikrein is activated during the natural event. Even so, it is still hard to prove that kallidin is essential, because a similar mechanism, such as the release of histamine, might work in parallel. In some important reactions the body has more than one means of achieving the required effect—like a man wearing both a belt and suspenders to keep his pants up. In this situation it is hard to say which is the essential device.

Research workers would be helped in getting the evidence needed to make the role of kallidin clear if they had drugs that more potently and specifically stopped its being inactivated in the body and others that antagonized its main biological actions. Meanwhile speculation on the possible role of kinins is a useful step toward finding the end of the main thread.

TEST OBJECT	ACTION	DOSE OR CONCENTRATION
ISOLATED RAT UTERUS	SMOOTH-MUSCLE CONTRACTION	.1 NANOGRAM PER MILLILITER
ISOLATED RAT DUODENUM	SMOOTH-MUSCLE RELAXATION	.8 NANOGRAM PER MILLILITER
WHOLE GUINEA PIG	CONSTRICTION OF BRONCHIOLES	.5 MICROGRAM PER KILOGRAM (INTRAVENOUS)
HUMAN FOREARM	DILATION OF BLOOD VESSELS	100 NANOGRAMS (INTRA-ARTERIAL)
WHOLE CAT	LOWERED BLOOD PRESSURE	400 NANOGRAMS PER KILOGRAM (INTRAVENOUS)
GUINEA PIG SKIN	INCREASED CAPILLARY PERMEABILITY	.1 TO 1 NANOGRAM (INTRADERMAL)
HUMAN BLISTER BASE	PAIN	.1 TO 1 MICROGRAM PER MILLILITER

POTENCY OF PURE BRADYKININ is shown by the extremely small dosages or highly dilute concentrations needed to evoke its principal effects in a variety of test objects.

12

The Control of Growth in Plant Cells

F. C. STEWARD

October 1963

For all sexually reproducing organisms, plant or animal, the zygote, or fertilized egg, is the bridge between one generation and the next. As such it seems to fulfill a unique role. The division of this single cell starts the building of a new organism. It contains in its nucleus a molecular blueprint (the structure of its DNA) that will determine the constitution of the entire organism, and the blueprint is faithfully reproduced in each of the millions of cells that constitute the new organism. Yet notwithstanding this fixed set of instructions, most of the cells stop dividing and eventually differentiate to form a great variety of tissues and organs.

The mystery of what makes some cells go on growing while in others growth subsides is one of the most challenging present problems in biology. Is there something altogether special about embryonic cells, something inherent that sets them apart from mature cells in their ability to grow? Or is the fate of cells decided largely by external factors—controlling factors in their environment?

Recent work with plant cells, which will be described in this article, has shown the latter to be the case. By supplying certain chemical factors we have been able to stimulate adult cells to grow again—even to grow entire plants from single rejuvenated cells! The investigations lead to the conclusion that the zygote, far from possessing unique properties, is perhaps the least specialized of all the cells in the plant. Its ability to grow is a common property that, under suitable conditions, is displayed by many other kinds of cells.

To understand these experiments we must first look into some of the details of how a flowering plant reproduces. In a flowering plant the process begins in two separate organs of the flower: the anther (at the tip of the stamen), where the male part of the sexual cycle begins, and the ovule (within the ovary), where the female part of the cycle begins. The first step, as in animals, is meiosis: the division of diploid cells (cells with a double set of chromosomes) into haploid cells (cells with a single set).

In plants the haploid cells that result from meiosis are called spores. These cells (or their nuclei) can divide many times before they give rise to gametes: male and female sex cells. The spores that give rise to the male sexual cycle are called microspores; those that give rise to the female sexual cycle, megaspores. Ordinarily spores can grow independently, but a gamete will do so only if it fuses with a gamete of the opposite sex.

In the anthers microspores develop into pollen, and a pollen tube, with two male nuclei in its tip, grows down the style of the flower toward the ovule [see top illustration, page 115]. Meanwhile in the ovule megaspores have formed an embryo sac that may contain as many

CULTURE FLASK viewed from top contains carrot tissue in a growth medium. Slow rotation of flask shakes individual cells loose; some can be stimulated to produce new plants.

as eight nuclei. When the tip of the pollen tube penetrates this sac, it discharges its two male nuclei. One of these fuses with a female nucleus in the sac, and the result is a zygote.

The act of fertilization itself is a great stimulus to the growth of the egg, but the zygote gets another type of stimulus from its environment in the ovule. The second male nucleus, although it is not a party to the sexual union, turns out to have a crucial role to play. This nucleus combines with a diploid nucleus composed of two nuclei in the embryo sac, and the fused nucleus produces a nutritive tissue called endosperm. The endosperm often develops in advance of the embryo and stores food that nourishes and stimulates the growth of the embryo from the zygote. The first specialized leaves of the young embryo, called cotyledons, absorb food and growth stimulants from the endosperm.

Thus the zygote's built-in capacity for growth gets indispensable help from its environment. As the young plant develops, its growth soon becomes highly localized. Surprisingly few of its cells continue to multiply; the ones that do are primarily those at the extreme tips of the shoots and roots. The main growth of the shoot takes place in a small dome of tissue on its apex less than a millimeter in diameter. Here the dividing cells form bulges that become leaves; in the mint plant, for example, two leaves form on opposite sides of the stem. Other pairs of leaves are present at intervals along the axis. And in the notches between the stem and the leaves small islands of growing cells form buds that later become branches.

Certain tissues of a plant may be able to grow indefinitely. An outstanding example is the cambium of a tree: the tissue that gives rise to the tree's annual rings and causes the trunk and branches to grow in girth. There are sequoia trees in California in which the cambium has been growing, with annual periods of rest or dormancy, for 4,000 years or more, which is as close an approximation of eternal life as occurs on this planet.

But just as remarkable as the continuation of cell growth is its cessation. What is it that makes the still living cells of the pith and bark of a plant stop dividing and remain quiescent? Why does the growth of an organ such as a potato tuber or a carrot root come to a halt even though it is supplied with an abundance of food and water? If a potato tuber or a carrot root is cut and kept in moist air, its surface cells will start dividing,

SUCCESSFUL EXPERIMENT created a new carrot plant in the laboratory from ordinarily nongrowing cells of a carrot root. The flask contains a carrot plant produced in that way.

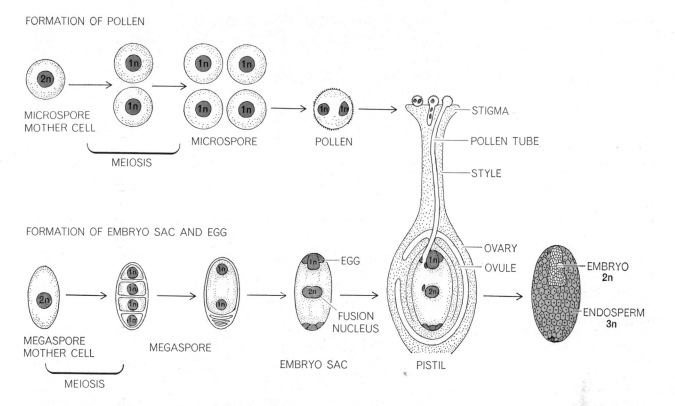

FORMATION OF POLLEN

MICROSPORE MOTHER CELL

MEIOSIS

MICROSPORE

POLLEN

STIGMA

POLLEN TUBE

STYLE

FORMATION OF EMBRYO SAC AND EGG

MEGASPORE MOTHER CELL

MEIOSIS

MEGASPORE

EGG

FUSION NUCLEUS

EMBRYO SAC

PISTIL

OVARY

OVULE

EMBRYO 2n

ENDOSPERM 3n

NORMAL REPRODUCTION IN FLOWERING PLANTS occurs as depicted here. Sequence at top left shows development of pollen after formation in anther, beginning with a 2n microspore mother cell (meaning that it is diploid, or contains two sets of chromosomes) and progressing through several divisions until one pollen grain lodges on a stigma and gives rise to a pollen tube. Meanwhile, as shown in sequence at bottom left, an embryo sac containing an egg similarly develops from a megaspore mother cell. On the pistil two of the nuclei that have developed in pollen grain start down pollen tube. One nucleus joins the egg to accomplish fertilization; one joins fusion nucleus to create endosperm, a nutritive stimulant to embryo growth. End product is seed containing embryo.

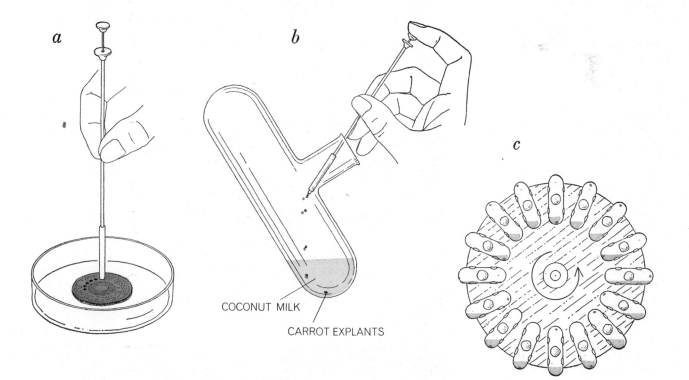

a

b

c

COCONUT MILK

CARROT EXPLANTS

EXPERIMENT BEGINS when, as shown at left, a thin metal tube is used to cut small carrot segments, or explants, which are then placed in a tube containing a growth medium that includes coconut milk. The medium thus imitates the nutritive functions of the endosperm. Several tubes are then rotated on a wheel, as shown at right, to provide a precise mixture of air and the growth medium.

but this growth stops as soon as the wound is healed.

All the cells of a plant receive the same genetic information. We must ask, therefore, what is it that turns a cell's built-in capacity for growth on or off as the case may be? Plainly this controlling signal or stimulus must come from outside the cell itself. In the living, intact plant the signal is evidently supplied by some chemical factor in the neighborhood of the cells in question, as the effect of the endosperm on the embryo suggests. To track down the responsible factor or factors a series of controlled experiments with cultures of plant tissues and individual cells have been performed.

At the turn of the century the Austrian botanist G. Haberlandt envisioned the possibility of growing plants from single cells and discovering their requirements in this way. The work in our laboratory at Cornell University has been toward this goal.

The first question investigated was whether or not a mature, quiescent plant tissue could be forced into active growth by exposing it to a variety of natural and unnatural materials. It turned out that endosperm, which was known to promote the growth of young embryos, was particularly effective. For the tissue to be tested the carrot root was chosen.

From thin cross-sectional slices of the carrot small cylindrical pieces (two to three milligrams in size) were taken from a nongrowing region of the root, a millimeter or two from the cambial ring [*see bottom illustration on preceding page*]. All the operations and manipulations of the tissue had to be done aseptically, with the precautions of a surgical operation. One to three of the tissue pieces were then placed in a nutrient medium in a special glass tube. Air can diffuse into the tube via a cotton plug in a side neck, and the tube was slowly rotated around a horizontal shaft (at one revolution per minute) so that the tissue, clinging to the wall of the tube, was alternately submerged in the liquid and exposed to air. The relative periods of exposure to the nutrient and to air proved to be important, and optimal exposure times were arranged by careful attention to the dimensions of the tube and the relative volume of the liquid medium.

The basic medium was a standard nutrient solution for plant tissue culture. To this was added various plant extracts and other substances that might stimulate the tissue to grow. Although many substances were tried, the greatest suc-

cess came with coconut milk, or coconut "water," as it is often called.

Coconut milk is the liquid endosperm that nourishes the embryo that grows inside the coconut. It was therefore a logical as well as convenient material to try as a possible stimulator of growth in our tissue culture. But we were hardly prepared for its dramatic effect on the quiescent carrot cells [*see upper illustration on page 119*]. The tissue began to grow rapidly, and in 20 days it had multiplied its weight approximately eightyfold!

To measure the effect on the cells themselves the tissues were treated in a mixture of chromic and hydrochloric acids. This procedure separated the cells so that they could be counted in much the same way as blood cells are counted. It then became possible to estimate the average size of the cells (by dividing the weight of a sample of tissue by the number of cells). This analysis, made at various growth stages, showed that at first the cells grew in size without dividing; then, as cell division got under way, their average size became smaller, and finally, as the rate of division subsided, the cell size tended to increase again.

The unleashing of the growth of these otherwise resting cells, which in the carrot root's natural condition would not have grown again, was a startling phenomenon. It was as if the coconut milk had acted like a clutch, putting the cell's idling engine of growth into gear and thereby enabling the cell to use its available fuel to grow again. Something in the coconut milk had turned on the built-in capacity of the carrot root cells for growth.

Certain other cells, however, did not respond to coconut milk in this way. Coconut milk alone failed, for example, to stimulate growth in the potato tuber. Experiments showed that the cells of some organs, for example the onion bulb and the dormant bud of the maple tree, contain substances that counteract the effect of coconut milk. The buds of the maple (and of other deciduous trees) become dormant in late summer. Extracts from these buds prevented the growth of carrot cells when they were added to the medium containing coconut milk. When the dormancy of the buds was broken by winter cold, however, even comparable extracts no longer inhibited the growth-promoting effect of

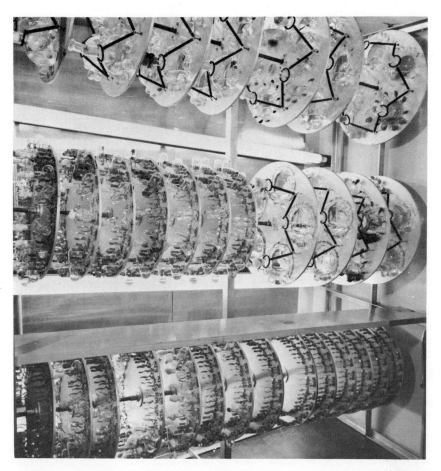

TUBES AND FLASKS are mounted on revolving apparatus in the laboratory. System was devised to provide a regulated alternation of air and liquid for carrot explants in tubes.

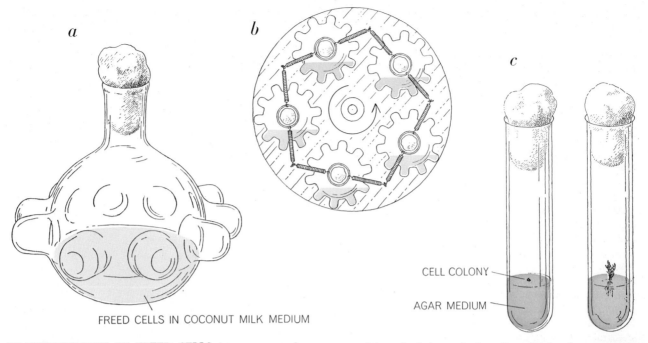

a   *b*   *c*

CELL COLONY

AGAR MEDIUM

FREED CELLS IN COCONUT MILK MEDIUM

TRANSFORMATION OF FREED CELLS into a carrot plant that is wholly a laboratory creation begins with free cells in a culture flask (*left*), which is then mounted with similar flasks on a revolving wheel (*center*). As cells multiply, clusters are removed and put into an agar medium (*right*). Some cells grow into normal carrot plants similar to those that are raised from seed.

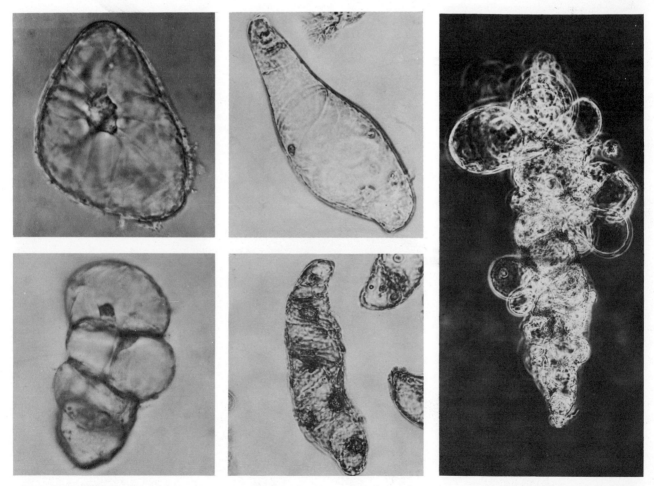

GROWTH OF CELLS in the author's experiments is shown in these photographs. The top photograph at left shows a freed cell, the bottom photograph an older cell after it has begun to grow by dividing. Similarly, the top and bottom photographs in the center panel show other stages in the development of a single freed cell, although with division taking place in a different manner. The photograph at right shows a cluster of cells beginning to assume the polarity characteristic of organized carrot plants.

coconut milk; evidently the chilling had inactivated the inhibitor that causes the buds to be dormant.

There are, however, substances that enhance the growth-stimulating effect of coconut milk. Such substances, which are not effective alone but display an effect when combined with another substance, are called synergists. It was found that coconut milk required the help of an appropriate synergist to initiate growth in certain resting cells. A number of synergists that can augment the effect of coconut milk have since been identified. The first of many was the well-known herbicide 2,4-D (2,4-dichlorophenoxyacetic acid); it speeded up the growth of potato tuber cells when it was added in the proportion of six parts per million to the medium that also contained coconut milk.

Thus the experiments graphically demonstrated that all cells have an inherent ability to grow that is controlled by a delicately poised system of chemical controls. Whether or not a given cell will grow depends not only on the general growing conditions (its food and water supply, temperature and so on) but also on the stimulating or inhibiting complex of substances to which it is exposed.

It follows that mature cells may often start to grow abnormally when their normal chemical balance is disturbed. This is well known in the occurrence of plant tumors; an example is the crown-gall tumor on the stem of the Kalanchoe plant. Extracts from these tumors proved to be capable of stimulating growth in our carrot explants, just as coconut milk did. Only the altered tumor cells contained the stimulating substance; extracts from normal stem tissue of the plant, and from the microorganism that changes the normal cell chemistry and gives rise to the tumor, failed to show the growth-promoting effect.

When pieces of carrot root were stimulated to grow in this way, the new growth had all the characteristics of the explanted tissue: it consisted of unspecialized living cells. But very different events were observed when the tissue was cultured in coconut milk and so treated that cells separated from its surface and were able to grow independently.

This was done in another type of flask consisting of a number of nipples radiating from the central container. The flask was actually designed to grow many carrot explants (up to 100) in a single vessel. As the flask was rotated individual cells were gently loosened from

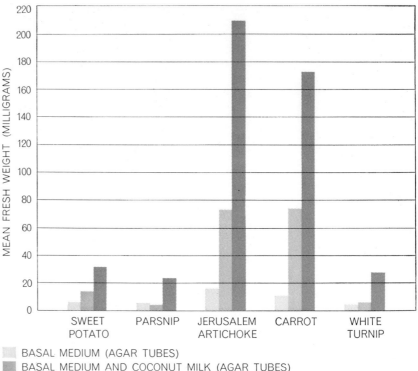

CONTRASTING RESULTS occurred when explants from various plants were stimulated with growth medium containing coconut milk. Each group of bars shows, from left to right, effect of basal control medium and various supplements on different explants over 21 days.

the tissue at its edges. These freed cells were then transplanted into fresh coconut milk growth medium in new flasks just as bacteria are commonly grown by inoculation of a medium.

Freed from the restricting influence of the organized root tissue, the individual carrot cells now began to grow in a variety of different ways. Some grew to giant size, with many nuclei, and showed active protoplasmic streaming. Others put forth tubular outgrowths that became filaments and then divided. Some formed small, uniform buds, almost like the growth of yeast cells. Eventually some of them partitioned themselves into a clump of cells resembling an early carrot embryo.

This striking development was observed when free cells, on dividing, often grew into aggregates that spontaneously formed rootlets. Transferred to an agar medium containing coconut milk, such clusters of cells would then grow shoots opposite the root; that is, they became plantlets very similar to the normal embryo of a carrot plant. Such plantlets, carefully nursed along on the agar medium and then successively transplanted to vermiculite and soil, would eventually grow into mature carrot plants, with normal roots, stalks, flowers and seeds. In short, Haberlandt's old

dream was finally realized: complete, normal plants were grown in culture from free single cells.

Quite recent work in our laboratory has proceeded further along the same line. If the embryo is dissected from the ovary of the carrot flower, it can of course be cultured as an already organized plantlet. This can easily be done in a medium that contains coconut milk. If, however, a very young embryo is made to proliferate so that cells can be removed from its surface, these freed cells can be grown suspended in liquid in the manner already described. The free cells of embryo origin multiply under these culture conditions, and when a sample of them is spread evenly on an agar medium containing coconut milk in a Petri dish, each cell or small cluster grows. It was estimated that more than 100,000 embryoids, remarkably like true, or zygotic, embryos, occurred on a plate inoculated from a cell suspension derived from one carrot embryo. This obviously means that virtually every cell of the young embryo was itself capable of developing into an embryo and that every cell could, under the right nutritional conditions, behave faithfully like a fertilized egg.

Thus a mature cell taken from the differentiated tissue of a carrot has been made to behave like the fertilized egg cell, and the stages of its development into a full plant bear a striking resemblance to the normal growth of a carrot embryo [*see bottom illustration on the next page*]. Experiments showed that the alteration of the adult cell's behavior can be brought about by two essential conditions: (1) removing the cell from its specialized environment and allow-

ing it to grow as a free cell, and (2) supplying it with the kind of substances from endosperm that normally nourish young embryos. In other words, given the right medium and space in which to grow, the adult cell and the embryonic cell behave in the same way.

From this point of view a differentiated cell can be regarded as one that has all the capacities of the fertilized egg but is allowed to use only part of the

information and directions that are stored in its genetic material. The limitations on its behavior result from its position in the special organ of the plant body in which it is incorporated. These controls now need to be interpreted in chemical terms. What are the specific substances that exercise these controls, turning on and off the action of the genes?

Before we get into this important

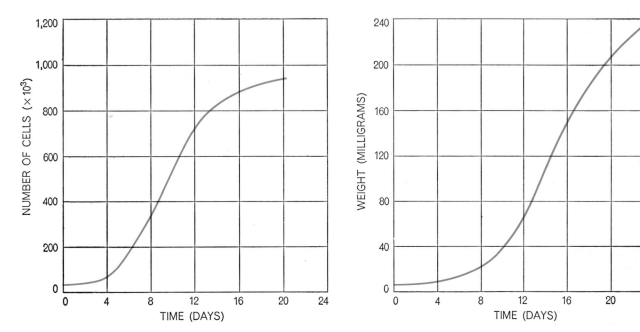

DRAMATIC GROWTH of explants from a part of the carrot root where growth under normal circumstances had ceased is reflected in these curves. Each relates to a single explant; curve at left shows example of cell increase; that at right, of weight increase.

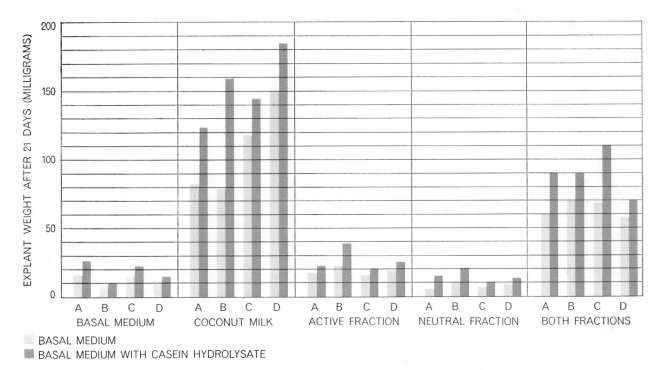

GROWTH-STIMULATING SUBSTANCES in coconut milk were separated into "active" and "neutral" fractions. Panel at left shows growth of four sets of carrot cultures in a basal medium with and without nitrogen in the form of casein hydrolysate; succeeding panels, what happened to similar groups of cultures when coconut milk or its fractions were added to those growth media.

question, we might note some other interesting findings about cell growth.

Armin C. Braun of the Rockefeller Institute has accomplished another important transformation: he has succeeded in converting growing tumor cells into normal tissue. Braun worked with a crown-gall tumor on the tobacco plant. After breaking down the tumor tissue into free cells he cultured these cells separately. A single cell grew into a cluster that Braun then grafted onto the normal shoot of a tobacco plant; after several successive grafts the group of tumor cells grew into a normal shoot. Thus under the powerful influence of the normal plant the tumor cells had been induced to behave again as normal, differentiated shoot cells.

The chromosomal events in cells stimulated to grow by coconut milk have also been investigated in our laboratory. In free-growing cells a number of events occur; some are highly unusual and some, although unexpected in such biological material, are normally associated with phases of reproductive growth. Sometimes the carrot cells grow into giant forms with nuclei containing several times the normal carrot diploid complement of 18 chromosomes. Other cells show distortions of the chromosomes such as are produced by ionizing radiation. Occasionally a cell division produces daughters with only nine chromosomes—the haploid number characteristic of the spores that initiate the sexual part of the life cycle. Indeed, we have seen quartets of cells that look very much like microspores. In cell cultures of the common Western weed *Haplopappus gracilis*, which has only four chromosomes in the diploid cell, we have even seen the exchange of parts of chromosomes that is known as "crossing over," a fairly common occurrence in the normal meiotic division of cells. All this emphasizes that when they can grow free, even adult cells can behave like reproductive cells.

It is now time to look into the all-important question: What are the specific substances that possess this remarkable power of activating the cell's built-in growth mechanism, and how do they act?

First of all it should be noted that the effects in question are not peculiar to carrots and coconuts. Coconut milk will stimulate growth not only in carrot tissue but also in artichoke tubers and many other plant tissues; with the assistance of a synergist it can even induce the cells of the potato tuber to grow continuously. And there are plant materials other

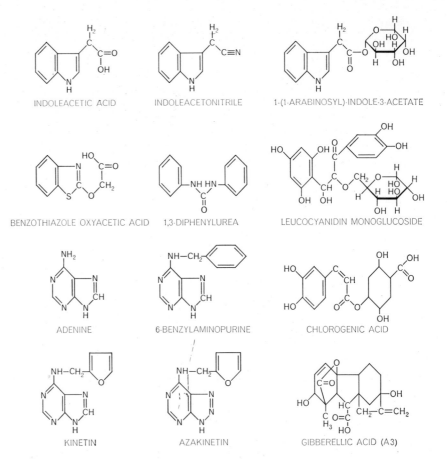

MOLECULAR STRUCTURE of various growth-promoting substances is shown in these drawings. The only obvious feature common to them is their complex cyclical configuration.

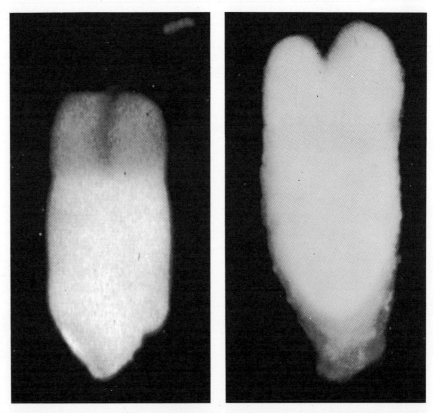

NATURAL AND CULTURED embryos (*greatly magnified*) show marked likeness. At left is young embryo dissected from carrot seed; at right, embryo grown from free cell culture.

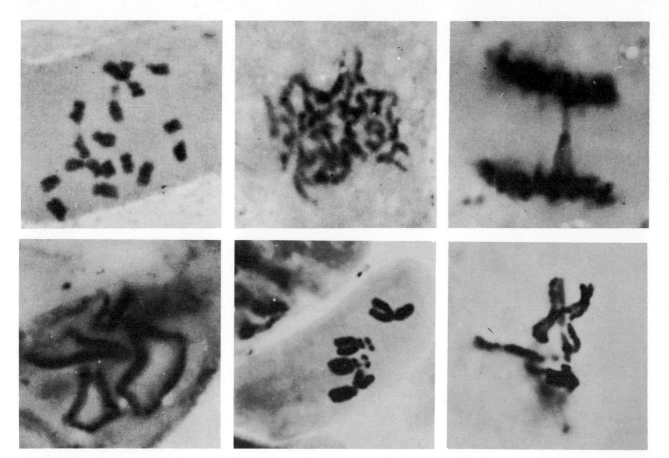

CHROMOSOMAL CHANGES occurred in cultured cells. At top, left to right, are normal diploid carrot cell with 18 chromosomes, polyploid nucleus in giant cultured cell and chromosome bridge due to failure to separate cleanly. At bottom are cultured carrot cell with nine chromosomes, normal diploid *Haplopappus* cell with four chromosomes and "crossing over" in cultured *Haplopappus*.

than coconut milk that have the same growth-stimulating effect; among them are extracts from the grains of corn in an immature stage (the "milk stage"), from immature walnuts and from immature horse chestnuts of the species *Aesculus woerlitzensis.*

These various materials have now been fractionated and analyzed to identify specific stimulating substances. The analysis indicates that the growth stimulation requires three types of compound, acting jointly: (1) highly active materials that specifically induce cell division, (2) a neutral fraction that acts as a kind of synergist or catalyst for the active fraction and (3) a source of "reduced" (organic) nitrogen.

The third requirement can be supplied most readily by amino acids or by the decomposition products (hydrolysate) of a protein, conveniently a hydrolysate of casein (the milk protein). The casein fraction has been found to be essential or at least helpful to the action of certain other ingredients in the growth-promoting system.

The second requirement, the neutral fraction, consists of sugar alcohols and the alcohols called inositols. Coconut milk contains the sugar alcohols D-sorbitol (200 grams of it was extracted from 20 liters of the fluid) and mannitol; it also contains the inositols myo-inositol and scyllo-inositol. Although the inositols are present in smaller amounts than the sugar alcohols, the inositols are the more important. Without the neutral fraction, the active fraction of coconut milk shows little or no growth-stimulating activity.

As for the ingredients that promote cell division, several active compounds have been isolated in purified or nearly purified form. Coconut milk and the other growth-promoting materials mentioned contain as somewhat active ingredients certain phenolic substances that are the colorless precursors of reddish pigments in plants. From one large batch of coconut milk, 1,3-diphenylurea was isolated as an active compound. From corn a compound of indoleacetic acid (IAA) and the sugar arabinose that is undoubtedly active in stimulating growth was obtained in a pure state. Indoleacetic acid is an auxin (plant hormone) that is known to promote the growth of cells by enlargement. The synthetic auxin 2,4-D, in combination with the active components of coconut milk, was found to stimulate growth in many tissues that were not susceptible to coconut milk alone. Another synthetic substance, 2-benzthiazolyloxyacetic acid (BTOA), showed a curious ability to stimulate the growth of carrot root and many other tissues in the manner of coconut milk. A synthetic purine known as kinetin (technically 6-furfurylaminopurine), isolated from heated nucleic acid by Folke Skoog and his colleagues at the University of Wisconsin, proved to be effective in combination with IAA in stimulating division of giant tobacco cells and also, to a smaller extent, carrot cells. On the other hand, the well-known growth-promoting substances called the gibberellins have, so far at least, shown only small effects on carrot-cell division.

The list of substances that have been investigated is already long, and the end is not yet in sight. They constitute an array of compounds, natural and artificial, with quite different kinds of activity, and in the present state of knowledge it is difficult to see any common feature that might distinguish those that can promote cell division. One thing they seem to have in common is their molecular architecture: they are composed of five-atom or six-atom rings, in some cases joined by short, three-atom links. Perhaps some subtle feature of their geometry accounts for their ability to stimulate cell division.

We know something about how the substances that cause the cells to divide function chemically in the cell. Most prominently, they promote the synthesis of proteins. In particular they seem to be concerned with producing a type of protein that does not metabolize but simply converts the amino acid proline into hydroxyproline, which is contained in this protein in larger quantities than is usual in plants. This purely structural protein appears to have some special significance in dividing cells. But a growing cell also differs from a quiescent one in many other aspects of its metabolism, so that it is doubtful that this one peculiarity is solely responsible for the cell's distinctive behavior. Significantly, carrot cells and cultured carrot explants, when stimulated to grow by coconut milk, turn green and become capable of photosynthesis. This is another aspect of their capacity for independent development.

To sum up, the fertilized egg, which initiated the development of an organism, is endowed with a hereditary blueprint and a built-in capacity for growth. This is, as it were, the organism's guidance system. Like the guidance system of a missile, the cell's built-in instructions are modulated and controlled by factors in the environment as the organism proceeds on its path through time and space. The initial thrust for its growth comes from powerful stimuli in the endosperm—stimuli so potent that they can even restore adult, differentiated cells to active division and growth. But the embryonic organism could not grow in an orderly, organized way if its cells merely went on multiplying without limitation. Its growth is therefore controlled by a delicately balanced complex of synergists and stimulating and inhibiting substances.

Thus the sequence of development that converts a zygote into an embryo and the embryo into a mature organism is determined by both the hereditary "nature" of the cell and the special "nurture" it receives. The problem of understanding how an organism develops, and the aim of the work discussed in this article, is to discover the details of the chemical mechanisms that control the inherited instructions and equipment of the cell.

13

Pheromones

EDWARD O. WILSON

May 1963

It is conceivable that somewhere on other worlds civilizations exist that communicate entirely by the exchange of chemical substances that are smelled or tasted. Unlikely as this may seem, the theoretical possibility cannot be ruled out. It is not difficult to design, on paper at least, a chemical communication system that can transmit a large amount of information with rather good efficiency. The notion of such a communication system is of course strange because our outlook is shaped so strongly by our own peculiar auditory and visual conventions. This limitation of outlook is found even among students of animal behavior; they have favored species whose communication methods are similar to our own and therefore more accessible to analysis. It is becoming increasingly clear, however, that chemical systems provide the dominant means of communication in many animal species, perhaps even in most. In the past several years animal behaviorists and organic chemists, working together, have made a start at deciphering some of these systems and have discovered a number of surprising new biological phenomena.

In earlier literature on the subject, chemicals used in communication were usually referred to as "ectohormones." Since 1959 the less awkward and etymologically more accurate term "pheromones" has been widely adopted. It is used to describe substances exchanged among members of the same animal species. Unlike true hormones, which are secreted internally to regulate the organism's own physiology, or internal environment, pheromones are secreted externally and help to regulate the organism's external environment by influencing other animals. The mode of influence can take either of two general forms. If the pheromone produces a more or less immediate and reversible change

in the behavior of the recipient, it is said to have a "releaser" effect. In this case the chemical substance seems to act directly on the recipient's central nervous system. If the principal function of the pheromone is to trigger a chain of physiological events in the recipient, it has what we have recently labeled a "primer" effect. The physiological changes, in turn, equip the organism with a new behavioral repertory, the components of which are thenceforth evoked by appropriate stimuli. In termites, for example, the reproductive and soldier castes prevent other termites from developing into their own castes by secreting substances that are ingested and act through the *corpus allatum,* an endocrine gland controlling differentiation [see "The Termite and the Cell," by Martin Lüscher; SCIENTIFIC AMERICAN, May, 1953].

These indirect primer pheromones do not always act by physiological inhibition. They can have the opposite effect. Adult males of the migratory locust *Schistocerca gregaria* secrete a volatile substance from their skin surface that accelerates the growth of young locusts. When the nymphs detect this substance with their antennae, their hind legs, some of their mouth parts and the antennae themselves vibrate. The secretion, in conjunction with tactile and visual signals, plays an important role in the formation of migratory locust swarms.

A striking feature of some primer pheromones is that they cause important physiological change without an immediate accompanying behavioral response, at least none that can be said to be peculiar to the pheromone. Beginning in 1955 with the work of S. van der Lee and L. M. Boot in the Netherlands, mammalian endocrinologists have discovered several unexpected effects on the female

mouse that are produced by odors of other members of the same species. These changes are not marked by any immediate distinctive behavioral patterns. In the "Lee-Boot effect" females placed in groups of four show an increase in the percentage of pseudopregnancies. A completely normal reproductive pattern can be restored by removing the olfactory bulbs of the mice or by housing the mice separately. When more and more female mice are forced to live together, their oestrous cycles become highly irregular and in most of the mice the cycle stops completely for long periods. Recently W. K. Whitten of the Australian National University has discovered that the odor of a male mouse can initiate and synchronize the oestrous cycles of female mice. The male odor also reduces the frequency of reproductive abnormalities arising when female mice are forced to live under crowded conditions.

A still more surprising primer effect has been found by Helen Bruce of the National Institute for Medical Research in London. She observed that the odor of a strange male mouse will block the pregnancy of a newly impregnated female mouse. The odor of the original stud male, of course, leaves pregnancy undisturbed. The mouse reproductive pheromones have not yet been identified chemically, and their mode of action is only partly understood. There is evidence that the odor of the strange male suppresses the secretion of the hormone prolactin, with the result that the *corpus luteum* (a ductless ovarian gland) fails to develop and normal oestrus is restored. The pheromones are probably part of the complex set of control mechanisms that regulate the population density of animals [see "Population Density and Social Pathology," by John B. Calhoun; SCIENTIFIC AMERICAN, February, 1962].

Pheromones that produce a simple releaser effect—a single specific response mediated directly by the central nervous system—are widespread in the animal kingdom and serve a great many functions. Sex attractants constitute a large and important category. The chemical structures of six attractants are shown on page 130. Although two of the six—the mammalian scents muskone and civetone—have been known for some 40 years and are generally assumed to serve a sexual function, their exact role has never been rigorously established by experiments with living animals. In fact, mammals seem to employ musklike compounds, alone or in combination with other substances, to serve several functions: to mark home ranges, to assist in territorial defense and to identify the sexes.

The nature and role of the four insect sex attractants are much better understood. The identification of each represents a technical feat of considerable magnitude. To obtain 12 milligrams of esters of bombykol, the sex attractant of the female silkworm moth, Adolf F. J. Butenandt and his associates at the Max Planck Institute of Biochemistry in Munich had to extract material from 250,000 moths. Martin Jacobson, Morton Beroza and William Jones of the U.S. Department of Agriculture processed 500,000 female gypsy moths to get 20 milligrams of the gypsy-moth attractant gyplure. Each moth yielded only about .01 microgram (millionth of a gram) of gyplure, or less than a millionth of its body weight. Bombykol and gyplure were obtained by killing the insects and subjecting crude extracts of material to chromatography, the separation technique in which compounds move at different rates through a column packed with a suitable adsorbent substance. Another technique has been more recently developed by Robert T. Yamamoto of the U.S. Department of Agriculture, in collaboration with Jacobson and Beroza, to harvest the equally elusive sex attractant of the American cockroach. Virgin females were housed in metal cans and air was continuously drawn through the cans and passed through chilled containers to condense any vaporized materials. In this manner the equivalent of 10,000 females were "milked" over a nine-month period to yield 12.2 milligrams of what was considered to be the pure attractant.

The power of the insect attractants is almost unbelievable. If some 10,000 molecules of the most active form of bombykol are allowed to diffuse from a source one centimeter from the antennae of a male silkworm moth, a characteristic sexual response is obtained in most cases. If volatility and diffusion rate are taken into account, it can be estimated that the threshold concentration is no more than a few hundred molecules per cubic centimeter, and the actual number required to stimulate the male is probably even smaller. From this one can calculate that .01 microgram of gyplure, the minimum average content of a single female moth, would be theoretically adequate, if distributed with maximum efficiency, to excite more than a billion male moths.

In nature the female uses her powerful pheromone to advertise her presence over a large area with a minimum expenditure of energy. With the aid of published data from field experiments and newly contrived mathematical models of the diffusion process, William H. Bossert, one of my associates in the Biological Laboratories at Harvard University, and I have deduced the shape and size of the ellipsoidal space within which male moths can be attracted under natural conditions [*see the bottom illustration on page 126*]. When a moderate wind is blowing, the active space has a long axis of thousands of meters and a transverse axis parallel to the ground of more than 200 meters at the widest point. The 19th-century French naturalist Jean Henri Fabre, speculating on sex attraction in insects, could not bring himself to believe that the female moth could communicate over such great distances by odor alone, since "one might as well expect to tint a lake with a drop of carmine." We now know that Fabre's conclusion was wrong but that his analogy was exact: to the male moth's powerful chemoreceptors the lake is indeed tinted.

One must now ask how the male moth, smelling the faintly tinted air, knows which way to fly to find the source of the tinting. He cannot simply fly in the direction of increasing scent; it can be shown mathematically that the attractant is distributed almost uniformly after it has drifted more than a few meters from the female. Recent experiments by Ilse Schwinck of the University of Munich have revealed what is probably the alternative procedure used. When male moths are activated by the pheromone, they simply fly upwind and thus inevitably move toward the female. If by accident they pass out of the active zone, they either abandon the search or fly about at random until they pick up the scent again. Eventually, as they approach the female, there is a slight increase in the concentration of the chemical attractant and this can serve as a guide for the remaining distance.

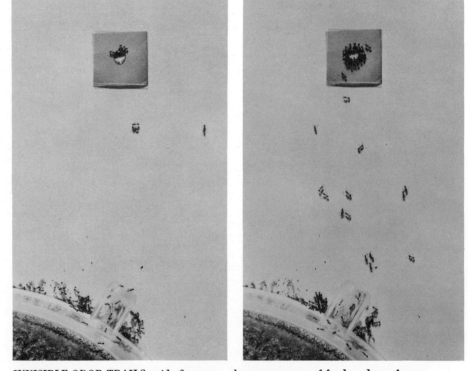

INVISIBLE ODOR TRAILS guide fire ant workers to a source of food: a drop of sugar solution. The trails consist of a pheromone laid down by workers returning to their nest after finding a source of food. Sometimes the chemical message is reinforced by the touching of antennae if a returning worker meets a wandering fellow along the way. This is hap-

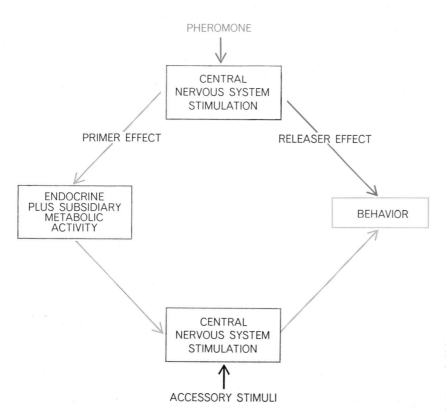

PHEROMONES INFLUENCE BEHAVIOR directly or indirectly, as shown in this schematic diagram. If a pheromone stimulates the recipient's central nervous system into producing an immediate change in behavior, it is said to have a "releaser" effect. If it alters a set of long-term physiological conditions so that the recipient's behavior can subsequently be influenced by specific accessory stimuli, the pheromone is said to have a "primer" effect.

If one is looking for the most highly developed chemical communication systems in nature, it is reasonable to study the behavior of the social insects, particularly the social wasps, bees, termites and ants, all of which communicate mostly in the dark interiors of their nests and are known to have advanced chemoreceptive powers. In recent years experimental techniques have been developed to separate and identify the pheromones of these insects, and rapid progress has been made in deciphering the hitherto intractable codes, particularly those of the ants. The most successful procedure has been to dissect out single glandular reservoirs and see what effect their contents have on the behavior of the worker caste, which is the most numerous and presumably the most in need of continuing guidance. Other pheromones, not present in distinct reservoirs, are identified in chromatographic fractions of crude extracts.

Ants of all castes are constructed with an exceptionally well-developed exocrine glandular system. Many of the most prominent of these glands, whose function has long been a mystery to entomologists, have now been identified as the source of pheromones [see illustra-

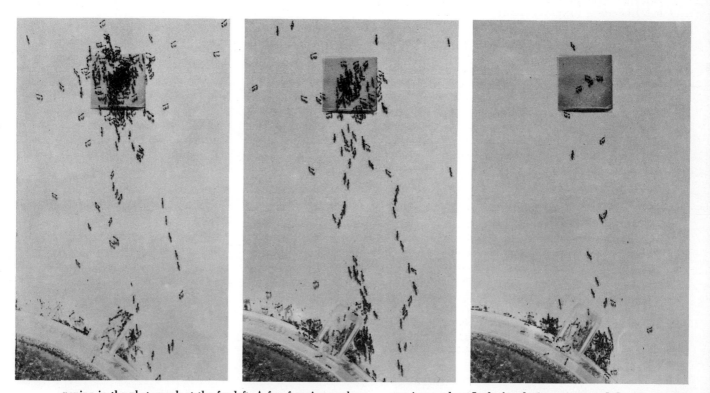

pening in the photograph at the far left. A few foraging workers have just found the sugar drop and a returning trail-layer is communicating the news to another ant. In the next two pictures the trail has been completed and workers stream from the nest in in- creasing numbers. In the fourth picture unrewarded workers return to the nest without laying trails and outward-bound traffic wanes. In the last picture most of the trails have evaporated completely and only a few stragglers remain at the site, eating the last bits of food.

tion on page 128]. The analysis of the gland-pheromone complex has led to the beginnings of a new and deeper understanding of how ant societies are organized.

Consider the chemical trail. According to the traditional view, trail secretions served as only a limited guide for worker ants and had to be augmented by other kinds of signals exchanged inside the nest. Now it is known that the trail substance is extraordinarily versatile. In the fire ant (Solenopsis saevissima), for instance, it functions both to activate and to guide foraging workers in search of food and new nest sites. It also contributes as one of the alarm signals emitted by workers in distress. The trail of the fire ant consists of a substance secreted in minute amounts by Dufour's gland; the substance leaves the ant's body by way of the extruded sting, which is touched intermittently to the ground much like a moving pen dispensing ink. The trail pheromone, which has not yet been chemically identified, acts primarily to attract the fire ant workers. Upon encountering the attractant the workers move automatically up the gradient to the source of emission. When the substance is drawn out in a line, the workers run along the direction of the line away from the nest. This simple response brings them to the food source or new nest site from which the trail is laid. In our laboratory we have extracted the pheromone from the Dufour's glands of freshly killed workers and have used it to create artificial trails. Groups of workers will follow these trails away from the nest and along arbitrary routes (including circles leading back to the nest) for considerable periods of time. When the pheromone is presented to whole colonies in massive doses, a large portion of the colony, including the queen, can be drawn out in a close simulation of the emigration process.

The trail substance is rather volatile, and a natural trail laid by one worker diffuses to below the threshold concentration within two minutes. Consequently outward-bound workers are able to follow it only for the distance they can travel in this time, which is about 40 centimeters. Although this strictly limits the distance over which the ants can communicate, it provides at least two important compensatory advantages. The more obvious advantage is that old, useless trails do not linger to confuse the hunting workers. In addition, the intensity of the trail laid by many workers provides a sensitive index of the amount of food at a given site and the rate of its depletion. As workers move to and from

ANTENNAE OF GYPSY MOTHS differ radically in structure according to their function. In the male (*left*) they are broad and finely divided to detect minute quantities of sex attractant released by the female (*right*). The antennae of the female are much less developed.

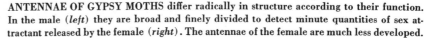

A = 108 METERS
B = 215 METERS
C = 4,560 METERS

A = 62.5 METERS
B = 125 METERS
C = 2,420 METERS

A = 48.5 METERS
B = 97 METERS
C = 1,820 METERS

ACTIVE SPACE of gyplure, the gypsy moth sex attractant, is the space within which this pheromone is sufficiently dense to attract males to a single, continuously emitting female. The actual dimensions, deduced from linear measurements and general gas-diffusion models, are given at right. Height (*A*) and width (*B*) are exaggerated in the drawing. As wind shifts from moderate to strong, increased turbulence contracts the active space.

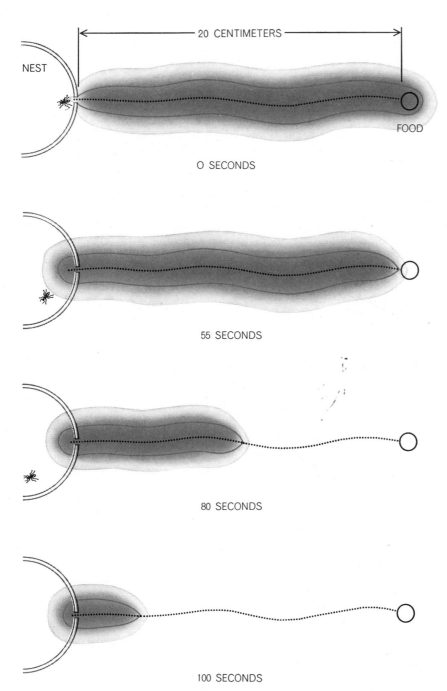

FIRE ANT WORKER lays an odor trail by exuding a pheromone along its extended sting. The sting is touched to the ground periodically, breaking the trail into a series of streaks.

20 CENTIMETERS

NEST

FOOD

O SECONDS

55 SECONDS

80 SECONDS

100 SECONDS

ACTIVE SPACE OF ANT TRAIL, within which the pheromone is dense enough to be perceived by other workers, is narrow and nearly constant in shape with the maximum gradient situated near its outer surface. The rapidity with which the trail evaporates is indicated.

the food finds (consisting mostly of dead insects and sugar sources) they continuously add their own secretions to the trail produced by the original discoverers of the food. Only if an ant is rewarded by food does it lay a trail on its trip back to the nest; therefore the more food encountered at the end of the trail, the more workers that can be rewarded and the heavier the trail. The heavier the trail, the more workers that are drawn from the nest and arrive at the end of the trail. As the food is consumed, the number of workers laying trail substance drops, and the old trail fades by evaporation and diffusion, gradually constricting the outward flow of workers.

The fire ant odor trail shows other evidences of being efficiently designed. The active space within which the pheromone is dense enough to be perceived by workers remains narrow and nearly constant in shape over most of the length of the trail. It has been further deduced from diffusion models that the maximum gradient must be situated near the outer surface of the active space. Thus workers are informed of the space boundary in a highly efficient way. Together these features ensure that the following workers keep in close formation with a minimum chance of losing the trail.

The fire ant trail is one of the few animal communication systems whose information content can be measured with fair precision. Unlike many communicating animals, the ants have a distinct goal in space—the food find or nest site—the direction and distance of which must both be communicated. It is possible by a simple technique to measure how close trail-followers come to the trail end, and, by making use of a standard equation from information theory, one can translate the accuracy of their response into the "bits" of information received. A similar procedure can be applied (as first suggested by the British biologist J. B. S. Haldane) to the "waggle dance" of the honeybee, a radically different form of communication system from the ant trail [see "Dialects in the Language of the Bees," by Karl von Frisch; this is available as Offprint #130]. Surprisingly, it turns out that the two systems, although of wholly different evolutionary origin, transmit about the same amount of information with reference to distance (two bits) and direction (four bits in the honeybee, and four or possibly five in the ant). Four bits of information will direct an ant or a bee into one of 16 equally probable sectors of a circle and two bits will identify one of four equally probable distances. It is conceivable that these information values represent the maximum that can be achieved with the insect brain and sensory apparatus.

Not all kinds of ants lay chemical trails. Among those that do, however, the pheromones are highly species-specific in their action. In experiments in which artificial trails extracted from one species were directed to living colonies of other species, the results have almost always been negative, even among related species. It is as if each species had its own private language. As a result there is little or no confusion when the trails of two or more species cross.

Another important class of ant pheromone is composed of alarm substances. A simple backyard experiment will show that if a worker ant is disturbed by a clean instrument, it will, for a short time, excite other workers with whom it comes in contact. Until recently most students of ant behavior thought that the alarm was spread by touch, that one worker simply jostled another in its excitement or drummed on its neighbor with its antennae in some peculiar way. Now it is known that disturbed workers discharge chemicals, stored in special glandular reservoirs, that can produce all the characteristic alarm responses solely by themselves. The chemical structure of four alarm substances is shown on page 132. Nothing could illustrate more clearly the wide differences between the human perceptual world and that of chemically communicating animals. To the human nose the alarm substances are mild or even pleasant, but to the ant they represent an urgent tocsin that can propel a colony into violent and instant action.

As in the case of the trail substances, the employment of the alarm substances appears to be ideally designed for the purpose it serves. When the contents of the mandibular glands of a worker of the harvesting ant (*Pogonomyrmex badius*) are discharged into still air, the volatile material forms a rapidly expanding sphere, which attains a radius of about six centimeters in 13 seconds. Then it contracts until the signal fades out completely some 35 seconds after the moment of discharge. The outer shell of the active space contains a low concentration of pheromone, which is actually attractive to harvester workers. This serves to draw them toward the point of disturbance. The central region of the active space, however, contains a concentration high enough to evoke the characteristic frenzy of alarm. The "alarm sphere" expands to a radius of about three centimeters in eight seconds and, as might be expected, fades out more quickly than the "attraction sphere."

The advantage to the ants of an alarm signal that is both local and short-lived becomes obvious when a *Pogonomyrmex* colony is observed under natural conditions. The ant nest is subject to almost innumerable minor disturbances. If the

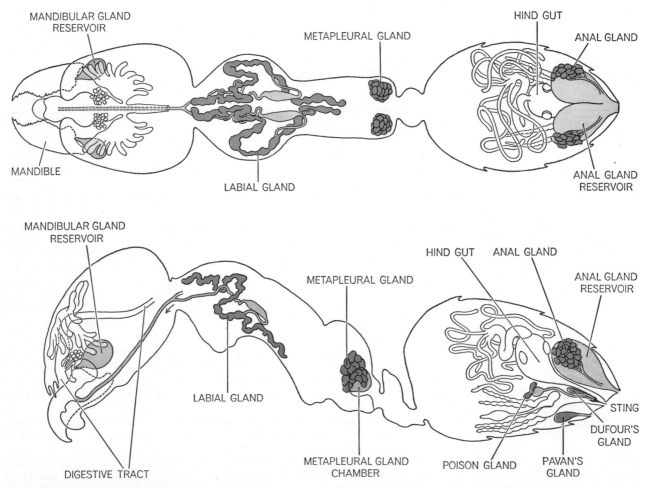

EXOCRINE GLANDULAR SYSTEM of a worker ant (*shown here in top and side cutaway views*) is specially adapted for the production of chemical communication substances. Some pheromones are stored in reservoirs and released in bursts only when needed; others are secreted continuously. Depending on the species, trail substances are produced by Dufour's gland, Pavan's gland or the poison glands; alarm substances are produced by the anal and mandibular glands. The glandular sources of other pheromones are unknown.

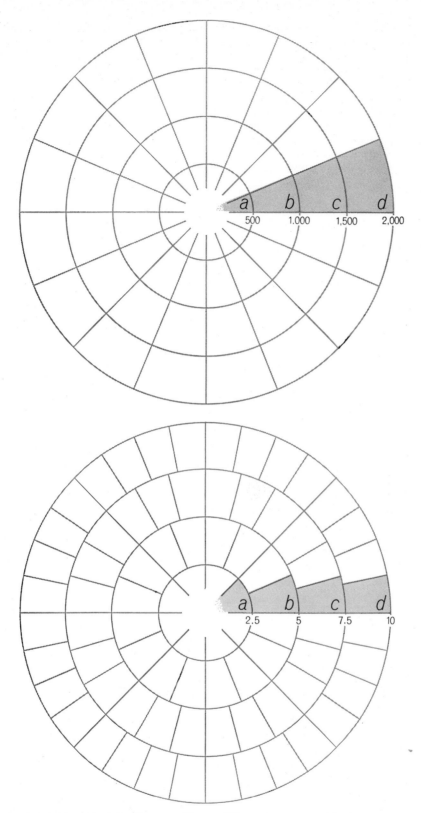

FORAGING INFORMATION conveyed by two different insect communication systems can be represented on two similar "compass" diagrams. The honeybee "waggle dance" (*top*) transmits about four bits of information with respect to direction, enabling a honeybee worker to pinpoint a target within one of 16 equally probable angular sectors. The number of "bits" in this case remains independent of distance, given in meters. The pheromone system used by trail-laying fire ants (*bottom*) is superior in that the amount of directional information increases with distance, given in centimeters. At distances *c* and *d*, the probable sector in which the target lies is smaller for ants than for bees. (For ants, directional information actually increases gradually and not by jumps.) Both insects transmit two bits of distance information, specifying one of four equally probable distance ranges.

alarm spheres generated by individual ant workers were much wider and more durable, the colony would be kept in ceaseless and futile turmoil. As it is, local disturbances such as intrusions by foreign insects are dealt with quickly and efficiently by small groups of workers, and the excitement soon dies away.

The trail and alarm substances are only part of the ants' chemical vocabulary. There is evidence for the existence of other secretions that induce gathering and settling of workers, acts of grooming, food exchange, and other operations fundamental to the care of the queen and immature ants. Even dead ants produce a pheromone of sorts. An ant that has just died will be groomed by other workers as if it were still alive. Its complete immobility and crumpled posture by themselves cause no new response. But in a day or two chemical decomposition products accumulate and stimulate the workers to bear the corpse to the refuse pile outside the nest. Only a few decomposition products trigger this funereal response; they include certain long-chain fatty acids and their esters. When other objects, including living workers, are experimentally daubed with these substances, they are dutifully carried to the refuse pile. After being dumped on the refuse the "living dead" scramble to their feet and promptly return to the nest, only to be carried out again. The hapless creatures are thrown back on the refuse pile time and again until most of the scent of death has been worn off their bodies by the ritual.

Our observation of ant colonies over long periods has led us to believe that as few as 10 pheromones, transmitted singly or in simple combinations, might suffice for the total organization of ant society. The task of separating and characterizing these substances, as well as judging the roles of other kinds of stimuli such as sound, is a job largely for the future.

Even in animal species where other kinds of communication devices are prominently developed, deeper investigation usually reveals the existence of pheromonal communication as well. I have mentioned the auxiliary roles of primer pheromones in the lives of mice and migratory locusts. A more striking example is the communication system of the honeybee. The insect is celebrated for its employment of the "round" and "waggle" dances (augmented, perhaps, by auditory signals) to designate the location of food and new nest sites. It is not so widely known that chemical signals play equally important roles in other aspects of honeybee life. The mother queen regulates the reproductive cycle of the colony by secreting from her mandibular glands a substance recently identified as 9-ketodecanoic acid. When this pheromone is ingested by the worker bees, it inhibits development of their ovaries and also their ability to manufacture the royal cells in which new queens are reared. The same pheromone serves as a sex attractant in the queen's nuptial flights.

Under certain conditions, including the discovery of new food sources, worker bees release geraniol, a pleasant-smelling alcohol, from the abdominal Nassanoff glands. As the geraniol diffuses through the air it attracts other workers and so supplements information contained in the waggle dance. When a worker stings an intruder, it discharges, in addition to the venom, tiny amounts of a secretion from clusters of unicellular

glands located next to the basal plates of the sting. This secretion is responsible for the tendency, well known to beekeepers, of angry swarms of workers to sting at the same spot. One component, which acts as a simple attractant, has been identified as isoamyl acetate, a compound that has a banana-like odor. It is possible that the stinging response is evoked by at least one unidentified alarm substance secreted along with the attractant.

Knowledge of pheromones has advanced to the point where one can make some tentative generalizations about their chemistry. In the first place, there appear to be good reasons why sex attractants should be compounds that contain between 10 and 17 carbon atoms and that have molecular weights between about 180 and 300—the range actually observed in attractants so far identified. (For comparison, the weight of a single

carbon atom is 12.) Only compounds of roughly this size or greater can meet the two known requirements of a sex attractant: narrow specificity, so that only members of one species will respond to it, and high potency. Compounds that contain fewer than five or so carbon atoms and that have a molecular weight of less than about 100 cannot be assembled in enough different ways to provide a distinctive molecule for all the insects that want to advertise their presence.

It also seems to be a rule, at least with insects, that attraction potency increases with molecular weight. In one series of esters tested on flies, for instance, a doubling of molecular weight resulted in as much as a thousandfold increase in efficiency. On the other hand, the molecule cannot be too large and complex or it will be prohibitively difficult for the insect to synthesize. An equally important limitation on size is

BOMBYKOL (SILKWORM MOTH)

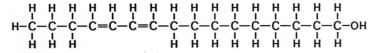

GYPLURE (GYPSY MOTH)

2,2-DIMETHYL-3-ISOPROPYLIDENECYCLOPROPYL PROPIONATE (AMERICAN COCKROACH)

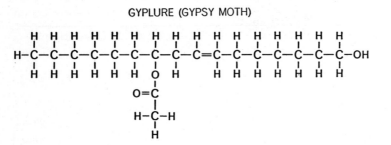

HONEYBEE QUEEN SUBSTANCE

CIVETONE (CIVET)

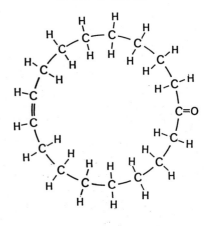

MUSKONE (MUSK DEER)

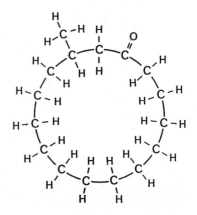

SIX SEX PHEROMONES include the identified sex attractants of four insect species as well as two mammalian musks generally believed to be sex attractants. The high molecular weight of most sex pheromones accounts for their narrow specificity and high potency.

the fact that volatility—and, as a result, diffusibility—declines with increasing molecular weight.

One can also predict from first principles that the molecular weight of alarm substances will tend to be less than those of the sex attractants. Among the ants there is little specificity; each species responds strongly to the alarm substances of other species. Furthermore, an alarm substance, which is used primarily within the confines of the nest, does not need the stimulative potency of a sex attractant, which must carry its message for long distances. For these reasons small molecules will suffice for alarm purposes. Of seven alarm substances known in the social insects, six have 10 or fewer carbon atoms and one (dendrolasin) has 15. It will be interesting to see if future discoveries bear out these early generalizations.

Do human pheromones exist? Primer pheromones might be difficult to detect, since they can affect the endocrine system without producing overt specific behavioral responses. About all that can be said at present is that striking sexual differences have been observed in the ability of humans to smell certain

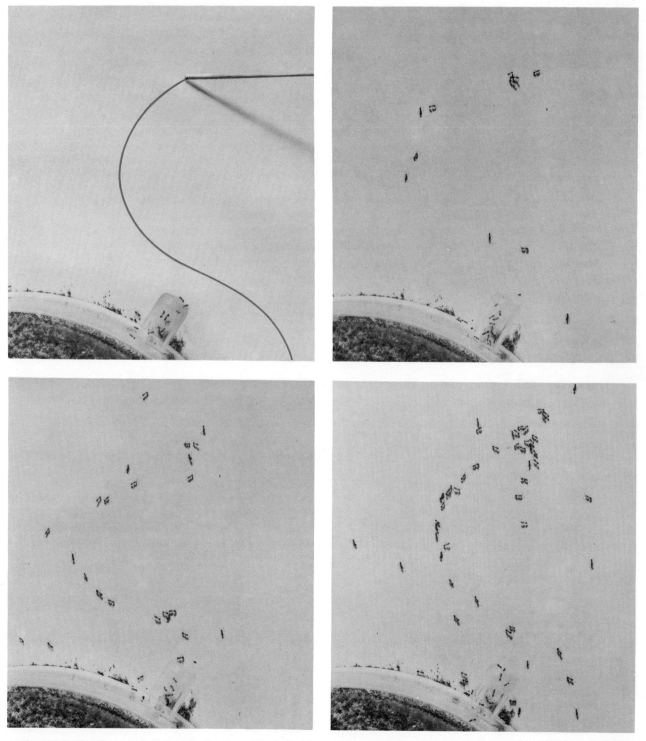

ARTIFICIAL TRAIL can be laid down by drawing a line (*colored curve in frame at top left*) with a stick that has been treated with the contents of a single Dufour's gland. In the remaining three frames, workers are attracted from the nest, follow the artificial route in close formation and mill about in confusion at its arbitrary terminus. Such a trail is not renewed by the unrewarded workers.

DENDROLASIN (*LASIUS FULIGINOSUS*)

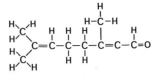

CITRAL (*ATTA SEXDENS*)

CITRONELLAL (*ACANTHOMYOPS CLAVIGER*)

2-HEPTANONE (*IRIDOMYRMEX PRUINOSUS*)

FOUR ALARM PHEROMONES, given off by the workers of the ant species indicated, have so far been identified. Disturbing stimuli trigger the release of these substances from various glandular reservoirs.

substances. The French biologist J. Le-Magnen has reported that the odor of Exaltolide, the synthetic lactone of 14-hydroxytetradecanoic acid, is perceived clearly only by sexually mature females and is perceived most sharply at about the time of ovulation. Males and young girls were found to be relatively insensitive, but a male subject became more sensitive following an injection of estrogen. Exaltolide is used commercially as a perfume fixative. LeMagnen also reported that the ability of his subjects to detect the odor of certain steroids paralleled that of their ability to smell Exaltolide. These observations hardly represent a case for the existence of human pheromones, but they do suggest that the relation of odors to human physiology can bear further examination.

It is apparent that knowledge of chemical communication is still at an early stage. Students of the subject are in the position of linguists who have learned the meaning of a few words of a nearly indecipherable language. There is almost certainly a large chemical vocabulary still to be discovered. Conceiv-

ably some pheromone "languages" will be found to have a syntax. It may be found, in other words, that pheromones can be combined in mixtures to form new meanings for the animals employing them. One would also like to know if some animals can modulate the intensity or pulse frequency of pheromone emission to create new messages. The solution of these and other interesting problems will require new techniques in analytical organic chemistry combined with ever more perceptive studies of animal behavior.

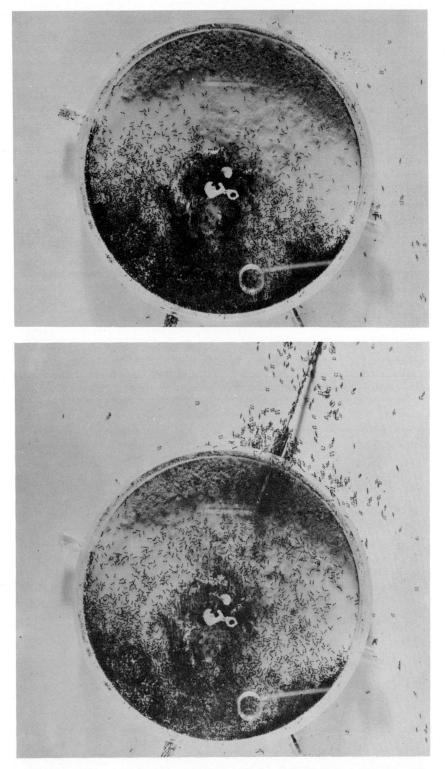

MASSIVE DOSE of trail pheromone causes the migration of a large portion of a fire ant colony from one side of a nest to another. The pheromone is administered on a stick that has been dipped in a solution extracted from the Dufour's glands of freshly killed workers.

14

Insect Attractants

MARTIN JACOBSON AND MORTON BEROZA

August 1964

Man's efforts to control harmful insects are increasingly encumbered by an awkward dilemma. There is rising protest that pesticides are destroying harmless wildlife and endangering the health of man himself. Hardly a week now passes without a new alarm about the killing of fish or birds or the contamination of food and water. Yet any significant retreat from the use of insecticides would bring even more alarming consequences. According to the World Health Organization insect pests are responsible for half of all human deaths and deformities due to disease. Insects consume or destroy about a third of everything that man grows or stores. The agricultural revolution in the U.S. that enables a small proportion of the population to raise more than enough food for the whole nation has been made possible largely by the extensive use of modern pesticides. Without them the U.S. could not maintain its present standard of living.

Unfortunately pesticides frequently generate increasing immunity among their intended victims. To this food-raisers are responding with heavier applications and pleas for more potent new chemicals. At the same time health authorities are becoming more sensitive to the dangers of toxic residues and more alert to the detection of these residues in food and water, even in concentrations as small as parts per trillion. Thus the designers of the weapons for the control of insects—that is, economic entomologists and chemists—find themselves in an embarrassing cross fire: on the one side from the farmers demanding more potent insecticides and on the other from the health agencies demanding less toxic residue.

Irreconcilable though these demands may seem, it now appears that there is a good chance that both of them can be satisfied by new methods of attack. One method that has already made a promising start involves the use of odorous chemicals to lure insects into lethal traps.

Many insects find their food, their partners for mating and favorable sites in which to deposit their eggs by means of automatic responses to various scent cues. Male moths, for example, can smell potential sexual partners at a considerable distance. Not surprisingly, each species tends to have its own distinctive odor, which facilitates the meeting of partners capable of mating with each other.

This behavior makes the odor-baited lure a most promising means of getting rid of malignant species of insects. Instead of spraying the whole countryside with insecticide, one could attract the unwanted insects to traps where they would make contact with an appropriate insecticide, with a sterilizing chemical or with some other exterminating device. Females could be induced to lay their eggs not on nourishing plants but in places where the emerging larvae would starve for lack of food. The odorous lures and the lethal chemicals could be applied only at the most effective time and place. Any new infestation of insects could be detected early and eliminated before it had a chance to spread. In sum, the battle against harmful insects would be much less costly and more efficient, and the problem of the contamination of the environment by toxic materials would be vastly reduced.

The principal difficulties in such a program are the problem of identifying the specific odorous substances to which various insect pests respond and, in the case of the natural sex lures, the task of obtaining large enough amounts of these substances to carry out the program. Until about a decade ago the prospects for the effective employment of attractants on any large scale did not look bright. In recent years, however, the method has scored an impressive success in the U.S. by helping to eradicate the Mediterranean fruit fly from a million infested acres in Florida. On the strength of this demonstration and a wealth of information acquired by intensive research, it can be said that the outlook for eradicating insect pests by means of attractants is now much more encouraging.

The investigation of insect attractants goes back to discoveries made in the 19th century by Jean Henri Fabre, the French naturalist to whose endless curiosity we owe many other insights into the lives and habits of insects. Fabre had been looking for years for a certain moth whose larvae fed on oak leaves, and one day he finally found a cocoon of the insect on a leaf. From this there soon emerged a female moth. Fabre placed his prize in a cloth cage near an open window in his house. Within 15 hours no fewer than 60 males of this previously elusive species came out of the woods and collected around the cage containing the virgin female.

Fabre began a series of experiments to try to discover what had attracted the males. When he placed the female in a tightly closed transparent container, where the moth could be seen but not smelled, no males appeared. On the other hand, an open container recently occupied by the female was strongly attractive to the males, although the female was no longer there. They made their way to the container in spite of the presence in the room of strong odors

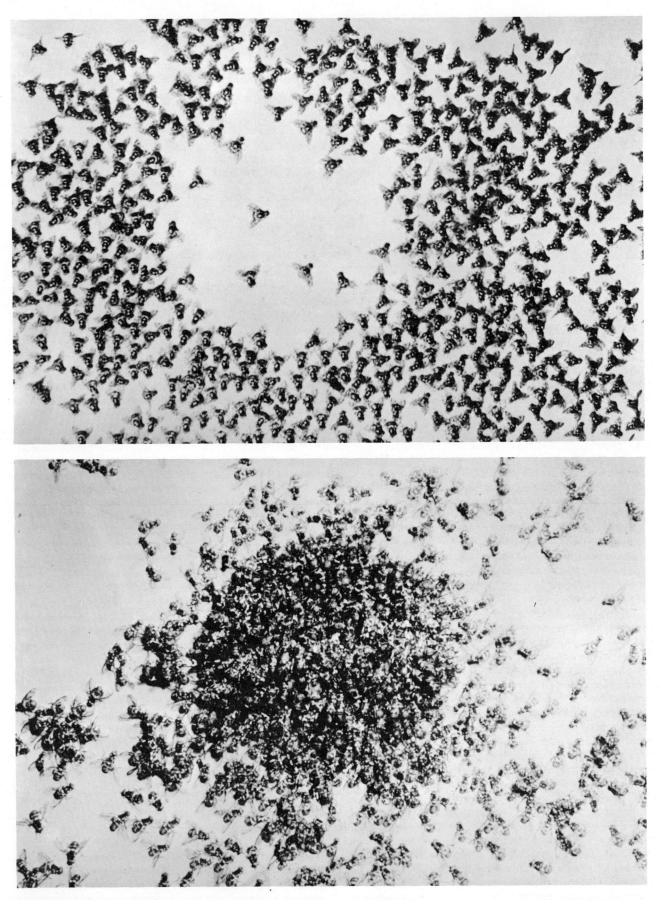

SYNTHETIC ATTRACTANTS vary in their action. One compound that normally attracts Mediterranean fruit flies will repel them instead if the concentration is too high (*center area of top photograph*). The lure that attracts oriental fruit flies is effective in both high and low concentrations (*bottom photograph*). Used with an insecticide, it has entirely rid one Pacific island of fruit flies.

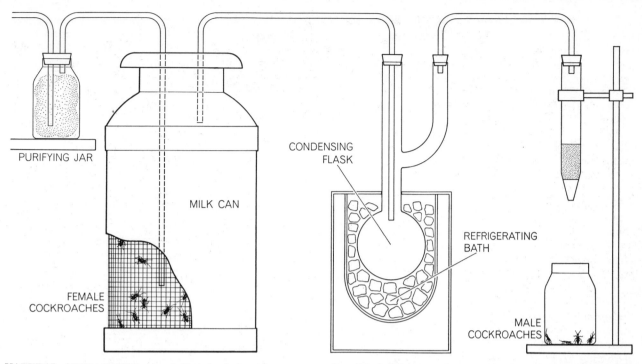

PURIFYING JAR

MILK CAN

FEMALE
COCKROACHES

CONDENSING
FLASK

REFRIGERATING
BATH

MALE
COCKROACHES

NATURAL ATTRACTANT, a sexually stimulating pheromone that is produced by virgin female cockroaches, was concentrated by passing air through a container filled with females and then liquefying the attractant vapor in a dry-ice trap. Males (*right*) served as monitors. The experimenters needed nine months' time and 10,000 females to isolate 12.2 milligrams of pure attractant.

from naphthalene, hydrogen sulfide or tobacco smoke. Fabre extended the same tests to the emperor moth and got the same results. A female emperor moth placed in a gauze bag on a table in his study lured about 40 males in a single evening. For eight successive nights, as Fabre wrote, "males seemed to take possession of the house." They hovered around the female's resting place even when it was hidden from sight in a drawer.

The experiments certainly indicated strongly that the females of both species attracted the males by odor (although the human nose could not detect it). Yet Fabre could not bring himself to believe that odor could draw moths from hundreds of yards or even miles away. He thought it quite unlikely that odorous vapor from the source could reach to such distances in any detectable amount. Fabre's guess was that some sort of vibration produced by the female moth generated waves that traveled through the air and were received by the male moth's antennae. He determined, in fact, that males deprived of their antennae seldom found the female.

Fabre was correct in identifying the antennae as the receptor organs but wrong in his conclusion that the message was not carried by odor. It was eventually proved beyond doubt that male moths are indeed guided to females by their sense of smell, that their odor-sensitive organs are located in their antennae and that they can detect the female scent in fantastically small amounts. The sex attractants of insects are probably the most potent physiological substances known; in some cases reception of just a few hundred molecules or less by the sensitive cells of the antennae is enough to stimulate the male [see "Pheromones," by Edward O. Wilson, which is included in this volume, page 123].

That scent plays an important part in sexual attraction throughout the animal kingdom has, of course, long been suspected. The details of its operation in individual species, however, still constitute one of nature's best-kept secrets. Not only is the attracting substance itself extremely difficult to identify; its effects usually elude discovery because they vary with different mating habits. This point is well illustrated by the moth of the European corn borer. Even when the population of corn borers is very sparse in a field, all the adult females in the moth stage somehow manage to mate. Yet experiments with a caged female failed to show any sign of a lure to males—until observations were made at night. In a darkened laboratory room (where the female was observed by means of an infrared light) males were attracted to the cage, so that the attraction must have been the emission of a scent. The answer was elementary: corn borer moths usually mate at night. Experiments have now established the fact that some species of moths mate only between 11:00 P.M. and 4:00 A.M. (presumably releasing their scents only during those hours), whereas others always mate between 2:00 A.M. and 6:00 A.M. Indeed, the moths are nocturnal. For example, although the male gypsy moth locates its partner during daylight hours, mating takes place in twilight or darkness.

Moths and butterflies—the insect order Lepidoptera—have been the main subjects in the investigation of sex attractants. The most remarkable finding is the great distances at which their lures are effective. Experiments with marked male gypsy moths have shown that they are attracted to a female up to half a mile away. Males of the saturniid and lasiocampid families (which include silkworms, tent caterpillars and eggars) have been reported to be lured to females from distances as great as two and a half miles. The extraordinary potency of insect sex lures was also demonstrated by an experiment in which a single caged female pine sawfly—a member of the order Hymenoptera—attracted more than 11,000 males!

Another notable feature of the sex lures is their sharp specificity. In most cases the female's scent attracts only males of the same species. There are, to be sure, a few exceptions, which only emphasize the rule. For example, the scent of the female tobacco moth has been found to excite male Indian meal moths and Mediterranean flour moths to make attempts at mating although anatomical differences make mating between them and the tobacco moth female impossible.

A typical virgin female of a lure-producing species of moth secretes the odorous substance from a pair of glands located between the last two segments of its abdomen. It releases the attractant by protruding these glands in what is termed the calling position. The attracted male, on arrival, begins to circle the female with its abdomen bent in the female's direction and its wings vibrating rapidly in what is called a whirring dance. In many species the male moth in turn excites the female with an aphrodisiac scent of its own, produced in glands under its wings and scattered around the female by its wing vibrations. The male scents of many species of insects can be detected by the human sense of smell and have been variously likened to pineapple, chocolate, lemon oil, musk, flower fragrances and other odors. One of these substances, a clear fluid with a cinnamon-like odor secreted by a tropical water bug, has long been used as a spice by inhabitants of southeast Asia. In 1957 the German biochemist Adolf Butenandt and his associate Nguyen Dang Tam isolated the odorous substance in pure form and identified it as *trans*-2-hexenyl acetate. They then succeeded in synthesizing the compound, and the synthetic product is now sold as a spice in Asia.

The story of the conversion of sex attractants into a weapon against insects begins with the gypsy moth. This insect, a European species similar to the silkworm moth, was brought to the U.S. in 1869 in a misguided effort to found a silk-growing industry. Leopold Trouvelot, a French artist, naturalist and astronomer, thought that by crossing the gypsy moth with the silkworm moth he might breed a hardy new race of silkworms that would thrive in New England. His attempt did not succeed, and unfortunately in the course of his experiments some of the gypsy moth eggs or caterpillars escaped and the insect proceeded to multiply at a prodigious rate. Eventually it infested all New England. The hairy, mottled caterpillar of the gypsy moth feeds voraciously on tree leaves and has done millions of dollars' worth of damage.

The use of a sex lure to trap the gypsy moth was begun many years ago. The female cannot fly and is therefore completely dependent on its scent to attract males. It was discovered that an extract from the abdomens of virgin females, prepared by using benzene as a solvent, could serve as an attractant for baiting traps. The U.S. Department of Agriculture also tested many laboratory chemicals, by the same kind of screening methods that have been used to search for medical drugs, in the hope of finding an attractant that would be available in substantial quantity. More than 2,000 chemicals were screened, and surprisingly several turned out to be at-

MALE ROACHES are sexually excited by an infinitesimal amount of attractant. Thus they serve to detect any leakage from the collection apparatus (*see illustration on opposite page*).

tractive to the male gypsy moth. All of these were alcohols with a straight-chain backbone of 16 carbon atoms.

Meanwhile the Department of Agriculture pursued intensive efforts to isolate the pure attractant from the female moth. The crude extract was not too reliable as a lure and was obtainable only in small amounts. The laboratory substitutes were only weakly attractive—less than a millionth as potent as the natural lure. For any large-scale trapping campaign against the gypsy moth it would be necessary to isolate and identify the natural compound and then try to synthesize it in quantity.

After 30 years of painstaking chemical work the gypsy moth sex attractant was at last identified in 1960 by three of us in the Department of Agriculture: the authors of this article and W. A. Jones. It took the abdomens of 500,000 female gypsy moths to yield 20 milligrams—less than a thousandth of an ounce—of the pure attracting substance. We identified it as the dextrorotatory form of a compound that in chemical terms is described as 10-acetoxy-*cis*-7-hexadecen-1-ol [*see illustration on page 139*]. In laboratory tests it was found that a male gypsy moth would curve its abdomen and make copulatory motions when exposed to as little as a trillionth of a microgram of this substance! And a trap in the field baited with only one ten-millionth of a microgram would lure males to it.

In the same year Butenandt and a team of chemists at the Max Planck Institute for Biochemistry in Munich isolated the sex attractant of the female silkworm moth. They too had had to extract the abdomens of 500,000 virgin females to obtain a tiny amount (12 milligrams) of the pure substance. Their "bombykol" (from *Bombyx*, the generic name of the commercial silkworm) is as potent as the gypsy moth's attractant and also remarkably like it in chemical structure: the description of bombykol is *trans*-10, *cis*-12-hexadecadien-1-ol. Very likely the sex attractants of other species of moths will be found to be chemically similar to these; yet with rare exceptions each attracts only its own species.

Fifteen years ago it would have been virtually impossible to isolate and identify minute amounts of sex attractant. That it is now possible is owing to the evolution of electronic instruments and their application in chemical technology. The new tools (such as infrared and ultraviolet spectrometry, mass spectrometry, gas chromatography and nuclear magnetic resonance) enable chemists to work with substances available only in milligram or even microgram amounts.

Once we had discovered the molecular structure of the gypsy moth attractant we soon succeeded in synthesizing it. We could not resist the temptation then to try to improve on nature and produce a still more effective lure for the male gypsy moth. Our first thought was that if we reduced the size of the molecule, say by shortening the chain from 16 carbon atoms to 14, the compound might be made more volatile and perhaps more attractive. This alteration did not work: the altered product failed to attract the males. Trying various other modifications, we found that a product in which the carbon chain was *lengthened* by two carbons was just as attractive to male moths as the natural lure [*see illustration on page 139*]. This 18-carbon analogue (which, as it happens, is closely related to an ingredient of castor oil) is much easier to synthesize than the natural substance, and it has been adopted by the Department of Agriculture as the agent for trapping the gypsy moth. It has been named gyplure.

For several summers now male gypsy moths have been flying enthusiastically into traps baited with gyplure. About 50,000 such traps are set out each year throughout New England and adjacent areas to check on the whereabouts of the insect. As the moth moves into new areas, control measures are applied promptly to prevent its spread. So far the campaign against the gypsy moth has been a holding action: a vigorous effort to confine the insect to a limited area, where it is so prevalent that a monumental attack would be necessary to eradicate it. Thanks to the use of the sex attractant, the moth has been prevented from spreading outside the northeastern U.S.

In the areas where the gypsy moth is strongly entrenched gyplure is now being tried as a subtle means of birth control. Granules containing the attractant are sprinkled in the woods to confuse the male moths in their odor-controlled search for mates. The tactic, called Operation Confusion, has not worked well in its trials so far because of unforeseen difficulties, but better results are expected in a new trial this summer in which gyplure-scented traps are being used [*see bottom illustration on page 140*].

The idea that food or food substances might be used as bait to trap insects is an old one and has long been investigated in a number of different ways. Experimenters have found that various insects are attracted to stale beer, rum, fermenting sugar solutions, cereal products, bacterial cultures, sliced cucumbers, crushed bananas, beef liver in water and fish meal. Plant extracts also have been extensively tested. The food lure has two aspects: it may draw adult insects simply as something

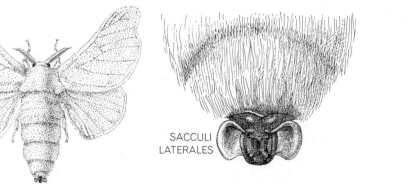

SACCULI
LATERALES

FEMALE SILKWORM MOTH (*extreme left*) emits a sexual pheromone from a pair of sacs that extrude from the abdomen (*detail second from left*). The male (*center*) receives the stimulus, which may consist of no more than a few hundred molecules of the attractant, by means of its antennae (*shown in detail at increasing magnifications*). Sensory studies by the German physiologist

SOME MALE INSECTS can produce sex attractants. When court-ing, a male queen butterfly approaches the female and extrudes a pair of "scent pencils" (*left*) that bush out (*right*) and disperse a pheromone. The attractant renders the female sexually receptive.

on which they can feed themselves, or it may attract egg-laying females because it will provide food for the young when they hatch.

For baiting traps to catch specific insects, food per se or chemicals derived from foodstuffs have proved disappointing. Their drawing power is short-lived, unpredictable and likely to attract insects indiscriminately rather than the particular species one seeks to trap. Derivatives that have been identified are ammonia, certain amines, fatty acids and sulfides. Ammonium carbonate, for

example, has been found to be attractive to female houseflies, which suggests that for the housefly the odor of the chemical indicates a favorable place for depositing its eggs. Some fermentation wastes are attractive to the Mexican fruit fly.

For many years the Entomology Research Division in the Department of Agriculture has been conducting a systematic program of screening plant substances as possible insect lures. Our laboratory uses a standard procedure in this search. First a specific part of a

plant (the flower, seeds, stem or root) is minced and dried, and the material is then put through a series of extractions with certain solvents, in this order: petroleum ether, ether, chloroform, ethanol and finally water. Each extracted fraction is tested for its attractiveness to insects. When an extract proves to be attractive, it is purified and tested in successive steps until the active substance is finally isolated.

In recent years we have searched for pure chemical compounds that will act as strong lures for specific insects. One

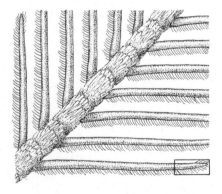

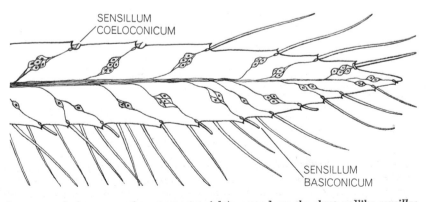

SENSILLUM COELOCONICUM

SENSILLUM BASICONICUM

Dietrich Schneider and his associates have demonstrated that either or both of two antenna organs may act as the chemoreceptors. First are the pitlike *sensillae coeloconicae* (*upper surface of cross section at extreme right*); second are the short rodlike *sensillae basiconicae* (*lower surface*). Relatives of the silkworm moth can be lured from more than two miles away by such sexual pheromones.

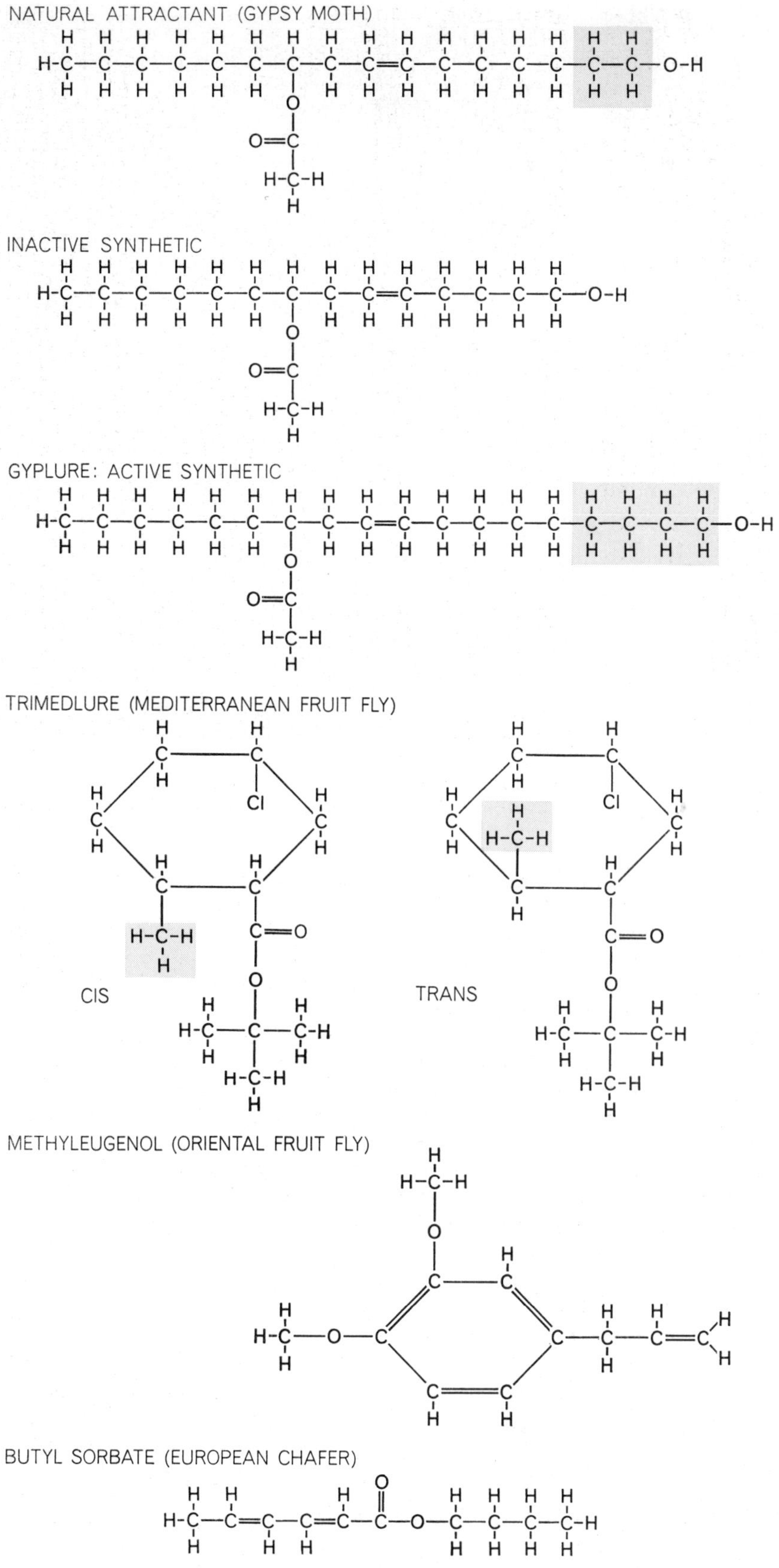

NATURAL ATTRACTANT (GYPSY MOTH)

INACTIVE SYNTHETIC

GYPLURE: ACTIVE SYNTHETIC

TRIMEDLURE (MEDITERRANEAN FRUIT FLY)

CIS

TRANS

METHYLEUGENOL (ORIENTAL FRUIT FLY)

BUTYL SORBATE (EUROPEAN CHAFER)

MOLECULAR STRUCTURES of attractants that affect four insect species contain 11 to 20 carbon atoms. To increase the volatility of the natural gypsy moth substance, the authors removed two carbons from the chain (*color in top diagram*) and found they had rendered it inactive. When, instead, they added two carbons (*color in diagram third from top*), the result, named gyplure, proved to be as attractive as the natural form. In the case of two trimedlure isomers, a *trans*- configuration (*right*) proved to be more potent than a *cis*- (*left*).

such compound proved to be strongly attractive to the male Mediterranean fruit fly. The discovery was exciting because this European insect had recently invaded Florida (which in these days of incessant air travel is difficult to prevent) and infested a million acres of that fruit-growing state. Having found a substance that would lure the fruit fly, we went on to improve its attractive power by tinkering with the molecule. This work culminated in the discovery of trimedlure [*see illustration at left*]. Trimedlure has eight possible isomers (spatial arrangements), and they differ considerably in attraction for the insect: the fly is much more strongly drawn to versions in which the methyl and ester groups are on opposite sides of the ring (*trans*) than to those with the groups on the same side (*cis*). We tested 46 analogues of the compound before selecting trimedlure as the best.

In 1957 traps baited with these attractants, mixed with a volatile, fast-acting insecticide, were set out throughout the infested areas of Florida, and by pinpointing pockets of infestation they helped to eradicate the Mediterranean fruit fly. Since then trimedlure has been used to detect and suppress reinfestations by the same insect. The entire program has cost about $10 million, which is a small investment considering the damage the insect could have done to Florida's fruit crops.

That successful campaign became the forerunner of others. The Department of Agriculture, in collaboration with state agencies, is now protecting fruit-growing areas with triple traps containing lures designed to detect invasions by three different foreign insects: the Mediterranean fruit fly, the oriental fruit fly and the melon fly. A trap baited with another attractant is helping to prevent the Mexican fruit fly from becoming established in California. The European chafer is being kept under surveillance by traps baited with butyl sorbate, and control measures are applied where necessary. All these campaigns illustrate the kind of situation in which attractants are most effective: early detection of the introduction of a destructive insect, prevention of its spread into a new area and its prompt eradication while the numbers involved are still small.

Elimination of an insect from a large area in which it is already well established is a much more difficult problem. An important success has recently been reported, however. Rota, a 35-square-mile island in the Mariana group of the

Pacific, was heavily infested with the oriental fruit fly. As a test the Honolulu Fruit Fly Laboratory of the Department of Agriculture dispersed over the island from the air small absorbent boards containing a lure (methyleugenol) and an insecticide. The attack eradicated the fly from the entire island at a cost of only 50 cents per acre. This demonstration has raised the hope that perhaps the insect can be eliminated from the Hawaiian Islands and other such areas.

Steady progress in the discovery of insect attractants is continuing. Last year the authors identified the sex attractant of the American cockroach. The source of the substance has not yet been located in the cockroach's body, but it has been isolated from a vapor emitted by virgin female roaches. Robert T. Yamamoto of our division ran a stream of air through large cans containing thousands of females for a nine-month period, trapping the vapor by freezing it with dry ice. From the condensate we obtained 12.2 milligrams of the pure attractant. It turned out to be a volatile yellow substance with a strong floral odor. Male cockroaches responded to the odor with intense excitement, raising their wings and making mating attempts [see illustration on page 136].

The identification and testing of attractants is a sophisticated art. We have already mentioned that in many insects the lure is released only at certain times of the day or night. The strength of the odor is important: we have found that in very strong concentration some lures may repel rather than attract. Conditions such as the amount of light, humidity, temperature and air movement are likely to affect insects' responses. Much thought and experimental effort have been devoted to the design of traps for the various insects [see illustration at right].

With the sensitive devices that chemists now have for analyzing extremely tiny amounts of material, the prospects for fighting the insects with their own lures and for investigating their behavior have suddenly become much brighter than they have been in the past. We can now mark insects and recall them at some later time by means of attractants. Thus armed with the ability to follow the lives of individual insects, we are in a position to learn more about the ecology, flight habits, longevity and other attributes of the insects, which in number of species constitute four-fifths of the animals that inhabit the earth.

FEMALE MEXICAN FRUIT FLY buries the tip of its ovipositor in a lemon. Attractant-baited traps are widely distributed in California groves to detect infestations of this fly.

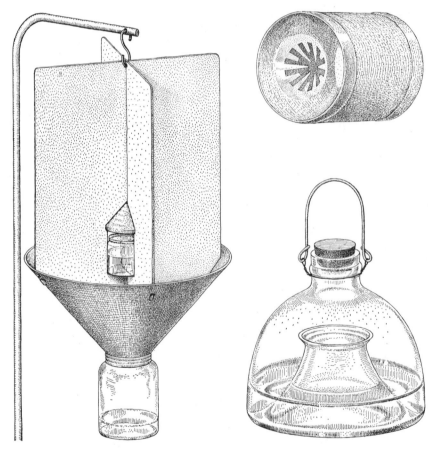

TRAPS FOR DIFFERENT PURPOSES use different attractants. At left butyl sorbate is placed at the intersection of twin baffles above a collecting cone. The European chafer, a heavy beetle, strikes the baffle and falls into the poison jar. At lower right a glass trap with an open bottom contains a liquid lure that attracts Mexican fruit flies. These McPhail traps are not used to control the flies; instead they are placed in suspect areas and checked regularly to see if an infestation has occurred. At the upper right is a cardboard trap with a plastic one-way entrance at each end. Sticky on the inside, it is baited with a synthetic analogue of the female gypsy moth's natural sex attractant. Air-dropped into infested areas, these traps are designed to attract male gypsy moths, which thus will be kept from mating.

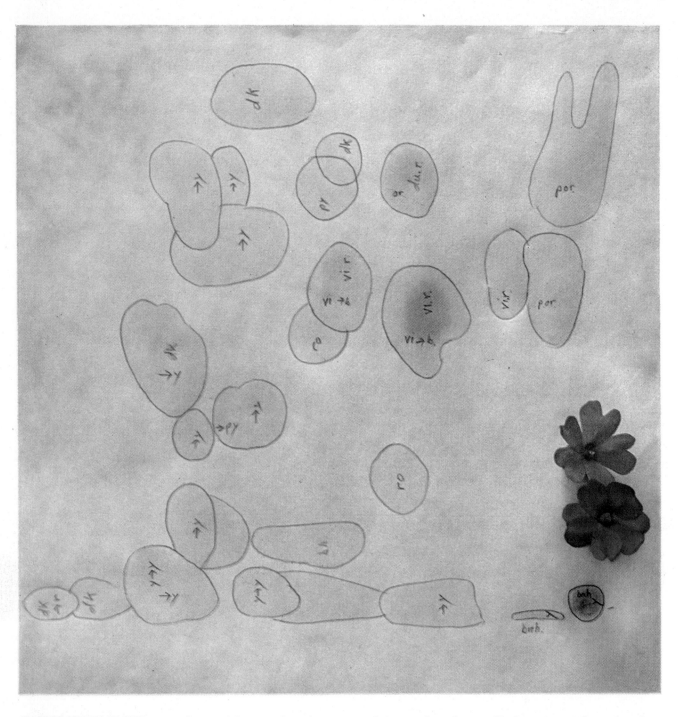

IN THIS PHOTOGRAPH are two flowers of the genus *Impatiens* (*lower right*). The magenta flower is *I. platypetala*, found in Java and Sumatra; the species of the orange flower, which grows on the nearby island of Celebes, is not certain. Because the two plants are so similar some taxonomists consider the second to be a variety of the first; others maintain that the second is a separate species and should be recognized as *I. aurantiaca*. Analysis of the flower pigments by the technique of paper chromatography strengthens the second viewpoint. A solution containing a mixture of pigments from flowers of both species was dropped on the spot just below the magenta flower. The right edge of the paper was then hung from a trough holding a solvent and the pigments descended in a line at different rates. The bottom edge of the paper was then placed in another solvent and the pigments ascended, again at different rates. The spots at which the various pigments stopped migrating are outlined in pencil. Some of the spots derived from *I. aurantiaca* do not appear in the chromatogram of *I. platypetala* alone.

15

Flower Pigments

SARAH CLEVENGER

June 1964

The rich variety of colors displayed by flowers has presented a challenge to both the chemist and the biologist. It has proved no easy matter to answer all the questions that may be asked. Why do the brilliant colors of the plant tend to be concentrated in the flower? Are many pigments involved or only a few, modified in various ways? How are the pigments synthesized in the plant? What function do they serve? Questions such as these have provided new insights into the intricacies as well as the beauties of nature.

Current studies of flower pigments and their control by genes can be traced to two seemingly unrelated researches of about 100 years ago. One was the experiments of Gregor Mendel, who worked out the basic laws of inheritance in his classic studies of the garden pea. The other was the synthesis by a young English chemist, William Henry Perkin, of the first coal-tar dye, mauveine. Perkin's success inspired an intensive investigation of pigments, both natural and synthetic. In the late 19th century and the early years of the 20th chemists such as Richard Willstätter and Stanislaus von Kostanecki in Germany and Robert and Gertrude Robinson in Britain identified many flower pigments and worked out their molecular structure.

The rediscovery of Mendel's work in 1900 stimulated research on the inheritance of flower color. A group of geneticists at the John Innes Horticultural Institution near London were early leaders in this field. Although many plant geneticists had examined the inheritance of flower color, Muriel Wheldale Onslow of the University of Cambridge was the first to realize that here might be a way to investigate the chemical events controlled by Mendelian factors. She reasoned that the presence of a simple bio-chemical substance—such as a pigment—might be correlated with a change in a single gene. Working in association with H. L. Bassett, she showed that this correlation did indeed exist in snapdragons, in spite of the fact that the identification of the pigments was incomplete. This work initiated the biochemical-genetic approach to the problem of plant pigments. It was also the first clear-cut demonstration of a link between a single gene and a biochemical entity.

Later in the 1930's Rose Scott-Moncrieff, a student of Muriel Onslow's, noted certain basic patterns of inheritance in the course of working with genetic varieties of many different plant species. Building on these classic studies, with the advantage of new analytic techniques such as paper chromatography, plant biochemists and geneticists have in recent years learned much more about the nature of the pigments and their production by the living cell.

Flower pigments are easily divided into two groups: the water-soluble flavonoids found in the cell vacuole, which give rise to red, blue and yellow colors, and the fat-soluble carotenoids located in the plastid bodies of the cell, which are red, orange or yellow. Although the carotenoids make a substantial contribution to the coloring of flowers, this article will deal only with the flavonoids. These pigments have a basic chemical structure consisting of two six-carbon-atom benzene rings linked together by a chain of three carbon atoms. This basic molecular structure of 15 carbon atoms is sometimes written C_6—C_3—C_6.

The various groups of flavonoid pigments are differentiated by the level of oxidation of the three-carbon chain. Two of the more common flavonoids are the anthocyanins (from the Greek for "blue flowers"), which come in shades of blue, purple or red, and the flavonols (from the Latin for "yellow"), which are yellow or ivory. The anthocyanins have fewer chemical variations than the flavonols.

In the cells of the flower the pigment is usually bound to one or more units of sugar, which make the molecule more soluble in water. When the sugar is attached, the pigment is known as an anthocyanin; the pigment without the sugar is called an anthocyanidin.

Six common and seven rare anthocyanidins have been isolated from flowers. The illustration on page 146 shows the chemical structure of the common ones. It will be seen that they differ in the number and arrangement of chemical groups attached to the "B" ring of the molecule. This ring may carry one, two or three hydroxyl groups (OH). Occasionally a methyl group (CH_3) replaces the hydrogen atom of a hydroxyl group.

Cyanidin, the most common anthocyanidin, was first isolated from *Centaurea cyanus*, the blue cornflower, which gave the pigment its name. Other anthocyanidins were similarly named. The red pigment pelargonidin was originally found in a bright red geranium of the genus *Pelargonium*. The deep purple pigment delphinidin was isolated from a member of the genus *Delphinium*. These three pigments differ from one another by the number of hydroxyl groups found on the B ring.

Another related group of pigments differ in the number of methyl subunits on the B ring. This group includes the purple pigment petunidin (isolated from petunias), the rosy red pigment peonidin (found in peonies) and the mauve pigment malvidin (discovered in a member of the mallow family, *Malvaceae*).

llhhpp

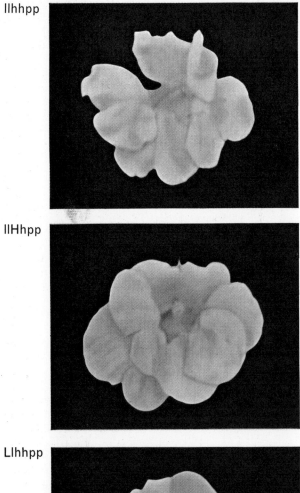

llhhPp

llHhpp

llHhPp

LlhhPp

Llhhpp

LlHhpp

LlHhPp

EIGHT GENOTYPES of the flower *Impatiens balsamina* are portrayed here with the symbols of the genes that determine their pigmentation. Uppercase letters signify dominant genes, lowercase letters recessive genes. Gene designated by *L* (or *l*) governs the production of purple pigment and that designated by *H* (or *h*) governs the production of red pigment. *P* (or *p*) denotes a gene that regulates the amount of pigment produced. A table of the pigments present in the four flowers at right appears on page 145.

An increase in the number of hydroxyl groups on the *B* ring makes the pigment bluer, whereas an increase in methyl groups makes the pigment redder.

The wide variety of flower colors is due not only to the different pigment molecules but also to the different cellular environments in which the pigments are found. Anthocyanins, for example, change color when they accept or release hydrogen ions, depending on the environmental conditions. In a slightly acid environment, which contains an excess of hydrogen ions, the pigment is reddish. As the hydrogen-ion concentration falls, the pigment becomes bluish, then colorless and finally decomposes in a basic solution. The color may also change when the anthocyanins form complexes with tannins and other pigments. Metallic ions, such as iron or aluminum, can also form complexes with the pigment to produce different colors. Thus a few pigments under a variety of environmental conditions are able to produce a wide spectrum of flower colors.

Often associated with the anthocyanidin pigments are the colorless compounds known as leucoanthocyanins. Only leucopelargonidin, leucocyanidin and leucodelphinidin occur frequently, and these are more often found in the woody portion of the plant than in the more highly colored portions.

Since flower color is determined not only by the pigments present but also to some extent by the cellular environment, it is possible for different pigments to produce the same color. Although some pigments produce characteristic colors,

the only sure way to identify the pigments present is by extraction and separation. Pigments can be extracted from flowers with alcohol that has been slightly acidified to keep the pigment from decolorizing. The sugar groups are removed by boiling the pigment with dilute acid. To this solution is then added a small amount of isoamyl alcohol, which rises to the top, carrying the pigment with it.

The mixture of pigments can then be separated by paper chromatography. In this technique pigments of different chemical compositions migrate at different speeds when placed on absorbent paper and exposed to the action of solvents [*see illustration on page 149*]. During the first run of a chromatogram the pigments are spread out along one line and may be overlapping, which makes identification difficult. After the chromatogram has dried it is run in the second direction with the line of pigments along the bottom of the sheet. The resulting pattern of spots is spread over two dimensions and is usually quite faint, but it can be intensified by the use of appropriate sprays. Several pigments fluoresce characteristically under ultraviolet radiation, and this also aids in the identification. A certain amount of information can be derived about an unknown anthocyanidin by comparing its performance in a two-dimensional chromatogram with that of pigments of known configuration. Thus the isolation, separation and identification of flower pigments can be achieved with a high degree of accuracy.

To determine the forms of the pigments as they occur naturally in the cell, a simple alcohol extract of the pig-

ments is applied to chromatography paper. A two-dimensional chromatogram of such an extract is shown in the color photograph on page 142.

Although it is not easy to isolate and identify the various plant pigments, it is a far more difficult problem to discover how the plant produces them. Green plants can synthesize all organic compounds—both simple and complex—from a few inorganic substances. The metabolic pathway of any one compound is very hard to follow. Some success in elucidating the synthesis of the flavonoid pigments has, however, been gained by two methods, one biochemical, the other genetic.

In the first method the metabolic pathway is followed with the help of molecules labeled with radioactive carbon atoms. Using this technique J. E. Watkin, E. W. Underhill and A. C. Neish of the National Research Council of Canada and others have established the broad outline of the biosynthetic pathway of the flavonoids. The Canadian group studied the formation of the flavonol quercetin in buckwheat. They found that the *A* and *B* rings of the molecule are synthesized by different pathways. Ring *B* and the three-carbon chain are formed by the condensation of a seven-carbon sugar with a three-carbon molecule of pyruvic acid. After several changes, in which one carbon atom is lost, the resulting product is phenylpyruvic acid, a C_6–C_3 molecule. This molecule then condenses with three molecules of acetic acid, which are the precursors of ring *A*, to yield the C_6–C_3–C_6 backbone of the flavonoid pigments.

It is not clear at what point in the synthesis the hydroxyl and methyl groups are introduced into the structure. Judging from the relative distribution in nature, the more primitive, or basic, structure carries two hydroxyl groups on the *B* ring. This form or its precursor is modified by the addition or removal of a hydroxyl group. Probably one of the late steps is the addition of methyl groups to form the methoxyl groups. Often delphinidin, petunidin and malvidin are present together in a flower; this would be expected if malvidin is formed by the stepwise methylation of delphinidin or its precursor.

The second—the genetic—approach to studying pigment biosynthesis is a method that has been successful in elucidating biosynthetic processes in microorganisms. The method involves the use

GENOTYPE	PIGMENTS		FLOWER COLOR
	ANTHOCYANIDINS	FLAVONOLS	
IIhhPp	PELARGONIDIN	KAMPFEROL	PINK
IIHhPp	PELARGONIDIN LEUCOPELARGONIDIN	KAMPFEROL	RED
LIhhPp	MALVIDIN	KAMPFEROL MYRICETIN	PURPLE
LIHhPp	MALVIDIN PELARGONIDIN LEUCOPELARGONIDIN	KAMPFEROL MYRICETIN	MAGENTA

FLAVONOID PIGMENTS found in the petals of four genotypes of the flower *Impatiens balsamina* include anthocyanidins (from the Greek for "blue flowers") and flavonols (from the Latin for "yellow"). Anthocyanidins can color petals blue, purple or red depending on their chemical environment. Flavonols contribute yellow or ivory shades.

BASIC STRUCTURE

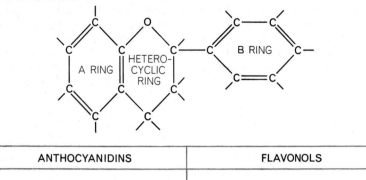

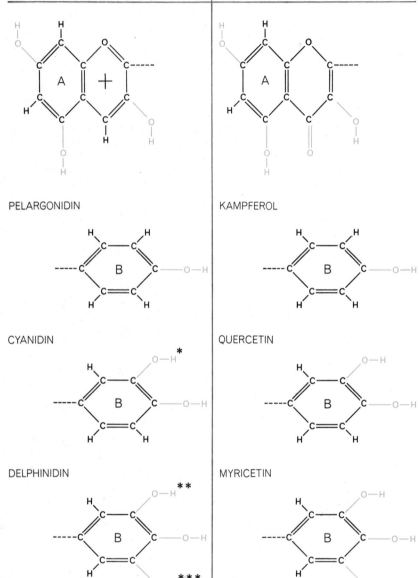

ANTHOCYANIDINS	FLAVONOLS

PELARGONIDIN

KAMPFEROL

CYANIDIN

QUERCETIN

DELPHINIDIN

MYRICETIN

CHEMICAL STRUCTURES of the common anthocyanidin and flavonol pigments are variations of a basic configuration (*top*), in which two six-carbon-atom benzene rings (*A and B*) are linked by a smaller three-carbon-atom structure known as a heterocyclic ring. What distinguishes the anthocyanidins from the flavonols is the level of oxidation of the heterocyclic ring; the flavonols have a doubly bonded oxygen atom there. Differences in hues within each family depend mainly on groups of atoms attached to the *B* ring. The pigments produced by the addition of one, two and three hydroxyl groups (OH) to certain positions on the *B* ring are shown at bottom. If a methyl group (CH_3) were substituted for the hydrogen atom in the hydroxyl group indicated by an asterisk, the result would be a rosy red pigment called peonidin. A similar methyl substitution at the double asterisk would produce petunidin and at the double and triple asterisks malvidin.

of mutant forms and is therefore more difficult to apply to higher plants, which have longer generation times and a more varied metabolism. Nevertheless, the method has contributed significantly to the knowledge of pigment synthesis.

A genetic study of this type has been carried out with members of the genus *Impatiens*. The generic name of these plants is derived from the characteristic fruit, which opens violently when mature and in the process projects the seeds some distance. Because this can happen if the capsule is merely touched, the plant is known as touch-me-not in many lands and in many languages. Among the members of the genus are the jewelweeds of eastern North America and the popular house plant often called sultana after the Sultan of Zanzibar, in whose country the plant was collected.

A group of plant physiologists at Indiana University headed by Charles W. Hagen, Jr., has been studying the genetic control of the flower pigments of *Impatiens balsamina*, the common garden balsam. Its flowers vary in color from white and pastel shades to deep purple or bright red. The mode of inheritance of these flower colors was determined several years ago by D. W. Davis and his co-workers at the College of William and Mary. The identification of the anthocyanidin pigments present in the different hereditary strains was made recently by Ralph Alston and Hagen and the flavonols were identified by me.

The formation of flower color in balsams is controlled by three separate sets of genes. Two genes, *L* and *H*, determine the kinds of pigment produced; the third gene, *P*, determines the amount. One form of this third gene suppresses pigment production and the flowers are very pale. Another form of the gene acts as an intensifier and the flowers are brightly colored.

Analysis of the petal pigments present in the various strains has provided some interesting correlations [*see the table on preceding page*]. When the gene *L* is present, the flower contains malvidin and myricetin, a flavonol resembling delphinidin. Since both pigments carry three groups on the *B* ring, it seems that *L* is associated with the addition of the third hydroxyl group. A similar correlation between the gene *H* and the presence of pelargonidin and leucopelargonidin suggests that *H* is associated with the formation of a single hydroxyl group on the *B* ring. Inasmuch as the synthesis of anthocyanidins, flavonols and leucoanthocyanins are all affected by the two genes, it is probable that these compounds are synthesized along similar pathways. The pigmented sepals contain a different complement of pigments from that found in the petals.

In order to study pigment development under more uniform conditions than those found in the greenhouse, Attila O. Klein of the Indiana group developed a method of growing detached petals in a nutrient culture solution. Light is needed both for the pro-

duction of the anthocyanins and the expansion of the petals. One unexpected result of this work revealed that the petals in culture are able to synthesize certain pigments (cyanidin, peonidin and quercetin) that are normally found in the colored sepals of these strains but

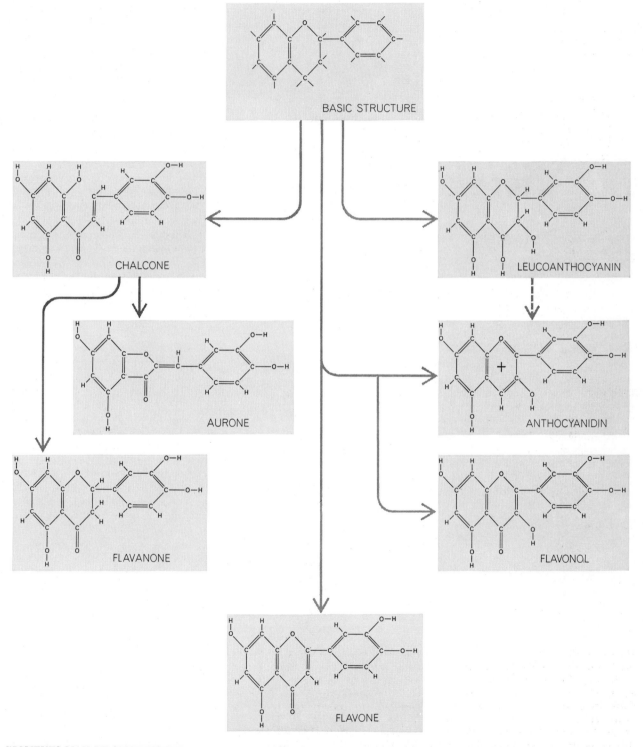

PIGMENTS MAY BE SYNTHESIZED in the flower at different stages along a multibranched, metabolic pathway as successive variations are introduced to the basic flavonoid molecule (*top*). One branch leads to the formation of the anthocyanidins, pos-

sibly by way of the colorless leucoanthocyanins (*broken arrow*). Other branches lead to the flavonols and other flavonoids. Slight chemical variations among the flavonoid pigments contribute to the full spectrum of colors displayed by the world of flowers.

not usually in the petals. This is further evidence that the action of a gene depends on the chemical, physical and genetic environment in which it acts. The cells of the cultured petals are able to produce substances that intact petals normally do not synthesize.

By pooling such information from various laboratories, one can speculate concerning the possible pathway for the synthesis of the flavonoid pigments —a multibranched pathway leading to many variations of the basic $C_6-C_3-C_6$ skeleton. One branch leads to the formation of the anthocyanidins, perhaps by way of the colorless leucoanthocyanins. Other branches lead to other flavonoids, such as the chalcones, the flavonols and the aurones. The differences between these various groups are slight; they involve the level of oxidation of the three-carbon chain and the number, kind and position of additional groups. Yet these slight variations contribute to the full spectrum of colors displayed by the plant world.

The comparison of the pigment complement present in different species of the same genus gives valuable information concerning the evolution of species within the genus as well as about the genetic control of pigment synthesis. Within any genus the differences between species have evolved gradually over the years through mutation and selection of genes. Undoubtedly some of these genetic changes have affected the synthesis of pigments. Consequently a comparison of the pigments in closely related species should shed light on the fine-scale evolution of pigment synthesis.

The genus *Impatiens* is well suited to such a study because it contains a great many species with a wide variety of flower colors. The greatest number of species are found in the tropical areas of the Eastern Hemisphere. Two somewhat similar plants I have investigated provide an excellent illustration of the possibilities offered by the comparative study of pigments. Both plants are native to Indonesia. *Impatiens platypetala,* found in Java and Sumatra, has large, showy magenta flowers. On the nearby island of Celebes grows an *Impatiens* with bright yellow-orange flowers. Because the two plants are so similar some taxonomists consider the second to be a variety of the first and call it *I. platypetala* var. *aurantiaca*. Others maintain that the second is a separate species and should be recognized as *I. aurantiaca*.

An analysis of the flower pigments strengthens the second viewpoint. The magenta petals of *I. platypetala* contain mainly malvidin, but the orange flowers of *I. aurantiaca* contain an apparently unrelated anthocyanidin not previously found in nature. The structure of the new pigment, called aurantinidin, is now being worked out by J. B. Harborne of the John Innes Institute. The pigment seems to resemble another rare anthocyanidin called luteolinidin. Since the two groups of plants synthesize such widely differing pigments, it seems unlikely that they are closely related, and so one can conclude that their resemblance is superficial rather than fundamental. A mixture of pigments from the flowers of these two species was used to make the chromatogram shown on the cover.

So far only a small percentage of the known species of the genus *Impatiens* has been analyzed. Cyanidin and malvidin are the most common pigments in the petals; cyanidin is the most common in the sepals and stems. From a morphological point of view one would expect the petal to be more highly evolved than the sepal, and sepals, in turn, to be more complex than the stem. It appears that this ordering may also be true for the pigments if one assumes that the nonmethylated pigments are the more primitive and the methylated pigments the more elaborate.

This suggests that the biosynthetic sequence leading to the production of anthocyanidins, at least as far as the *B* ring is concerned, proceeds as follows: first, two hydroxyl groups are added as in cyanidin, then a third as in delphinidin; finally stepwise methylation produces first petunidin, then malvidin. At times methylated pigments appear with small amounts of their unmethylated counterparts, indicating that such a stepwise procedure is plausible. These separate steps appear to be under the control of different genes; the pigment produced in any given cell depends on whether a particular gene functions or is prevented from functioning.

In spite of the abundance of the flavonoids in nature, they represent an unresolved area of plant metabolism. One of the more important unanswered questions about anthocyanins in particular and flavonoids in general concerns their function in the living plant. Many roles in metabolism have been postulated but none has actually been shown to obtain in the plant. These substances may be end products of metabolism

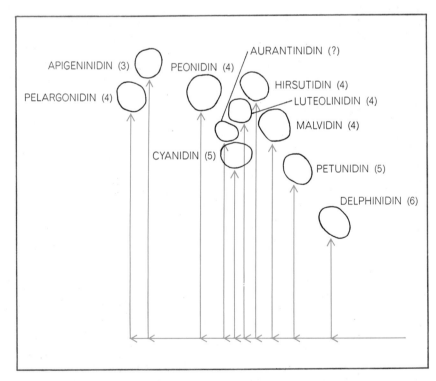

TWO-DIMENSIONAL PAPER CHROMATOGRAM, similar to the one on page 142, is made by first hanging the spotted paper and allowing the solution containing the pigments to descend; an edge is then placed in a different solvent and the solution ascends. In this schematic drawing the general areas in which the various anthocyanidin pigments are deposited are indicated. The number in parentheses after the name of each pigment denotes the number of free hydroxyl groups on a molecule of that pigment.

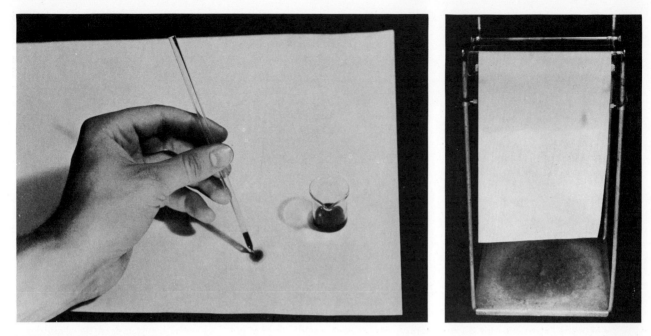

PIGMENTS ARE ANALYZED by a technique known as paper chromatography. A solution of alcohol and dilute mineral acid containing several pigments from one flower is spotted on the corner of a sheet of paper (*left*). The paper is then hung from a trough that contains a solvent (*right*). As the solvent travels down the paper (*darker area at top*) different pigments will be de-posited at different distances from the point of origin, depending on their chemical structure. The pigments can be further separated by rehanging the paper from its edge and using a different solvent. The solution can also be made to ascend the paper from a trough of solvent at the bottom; the chromatogram on page 142 was made by a combination of the two methods.

that gradually build up in the cell; they may act as agents of oxidation and reduction; they may be waste products that serve little or no use, or perhaps they act as antifungal agents.

Undoubtedly one of the functions of the pigments in the flowers is to attract the pollinating agents. Although it is quite clear that flower pigments do perform this function, it is probably a function that developed only secondarily; anthocyanins are found in plants that are not dependent on attracting pollinating agents. Bright red and red-orange flowers, particularly prevalent in the Tropics, attract birds. Bees favor yellow and blue flowers. Day-flying butterflies pollinate brightly colored flowers, whereas their night-flying counterparts, the moths, choose the white or pale flowers, which are more noticeable during the poorly lighted hours. In addition to attracting pollinators by the conspicuousness of their coloring, most flowers have streaks, dots or lines known as pollen guides to help orient the alighting visitor in search of nectar.

Since flower pigments are so widely distributed, one feels that they must have other important functional roles. With the wide appeal that this subject has for plant physiologists, geneticists, biochemists and taxonomists, it is certain that a great deal of new information on the subject of flower pigments will be produced in the next few years. However one looks at these pigments, they are a most attractive subject for investigation.

16

The Stereochemical Theory of Odor

JOHN E. AMOORE, JAMES W. JOHNSTON, JR., AND MARTIN RUBIN

February 1964

A rose is a rose and a skunk is a skunk, and the nose easily tells the difference. But it is not so easy to describe or explain this difference. We know surprisingly little about the sense of smell, in spite of its important influence on our daily lives and the voluminous literature of research on the subject. One is hard put to describe an odor except by comparing it to a more familiar one. We have no yardstick for measuring the strength of odors, as we measure sound in decibels and light in lumens. And we have had no satisfactory general theory to explain how the nose and brain detect, identify and recognize an odor. More than 30 different theories have been suggested by investigators in various disciplines, but none of them has passed the test of experiments designed to determine their validity.

The sense of smell obviously is a chemical sense, and its sensitivity is pro-verbial; to a chemist the ability of the nose to sort out and characterize substances is almost beyond belief. It deals with complex compounds that might take a chemist months to analyze in the laboratory; the nose identifies them instantly, even in an amount so small (as little as a ten-millionth of a gram) that the most sensitive modern laboratory instruments often cannot detect the substance, let alone analyze and label it.

Two thousand years ago the poet Lucretius suggested a simple explanation of the sense of smell. He speculated that the "palate" contained minute pores of various sizes and shapes. Every odorous substance, he said, gave off tiny "molecules" of a particular shape, and the odor was perceived when these molecules entered pores in the palate. Presumably the identification of each odor depended on which pores the molecules fitted.

It now appears that Lucretius' guess was essentially correct. Within the past few years new evidence has shown rather convincingly that the geometry of molecules is indeed the main determinant of odor, and a theory of the olfactory process has been developed in modern terms. This article will discuss the stereochemical theory and the experiments that have tested it.

The nose is always on the alert for odors. The stream of air drawn in through the nostrils is warmed and filtered as it passes the three baffle-shaped turbinate bones in the upper part of the nose; when an odor is detected, more of the air is vigorously sniffed upward to two clefts that contain the smelling organs [see illustration on opposite page]. These organs consist of two patches of yellowish tissue, each about one square inch in area. Embedded in the tissue are two types of nerve fiber whose endings receive and detect the odorous molecules. The chief type is represented by the fibers of the olfactory nerve; at the end of each of these fibers is an olfactory cell bearing a cluster of hairlike filaments that act as receptors. The other type of fiber is a long, slender ending of the trigeminal nerve, which is sensitive to certain kinds of molecules. On being stimulated by odorous molecules, the olfactory nerve endings send signals to the olfactory bulb and thence to the higher brain centers where the signals are integrated and interpreted in terms of the character and intensity of the odor.

From the nature of this system it is obvious at once that to be smelled at all a material must have certain basic properties. In the first place, it must be volatile. A substance such as onion soup, for example, is highly odorous because it continuously gives off vapor that can reach the nose (unless the soup is im-

PRIMARY ODOR	CHEMICAL EXAMPLE	FAMILIAR SUBSTANCE
CAMPHORACEOUS	CAMPHOR	MOTH REPELLENT
MUSKY	PENTADECANOLACTONE	ANGELICA ROOT OIL
FLORAL	PHENYLETHYL METHYL ETHYL CARBINOL	ROSES
PEPPERMINTY	MENTHONE	MINT CANDY
ETHEREAL	ETHYLENE DICHLORIDE	DRY-CLEANING FLUID
PUNGENT	FORMIC ACID	VINEGAR
PUTRID	BUTYL MERCAPTAN	BAD EGG

PRIMARY ODORS identified by the authors are listed, together with chemical and more familiar examples. Each of the primary odors is detected by a different receptor in the nose. Most odors are composed of several of these primaries combined in various proportions.

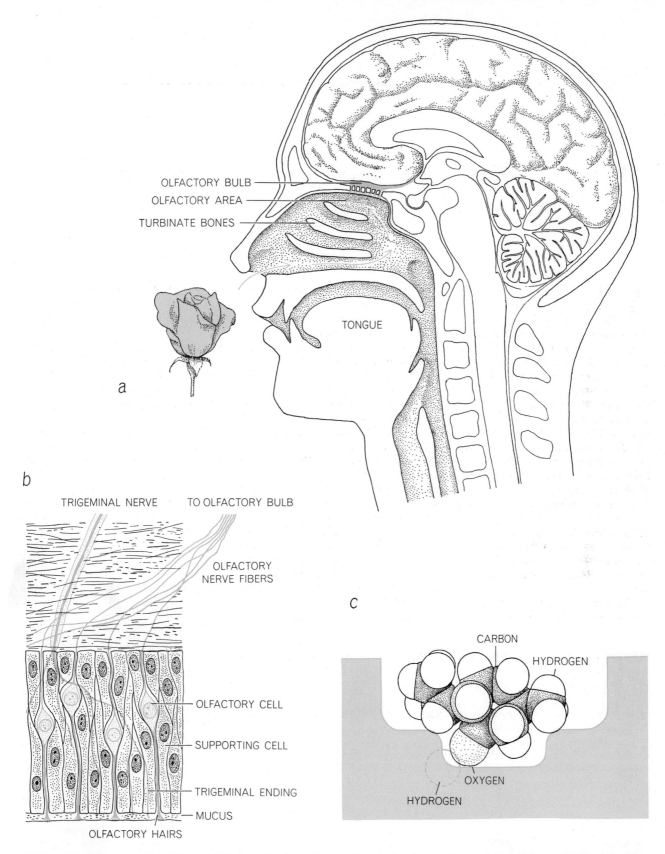

OLFACTORY BULB

OLFACTORY AREA

TURBINATE BONES

TONGUE

a

b

TRIGEMINAL NERVE   TO OLFACTORY BULB

OLFACTORY
NERVE FIBERS

c

OLFACTORY CELL

SUPPORTING CELL

TRIGEMINAL ENDING

MUCUS

OLFACTORY HAIRS

CARBON

HYDROGEN

OXYGEN

HYDROGEN

ANATOMY of the sense of smell is traced in these drawings. Air carrying odorous molecules is sniffed up past the three baffle-shaped turbinate bones to the olfactory area (*a*), patches of epithelium in which are embedded the endings of large numbers of olfactory nerves (*color*). A microscopic section of the olfactory epithelium (*b*) shows the olfactory nerve cells and their hairlike endings, trigeminal endings and supporting cells. According to the stereochemical theory different olfactory nerve cells are stimulated by different molecules on the basis of the size and shape or the charge of the molecule; these properties determine which of various pits and slots on the olfactory endings it will fit. A molecule of *l*-menthone is shown fitted into the "pepperminty" cavity (*c*).

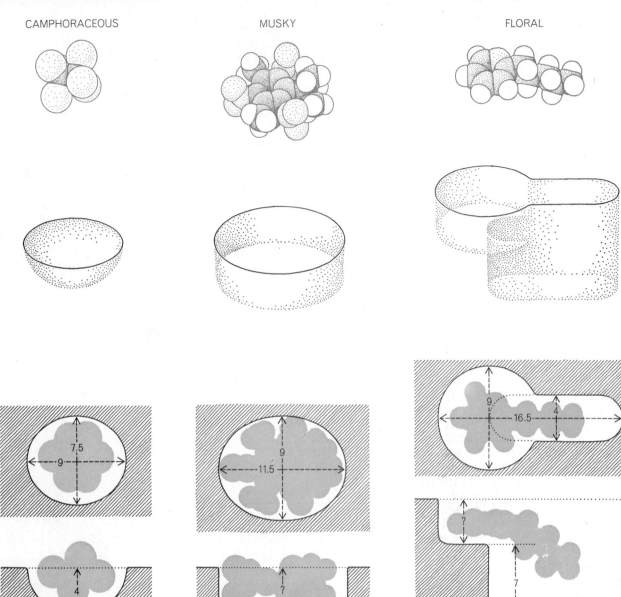

CAMPHORACEOUS   MUSKY   FLORAL

OLFACTORY RECEPTOR SITES are shown for each of the primary odors, together with molecules representative of each odor. The shapes of the first five sites are shown in perspective and (with the molecules silhouetted in them) from above and the side;

prisoned in a sealed can). On the other hand, at ordinary temperatures a substance such as iron is completely odorless because it does not evaporate molecules into the air.

The second requirement for an odorous substance is that it should be soluble in water, even if only to an almost infinitesimal extent. If it is completely insoluble, it will be barred from reaching the nerve endings by the watery film that covers their surfaces. Another common property of odorous materials is solubility in lipids (fatty substances); this enables them to penetrate the nerve endings through the lipid layer that

forms part of the surface membrane of every cell.

Beyond these elementary properties the characteristics of odorous materials have been vague and confusing. Over the years chemists empirically synthesized a wealth of odorous compounds, both for perfumers and for their own studies of odor, but instead of clarifying the properties responsible for odor these compounds seemed merely to add to the confusion. A few general principles were discovered. For instance, it was found that adding a branch to a straight chain of carbon atoms in a perfume molecule markedly increased the po-

tency of the perfume. Strong odor also seemed to be associated with chains of four to eight carbon atoms in the molecules of certain alcohols and aldehydes. The more chemists analyzed the chemical structure of odorous substances, however, the more puzzles emerged. From the standpoint of chemical composition and structure the substances showed some remarkable inconsistencies.

Curiously enough, the inconsistencies themselves began to show a pattern. As an example, two optical isomers—molecules identical in every respect except that one is the mirror image of the other —may have different odors. As another

PEPPERMINTY

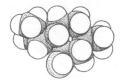

ETHEREAL

PUNGENT

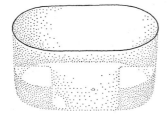

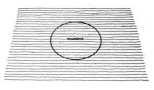

PUTRID

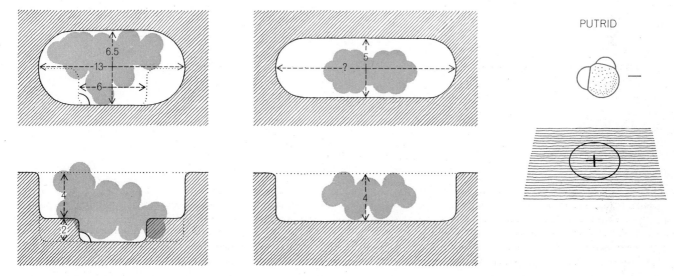

known dimensions are given in angstrom units. The molecules are *(left to right)* **hexachloroethane, xylene musk, alpha-amylpyridine,** *l*-menthol and diethyl ether. Pungent (formic acid) and putrid (hydrogen sulfide) molecules fit because of charge, not shape.

example, in a compound whose molecules contain a small six-carbon-atom benzene ring, shifting the position of a group of atoms attached to the ring may sharply change the odor of the compound, whereas in a compound whose molecules contain a large ring of 14 to 19 members the atoms can be rearranged considerably without altering the odor much. Chemists were led by these facts to speculate on the possibility that the primary factor determining the odor of a substance might be the over-all geometric shape of the molecule rather than any details of its composition or structure.

In 1949 R. W. Moncrieff in Scotland gave form to these ideas by proposing a hypothesis strongly reminiscent of the 2,000-year-old guess of Lucretius. Moncrieff suggested that the olfactory system is composed of receptor cells of a few different types, each representing a distinct "primary" odor, and that odorous molecules produce their effects by fitting closely into "receptor sites" on these cells. His hypothesis is an application of the "lock and key" concept that has proved fruitful in explaining the interaction of enzymes with their substrates, of antibodies with antigens and of deoxyribonucleic acid with the "messenger" ribonucleic acid that presides at the synthesis of protein.

To translate Moncrieff's hypothesis into a practical approach for investigating olfaction, two specific questions had to be answered. What are the "primary odors"? And what is the shape of the receptor site for each one? To try to find answers to these questions, one of us (Amoore, then at the University of Oxford) made an extensive search of the literature of organic chemistry, looking for clues in the chemical characteristics of odorous compounds. His search resulted in the conclusion that there were seven primary odors, and in 1952 his findings were summed up in a stereochemical theory of olfaction that identified the seven odors and gave a detailed description of the size, shape and chemical affinities of the seven corresponding receptor sites.

To identify the primary odors Amoore started with the descriptions of 600 organic compounds noted in the literature as odorous. If the receptor-site hypothesis was correct, the primary odors should be recognized much more frequently than mixed odors made up of two or more primaries. And indeed, in the chemists' descriptions certain odors turned up much more commonly than others. For instance, the descriptions mentioned more than 100 compounds as having a camphor-like odor, whereas only about half a dozen were put in the category characterized by the odor of cedarwood. This suggested that in all likelihood the camphor odor was a primary one. By this test of frequency, and from other considerations, it was possible to select seven odors that stand out as probable primaries. They are: camphoraceous, musky, floral, pepperminty, ethereal (ether-like), pungent and putrid.

From these seven primaries every known odor could be made by mixing them in certain proportions. In this respect the primary odors are like the three primary colors (red, green and blue) and the four primary tastes (sweet, salt, sour and bitter).

To match the seven primary odors there must be seven different kinds of olfactory receptors in the nose. We can picture the receptor sites as ultramicroscopic slots or hollows in the nerve-fiber membrane, each of a distinctive shape and size. Presumably each will accept a molecule of the appropriate configuration, just as a socket takes a plug. Some molecules may be able to fit into two different sockets—broadside into a wide receptor or end on into a narrow one. In such cases the substance, with its molecules occupying both types of receptor, may indicate a complex odor to the brain.

The next problem was to learn the shapes of the seven receptor sites. This was begun by examining the structural formulas of the camphoraceous compounds and constructing models of their molecules. Thanks to the techniques of modern stereochemistry, which explore the structure of molecules with the aid of X-ray diffraction, infrared spectroscopy, the electron-beam probe and other means, it is possible to build a three-dimensional model of the molecule of any chemical compound once its structural formula is known. There are rules for building these models; also available are building blocks (sets of atomic units) on a scale 100 million times actual size.

As the models of the camphoraceous molecules took form, it soon became clear that they all had about the same shape: they were roughly spherical. Not only that, it turned out that when the models were translated into molecular dimensions, all the molecules also had about the same diameter: approximately seven angstrom units. (An angstrom unit is a ten-millionth of a millimeter.) This meant that the receptor site for camphoraceous molecules must be a hemispherical bowl about seven angstroms in diameter. Many of the camphoraceous molecules are rigid spheres that would inevitably fit into such a bowl; the others are slightly flexible and could easily shape themselves to the bowl.

When other models were built, shapes and sizes of the molecules representing the other primary odors were found [see illustration on preceding two pages]. The musky odor is accounted for by molecules with the shape of a disk about 10 angstroms in diameter. The pleasant floral odor is caused by molecules that have the shape of a disk with a flexible tail attached—a shape somewhat like a kite. The cool pepperminty odor is produced by molecules with the shape of a wedge, and with an electrically polarized group of atoms, capable of forming a hydrogen bond, near the point of the wedge. The ethereal odor is due to rod-shaped or other thin molecules. In each of these cases the receptor site in the nerve endings presumably has a shape and size corresponding to those of the molecule.

The pungent and putrid odors seem to be exceptions to the Lucretian scheme of shape-matching. The molecules responsible for these odors are of indifferent shapes and sizes; what matters in their case is the electric charge of the molecule. The pungent class of odors is produced by compounds whose molecules, because of a deficiency of electrons, have a positive charge and a strong affinity for electrons; they are called electrophilic. Putrid odors, on the other hand, are caused by molecules

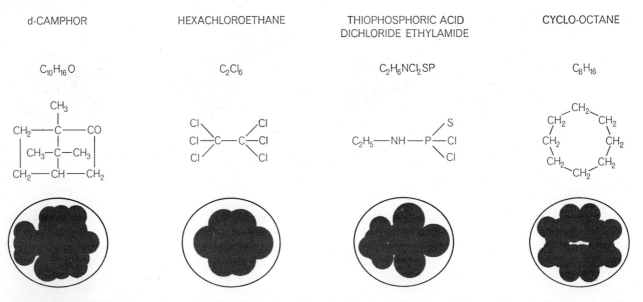

d-CAMPHOR   HEXACHLOROETHANE   THIOPHOSPHORIC ACID DICHLORIDE ETHYLAMIDE   CYCLO-OCTANE

$C_{10}H_{16}O$ C_2Cl_6 $C_2H_6NCl_2SP$ C_8H_{16}

UNRELATED CHEMICALS with camphor-like odors show no resemblance in empirical formulas and little in structural formulas. Yet, because the size and shape of their molecules are similar, they all fit the bowl-shaped receptor for camphoraceous molecules.

that have an excess of electrons and are called nucleophilic, because they are strongly attracted by the nuclei of adjacent atoms.

A theory is useful only if it can be tested in some way by experiment. One of the virtues of the stereochemical theory is that it suggests some very specific and unambiguous tests. It has been subjected to six severe tests of its accuracy so far and has passed each of them decisively.

To start with, it is at once obvious that from the shape of a molecule we should be able to predict its odor. Suppose, then, that we synthesize molecules of certain shapes and see whether or not they produce the odors predicted for them.

Consider a molecule consisting of three chains attached to a single carbon atom, with the central atom's fourth bond occupied only by a hydrogen atom [*see top illustration at right*]. This molecule might fit into a kite-shaped site (floral odor), a wedge-shaped site (pepperminty) or, by means of one of its chains, a rod-shaped site (ethereal). The theory predicts that the molecule should therefore have a fruity odor composed of these three primaries. Now suppose we substitute the comparatively bulky methyl group (CH_3) in place of the small hydrogen atom at the fourth bond of the carbon atom. The introduction of a fourth branch will prevent the molecule from fitting so easily into a kite-shaped or wedge-shaped site, but one of the branches should still be able to occupy a rod-shaped site. As a result, the theory predicts, the ether smell should now predominate.

Another of us (Rubin) duly synthesized the two structures in his laboratory at the Georgetown University School of Medicine. The third author (Johnston), also working at the Georgetown School of Medicine, then submitted the products to a panel of trained smellers. He used an instrument called the olfactometer, which by means of valves and controlled air streams delivers carefully measured concentrations of odors, singly or mixed, to the observer. The amount of odorous vapor delivered was measured by gas chromatography. A pair of olfactometers was used, one for each of the two compounds under test, and the observer was asked to sniff alternately from each.

The results verified the predictions. The panel reported that Compound A had a fruity (actually grapelike) odor, and that Compound B, with the methyl

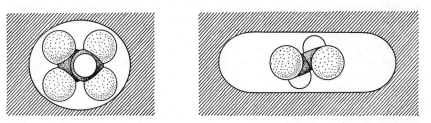

CHANGE IN SHAPE of a molecule changed its odor. The molecule at left smelled fruity because it fitted into three sites. When it was modified (*right*) by the substitution of a methyl group for a hydrogen, it smelled somewhat ethereal. Presumably the methyl branch made it fit two of the original sites less well but allowed it still to fit the ethereal slot.

SINGLE CHEMICAL has more than one primary odor if its molecule can fit more than one site. Acetylenetetrabromide, for example, is described as smelling both camphoraceous and ethereal. It turns out that its molecule can fit either site, depending on how it lies.

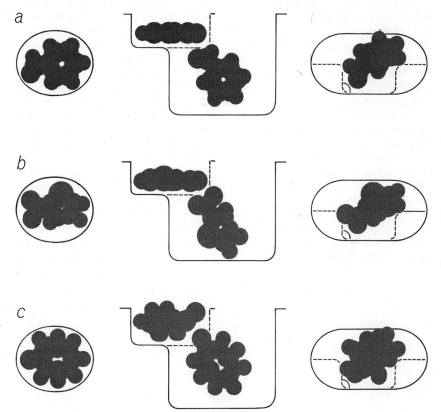

COMPLEX ODORS are made up of several primaries. Three molecules with an almond odor are illustrated: benzaldehyde (*a*), alpha-nitrothiophen (*b*) and cyclo-octanone (*c*). Each of them fits (*left to right*) camphoraceous, floral (with two molecules) and pepperminty sites.

group substituted for the hydrogen atom, had a pronounced tinge of the ether-like odor. This experiment, and the theory behind it, make understandable the earlier finding that the odor of certain benzene-ring compounds changes sharply when the position of a group of atoms is shifted. The change in odor is due to the change in the over-all shape of the molecule.

A second test suggested itself. Could a complex odor found in nature be matched by putting together a combination of primary odors? Taking the odor of cedarwood oil as a test case, Amoore found that chemicals known to possess this odor had molecular shapes that would fit into the receptor sites for the camphoraceous, musky, floral and pepperminty odors. Johnston proceeded to try various combinations of these four primaries to duplicate the cedarwood odor. He tested each mixture on eight trained observers, who compared the synthetic odor with that of cedarwood oil. After 86 attempts he was able to produce a blend that closely matched the natural cedarwood odor. With the same four primaries he also succeeded in synthesizing a close match for the odor of sandalwood oil.

The next two tests had to do with the identification of pure (that is, primary) odors. If the theory was correct, a molecule that would fit only into a receptor site of a particular shape and size, and no other, should represent a primary odor in pure form. Molecules of the same shape and size should smell very much alike; those of a different primary shape should smell very different. Human subjects were tested on this point. Presented with the odors from a pair of different substances whose molecules nonetheless had the same primary shape (for example, that of the floral odor), the subjects judged the two odors to be highly similar to each other. When the pair of

substances presented had the pure molecular traits of different categories (for instance, the kite shape of the floral odor and the nucleophilic charge characteristic of putrid compounds), the subjects found the odors extremely dissimilar.

Johnston went on to make the same sort of test with honeybees. He set up an experiment designed to test their ability to discriminate between two odors, one of which was "right" (associated with sugar sirup) and the other "wrong" (associated with an electric shock). The pair of odors might be in the same primary group or in different primary groups (for example, floral and pepperminty). At pairs of scented vials on a table near the hive, the bees were first conditioned to the fact that one odor of a pair was right and the other was wrong. Then the sirup bait in the vials was replaced with distilled water and freshly deodorized scent vials were substituted for those used during the training period. The visits of the marked bees to the respective vials in search of sirup were counted. It could be assumed that they would tend to visit the odor to which they had been favorably conditioned and to avoid the one that had been associated with electric shock, provided that they could distinguish between the two.

So tested, the honeybees clearly showed that they had difficulty in detecting a difference between two scents within the same primary group (say pepperminty) but were able to distinguish easily between different primaries (pepperminty and floral). In the latter case they almost invariably chose the correct scent without delay. These experiments indicate that the olfactory system of the honeybee, like that of human beings, is based on the stereochemical principle, although the bee's smelling organ is different; it smells not with a nose but with antennae. Apparently the receptor sites on the antennae are differentiated by shape in the same way as those in the human nose.

A fifth test was made with human observers trained in odor discrimination. Suppose they were presented with a number of substances that were very different chemically but whose molecules had about the same over-all shape. Would all these dissimilar compounds smell alike? Five compounds were used for the test. They belonged to three different chemical families differing radically from one another in the internal structure of their molecules but in all five cases had the disk shape characteristic of the molecules of musky-odored substances. The observers, exposed to

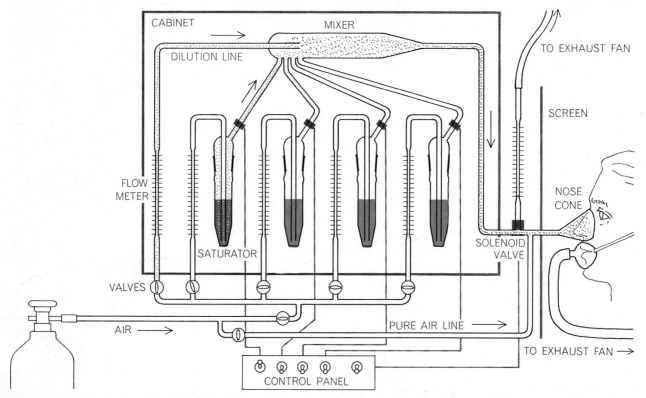

OLFACTOMETER developed by one of the authors (Johnston) mixes odors in precise proportions and delivers them to a nose cone for sampling. This schematic diagram shows the main elements. Air bubbles through a liquid in one of the saturators, picks up odorous molecules and is then diluted with pure air or mixed with air carrying other odors. The experimenter controls the solenoid valves.

the vapors of these five chemicals among many others by means of the olfactometer, did indeed pick out and identify all five as musky. By the odor test, however, they were often unable to distinguish these five quite different chemicals from one another.

Basically all this evidence in favor of the stereochemical theory was more or less indirect. One would like some sort of direct proof of the actual existence of differentiated receptor sites in the smelling organ. Recently R. C. Gesteland, then at the Massachusetts Institute of Technology, searched for such evidence. He devised a way to tap the electric impulses from single olfactory-nerve cells by means of microelectrodes. Applying his electrodes to the olfactory organ of the frog, Gesteland presented various odors to the organ and tapped the olfactory cells one by one to see if they responded with electric impulses. He found that different cells responded selectively to different odors, and his exploration indicated that the frog has about eight such different receptors. What is more, five of these receivers correspond closely to five of the odors (camphoraceous, musky, ethereal, pungent and putrid) identified as primary in the stereochemical theory! This finding, then, can be taken as a sixth and independent confirmation of the theory.

Equipped now with a tested basic theory to guide further research, we can hope for much faster progress in the science of osmics (smell) than has been possible heretofore. This may lead to unexpected benefits for mankind. For man the sense of smell may perhaps have become less essential as a life-and-death organ than it is for lower animals, but we still depend on this sense much more than we realize. One can gain some appreciation of the importance of smell to man by reflecting on how tasteless food becomes when the nose is blocked by a head cold and on how unpleasantly we are affected by a bad odor in drinking water or a closed room. Control of odor is fundamental in our large perfume, tobacco and deodorant industries. No doubt odor also affects our lives in many subtle ways of which we are not aware.

The accelerated research for which the way is now open should make it possible to analyze in fine detail the complex flavors in our food and drink, to get rid of obnoxious odors, to develop new fragrances and eventually to synthesize any odor we wish, whether to defeat pests or to delight the human nose.

CONSTANT-TEMPERATURE CABINET maintains the olfactometer parts at 77 degrees Fahrenheit. The photograph shows the interior of the cabinet, containing two units of the type diagramed on the opposite page. Several of the saturators are visible, as are two mixers (*horizontal glass vessels*), each of them connected by tubing to a nose cone at right.

17

Steroids

LOUIS F. FIESER

January 1955

The story of the steroids is one of the great epics of chemistry. Part of the story has come to public attention in the last few years as a result of the well-publicized struggle to synthesize the steroid hormone cortisone. But cortisone is only an episode in an enthralling history of research and discovery that has occupied more than half a century.

The steroids are a family of substances critically important to plant and animal life. They include the adrenal cortical hormones, the sex hormones, some of the vitamins, plant sterols such as ergosterol and animal sterols such as cholesterol. This array of substances, though so alike chemically that it is often difficult to tell them apart, exhibits a prodigious range of different activities.

The bile acids, for instance, aid digestion by emulsifying fats so that they can pass through the walls of the intestines. An interesting illustration of this function is that, if the normal flow of bile is obstructed by a tumor, the patient's blood does not absorb enough antihemorrhagic vitamin K_1 from his food, and an operation on such a patient is attended by the hazard that he may bleed to death unless he is given doses of the vitamin and bile salts to promote its absorption. A very different steroid function is illustrated by digitalis, a plant steroid obtained from foxglove, which stimulates the heart; still another example is a plant steroid alkaloid recently put on the market for treating high blood pressure. Certain other plant steroids rupture red blood cells and are therefore highly toxic to animals, even in extremely high dilutions. Yet many of these plant steroids, while capable of acting as powerful drugs in animals, seem to perform no direct function in the plants themselves.

Cholesterol presents a still more interesting question. This substance appears in nearly all the tissues of vertebrate animals; it is particularly abundant in the brain and spinal cord. The higher animals synthesize considerable amounts of cholesterol and have an efficient chemical mechanism for delivering it to the tissues by way of the blood. Hence it would be reasonable to suppose that cholesterol carries out some vital function. If any direct function exists, it has not yet been discovered—though cholesterol does seem to play a harmful role in hardening of the arteries. In the absence of evidence of any direct function, it has been assumed that cholesterol serves as a precursor for building the usable steroids.

Animals may obtain steroids by eating other animals, but not by eating plants, because plant sterols are not absorbed through the intestinal wall. However, an animal readily makes its own sterols. It is capable of rapidly synthesizing the complex cholesterol molecule even from simple compounds such as acetic acid.

A sterol is a white, solid, fatty sub-

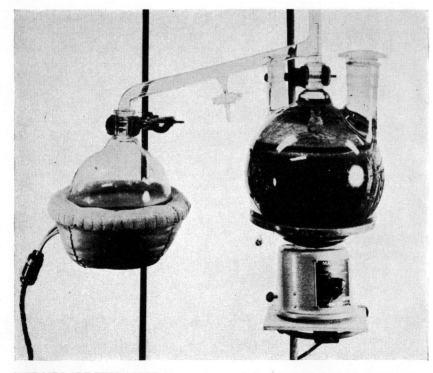

STEROIDS ARE EXTRACTED from a mixture of plant materials in the flask at the right. The flask at the left contains ether, in which steroids are soluble. When the flask at the left is heated, ether vapor rises in a distillation column above the flask at the right. As the ether condenses it flows through a tube to the bottom of the flask at the right and rises through the heavier plant material. It then fills the flask at the right and, bearing the steroids, overflows into the flask at the left. The cycle of extraction may be repeated for days.

stance—a crystalline alcohol—which can be extracted from animal or plant tissues by a process requiring several steps. First the tissues' lipids (fatty materials not soluble in water) are extracted by an oil solvent. This extract is then boiled with alkali, which splits some of the lipids into glycerol and soap The remaining "nonsaponifiable" lipids, which are principally sterols, are then captured by removal with an organic solvent. Cholesterol of about 98 per cent purity can be isolated with comparative ease from the brains or spinal cords of animals or from human gallstones, another rich source of the substance.

The subject of this article is the story of the achievement of chemists in elucidating the structure and shape of the various steroid molecules. The task presented a series of problems as baffling and complex as any encountered in the whole history of organic chemistry. Solution of the major problems came only after the concerted efforts of a large number of investigators working over a period of many years. The subject was so important and the achievements so brilliant that no fewer than six investigators in this field received Nobel prizes.

The Cholesterol Molecule

The father of sterol chemistry is Adolf Windaus of Germany, who, now 75 and retired, holds the admiration and affection of present workers in the field he pioneered. Beginning at the University of Freiburg in 1903, he devoted his career to sterol research. At the University of Göttingen he built up the world's leading school of sterol chemistry, and produced a succession of able students who, stimulated by his skill, enthusiasm and leadership, accounted for many of the discoveries and triumphs that followed his own.

Windaus started with cholesterol, partly because this substance had been isolated as early as 1770 and partly because it was the most easily obtainable of all the steroids. The formula of the cholesterol molecule is $C_{27}H_{46}O$. To understand the steroid problem it is necessary to picture the arrangement of this molecule and to review some of the fundamental concepts of organic chemistry. The cholesterol molecule is shown in the diagrams above, with the positions of its 27 carbon atoms numbered in the conventional way. (The numbering sequence is not entirely logical, because it was adopted at a time when the structure was not fully known.) Four rings of carbon atoms, plus a side chain branch-

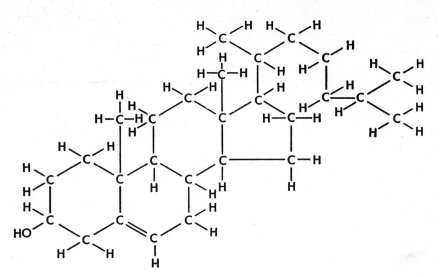

COMPLETE MOLECULAR STRUCTURE of cholesterol, a steroid abundant in the brain and spinal cord, consists of atoms of hydrogen (H), carbon (C) and oxygen (O). Seventeen of the 27 carbon atoms comprise the four rings that are characteristic of steroids.

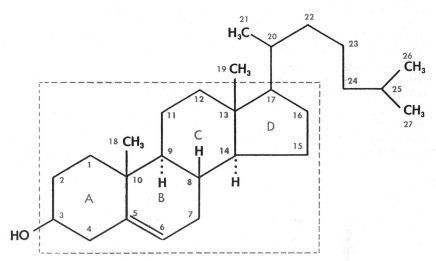

ABBREVIATED MOLECULAR STRUCTURE of cholesterol emphasizes its salient features. The four rings are labeled with letters and the 27 carbon atoms with numbers. The solid lines indicate bonds that project upward; the dotted lines, atoms projecting to rear.

ing from the fourth, form the skeleton of the molecule. One of the major complications of steroid research is that the same skeleton is present in a host of different sterols, which differ only in the way that hydrogen or oxygen atoms or groups of them are attached to the frame; indeed, there are many variants (isomers) of cholesterol with precisely the same total number of carbon, hydrogen and oxygen atoms.

In a carbon compound the four atoms or groups of atoms attached to each carbon atom are not in one plane but are angled from it in a three-dimensional arrangement; even in the simplest case, the methane molecule, they form a tetrahedral figure. Whenever the four atoms or groups attached to the four-valent carbon atom are all different, the mole-

cule can have two mirror-image forms, known as optical isomers. A good example is the existence of two forms of lactic acid (in milk and in muscle), which are identical in all properties except that one rotates plane-polarized light to the right and the other rotates it to exactly the same degree to the left [see models on page 161].

The cholesterol skeleton has eight centers of asymmetry where such variations may occur. As a result there are 256 possible optical isomers of this molecule.

Cholesterol itself has four groups of atoms projecting on the front side of the molecule (upward from the plane of the paper as it is diagrammed here) and two hydrogen atoms projecting to the rear. The array of projecting groups on the front side forms a canopy protecting the molecule on that side. Hence most of its chemical and biological reactions occur by attack from the rear.

Dismemberment of the Molecule

At the turn of the century Windaus attacked the problem of unraveling the then unknown cholesterol molecule by breaking it down with oxidizing reactions. He found that he could open the first two rings for exploration by oxidizing respectively the hydroxyl (OH) group in the first ring and the double bond in the second ring. He also discovered two methods of splitting the side chain attached to the fourth ring: first he split off the entire eight-carbon chain with one method of oxidation, and later he found a way to remove just the three-carbon fragment at the end of the chain [*see diagram below*].

The latter reaction left a molecule with a five-carbon acidic side chain. And here Windaus came to a common ground with Heinrich Wieland of Freiburg, who for several years had been investigating the structure of the bile acids of cattle. The two men discovered that the five-carbon side chain Windaus obtained when he split the end group from cholesterol was identical with the side chain of bile acid. The bile acids, indeed, proved to be like sterols in most respects, differing from the sterols with which Windaus had been working only in details of arrangement of functional groups in the various rings.

From this point on, Windaus' and Wieland's lines of research helped each other at every step forward. Although the road was hard and the going slow and uncertain, the two intrepid investigators held unwaveringly to their course. They indoctrinated a number of students

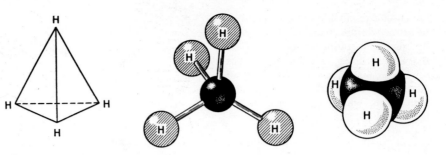

METHANE MOLECULE illustrates the fact that atoms attached to carbon project in three dimensions. The four hydrogen atoms of methane (CH_4) are arranged in a tetrahedron (*left*). The arrangement can be represented with pegs and balls (*center*) or with spheres made to conform to the known distances between the atoms of carbon and hydrogen (*right*).

in the new line of chemistry and made steady progress. By 1928 they were able to propose a tentative structural outline of the cholesterol molecule for which they jointly received the Nobel prize in chemistry.

Their formulation, as it turned out, was incorrect. The first indication that drastic revision was needed came from an unexpected source. Windaus and Wieland had supposed that the first three rings were clustered around a common carbon atom holding them together, which meant that the molecule should have a globular shape. But in 1932 the British physicist J. D. Bernal discovered by X-ray studies that the sterol molecule was long and thin. With this clue other English workers and Wieland himself were able by the end of the year to work out the correct structural formula.

Vitamins

By this time sterol chemistry had emerged from the realm of purely academic interest to a position of practical importance in medicine. It entered into medicine in connection with vitamin D,

the anti-rickets vitamin. It had been discovered that the active principle of this vitamin, found in fish-liver oils, was probably a steroid, and also that foods irradiated with sunlight could counteract a deficiency of the vitamin. The question arose: Would irradiation of an ordinary sterol convert it into an antirachitic steroid like the one in cod-liver oil?

Windaus and the Göttingen physicist R. Pohl attacked this problem with the help of ultraviolet spectroscopy, then just coming into use as a powerful tool for identifying molecular structures. They found that a substance present in minute amounts in some samples of cholesterol could be made active against rickets by irradiation, and that this activatable substance had an absorption spectrum very similar to that of ergosterol, a sterol in yeast. Windaus, and independently a research team at the National Institute for Medical Research in London, proceeded to isolate from irradiated ergosterol a new substance of high potency against rickets which was named vitamin D_2 [*see formulas on page 162*]. Irradiation of ergosterol effects a series of chemical changes yielding vari-

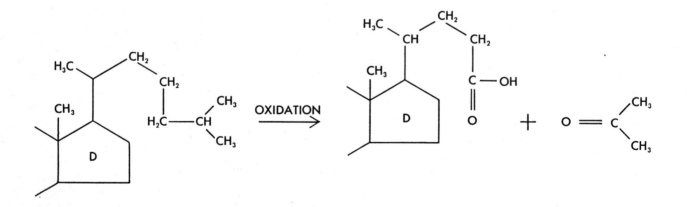

OXIDATION OF CHOLESTEROL provided much information about its structure. When cholesterol (*partly diagrammed at left*) was oxidized in one experiment, it yielded acetone (*right*) and a substance with an acid side chain of five carbon atoms (*center*).

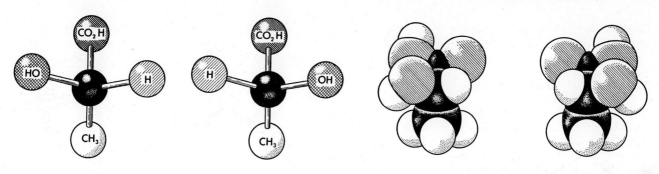

LACTIC ACID MOLECULES illustrate optical isomers. The peg-and-ball model at the left represents the molecule of lactic acid ($C_3H_6O_3$) as it is found in milk; the peg-and-ball model second from the left represents the molecule of lactic acid as it is found in muscle. The corresponding sphere models are third and fourth. The two molecules are chemically and physically identical except that one rotates plane-polarized light to the right and the other rotates it to the left. In short, the molecules are mirror images of each other.

ous isomers, of which only vitamin D_2 is active against rickets.

It seemed reasonable to suppose that D_2 was identical with the active principle in fish-liver oils, until Windaus and his associates showed that certain variants differing only slightly from D_2 were just about as potent. The most interesting variant was one prepared from cholesterol by a series of chemical operations which involved placing a double bond at the 7,8 position, as in ergosterol, and then irradiating this molecule (7-dehydrocholesterol). The product [*formula at lower right on next page*] had an antirachitic activity comparable in strength to that of D_2, as measured by bio-assay in rats. It was named vitamin D_3.

Was the natural vitamin in fish-liver oils more closely related to cholesterol than to ergosterol? This question, posed by Windaus' synthesis of D_3 and by biological investigations in the U. S., was brilliantly resolved in 1936 by Hans Brockmann of the Göttingen laboratory. By means of the sensitive method of chromatography, he isolated the vitamin of tuna-liver oil and proved that it was identical with Windaus' vitamin D_3.

Vitamins D_2, made from ergosterol, and D_3, made from cholesterol, have about the same activity against rickets in rats, but in chicks D_3 is far more potent. D_2 is still used for treating children with rickets, because it is easier to make and has satisfactory potency in human beings; however, for chickens, which are susceptible to rickets, D_3 is now manufactured in substantial quantities, both from cholesterol and from fish-oil concentrates.

The Sex Hormones

The road to chemical identification of the sex hormones was opened in 1927 when S. Aschheim and Bernhard Zondek, then in Berlin, discovered that the urine of pregnant women contained considerable amounts of a hormone which produced sexual heat when tested in mice or rats. Windaus was asked by a German chemical firm to explore this substance. Involved at the time in the vitamin D research, he elected to turn over the new problem to a promising young student named Adolf Butenandt. The student plunged into the task of iso-

lating the hormone with the help of a young biologist, Erika von Ziegner, who later became his wife. In the meantime Edward A. Doisy, of the St. Louis University School of Medicine, also set out to identify the active substance. Working independently, both Butenandt and Doisy succeeded in 1929 in isolating the first known sex hormone—estrone.

With keen insight Butenandt proceeded by a roundabout route to arrive at a shrewd guess concerning the chemical structure of estrone. In pregnancy urine there was found an inactive companion of estrone, called pregnanediol. Butenandt proved that pregnanediol was related to cholic acid, a component of bile, by breaking both down to a common product. Thus he showed that pregnanediol was a steroid. By further adroit experimentation he related its companion, estrone, to bile acid and then deduced the correct structure of estrone.

It developed that estrone was not the true estrogenic hormone secreted by the ovaries but a transformed product of it excreted in the urine. The actual hormone, first made from estrone and later isolated from sow ovaries by Doisy (who extracted 12 milligrams of the substance from four tons of ovaries), is believed to be estradiol [*see formulas at top of page 163*].

The discovery and analysis of the male sex hormone testosterone followed a similar pattern. In 1931 Butenandt and Kurt Tschering isolated from 15,000 liters of male urine 15 milligrams of a hormonal substance which they named androsterone. From this tiny pile of crystals, hardly enough to cover the tip of a small spatula, Butenandt derived a great deal of information about the nature of the molecule. He tentatively deduced its structure, and his deduction was independently proved correct by Leopold Ruzicka of Zurich, who produced androsterone by splitting off the eight-carbon side chain from a deriva-

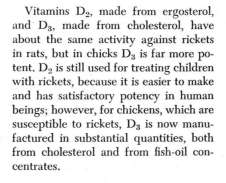

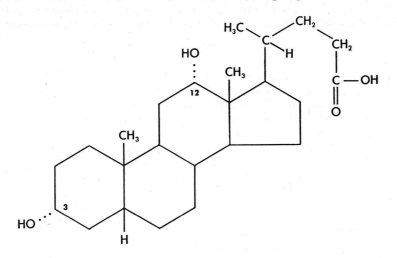

STRUCTURE OF CHOLIC ACID, found in the bile of cattle, includes the same side chain found in the oxidation product of cholesterol. The bile acids resemble steroids in other ways.

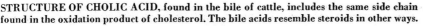

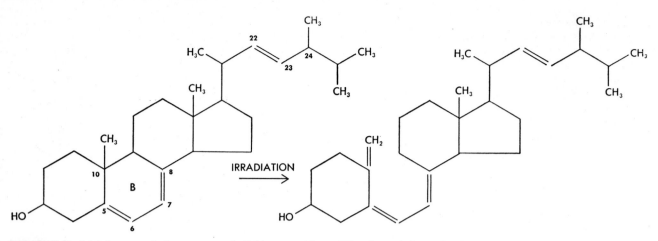

VITAMIN D₂ (*right*) was made from ergosterol (*left*), a steroid found in yeast, by exposing it to ultraviolet radiation. Ergosterol differs from cholesterol in having an extra methyl group (CH_3) at position 24 and double chemical bonds at positions 7, 8 and 22, 23.

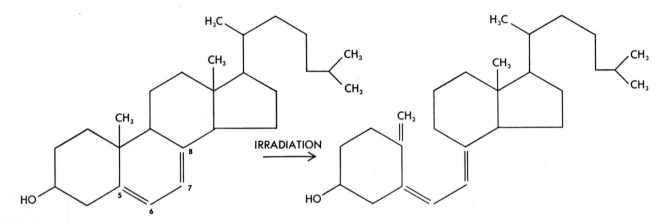

VITAMIN D₃ (*right*) was made from 7-dehydrocholesterol (*left*), also by exposing it to ultraviolet radiation. The 7-dehydro- cholesterol was prepared synthetically from cholesterol by a process adding a double chemical bond between positions 7 and 8.

tive of cholesterol through oxidation.

Androsterone was obtainable only in very small amounts, either by synthesis or by extraction from urine, but Butenandt, Ruzicka and others soon succeeded in synthesizing a related substance which could be produced in more plentiful yield. This substance, named dehydroepiandrosterone, was made from cholesterol by burning off the side chain while the essential hydroxyl group attached to the first ring and the double bond at the 5,6 position in the second ring were protected by stable chemical combinations at those positions. With the more plentiful working material at hand, the investigators were able to synthesize a number of interesting products, some of which proved more potent than androsterone in hormonal activity. Meanwhile Ernst Laqueur in Amsterdam reported that he had isolated from steer testes a potent hormone which he called testosterone. Butenandt and Ruzicka shortly afterward synthesized testosterone from dehydroepiandrosterone. It became clear that testosterone

was the true hormone; androsterone and dehydroepiandrosterone were metabolites of the hormone excreted in the urine [*formulas in center on opposite page*]. A practical method is now available for converting dehydroepiandrosterone into testosterone in 81 per cent yield.

In 1934 four research groups isolated from the corpus luteum tissue in sow ovaries the pregnancy hormone—progesterone. Butenandt obtained 20 milligrams of the hormone from the ovaries of 50,000 sows. The structure of progesterone, very similar to that of testosterone [*formulas at bottom of opposite page*], was soon inferred from its chemical properties and ultraviolet analysis. Butenandt promptly synthesized progesterone by two methods, one of which was the oxidation of a substance called pregnenolone, a by-product of the production of testosterone from cholesterol.

Hormones from Plants

At this dramatic point in the development of the chemistry of the sex hor-

mones, there came a break in another field which was to open a more fertile route for production of the hormones. The plant steroids had been relatively neglected, though Windaus and others had published occasional reports on them. After the establishment of the structure of cholesterol in 1932, however, the new surge of intensive research embraced active substances in plants as well as in animals. Attention was focused on the cardiac glycosides—extracts from plants which had been known for centuries as poisons. Particularly interesting was digitalis, the heart stimulant that had been used since 1785, when it was introduced as a treatment for dropsy. It was believed that a part of the active principle of this drug might be a steroid, and Windaus delegated the problem to one of his pupils, Rudolf Tschesche. At the Rockefeller Institute for Medical Research W. A. Jacobs and R. C. Elderfield also investigated the same question.

Within two years the two independent investigations established that steroids were indeed present in the active components of digitalis. The steroid here is attached to a sugar. Digitoxin, for example, contains a steroid of 24 carbon atoms to which is linked the rare sugar digitoxose (making the large molecule somewhat soluble in water). The steroid part has a skeleton like that of a bile acid, but one major difference is that the side chain is coiled into a ring [*see formula on next page*].

The digitalis steroids are rather special, but steroids with sugars attached are very common in the plant world. One class of these substances is known as the saponins, because water solutions of them foam like soap when shaken. The steroid part of a saponin is called a sapogenin. The structure of sapogenins, on which Windaus and his pupils and successors had worked for many years, was finally clarified by Russell E. Marker and his group at the Pennsylvania State College in an extraordinary series of studies between 1939 and 1947. The most interesting of these substances is diosgenin, which has a skeleton remarkably like that of cholesterol, with 27 carbon atoms and a double bond between the fifth and sixth carbons [*see formula, bottom of page 165*]. The discovery of this structure at once suggested that diosgenin would be useful for producing sex hormones, for which more and more uses had been found in medical therapy.

The possibility of manufacturing the hormones from plant extracts excited Marker. Production of these hormones from animal sources was still difficult and expensive, in spite of new methods of synthesis that had been discovered by various investigators. Diosgenin was abundantly available from yams (plants of the genus *Dioscorea*), and Marker in field trips to the southern U. S. and Mexico had found many other plant sapogenins (which he whimsically named for current friends and enemies: rockogenin for the late Dean Frank "Rocky" Whitmore of Pennsylvania State College, kammogenin for Oliver Kamm of Parke Davis & Company, nologenin for Carl R. Noller of Stanford University, fesogenin for the writer of this article).

Marker showed that diosgenin could easily be converted into pregnenolone, already known as a building material for progesterone. A Mexican firm named Syntex was set up to manufacture progesterone from Mexican yams. Before long Marker fell out with the management of the company and was replaced by Georg Rosenkranz, a young Hungarian-born chemist who had trained

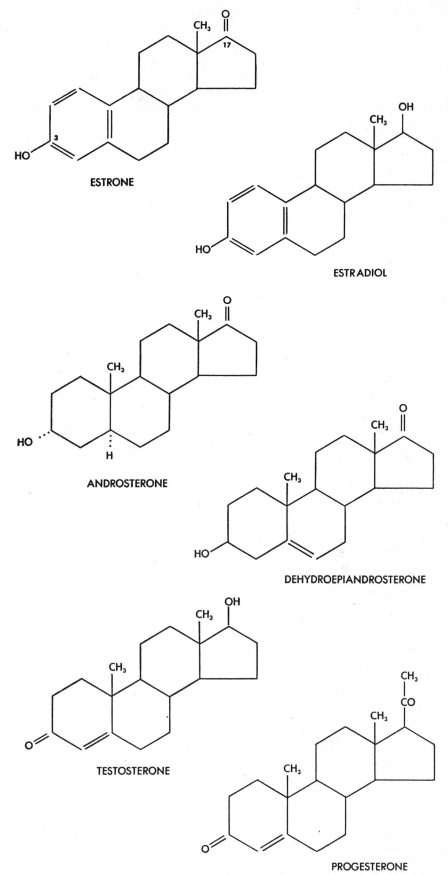

ESTRONE

ESTRADIOL

ANDROSTERONE

DEHYDROEPIANDROSTERONE

TESTOSTERONE

PROGESTERONE

SEX HORMONES share the steroid configuration. Estrone is a female hormone. Estradiol is a variant of it with higher potency. Androsterone, dehydroepiandrosterone and testosterone are male hormones. Progesterone is the female hormone found in pregnant women.

with Ruzicka in Zurich. Since Marker had not disclosed some of the essential bits of know-how to his associates, Rosenkranz had to work out the process anew. He succeeded in rediscovering the missing links, developed a system of chemical manufacture based on the training of unschooled young women to perform specific operations, and soon achieved production of progesterone on a scale surpassing previous performance. He also found a way to produce testosterone, as well as progesterone, from pregnenolone.

Rosenkranz recruited an able research staff of Mexican and foreign chemists, and he brought in as his lieutenant Carl Djerassi, a young chemist born in Bulgaria and trained at the University of Wisconsin. A first fruit of the pioneering research instituted by Rosenkranz and Djerassi was a new process for production of estrone, which involved conversion of the male hormone testosterone into the female hormone estradiol.

Cortisone

The story of the adrenal cortical hormones is so well known that I need not go into it at length here [see "Cortisone and ACTH," by George W. Gray; this is available as Offprint #14]. Ever since the most active of these substances, now known as cortisone, was isolated in the laboratory of E. C. Kendall at the Mayo Clinic in 1936, the key problem in its synthesis has been to find some nonlaborious way to place an oxygen

atom at the comparatively inaccessible 11 position in the third ring [see formula on page 166]. Several workable solutions are now at hand, but for close to a decade the armies of researchers who attacked the problem found it completely baffling.

In 1942 vague rumors (now known to be unfounded) that the Luftwaffe was employing adrenal cortical hormones to improve pilots' endurance and resistance to blackout prompted the National Research Council to contract with several laboratories for research on the synthesis of Compound E (cortisone). The first objective was to introduce oxygen at position 11. Desoxycholic acid from bile seemed the best starting material for this purpose, because it carries a hydroxyl group at position 12, offering the possibility that the oxygen atom might be transposed to the neighboring 11 position. A practicable method of effecting the transposition, involving some amazing new chemistry, was devised by Kendall and his group. This made feasible production of Kendall's Compound A, which contains oxygen at position 11 but does not have Compound E's added feature of a hydroxyl group at position 17. But when, after considerable effort and expense, Merck & Company produced a quantity of Compound A by this method, the substance proved completely useless in clinical tests.

Meanwhile Lewis H. Sarett, a young Princeton-trained chemist at Merck, devised a method of introducing oxygen at position 17 and succeeded in synthesizing cortisone. After more than two

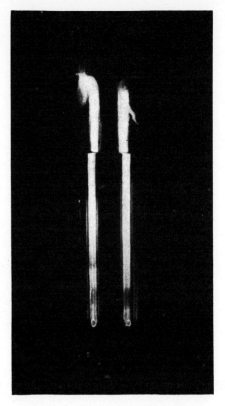

IRRADIATION of steroids is accomplished in vessel containing two ultraviolet lamps.

years of further research and chemical labor, Merck produced enough cortisone for medical trial. The result was the now classical investigation of Kendall and Philip S. Hench at the Mayo Clinic which produced dramatic relief of patients with rheumatoid arthritis.

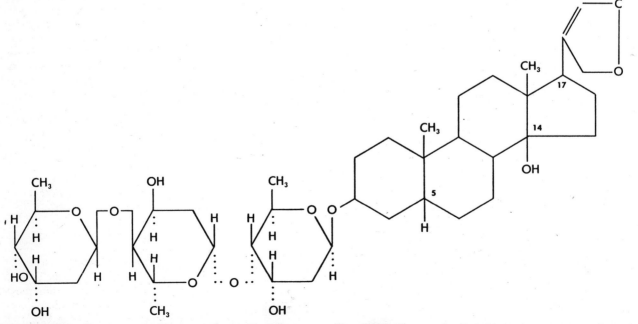

DIGITOXIN, a plant extract used in the treatment of heart disease, consists of a sugar (left) and a steroid (right). The steroid resembles a bile acid except that the side chain is a ring, and the carbon atom at position 14 bears an OH group and is differently oriented.

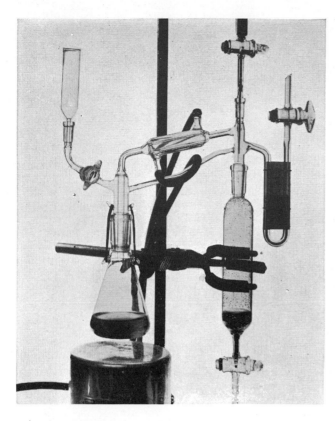

HYDROGENATION of a steroid in the vessel at left measures the number of double bonds, which take up hydrogen, in the molecule.

EXTRACTION of steroids in cranberry skins is accomplished in this apparatus. The skins are in the round vessels at upper right.

Although the yield of cortisone from animal bile was pitifully small, Merck at once undertook plant-scale production. The task was without precedent in modern chemical technology. The process, starting with bile acid and ending with pure cortisone, involved 32 separate steps. Max Tishler and his development group at Merck performed miracles of chemical technology, first to produce cortisone at all, and then to introduce a succession of improvements which reduced the price from $200 per gram to less than $20 per gram.

But the demand for cortisone increased and the supply of available bile began to run out. Consequently a problem already brilliantly solved had to be attacked again from some new angle. How synthesize cortisone from something other than a bile acid? Workers in the field grasped at a substance called sarmentogenin, which had been isolated in 1929 from some unknown plant seed. This molecule carries a hydroxyl group at the mystical position 11, and presumably it could be converted into cortisone without great difficulty. Expeditions to South Africa in search of sarmentogenin went out from the Swiss laboratory of Tadeus Reichstein, a leader in cortisone research, from the U. S. Public Health Service, from the National Institute of Medical Research in London, from the Merck laboratory. A plant source of sarmentogenin was found, and Reichstein recently reported its conversion to cortisone, but interest in it has diminished because of the emergence of more promising approaches.

Several groups sought a route to cortisone from the abundantly available natural sterols, particularly cholesterol, ergosterol and diosgenin. From these substances Windaus had produced certain compounds with double bonds at the 7,8 and 9,11 position. In retrospect it seems that it should have been easy to

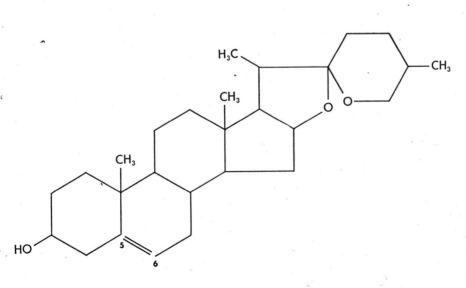

DIOSGENIN is also found in plants. Because the skeleton of its molecule is the same as that of cholesterol, it is uniquely useful for the synthetic production of animal hormones.

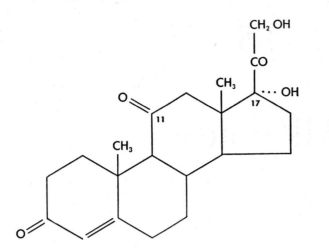

CORTISONE also has the steroid skeleton. It is characterized by the double-bonded oxygen atom attached at position 11 and by the OH group projecting to the rear at position 17.

make use of the double bond to attach an oxygen to the 11 position, but many chemists worked on the problem for two years before, in May, 1951, it suddenly broke. Within a few months success in attachment of oxygen at position 11 by various processes starting with Windaus' compounds was reported by five research teams—the writer's at Harvard University and groups at Merck, Syntex, Zurich and Glasgow.

In the same year Robert B. Woodward and his associates at Harvard made a break-through toward total synthesis of cortisone from simple materials. Woodward synthesized a steroid, the first ever manufactured outside a living organism, with a double bond at the 9,11 position. Then he carried the synthesis three steps further to form a type of molecule which,

as it happened, my associates S. Rajagopalan and Hans Heymann had already succeeded in endowing with an oxygen at the 11 position. From there it did not take long to achieve total synthesis of cortisone. A year later Sarett and his group at Merck reported another total synthesis, beautiful and efficient, which extends all the way from simple starting materials to synthetic cortisone identical in every respect with the natural hormone isolated from the adrenal gland.

But all these approaches yield at present to new processes which have enlisted microorganisms to do the critical work of placing oxygen at position 11. The Upjohn Company was the first to announce discovery of a specific fungus that converts steroids into 11-ketosteroids (oxygenated at the 11 position).

Then Syntex and E. R. Squibb & Sons found other microorganisms capable of the same performance.

The six chemists who received Nobel awards for their work in steroid research were Windaus, Wieland, Ruzicka, Butenandt, Kendall and Reichstein. Their efforts and those of the great army of their fellow workers, only a few of whom could be mentioned in this brief review, have cleared up the chemistry of practically all the known steroid hormones and vitamins.

An important unsolved problem is the function of cholesterol in the animal body. If cholesterol is the essential building material for the bile acids, steroid hormones and vitamin D_3, why does the body produce huge amounts of the precursor to make only trace amounts of the final products? Is cholesterol perhaps just an incidental by-product of the manufacture of the hormones and vitamins? There are some indications that cholesterol or a derivative of it may be involved in degenerative diseases. Cholesterol is found deposited along the walls of blood vessels in victims of hardening of the arteries and of atherosclerosis. Several recent reports suggest that a high level of cholesterol or of a cholesterol-protein complex in the blood may lead to this type of disease. Other lines of experimentation have suggested the possibility that under certain circumstances cholesterol or a companion substance may initiate cancerous growth.

It seems reasonable to hope that advances in the field of preventive medicine may emerge in the next chapter of steroid research.

18

Alkaloids

TREVOR ROBINSON

July 1959

The alkaloids are a class of compounds that are synthesized by plants and are distinguished by the fact that many of them have powerful effects on the physiology of animals. Since earliest times they have served man as medicines, poisons and the stuff that dreams are made of.

The alkaloid morphine, the principal extract of the opium poppy, remains even today "the one indispensable drug." It has also had an illicit and largely clandestine history in arts and letters, politics and crime. Quinine, from cinchona bark, cures or alleviates malaria; colchicine, from the seeds and roots of the meadow saffron, banishes the pangs of gout; reserpine, from snake root, tranquilizes the anxieties of the neurotic and psychotic. The coca-leaf alkaloid cocaine, like morphine, plays Jekyll and Hyde as a useful drug and sinister narcotic. In tubocurarine, the South American arrow poison, physicians have found a powerful muscle relaxant; atropine, said to have been a favorite among medieval poisoners, is now used to dilate the pupils of the eyes and (in minute doses!) to relieve intestinal spasms; physostigmine, employed by West African tribes in trials by ordeal, has come into use as a specific for the muscular disease myasthenia gravis. Aconitine is catalogued as too toxic to use except in ineffective doses. On the other hand, caffeine and nicotine, the most familiar of all alkaloids, are imbibed and inhaled daily by a substantial fraction of the human species.

Our self-centered view of the world leads us to expect that the alkaloids must play some comparably significant role in the plants that make them. It comes as something of a surprise, therefore, to discover that many of them have no identifiable function whatever. By and large they seem to be incidental or accidental products of the metabolism of plant tissues. But this conclusion somehow fails to satisfy our anthropocentric concern. The pharmacological potency of alkaloids keeps us asking: What are they doing in plants, anyway? Investigators have found that a few alkaloids actually function in the life processes of certain plants. But this research has served principally to illuminate the subtlety of such processes.

The pharmacology of alkaloids has inspired parallel inquiry in organic chemistry. Some of the greatest figures in the field first exercised their talents on these substances. But nothing in the composition of alkaloids has been found to give them unity or identity as a group. The family name, conferred in an earlier time, literally means "alkali-like." Many alkaloids are indeed mildly alkaline and form salts with acids. Yet some perfectly respectable alkaloids, such as ricinine (found in the castor bean), have no alkaline properties at all. Alkaloids are often described as having complex structures. The unraveling of the intricate molecules of strychnine and morphine has taught us much about chemical architecture in general. Yet coniine, the alkaloid poison in the draught of hemlock that killed Socrates, has a quite simple structure. Nor is there much distinction in the characterization of alkaloids as "nitrogen-containing compounds found in plants." Proteins and the amino acids from which they are made also fit this definition.

From the chemical point of view it begins to seem that alkaloids are in a class of compounds only because we do not know enough about them to file them under any other heading. Consider the vitamin nicotinamide, the plant hormone indoleacetonitrile and the animal hormone serotonin. All these compounds occur in plants, and all contain nitrogen. We would call them alkaloids except that we have learned to classify them in more descriptive ways. As we come to know the alkaloids better, we may select other substances from this formless group and assign them to more significantly defined categories.

Though all alkaloids come from plants, not all plants produce alkaloids. Some plant families are entirely innocent of them. Every species of the poppy family, on the other hand, produces alkaloids; the opium poppy alone yields some 20 of them. The Solanaceae present a mixed picture: tobacco and deadly nightshade contain quantities of alkaloids; eggplant, almost none; the potato accumulates alkaloids in its foliage and fruits but not in its tubers. Some structurally interrelated alkaloids, such as the morphine group, occur only in plants of a single family. Nicotine, by contrast, is found not only in tobacco but in many quite unrelated plants, including the primitive horsetails. Alkaloids are often said to be uncommon in fungi, yet the ergot fungus produces alkaloids, and we might classify penicillin as an alkaloid had we not decided to call it an antibiotic. However, alkaloids do seem to be somewhat commoner among higher plants than among primitive ones.

Some 50 years ago the Swiss chemist Amé Pictet suggested that alkaloids in plants, like urea and uric acid in animals, are simply wastes—end products of the metabolism of nitrogenous compounds. But the nitrogen economy of most plants is such that they husband the element, reprocessing nitrogenous compounds of all sorts, including substances such as ammonia which are poisonous to animals. Indeed, many plants have evolved elaborate symbiotic arrangements with bacteria to secure additional nitrogen from the air. From the evolutionary standpoint the tying-up of valuable nitrogen in alkaloids seems an inefficient arrangement.

More recently investigators have come to regard alkaloids not as end products but as by-products thrown off at various points along metabolic pathways, much as substandard parts are rejected on an assembly line. That is to say, alkaloids arise when certain substances in the plant cell cross signals and make an alkaloid instead of their normal product. This idea is certainly plausible when it is applied to the alkaloids formed by the action of the commonest enzymes on the commonest metabolites. The alkaloid trigonelline, for example, is found not only in many plant seeds but also in some species of sea urchins and jellyfish. It is merely nicotinic acid with a methyl group (CH_3) added to it. Now nicotinic acid is one of the commonest components of plant cells. Compounds that can donate methyl groups are also common, as are the enzymes that catalyze such donations. A "confused" enzyme, transferring a methyl group to nicotinic acid instead of to some other substance, could thus form trigonelline by mistake [see illustration at top of page 172]. Nicotine, which has an equally wide distribution, may likewise be produced by everyday biochemical processes.

The more frequent occurrence of alkaloids in higher plants suggests another idea. More highly evolved organisms have obviously made more experiments in metabolism. Some alkaloids may represent experiments that never quite worked. Others may have originated as intermediates in once-useful processes that are no longer carried to completion. Since most alkaloids seem neither to help nor to hurt the plant, natural selection has not operated for or against them. Thus the modern plant that produces alkaloids may do so for no other reason than the persistent pattern of its genes.

Such explanations for the presence of alkaloids in plant tissues find support in what we know about the synthesis of these substances. In 1917 the noted British chemist Sir Robert Robinson showed that the structures of scores of alkaloid molecules could be built up from amino acids by postulating reactions of a few simple types: dehydration, oxidation and so on. For example, he showed that the amino acid tyrosine could easily be transformed into the alkaloid hordenine. Even the complex molecule of reserpine could be built up,

according to his scheme, from tyrosine and the amino acid tryptophan, plus a methylene group [see illustrations on page 171]. More recently Robert B. Woodward of Harvard University has proposed that the same three substances, through another series of reactions, may yield the extremely complex molecule of strychnine.

During the past 40 years considerable experimental evidence has accumulated to show that these reactions are not just paper-and-pencil chemistry, but actually occur in nature. Robinson himself correctly predicted the structures of several highly complex alkaloids before these structures were worked out. Later experimenters have shown that enzyme-containing plant extracts can promote amino acid-alkaloid transformations such as the tyrosine-hordenine synthesis. Other investigators, by simply mixing together the postulated precursors of certain alkaloids, have obtained compounds of approximately the correct structure even in the absence of enzymes. Tracer experiments have furnished additional support for Robinson's scheme. If labeled amino acids are injected into alkaloid-producing plants, the plants produce labeled alkaloids. Moreover, the alkaloids contain labeled atoms at just the points that theory predicts.

We know, however, that many steps intervene between the introduction of a labeled precursor and the production of a labeled alkaloid. Moreover, a compound that yields an alkaloid when it is injected in high concentration may not be the normal precursor. Some intermediates go to form all sorts of things, and may only get to alkaloids by quite devious routes. The problem of alkaloid biosynthesis resolves itself into the task of establishing the point at which the alkaloid-producing process diverges from the other metabolic processes of the plant. In principle we might feed various labeled compounds to a plant and ascertain whether the labeled material shows up only in alkaloids or in other substances as well. But we must decide which intermediate compounds we are going to feed. It is fruitless to test a versatile intermediate like glucose, which enters into many processes. In a sense, therefore, we must know our intermediate before conducting the experiment that will identify it. One way of breaking out of this impasse may be to work backward by feeding the alkaloid itself to the plant. By building up high concentrations of alkaloid in the plant's tissues we can perhaps block the alkaloid "production line" and thus cause the im-

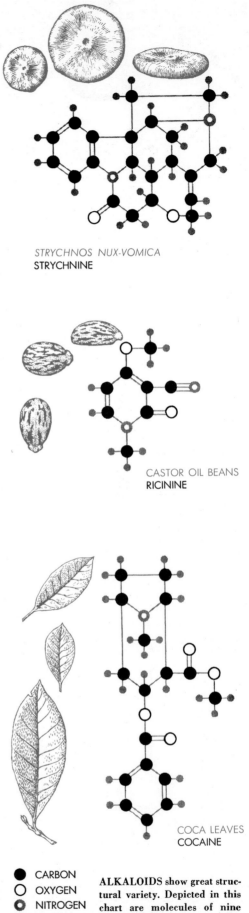

STRYCHNOS NUX-VOMICA
STRYCHNINE

CASTOR OIL BEANS
RICININE

COCA LEAVES
COCAINE

● CARBON
○ OXYGEN
◎ NITROGEN
✳ HYDROGEN

ALKALOIDS show great structural variety. Depicted in this chart are molecules of nine typical alkaloids together with

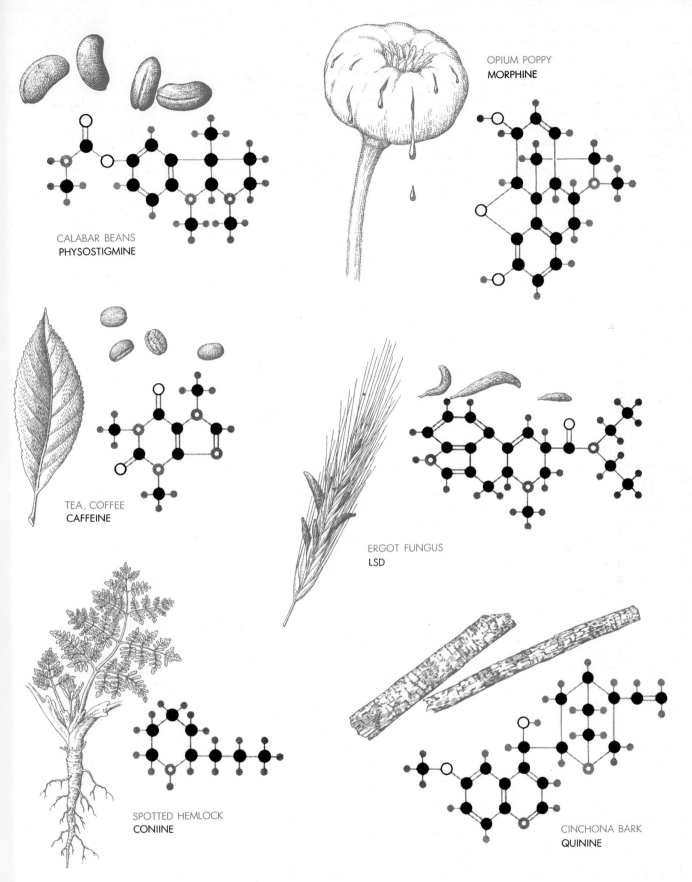

CALABAR BEANS
PHYSOSTIGMINE

OPIUM POPPY
MORPHINE

TEA, COFFEE
CAFFEINE

ERGOT FUNGUS
LSD

SPOTTED HEMLOCK
CONIINE

CINCHONA BARK
QUININE

the plants or plant substances from which they derive. At left is the key to these diagrams and those elsewhere in this article. Strychnine, a violent poison, is one of the most complex alkaloids; coniine, the poison which killed Socrates, one of the simplest. Physostigmine, a West African "ordeal poison," is now used to treat the muscular disease myasthenia gravis; LSD (lysergic acid diethylamide) produces delusions resembling those of schizophrenia. Ricinine is one of the few alkaloids that exert little effect on human beings.

mediate precursors of the alkaloid to accumulate to the point where they can be identified.

With this information in hand, we can go on to inquire which enzymes transform these precursors into alkaloids and whether these enzymes function only in alkaloid formation or in other metabolic processes as well. If we find, for example, that a certain enzyme catalyzes the transfer of a methyl group to an alkaloid precursor but does not function in other methylations, we will have to regard this alkaloid synthesis as a definitely programmed process, and not as a mere aberration. Our present sparse knowledge strongly suggests that at least some alkaloids are programmed. Thus ricinine contains a nitrile group (CN), which rarely occurs in living organisms. If the formation of this group is catalyzed by an enzyme that normally does some other job, we have no indication of what the other job might be. From intimate understanding of this kind we may yet help the plant physiologist to discover what there is about different plants that causes one to make reserpine, while another makes strychnine from the same starting materials.

Of course the study of any metabolic process involves not only the synthesis but also the breakdown of the substances involved. If a given alkaloid is just a waste product or by-product, it has no future and there is no breakdown to be considered. In this case it may simply accumulate in the plant's tissues. For example, quinine piles up in the bark of the cinchona tree, and nicotine in the leaves of the tobacco plant. Some ingenious grafting experiments have furnished additional evidence that many alkaloids, once synthesized, become inert and play no further role in the plant's metabolism. The tobacco plant, for example, manufactures nicotine in its roots, whence the alkaloid migrates to the leaves. However, if we graft the top of a tobacco plant to the roots of a tomato plant, which produces no nicotine, the tobacco flourishes despite the absence of the alkaloid. Conversely, a tomato top grafted to a tobacco root becomes impregnated with nicotine with no apparent ill effects.

But the alkaloids in plants are not always inactive. Hordenine, for example, is found in high concentrations in young barley plants, and gradually disappears as the plant matures. By the use of tracers Arlen W. Frank and Leo Marion of the National Research Council of Canada have found that the disappearing hordenine is converted into lignin,

GRAFTING EXPERIMENT indicates that nicotine has no effect on plants. Tobacco plant (*top left*) produces nicotine (*color*) in its roots; the alkaloid then migrates to the leaves. Tomato plant (*top right*) produces no nicotine. A tomato top grafted to a tobacco root (*bottom left*) becomes impregnated with nicotine with no apparent ill effects; tobacco top grafted to tomato root (*bottom right*) is unaffected by the absence of alkaloid. Similar grafting experiments with other alkaloid-producing plants have with few exceptions yielded similar results.

the "plastic" that binds the cellulose fibers in the structure of plants. To be sure, not all plants employ hordenine as an intermediate in making lignin [see "Lignin," by F. F. Nord and Walter J. Schubert; SCIENTIFIC AMERICAN, October, 1958]. But it is gratifying to find at least one case in which an alkaloid performs an identifiable function. Similarly, Edward Leete of the University of Minnesota has shown that in some plants nicotine serves as a "carrier" for methyl groups which it ultimately donates to other molecules.

Such modest findings are a far cry from the first grand-scale function assigned to alkaloids a century ago by the great German chemist Justus von Liebig. Since most alkaloids are alkaline, he proposed that plants use them to neu-

tralize deleterious organic acids by forming salts with them. Many alkaloids do, in fact, occur in plants as salts of organic acids. But no one could explain why alkaloid-producing plants should elaborate poisonous acids when closely related plants manage to get along without either the acids or their metabolic antagonists. The question "Why?" still persists. Today it stimulates more modest but sometimes quite intriguing proposals.

Some experiments by the French physiologist Clément Jacquiot suggest a variant of Liebig's neutralization theory. Jacquiot has shown that the tannin produced in cultures of oak cells inhibits cell growth. The alkaloid caffeine counteracts the effects of the tannin and allows growth to proceed. Unfortunately

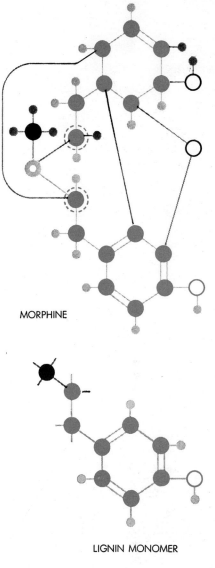

MORPHINE

TYROSINE

HORDENINE

LIGNIN MONOMER

TRYPTOPHAN

RESERPINE (PART)

AMINO ACIDS appear to be the source of most alkaloids. Thus the skeleton (*color*) of tyrosine, an amino acid, can be easily transformed into hordenine, an alkaloid; broken circles indicate the "labeled" atoms which confirm the synthesis. Two tyrosine skeletons similarly form morphine, as shown at right; the morphine molecule shown here is distorted (*see diagram on page 169*) to emphasize its derivation. Tyrosine and tryptophan, another amino acid, could join with a methylene group (*broken square*) to form part of the molecule of reserpine, an alkaloid tranquilizer. Hordenine is one of the few alkaloids known to undergo further metabolism in plants; it is converted into one of the units that form the long-chain molecules of lignin, an essential structural material in many plants. The complete structure of the lignin monomer is not known.

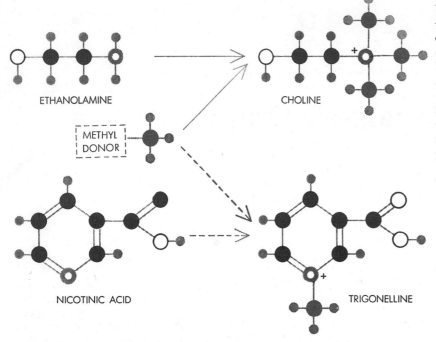

ETHANOLAMINE

METHYL DONOR

NICOTINIC ACID

CHOLINE

TRIGONELLINE

METABOLIC ACCIDENTS may account for the synthesis of some alkaloids. Changing one compound to another by adding methyl groups (*color*), as in the ethanolamine-choline transformation, is a common biochemical process. If a methyl group were added "by mistake" to nicotinic acid, a common plant substance, the alkaloid trigonelline would result.

More recently the concept of chelation, the process by which certain organic molecules "sequester" the atoms of metals, has suggested another possible alkaloid function. The structures of some alkaloids should permit them to act as chelating agents. The structure of nicotine is temptingly similar to that of dipyridyl, a common chelating agent for iron [see *illustration at bottom of this page*]. Such alkaloids might help a plant select one metal from the soil and reject others. Alternatively, they might facilitate the transport of the metal from the roots, where it is absorbed, to the leaves, where it is utilized. Quite a few alkaloids, including nicotine, migrate from roots to leaves, but no one has yet determined whether any of them carry metals along with them.

The structures of many alkaloids resemble those of hormones, vitamins and other metabolically active substances. This resemblance suggests that such alkaloids may function as growth regulators. In a way this hypothesis fits in with the chelation theory, since certain important growth regulators seem to owe their activity to their chelating capacity. Some alkaloids do affect growth processes: Alkaloids from the seeds of certain lupines can inhibit the germination of seeds of related species that produce no alkaloids. Presumably they help the former species to compete successfully with the latter. Similar alkaloids may function as "chemical rain gauges" which prevent germination until sufficient rain has fallen to leach them away and provide adequate moisture for plant growth. Many plants in arid and semiarid environments depend on such rain gauges for survival [see "Germination," by Dov Koller, which is available as Offprint #117].

this suggestion merely replaces one question with another, since the function of tannins in plants is itself unknown. The suggestion has another flaw in that oak cells produce no caffeine of their own. But here, at any rate, is one case in which caffeine is good for something other than providing a pleasant stimulant for coffee-drinkers.

Botanists and ecologists have speculated that the bitter taste of some alkaloids may discourage animals from eating a plant that contains them, and that poisonous alkaloids may kill off pathogenic organisms that attack the plant. One species of wild tomato does produce an alkaloid that protects it against Fusarium wilt, a common fungus disease of the cultivated tomato. However, the "protection" idea must be handled with caution because of its anthropocentric bias. What is unpalatable or poisonous to a man may be tasty and nourishing to a rabbit or a cutworm.

No one theory can account for the functions of so heterogeneous a group of compounds. The steroid compounds, a much smaller and structurally a far more homogeneous group, play a wide variety of physiological roles. Future research will probably reveal an even greater functional diversity among the alkaloids. Certainly we must learn a good deal more about the functions of a few alkaloids before we can safely propose generalizations about all of them.

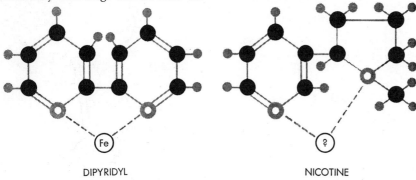

DIPYRIDYL

NICOTINE

STRUCTURE OF NICOTINE resembles that of dipyridyl, a compound that can "chelate" or bind atoms of iron. This similarity suggests that nicotine, and perhaps other alkaloids, may function as chelating agents in some plants. Whether they actually do so is not yet known.

19

Analgesic Drugs

MARSHALL GATES

November 1966

Early man, omnivorous and inquisitive, had discovered the use of opium by the time of the earliest written records. Babylonian and Egyptian writings contain many references to the value of opium preparations for the relief of pain. Hippocrates, Dioscorides, Galen and other early physicians formed a regard amounting to veneration for opium's almost miraculous power to "lull all pain and anger and bring relief to every sorrow." With the progress of medicine the respect of physicians for the drug increased. Thomas Sydenham, the 17th-century pioneer of English medicine, wrote: "Among the remedies which it has pleased Almighty God to give to man to relieve his sufferings, none is so universal and so efficacious as opium." Today, although opium is clearly no longer regarded as a universal remedy,

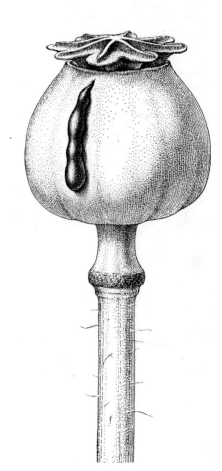

OPIUM POPPY (*Papaver somniferum*) is the source of morphine. The technique of obtaining the raw opium is to make a cut in the unripe seed capsule of the plant (*enlarged drawing at right*). The rubbery exudate that oozes from the cut is then collected and dried.

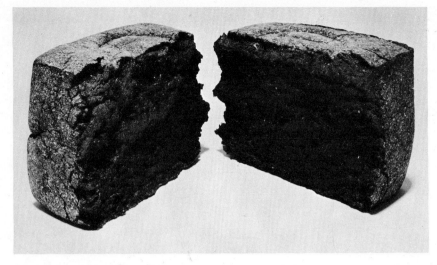

RAW OPIUM contains some 20 alkaloid substances, one of which is morphine. A typical yield of morphine from opium is 10 percent. The drug was first isolated from opium in 1805.

laudanum (an opium preparation) while he was a student at Oxford. Opiate addiction is too vast a subject to be discussed in detail here. For our purposes it is enough to note that prolonged use of an opiate generally leads to a physiological and psychological dependence on the drug, and this dependence is shown by the onset of highly unpleasant and sometimes dangerous symptoms when use of the drug is stopped. In addition to the opiates' addicting property, they have a depressing effect on respiration. It is no wonder, then, that in this century chemists and clinical investigators have conducted a tireless and expensive search for an analgesic that would be as potent as morphine but free of its dangerous effects.

its active principle, morphine, is still the drug that is most commonly prescribed by physicians for the relief of severe pain.

The defects of the drug have long been well known. The ancients could scarcely have been unaware of the addicting property of opium; it appears, however, that Thomas De Quincey's *Confessions of an English Opium Eater*, published in a magazine in 1821, was the first detailed description of opiate addiction. De Quincey was a brilliant man of letters who developed an addiction to

Opium is obtained from the opium poppy (*Papaver somniferum*) by scarifying the unripe seed capsule and collecting and drying the exudate. The dried material, pressed into bricks, is the opium of commerce. The substance is a complex mixture containing at least 20 alkaloids. Morphine, which constitutes about 10 percent of opium and is primarily responsible for its physiological effects, was first isolated in 1805 by Friedrich Sertürner, an apothecary's assistant in Paderborn, Germany. The isolation of this alkaloid was the beginning of alkaloid chemistry, which has yielded many important medicinal substances, including (to cite a recent example) the tranquilizing and blood-pressure-reducing drug reserpine, extracted from the Indian snakeroot (*Rauwolfia serpentina*).

Morphine itself became an object of increasingly intensive study. The unraveling of its structure is a fascinating story. The difficulty involved in the work is apparent from the fact that the correct basic structure of the alkaloid was not suggested until 120 years after the isolation of the drug. The workers who ascertained the structure in 1925 were John M. Gulland and Robert Robinson, then at the University of Manchester. Even at that time the subtleties of morphine's three-dimensional structure were largely unresolved.

The chemical investigations of morphine made available a number of substances closely related to it structurally. Many of them—including codeine (also occurring in opium), heroin, Dilaudid and Bentley's compound—were physiologically active [see illustration on opposite page]. Bentley's compound, recently prepared by the British chemist K. W. Bentley, is of particular interest. In tests on small animals it has proved to be 10,000 times more potent than

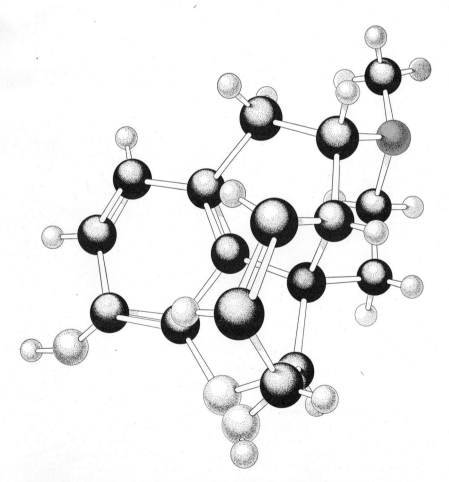

THREE-DIMENSIONAL MODEL of the morphine molecule shows the characteristic structure of the drug. The black balls in the model are carbon atoms, the dark-colored ball is a nitrogen atom, the light-colored balls are oxygens and the gray balls are hydrogens.

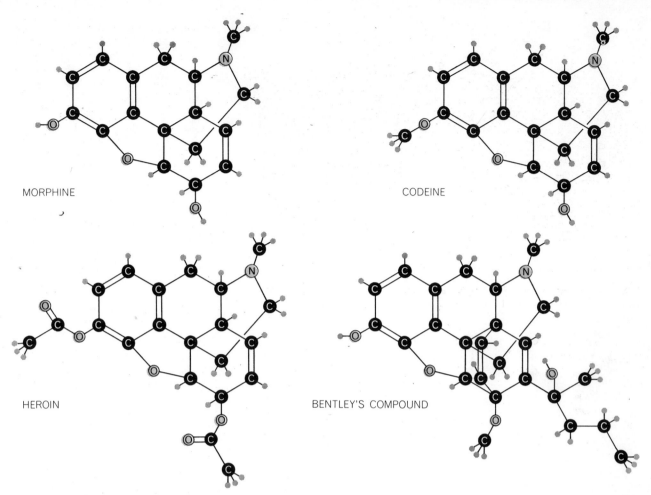

MORPHINE

CODEINE

HEROIN

BENTLEY'S COMPOUND

CHEMICAL STRUCTURES of morphine and several of its close relatives are markedly similar. Codeine, heroin and Bentley's com- pound were produced by altering the structure of morphine. In these two-dimensional diagrams the hydrogens are small gray dots.

morphine, and some of Bentley's preparations have been used to subdue elephants on African game preserves at doses of one milligram per elephant! Unfortunately the Bentley compounds have disappointed early hopes that they might, at analgesic doses, produce less respiratory depression than morphine, and they have also given evidence that they are dangerously addicting.

Of the many fragments or synthetic assemblies of fragments of the morphine molecule that have been studied, only a few have shown a significant degree of analgesic activity [*see top and middle illustrations on next page*]. And in these compounds, whose structure is sometimes only vaguely related to that of morphine, addiction liability seems to parallel analgesic activity. Only the substances with very mild analgesic activity are nonaddicting.

What general principles might be drawn from these analytic studies? In 1955 Nathan B. Eddy of the National Institutes of Health, examining the experimental results, attempted to iden- tify the structural features that might account for the analgesic activity of a drug of the morphine type. The most active drugs, he noted, all seemed to be characterized by (1) the presence of a tertiary or trisubstituted amine with a small group attached to the nitrogen atom, (2) a central carbon atom, none of whose valences was occupied by a hydrogen atom, (3) a phenyl or closely analogous group attached to the central carbon atom and (4) separation of the tertiary or trisubstituted amino group from the central carbon atom by an intervening string of two carbon atoms. Events later showed that this categorical description missed the mark. Since 1955 it has been found that all four of these criteria can be violated without destroying analgesic activity.

Although a satisfactory theory of analgesic structure or action still eludes us, experimenters have developed a number of useful synthetic analgesics related to the morphine model. The oldest and perhaps the best-known is pethidine (also called meperidine, Demerol and by some 40 other names). It was synthesized in 1939 by Otto Eisleb of Germany. Less potent than morphine, pethidine is widely used for the relief of postoperative pain and in obstetrics. It was acclaimed originally as a nonaddicting drug but was soon found to have dangerous addiction liability—a constantly recurring theme in the field of analgesic drugs. (Even heroin was originally introduced as a nonaddicting substitute for morphine.) Analgesics related to pethidine have since been prepared in great variety and in widely varying potency; pethidine itself, however, remains the most widely used of these substances.

Another family of synthetic analgesics, less closely related to morphine, is the one based on methadone, which b... recently as a relati... tute for heroin i... management of ... recently develo... of the Nation... the group of ... morphans. ... this group ...

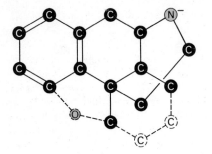

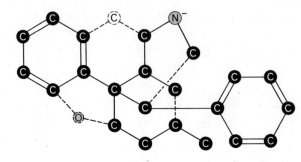

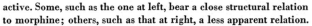

STRUCTURAL ALTERATIONS of the morphine molecule have produced several fragments that have proved to be analgesically active. Some, such as the one at left, bear a close structural relation to morphine; others, such as that at right, a less apparent relation.

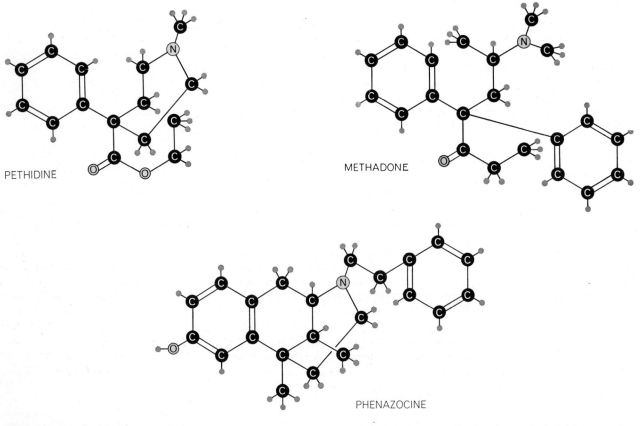

PETHIDINE

METHADONE

PHENAZOCINE

SYNTHETIC ANALGESICS have been developed by various experimenters. Pethidine, the oldest, most closely resembles the structure of morphine. Methadone is less like morphine structurally. Phenazocine, a recent development, is the best-known member of a group of substances called benzomorphans. Phenazocine is more effective than morphine against pain but is highly addicting.

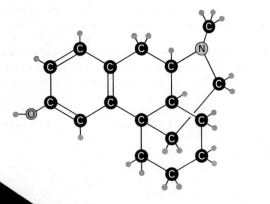

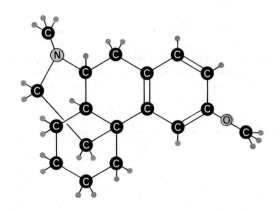

IMAGE MOLECULES proved to have notably different ...nthetic drug levorphan (*left*), with a morphine-like ...potent than morphine against pain and also is strongly addicting. Dextrorphan (*right*), the right-handed form of the molecule, is neither analgesic nor addicting. The difference indicates the importance of molecular geometry in analgesic activity.

times more potent than morphine as an analgesic and possesses some other advantages, but like morphine it is dangerously addicting.

That analgesic activity depends quite specifically on molecular geometry is strikingly illustrated by the synthetic drug levorphan, a member of the group called the morphinans, which are closely akin to morphine in structure [*see bottom illustration on opposite page*]. Levorphan is several times more potent than morphine and is strongly addicting. Curiously the mirror image of this molecule (that is, the dextrorotatory, or right-handed, form) has no analgesic activity or addiction liability. (Slightly modified by the substitution of a methyl ether group for the hydroxyl group in the molecule, the dextrorotatory form has been found to be a useful cough-suppressing drug without narcotic properties and seems likely to supplant codeine for that purpose.) The geometric specificity exhibited by levorphan has been demonstrated to apply also to morphine, whose molecule is levorotatory. There is no mirror image of morphine in nature, but the Japanese chemist Kakuji Goto has synthesized a dextrorotatory counterpart of the molecule, using a method developed in my laboratory at the University of Rochester, and found that the mirror form possesses none of morphine's properties.

I have cited only a few representative examples of the synthetic analgesics; there are now a great number of them. Many have certain advantages over morphine, but none has supplanted morphine as the mainstay of physicians for the control of severe pain. The continued preference for morphine stems in part from the confidence developed from long experience with the drug; fundamentally, however, the fact remains that there is not yet available a fully satisfactory substitute that avoids morphine's principal shortcomings. Indeed, the properties of analgesic activity, addiction liability and depression of respiration seem to go together, and until recently there appeared to be no hope of separating one of these properties from another.

We now come to a most interesting development in the story. Its beginning actually goes back to a rather old discovery. Nearly 50 years ago Julius Pohl of the University of Breslau reported he had prepared a substance that suppressed the respiratory depression produced by morphine. The substance was a modification of codeine: in place of the methyl group (CH_3) attached to the nitrogen atom in codeine he substituted the unsaturated allyl group ($CH_2CH{=}CH_2$), forming a compound called N-allyl-nor-codeine. This drug, administered to an experimental animal that had received a narcotic dose of morphine, reversed morphine's respiration-depressing effect.

The significance of Pohl's finding was overlooked at the time, and it lay largely unnoticed for 27 years. In 1942 John Weijlard and A. E. Erickson at the laboratories of Merck & Co. took up this old lead and performed the same operation on the morphine molecule itself, substituting the allyl group for the methyl group. Their product, nalorphine, proved to be capable of counteracting most of the physiological effects of morphine. It not only reversed the respiratory depression but also acted as an antidote for acute morphine poisoning, and when administered to a narcotics addict it rapidly precipitated a severe withdrawal syndrome. In addition, screening tests on small animals indicated that nalorphine, in contrast to morphine, had no analgesic effect.

A surprising finding emerged, however, when nalorphine was administered to human patients. In 1954 Henry K. Beecher and Louis Lasagna conducted an experiment to examine the possibility that nalorphine, given with morphine, might reduce morphine's respiratory depression without weakening its analgesic activity. At the Massachusetts General Hospital they gave one group of patients both morphine and nalorphine and gave a control group only nalorphine. Unexpectedly nalorphine alone proved to be as effective in relieving pain in the control group as the combination of morphine and nalorphine was in the test group. This finding was quickly confirmed in experiments by Arthur S. Keats and Jane R. Telford of the Baylor University Medical School. Harris Isbell at the Addiction Research Center of the National Institute of Mental Health then proceeded to demonstrate by further tests with human subjects that nalorphine is not addicting in man.

For the first time analgesia had been divorced from addiction liability. The new drug, however, produced hallucinations when given at analgesic doses. Perhaps for this reason it did not immediately precipitate the rash of new investigations that might have been expected to follow so promising a lead. For some time only Keats and his group at Baylor actively pursued the study of nalorphine and related morphine antagonists.

In 1958 Sydney Archer and his coworkers at the Sterling-Winthrop Institute for Therapeutic Research undertook to seek nonaddicting analgesics among morphine antagonists structurally related to the benzomorphans (represented by phenazocine). Their attack was based on the supposition that the D'Amour-Smith rat-tail-flick test, one of the most widely used means of determining the analgesic effectiveness of drugs in animals, was at least as good a test for addiction liability as for analgesic activity. Therefore they reasoned that any substance active in the test should be discarded. In the test an intense beam of light is used as the pain stimulus. Normally when the light is focused on a rat's tail the animal quickly flicks its tail out of the beam; this reaction is delayed, however, if the rat has been given an analgesic drug. The test has been found to give a good measure of a drug's analgesic potency. Moreover, the results of this test on rats usually correlate well with the clinical effectiveness of a drug in man (although they failed to do so in the case of nalorphine).

From the benzomorphans Archer and his group succeeded in preparing a number of derivatives that combine analgesic activity with some degree of antagonism to morphine. Among these products is cyclazocine, an extremely interesting substance that is one of the most potent morphine antagonists discovered so far [*see illustration on next page*].

In January, 1959, our laboratory independently began a search for a nonaddicting drug among the morphine antagonists. We thought it might be possible, by modifying the allyl group in the nalorphine molecule, to transform it into a more acceptable analgesic, although perhaps somewhat less active as an antagonist of addicting drugs. As a replacement for the allyl group we chose the cyclopropylmethyl group, which is well known to affect the chemical and physical properties of a substance in much the same way as the allyl group (and which is the distinguishing feature of cyclazocine). Thomas Montzka, a graduate student working in our laboratory, prepared a number of cyclopropylmethyl derivatives of morphine-type drugs, and these substances were screened in small animals for us by Louis S. Harris, then at the Sterling-Winthrop Institute, and by Charles A.

STRUCTURE	NAME	RELATIVE ACTIVITY
	NALORPHINE	1.00
	LEVALLORPHAN	2.6
	NALOXONE	18
	CYCLAZOCINE	28
	PENTAZOCINE	1/30
	N-CYCLOPROPYLMETHYL-NOR DIHYDROMORPHINONE	10
	CYCLORPHAN	4
	N-CYCLOPROPYLMETHYL-NOR MORPHINE	3

ANTAGONISTS TO MORPHINE suppress the addicting effects of the drug without imped-
ing its analgesic effects. Indeed, several of them have analgesic properties in addition to
their counteraction against morphine, as shown in the column headed "Relative activity."

Winter of the Merck Institute for Therapeutic Research.

The new series of substances proved
to be highly active antagonists of morphine and pethidine. We selected one,
which we call cyclorphan, for further
study. It is a considerably more potent
morphine antagonist than nalorphine
and appears to have pharmacological
properties quite similar to those of
cyclazocine.

Both cyclazocine and cyclorphan
have been found to be capable, at very
low doses, of precipitating the withdrawal syndrome in monkeys that have
been addicted to narcotics and also in
human addicts. This capability can be
taken as good evidence that the drugs
will not produce addiction in man. William R. Martin, who has studied the
addiction liability of cyclazocine with
subjects at the Addiction Research Center of the National Institute of Mental
Health, reports that it generates a mild,
typical dependence that does not seem
very likely to lead to serious consequences.

Cyclazocine and cyclorphan have also
been examined clinically, cyclazocine
extensively, cyclorphan in preliminary
fashion. Both drugs have been found to
be potent analgesics, perhaps 30 to 50
times more potent than morphine on a
weight basis. Both, however, produce
hallucinations, much less commonly
than nalorphine does but still frequently enough to raise some question as
to their acceptability as drugs for general use.

Perhaps the most promising of the
new analgesics discovered so far is pentazocine, one of the morphine antagonists prepared from the benzomorphans
by workers at the Sterling-Winthrop Institute. Although it is only weakly an-
tagonistic to morphine, pentazocine has
been shown in exhaustive clinical tests
to be devoid of addiction liability. Yet
it is as effective as morphine in controlling postoperative pain, labor pains,
the pains of terminal cancer, cardiac
pain and traumatic pains. Thus pentazocine is the first really potent analgesic that has proved in practice to be
nonaddicting. It does, however, produce
respiratory depression, and so it cannot
be said to be the last word.

What can be said with reasonable
confidence is that, in view of the recent
demonstrations that analgesic potency
can be separated from addiction liability, it seems not too much to hope that
we shall soon have an ideal analgesic:
effective, free of side effects such as
respiratory depression and hallucinogenic activity—and nonaddicting.

20

The Hallucinogenic Drugs

FRANK BARRON, MURRAY E. JARVIK, AND STERLING BUNNEL, JR.

April 1964

Human beings have two powerful needs that are at odds with each other: to keep things the same, and to have something new happen. We like to feel secure, yet at times we like to be surprised. Too much predictability leads to monotony, but too little may lead to anxiety. To establish a balance between continuity and change is a task facing all organisms, individual and social, human and nonhuman.

Keeping things predictable is generally considered one of the functions of the ego. When a person perceives accurately, thinks clearly, plans wisely and acts appropriately—and represses maladaptive thoughts and emotions—we say that his ego is strong. But the strong ego is also inventive, open to many perceptions that at first may be disorganizing. Research on the personality traits of highly creative individuals has shown that they are particularly alert to the challenge of the contradictory and the unpredictable, and that they may even court the irrational in their own make-up as a source of new and unexpected insight. Indeed, through all recorded history and everywhere in the world men have gone to considerable lengths to seek unpredictability by disrupting the functioning of the ego. A change of scene, a change of heart, a change of mind: these are the popular prescriptions for getting out of a rut.

Among the common ways of changing "mind" must be reckoned the use of intoxicating substances. Alcohol has quite won the day for this purpose in the U.S. and much of the rest of the world. Consumed at a moderate rate and in sensible quantities, it can serve simultaneously as a euphoriant and tranquilizing agent before it finally dulls the faculties and puts one to sleep. In properly disposed individuals it may dissolve sexual inhibitions, relieve fear and anxiety, or stimulate meditation on the meaning of life. In spite of its costliness to individual and social health when it is used immoderately, alcohol retains its rank as first among the substances used by mankind to change mental experience. Its closest rivals in popularity are opium and its derivatives and various preparations of cannabis, such as hashish and marijuana.

This article deals with another group of such consciousness-altering substances: the "hallucinogens." The most important of these are mescaline, which comes from the peyote cactus *Lophophora williamsii;* psilocybin and psilocin, from such mushrooms as *Psilocybe mexicana* and *Stropharia cubensis;* and d-lysergic acid diethylamide (LSD), which is derived from ergot (*Claviceps purpurea*), a fungus that grows on rye and wheat. All are alkaloids more or less related to one another in chemical structure.

Various names have been applied to this class of substances. They produce distinctive changes in perception that are sometimes referred to as hallucinations, although usually the person under the influence of the drug can distinguish his visions from reality, and even when they seem quite compelling he is able to attribute them to the action of the drug. If, therefore, the term "hallucination" is reserved for perceptions that the perceiver himself firmly believes indicate the existence of a corresponding object or event, but for which other observers can find no objective basis, then the "hallucinogens" only rarely produce hallucinations. There are several other names for this class of drugs. They have been called "psychotomimetic" because in some cases the effects seem to mimic psychosis [see "Experimental Psychoses," by Six Staff Members of the Boston Psychopathic Hospital; SCIENTIFIC AMERICAN, June, 1955]. Some observers prefer to use the term "psychedelic" to suggest that unsuspected capacities of the imagination are sometimes revealed in the perceptual changes.

The hallucinogens are currently a subject of intense debate and concern in medical and psychological circles. At issue is the degree of danger they present to the psychological health of the person who uses them. This has become an important question because of a rapidly increasing interest in the drugs among laymen. The recent controversy at Harvard University, stemming at first from methodological disagreements

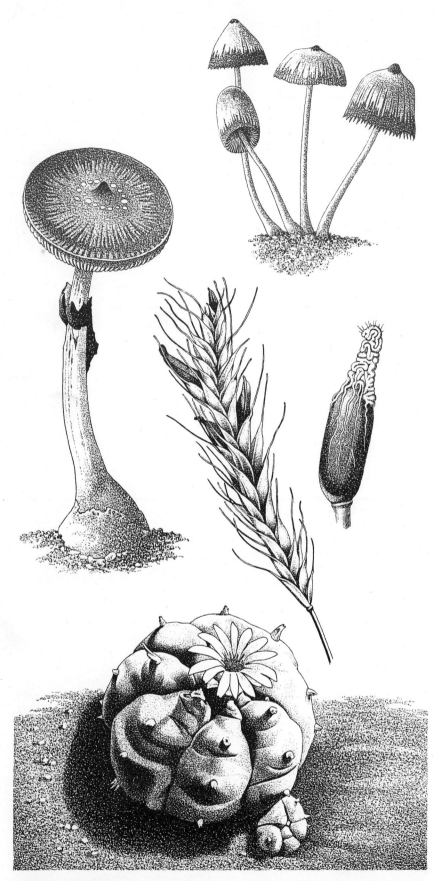

among investigators but subsequently involving the issue of protection of the mental health of the student body, indicated the scope of popular interest in taking the drugs and the consequent public concern over their possible misuse.

There are, on the other hand, constructive uses of the drugs. In spite of obvious differences between the "model psychoses" produced by these drugs and naturally occurring psychoses, there are enough similarities to warrant intensive investigation along these lines. The drugs also provide the only link, however tenuous, between human psychoses and aberrant behavior in animals, in which physiological mechanisms can be studied more readily than in man. Beyond this many therapists feel that there is a specialized role for the hallucinogens in the treatment of psychoneuroses. Other investigators are struck by the possibility of using the drugs to facilitate meditation and aesthetic discrimination and to stimulate the imagination. These possibilities, taken in conjunction with the known hazards, are the bases for the current professional concern and controversy.

In evaluating potential uses and misuses of the hallucinogens, one can draw on a considerable body of knowledge from such disciplines as anthropology, pharmacology, biochemistry, psychology and psychiatry.

In some primitive societies the plants from which the major hallucinogens are derived have been known for millenniums and have been utilized for divination, curing, communion with supernatural powers and meditation to improve self-understanding or social unity; they have also served such mundane purposes as allaying hunger and relieving discomfort or boredom. In the Western Hemisphere the ingestion of hallucinogenic plants in pre-Columbian times was limited to a zone extending from what is now the southwestern U.S. to the northwestern basin of the Amazon. Among the Aztecs there were professional diviners who achieved inspiration by eating either peyote, hallucinogenic mushrooms (which the Aztecs called *teo-nanacatyl*, or "god's flesh") or other hallucinogenic plants. *Teo-nanacatyl* was said to have been distributed at the coronation of Montezuma to make the ceremony seem more spectacular. In the years following the conquest of Mexico there were reports of communal mushroom rites among the Aztecs and other Indians of southern Mexico. The communal use has almost died out today, but in several

NATURAL SOURCES of the main hallucinogens are depicted. Psilocybin comes from the mushrooms *Stropharia cubensis* (*top left*) and *Psilocybe mexicana* (*top right*). LSD is synthesized from an alkaloid in ergot (*Claviceps purpurea*), a fungus that grows on cereal grains; an ergot-infested rye seed head is shown (*center*) together with a larger-scale drawing of the ergot fungus. Mescaline is from the peyote cactus *Lophophora williamsii* (*bottom*).

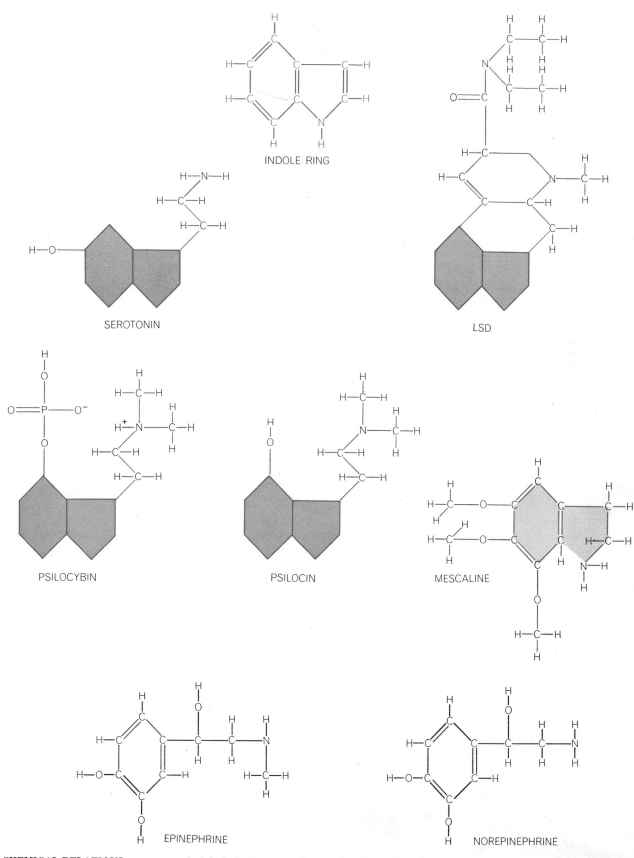

INDOLE RING

SEROTONIN

LSD

PSILOCYBIN

PSILOCIN

MESCALINE

EPINEPHRINE

NOREPINEPHRINE

CHEMICAL RELATIONS among several of the hallucinogens and neurohumors are indicated by these structural diagrams. The indole ring (*in color at top*) is a basic structural unit; it appears, as indicated by the colored shapes, in serotonin, LSD, psilocybin and psilocin. Mescaline does not have an indole ring but, as shown by the light color, can be represented so as to suggest its relation to the ring. The close relation between mescaline and the two catechol amines epinephrine and norepinephrine is also apparent here.

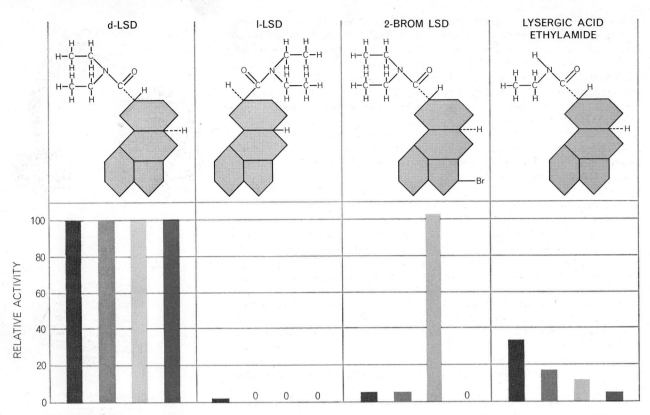

SLIGHT CHANGES in LSD molecule produce large changes in its properties. Here LSD (*left*) is used as a standard, with a "relative activity" of 100 in toxicity (*dark gray bar*), fever-producing effect (*light gray*), ability to antagonize serotonin (*light color*) and typical psychotomimetic effects (*dark color*). The stereoisomer of LSD (*second from left*) in which the positions of the side chains are reversed, shows almost no activity; the substitution of a bromine atom (*third from left*) reduces the psychotomimetic effect but not the serotonin antagonism; the removal of one of the two ethyl groups (*right*) sharply reduces activity in each of the areas.

tribes the medicine men or women (*curanderos*) still partake of *Psilocybe* and *Stropharia* in their rituals.

In the arid region between the Rio Grande and central Mexico, where the peyote cactus grows, the dried tops of the plants ("peyote buttons") were eaten by Indian shamans, or medicine men, and figured in tribal rituals. During the 19th century the Mescalero Apaches acquired the plant and developed a peyote rite. The peyotism of the Mescaleros (whence the name mescaline) spread to the Comanches and Kiowas, who transformed it into a religion with a doctrine and ethic as well as ritual. Peyotism, which spread rapidly through the Plains tribes, became fused with Christianity. Today its adherents worship God as the great spirit who controls the universe and put some of his power into peyote, and Jesus as the man who gave the plant to the Indians in a time of need. Saturday-night meetings, usually held in a traditional tepee, begin with the eating of the sacramental peyote; then the night is spent in prayer, ritual singing and introspective contemplation, and in the morning there is a communion breakfast of corn, game and fruit.

Recognizing the need for an effective organization to protect their form of worship, several peyote churches joined in 1918 to form the Native American Church, which now has about 225,000 members in tribes from Nevada to the East Coast and from the Mexican border to Saskatchewan. It preaches brotherly love, care of the family, self-reliance and abstinence from alcohol. The church has been able to defeat attempts, chiefly by the missionaries of other churches, to outlaw peyote by Federal legislation, and it has recently brought about the repeal of antipeyote legislation in several states.

The hallucinogens began to attract scholarly interest in the last decade of the 19th century, when the investigations and conceptions of such men as Francis Galton, J. M. Charcot, Sigmund Freud and William James introduced a new spirit of serious inquiry into such subjects as hallucination, mystical experience and other "paranormal" psychic phenomena. Havelock Ellis and the psychiatrist Silas Weir Mitchell wrote accounts of the subjective effects of peyote, or Anhalonium, as it was then called. Such essays in turn stimulated

the interest of pharmacologists. The active principle of peyote, the alkaloid called mescaline, was isolated in 1896; in 1919 it was recognized that the molecular structure of mescaline was related to the structure of the adrenal hormone epinephrine.

This was an important turning point, because the interest in the hallucinogens as a possible key to naturally occurring psychoses is based on the chemical relations between the drugs and the neurohumors: substances that chemically transmit impulses across synapses between two neurons, or nerve cells, or between a neuron and an effector such as a muscle cell. Acetylcholine and the catechol amines epinephrine and norepinephrine have been shown to act in this manner in the peripheral nervous system of vertebrates; serotonin has the same effect in some invertebrates. It is frequently assumed that these substances also act as neurohumors in the central nervous system; at least they are present there, and injecting them into various parts of the brain seems to affect nervous activity.

The structural resemblance of mescaline and epinephrine suggested a possible link between the drug and mental illness: Might the early, excited stage of schizophrenia be produced or at least triggered by an error in metabolism that produced a mescaline-like substance? Techniques for gathering evidence on this question were not available, however, and the speculation on an "M-substance" did not lead to serious experimental work.

When LSD was discovered in 1943, its extraordinary potency again aroused interest in the possibility of finding a natural chemical activator of the schizophrenic process. The M-substance hypothesis was revived on the basis of reports that hallucinogenic effects were produced by adrenochrome and other breakdown products of epinephrine, and the hypothesis appeared to be strengthened by the isolation from human urine of some close analogues of hallucinogens. Adrenochrome has not, however, been detected in significant amounts in the human body, and it seems unlikely that the analogues could be produced in sufficient quantity to effect mental changes.

The relation between LSD and serotonin has given rise to the hypothesis that schizophrenia is caused by an imbalance in the metabolism of serotonin, with excitement and hallucinations resulting from an excess of serotonin in certain regions of the brain, and depressive and catatonic states resulting from a deficiency of serotonin. The idea arose in part from the observation that in some laboratory physiological preparations LSD acts rather like serotonin but in other preparations it is a powerful antagonist of serotonin; thus LSD might facilitate or block some neurohumoral action of serotonin in the brain.

The broad objection to the serotonin theory of schizophrenia is that it requires an oversimplified view of the disease's pattern of symptoms. Moreover, many congeners, or close analogues, of LSD, such as 2-brom lysergic acid, are equally effective or more effective antagonists of serotonin without being significantly active psychologically in man. This does not disprove the hypothesis, however. In man 2-brom LSD blocks the mental effects of a subsequent dose of LSD, and in the heart of a clam it blocks the action of both LSD and serotonin. Perhaps there are "keyholes" at the sites where neurohumors act; in the case of those for serotonin it may be that LSD fits the hole and opens the lock, whereas the psychologically inactive analogues merely occupy the keyhole, blocking the action of serotonin or LSD without mimicking their effects. Certainly the re-

semblance of most of the hallucinogens to serotonin is marked, and the correlations between chemical structure and pharmacological action deserve intensive investigation. The serotonin theory of schizophrenia is far from proved, but there is strong evidence for an organic factor of some kind in the disease; it may yet turn out to involve either a specific neurohumor or an imbalance among several neurohumors.

The ingestion of LSD, mescaline or psilocybin can produce a wide range of subjective and objective effects. The subjective effects apparently depend on at least three kinds of variable: the properties and potency of the drug itself; the basic personality traits and current mood of the person ingesting it, and the social and psychological context, including the meaning to the individual of his act in taking the drug and his interpretation of the motives of those who made it available. The discussion of subjective effects that follows is compiled from many different accounts of the drug experience; it should be considered an inventory of possible effects rather than a description of a typical episode.

One subjective experience that is frequently reported is a change in visual perception. When the eyes are open, the perception of light and space is affected: colors become more vivid and seem to glow; the space between objects becomes more apparent, as though space itself had become "real," and surface details appear to be more sharply defined. Many people feel a new awareness of the physical beauty of the world, particularly of visual harmonies, colors, the play of light and the exquisiteness of detail.

The visual effects are even more striking when the eyes are closed. A constantly changing display appears, its content ranging from abstract forms to dramatic scenes involving imagined people or animals, sometimes in exotic lands or ancient times. Different individuals have recalled seeing wavy lines, cobweb or chessboard designs, gratings, mosaics, carpets, floral designs, gems, windmills, mausoleums, landscapes, "arabesques spiraling into eternity," statuesque men of the past, chariots, sequences of dramatic action, the face of Buddha, the face of Christ, the Crucifixion, "the mythical dwelling places of the gods," the immensity and blackness of space. After taking peyote Silas Weir Mitchell wrote: "To give the faintest idea of the perfectly satisfying intensity and purity of these gorgeous color fruits

WATER COLORS were done, while under the influence of a relatively large dose of a hallucinogenic drug, by a person with no art training. Originals are bright yellow, purple, green and red as well as black.

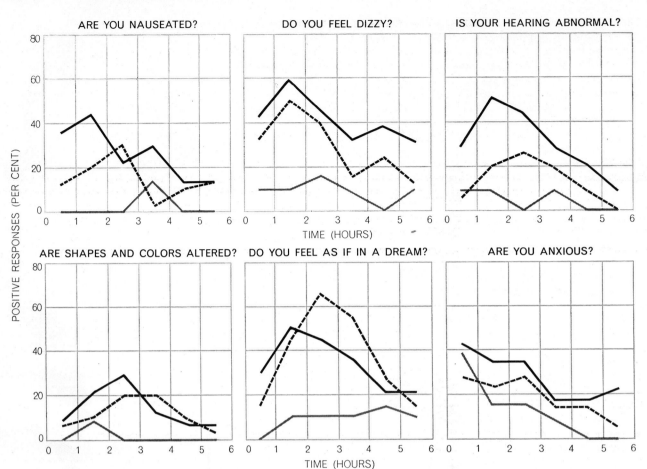

ARE YOU NAUSEATED? DO YOU FEEL DIZZY? IS YOUR HEARING ABNORMAL?

ARE SHAPES AND COLORS ALTERED? DO YOU FEEL AS IF IN A DREAM? ARE YOU ANXIOUS?

POSITIVE RESPONSES (PER CENT)

TIME (HOURS)

SUBJECTIVE REPORT on physiological and perceptual effects of LSD was obtained by means of a questionnaire containing 47 items, the results for six of which are presented. Volunteers were questioned at one-hour intervals beginning half an hour after they took the drug. The curves show the per cent of the group giving positive answers at each time. The gray curves are for those given an inactive substance, the broken black curves for between 25 and 75 micrograms and the solid black curves for between 100 and 225.

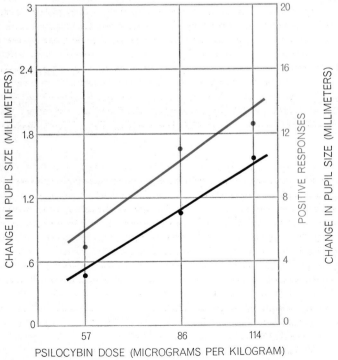

CHANGE IN PUPIL SIZE (MILLIMETERS)

POSITIVE RESPONSES

PSILOCYBIN DOSE (MICROGRAMS PER KILOGRAM)

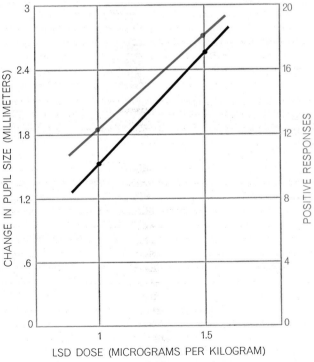

CHANGE IN PUPIL SIZE (MILLIMETERS)

POSITIVE RESPONSES

LSD DOSE (MICROGRAMS PER KILOGRAM)

OBJECTIVE AND SUBJECTIVE effects vary with dosage as shown here. The data plotted in black are for the increase in size of pupil; the number of positive responses to questions like the ones at the top of the page are shown in color. The objective and subjective measures vary in a similar manner. The data are from an experiment done by Harris Isbell of the University of Kentucky.

is quite beyond my power." A painter described the waning hours of the effects of psilocybin as follows: "As the afternoon wore on I felt very content to simply sit and stare out of the window at the snow and the trees, and at that time I recall feeling that the snow, the fire in the fireplace, the darkened and book-lined room were so perfect as to seem almost unreal."

The changes in visual perception are not always pleasant. Aldous Huxley called one of his books about mescaline *Heaven and Hell* in recognition of the contradictory sensations induced by the drug. The "hellish" experiences include an impression of blackness accompanied by feelings of gloom and isolation, a garish modification of the glowing colors observed in the "heavenly" phase, a sense of sickly greens and ugly dark reds. The subject's perception of his own body may become unpleasant: his limbs may seem to be distorted or his flesh to be decaying; in a mirror his face may appear to be a mask, his smile a meaningless grimace. Sometimes all human movements appear to be mere puppetry, or everyone seems to be dead. These experiences can be so disturbing that a residue of fear and depression persists long after the effects of the drug have worn off.

Often there are complex auditory hallucinations as well as visual ones: lengthy conversations between imaginary people, perfectly orchestrated musical compositions the subject has never heard before, voices speaking foreign languages unknown to the subject. There have also been reports of hallucinatory odors and tastes and of visceral and other bodily sensations. Frequently patterns of association normally confined to a single sense will cross over to other senses: the sound of music evokes the visual impression of jets of colored light, a "cold" human voice makes the subject shiver, pricking the skin with a pin produces the visual impression of a circle, light glinting on a Christmas tree ornament seems to shatter and to evoke the sound of sleigh bells. The time sense is altered too. The passage of time may seem to be a slow and pleasant flow or to be intolerably tedious. A "sense of timelessness" is often reported; the subject feels outside of or beyond time, or time and space seem infinite.

In some individuals one of the most basic constancies in perception is affected: the distinction between subject and object. A firm sense of personal identity depends on knowing accurately the borders of the self and on being able to distinguish what is inside from what is outside. Paranoia is the most vivid pathological instance of the breakdown of this discrimination; the paranoiac attributes to personal and impersonal forces outside himself the impulses that actually are inside him. Mystical and transcendental experiences are marked by the loss of this same basic constancy. "All is one" is the prototype of a mystical utterance. In the mystical state the distinction between subject and object disappears; the subject is seen to be one with the object. The experience is usually one of rapture or ecstasy and in religious terms is described as "holy." When the subject thus achieves complete identification with the object, the experience seems beyond words.

Some people who have taken a large dose of a hallucinogenic drug report feelings of "emptiness" or "silence," pertaining either to the interior of the self or to an "interior" of the universe—or to both as one. Such individuals have a sense of being completely undifferentiated, as though it were their personal consciousness that had been "emptied," leaving none of the usual discriminations on which the functioning of the ego depends. One man who had this experience thought later that it had been an anticipation of death, and that the regaining of the basic discriminations was like a remembrance of the very first days of life after birth.

The effect of the hallucinogens on sexual experience is not well documented. One experiment that is often quoted seemed to provide evidence that mescaline is an anaphrodisiac, an inhibitor of sexual appetite; this conclusion seemed plausible because the drugs have so often been associated with rituals emphasizing asceticism and prayer. The fact is, however, that the drugs are probably neither anaphrodisiacs nor aphrodisiacs—if indeed any drug is. There is reason to believe that if the drug-taking situation is one in which sexual relations seem appropriate, the hallucinogens simply bring to the sexual experience the same kind of change in perception that occurs in other areas of experience.

The point is that in all the hallucinogen-produced experiences it is never the drug alone that is at work. As in the case of alcohol, the effects vary widely depending on when the drug is taken, where, in the presence of whom, in what dosage and—perhaps most important of all—by whom. What happens to the individual after he takes the drug, and his changing relations to the setting and the people in it during the episode, will further influence his experience.

Since the setting is so influential in these experiments, it sometimes happens that a person who is present when someone else is taking a hallucinogenic drug, but who does not take the drug himself, behaves as though he were under the influence of a hallucinogen. In view of this effect one might expect that a person given an inactive substance he thought was a drug would respond as though he had actually received the drug. Indeed, such responses have sometimes been noted. In controlled experiments, however, subjects given an inactive substance are readily distinguishable from those who take a drug; the difference is apparent in their appearance and behavior, their answers to questionnaires and their physiological responses. Such behavioral similarities as are observed can be explained largely by a certain apprehension felt by a person who receives an inactive substance he thinks is a drug, or by anticipation on the part of someone who has taken the drug before.

In addition to the various subjective effects of the hallucinogens there are a number of observable changes in physiological function and in performance that one can measure or at least describe objectively. The basic physiological effects are those typical of a mild excitement of the sympathetic nervous system. The hallucinogens usually dilate the pupils, constrict the peripheral arterioles and raise the systolic blood pressure; they may also increase the excitability of such spinal reflexes as the knee jerk. Electroencephalograms show that the effect on electrical brain waves is usually of a fairly nonspecific "arousal" nature: the pattern is similar to that of a normally alert, attentive and problem-oriented subject, and if rhythms characteristic of drowsiness or sleep have been present, they disappear when the drug is administered. (Insomnia is common the first night after one of the drugs has been taken.) Animal experiments suggest that LSD produces these effects by stimulating the reticular formation of the midbrain, not directly but by stepping up the sensory input.

Under the influence of one of the hallucinogens there is usually some reduction in performance on standard tests of reasoning, memory, arithmetic, spelling and drawing. These findings may not indicate an inability to perform well; after taking a drug many people simply refuse to co-operate with the tester. The very fact that someone should want to

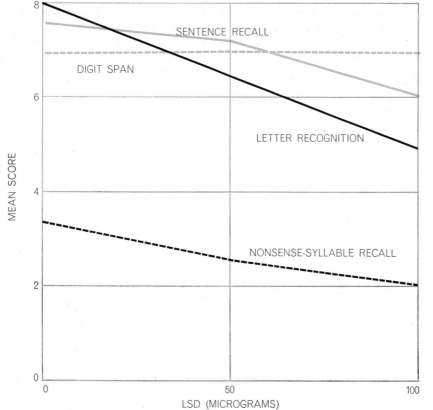

EFFECT OF LSD on memory was determined with standard tests. Curves show results of four tests for subjects given an inactive substance, 50 micrograms of the drug and 100 micrograms respectively. Effect of LSD was to decrease scores except in a test of digit-recall ability.

test them may seem absurd and may arouse either hostility or amusement. Studies by one of the authors in which tests of attention and concentration were administered to subjects who had been given different doses of LSD indicated that motivation was perhaps as important in determining scores as the subject's intellectual capacity.

The hallucinogenic drugs are not addictive—if one means by addiction that physiological dependence is established and the drug becomes necessary, usually in increasing amounts, for satisfactory physiological functioning. Some individuals become psychologically dependent on the drugs, however, and develop a "habit" in that sense; indeed, there is a tendency for those who ingest hallucinogens habitually to make the drug experience the center of all their activities. LSD, mescaline and psilocybin do produce physiological tolerance. If the same quantity of LSD is administered on three successive days, for example, it will not suffice by the third day to produce the same subjective or physiological effects; tolerance develops more slowly and less completely with mescaline and psilocybin. When an individual becomes tolerant to a given dos-

age of LSD, the ordinarily equivalent dose of psilocybin produces reduced effects. This phenomenon of cross-tolerance suggests that the two drugs have common pathways of action. Any tolerance established by daily administration of the drugs wears off rather rapidly, generally being dissipated within a few days if the drug is not taken.

The three major hallucinogens differ markedly in potency. The standard human doses—those that will cause the average adult male weighing about 150 pounds to show the full clinical effects—are 500 milligrams of mescaline, 20 milligrams of psilocybin and .1 milligram of LSD. It is assumed that in a large enough dose any of the hallucinogens would be lethal, but there are no documented cases of human deaths from the drugs alone. Death has been brought on in sensitive laboratory animals such as rabbits by LSD doses equivalent to 120 times the standard human dose. Some animals are much less susceptible; white rats have been given doses 1,000 times larger than the standard human dose without lasting harm. The maximum doses known by the authors to have been taken by human beings are 900 milligrams of mescaline, 70 milligrams

of psilocybin and two milligrams of LSD. No permanent effects were noted in these cases, but obviously no decisive studies of the upper limits of dosage have been undertaken.

There are also differences among the hallucinogens in the time of onset of effects and the duration of intoxication. When mescaline is given orally, the effects appear in two or three hours and last for 12 hours or more. LSD acts in less than an hour; some of its effects persist for eight or nine hours, and insomnia can last as long as 16 hours. Psilocybin usually acts within 20 or 30 minutes, and its full effect is felt for about five hours. All these estimates are for the standard dose administered orally; when any of the drugs is given intravenously, the first effects appear within minutes.

At the present time LSD and psilocybin are treated by the U.S. Food and Drug Administration like any other "experimental drug," which means that they can be legally distributed only to qualified investigators who will administer them in the course of an approved program of experimentation. In practice the drugs are legally available only to investigators working under a Government grant or for a state or Federal agency.

Nevertheless, there has probably been an increase during the past two or three years in the uncontrolled use of the drugs to satisfy personal curiosity or to experience novel sensations. This has led a number of responsible people in government, law, medicine and psychology to urge the imposition of stricter controls that would make the drugs more difficult to obtain even for basic research. These people emphasize the harmful possibilities of the drugs; citing the known cases of adverse reactions, they conclude that the prudent course is to curtail experimentation with hallucinogens.

Others—primarily those who have worked with the drugs—emphasize the constructive possibilities, insist that the hallucinogens have already opened up important leads in research and conclude that it would be shortsighted as well as contrary to the spirit of free scientific inquiry to restrict the activities of qualified investigators. Some go further, questioning whether citizens should be denied the opportunity of trying the drugs even without medical or psychological supervision and arguing that anyone who is mentally competent should have the right to explore the varieties of conscious experience if he can do so without harming himself or others.

The most systematic survey of the incidence of serious adverse reactions to hallucinogens covered nearly 5,000 cases, in which LSD was administered on more than 25,000 occasions. Psychotic reactions lasting more than 48 hours were observed in fewer than two-tenths of 1 per cent of the cases. The rate of attempted suicides was slightly over a tenth of 1 per cent, and these involved psychiatric patients with histories of instability. Among those who took the drug simply as subjects in experiments there were no attempted suicides and the psychotic reactions occurred in fewer than a tenth of 1 per cent of the cases.

Recent reports do indicate that the incidence of bad reactions has been increasing, perhaps because more individuals have been taking the hallucinogens in settings that emphasize sensation-seeking or even deliberate social delinquency. Since under such circumstances there is usually no one in attendance who knows how to avert dangerous developments, a person in this situation may find himself facing an extremely frightening hallucination with no one present who can help him to recognize where the hallucination ends and reality begins. Yet the question of what is a proper setting is not a simple one. One of the criticisms of the Harvard experiments was that some were conducted in private homes rather than in a laboratory or clinical setting. The experimenters defended this as an attempt to provide a feeling of naturalness and "psychological safety." Such a setting, they hypothesized, should reduce the likelihood of negative reactions such as fear and hostility and increase the positive experiences. Controlled studies of this hypothesis have not been carried out, however.

Many psychiatrists and psychologists who have administered hallucinogens in a therapeutic setting claim specific benefits in the treatment of psychoneuroses, alcoholism and social delinquency. The published studies are difficult to evaluate because almost none have employed control groups. One summary of the available statistics on the treatment of alcoholism does indicate that about 50 per cent of the patients treated with a combination of psychotherapy and LSD abstained from alcohol for at least a year, compared with 30 per cent of the patients treated by psychotherapy alone.

In another recent study the results of psychological testing before and after

LSD therapy were comparable in most respects to the results obtained when conventional brief psychotherapy was employed. Single-treatment LSD therapy was significantly more effective, however, in relieving neurotic depression. If replicated, these results may provide an important basis for more directed study of the treatment of specific psychopathological conditions.

If the hallucinogens do have psychotherapeutic merit, it seems possible that they work by producing a shift in personal values. William James long ago noted that "the best cure for dipsomania is religiomania." There appear to be religious aspects of the drug experience that may bring about a change in behavior by causing a "change of heart." If this is so, one might be able to apply the hallucinogens in the service of moral regeneration while relying on more conventional techniques to give the patient insight into his habitual behavior patterns and motives.

In the light of the information now available about the uses and possible abuses of the hallucinogens, common sense surely decrees some form of social control. In considering such control it should always be emphasized that the reaction to these drugs depends not only on their chemical properties and biological activity but also on the context in which they are taken, the meaning of the act and the personality and mood of the individual who takes them. If taking the drug is defined by the group or individual, or by society, as immoral or criminal, one can expect guilt and aggression and further social delinquency to result; if the aim is to help or to be helped, the experience may be therapeutic and strengthening; if the subject fears psychosis, the drug could induce psychosis. The hallucinogens, like so many other discoveries of man, are analogous to fire, which can burn down the house or spread through the house life-sustaining warmth. Purpose, planning and constructive control make the difference. The immediate research challenge presented by the hallucinogens is a practical question: Can ways be found to minimize or eliminate the hazards, and to identify and develop further the constructive potentialities, of these powerful drugs?

NATIVE AMERICAN CHURCH members take part in a peyote ceremony in Saskatchewan, Canada. Under the influence of the drug, they gaze into the fire as they pray and meditate.

21

Barbiturates

ELIJAH ADAMS

January 1958

The barbiturates are the most versatile of all depressant drugs. They can produce the whole range of effects from mild sedation to deep anesthesia—and death. They are among the oldest of the modern drugs. Long before reserpine and chlorpromazine, the barbiturates were being used as tranquilizers. Indeed, phenobarbital has been called "the poor man's reserpine." Had phenobarbital been introduced five years ago instead of half a century ago, it might have evoked the same burst of popular enthusiasm as greeted Miltown and its fashionable contemporaries. Not that the vogue of the barbiturates is any less spectacular, in terms of total production and consumption. The U. S. people take an estimated three to four billion doses of these drugs per year, on prescription by their physicians. The barbiturates rank near the top of the whole pharmacopoeia in value to medicine. They are also a national problem.

It was nearly a century ago that a young assistant of the great chemist August Kekulé in Ghent made the first of these compounds. In 1864 this young man, Adolf von Baeyer, combined urea (an animal waste product) with malonic acid (derived from the acid of apples) and obtained a new synthetic which was named "barbituric acid." There are several stories about how it got this name. The least apocryphal version relates that von Baeyer and his fellow chemists went to celebrate the discovery in a tavern where the town's artillery garrison was also celebrating the day of Saint Barbara, the saint of artillerists. An artillery officer is said to have christened the new substance by amalgamating "Barbara" with "urea."

Chemists proceeded to produce a great variety of derivatives of barbituric acid. The medical value of the substances was not realized, however, until 1903, when two other luminaries of German organic chemistry, Emil Fischer and Joseph von Mering, discovered that one of the compounds, diethylbarbituric acid, was very effective in putting dogs to sleep. Von Mering, it is said, promptly proposed that the substance be called veronal, because the most peaceful place he knew on earth was the city of Verona.

Within a few months of their report, "A New Class of Sleep-Inducers," physicians in Europe and the U. S. took up the new drugs enthusiastically. More and more uses for them were discovered. Veronal (barbital) was soon followed by phenobarbital, sold under the trade name Luminal. In all, more than 2,500 barbiturates were synthesized in the next half-century, and of these some two dozen won an important place in medicine. By 1955 the production of barbiturates in the U. S. alone amounted to 864,000 pounds—more than enough to provide 10 million adults with a sleeping pill every night of the year.

As is true of most drugs, we still do not know how the barbiturates work or exactly how their properties are related to their chemistry. The basic structure is a ring composed of four carbon atoms and two nitrogens [see diagrams on page 191]. Certain side chains added to the ring increase the drug's potency; in some instances the addition of a single carbon atom transforms an inactive form of the compound into an active one. Empirical analysis of the thousands of barbiturates has given us some practical information about relations between structure and activity. But by and large the mode of action of the drugs is an unsolved problem.

We know a great deal, however, about the action itself. We can follow it best by examining the successive stages of the drugs' depressant effect on the central nervous system [see "Anesthesia," by Henry K. Beecher; SCIENTIFIC AMERICAN, January, 1957]. From this standpoint the barbiturates can be considered together as a group, for the differences among them are not fundamental and concern such matters as the speed and duration of the effect.

In small doses these drugs are sedatives, acting to reduce anxiety and to relieve psychogenic disorders—for example, certain types of hypertension and gastrointestinal pain. In this respect the barbiturates are yesterday's tranquilizers. They have now taken second place in popularity as sedatives to the newer tranquilizers.

At three to five times the sedative dose, the same barbiturate produces sleep. Barbiturates are still by far the most widely used drugs for this purpose, as millions of us know. Hardly any hospital patient has escaped his yellow or red capsule at evening, for it is an article of clinical faith that the patient needs chemical assistance to achieve sleep in his new environment. Another large block of users are the chronic travelers by plane and train. Finally there are the thousands of sufferers from insomnia who take the drugs habitually.

Many persons find barbiturate-induced sleep as refreshing as natural sleep. Others awake with a hangover, feeling drowsy, dizzy and suffering a headache. Tests show that, with or without symptoms, the barbiturates reduce efficiency: six to eight hours after a sleeping dose of sodium pentobarbital (Nembutal) the subjects perform below par on mental and memory tests. The various drugs act differently as sleep-

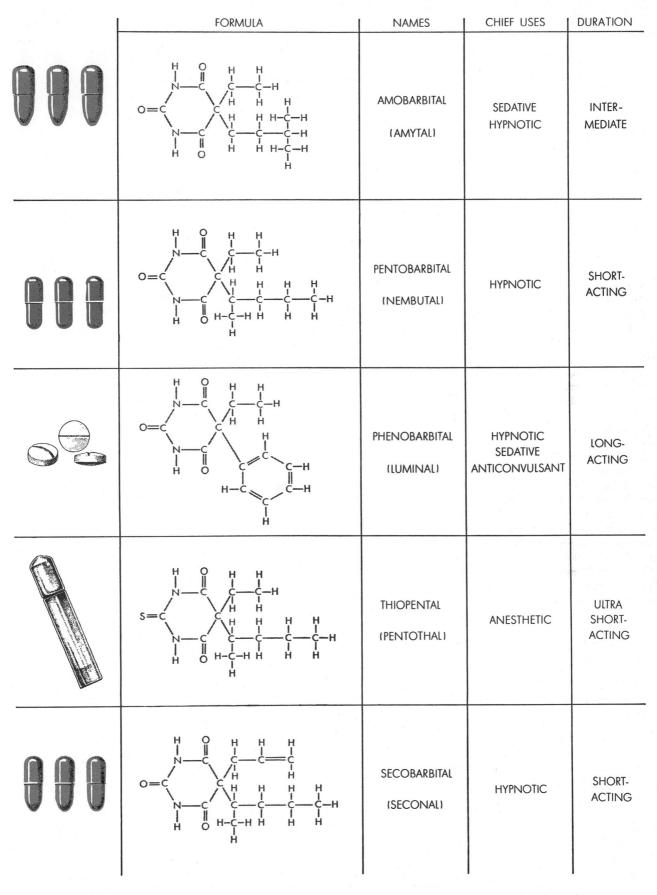

	FORMULA	NAMES	CHIEF USES	DURATION
		AMOBARBITAL (AMYTAL)	SEDATIVE HYPNOTIC	INTER-MEDIATE
		PENTOBARBITAL (NEMBUTAL)	HYPNOTIC	SHORT-ACTING
		PHENOBARBITAL (LUMINAL)	HYPNOTIC SEDATIVE ANTICONVULSANT	LONG-ACTING
		THIOPENTAL (PENTOTHAL)	ANESTHETIC	ULTRA SHORT-ACTING
		SECOBARBITAL (SECONAL)	HYPNOTIC	SHORT-ACTING

FIVE BARBITURATES are depicted at the left as they are commonly manufactured. As shown in the column of chemical structures, four of these drugs differ only in the chains of atoms attached to the carbon atom at the right side of their basic ring structure. The permutability of the basic barbiturate structure makes possible variations in speed and duration of its effect on the body.

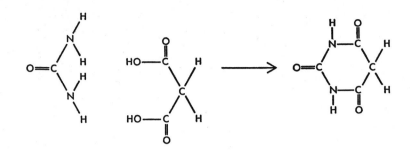

BARBITURIC ACID (*right*), is made by combining urea (*left*) and malonic acid (*right*) with the elimination of water (*colored rectangles*). The barbiturate families arise from substitution of other substances for hydrogens at position 5 in the basic barbiturate structure.

producers. Some last for only three hours or less, others for six hours or more. The shorter-acting barbiturates (sodium pentobarbital, secobarbital) are appropriate for insomniacs who have trouble falling asleep; the longer-acting ones (barbital, phenobarbital) for people who go to sleep easily but awake after four to six hours. The latter drugs, however, are more likely to produce a hangover.

In large doses a barbiturate acts as an anesthetic. Not only does the patient become unconscious, but his spinal cord reflexes are depressed so that the muscles are relaxed and manageable for surgery. Like the gaseous anesthetics, the barbiturates depress the cerebral cortex first, then lower brain centers, next the spinal cord centers and finally the medullary centers controlling blood pressure and respiration.

The fast-acting barbiturates produce anesthesia more rapidly than ether: the patient passes from the waking state to anesthetic coma in a few moments. Sodium thiopental is the most widely used. It has important advantages over a gaseous anesthetic such as ether. Injected intravenously, it works rapidly, avoids the sense of suffocation, requires no special equipment, is free from the explosion hazard and from respiratory complications. A barbiturate anesthetic has, however, an outstanding disadvantage: the dose necessary for good muscular relaxation may seriously reduce oxygen supply to the tissues by depressing the brain center that drives respiration. Consequently for a long operation the barbiturate is often combined with a gaseous anesthetic; for a short one the dose is reduced and combined with a specific muscle-relaxing drug that has no brain-depressant action.

There are two other interesting uses of the barbiturates. One of them is in the field of psychology. As Henry Beecher observed in his article on anes-thesia in SCIENTIFIC AMERICAN, an anesthetic can provide "planned access to levels of consciousness not ordinarily attainable except perhaps in dreams, in trances or in the reveries of true mystics." During World War II the barbiturates, particularly thiopental, were used for analysis and therapy for many thousands of GIs, who by this means relived and verbalized traumatic battle experiences which had been buried beyond voluntary recollection. The inhibition-relieving action of these drugs has also been employed by the police—in which application the press has given them the name of "truth serum," although they are neither a serum nor a guaranteed truth-producer.

The other important use of the drugs is for the control of epileptic convulsions. Certain of the barbiturates—phenobarbital, mephobarbital and methabarbital —can prevent or stop these seizures by depressing brain activity. Barbiturates can control not only the generalized convulsions of genuine (idiopathic) epilepsy—a disease afflicting almost a million persons in the U. S.—but also seizures induced by stimulating drugs or by bacterial toxins such as tetanus. The barbiturates and the convulsant drugs act in opposite fashion, and, curiously, each is used as an antidote for the other. Acute barbiturate poisoning is often treated with a stimulating drug such as pentylenetetrazol (Metrazol) or picrotoxin to bring the patient out of his coma; if the dose of the stimulant turns out to be too strong, producing convulsions, this in turn is treated with a dose of a fast-acting barbiturate!

The toxic effects of barbiturates are subtle and sometimes unpredictable. For some patients even a comparatively small dose may be dangerous. The body gets rid of barbital and phenobarbital chiefly by excretion in the urine; for a person with damaged kidneys, therefore, these drugs become toxic. Pentobarbital and secobarbital, two of the most widely used barbiturates, are broken down in the liver. Given to a patient with a poorly functioning liver, they may produce a far longer sleep than desired.

Next to carbon monoxide, the barbiturates are the most popular suicide poison in the U. S. They account for one fifth of all the cases of acute drug poisoning, and most of these are suicide attempts. The barbiturates are not, as a matter of fact, a very efficient suicide agent: only about 8 per cent of those poisonees who arrive at hospitals die. But they are widely known and readily available, and they produce from 1,000 to 1,500 deaths in the U. S. each year.

Some of these deaths, though self-inflicted, are accidental. A British physician first called attention some years ago to a specific and probably common hazard. The person takes a small dose to go to sleep, and later, half asleep and confused, he swallows another, lethal dose. Some physicians now warn barbiturate-users not to keep their bottle of tablets on a night table, where they may stretch out a hand to take more while in the comatose state.

There is a comfortable margin of safety between the ordinary sleeping dose (a tenth of a gram for the average adult) and a definitely toxic dose (more than half a gram). The lethal dose is usually a gram and a half or more. Acute barbiturate poisoning has to be treated promptly. Unfortunately it is often not recognized in time, because the victim is thought to be merely in a deep sleep. The first step in treatment is to strengthen the victim's breathing, in a respirator if necessary. And a stimulant may have to be administered to restore the activity of the brain centers.

Are the barbiturates habit-forming? This much-debated question has been answered rather conclusively by recent studies. They can indeed produce addiction and chronic intoxication. The two chief criteria of addiction to a drug are a heightened tolerance to it and physical dependence on it, so that removal of the drug produces withdrawal symptoms. A morphine addict, for example, may be able to take many times the dose that would be lethal for a normal person, and he becomes acutely sick if the drug is stopped. Several years ago Havelock Fraser, Harris Isbell and their associates at the U. S. Public Health Service hospital for drug addicts in Lexington, Ky., made a thorough study of whether the barbiturates had these properties. Their investigation included experiments with human subjects who were given large doses of barbiturates over a period of months and then abruptly taken off the drug.

They found that the barbiturates acted as addicting drugs in every respect—physical and psychic. The men behaved like chronic alcoholics: they neglected their appearance and hygiene, became confused and quarrelsome, showed unpredictable mood swings and lost physical coordination and the mental discipline necessary for simple games. After abrupt withdrawal of the drug, the subjects began within a few hours to show signs of increasing apprehension and developed weakness, tremors, nausea and vomiting. In the next five days most of the subjects had convulsions like those of epilepsy and an acute psychosis such as alcoholics suffer, with delirium and violent hallucinations.

The Lexington investigators also made similar tests on dogs. They too exhibited withdrawal symptoms. In their "canine delirium" the dogs would stare at a blank wall and move their heads, eyes and ears as if responding to imaginary animals, people or objects; even while alone in a cage a dog would growl as if being attacked.

Stories in the press have greatly exaggerated the extent of barbiturate addiction in the U. S. "Thrill pills," "goof balls," "wild geronimos," "red devils" (secobarbital), "yellow jackets" (sodium pentobarbital), "blue heaven" (amobarbital)—all these terms certainly have a currency in a limited circle of addicts, but the number of addicts is not nearly so large as some of the stories have alleged. There are probably not more than 50,000 barbiturate addicts, compared with a million chronic alcoholics. Never-

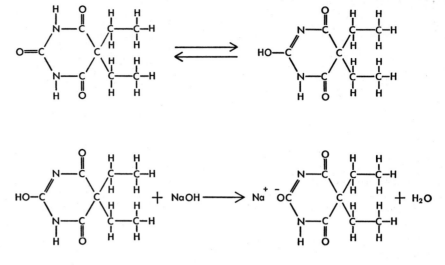

SODIUM BARBITAL (*lower right*) can be made from barbital (*shown at top of diagram in its two forms*) by addition of sodium hydroxide (NaOH) and the elimination of water.

theless, in view of the easy access to the barbiturates, the public does need to be alerted to their addictive property.

The saving fact is that it takes extraordinarily heavy use of these drugs to produce addiction. Subjects who have taken a fifth of a gram (twice the usual sleeping dose) every night for a year have shown no withdrawal symptoms after stopping the drug. In contrast, morphine, taken in the usual hospital doses for as short a time as 30 days, produces definite physical dependence. Moderate use of the barbiturates, in the doses prescribed by physicians, will not lead to addiction. Those who become addicts are probably, in the main, drug-users who turn to the barbiturates because they cannot get narcotics, alcoholics who

seek relief from alcohol withdrawal and, in general, abnormal personalities who are addiction risks for any intoxication that will give psychic relief. Whether stricter Federal laws are needed to control misuse of the barbiturates has been a matter of considerable controversy.

Biologists look forward to the day when progress in medicine will make all present drugs, including the barbiturates, obsolete. Better understanding and treatment of the personal and social causes of anxiety should reduce our present reliance on chemical aids to tranquility and sleep. Meanwhile the barbiturates can teach us much about the functions of the brain and so help lead toward that more tranquil day.

BARK OF WILLOW
(SALIX)
(EFFECT ON MALARIA; 1763, STONE)

MEADOWSWEET FLOWER
(SPIRAEA)

OIL OF WINTERGREEN
(GAULTHERIA)

EXTRACTION;
1826–1829, BRUGNATELLI, FONTANA; LEROUX

DISTILLATION;
1831, PAGENSTECHER

EXTRACTION;
1843, PROCTER; CAHOURS

—CH₂OH
—OC₆H₁₁O₅

—CHO
—OH

—COOCH₃
—OH

SALICIN
(EFFECT ON RHEUMATIC FEVER;
1874–1876, MACLAGAN)

SALICYLALDEHYDE

METHYL SALICYLATE

HYDROLYSIS AND OXIDATION;
1838, PIRIA

OXIDATION;
1835, LOWIG

HYDROLYSIS;
1843, CAHOURS

SYNTHESIS;
1852, GERLAND;
1860, KOLBE, LAUTEMANN

—COOH
—OH

—COONa
—OH

SALICYLIC ACID ("SPIRSÄURE")
(EFFECT ON RHEUMATIC FEVER;
1876, RIESS, STRICKER)

SODIUM SALICYLATE
(EFFECT ON GOUT, ARTHRITIS,
NEURALGIA; 1877, SEE)

ACETYLATION;
1853, GERHARDT; 1893, HOFMANN

—COOH
—OCOCH₃

ACETYLSALICYLIC ACID (ASPIRIN)
(EFFECT ON RHEUMATIC FEVER
1899, WITTHAUER, WOHLGEMUT
ON PAIN; 1900, WITTHAUER)

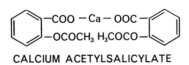

—COO—Ca—OOC—
—OCOCH₃ H₃COCO—

CALCIUM ACETYLSALICYLATE

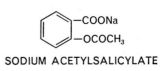

—COONa
—OCOCH₃

SODIUM ACETYLSALICYLATE

22

Aspirin

H. O. J. COLLIER

November 1963

The most widely used drug in the world—if we accept one medical dictionary's definition of a drug as "any substance employed as a medicine in the treatment of disease" and consider disease to imply all the minor aches, pains and chills that flesh is heir to—is aspirin. Even if we expand the definition of a drug to include the active principles of alcoholic drinks, coffee, tea and tobacco, aspirin would follow grain alcohol, caffeine, nicotine and possibly other substances consumed as chemical comforts rather than medicaments in the number of effective doses taken. In 1962 the production of aspirin in the U.S. alone was 27.2 million pounds. The consumption of aspirin tablets was 15 billion, plus a somewhat larger number containing aspirin mixed with caffeine, codeine or other substances. In spite of this massive acceptance of aspirin as an analgesic, or mitigator of pain, its exact mode of action within the body remains obscure. Evidently it works not by blocking some agent of disease but by moderating such aspects of the body's defensive response as fever, pain and inflammation.

CHEMICAL ANCESTRY of acetylsalicylic acid, the chemical now known as aspirin, is traced on opposite page to plants in which salicylates were found. Formulas for the chemical relatives of salicylic acid are given below, with techniques used in isolating it, the chemists who performed the steps and physicians who reported medical uses of the drug. A method of acetylating salicylic acid to weaken its acidity was devised as early as 1853, but only in the last decade of the century was the process refined to make possible large-scale manufacture. The salts of aspirin (*bottom*) are more soluble, are more quickly absorbed into the bloodstream and are less injurious to the digestive tract.

The chemical name of aspirin is acetylsalicylic acid; this compound and its various salts appear under 56 proprietary names in the current *Pharmacological and Chemical Synonyms*. One of these is "Aspirin," the name under which the compound was introduced for medicinal purposes by the German firm of Bayer in 1899. Since that time wars and widespread usage have negated the effect of trade-mark laws in some countries and have deprived the name of its proprietary exclusiveness. In Germany, however, "Aspirin" remains the valuable trade-mark of the original manufacturer.

The name itself, a roundabout contraction of acetylsalicylic acid, represents one of the first exercises in the peculiar art of applied etymology that the merchandising specialists of the pharmaceutical industry have brought to such a high point of elaboration today. The prefix "a-" stands for the acetyl group that Charles Frédéric Gerhardt of Strasbourg first added to salicylic acid in 1853. The root, "spir," stands for *spirsäure*, the name given by Karl Jakob Löwig of Germany to the acid he prepared in 1835 from an aldehyde that Johann S. F. Pagenstecher, a Swiss pharmacist, had distilled several years earlier from the flowers of the meadowsweet (*Spiraea ulmaria*). Löwig's *spirsäure* is salicylic acid, a substance occurring in the form of esters in several plants. The diversity of natural sources of the acid resulted in more than one line of descent in the pharmacopoeia [*see illustration on opposite page*].

On June 2, 1763, a paper entitled "An Account of the Success of the Bark of the Willow in the Cure of Agues" was read to the Royal Society of London. The authorship of this first description of

the effects of salicylic acid was recorded inaccurately. At the head of the paper, as printed in the *Philosophical Transactions of the Royal Society of London*, the author is named Edmund Stone; at the foot he has become Edward Stone [*see illustration on next page*]. The original manuscript bears the abbreviated signature of either "Edwd" or "Edm^d." An Edmund Stone was elected to the Royal Society in 1725 and was still a fellow in 1763, but he was a mathematician. A protégé of the Duke of Argyll, on whose estate he had been a gardener, Edmund's gifts came to light accidentally when the duke found that his gardener possessed a copy of Newton's *Principia* and was conversant with its contents. It is probable, however, that the author of the "Account of the Success of the Bark of the Willow" was one Edward Stone, a clergyman of Chipping Norton in Oxfordshire. The printer of the *Philosophical Transactions* apparently confused him with the better-known Edmund.

Edward Stone recommended a decoction of the bark of the white willow for treating "aguish and intermitting disorders," a description of malaria. Two coincidences bolstered Stone's proposal to try willow bark against malaria. First, the bark tasted extraordinarily bitter, as does cinchona, the Peruvian bark that was then acknowledged to be the sovereign remedy for malaria. Second, the willow grows in damp and marshy places, which in Stone's day were often malarial and where, in accordance with the contemporary medical "doctrine of signatures," he would have expected to find a cure for the disease.

Stone's decoction did indeed relieve the feverish symptoms of malaria because, as chemists later learned, it contains salicylic acid, an antipyretic compound. It did not cure the disease, however, because willow bark does not contain quinine, the ingredient in cinchona bark that acts directly against the malarial parasite. Stone's recommendation of willow bark unfortunately led to the adulteration of cinchona bark with a less curative (and less expensive) material.

In 1829 a French pharmacist named H. Leroux isolated from a willow-bark extract salicin, a compound of glucose and salicyl alcohol. Salicylic acid itself was derived from this compound in 1838 by Raffaele Piria of Naples three years after Löwig had extracted the same acid from meadowsweet flowers. In 1842 William Procter of the U.S. and Auguste Cahours of France obtained methyl salicylate from oil of wintergreen; Cahours later carried the isolation a step further to salicylic acid. Since then the chemical relatives of salicylic acid have turned up in many plants. A salicylate has also been found in the secretion of the beaver's prepuce that is known as castoreum; the substance is perhaps derived from the bark of trees on which beavers subsist.

The purification and identification of salicylates occurring in nature facilitated their synthesis in the laboratory. In 1852 H. Gerland synthesized salicylic acid, and by the end of the decade Hermann Kolbe and E. Lautemann had developed a practical method of preparing it in sufficient quantity for therapeutic use. As chemists had been encouraged to synthesize salicylates by reports of medical interest, physicians were now aided in their research by the availability of salicylic acid and its purified esters.

In 1874, more than a century after Edward Stone's communication to the Royal Society, a Scottish physician named T. J. MacLagan echoed Stone's original proposal. He wrote: "Nature seeming to produce the remedy under climatic conditions similar to those which give rise to the disease...among the Salicaceae...I determined to search for a remedy for acute rheumatism. The bark of many species of willow contains a bitter principle called salicin. This principle was exactly what I wanted."

MacLagan did not, however, have to make his own decoction from the willow bark. With salicin available in pure form, he proceeded to a historic experiment: "I had at the time under my care a well-marked case of the disease which was being treated by alkalies but was not improving. I determined to give him salicin; but before doing so, took myself first five, then ten, and then thirty grains without experiencing the least inconvenience or discomfort. Satisfied as to the safety of its administration, I gave to the patient referred to twelve grains every three hours. The results exceeded my most sanguine expectations."

History was repeating itself, not only in the invocation of the doctrine of signatures that gave rise to the discovery but also in the way the remedy worked, because salicin and its derivatives no more destroy the infecting bacteria that initiate the immunological process culminating in rheumatic fever (as acute rheumatism is now often called) than they kill the malaria parasite that caused Stone's agues. Salicylates act by lessening the fever and painful inflammation that form part of the body's immunological response to some substance produced by the infecting bacteria.

MacLagan was the first physician to treat rheumatic fever successfully with salicylates, but a few months before his paper on salicin appeared in *The Lancet* of March 4, 1876, L. Riess and S. Stricker had separately reported in Berlin that

---

[195]

XXXII. *An Account of the Success of the Bark of the Willow in the Cure of Agues. In a Letter to the Right Honourable* George Earl *of* Macclesfield, *President of R. S. from the Rev. Mr.* Edmund Stone, *of* Chipping-Norton *in* Oxfordshire.

My Lord,

Read June 2d, 1763. A Mong the many useful discoveries, which this age hath made, there are very few which, better deserve the attention of the public than what I am going to lay before your Lordship.

There is a bark of an English tree, which I have found by experience to be a powerful astringent, and very efficacious in curing aguish and intermitting disorders.

About six years ago, I accidentally tasted it, and was surprised at its extraordinary bitterness; which immediately raised me a suspicion of its having the properties of the Peruvian bark. As this tree delights in a moist or wet soil, where agues chiefly abound, the general maxim, that many natural maladies carry their cures along with them, or that their remedies lie not far from their causes, was so very apposite to this particular case, that I could not help applying it;

[200]

cinnamon or lateritious colour, which I believe is the case with the Peruvian bark and powders.

I have no other motives for publishing this valuable specific, than that it may have a fair and full trial in all its variety of circumstances and situations, and that the world may reap the benefits accruing from it. For these purposes I have given this long and minute account of it, and which I would not have troubled your Lordship with, was I not fully persuaded of the wonderful efficacy of this Cortex Salignus in agues and intermitting cases, and did I not think, that this persuasion was sufficiently supported by the manifold experience, which I have had of it.

I am, my Lord,

with the profoundest submission and respect,

Chipping-Norton, Oxfordshire, April 25, 1763.

your Lordship's most obedient humble Servant

Edward Stone.

UNCERTAIN AUTHORSHIP of first paper to describe medicinal effects of willow-bark extract can be traced to a printer's error in the *Philosophical Transactions* of 1763. At top of paper (*left*) the author is named Edmund Stone. At bottom (*right*) the name is Edward. "Doctrine of signatures" is synopsized in the proposition that "many natural maladies carry their cures along with them...."

salicylic acid was effective in treating the disease. In the following year Germain Sée announced in Paris that salicylates also relieved chronic rheumatoid arthritis and gout. By this time several physicians had noted that salicylates detectably but not dramatically lessened certain nonrheumatic pains such as neuralgia and headache.

Although salicylic acid was probably the wonder drug of its day, its success was diminished by the irritation and damage it caused to the moist membranes lining the mouth, gullet and stomach. The molecule of the acid contains a hydroxyl group (OH) and a carboxyl group (COOH) extending from the six-carbon-atom benzene ring. The carboxyl group can dissociate on contact with the moist lining of the stomach wall to yield a hydrogen ion. The resulting acidity can be neutralized by replacing the hydrogen atom of the carboxyl group with an atom of a metal such as sodium. This salt, sodium salicylate, was less irritating than the acid and was prescribed by physicians, but it had to be administered in a solution that many people found to have an "obnoxious sweetish taste." Thus although the great potential of salicylic acid had been demonstrated as early as 1876, many of those to whom it was administered were distressed by its damaging effect on the lining of the digestive tract or by the unpleasant taste of the sodium salt.

Ironically the key step in successfully improving the drug's palatability had been demonstrated in 1853 by Gerhardt. He had replaced the hydrogen atom of the hydroxyl group with an acetyl group (COCH₃), but his method was cumbersome enough to discourage further investigation for some time. It was 40 years before Felix Hofmann, a Bayer chemist, found a simpler way to make the acetyl compound of salicylic acid. Hofmann had a personal interest in the task because his father was one of those sufferers from rheumatism who could not stomach sodium salicylate. After Hofmann's successful acetylation, his colleague Heinrich Dreser conducted an impressive exploration of the properties of acetylsalicylic acid.

"It is self-evident," he wrote, "that only a salicylate compound which is split as soon as possible in the blood with liberation of salicylic acid has medicinal value." Dreser performed several experiments on the breakdown of acetylsalicylic acid in the body, including some on himself. He swallowed a solution containing one gram of sodium acetylsalicylate, a salt in which the hydrogen

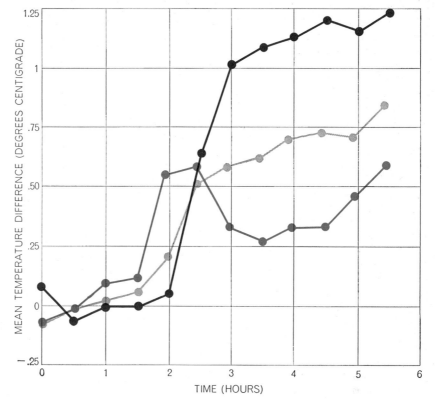

ANTIPYRETIC EFFECT of aspirin is graphed by plotting against time the rise in fever (*vertical axis*) of rabbits treated with pyrogen and aspirin. Dark-colored curve shows fever of rabbits receiving 66.7 milligrams of aspirin per kilogram of body weight. Light-colored curve depicts 22.2 milligrams per kilogram dose. Control animals (*black curve*) got no aspirin.

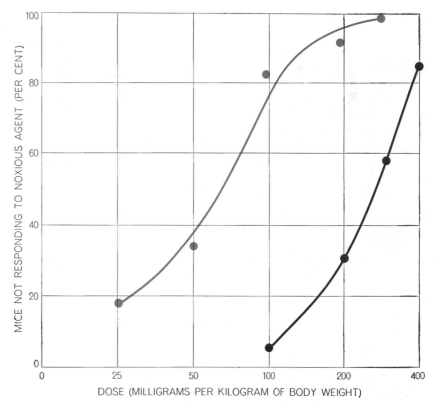

ANALGESIC EFFECT of aspirin (*colored curve*) is shown to exceed that of free salicylate. On horizontal axis is dosage of each drug given to mice before injection of phenylquinone, a noxious chemical. Vertical axis shows per cent that did not manifest any pain thereafter. Experiment was performed by L. C. Hendershot and J. A. Forsaith at Dow Chemical Company.

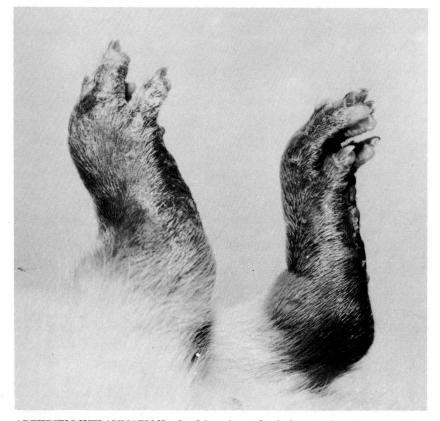

ARTHRITIC INFLAMMATION in hind feet of a rat that had received an injection of dead tubercle bacilli 13 days earlier is shown in this photograph. Precise nature of the swelling and response of arthritic rats to drugs provide a "model" of human rheumatoid arthritis.

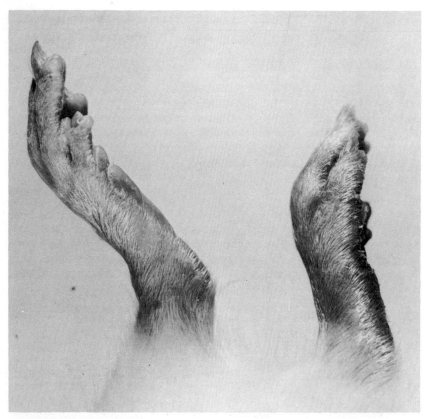

ANTIRHEUMATIC EFFECT of aspirin is evident in this photograph of hind feet of a rat that had received daily doses of aspirin starting one day before the injection of tubercle bacilli. Photographs were made by B. B. Newbould of Imperial Chemical Industries.

atom of the carboxyl group has been replaced by a sodium atom and the hydroxyl group by an acetyl group. After 22 minutes the chemist tested a sample of his own urine for the presence of acetylsalicylate and free salicylate. The latter was present, but the urine gave no reaction for the acetyl compound. Over the next 12 hours the urine gave the same reactions, and Dreser concluded that acetylsalicylates readily decomposed in the body, liberating the therapeutically active salicylate. Observing that acetylsalicylic acid had "a pleasant sharp taste" instead of the sweet, nauseating flavor of sodium salicylate, and that it "acted more gently on the walls of the stomach," Dreser recommended it as a pharmaceutical preparation.

The first physicians to describe the medicinal uses of aspirin were Kurt Witthauer and Julius Wohlgemut of Germany. Their 1899 papers did not suggest that aspirin, either as a solid or as a liquid, had therapeutic effects greater than those of earlier salicin derivatives. Instead they emphasized the pharmaceutical advantages cited by Dreser, such as acceptable taste and decreased irritation of the stomach lining.

Only a year later—following the production of aspirin tablets "so cheap that no obstacle stands in the way of their use" and a small explosion of papers on aspirin in the medical journals—Witthauer wrote a second paper in which he described the unexpected potency of aspirin as a relief for pain in such varied conditions as migraine, persistent headache and inoperable carcinoma. Patients and their physicians had discovered in aspirin an analgesic so effective that its success misled them into extravagant optimism.

Witthauer himself warned that tablets "should not be swallowed whole but allowed to disintegrate first in a little sugar water flavored with 2 drops of lemon juice." Many ignored his advice and swallowed crude tablets of aspirin, which, disintegrating slowly and unevenly in the stomach, brought lumps of acetylsalicylic acid into contact with the stomach wall, with damaging results. Most modern aspirin tablets are designed to promote quick dissolution and so reduce the time in which an acidic lump can touch the stomach wall. Some tablets form the soluble calcium salt of acetylsalicylic acid as they dissolve in the stomach juices, whereas others yield a solution of the sodium salt in a glass of water prior to administration. Some capsules enclose the drug in a coat that resists the acid of the stomach and dissolves in the alkaline juice of the small intestine. Although each of these is less likely to injure the stomach than the plain aspirin tablet, a real risk remains, as is indicated by the gastrointestinal bleeding that in some individuals can follow the taking of aspirin and by the fact that acetylsalicylic acid and its chemical relatives can produce stomach ulcers in rats, even when these drugs are injected under the skin rather than swallowed.

In some people aspirin induces an allergic hypersensitivity; thereafter a small dose has been known to provoke a fatal reaction. Because aspirin is incorporated in many medicaments, the occasional sufferer of the allergic reaction must be wary of this hazard. An interesting footnote to the "dangers" of aspirin is the listing in a chemical index of four of its helpful effects ("analgesic, antipyretic, antirheumatic, uricosuric") and 31 hazardous effects.

It has always been easier to catalogue the wide application of aspirin to man's commonest ills than to explain its mode of action. As an analgesic it relieves pain rapidly, inexpensively and effectively. Unlike morphine, it does not give rise to physiological dependence and may therefore be used freely for everyday aches, pains and malaises: headache, dysmenorrhea, hangover and so on. As an antipyretic, aspirin brings fever down by increasing sweating and the flow of blood through the skin. As an antirheumatic, it reduces the inflammation and pain in the joints and permits increased mobility. As a treatment for gout, it has both these effects and induces the excretion of uric acid, thus lessening the deposits of urate that form in the joints. There is no doubt about the usefulness of the drug. If the precise nature of its biochemical action remains a mystery, it is because so little is known about the biochemistry of the defensive responses, such as pain, fever and inflammation, evoked in the body by disease.

Early clinical studies indicated that the dose of aspirin for effective treatment of rheumatic fever, rheumatoid arthritis or gout virtually equaled that of sodium salicylate. This supported Dreser's view that aspirin acts by liberating salicylate within the body. When it came to the relief of pain, however, the situation soon appeared to be different: aspirin seemed more effective than sodium salicylate. Some investigators began to wonder what role

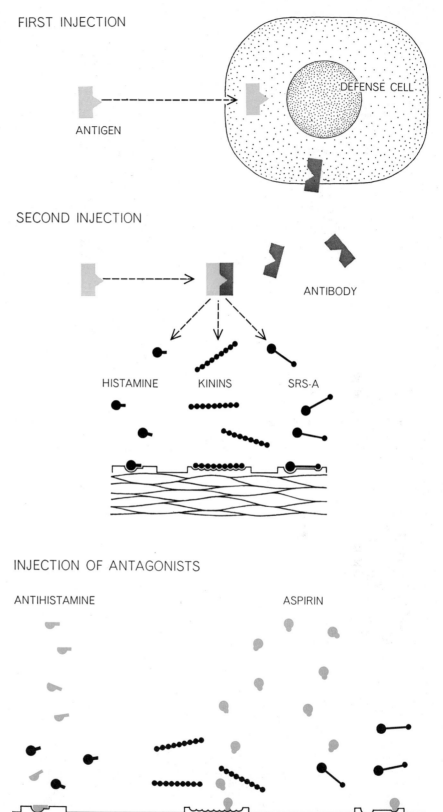

FIRST INJECTION

ANTIGEN

DEFENSE CELL

SECOND INJECTION

ANTIBODY

HISTAMINE   KININS   SRS-A

INJECTION OF ANTAGONISTS

ANTIHISTAMINE   ASPIRIN

A MODE OF ACTION FOR ASPIRIN is suggested at bottom of this generalized view of bronchospasm in guinea pigs. An injection of antigen (*top*) signals antibody production. After a second injection the antigens react with antibodies to form histamine, kinins and the substance designated SRS-A, all of which induce a constriction of the bronchioles. This bronchospasm can be stopped if animal is treated with antihistamine, shown at bottom to block the action of histamine, and aspirin, which in this case antagonizes kinins and SRS-A.

the liberation of salicylate could play if aspirin itself was the more potent of the two substances.

The problem assumed clearer shape when in 1946 David Lester, Giorgio Lolli and Leon A. Greenberg of Yale University reported the results of their examination of the substances present in the blood plasma of volunteers who had taken a single oral dose of aspirin. As much as a quarter of the total dose, with the acetyl group still attached to the compound, could be detected in the blood for one to two hours after ingestion. The period during which aspirin was present intact in the blood corresponded with the duration of its analgesic action; hence the Yale workers argued that aspirin had an analgesic action independent of the salicylate it might release on decomposing.

In order to bring these findings back into line with Dreser's view it was suggested that some special characteristics of the distribution of aspirin to the tissues enabled it to liberate salicylate at sites of action that this substance alone could not reach. Doubt has been cast on this explanation by the discovery of other situations in which the potency of aspirin greatly exceeds that of the salicylate. One of these, which will serve as an example, involves thurfyl nicotinate, a substance that is sometimes applied to the skin as a counterirritant in muscular pain, sciatica and neuralgia.

When a cream that contains thurfyl nicotinate is rubbed into the skin, it evokes reddening and wealing. This is probably a local expression of the generalized skin flush that follows the swallowing of a tablet of nicotinic acid. In 1952 J. R. Nassim and H. Banner reported that the usual skin reaction to thurfyl nicotinate was not observed in patients with rheumatoid arthritis. For some years this was taken to be a sign of the disease. In 1959 L. H. Truelove and J. J. R. Duthie of the Northern General Hospital in Edinburgh showed that the effect was caused not by arthritis but by the aspirin with which the patients were regularly treated. In normal volunteers a single 10-grain (650 milligram) dose of aspirin delayed the reddening and abolished the swelling after thurfyl nicotinate was rubbed into the skin.

At the Salicylate Symposium in London in 1962 S. S. Adams and R. Cobb of the Boots Pure Drug Company described how they had tested the ability of several antirheumatic drugs to modify the skin response to thurfyl nicotinate. They found aspirin to be surprisingly potent: a single dose of 3.5 grains (225 milligrams) by mouth was detectably effective, and a 10-grain dose inhibited the skin response for several days. Neither sodium salicylate nor phenylbutazone, both useful antirheumatic drugs, was active at the dosage tested; taking into account the fact that decomposition in the bloodstream will allow no more than a quarter of the aspirin to reach the skin as the acetyl compound, it can be estimated that acetylsalicylic acid is at least 12 times more potent than sodium salicylate against thurfyl nicotinate.

This experiment indicates that acetylsalicylate has a medicinal effect in its own right, without having to be broken down first to salicylate as Dreser supposed. It does not show that the actions of the two drugs are qualitatively different, since a still larger dose of sodium salicylate might have shown activity.

A powerful stimulus to the study of how aspirin exerts its effects has been the desire of pharmaceutical manufacturers to find new drugs that have the therapeutic virtues of aspirin without its disadvantages. Here laboratory models of disease, or the body's various responses to disease, play a fundamental role. These models are set up in animals or in isolated living tissue. To be valid they must not only resemble the human disease and its symptoms but also react comparably to drugs.

Fever, rheumatoid arthritis and pain can be fairly well approximated in experimental animals. Of these, fever has proved the simplest to reproduce. Fevers in man usually arise during microbial infections, in which the invaders liberate minute quantities of substances called pyrogens. Pyrogens can be extracted from bacterial cultures, and they produce fevers when injected into laboratory animals. For example, the injection of half a microgram (half a millionth of a gram) of pyrogen extracted from cultures of *Bacillus proteus* will raise the rectal temperature of a rabbit by one to two degrees centigrade within an hour or two. This fever can be prevented by a relatively small dose of aspirin.

The main manifestation of rheumatoid arthritis is an inflammation of the joints, more simply "arthritis." An apparently close approximation of this condition can be induced in rats. In 1954 H. C. Stoerk, T. C. Bielinski and T. Budzilovich of the Merck Institute observed that rats developed a chronic arthritis when they were injected with emulsions of spleen cells suspended in an adjuvant consisting of dead tubercle bacilli in liquid paraffin, commonly used by pathologists to intensify the action of injected cells or bacteria. A few weeks after the injection swelling appeared in some of the joints of about half of the animals treated. Tails as well as limb joints were affected, and the swellings lasted, with occasional temporary lessening, for many months [see illustrations on page 195]. Under the microscope the swelling was seen to be caused by inflammation like that in human rheumatoid arthritis.

Stoerk and his colleagues attributed this chronic arthritis to the spleen cells injected into their rats. In 1956, however, Carl M. Pearson of the University of California School of Medicine in Los Angeles showed that the adjuvant alone, without any spleen cells suspended in it, would produce the same effect. Later Pearson and Fae D. Wood found that dead bacteria of other species of the genus *Mycobacterium,* to which the human tubercle bacillus belongs, were also effective, although bacteria of other genera were not. Even chemical extracts of tubercle bacilli can elicit this chronic arthritis in rats. The disease seems therefore to be an ultimate immunological response of the animal to a foreign chemical derived from a particular kind of bacterium. Conceivably rheumatoid arthritis arises from similar causes in man.

In the treatment of arthritis the hormones of the adrenal cortex and other steroid hormones have proved to be most effective in both human beings and rats. Recently B. B. Newbould of the Imperial Chemical Industries has found that acetylsalicylic acid, sodium salicylate, phenylbutazone, aminopyrine and flufenamic acid, the most effective types of nonsteroidal agents in the treatment of human rheumatoid arthritis, show corresponding potencies when administered to rats. Newbould's research indicates that among drugs known to be effective against the human disease only the quinoline antimalarials are ineffective against the rat arthritis. His experiments thus affirm the similarity between the laboratory model of arthritis and the human disease and demonstrate the powerful anti-inflammatory action of aspirin and related drugs.

It has proved difficult to develop equally persuasive laboratory models of pain and the objective measurement of the analgesic effect that motivates most use of aspirin. In a few animal experiments aspirin could be shown to raise the intensity of noxious stimulation needed to elicit a protective response, but the magnitude of the effect was small and the dose required correspondingly large. In 1956, however, Christine Vander Wende and Sol Margolin of the Schering Corporation described a model pain situation in which the injection of a noxious chemical solution into the abdominal cavity of rats or mice produces a characteristic constriction of the abdominal wall followed by extension of the hind legs. The response, which has been termed "stretching" or "writhing," was usually repeated several times after the injection. The inference that this response signifies pain is supported by the actions of drugs. Local anesthetics suppress the response when they are injected at the site, and analgesics suppress it when they are administered by any route. In a mouse a dose of about 20 micrograms of morphine effectively reduces writhing, and a dose of about one milligram of aspirin is correspondingly active. For this model situation, then, it can be said that aspirin has about a fiftieth of the analgesic effect of morphine. This corresponds with human experience; on the subjective testimony of patients it is said that 300 to 1,000 milligrams of aspirin relieves pain about as well as 10 to 30 of morphine.

The suggestion has been made that aspirin acts in mice and men by antagonizing natural pain substances such as the peptides called kinins, which are released locally in the blood and tissues at the site of injury [see "Kinins," by H. O. J. Collier; reprinted in this volume, page 105]. Robert K. S. Lim and his co-workers at the Miles Laboratories have performed ingenious experiments in dogs showing that aspirin blocks the action of one of these kinins (bradykinin) and suppresses its excitation of the nerve endings in the viscera that promote pain sensation. Bradykinin also evokes the writhing response when it is injected into the abdominal cavity of mice, and this too is blocked by aspirin. It has not been established that aspirin blocks the pain evoked by bradykinin more effectively than it blocks pain signaled by other substances; nor has aspirin been found to block all the types of pain caused by bradykinin. For example, bradykinin injected into the skin of guinea pigs elicits scratching and licking at the site of the injection; aspirin does not prevent these responses, although morphine does.

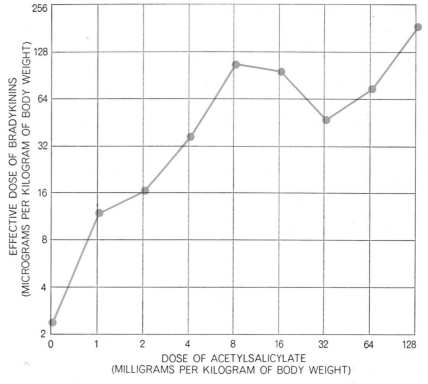

ANTAGONISM of bradykinin inducing bronchospasm in the guinea pig is graphed by plotting the dosage of acetylsalicylate injected (*horizontal axis*) against the quantity of bradykinin needed to cause constriction of the bronchioles (*vertical axis*). Experiment was performed by the author and Patricia G. Shorley at Parke, Davis & Company in England.

In the most illustrative experiments exploring aspirin's mode of action on the molecular level, the disease duplicated in the laboratory was bronchial asthma. Significantly, a disease can be described in terms of various elements, such as the invading agent (for example the influenza virus), the body's response (rheumatic fever) or the ultimate damage inflicted (infantile paralysis). Human bronchial asthma, which fits the second descriptive category, is the reaction of the bronchioles to the inhalation of a small amount of a specific antigen, usually a foreign protein present in a pollen or in the dander of an animal. Like fever, pain or arthritic inflammation, then, asthma represents the type of unwarranted or excessive bodily response to an invading agent that aspirin seems able to mitigate.

A crude example of asthma in the guinea pig has been observed for half a century. If a single dose of foreign protein such as egg white or horse serum is injected, it does little harm to the guinea pig. But a second dose a few weeks later causes an intense reaction in which the muscular walls of the bronchioles contract violently. The resulting constriction of the bronchioles, or bronchospasm, usually hinders breathing so

drastically as to be fatal. This is one of the more familiar and extreme forms of the distorted immunological response known as anaphylactic shock. In response to the first injection of antigen, defense cells produce an antibody tailored to fit the substance [see "The Mechanism of Immunity," by Sir Macfarlane Burnet; available as Offprint #78]. When the antigen is injected a second time, it reacts with the antibody to produce anaphylactic shock [*see illustration on page 197*].

Human bronchial asthma is a much milder reaction of the bronchioles to inhalation of a dust containing a small amount of antigen to which the sufferer has become sensitized. An equivalent of human asthma in the guinea pig was achieved in 1952 by Herbert Herxheimer, then at the University College Hospital Medical School in London, who caused animals previously sensitized to egg albumen to inhale a solution of it in a fine mist.

As long ago as 1910, at the Wellcome Physiological Research Laboratories in England, Sir Henry Dale and Sir Patrick P. Laidlaw had observed that the injection of histamine, a substance released by injured tissues, produces a bronchospasm like that of anaphylactic shock. Histamine had not long been synthesized at that time and was still known under its chemical name of beta-imidazolylethylamine. After comparing many responses of various animals to histamine and to anaphylactic shock, Dale and Laidlaw wrote: "We content ourselves with recording, as a point of interest and possible significance, the fact that the immediate symptoms with which an animal responds to an injection of a normally inert protein, to which it has been sensitized, are to a large extent these of poisoning by beta-imidazolylethylamine."

This comment had a powerful influence on later investigations. In 1932 several teams of workers in different parts of the world showed that histamine is released during anaphylactic shock in the guinea pig. Then in 1937 Daniel Bovet and A.-M. Staub, working at the Pasteur Institute in Paris, described the first antihistamine drug, 929F. This drug not only protected guinea pigs against constriction of the bronchioles caused by inhaling histamine solution in a fine mist but also protected them to some extent against anaphylactic shock. Many other antihistamines followed 929F; all of them lessened anaphylactic bronchospasm but none abolished it altogether. This confirmed that the histamine released in anaphylactic shock played a part in constricting the bronchioles, but it also implied that some other factor was involved.

A search for other substances that are released during anaphylactic shock and might play a part in constricting the bronchioles in the guinea pig has so far implicated two. In 1940 C. H. Kellaway and E. R. Trethewie found a substance that has not yet been purified

and chemically identified and is known by the awkward name of Slow Reacting Substance in Anaphylaxis, or SRS-A. The other substance is the family group of kinins, as W. E. Brocklehurst and S. C. Lahiri of the University of Edinburgh demonstrated in 1961.

Previously John A. Holgate, Mel Schachter, Patricia G. Shorley and I, working at the laboratories of Parke, Davis & Company in England and at University College London, had shown that intravenous injection of kinin into normal guinea pigs causes constriction of the bronchioles, and in 1962 P. A. Berry, Holgate and I showed that SRS-A acts in a similar way. We also found that the bronchospasm induced by either kinins or SRS-A can be completely prevented by the administration of a small dose of aspirin a few minutes before the injection.

Although aspirin has no such effect on the action of histamine, it appears to act as a specific chemical antagonist of kinins and SRS-A, just as antihistamines antagonize histamine. If the three substances are jointly responsible for the bronchospasm, one might expect that treatment with both aspirin and antihistamine would prevent it and that either drug alone would be partly effective. Within the past year Alexander R. Hammond, Barbara Whiteley and I have found strong evidence in support of this prediction. In this particular model of asthma, at least, it appears that aspirin acts as a pharmacological antagonist of kinins and SRS-A. This effect is probably achieved by the molecules of aspirin blocking a reaction between the molecules of kinin, SRS-A and the bronchial muscle they stimulate.

The question of how closely the guinea pig model of asthma resembles

the human counterpart has occupied more than a generation of research workers. In 1951 H. O. Schild, Denis F. Hawkins, Jack L. Mongar and Herxheimer, working at University College London, showed that a piece of human bronchial muscle, removed from an asthma sufferer during a surgical operation and suspended in a suitable saline medium, released histamine when it was exposed to the pollen to which the patient was hypersensitive. In 1955 Brocklehurst, then working at the National Institute for Medical Research in London, found that contact with the appropriate antigen also released SRS-A from isolated fragments of a human asthmatic lung. Recently Herxheimer and E. Stresemann, working at the Free University of West Berlin, have demonstrated that when volunteers susceptible to asthma inhale a solution of either bradykinin or SRS-A in a fine mist, an asthmatic attack follows. From clinical experience it is known that aspirin and antihistamines, when taken separately, ameliorate asthma slightly in some human patients, although aspirin may elicit asthma in other hypersensitive people. But it is not yet established that the two drugs, taken together, would have a stronger effect, or that aspirin acts as a pharmacological antagonist of kinins or SRS-A in the human lung.

Whether aspirin, in its vast consumption, is taken as an antipyretic, analgesic or antirheumatic, its general function seems to be the moderation of the defensive reactions to various forms of disease. It would appear that the human body has an unwieldy defense establishment that aspirin fortunately can help to control.

SECTION III

Chemical Biodynamics

III

Chemical Biodynamics

INTRODUCTION

In this last section we have collected only a few of the many available articles on the relation between the dynamic function of both the small and the large organic molecules and the behavior of the organisms of which they are a part. The first of these, on chemical fossils, not only discusses the historical sequence of structural evolution but provides a basis for understanding the present dynamic structure of living organisms. The next two, on photosynthesis and on energy transfer, discuss the ways in which both the green-plant cell and the animal cell collect, store, and transform energy. The following articles — David Green on fats and Hans Neurath on enzymes—give us some insight into the ways in which cells transform molecules, a basic function of all living organisms.

The discussion by Ruth Hubbard and Alfred Kropf on the carotenoids involved in vision and the simple molecular photochemical processes that seem to be the basis of this highly important function in all animals—from the most simple unicellular organisms to man—give us some clue to the operation of the sensory transducers that initiate the input of information into the higher animals. This is discussed at a much higher level by Bernard Agranoff in his article on memory and protein synthesis, which is addressed not so much to the solution of the problem of sensory transducers and input as it is to the mechanism by which this input is stored in the living system of the higher organism and is found again at the proper moment. The remaining three articles deal with the action of the control mechanisms of nucleic acids on the structure of living organisms through their coding of specific protein structures, and with one way in which this kind of information storage is effected, that is, through the action of ultraviolet radiation on the structure of nucleic acids.

It is clear that this selection of articles on chemical biodynamics is only a sampling—a sampling based primarily on the amount of chemical information about the dynamic behavior of a living organism that each article contained, and the degree to which principles, rather than specific studies, were elucidated. The progress in this field is so rapid that we can expect specific knowledge of the molecular mechanisms that affect the dynamic behavior of living organisms to be outdated rapidly; the principles, however, should remain valid.

Additional articles, very closely related chemically in subject matter to those chosen as representatives for this section, are the following: P. H. Abelson, *Paleobiochemistry* (June 1956, offprint 101); E. Frieden, *The Chemistry of Amphibian Metamorphosis* (November 1963, offprint 170); G. Wald, *Life and Light* (October 1959, offprint 61); E. I. Rabinowitch and Govindjee, *The Role of*

Chlorophyll in Photosynthesis (July 1965, offprint 1016); D. I. Arnon, *The Role of Light in Photosynthesis* (November 1960, offprint 75); W. D. McElroy and H. H. Seliger, *Biological Luminescence* (December 1962, offprint 141); M. Papa, *Electric Currents in Organic Crystals* (January 1967); M. J. Dawkins and D. Hall, *The Production of Heat by Fat* (August 1965, offprint 1018); A. Lehninger, *How Cells Transform Energy* (September 1961, offprint 91); D. E. Green, *The Synthesis of Fats* (February 1960, offprint 67); J. Changeux, *The Control of Biochemical Reactions* (April 1965, offprint 1008); L. E. Hokin and M. R. Hokin, *The Chemistry of Cell Membranes* (October 1965, offprint 1022); M. A. Amerine, *Wine* (August 1964, offprint 190); F. H. C. Crick, *The Genetic Code* (October 1962, offprint 123); F. H. C. Crick, *The Genetic Code III* (October 1966, offprint 1052); C. Yanofsky, *Gene Structure and Protein Structure* (May 1967); P. C. Hanawalt and R. H. Haynes, *The Repair of DNA* (February 1967, offprint 1061); F. Verzar, *The Aging of Collagen* (April 1963, offprint 155).

23

Chemical Fossils

GEOFFREY EGLINTON AND MELVIN CALVIN

January 1967

If you ask a child to draw a dinosaur, the chances are that he will produce a recognizable picture of such a creature. His familiarity with an animal that lived 150 million years ago can of course be traced to the intensive studies of paleontologists, who have been able to reconstruct the skeletons of extinct animals from fossilized bones preserved in ancient sediments. Recent chemical research now shows that minute quantities of organic compounds—remnants of the original carbon-containing chemical constituents of the soft parts of the animal—are still present in some fossils and in ancient sediments of all ages, including some measured in billions of years. As a result of this finding organic chemists and geologists have joined in a search for "chemical fossils": organic molecules that have survived unchanged or little altered from their original structure, when they were part of organisms long since vanished.

This kind of search does not require the presence of the usual kind of fossil—a shape or an actual hard form in the rock. The fossil molecules can be extracted and identified even when the organism has completely disintegrated and the organic molecules have diffused into the surrounding material. In fact, the term "biological marker" is now being applied to organic substances that show pronounced resistance to chemical change and whose molecular structure gives a strong indication that they could have been created in significant amounts only by biological processes.

One might liken such resistant compounds to the hard parts of organisms that ordinarily persist after the soft parts have decayed. For example, hydrocarbons, the compounds consisting only of carbon and hydrogen, are comparatively resistant to chemical and biological attack. Unfortunately many other biologi-

cally important molecules such as nucleic acids, proteins and polysaccharides contain many bonds that hydrolyze, or cleave, readily; hence these molecules rapidly decompose after an organism dies. Nevertheless, several groups of workers have reported finding constituents of proteins (amino acids and peptide chains) and even proteins themselves in special well-protected sites, such as between the thin sheets of crystal in fossil shells and bones [see "Paleobiochemistry," by Philip H. Abelson; available as Offprint #101].

Where complete destruction of the organism has taken place one cannot, of course, visualize its original shape from the nature of the chemical fossils it has left behind. One may, however, be able to infer the biological class, or perhaps even the species, of organism that gave rise to them. At present such deductions must be extremely tentative because they involve considerable uncertainty. Although the chemistry of living organisms is known in broad outline, biochemists even today have identified the principal constituents of only a few small groups of living things. Studies in comparative biochemistry or chemotaxonomy are thus an essential parallel to organic geochemistry. A second uncertainty involves the question of whether or not the biochemistry of ancient organisms was generally the same as the biochemistry of present-day organisms. Finally, little is known of the chemical changes wrought in organic substances when they are entombed for long periods of time in rock or a fossil matrix.

In our work at the University of California at Berkeley and at the University of Glasgow we have gone on the assumption that the best approach to the study of chemical fossils is to analyze geological materials that have had a relatively simple biological and geological history.

The search for suitable sediments requires a close collaboration between the geologist and the chemist. The results obtained so far augur well for the future.

Organic chemistry made its first major impact on the earth sciences in 1936, when the German chemist Alfred Treibs isolated metal-containing porphyrins from numerous crude oils and shales. Certain porphyrins are important biological pigments; two of the best-known are chlorophyll, the green pigment of plants, and heme, the red pigment of the blood. Treibs deduced that the oils were biological in origin and could not have been subjected to high temperatures, since that would have decomposed some of the porphyrins in them. It is only during the past decade, however, that techniques have been available for the rapid isolation and identification of organic substances present in small amounts in oils and ancient sediments. Further refinements and new methods will be required for detailed study of the tiny amounts of organic substances found in some rocks. The effort should be worthwhile, because such techniques for the detection and definition of the specific architecture of organic molecules should not only tell us much more about the origin of life on the earth but also help us to establish whether or not life has developed on other planets. Furthermore, chemical fossils present the organic chemist with a new range of organic compounds to study and may offer the geologist a new tool for determining the environment of the earth in various geological epochs and the conditions subsequently experienced by the sediments laid down in those epochs.

If one could obtain the fossil molecules from a single species of organism, one would be able to make a direct correlation between present-day biochemistry and organic geochemistry. For example, one could directly compare the lipids, or fatty compounds, isolated from a living organism with the lipids of its fossil ancestor. Unfortunately the fossil lipids and other fossil compounds found in sediments almost always represent the chemical debris from many organisms.

The deposition of a compressible fine-grained sediment containing mineral particles and disseminated organic matter takes place in an aquatic environment in which the organic content can be partially preserved; an example would be the bottom of a lake or a delta. The organic matter makes up something less than 1 percent of many ancient sediments. The small portion of this carbon-containing material that is soluble in organic solvents represents a part of the original lipid content, more or less modified, of the organisms that lived and died while the sediment was being deposited.

The organic content presumably consists of varying proportions of the components of organisms—terrestrial as well as aquatic—that have undergone chemical transformation while the sediment was being laid down and compressed. Typical transformations are reduction, which has the effect of removing oxygen from molecules and adding hydrogen, and decarboxylation, which removes the carboxyl radical (COOH). In addition, it appears that a variety of reactive unsaturated compounds (compounds having available chemical bonds) combine to form an insoluble amorphous material known as kerogen. Other chemical changes that occur with the passage of time are related to the temperature to which the rock is heated by geologic processes. Thus many petroleum chemists and geologists believe petroleum is created by progressive degradation, brought about by heat, of the organic matter that is finely disseminated throughout the original sediment. The organic matter that comes closest in structure to the chains and rings of carbon atoms found in the hydrocarbons of petroleum is the matter present in the lipid fraction of organisms. Another potential source of petroleum hydrocarbons is kerogen itself, presumably formed from a wide variety of organic molecules; it gives off a range of straight-chain, branched-chain and ring-containing hydrocarbons when it is strongly heated in the laboratory. One would also like to know more about the role of bacteria in the early steps of sediment formation. In the upper layers of most newly formed sediments there is strong bacterial activity, which must surely re-

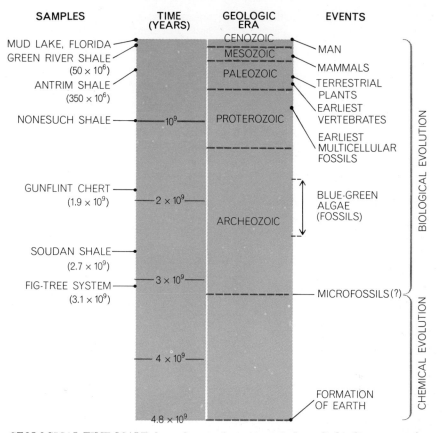

GEOLOGICAL TIME SCALE shows the age of some intensively studied sedimentary rocks (*left*) and the sequence of major steps in the evolution of life (*right*). The stage for biological evolution was set by chemical evolution, but the period of transition is not known.

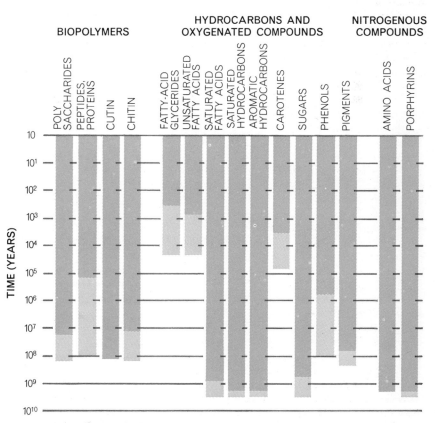

ORGANIC COMPOUNDS originally synthesized by living organisms and more or less modified have now been found in many ancient rocks that began as sediments. The dark bars indicate reasonably reliable identification; the light bars, unconfirmed reports. Cutin and chitin are substances present respectively in the outer structures of plants and of insects.

sult in extensive alteration of the initially deposited organic matter.

In this article we shall concentrate on the isolation of fossil hydrocarbons. The methods must be capable of dealing with the tiny quantity of material available in most rocks. Our general procedure is as follows.

After cutting off the outer surface of a rock specimen to remove gross contaminants, we clean the remaining block with solvents and pulverize it. We then place the powder in solvents such as benzene and methanol to extract the organic material. Before this step we sometimes dissolve the silicate and carbonate minerals of the rock with hydrofluoric and hydrochloric acids. We separate the organic extract so obtained into acidic, basic and neutral fractions. The compounds in these fractions are converted, when necessary, into derivatives that make them suitable for separation by the technique of chromatography. For the initial separations we use column chromatography, in which a sample in solution is passed through a column packed with alumina or silica. Depending on their nature, compounds in the sample pass through the column at different speeds and can be collected in fractions as they emerge.

In subsequent stages of the analysis finer fractionations are achieved by means of gas-liquid chromatography. In this variation of the technique, the sample is vaporized into a stream of light gas, usually helium, and brought in contact with a liquid that tends to trap the compounds in the sample in varying degree. The liquid can be supported on an inorganic powder, such as diatomaceous earth, or coated on the inside of a capillary tube. Since the compounds are alternately trapped in the liquid medium and released by the passing stream of gas they progress through the column at varying speeds, with the result that they are separated into distinct fractions as they emerge from the tube. The temperature of the column is raised steadily as the separation proceeds, in order to drive off the more strongly trapped compounds.

The initial chromatographic separation is adjusted to produce fractions that consist of a single class of compound, for example the class of saturated hydrocarbons known as alkanes. Alkane molecules may consist either of straight chains of carbon atoms or of chains that include branches and rings. These subclasses can be separated with the help of molecular sieves: inorganic substances, commonly alumino-silicates, that have a fine honeycomb structure. We use a sieve whose mesh is about five angstrom units, or about a thousandth of the wavelength of green light. Straight-chain alkanes, which resemble smooth flexible rods about 4.5 angstroms in diameter, can enter the sieve and are trapped. Chains with branches and rings are too big to enter and so are held back. The straight-chain alkanes can be liberated from the sieve for further analysis by dissolving the sieve in hydrofluoric acid. Other families of molecules can be trapped in special crystalline forms of urea and thiourea, whose crystal lattices provide cavities with diameters of five angstroms and seven angstroms respectively.

The families of molecules isolated in this way are again passed through gas chromatographic columns that separate the molecular species within the family. For example, a typical chromatogram of straight-chain alkanes will show that molecules of increasing chain length emerge from the column in a regularly spaced sequence that parallels their increasing boiling points, thus producing a series of evenly spaced peaks. Although the species of molecule in a particular peak can often be identified tentatively on the basis of the peak's position, a more precise identification is usually desired. To obtain it one must collect the tiny amount of substance that produced the peak—often measured in micrograms—and examine it by one or more analytical methods such as ultraviolet and infrared

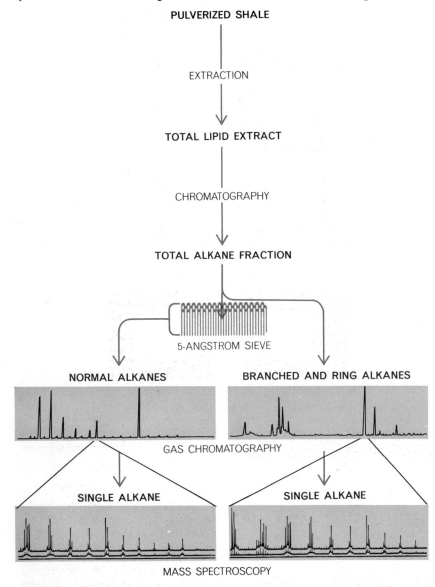

PULVERIZED SHALE

EXTRACTION

TOTAL LIPID EXTRACT

CHROMATOGRAPHY

TOTAL ALKANE FRACTION

5-ANGSTROM SIEVE

NORMAL ALKANES   **BRANCHED AND RING ALKANES**

GAS CHROMATOGRAPHY

SINGLE ALKANE   **SINGLE ALKANE**

MASS SPECTROSCOPY

ANALYTICAL PROCEDURE for identifying chemical fossils begins with the extraction of alkane hydrocarbons from a sample of pulverized shale. In normal alkanes the carbon atoms are arranged in a straight chain. (Typical alkanes are illustrated on page 208.) Molecular sieves are used to separate straight-chain alkanes from alkanes with branched chains and rings. The two broad classes are then further fractionated. Compounds responsible for individual peaks in the chromatogram are identified by mass spectrometry and other methods.

spectroscopy, mass spectrometry or nuclear magnetic resonance. In one case X-ray crystallography is being used to arrive at the structure of a fossil molecule.

A new and useful apparatus is one that combines gas chromatography and mass spectrometry [*see illustration at right*]. The separated components emerge from the chromatograph and pass directly into the ionizing chamber of the mass spectrometer, where they are broken into submolecular fragments whose abundance distribution with respect to mass is unique for each component. These various analytical procedures enable us to establish a precise structure and relative concentration for each organic compound that can be extracted from a sample of rock.

How is it that such comparatively simple substances as the alkanes should be worthy of geochemical study? There are several good reasons. Alkanes are generally prominent components of the soluble lipid fraction of sediments. They survive geologic time and geologic conditions well because the carbon-hydrogen and carbon-carbon bonds are strong and resist reaction with water. In addition, alkane molecules can provide more information than the simplicity of their constitution might suggest; even a relatively small number of carbon and hydrogen atoms can be joined in a large number of ways. For example, a saturated hydrocarbon consisting of 19 carbon atoms and 40 hydrogen atoms could exist in some 100,000 different structural forms that are not readily interconvertible. Analysis of ancient sediments has already shown that in some cases they contain alkanes clearly related to the long-chain carbon compounds of the lipids in present-day organisms [*see illustration on next page*]. Generally one finds a series of compounds of similar structure, such as the normal, or straight-chain, alkanes (called *n*-alkanes); the compounds extracted from sediments usually contain up to 35 carbon atoms. Alkanes isolated from sediments may have been buried as such or formed by the reduction of substances containing oxygen.

The more complicated the structure of the molecule, the more valuable it is likely to be for geochemical purposes: its information content is greater. Good examples are the alkanes with branches and rings, such as phytane and cholestane. It is unlikely that these complex alkanes could be built up from small subunits by processes other than biological ones, at least in the proportions found. Hence we are encouraged to look

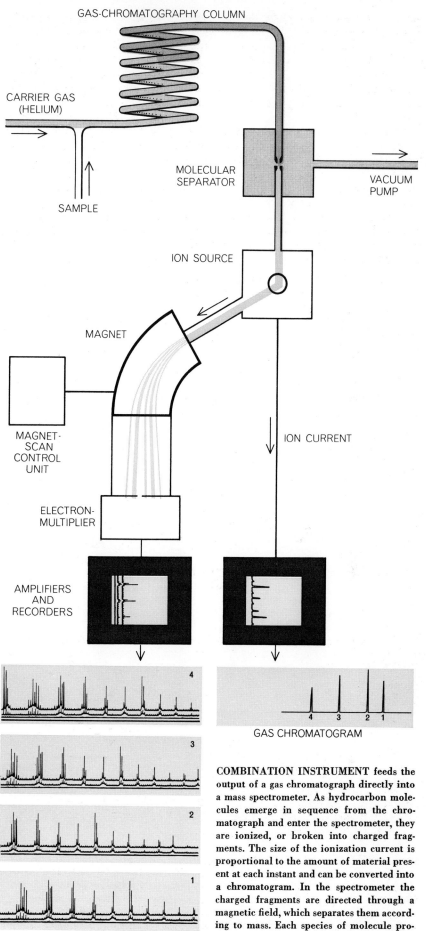

COMBINATION INSTRUMENT feeds the output of a gas chromatograph directly into a mass spectrometer. As hydrocarbon molecules emerge in sequence from the chromatograph and enter the spectrometer, they are ionized, or broken into charged fragments. The size of the ionization current is proportional to the amount of material present at each instant and can be converted into a chromatogram. In the spectrometer the charged fragments are directed through a magnetic field, which separates them according to mass. Each species of molecule produces a unique mass-distribution pattern.

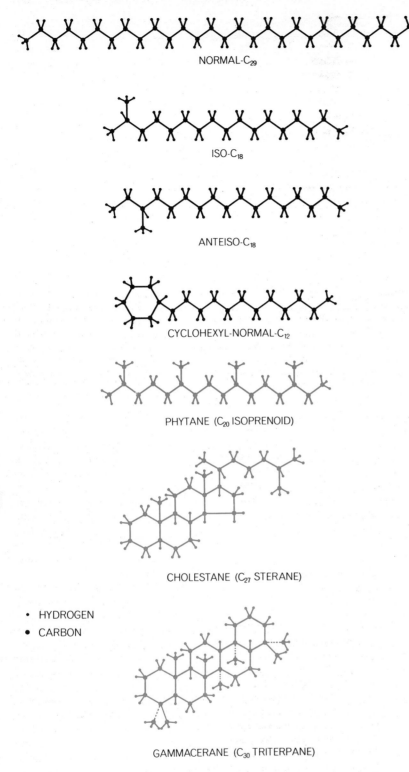

NORMAL-C$_{29}$

ISO-C$_{18}$

ANTEISO-C$_{18}$

CYCLOHEXYL-NORMAL-C$_{12}$

PHYTANE (C$_{20}$ ISOPRENOID)

CHOLESTANE (C$_{27}$ STERANE)

· HYDROGEN
● CARBON

GAMMACERANE (C$_{30}$ TRITERPANE)

CAROTANE (C$_{40}$ TETRATERPANE)

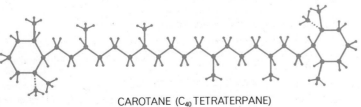

ALKANE HYDROCARBON MOLECULES can take various forms: straight chains (which are actually zigzag chains), branched chains and ring structures. Those depicted here have been found in crude oils and shales. The molecules shown in color are so closely related to well-known biological molecules that they are particularly useful in bespeaking the existence of ancient life. The broken lines indicate side chains that are directed into the page.

for biological precursors with appropriate preexisting carbon skeletons.

In conducting this kind of search one makes the assumption, at least at the outset, that the overall biochemistry of past organisms was similar to that of present-day organisms. When lipid fractions are isolated directly from modern biological sources, they are generally found to contain a range of hydrocarbons, fatty acids, alcohols, esters and so on. The mixture is diverse but by no means random. The molecules present in such fractions have structures that reflect the chemical reaction pathways systematically followed in biological organisms. There are only a few types of biological molecule wherein long chains of carbon atoms are linked together; two examples are the straight-chain lipids, the end groups of which may include oxygen atoms, and the lipids known as isoprenoids.

The straight-chain lipids are produced by what is called the polyacetate pathway [see illustration on opposite page]. This pathway leads to a series of fatty acids with an even number of carbon atoms; the odd-numbered molecules are missing. One also finds in nature straight-chain alcohols (n-alkanols) that likewise have an even number of carbon atoms, which is to be expected if they are formed by simple reduction of the corresponding fatty acids. In contrast, the straight-chain hydrocarbons (n-alkanes) contain an odd number of carbon atoms. Such a series would be produced by the decarboxylation of the fatty acids.

The second type of lipid, the isoprenoids, have branched chains consisting of five-carbon units assembled in a regular order [see illustration on page 210]. Because these units are assembled in head-to-tail fashion the side-chain methyl groups (CH$_3$) are attached to every fifth carbon atom. (Tail-to-tail addition occurs less frequently but accounts for several important natural compounds, for example beta-carotene.) When the isoprenoid skeleton is found in a naturally occurring molecule, it is reasonable to assume that the compound has been formed by this particular biological pathway.

Chlorophyll is possibly the most widely distributed molecule with an isoprenoid chain; therefore it must make some contribution to the organic matter in sediments. Its fate under conditions of geological sedimentation is not known, but it may decompose into only two or three large fragments [see illustration on page 211]. The molecule of chlorophyll a consists of a system of interconnected rings and a phytyl side chain, which is an isoprenoid. When chlorophyll is decomposed, it seems likely that the phytyl chain is split off and converted to phytane (which has the same number of carbon atoms) and pristane (which is shorter by one carbon atom). When both of these branched alkanes are found in a sediment, one has reasonable presumptive evidence that chlorophyll was once present. The chlorophyll ring system very likely gives rise to the metal-containing porphyrins that are found in many crude oils and sediments.

Phytane and pristane may actually enter the sediments directly. Max Blumer of the Woods Hole Oceanographic Institution showed in 1965 that certain species of animal plankton that eat the plant plankton containing chlorophyll store quite large quantities of pristane and related hydrocarbons. The animal plankton act in turn as a food supply for bigger marine animals, thereby accounting for the large quantities of pristane in the liver of the shark and other fishes.

An indirect source for the isoprenoid alkanes could be the lipids found in the outer membrane of certain bacteria that live only in strong salt solutions, an environment that might be found where ancient seas were evaporating. Morris Kates of the National Research Council of Canada has shown that a phytyl-containing lipid (diphytyl phospholipid) is common to bacteria with the highest salt requirement but not to the other bacteria examined so far.

This last example brings out the point that in spite of the overall oneness of present-day biochemistry, organisms do differ in the compounds they make. They also synthesize the same compounds in different proportions. These differences are making it possible to classify living species on a chemotaxonomic, or chemical, basis rather than on a morphological, or shape, basis. Eventually it may be possible to extend chemical classification to ancient organisms, creating a discipline that could be called paleochemotaxonomy.

Our study of chemical fossils began in 1961, when we decided to probe the sedimentary rocks of the Precambrian period in a search for the earliest signs of life. This vast period of time, some four billion years, encompasses the beginnings of life on this planet and its early development to the stage of organisms consisting of more than one cell [see illustrations on page 205]. We hoped that our study would complement the efforts being made by a number of work-

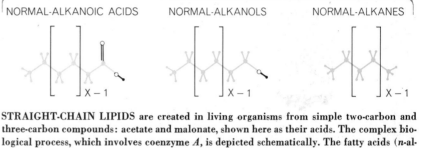

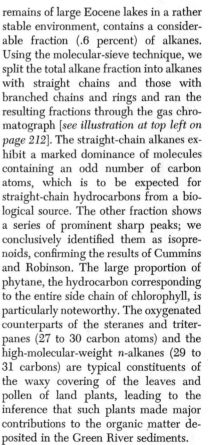

• HYDROGEN
• CARBON
○ OXYGEN

ACETIC ACID   MALONIC ACID

NORMAL-ALKANOIC ACIDS   NORMAL-ALKANOLS   NORMAL-ALKANES

X − 1   X − 1   X − 1

STRAIGHT-CHAIN LIPIDS are created in living organisms from simple two-carbon and three-carbon compounds: acetate and malonate, shown here as their acids. The complex biological process, which involves coenzyme A, is depicted schematically. The fatty acids (*n*-alkanoic acids) and fatty alcohols (*n*-alkanols) produced in this way have an even number of carbon atoms. The removal of carbon dioxide from the fatty acids, the net effect of decarboxylation, would give rise to a series of *n*-alkanes with an odd number of carbon atoms.

ers, including one of us (Calvin), to imitate in the laboratory the chemical evolution that must have preceded the appearance of life on earth. We also saw the possibility that our work could be adapted to the study of meteorites and of rocks obtained from the moon or nearby planets. Thus it even includes the possibility of uncovering exotic and alien biochemistries. The exploration of the ancient rocks of the earth provides a testing ground for the method and the concepts involved.

We chose the alkanes because one might expect them to resist fairly high temperatures and chemical attack for long periods of time. Moreover, J. G. Bendoraitis of the Socony Oil Company, Warren G. Meinschein of the Esso Research Laboratory and others had already identified individual long-chain alkanes, including a range of isoprenoid types, in certain crude oils. Even more encouraging, J. J. Cummins and W. E. Robinson of the U.S. Bureau of Mines had just made a preliminary announcement of their isolation of phytane, pristane and other isoprenoids from a relatively young sedimentary rock: the Green River shale of Colorado, Utah and Wyoming. Thus the alkanes seemed to offer the biological markers we were seeking. Robinson generously provided our laboratory with samples of the Green River shale, which was deposited some 50 million years ago and constitutes the major oil-shale reserve of the U.S.

The Green River shale, which is the

remains of large Eocene lakes in a rather stable environment, contains a considerable fraction (.6 percent) of alkanes. Using the molecular-sieve technique, we split the total alkane fraction into alkanes with straight chains and those with branched chains and rings and ran the resulting fractions through the gas chromatograph [see illustration at top left on page 212]. The straight-chain alkanes exhibit a marked dominance of molecules containing an odd number of carbon atoms, which is to be expected for straight-chain hydrocarbons from a biological source. The other fraction shows a series of prominent sharp peaks; we conclusively identified them as isoprenoids, confirming the results of Cummins and Robinson. The large proportion of phytane, the hydrocarbon corresponding to the entire side chain of chlorophyll, is particularly noteworthy. The oxygenated counterparts of the steranes and triterpanes (27 to 30 carbon atoms) and the high-molecular-weight *n*-alkanes (29 to 31 carbons) are typical constituents of the waxy covering of the leaves and pollen of land plants, leading to the inference that such plants made major contributions to the organic matter deposited in the Green River sediments.

Although the gross chemical structure (number of rings and side chains) of the steranes and triterpanes was established in this work, it was only recently that the precise structure of one of these hydrocarbons was conclusively established. E. V. Whitehead and his associates in the British Petroleum Company and Robinson and his collaborators in the Bureau of Mines have shown that one of the triterpanes extracted from the Green River shale is identical in all respects with gammacerane [*see illustration on page 208*]. Conceivably it is produced by the reduction of a compound known as gammaceran-3-beta-ol, which was recently isolated from the common protozoon *Tetrahymena pyriformis*. Other derivatives of gammacerane are rather widely distributed in the plant kingdom.

At our laboratory in Glasgow, Sister Mary T. J. Murphy and Andrew McCormick recently identified several steranes and triterpanes and also the tetraterpane called perhydro-beta-carotene, or carotane [*see top illustration on page 215*]. Presumably carotane is derived by reduction from beta-carotene, an important red pigment of plants. A similar reduction process could convert the familiar biological compound cholesterol into cholestane, one of the steranes found in the Green River shale [*see same illustration on page 215*]. The mechanism and sedimentary site of such geochemical reduction processes is an important problem awaiting attack.

W. H. Bradley of the U.S. Geological Survey has sought a contemporary counterpart of the richly organic ooze that presumably gave rise to the Green River shale. So far he has located only four lakes, two in the U.S. and two in Africa, that seem to be reasonable candidates. One of them, Mud Lake in Florida, is now being studied closely. A dense belt of vegetation surrounding the lake filters out all the sand and silt that might otherwise be washed into it from the land. As a result the main source of sedimentary material is the prolific growth of microscopic algae. The lake bottom uniformly consists of a grayish-green ooze about three feet deep. The bottom of the ooze was deposited about 2,300 years ago, according to dating by the carbon-14 technique.

Microscopic examination of the ooze shows that it consists mainly of minute fecal pellets, made up almost exclusively of the cell walls of blue-green algae. Some pollen grains are also present. Decay is surprisingly slow in spite of the ooze's high content of bound oxygen and the temperatures characteristic of Florida. Chemical analyses in several laboratories, reported this past November at a meeting of the Geological Society of America, indicate that there is indeed considerable correspondence between the lipids of the Mud Lake ooze and those of the Green River shale. Eugene McCarthy of the University of California at Berkeley has also found beta-carotene in samples of Mud Lake ooze that are about 1,100 years old. The high oxygen content of the Mud Lake ooze seems inconsistent, however, with the dominance of oxygen-poor compounds in the Green River shale. The long-term geological mechanisms that account for the loss of oxygen may have to be sought in sediments older than those in Mud Lake.

Sediments much older than the Green River shale have now been examined by our groups in Berkeley and Glasgow, and by workers in other universities and in oil-industry laboratories. We find that the hydrocarbon fractions in these more ancient samples are usually more complex than those of the Green River shale; the gas chromatograms of the older samples tend to show a number of partially resolved peaks centered around a single maximum. One of the older sediments we have studied is the Antrim shale of Michigan. A black shale probably 350 million years old, it resembles other shales of the Chattanooga type that underlie many thousands of square miles of the eastern U.S. Unlike the Green River shale, the straight-chain alkane fraction of the Antrim shale shows little or no predominance of an odd number of carbon atoms over an even number [*see middle illustration of three at top of pages 212 and 213*]. The alkanes with branched chains and rings, however, continue to be rich in isoprenoids.

The fact that alkanes with an odd number of carbon atoms are not predominant in the Antrim shale and sediments of comparable antiquity may be owing to the slow cracking by heat of carbon chains both in the alkane component and in the kerogen component. The effect can be partially reproduced in the laboratory by heating a sample of the Green River shale for many hours above 300 degrees centigrade. After such treatment the straight-chain alkanes show a reduced dominance of odd-carbon molecules and the branched-chain-and-ring fraction is more complex.

The billion-year-old shale from the Nonesuch formation at White Pine, Mich., exemplifies how geological, geochemical and micropaleontological techniques can be brought to bear on the problem of detecting ancient life. With the aid of the electron microscope Elso S. Barghoorn and J. William Schopf of Harvard University have detected in the Nonesuch shale "disaggregated particles of condensed spheroidal organic matter." In collaboration with Meinschein the Harvard workers have also found evidence that the Nonesuch shale contains isoprenoid alkanes, steranes and porphyrins. Independently we have analyzed the Nonesuch shale and found that it contains pristane and phytane, in addition to iso-alkanes, anteiso-alkanes and cyclohexyl alkanes.

Barghoorn and S. A. Tyler have also detected microfossils in the Gunflint chert of Ontario, which is 1.9 billion years old, almost twice the age of the

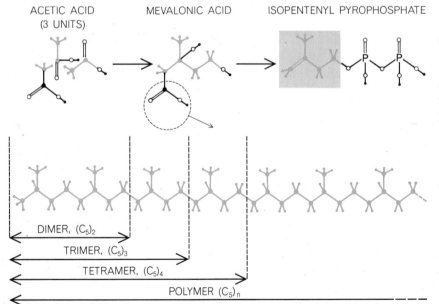

ACETIC ACID (3 UNITS)   MEVALONIC ACID   ISOPENTENYL PYROPHOSPHATE

DIMER, (C₅)₂

TRIMER, (C₅)₃

TETRAMER, (C₅)₄

POLYMER (C₅)ₙ

BRANCHED-CHAIN LIPIDS are produced in living organisms by an enzymatically controlled process, also depicted schematically. In this process three acetate units link up to form a six-carbon compound (mevalonic acid), which subsequently loses a carbon atom and is combined with a high-energy phosphate. "Head to tail" assembly of the five-carbon subunits produces branched-chain molecules that are referred to as isoprenoid structures.

Nonesuch shale. They have reported that the morphology of the Gunflint microfossils "is similar to that of the existing primitive filamentous blue-green algae."

One of the oldest Precambrian sediments yet analyzed is the Soudan shale of Minnesota, which was formed about 2.7 billion years ago. Although its total hydrocarbon content is only .05 percent, we have found that it contains a mixture of straight-chain alkanes and branched-chain-and-ring alkanes not unlike those present in the much younger Antrim shale [*see third illustration of three at top of next two pages*]. In the branched-chain-and-ring fraction we have identified pristane and phytane. Steranes and triterpanes also seem to be present, but we have not yet established their precise three-dimensional structure. Preston E. Cloud of the University of California at Los Angeles has reported that the Soudan shale contains microstructures resembling bacteria or blue-green algae, but he is not satisfied that the evidence is conclusive.

A few reports are now available on the most ancient rocks yet examined: sediments from the Fig Tree system of Swaziland in Africa, some 3.1 billion years old. An appreciable fraction of the alkane component of these rocks consists of isoprenoid molecules. If one assumes that isoprenoids are chemical vestiges of chlorophyll, one is obliged to conclude that living organisms appeared on the earth only about 1.7 billion years after the earth was formed (an estimated 4.8 billion years ago).

Before reaching this conclusion, however, one would like to be sure that the isoprenoids found in ancient sediments have the precise carbon skeleton of the biological molecules from which they are presumed to be derived. So far no sample of pristane or phytane—the isoprenoids that may be derived from the phytyl side chain of chlorophyll—has been shown to duplicate the precise three-dimensional structure of a pure reference sample. Vigorous efforts are being made to clinch the identification.

Assuming that one can firmly establish the presence of biologically structured isoprenoid alkanes in a sediment, further questions remain. The most serious one is: Were the hydrocarbons or their precursors deposited when the sediment was formed or did they seep in later? This question is not easily answered. A sample can be contaminated at any point up to—and after—the time it reaches the laboratory bench. Fossil fuels, lubricants and waxes are omnipresent, and laboratory solvents contain

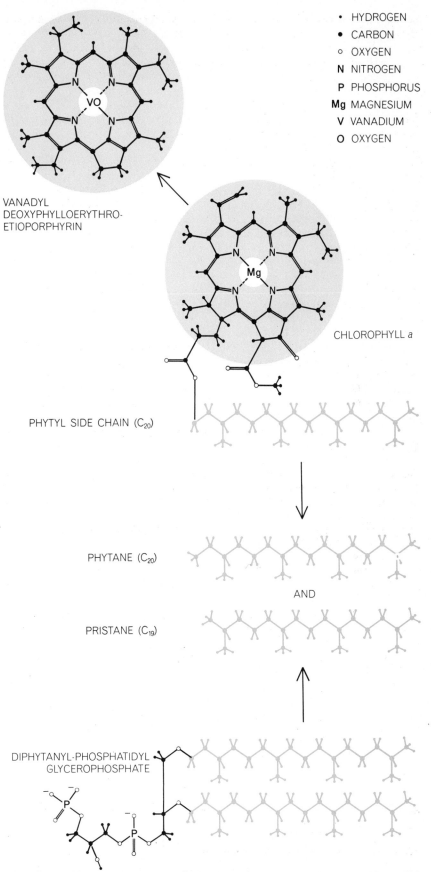

- • HYDROGEN
- • CARBON
- ○ OXYGEN
- N NITROGEN
- P PHOSPHORUS
- Mg MAGNESIUM
- V VANADIUM
- O OXYGEN

VANADYL DEOXYPHYLLOERYTHRO-ETIOPORPHYRIN

CHLOROPHYLL *a*

PHYTYL SIDE CHAIN (C₂₀)

PHYTANE (C₂₀)

AND

PRISTANE (C₁₉)

DIPHYTANYL-PHOSPHATIDYL GLYCEROPHOSPHATE

DEGRADATION OF CHLOROPHYLL *A*, the green pigment in plants, may give rise to two kinds of isoprenoid molecules, phytane and pristane, that have been identified in many ancient sediments. It also seems likely that phytane and pristane can be derived from the isoprenoid side chains of a phosphate-containing lipid (*bottom structure*) that is a major constituent of salt-loving bacteria. The porphyrin ring of chlorophyll *a* is the probable source of vanadyl porphyrin (*upper left*) that is widely found in crude oils and shales.

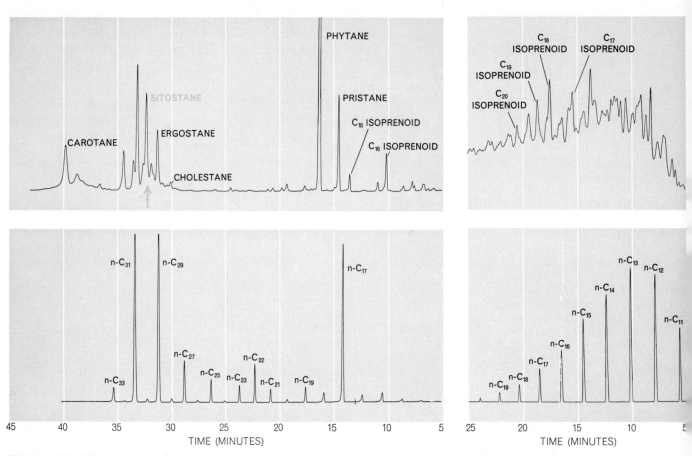

HYDROCARBONS IN YOUNG SEDIMENT, the 50-million-year-old Green River shale, produced these chromatograms. Alkanes with branched chains and rings appear in the top curve, normal alkanes in the bottom curve. The alkanes in individual peaks were identified by mass spectrometry and other methods. Such alkanes as phytane and pristane and the predominance of normal alkanes with an odd number of carbon atoms affirm that the hydrocarbons are biological in origin. The bimodal distribution of the curves is also significant.

OLDER SEDIMENTS are represented by the Antrim shale (*left*), which is 350 million years old, and by the Soudan shale (*right*), which is 2.7 billion years old. Alkanes with branched chains and rings again are shown in the top curves, normal alkanes

tiny amounts of pristane and phytane unless they are specially purified.

One way to determine whether or not rock hydrocarbons are indigenous is to measure the ratio of the isotopes carbon 13 and carbon 12 in the sample. (The ratio is expressed as the excess of carbon 13 in parts per thousand compared with

the isotope ratio in a standard: a sample of a fossil animal known as a belemnite.) The principle behind the test is that photosynthetic organisms discriminate against carbon 13 in preference to carbon 12. Although we have few clues to the abundance of the two isotopes throughout the earth's history, we can

at least test various hydrocarbon fractions in a given sample to see if they have the same isotope ratio. As a simple assumption, one would expect to find the same ratio in the soluble organic fraction as in the insoluble kerogen fraction, which could not have seeped into the rock as kerogen.

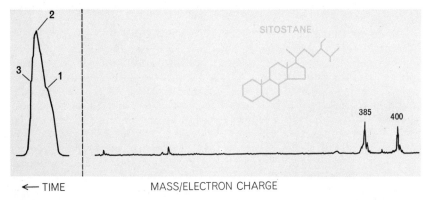

IDENTIFICATION OF SITOSTANE in the Green River shale was accomplished by "trapping" the alkanes that produced a major peak in the chromatogram (*colored arrow at top left on this page*) and passing them through the chromatograph-mass spectrometer. As the chromatograph drew the curve at the left, three scans were made with the spectrometer. Scan 1 (*partially shown at right*) is identical with the scan produced by pure sitostane.

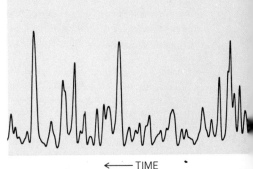

NINETEEN-CARBON ISOPRENOID was identified in the Antrim shale by using a coinjection technique together with a high-resolution gas chromatograph. These two high-resolution curves, each taken from a

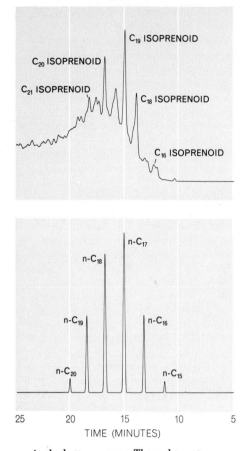

in the bottom curves. These chromatograms lack a pronounced bimodal distribution and the normal alkanes do not show a predominance of molecules with an odd number of carbon atoms. Nevertheless, the prevalence of isoprenoids argues for a biological origin.

Philip H. Abelson and Thomas C. Hoering of the Carnegie Institution of Washington have made such measurements on sediments of various geological ages and have found that the isotope ratios for soluble and insoluble fractions in most samples agree reasonably well. In some of the oldest samples, however,

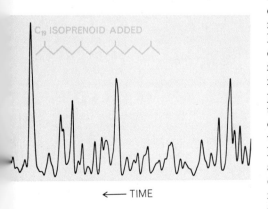

much longer trace, show the change in height of a specific peak when a small amount of pure 19-carbon isoprenoid was coinjected with the sample. Other peaks can be similarly identified by coinjecting known alkanes.

there are inconsistencies. In the Soudan shale, for example, the soluble hydrocarbons have an isotope ratio expressed as −25 parts per thousand compared with −34 parts per thousand for the kerogen. (In younger sediments and in present-day marine organisms the ratio is about midway between these two values: −29 parts per thousand.) The isotope divergence shown by hydrocarbons in the Soudan shale may indicate that the soluble hydrocarbons and the kerogen originated at different times. But since nothing is known of the mechanism of kerogen formation or of the alterations that take place in organic matter generally, the divergence cannot be regarded as unequivocal evidence of separate origin.

On the other hand, there is some reason to suspect that the isoprenoids did indeed seep into the Soudan shale sometime after the sediments had been laid down. The Soudan formation shows evidence of having been subjected to temperatures as high as 400 degrees C. The isoprenoid hydrocarbons pristane and phytane would not survive such conditions for very long. But since the exact date, extent and duration of the heating of the Soudan shale are not known, one can only speculate about whether the isoprenoids were indigenous and survived or seeped in later. In any event, they could not have seeped in much later because the sediment became compacted and relatively impervious within a few tens of millions of years.

A still more fundamental issue is whether or not isoprenoid molecules and others whose architecture follows that of known biological substances could have been formed by nonbiological processes. We and others are studying the kinds and concentrations of hydrocarbons produced by both biological and nonbiological sources. Isoprene itself, the hydrocarbon whose polymer constitutes natural rubber, is easily prepared in the laboratory, but no one has been able to demonstrate that isoprenoids can be formed nonbiologically under geologically plausible conditions. Using a computer approach, Margaret O. Dayhoff of the National Biomedical Research Foundation and Edward Anders of the University of Chicago and their colleagues have concluded that under certain restricted conditions isoprene should be one of the products of their hypothetical reactions. But this remains to be demonstrated in the laboratory.

It is well known, of course, that complex mixtures of straight-chain, branched-chain and even ring hydrocarbons can readily be synthesized in the

laboratory from simple starting materials. For example, the Fischer-Tropsch process, used by the Germans as a source of synthetic fuel in World War II, produces a mixture of saturated hydrocarbons from carbon monoxide and water. The reaction requires a catalyst (usually nickel, cobalt or iron), a pressure of about 100 atmospheres and a temperature of from 200 to 350 degrees C. The hydrocarbons formed by this process, and several others that have been studied, generally show a smooth distribution of saturated hydrocarbons. Many of them have straight chains but lack the special characteristics (such as the predominance of chains with an odd number of carbons) found in the similar hydrocarbons present in many sediments. Isoprenoid alkanes, if they are formed at all, cannot be detected.

Paul C. Marx of the Aerospace Corporation has made the ingenious suggestion that isoprenoids may be produced by the hydrogenation of graphite. In the layered structure of graphite the carbon atoms are held in hexagonal arrays by carbon-carbon bonds. Marx has pointed out that if the bonds were broken in certain ways during hydrogenation, an isoprenoid structure might result. Again a laboratory demonstration is needed to support the hypothesis. What seems certain, however, is that nonbiological syntheses are extremely unlikely to produce those specific isoprenoid patterns found in the products of living cells.

Another dimension is added to this discussion by the proposal, made from time to time by geologists, that certain hydrocarbon deposits are nonbiological in origin. Two alleged examples of such a deposit are a mineral oil found enclosed in a quartz mineral at the Abbott mercury mine in California and a bitumen-like material called thucolite found in an ancient nonsedimentary rock in Ontario. Samples of both materials have been analyzed in our laboratory at Berkeley. The Abbott oil contains a significant isoprenoid fraction and probably constitutes an oil extracted and brought up from somewhat older sediments of normal biological origin. The thucolite consists chiefly of carbon from which only a tiny hydrocarbon fraction can be extracted. Our analysis shows, however, that the fraction contains trace amounts of pristane and phytane. Recognizing the hazards of contamination, we are repeating the analysis, but on the basis of our preliminary findings we suspect that the thucolite sample represents an oil of biological origin that has been almost completely carbonized. We are aware, of course, that one runs the risk of invoking circular arguments in such discussions. Do isoprenoids demonstrate biological origin (as we and others are suggesting) or does the presence of isoprenoids in such unlikely substances indicate that they were formed nonbiologically? The debate may not be quickly settled.

There is little doubt, in any case, that organic compounds of considerable variety and complexity must have accumulated on the primitive earth during the prolonged period of nonbiological chemical development—the period of chemical evolution. With the appearance of the first living organisms biological evolution took command and presumably the "food stock" of nonbiological compounds was rapidly altered. If the changeover was abrupt on a geological time scale, one would expect to find evidence of it in the chemical composition of sediments whose age happens to bracket the period of transition. Such a discontinuity would make an intensely exciting find for organic geochemistry. The transition from chemical to biological evolution must have occurred earlier than three billion years ago. As yet, however, no criteria have been established for distinguishing between the two types of evolutionary process.

We suggest that an important distinction should exist between the kinds of molecules formed by the two processes. In the period of chemical evolution autocatalysis must have been one of the dominant mechanisms for creating large molecules. An autocatalytic system is one in which a particular substance promotes the formation of more of itself. In biological evolution, on the other hand, two different molecular systems are involved: an information-bearing system based on nucleic acids and a catalytic system based on proteins. The former directs the synthesis of the latter. A major problem, subject to laboratory experiment, is visualizing how the two systems originated and were linked.

The role of lipids in the transition may have been important. Today lipids form an important part of the membranes of all living cells. A. I. Oparin, the Russian investigator who was among the first to discuss in detail the chemical origin of life, has suggested that an essential step in the transition from chemical to biological evolution may have been the formation of membranes around droplets, which could then serve as "reaction vessels." Such self-assembling membranes might well have required lipid constituents for their function, which would be to allow some compounds to enter and leave the "cell" more readily than others. These membranes might have been formed nonbiologically by the polymerization of simple two-carbon and three-carbon units. According to this line of reasoning, the compounds that are now prominent constituents of living things are prominent precisely because they were prominent products of chemical evolution. We scarcely need add that this is a controversial and therefore stimulating hypothesis.

What one can say with some confidence is that autocatalysis alone seems unlikely to have been capable of producing the distribution pattern of hydrocarbons observed in ancient Precambrian rocks, even when some allowance is made for subsequent reactions over the course of geologic time. That it could have produced compounds of the observed type is undoubtedly possible, but

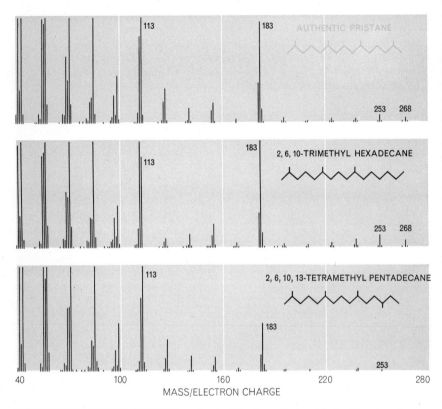

SIMILARITY OF MASS SPECTRA makes it difficult to distinguish the 19-carbon isoprenoid pristane from two of its many isomers (molecules with the same number of carbon and hydrogen atoms). The three records shown here are replotted from the actual tracings produced by pure compounds. When the sample contains impurities, as is normally the case, the difficulty of identifying authentic pristane by mass spectrometry is even greater.

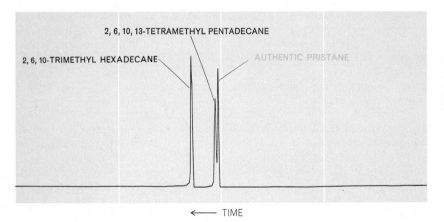

IDENTIFICATION OF PRISTANE can be done more successfully with the aid of a high-resolution gas chromatograph. When pure pristane and the isomers shown in the illustration above are fed into such an instrument, they produce three distinct peaks. This curve and the mass spectra were made by Eugene McCarthy of the University of California at Berkeley. He also made the isoprenoid study shown at the bottom of preceding two pages.

it seems to us that the observed pattern could not have arisen without the operation of those molecular systems we now recognize as the basis of living things. Eventually it should be possible to find in the geological record certain molecular fossils that will mark the boundary between chemical and biological evolution.

Another and more immediate goal for the organic geochemist is to attempt to trace on the molecular level the direction of biological evolution. For such a study one would like to have access to the actual nucleic acids and proteins synthesized by ancient organisms, but these are as yet unavailable (except perhaps in rare instances). We must therefore turn to the geochemically stable compounds, such as the hydrocarbons and oxygenated compounds that must have derived from the operation of the more perishable molecular systems. These "secondary metabolites," as we have referred to them, can be regarded as the signatures of the molecular systems that synthesized them or their close relatives.

It follows that the carbon skeletons found in the secondary metabolites of present-day organisms are the outcome of evolutionary selection. Thus it should be possible for the organic geochemist to arrange in a rough order of evolutionary sequence the carbon skeletons found in various sediments. There are some indications that this may be feasible. G. A. D. Haslewood of Guy's Hospital Medical School in London has proposed that the bile alcohols and bile acids found in present-day vertebrates can be arranged in an evolutionary sequence: the bile acids of the most primitive organisms contain molecules nearest chemically to cholesterol, their supposed biosynthetic precursor.

Within a few years the organic geochemist will be presented with a piece of the moon and asked to describe its organic contents. The results of this analysis will be awaited with immense curiosity. Will we find that the moon is a barren rock or will we discover traces of organic compounds—some perhaps resembling the complex carbon skeletons we had thought could be produced only by living systems? During the 1970's and 1980's we can expect to receive reports from robot sampling and analytical instruments landed on Mars, Venus and perhaps Jupiter. Whatever the results and their possible indications of alien forms of life, we shall be very eager to learn what carbon compounds are present elsewhere in the solar system.

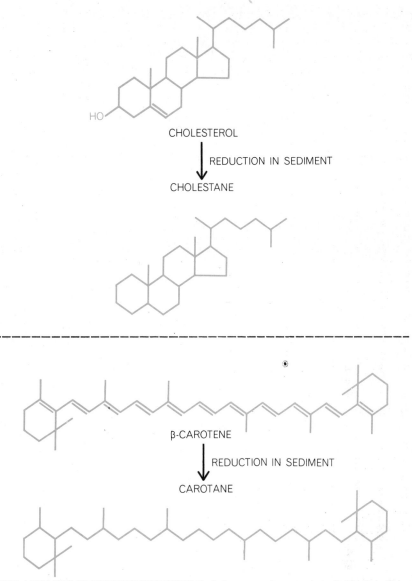

TWO ALKANES IN GREEN RIVER SHALE, cholestane and carotane, probably have been derived from two well-known biological substances: cholesterol and beta-carotene. The former is closely related to the steroid hormones; the latter is a red pigment widely distributed in plants. These two natural substances can be converted to their alkane form by reduction: a process that adds hydrogen at the site of double bonds and removes oxygen.

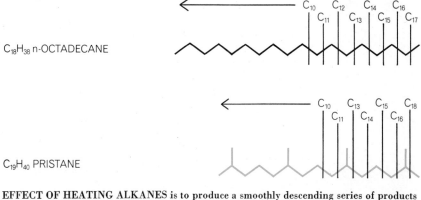

EFFECT OF HEATING ALKANES is to produce a smoothly descending series of products (normal alkenes) if the starting material is a straight-chain molecule such as *n*-octadecane. (The term "alkene" denotes a hydrocarbon with one carbon-carbon double bond.) If, however, the starting material is an isoprenoid such as pristane, heating it to 600 degrees centigrade for .6 second produces an irregular series of alkenes because of the branched chain. Such degradation processes may take place in deeply buried sediments. These findings were made by R. T. Holman and his co-workers at the Hormel Institute in Minneapolis, Minn.

THREE CULTURE TUBES are part of the continuous-culture apparatus used by the Bio-Organic Chemistry Group at the University of California to grow green algae under constant conditions in an aqueous medium. Two tubes are empty; the third contains algae.

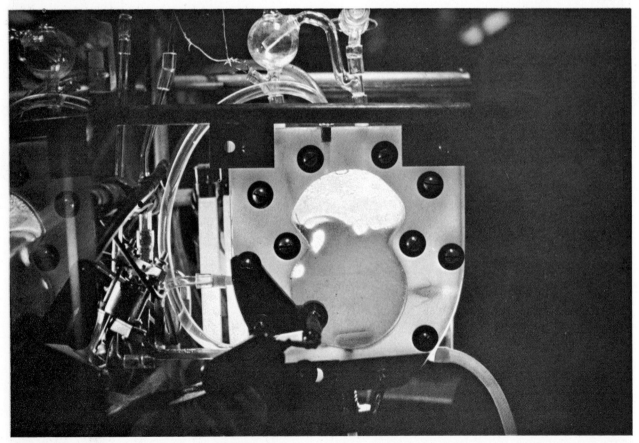

"LOLLIPOP" is a thin, transparent vessel to which algae are transferred from culture tubes. Carbon dioxide containing radioactive carbon is bubbled through the algae suspension in experiments to determine the path taken by carbon in the photosynthetic process.

24

The Path of Carbon in Photosynthesis

J. A. BASSHAM

June 1962

The processes of life consist ultimately of the synthesis and breakdown of carbon compounds. Because a carbon atom can bind four other atoms to itself at a time and is thereby able to link up with other atoms—especially other carbon atoms—in chains and rings, carbon lends itself to the construction of a virtually endless variety of molecules. These molecules derive their physical characteristics and chemical activity not only from their composition but also from their size and intricacy of structure. The rich variety of life suggests in turn that living cells have gone far in the elaboration of such compounds and the processes that make and unmake them. All these processes depend in the end on a first one. This is the process of photosynthesis, which takes carbon and several other common elements from the environment and builds them into the substances of life.

The plant finds most of these elements already bonded to oxygen in oxides such as carbon dioxide (CO_2), water (H_2O), nitrate (NO_3^-) and sulfate (SO_4^{--}). Before the plant can bind the elements other than oxygen together as organic compounds, it must remove some of the excess oxygen as oxygen gas (O_2), and this accomplishment takes a large amount of energy.

In the simplest terms photosynthesis is the process by which green plants trap the energy of sunlight by using that energy to break strong bonds between oxygen and other elements, while forming weaker bonds between the other elements and forcing oxygen atoms to pair as oxygen gas. For example, to make the sugar glucose ($C_6H_{12}O_6$) the plant must split out six molecules of oxygen in order to combine the carbon and half the oxygen of six carbon dioxide molecules with the hydrogen of six water molecules.

The glucose and other organic compounds taken up in the chemical machinery of the plants and the animals that live on plants serve both as fuel and as the raw materials for the synthesis of higher organic compounds. That considerable solar energy is bound by photosynthesis becomes apparent when wood or coal is burned. In living cells the controlled combustion of respiration extracts this energy to power the other processes of life. Both kinds of combustion take oxygen from the air and break down organic compounds to carbon dioxide and water again. In its end result photosynthesis can be defined as the opposite of respiration. Together these complementary processes drive the cyclic flow of matter and the noncyclic flow of energy through the living world [*see illustration below*].

From such generalizations about the effect and function of photosynthesis in nature it is a long step to the explanation of how photosynthesis works. Yet much of the explanation is now complete. The work has been greatly facilitated by the earlier and more nearly complete resolution of the chemistry of respiration. The two processes, it turns out, are in some ways complementary on the molecular scale, just as they are on the grand scale in the biosphere. Each involves some 20 to 30 discrete reactions and as many intermediate compounds; half a dozen of these reactions and their intermediates are common to both photosynthesis and respiration. Only the first few steps in photosynthesis are driven directly by light. The energy of light is trapped in the bonds of a few specific compounds. These energy carriers deliver the energy in discrete units to the steps of synthesis that follow. The same or closely similar carriers perform corresponding operations in respiration, picking up energy from the stepwise dismemberment of the fuel molecule and

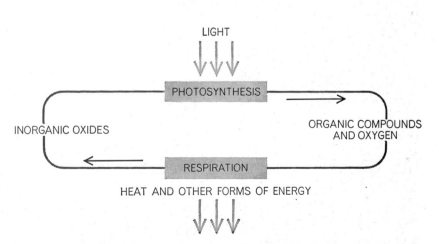

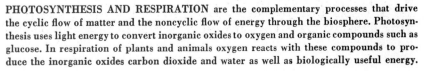

PHOTOSYNTHESIS AND RESPIRATION are the complementary processes that drive the cyclic flow of matter and the noncyclic flow of energy through the biosphere. Photosynthesis uses light energy to convert inorganic oxides to oxygen and organic compounds such as glucose. In respiration of plants and animals oxygen reacts with these compounds to produce the inorganic oxides carbon dioxide and water as well as biologically useful energy.

delivering it to the energy-consuming processes of the cell. Although the first, energy-trapping stage in photosynthesis remains to be clarified, it is now possible to trace the path of carbon from the very first step in which a single atom of carbon is captured in the bonds of an evanescent intermediate compound.

The term "carbohydrate" recalls the deduction of early 19th-century investigators that photosynthesis made glucose directly by combining atoms of carbon with molecules of water, as the formula for glucose suggests. In line with this idea it was thought that the oxygen transpired by green leaves came from the splitting of carbon dioxide. The progress of chemistry, however, failed to disclose any processes that would accomplish these results so simply. Accumulat-

ing evidence to the contrary became convincing some 30 years ago, when C. B. van Niel of Stanford University discovered that certain bacteria produce organic compounds by a process of photosynthesis similar to that in plants but with one important difference. These bacteria use hydrogen sulfide (H_2S) instead of water and liberate elemental sulfur instead of gaseous oxygen. The

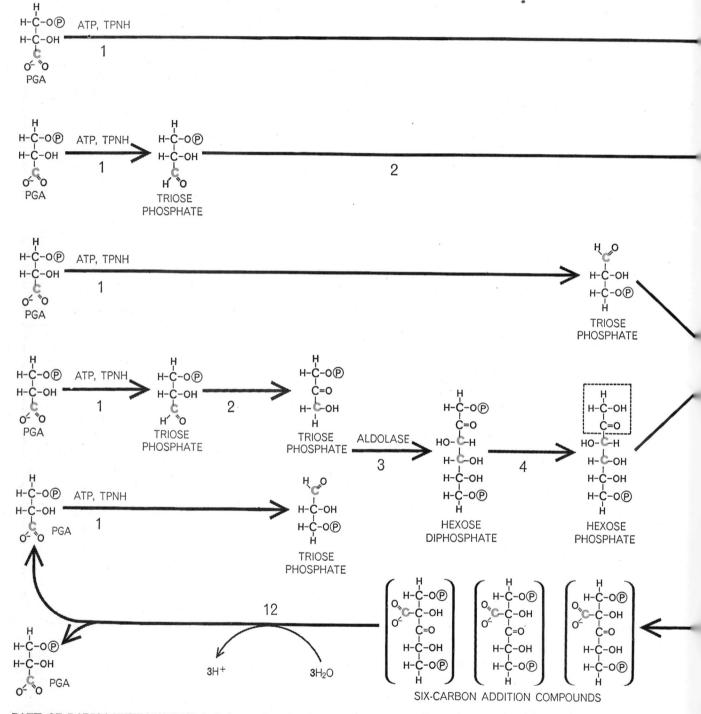

PATH OF RADIOACTIVE CARBON (*color*) was determined from experiments described in the text. Five molecules of PGA, the first stable intermediate product to appear, are reduced (*1*) by cofactors ATP and TPNH to five triose phosphate molecules. A circled *P* represents a phosphate group (—HPO_3^-). Two of these are converted to a different type of triose phosphate (*2*); the subsequent condensation of one of each kind of triose into hexose diphosphate (*3*) is mediated by the enzyme aldolase. Hexose diphosphate then loses a phosphate group (*4*). Transketolase, another enzyme, removes two carbons from the hexose and adds them to a triose

otherwise complete similarity of the two processes strongly suggested that the oxygen evolved by green plants must come from the splitting of water.

The Capture of Light

Photosynthesis could now be described in terms of familiar chemistry. The splitting of water would be accomplished by the process of oxidation (which means the removal of hydrogen atoms from a molecule), with oxygen gas as the product of the reaction. The free hydrogen atoms would then be available to carry through the equally familiar and opposite process of reduction (which means the addition of hydrogen atoms to a molecule). By the addition of hydrogen atoms (or electrons plus hydrogen ions) the carbon dioxide would be reduced to an organic compound.

It is during the first, energy-converting stage of photosynthesis that the water molecule is split. Initially the energy of light impinging on the plant cell is transformed into the chemical potential energy of electrons excited from their normal orbits in molecules of the green pigment chlorophyll and other plant pig-

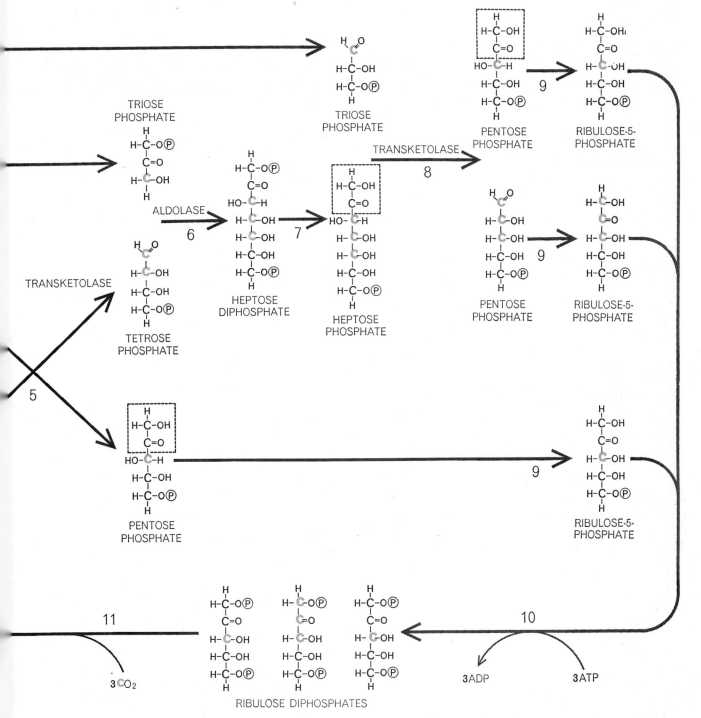

phosphate (5), making one tetrose and one pentose phosphate. The tetrose condenses with a triose (6) to form a heptose diphosphate, which then loses a phosphate group (7). Transketolase removes two carbons from the heptose and adds them to a triose (8), making two more pentose phosphates for a total of three; these are converted to ribulose-5-phosphate (9), then to ribulose diphosphate (10). Addition of three carbon dioxide molecules (11) produces three unstable compounds (*brackets indicate unknown structure*) that begin the cycle again. Addition of three water molecules (12) results in six PGA molecules for a net gain of one in the cycle.

ments. A large part of this energy eventually goes into the splitting of water as electrons and hydrogen ions are transferred from water to the substance triphosphopyridine nucleotide (TPN⁺), which is thereupon reduced to the form designated TPNH. The TPNH thus becomes not only a carrier of energy but also the bearer of electrons for the subsequent reduction of carbon dioxide. Along with the movement of electrons from water to TPNH, some energy goes to charging the energy-carrying molecule adenosine triphosphate (ATP), specifically by promoting the attachment of a third phosphate group (−OPO₃⁻⁻) to adenosine diphosphate (ADP), the discharged form of the carrier. Both ATP and TPNH belong to the family of compounds known as cofactors or coenzymes, which work with enzymes in the catalysis of chemical reactions. ATP, the universal currency of energy transactions in the cell, plays a significant role in respiration as well as in photosynthesis.

Needless to say, the manufacture of each of these cofactors involves an intricate cycle of reactions [see "The Role of Light in Photosynthesis," by Daniel I. Arnon, which is available as Offprint #75]. Although the cycles are not yet fully understood, it is enough for the purpose of the present discussion to know that ATP and TPNH, or closely similar compounds, furnish the energy

for the second stage of photosynthesis, during which the carbon atom of carbon dioxide is reduced and joined to a hydrogen atom and a carbon atom in place of an oxygen.

The process of reduction goes forward in small steps. Each reaction brings about some change in a carbon compound until the starting material is at last transformed to the final product. For each reaction there is therefore an intermediate compound. Since every life process involves a more or less extended series of intermediates, cells typically contain a large number of intermediates. Many of them turn up in two or more pathways leading to different end products. The tracing of the path of carbon in photosynthesis required first of all a technique for identifying the intermediates proper to it and for establishing their sequence along the path.

Samuel Ruben and Martin D. Kamen, then at the University of California, met this need some 20 years ago by their discovery of the radioactive isotope of carbon with a mass number of 14. This isotope has a conveniently long half life of more than 5,000 years; over the time period of an experiment, therefore, carbon 14 has an effectively constant radioactivity. Ruben and his colleagues recognized at once the potential usefulness of this isotope as a label for the identification of compounds in biological processes. They prepared carbon dioxide in

which the carbon atoms were carbon 14. When they exposed green plants to an atmosphere containing this gas instead of normal carbon dioxide (C¹²O₂), the plants took up the C¹⁴O₂ and made compounds from it. The presence of the carbon 14 in these compounds could be detected by various devices, such as the Geiger-Müller counter, and by radioautography on X-ray film. Unfortunately this work was cut short by the war and by Ruben's death in a laboratory accident.

In 1946 Melvin Calvin organized a new group at the Lawrence Radiation Laboratory of the University of California with the primary objective of tracing the path of carbon in photosynthesis with C¹⁴O₂ as one of its principal tools. Starting as a graduate student in 1947, I had the good fortune to participate in this work with Calvin, Andrew A. Benson and others.

The early experiments were quite simply contrived. We used leafy plants and often just the leaves of plants. After allowing a leaf to photosynthesize for a given length of time in an atmosphere of C¹⁴O₂ in a closed chamber, we would bring biochemical activity to a halt by immersing the leaf in alcohol. With the enzymes inactivated, the reactions converting one intermediate compound into another would stop, and the pattern of labeling would be "frozen" at that point. We soon discovered, however, that photosynthesis proceeds too rapidly for completely reliable observation by such a procedure. With a few seconds' delay in the penetration of alcohol into the cell, for example, the labeling pattern would be disarrayed and no longer representative of the stage at which we tried to halt the photosynthesis.

Since rapid and precisely timed killing of the plant is important, we adopted single-celled algae—*Chlorella pyrenoidosa* and *Scenedesmus obliquus*—as the subject for many of our experiments. In both species the plant consists of a single cell so small that it can be seen only with a microscope. Alcohol can quickly penetrate the cell wall and deactivate the enzymes. The algae offer another advantage: they can be grown in continuous cultures, assuring us a supply of material with highly constant properties.

An experimental sample is taken from the culture in a thin-walled, transparent closed vessel. Illuminated through the walls of the vessel and supplied with a stream of ordinary carbon dioxide, which is bubbled through the suspension, the algae photosynthesize at the normal rate. We shut off the supply of carbon dioxide and inject a solution of

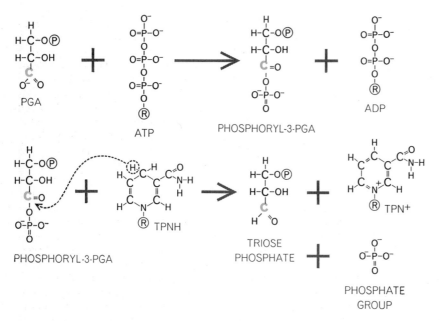

REDUCTION OF PGA to triose phosphate requires both ATP and TPNH. At top ATP gives up its terminal phosphate group to PGA to produce phosphoryl-3-PGA. At bottom TPNH donates a hydrogen atom and an electron (*broken circle and arrow*), thereby displacing a phosphate group and forming triose phosphate. The second step is in reality more complex than shown here and involves other cofactors in addition to TPNH.

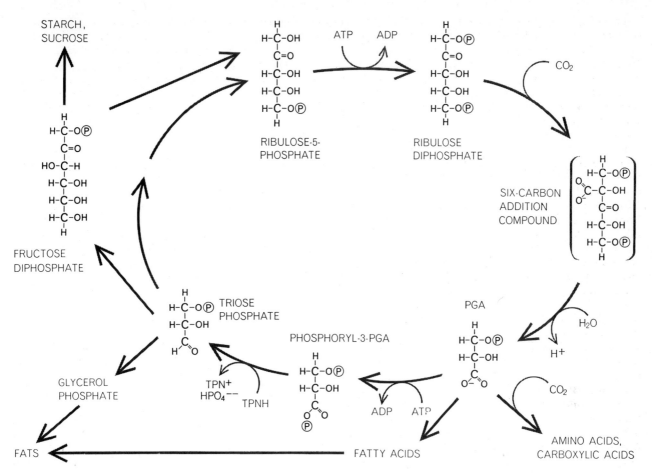

END PRODUCTS OF PHOTOSYNTHESIS are not limited to carbohydrates (e.g., sucrose and starch), as first thought, but include, among other things, fatty acids, fats, carboxylic acids and amino acids. Carbon cycle shown here is highly simplified; it involves at least 12 discrete reactions. Moreover, the steps from PGA to fatty acids and to amino and carboxylic acids have not been indicated.

radioactive bicarbonate ion (carbon dioxide dissolved in our algae culture medium is mostly converted into bicarbonate ion). After a few seconds or minutes the cells are killed. We then extract the soluble radioactive compounds from the plant material and analyze them.

The Reduction of CO₂

Calvin and his colleagues soon found that the carbon 14 label was distributed among several classes of biochemical compounds, including not only sugars but also amino acids: the subunits of proteins. As the exposure time was reduced to a few seconds, the first stable intermediate product of photosynthesis was found to be the three-carbon compound 3-phosphoglyceric acid (PGA).

The next step was to determine which of the three carbon atoms in the first generation of PGA molecules synthesized in the presence of radioactive carbon dioxide bears the carbon 14 label. We first removed from PGA the phosphate group [see illustration on

opposite page] and then diluted the free glyceric acid with glyceric acid containing the stable carbon 12 isotope in order to have enough material for analysis by ordinary chemical methods. Treatment with reagents that severed the bonds between the carbons produced three different products, one from each carbon atom. By measuring the radioactivity of each of the products we were able to identify the labeled carbon.

In PGA from plants that had been exposed to labeled carbon dioxide for only five seconds we found that virtually all the carbon 14 was located in the carboxyl atom, the carbon at one end of the chain that is bound to two oxygens. This was not surprising because the carboxyl group most nearly resembles carbon dioxide. The carbon is bound to the oxygens by three bonds, however, instead of four; the fourth bond now ties it to the middle carbon in the PGA chain. The transfer of this bond from one of the oxygens to a carbon constitutes the first step in the reduction of the carbon dioxide. This was evidence also that the re-

duction is accomplished by some sort of carboxylation reaction, a reaction in which carbon dioxide is added to some organic compound. Ultimately, of course, the two other carbons of PGA must come from carbon dioxide. But it was some time before investigation disclosed the specific compound that picks up the carbon dioxide and the cyclic pathway that makes this carbon dioxide acceptor from PGA.

The discovery of the pathway intermediates was made much easier by a then comparatively new technique: two-dimensional paper chromatography, developed by the British chemists A. J. P. Martin and R. L. M. Synge. Closely similar compounds can be distinguished in this procedure by slight differences in their relative solubility in an organic solvent and in water. The extract from the plant is dropped on a sheet of filter paper near one corner. An edge of the paper adjacent to the corner is immersed in a trough containing an organic solvent; the paper is held taut by a weight and the whole assembly is placed in a water-saturated atmosphere in a vapor-tight box. The solvent traveling through the paper by capillarity dissolves the compounds and carries them along with it. As they move along in the solvent, however, the compounds tend to distribute themselves between the solvent and the water absorbed by the fibers of the paper. In general the more soluble the compound is in water compared with the organic solvent, the slower it travels. If the compound is also absorbed to some extent by the cellulose fibers, its movement will be even slower. As a result the compounds are distributed in a row in one dimension. Depending on the solubility of the compounds and the nature of the solvent used, some compounds may still overlap one another. Repetition of the procedure, with a different solvent traveling at right angles

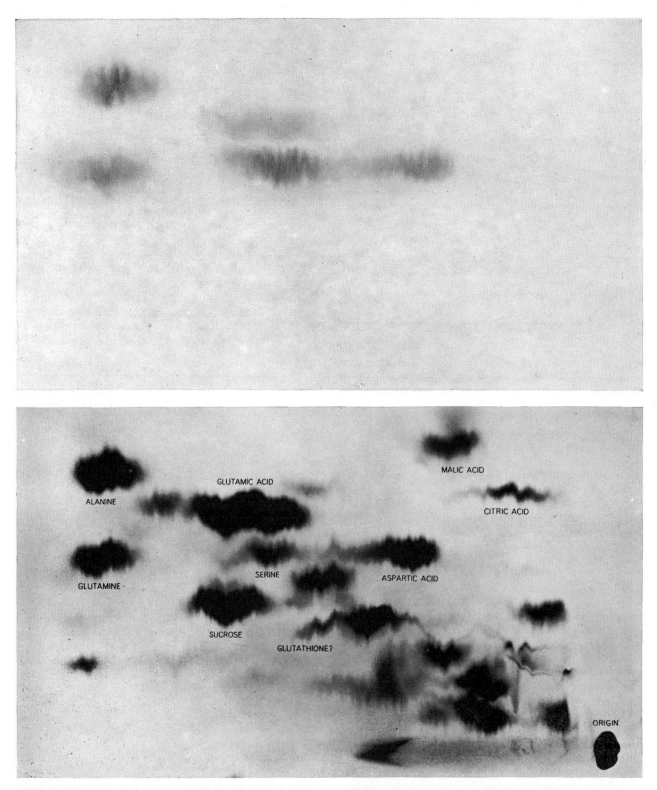

CHROMATOGRAM AND RADIOAUTOGRAPH used to corroborate the identity of amino acids produced by photosynthesizing algae appear at top and bottom respectively. The method of identifying such substances is described in the text. Areas of the radioautograph corresponding to colored areas in the chromatogram are alanine, glutamine, glutamic acid, serine and aspartic acid.

to the direction of the first run, will usually separate these compounds in a second dimension.

Since most of the compounds are colorless, special techniques are needed to locate them on the paper. Those that are radioactive will locate themselves, however, if the chromatographic paper is placed in contact with a sheet of X-ray film for a few days. The resulting radioautograph will show as many as 20 or 30 radioactive compounds in the substances extracted from algae exposed to carbon 14 for only 30 seconds [see illustration at right]. Clearly the synthetic apparatus of the plant works rapidly.

Chromatographs and Radioautographs

In order to identify these compounds we prepared a chromatographic map by running samples of many known compounds through the same chromatographic system and recording the locations at which we found them on the paper. The locations can be made visible in these cases by spraying the paper with a mist of some chemical that is known to react with the compound to produce a colored spot. Comparison of the radioautograph of an unknown compound with the map yields a first clue to its identity. This can be corroborated by washing the radioactive compound out of the paper with water and mixing it with a larger sample of the suspected authentic substance. The mixture is applied to a new piece of filter paper and chromatographed. With enough of the authentic material to yield a colored spot, comparison with a radioautograph of the same paper now shows whether or not the radioactive and the authentic material really coincide. The possibility that the authentic material and the radioactive material are still not the same can be tested by using different solvent systems in the preparation of the chromatograph and by other means.

Over the years these procedures have established the identity of a great many of the intermediate and end products of photosynthesis. Some of the sugar phosphates labeled by carbon 14 proved to be well-known derivatives of triose (three-carbon) and hexose (six-carbon) sugars. Others were discovered for the first time among the intermediates produced by our algae. Benson showed that among these are a seven-carbon sugar phosphate and also five-carbon phosphates, including in particular ribulose-1,5-diphosphate.

The rapid building of carbon 14 into the more familiar triose and hexose phosphates suggested certain biochemi-

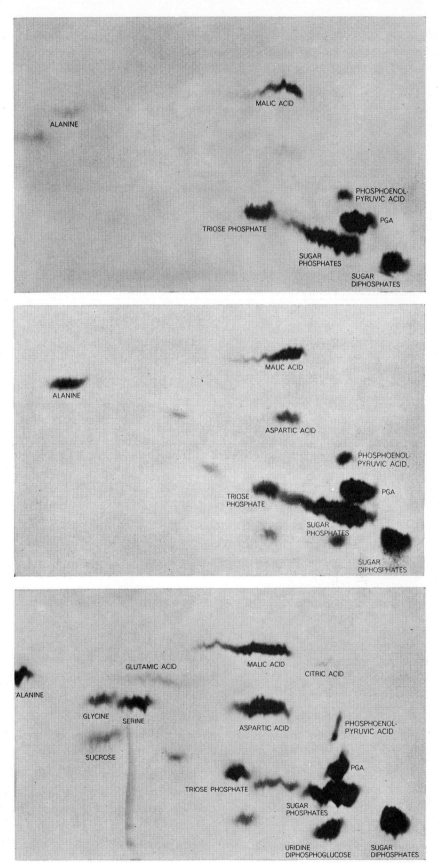

THREE RADIOAUTOGRAPHS reveal the compounds containing radioactive carbon that were produced by *Chlorella* algae during five (*top*), 10 (*middle*) and 30 seconds (*bottom*) of photosynthesis. Alanine, the first amino acid to appear in the process, shows up very faintly at first (*top*); glycine, serine, glutamic acid and aspartic acid appear as photosynthesis progresses. These radioautographs were made at the author's laboratory by exposing X-ray-sensitive film to chromatograms of compounds extracted from three samples of algae.

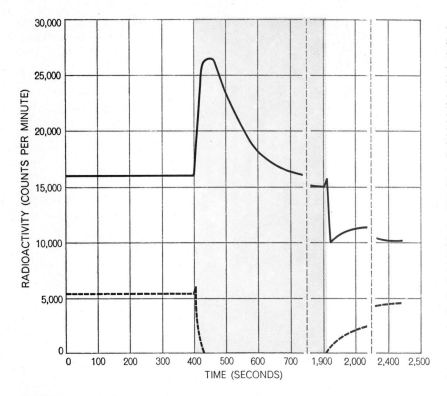

EFFECT OF SUDDEN DARKNESS on PGA (*solid curve*) and ribulose diphosphate (*broken curve*) is shown here. The conversion of ribulose diphosphate to PGA continues after the light is turned off (*colored area*), so that the ribulose concentration drops to zero. The concentration of PGA, which is no longer reduced to triose phosphate by ATP and TPNH, increases momentarily before it is used up in the production of other compounds.

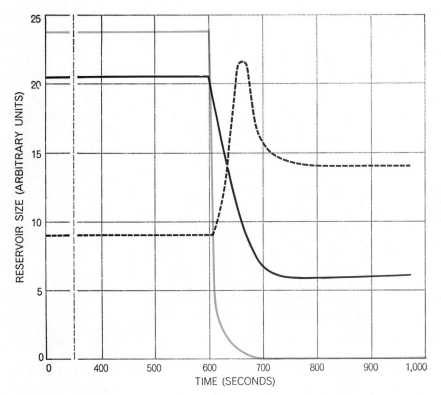

SUDDEN DEPLETION OF CARBON DIOXIDE (*colored curve*) slows the carboxylation of ribulose diphosphate to PGA. Because the light remains on after depletion, ribulose diphosphate (*broken curve*) continues to be formed and its concentration rises. PGA (*black curve*) is still reduced to triose phosphate, so that its concentration drops. "Reservoir size" refers to the average size of the "pool" of any one compound per unit quantity of algae.

cal pathways already established in studies of respiration. It seemed likely that PGA might be linked to these phosphates by the reverse of a sequence of respiratory reactions first mapped many years ago by the German chemists Otto Meyerhof, Gustav Embden and Jakob Parnas. In the respiratory pathway hexose phosphate is split into two molecules of triose phosphate, with the split occurring between the two carbon atoms in the middle of the chain. The triose phosphate is then oxidized to give PGA. The electrons from this energy-yielding operation are picked up by diphosphopyridine nucleotide (DPN^+), which is thereupon reduced to DPNH. The DPN^+ is a close relative of the TPN^+ that turns up in photosynthesis. In addition this oxidation yields enough energy to make a molecule of ATP from ADP and phosphate ion.

In the reverse pathway of these reactions in photosynthesis, Calvin concluded, the plant uses the cofactors ATP and TPNH, made earlier by the transformation of the energy of light, to bring about the reduction of PGA to triose phosphate. In the first step the terminal phosphate group of ATP is transferred to the carboxyl group of PGA to form a "carboxyl phosphate" (really an acyl phosphate). Some of the chemical potential energy that was stored in ATP is now stored in the acyl phosphate, making the new intermediate compound highly reactive. It is now ready for reduction by TPNH. This reducing agent donates two electrons to the reactive intermediate. One carbon-oxygen bond is thereby severed and the oxygen atom, carried off with the phosphate group, is replaced by a hydrogen atom. In this way the carboxyl carbon atom is reduced to an aldehyde carbon atom; that is, it now has two bonds to oxygen instead of three and one bond each to carbon and hydrogen [*see illustration on page 220*]. This is the point in the cycle at which the major portion of the solar energy captured in the first stage of photosynthesis is applied to the reduction of carbon.

The Unstable Intermediate

The next development in the plotting of the carbon pathway came from a series of experiments first performed in our laboratory by Peter Massini. He hoped to see which intermediates would be most strongly increased or decreased in concentration by turning off the light and allowing the synthetic process to go on for a while in the dark. In order to establish the concentration of the various intermediates when the reaction proceeds in the light, he bubbled radioactive carbon dioxide through the culture for more than half an hour. At the end of this period every intermediate was as highly radioactive as the incoming carbon dioxide. The radioactivity from each compound therefore gave a measure of the concentration of the compound. He then turned off the light and after a few seconds took another sample of algae in which he measured the relative concentration of compounds by the same technique. Comparison with the compounds sampled in the light showed that the concentration of PGA was greatly increased. This finding could be readily explained: turning off the light stopped the production of the ATP and TPNH required to reduce PGA to triose phosphate.

Of the sugar phosphates present, only one, the five-carbon ribulose diphosphate, was found to have changed significantly; its concentration dropped to zero. Because the PGA had simultaneously increased in concentration, it was apparent that ribulose diphosphate was consumed in the production of PGA. This finding was of great significance because it indicated for the first time that

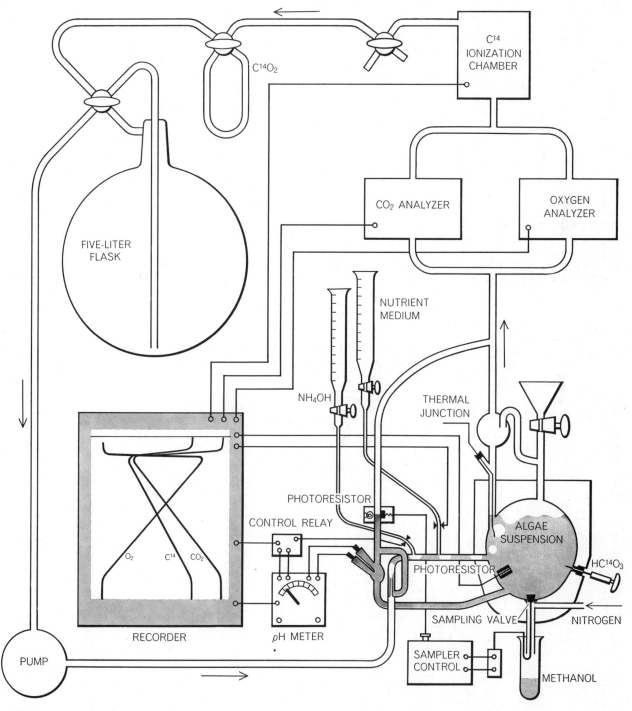

STEADY-STATE APPARATUS permits experimental control and study of photosynthesis. The algae are suspended in nutrient in a transparent vessel (*lower right*). A gas pump circulates a mixture of air, ordinary carbon dioxide and labeled carbon dioxide (when needed) to the vessel, where it bubbles through the suspensions.

Labeled carbon can also be added in the form of bicarbonate ($HC^{14}O_3$). Measurements of the oxygen, carbon dioxide and labeled carbon levels in the gas are recorded continuously. The pH is maintained at a constant value by means of the pH meter. The sampler control allows removal of samples into the test tube.

ribulose diphosphate is the intermediate to which carbon dioxide is attached by the carboxylation reaction.

For this reaction ribulose diphosphate is prepared by an earlier reaction that goes on in the light and in which ATP donates its terminal phosphate group to ribulose monophosphate. The more reactive diphosphate molecule now adds one molecule of carbon dioxide by carboxylation. The details of this reaction remain obscure because the resulting six-carbon intermediate is so unstable that we have not been able to detect it

by our methods of analysis. As its first stable product this sequence of events yields two three-carbon PGA molecules.

Massini's experimental results were confirmed by a parallel experiment devised by Alex Wilson, then a graduate student in our laboratory. Instead of turning out the light Wilson shut off the supply of carbon dioxide. In this situation one might expect to find an increase in the concentration of the compound that is consumed in the carboxylation reaction; ribulose diphosphate showed such an increase. Correspondingly, one

would look for a decrease in the concentration of the product of this reaction; PGA did in fact decrease in concentration.

The first steps along the path were thus established. The photosynthesizing plant starts with ribulose monophosphate and converts it to ribulose diphosphate, using chemical potential energy trapped from the light in the terminal phosphate bond of ATP. Carbon dioxide is joined to this compound, and the resulting six-carbon intermediate splits to two molecules of PGA. With energy and

EXPERIMENT to determine the path of carbon in photosynthesis is outlined. After removal of an algae sample from its culture tube, the sample is placed in a transparent vessel (*top left*). At start of experiment labeled bicarbonate is injected into the vessel (*second from*

top left). A sample is then removed by pressing a button on the sampler control (*third from top left*); alcohol in the test tube kills the algae. The sample is concentrated by evaporation in a special flask to which a vacuum has been applied (*top right*)

electrons supplied by ATP and TPNH, PGA is reduced to triose phosphate. In the next step, it was apparent, two triose phosphates must be joined end to end in the reverse of a familiar respiratory pathway to form a hexose phosphate. The pathway from hexose to pentose phosphate remained to be uncovered.

We continued the carbon-by-carbon dissection and analysis of these chains by the methods that had earlier shown the carbon 14 in PGA to be located first in the carboxyl carbon. In the hexose molecules we had found the labeled carbon concentrated in the two middle carbons, just where it should be if two triose molecules made from PGA were linked together by their labeled ends. We also took apart the seven-carbon and five-carbon sugar phosphates to establish the position of the carbon 14 atoms in their chains. As the result of these degradations we were able to show that the overall economy of the photosynthetic process starts with five three-carbon PGA's, variously transforms them through three-, six-, four- and seven-carbon phosphate intermediates and returns three five-carbon ribulose diphosphates to the starting point [*see illustrations on pages 218 and 219*]. From the carboxylation of these three chains and their immediate bisection, the cycle at last yields six PGA molecules. The net result, therefore, is the conversion of three carbon dioxide molecules to one PGA molecule.

The Calvin Cycle

With these steps filled in, the carbon reduction cycle in photosynthesis, called the Calvin cycle, was complete. The in-

and the extract applied to chromatogram paper (*bottom left*). The paper is placed in a trough of chromatographic solvent (*second from bottom left*), which diffuses through the paper; after eight hours the paper is turned at right angles and the process is repeated. A radioautograph is made by exposing X-ray-sensitive film to the chromatogram (*third from bottom left*). The radioactivity of the compounds in the chromatogram is then measured (*bottom right*), using the radioautograph as a guide to their location.

termediates formed in the cycle depart from it on various pathways to be converted to the end products of photosynthesis. From triose phosphate, for example, one sequence of reactions leads to the six-carbon sugar glucose and the large family of carbohydrates.

Because the cycle had been established primarily by experiments with algae and the leaves of a few higher plants, it was important to see whether or not the cycle prevailed throughout the plant kingdom. Calvin and Louisa and Richard Norris carried out experiments with a wide variety of photosynthetic organisms. In every case, although they found variation in the amounts of particular intermediates formed, the pattern was qualitatively the same.

It also had to be shown that the pathway we had traced out is quantitatively the most important route of carbon reduction in photosynthesis. To this end

Martha Kirk and I undertook an intensive study of the kinetics of the flow of carbon in photosynthesis. Our study has helped to solve other general problems, particularly the question of how carbon enters into the pathways leading to the synthesis of proteins and fats. The biological materials for this work are supplied by an algae culture system under automatic feedback control. In this apparatus we are able to maintain the photosynthetic process in a steady state, with nutrients supplied at a constant rate and with temperature, density, salinity and acidity held within narrow limits.

At the start of a run we inject radioactive bicarbonate ion into the culture medium along with radioactive carbon dioxide gas and so bring the ratio of carbon 14 to carbon 12 immediately to its final level in both the gas and the liquid phase. An automatic recorder measures the rate at which carbon is absorbed by the photosynthesizing cells. We take samples every few seconds and kill the cells immediately by immersing them in alcohol. After we have chromatographed the photosynthetic intermediates and measured their radioactivity we then plot the appearance of labeled carbon

in each of these compounds as a function of time.

By the end of three to five minutes, our records show, all the stable intermediates of the cycle are saturated with carbon 14. Taking the total amount of carbon thus fixed in compounds and comparing it with the rate of uptake of carbon in the culture, we found that the cycle accounts for more than 70 per cent of the total carbon fixed by the algae. A small but significant amount is also taken up by the addition of carbon dioxide to a three-carbon compound, phosphoenōlpyruvic acid, to give four-carbon compounds.

From the earliest work with carbon 14 in our laboratory, it had been apparent that carbon dioxide finds its way rather quickly into products other than carbohydrates in the photosynthesizing plant. This was at variance with traditional ideas about photosynthesis that regarded carbohydrates as the sole organic products of the process. It was important to ask, therefore, whether fats and amino acids could be formed directly from the cycle as products of its intermediates or whether these noncarbohydrates were synthesized only from the carbohydrate end products of photosynthesis. Our kinetic studies show that certain amino acids must indeed be formed from the intermediates and must therefore be regarded as true products of photosynthesis. The amino acid alanine, for example, shows up labeled by carbon 14 at least as rapidly as any carbohydrate; it would be labeled with carbon 14 much more slowly if it were made from carbohydrate, since the carbohydrate would have to be labeled first. We have been able to show that more than 30 per cent of the carbon taken up by the algae in our steady-state system is incorporated directly into amino acids. There is some evidence that fats may also be formed as products of the cycle.

The discovery that plants make these other compounds as direct products of photosynthesis lends new interest and importance to the chloroplast, the subcellular compartment of green cells that contains pigments and the rest of the photosynthetic apparatus. It has been known for some time that this highly structured organelle is responsible for the absorption of light, the splitting of water and the formation of the cofactors for carbon reduction. More recent studies have shown that it is the site of the entire carbon-reduction cycle. Now the chloroplast emerges as a complete photosynthetic factory for the production of just about everything necessary to the plant's growth and function.

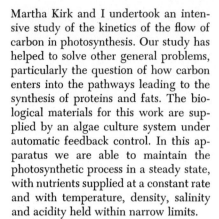

1 HEXOSE AND HEPTOSE
  MONOPHOSPHATES

2 PGA

3 SUCROSE

4 HEXOSE AND HEPTOSE
  DIPHOSPHATES

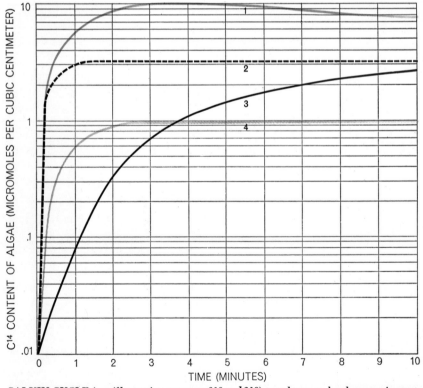

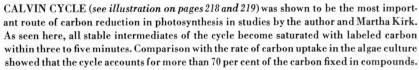

CALVIN CYCLE (*see illustration on pages 218 and 219*) was shown to be the most important route of carbon reduction in photosynthesis in studies by the author and Martha Kirk. As seen here, all stable intermediates of the cycle become saturated with labeled carbon within three to five minutes. Comparison with the rate of carbon uptake in the algae culture showed that the cycle accounts for more than 70 per cent of the carbon fixed in compounds.

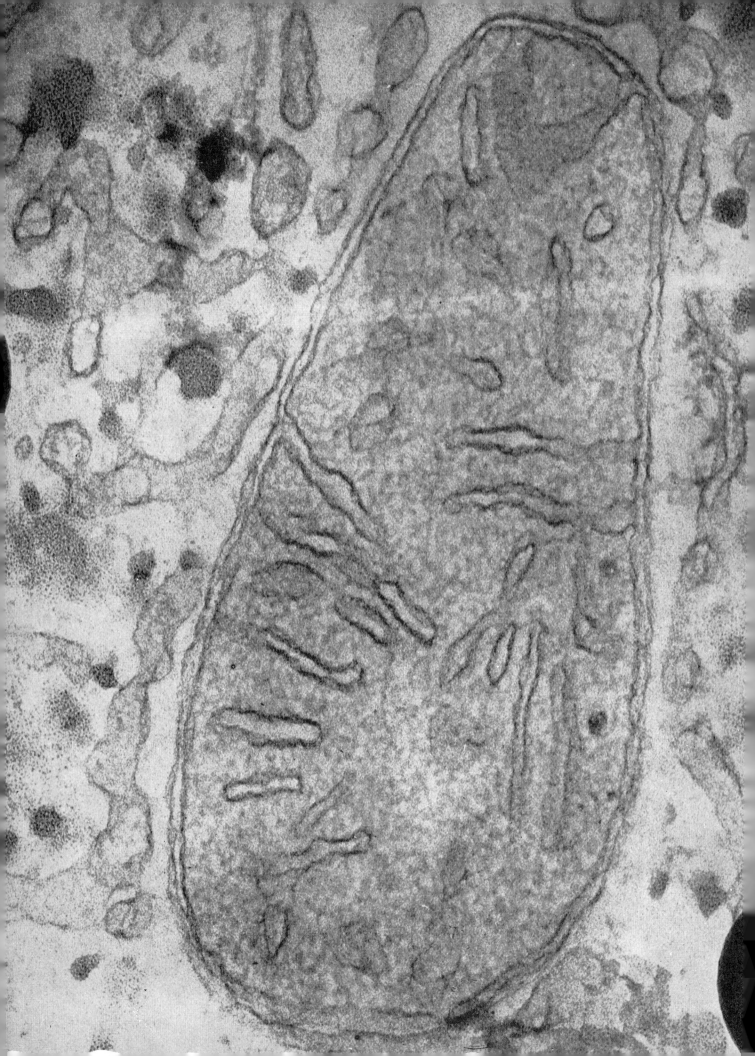

25

Energy Transformation in the Cell

ALBERT L. LEHNINGER

May 1960

A flame and a living cell both burn fuel to yield energy, carbon dioxide and water. The flame, in one step, transforms the chemical energy of the fuel into heat. The cell, in many steps and with little loss to heat, converts this chemical energy into a variety of forms: into the energy of the chemical bonds in the molecules of its own substance, into the mechanical energy of muscle contraction, into the electrical energy of the nerve impulse. In luminescent organisms special cells transform the energy into light.

From the standpoint of thermodynamics the very existence of living things, with their marvelous diversity and complexity of structure and function, is improbable. The laws of thermodynamics say that energy must run "downhill," as in a flame, and that all systems of atoms and molecules must ultimately and inevitably assume the most random configurations with the least energy-content. Continuous "uphill" work is necessary to create and maintain the structure of the cell. It is the capacity to extract energy from its surroundings and to use this energy in an orderly and directed manner that distinguishes the living human organism from the few dollars' (actually $5.66 in today's inflated market) worth of common chemical elements of which it is composed.

The past few years have seen great advances in the investigation of the transformation of energy by the cell. This historic enterprise has engaged the talents of some of the ablest investigators of the century. In its present stage our understanding encompasses not only some of the chemical and physical aspects of the process, but has begun to take in the arrangement of the molecules in the cell that conduct it. Many of the active molecules—the enzymes—have been identified. The intricate chains and cycles of activity by which they extract, trap, exchange and distribute energy have been worked out in sufficient detail to illuminate their principles of operation. And the molecular machinery of these energy-transforming functions has been securely located in the mitochondria, structures found in all cells that burn their fuel in oxygen.

It is, of course, the food intake of the organism that supplies the fuel—sugars, fats and proteins—to the energy-transforming system of the cell. Every student of elementary chemistry learns that a given weight of an organic compound contains a fixed amount of potential energy locked up in the bonds between the atoms of its molecule; for example, the bonds between the carbon, hydrogen and oxygen atoms in the sugar glucose. The energy can be liberated by burning the sugar in oxygen, with the carbon and hydrogen evolving from the flame in the relatively simple, energy-poor molecules of carbon dioxide (CO_2) and water (H_2O). This oxidation yields 690,000 calories per mole of glucose. (A mole is the weight of a substance in grams that is numerically equal to its molecular weight. A mole of glucose weighs 180 grams.) Now it is one of the fundamental principles of thermodynamics that the same total amount of energy is always liberated upon combustion of a given weight of a substance, no matter what the mechanism or pathway of the process. Thus the cellular oxidation of glucose to carbon dioxide and water makes a total of 690,000 calories of energy available to the energy-harnessing activities of cells.

There is an important reason why oxidation in the cell, as contrasted with the uncontrolled combustion that goes on in a flame, must proceed under rigorous control. Living cells are unable to utilize heat in the performance of functions such as muscle contraction, because heat energy can do work only if it flows from a warm region to a cooler one. This is the principle of a heat engine, in which the temperature of the working fluid undergoes a large drop between the combustion chamber and the exhaust. For all practical purposes there is no such temperature differential in the living cell, and the cell cannot function as a heat engine. The cell recovers the energy liberated by the oxidation of foodstuff not primarily as heat, but rather as chemical energy, a form of energy that can do work in a constant-temperature system. To obtain energy in this useful form the cell oxidizes its fuel in a stepwise manner. The agents of this controlled combustion are the enzymes: large molecules that function as catalysts, or promoters of chemical reactions. The cell employs dozens of oxidative enzymes, each specialized to catalyze one reaction in the series that ultimately converts the fuel into carbon dioxide and water.

Investigators have broken down the

MITOCHONDRION, the site of energy transfer in the living cell, is enlarged some 235,000 diameters in this electron micrograph of a rat liver-cell. Cristae, the flattened infoldings of the lining membrane, have been cut at different angles. One lying almost in the plane of the cut forms the wide V at top. Several near the center, cut at right angles, project like fingers from the outer wall. The connections to the wall do not show in those cut at oblique angles. The micrograph was made by Michael L. Watson of the University of Rochester while conducting research under a contract from the Atomic Energy Commission and a grant from the National Institutes of Health.

labyrinthine succession of reactions into three major stages. In the first stage enzymes break down the sugar and fat molecules (and protein fragments) into a simpler unit that represents a kind of common denominator of the distinctly different structures of these fuels. In the next two stages other enzymes take this unit apart and oxidize carbon and hydrogen. But the biologically significant product of the whole chain of transactions is energy, not water and carbon dioxide, which are mere waste or exhaust products. As the energy is liberated in the breakdown and oxidation reactions, it is captured in the chemical bonds of a special energy-storing molecule and is delivered thereby to the energy-consuming activities of the cell.

The Stages of Oxidation

In the first-stage breakdown of the glucose molecule, which has six carbon atoms, the enzymes split it into two molecules of pyruvic acid, each of which has three carbon atoms. This conversion is not so simple as it sounds. It involves the sequential action of a dozen specific enzymes [see top illustration on pages 234 and 235]. Some 40 years of intensive research went into the resolution of the details of this process and the isolation of the enzymes in pure form.

The intermediate pyruvic acid molecules become the center of activity in the second stage. They are converted to the two-carbon compound acetic acid, in a combined or "activated" form with

coenzyme A, a substance that contains pantothenic acid, one of the B vitamins. It is at this point that fats and proteins—broken down to acetic acid by enzyme systems specifically adapted to their structures—also join the common pathway of oxidation. Another set of enzymes acting sequentially and cyclically links up acetic acid with oxalacetic acid, a four-carbon compound, to form citric acid, a six-carbon compound. The second stage is often called the citric acid cycle, after this important intermediate; it is also known as the Krebs cycle in recognition of Sir Hans Krebs of the University of Oxford, who first postulated it in 1937. As the cycle continues, the citric acid undergoes a series of rearrangements and degradations, in the

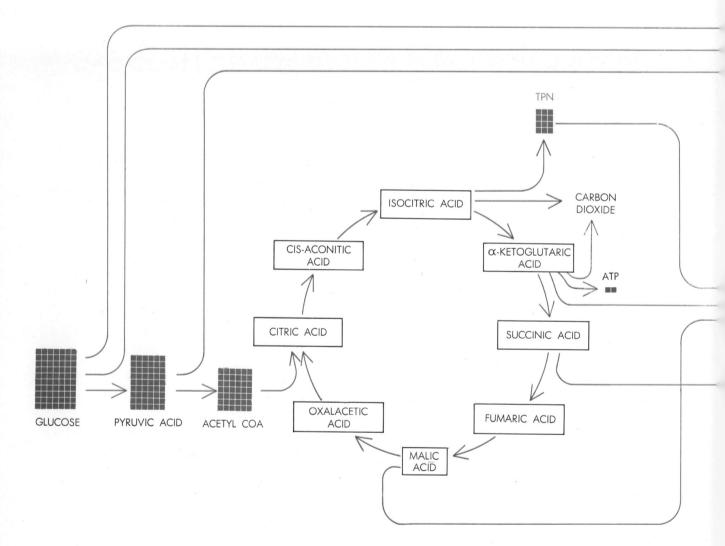

POTENTIAL ENERGY OF GLUCOSE (*far left*) is passed from compound to compound; finally more than 60 per cent is recovered in the form of adenosine triphosphate, or ATP (*top right*). Most of the energy is transferred by the citric acid cycle (*circle*) to en-

course of which oxalacetic acid is regenerated for the next round, and the two carbons from the acetic acid molecule are oxidized to form two molecules of carbon dioxide. Half of the task of oxidation is now completed.

Meanwhile, during the dismemberment of the pyruvic acid molecule in the citric acid cycle, intermediate compounds have picked up the pairs of hydrogen atoms that are attached to carbon atoms. The hydrogens are carried over into the third major multi-enzyme sequence to be combined with oxygen, which in higher animals is brought from the lungs via the bloodstream. This so-called respiratory cycle thus yields water, the second of the two end products of the biological oxidation.

As elementary as the combustion of hydrogen and oxygen may seem, the unraveling of the chain of enzyme activity in the respiratory cycle is the goal of a 50-year campaign of investigation. The contributions of Otto Warburg of Germany and David Keilin of England to this work place them among the major figures in biochemistry. The hydrogen atoms do not by any means enter directly into combination with the oxygen. They or their equivalent electrons, set free when the hydrogen is ionized, travel to this terminus along a chain of hydrogen- and electron-transferring enzyme molecules in the cell. Each of these enzymes possesses a characteristic and specific "active group" that is capable of accepting electrons

from the preceding member of the chain and of passing them along to the next. The chemical nature of the active groups explains why animals must have certain minerals and vitamins in their diet; all the groups contain either a metal, such as iron, or a vitamin, such as riboflavin (vitamin B_2). The lack of any of these essential activators may interrupt the chain and cause faulty or incomplete oxidation of foodstuff in the cell. Not all the links in the chain of enzymes have been identified. Recent work indicates that as many as three additional enzymes may be involved, one containing vitamin K (also essential to the clotting of blood); another containing tocopherol, or vitamin E (also essential to maintenance of muscle tone and to

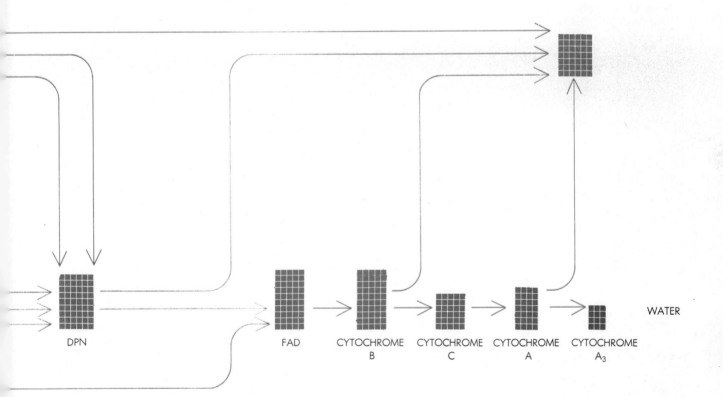

DPN   FAD   CYTOCHROME B   CYTOCHROME C   CYTOCHROME A   CYTOCHROME A₃   WATER

zymes of the respiratory chain (*TPN, DPN, FAD and the cytochromes*), which then pass it to ATP. Small gray squares, each representing approximately 10,000 calories, indicate the portions of the original 690,000 glucose calories that reach various compounds.

reproduction), and a third containing a newly isolated active group called ubiquinone, or coenzyme Q.

The Storage Battery

With the fuel completely oxidized, what has become of the potential energy it contained? This question began to yield to investigation in the late 1930's.

Herman M. Kalckar of Denmark and V. A. Belitser of the U.S.S.R. then independently recognized the significance of a chemical event that occurs along with the oxidation of the fuel. They incubated simple suspensions of ground muscle or kidney with glucose in the presence of oxygen and observed that phosphate ions present in the suspension medium disappeared as the glucose was oxidized.

Further investigation revealed that the phosphate was being incorporated into organic compounds, in particular the compound adenosine triphosphate. Biochemists at once recognized the great significance of this finding. Adenosine triphosphate, now universally known as ATP, had been identified a few years earlier as the energy source in the contraction of muscle. Today it is known

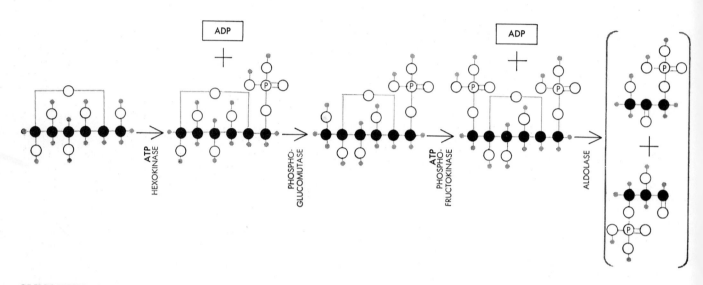

GLYCOLYSIS, the process by which glucose (*first molecule*) is broken down into two molecules of pyruvic acid (*last molecule*), requires the catalytic aid of many enzymes (*light-face type*). Two molecules of ATP are needed to prime the process, but four are

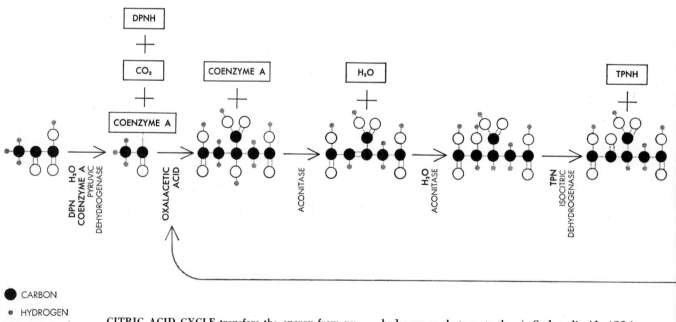

CARBON (●)
HYDROGEN (•)
OXYGEN (○)
PHOSPHORUS (Ⓟ)

CITRIC ACID CYCLE transfers the energy from pyruvic acid (*first molecule*) to the respiratory enzymes DPN, TPN and FAD by reducing them (*i.e.*, adding hydrogen or electrons to them). Carbon dioxide (CO_2) is released as a waste product. First pyruvic acid is converted to acetyl coenzyme A, an activated form of acetic

that ATP is the universal intracellular carrier of chemical energy.

ATP may be regarded literally as a fully charged storage battery. When the energy of this battery is withdrawn to make muscle contract, for example, the energy-rich ATP molecule transfers its energy to the contracting muscle by losing its terminal phosphate group. ATP thus becomes adenosine diphos-

phate (ADP)—the storage battery in its discharged state. To "recharge" the battery it is obviously necessary to supply a phosphate group plus the energy required to effect the uphill reaction that couples the phosphate to ADP. It was found that ADP as well as free phosphate ions disappear during biological oxidation, and that the two are combined in ATP. Kalckar postulated that this

coupled phosphorylation, often called oxidative phosphorylation, provides the means for converting the energy released by oxidation into a readily usable form. The energy-rich ATP molecule can travel wherever energy is needed in the cell to drive energy-consuming functions, from the contraction of muscle to the synthesis of protein.

This conversion of the energy liber-

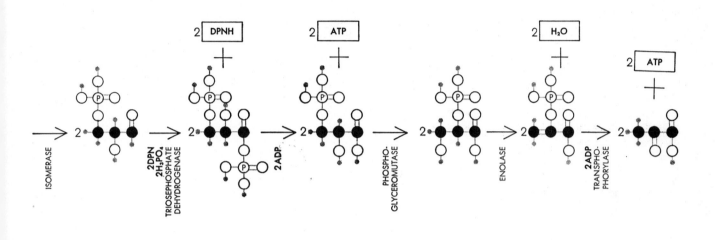

generated, yielding a net gain of two molecules of this energy-rich compound. Energy from glucose is also conserved by the reduction

of the respiratory coenzyme DPN to DPNH (*sixth step*). The glycolytic reactions are reversible with the aid of appropriate enzymes.

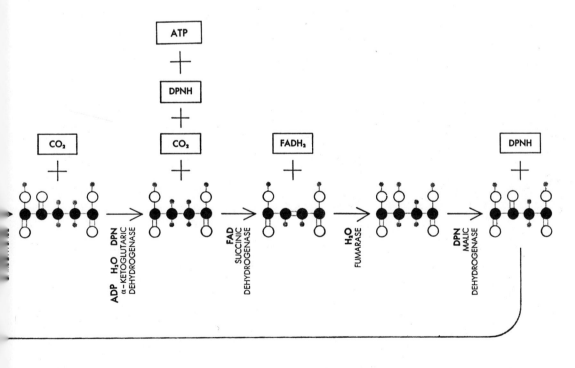

acid (*second molecule*). This reacts with oxalacetic acid to form citric acid (*third molecule*). After a series of rearrangements and oxidations, oxalacetic acid is regenerated (*last molecule*) and can

participate in the cycle again. The substances necessary for each step are named below the arrows (*catalytic enzymes are in light-face type*); side products of the reactions are shown in boxes.

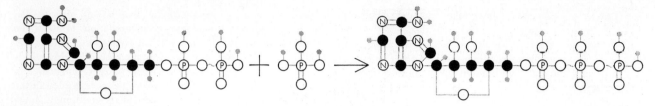

ADENOSINE DIPHOSPHATE, or ADP (*first molecule*), adds the phosphate group from phosphoric acid to generate adenosine tri-

phosphate, or ATP (*right of arrow*). Energy is required to forge the high-energy bond (*wavy line*) that links the phosphate groups.

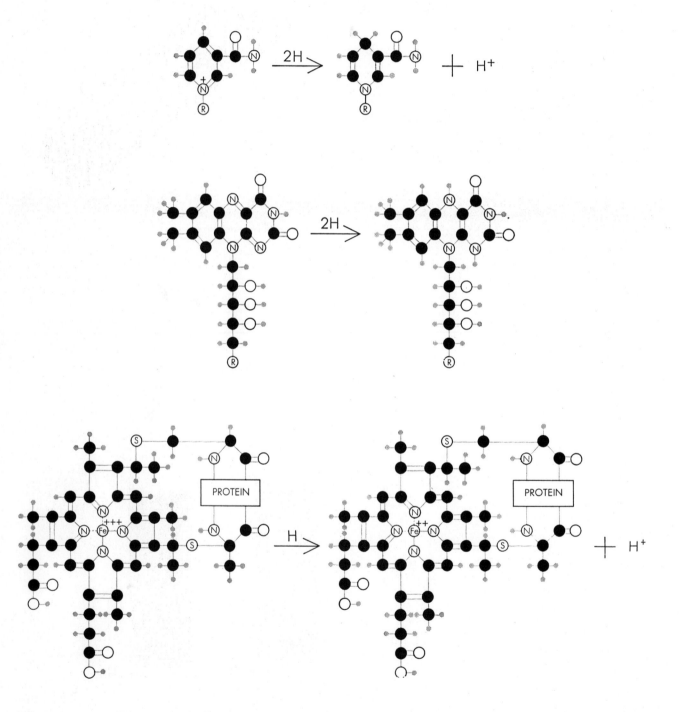

● CARBON   ● HYDROGEN
○ OXYGEN   Ⓝ NITROGEN
Ⓡ RADICAL   Ⓢ SULFUR
Ⓕ IRON

ACTIVE GROUPS of respiratory enzymes are shown oxidized (*left of arrows*) and reduced (*right*). "R" or "protein" indicates the rest of the molecule. In TPN or DPN (*top*) one hydrogen is joined to a carbon atom; the electron from the other neutralizes the charge on nitrogen. Riboflavin, the active group of FAD (*center*), adds hydrogens to two nitrogen atoms. The active group of cytochromes is heme (*bottom*); an electron from a hydrogen reduces the charge on iron.

ated by the combustion of fuel into the third phosphate bond of ATP proceeds with extraordinary efficiency. For each molecule of glucose completely oxidized to water and carbon dioxide in a tissue preparation, approximately 38 molecules of free phosphate and 38 molecules of ADP combine to form 38 molecules of ATP. In other words the oxidation of each mole of glucose produces 38 moles of ATP. It has been shown that the formation of one mole of ATP from ADP in this reaction as it occurs in the cell requires about 12,000 calories. The formation of 38 moles of ATP therefore requires the input of at least 38 times 12,000 calories, or about 456,000 calories. Since the oxidation of one mole of glucose yields a maximum of 690,000 calories, the recovery of 38 moles of ATP represents a conversion of 66 per cent of the energy. As a comparison, a modern steam-generating plant converts about 30 per cent of its energy input to useful work.

Just how the energy is transferred from the fuel molecules to ATP is a problem that has preoccupied many biochemists over the past 10 years. One early clue to the mechanism of oxidative phosphorylation came from the theoretical calculation of the energy exchanges at each major stage in the oxidation of glucose. Thermodynamics shows, for example, that the first stage in the process—the breakdown of glucose to pyruvic acid—yields little more than 5 per cent of the total energy. From such calculations Belitser predicted over 20 years ago that the combination of hydrogen with oxygen in the third phase—the respiratory cycle—must yield most of the energy. As a matter of fact, the oxidation of one mole of hydrogen to produce one mole of water releases some 52,000 calories. Since the biological oxidation of one mole of glucose reduces 12 atoms of oxygen in the respiratory cycle, the latter must account for 12 times 52,000 calories, or 624,000 calories—90 per cent of the total of 690,000 calories. Conclusive as these calculations seemed to be, it was another dozen years before direct evidence could be adduced to prove that the phosphorylation of ADP is coupled to the respiratory chain. In fact, experimental results seemed if anything to argue against this conclusion.

In 1951 our group, then at the University of Chicago, perfected an experiment that demonstrated unequivocally the presence of supplementary energy-converting enzymes at three points in the respiratory chain. These enzymes har-

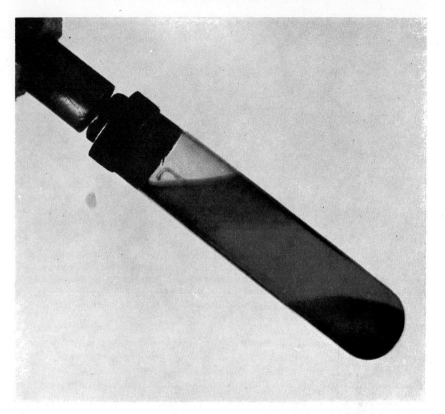

SEPARATION OF MITOCHONDRIA from disrupted cells requires centrifugation at high speed. The tube used for this is made of plastic and has a locking metal cap. The mitochondria are present in the pale middle layer of sediment. The dark layer at the bottom contains cell nuclei; the top layer contains microsomes, the smallest particles of the cell.

CYTOCHROME C in solution changes color visibly when it is oxidized (left) or reduced (right). A sensitive spectrophotometer measures the color differences accurately by registering the transmission of light of various wavelengths through the solution. Special quartz containers of high optical quality, here somewhat enlarged, are used in this instrument.

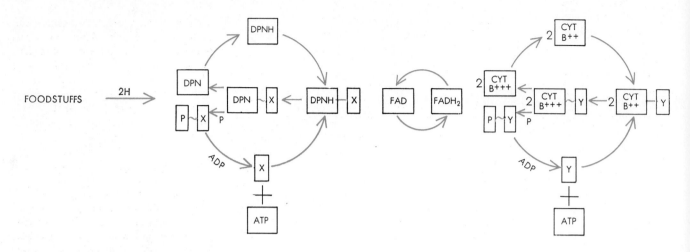

RESPIRATORY ENZYMES transfer energy by a series of cyclic reactions, each set in motion by the one preceding it, like a system of interlocking gears. A pair of hydrogen atoms released in the citric acid cycle reduces one enzyme; this is oxidized again by reducing the next enzyme, and so on. At the end of the chain the hydrogen combines with oxygen to form water. The known carriers in the chain are diphosphopyridine nucleotide (DPN), flavin adenine dinucleotide (FAD), attached to a protein, and four cytochromes. Coupled with the reduction-oxidation cycles of three carriers (DPN, cytochromes B and A) are reactions with unidenti-

ness the energy liberated by the passage of electrons from one link to the next in the chain to phosphorylate ADP to ATP. We found that the passage of each pair of hydrogen atoms or equivalent electrons yields one molecule of ATP at each of three enzymic energy-transfer stations. Since the oxidation of one molecule of glucose sets 12 pairs of hydrogen atoms moving down the chain, the total yield is three times 12, or 36, molecules of ATP. Two additional molecules of ATP are formed in the breakdown of glucose to pyruvic acid. The grand total is then 38 moles of ATP per mole of glucose. These findings fulfilled the prediction from thermodynamic considerations and satisfied the over-all energy balance-sheet of biological oxidation, showing that the respiratory chain is the primary site of energy conversion.

From more recent work we have been able to postulate the probable form of the mechanism by which the energy is coupled at each of the energy-transfer points in the respiratory chain [*see illustration above on these two pages*]. The chain is apparently a series of wheels within wheels, characterized by a cyclic process at each molecule in the chain. Each of these molecules is reduced by the addition of a hydrogen or an electron at one point, and is restored to its original form by oxidation when it delivers the hydrogen or electron to the next point. In three of the cycles there is an intermediate step by which the energy is transferred from the reaction to a coupled reaction that forms

ATP from ADP.

This picture has been modified by the finding that one pair of hydrogen atoms enters the respiratory chain at the middle, and so yields only two molecules of ATP. The deficit is made up, however, by the conversion of ADP to ATP in one of the reactions of the citric acid cycle. The respiratory chain nonetheless remains the primary site of energy conversion.

The purpose that is served by the stepwise character of the oxidation process in the cell now becomes clear. Na-

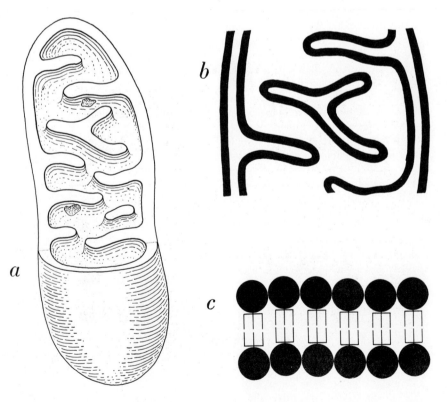

MITOCHONDRIAL STRUCTURE is basically that of a fluid-filled vessel with an involuted wall (*a*). Closer analysis shows that the wall consists of a double membrane (*b*). Each membrane approximates the thickness of a single layer of protein molecules (*spheres at c*),

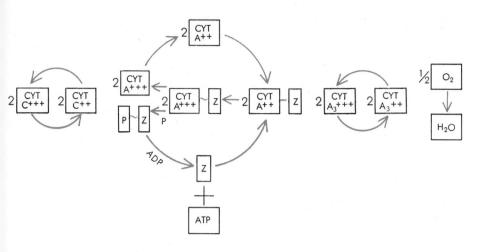

fied enzymes (*designated* X, Y *and* Z) that transfer energy released in the cycles to ATP. The transfer is not fully understood; it is believed to involve the formation of a high-energy bond (*wavy line*) to the transfer enzyme, then combination of this enzyme with a phosphate group (P) and finally the addition of the phosphate to ADP to form ATP. When two hydrogen atoms are passed down the whole chain, they give rise to three molecules of ATP.

Such a program of sequential and cyclic reactions requires that many different enzymes act in proper order and in an integrated, well-controlled way. This suggests that the participating enzymes, perhaps hundreds in number, must have a specific geometric orientation with respect to one another within the cell.

The Geometry of Oxidation

In 1948 Eugene P. Kennedy and I were able to show that enzymes involved in both the citric acid and the respiratory cycles are located in the mitochondria. These tiny oblong or rodlike structures, much smaller than the cell nucleus, occur in the cytoplasm: the extranuclear portion of the cell. A single liver-cell may contain several thousand such bodies; together they may account for about 20 per cent of the total weight of the cell. Earlier in 1948 George H. Hogeboom, Walter C. Schneider and George E. Palade of the Rockefeller Institute had perfected a method for isolating mitochondria intact and in large quantities by spinning down cell extracts in the ultracentrifuge.

ture usually chooses simple ways to do things, and it would be simpler to accomplish the combustion in one step. The many-membered respiratory chain serves, however, to break up or quantize the 52,000 calories liberated by the oxidation of each pair of hydrogens into three smaller packets. Each of these packets contains the approximate amount of energy, namely 12,000 calories, required to phosphorylate ADP to ATP. The process thus achieves efficient conversion of energy in terms of the energy currency of the cell.

When we incubated mitochondria with pyruvic acid and other intermediates of the citric acid cycle in the presence of oxygen, we found that all of the complex reactions of the citric acid and respiratory cycle proceeded at a high rate and in an orderly manner. On the other hand, we found that nuclei and other cell structures were incapable of conducting the oxidation process. We also discovered that the mitochondria carry out the vital energy-recovery process of oxidative phosphorylation, generating ATP from ADP. The mitochondria are thus the "power plants" of the cell.

These bodies are so small that they are barely recognizable as oblongs or rods when they are viewed in the light microscope. Yet recent advances in instrumentation have made it possible to sketch a molecular description of the mitochondrion and to discern at least dimly the spatial arrangement of the many enzymes concerned with biological oxidation.

The first approach was to look at the ultrastructure of the mitochondrion under the electron microscope. In 1952 Fritiof S. Sjöstrand in Sweden and Palade in New York began to apply a newly perfected means of obtaining ultrathin sections of tissue to study mitochondria. Their pictures of thin sections cut at different angles through

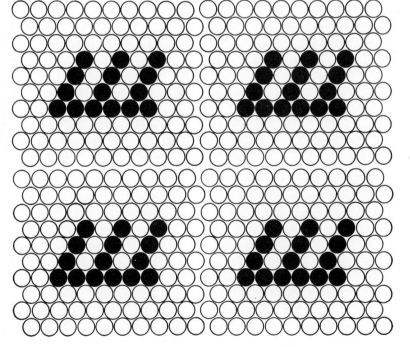

and the space between them equals the thickness of a double layer of fat molecules (*prongs*). The respiratory-chain enzymes (*black spheres at d*) form part of the membranes; they are evidently arranged in sets distributed at regular intervals in the membranes' protein layers.

single mitochondria demonstrated that the mitochondrion is not just an amorphous blob of protoplasm, but rather a highly organized structure with much fine detail—almost a cell within the cell. It consists of an outer enclosing membrane separated by a thin space from an inner membrane which at intervals apparently folds inward to form the so-called cristae. The semicompartmented space inside is filled with a semifluid "matrix."

From electron micrographs it is possible to estimate the dimensions of these structures. The membranes have a thickness of from 60 to 70 angstrom units. (An angstrom unit is a hundred millionth of a centimeter.) The space between the membranes and across the cristae measures about 60 angstroms. Mitochondria of all cells, regardless of the tissue or the species, have the same structural plan, in accord with their similarity of function.

The constant thickness of the membrane has significance from another point of view. It happens to approximate the dimension of a single protein molecule plus a lipid (fat) molecule. Chemical analysis shows that the membrane consists of about 65 per cent protein and 35 per cent lipid. These findings suggest that the membranes are arranged in a sandwich: The single layer of protein molecules that forms the outer membrane is apparently lined with oriented lipid molecules abutting a similar layer of lipid molecules on the outer surface of the layer of protein that forms the inner membrane.

When mitochondria are subjected to intense sound waves or to chemical agents such as detergents, the membranes break up, and the internal matrix escapes. The insoluble membrane fragments can easily be separated by centrifugation from the soluble matrix material, and the two fractions can then be analyzed separately. By these procedures we have found that the matrix contains most of the enzymes of the citric acid cycle, and that the enzymes of the respiratory cycle turn up exclusively in the membrane fragments.

Britton Chance of the University of Pennsylvania has employed spectroscopic techniques to study the respiratory enzymes in intact mitochondria. Each of the respiratory enzymes, having a characteristic active group, possesses a distinctive "color" and spectrum. Chance has succeeded in establishing not only the number of molecules of each type in the mitochondria but also the sequence in which the electrons move from one carrier to another in the respiratory chain.

The Enzymes Assembled

Such information, supplemented by our chemical studies, leads me to believe that the respiratory-chain enzymes are organized in assemblies or sets containing only one molecule of each of the enzymes. One such set would be made up of perhaps eight different molecules. Attached laterally to these would probably be six (perhaps nine) other catalytically

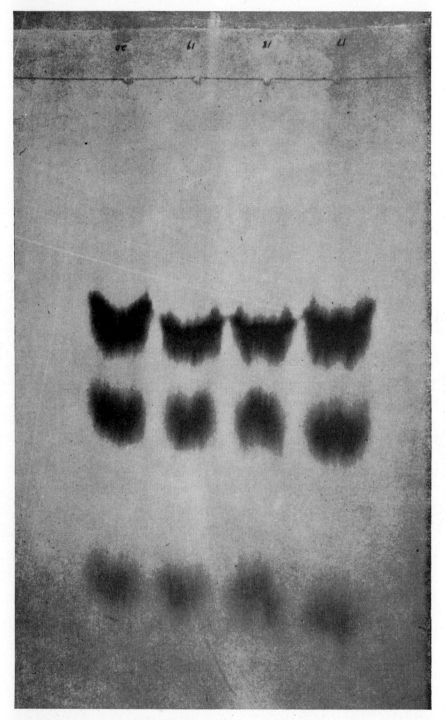

CHROMATOGRAM separates ATP (*top row of spots*) from ADP (*second row*) and AMP (*bottom*). These substances are hard to separate by other methods. In this experiment samples from a flask containing mitochondrial fragments incubated with ADP and DPNH were placed on the numbered marks. A solvent, allowed to flow downward from the top edge of the paper by capillary action, then carried the compounds with it at varying speeds. The paper was later viewed in ultraviolet radiation, under which the compounds show up at characteristic sites as dark spots against the fluorescent paper. ATP spots confirm that fragments formed ATP from ADP. Spots can be cut out and ATP dissolved for testing.

active protein molecules, the function of which is to carry out the coupled formation of ATP. A complete assembly would thus contain 15 or more active protein molecules arranged in close geometric array. An individual liver mitochondrion might contain several thousand such units. Since the total mass and the protein content of the mitochondrial membrane are known, it is possible to calculate that these assemblies comprise as much as 40 per cent of its substance. This calculation, along with our recent finding that the assemblies are evenly distributed in the membrane, show that the membrane is not an inert wall or container but an active molecular machine. The highly ordered arrangement of the specialized enzyme molecules determines the organization and pro-

gramming of the enzymatic activity of the living cell.

Mitochondria in intact cells have been observed to swell and shrink, apparently by the uptake of water from the cytoplasm. This activity may serve mainly to move water and other substances through the cell. In this connection we have made the interesting discovery that the membrane itself changes its dimensions in the course of its activity. Like a sheet of muscle tissue, it can relax or contract. We have found that this change in dimension is related to the concentration of ATP; the membrane contracts when the concentration is high and relaxes when it is low. This suggests that the rate of oxidation (and of energy recovery in the mitochondria) may be regulated by the local concentrations of

ATP and ADP, which occur in inverse relationship to each other. Overproduction of ATP may thus automatically throttle down this mechano-chemical system and gear its rate of power production to the demands of the cell. This same mechano-chemical system may also be responsible for "pumping" water and for the remarkable motility of mitochondria in some cells.

The integration of chemistry and geometry in the structure of the power plant of the cell poses new challenges to the investigator. It sets as the supreme goal not only the duplication of the catalytically active enzyme assemblies by proper linkage of the individual energy-transferring enzyme molecules, but also the reconstitution of the detailed structure of the mitochondrial membrane.

WARBURG APPARATUS is used in biochemical experiments to test for oxidative activity. Flasks containing the mitochondria and a solution of pyruvate are incubated inside the drumlike water bath. Each flask is connected to the top of one arm of a U-tube, containing colored fluid. As oxygen is used up by the test material, the change in gas pressure forces the fluid to rise in one arm and fall in the other. The rate and amount of oxygen consumption can be calculated by taking readings of the levels at various times.

26

The Metabolism of Fats

DAVID E. GREEN

January 1954

Animals generate nearly all their energy by oxidizing sugars and fats. Biochemists have known for some time how the body oxidizes sugars, but only within the past year have they filled in an equally detailed picture of how it oxidizes fats. It had taken some 50 years of intensive work in laboratories all over the world to complete the picture. Last month the Nobel prize committee recognized the importance of phases of that work when it awarded the 1953 prize in physiology and medicine to two men who had made key discoveries. The his-

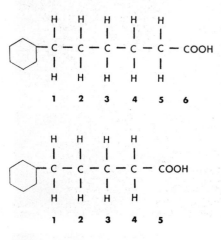

FATTY ACID is composed of a hydrocarbon chain with a carboxyl group at one end.

PHENYL FATTY ACIDS have even or odd number of carbons attached to benzene ring.

tory of the research on oxidation of fatty acids is one of the truly adventurous episodes in biochemistry.

The substances called fats consist of a combination of a fatty acid with an alcohol, such as glycerol. The part of this combination that the body burns for fuel is the fatty acid. It is a hydrocarbon—the kind of stuff man has been burning for fuel ever since he lit the first wax candle. A fatty acid is a hydrocarbon with a carboxyl group (COOH) attached at one end of the molecule [*see diagram at the left*]. In the common fatty acids the hydrocarbon chain is usually 16 to 20 carbon atoms long.

The process nature has developed for burning fatty acids in the body is roundabout, complex and under beautiful control. The only way a chemist can reconstruct it is from deductions based on examination of the combustion products, and the main problem has been to catch these products at the successive stages of the combustion.

In 1904 the German biochemist Franz Knoop opened the door to an understanding of fatty acid oxidation with a brilliantly thought-out experiment. He conceived the idea of attaching a fatty acid to a more obdurate substance, as one would fasten a piece of cheese to a wooden block, and then examining the products when the animal body so to speak "chopped off" (oxidized) successive slices of the "cheese." The block he used was the benzene ring. Attachment of a fatty acid to this ring forms what organic chemists call a phenyl fatty acid. Knoop synthesized two kinds of phenyl fatty acids—one with an even number of carbon atoms in the hydrocarbon chain, the other with an odd number. Then he fed them to experimental animals for oxidation and analyzed the animals' urine to find out how they had "de-

graded" (chopped down) the fatty acids.

As he had hoped, the odd-numbered and even-numbered phenyl fatty acids yielded different end products. The even-numbered chain was reduced to one carbon atom plus the carboxyl group, *i.e.*, two carbon atoms in all. This is phenyl acetic acid. The odd-numbered chain was degraded to just the carboxyl group, attached directly to the benzene ring, that is, benzoic acid. From these results Knoop, and independently the chemist Henry Dakin, concluded that fatty acids were chopped down two carbon atoms at a time. Each chop (oxidation) removed two carbon atoms, including the one in the carboxyl group, and then a new carboxyl group was formed at the cut end of the chain. The successive cleavages are shown in the series of diagrams on page 244. Chemists called the carbon atom that was cut from the chain the alpha atom and the one from which it was separated the beta atom, and the process became known as beta oxidation. Knoop and Dakin visualized each oxidation as taking place in four steps, shown in the formulas at the top of page 245.

Knoop's theory hit the mark almost exactly, but it took half a century to prove the theory correct and to identify the intermediate products formed in the four steps of beta oxidation. The difficulty was that only the final product appeared in the urine, and the intermediate stages could not be isolated. The number of investigators who beat their heads against this difficulty is legion. But occasionally an ingenious experimenter had a flash of inspiration, and one inspiration led to another.

In 1906 the German chemist Gustave Embden made the first break in the wall by studying fatty acid metabolism in a

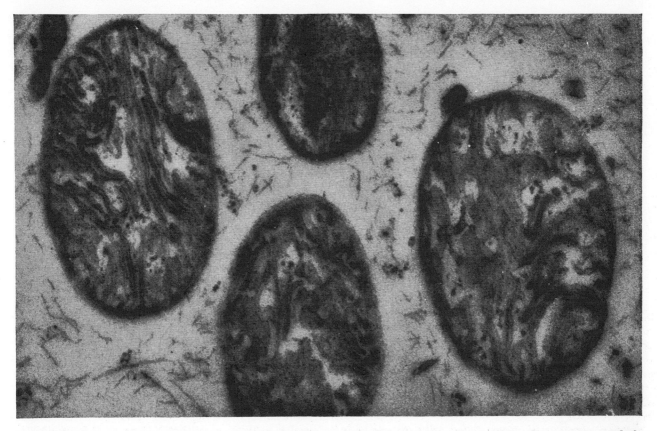

MITOCHONDRIA are particles where fats are oxidized. The four mitochondria in this electron micrograph of rat muscle are enlarged 75,000 diameters. The micrographs on this page were made by George E. Palade of the Rockefeller Institute for Medical Research.

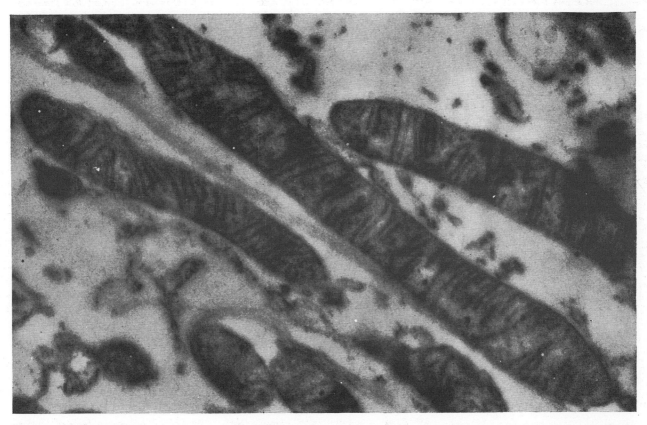

LONG MITOCHONDRIA in this electron micrograph of the proximal convoluted tubule of a rat kidney are enlarged 41,000 diameters. The mitochondria are shown in cross section by impregnating the tissue with plastic and cutting it with a glass knife.

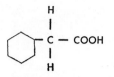

PHENYL ACETIC ACID is the end product of the oxidation of a phenyl fatty acid that has an even number of carbon atoms.

BENZOIC ACID is the end product of the similar oxidation of a phenyl fatty acid that possesses an odd number of carbon atoms.

EVEN-NUMBERED phenyl fatty acid is chopped down (*vertical lines*) two carbon atoms at a time, leaving phenyl acetic acid.

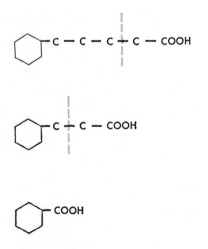

ODD-NUMBERED phenyl fatty acid is similarly chopped, leaving benzoic acid. The hydrocarbon hydrogens are omitted for clarity.

single organ instead of the whole animal. He separated the liver from an animal and kept it functioning by pumping nutrients into it through a closed circulation system. When he introduced fatty acids into the entering veins, he found that the isolated liver did indeed oxidize many kinds of fatty acids. But the only product he could recognize in the outgoing blood was diacetic acid—a combination of two molecules of acetic acid. This was one of the end products, not an intermediate. Yet Embden had begun to blaze the right path, though it took many years for investigators to follow it up. That path was to simplify the experimental conditions. In 1935 the English biochemist J. H. Quastel went a step further by examining fatty acid oxidation in thin slices of tissue, rather than in a whole organ. Although he obtained valuable information on the extent of combustion of fatty acids by various tissues, he too failed to isolate any intermediate products.

Then in 1939 Luis Leloir and J. M. Muñoz of Argentina reported an epoch-making discovery. They crushed liver cells and found that tiny granules from the cell, after being separated from the debris, were able to carry out fatty acid oxidation as effectively as the intact cell. No outsider can really appreciate what this meant to investigators: at last they were freed from the shackles of working with complex biological systems and could probe fatty acid oxidation at the molecular level.

At first the results were disappointing, because the oxidation products of the granules were essentially identical with those obtained in the more complex systems. But studies of the granules eventually opened a completely new approach. The cell granules, later identified as mitochondria, were found to house hundreds of enzymes which catalyzed fatty acid oxidation and other related processes. Most important, experiments with the mitochondrial system carried out in my laboratory disclosed that the fatty acids were not oxidized as such; they had to be converted to something else first. No oxidation took place unless an oxidizable substance called a "sparker" was added to the mitochondrial suspension. However, it soon became apparent that the oxidation of the fatty acid was sparked not by the oxidation of the sparker itself but by some event which accompanied this oxidation. The tracking down of that mysterious event involved the piecing together of clues from many different investigations.

One of the clues came from the discovery of the so-called citric acid or Krebs cycle by Hans A. Krebs of England (who for his discovery was awarded half of the 1953 Nobel prize in physiology). This cycle has to do with the oxidation of pyruvic acid (a breakdown product of sugar) into carbon dioxide and water, and it takes place in five separate oxidative steps. At each step the oxidation of the intermediate product is accompanied by the simultaneous conversion of inorganic phosphate into adenosine triphosphate (ATP)—that famous substance which triggers so many chemical reactions in the cell.

Now the mysterious role of the sparker in fatty acid oxidation began to unravel. Any one of the five oxidative steps in the citric acid cycle can spark fatty acid oxidation; thus the sparker could be any of the four substances formed from pyruvic acid during the operation of the cycle. It was apparent that the oxidation of the sparker led to the formation of ATP, and ATP in turn converted the fatty acid to something else. What that something was, and how it took part in the oxidative chopping down of the fatty acid, became the next important question to be answered. And here the chief clues stemmed from the work of Fritz A. Lipmann of Harvard University (winner of the other half of the 1953 Nobel physiology prize).

In 1945 Lipmann discovered in animal tissues a substance which was essential for the utilization of acetic acid in the body. He named it coenzyme A: a coenzyme is much smaller than an enzyme (about the relative size of the moon compared to the earth), is not a protein and is usually resistant to breakdown by heat. Lipmann and his group proceeded to purify and analyze coenzyme A. It was found to be made of three main building stones: (1) pantothenic acid (one of the B vitamins), (2) a phosphate related to ATP and (3) thioethanolamine (discovered by Esmond E. Snell of Wisconsin).

Lipmann recognized that the acetic acid participating in cell reactions is not the original form but a more reactive derivative. He and his colleagues found many signs pointing to the likelihood that acetic acid interacted with coenzyme A to form acetyl coenzyme A. But he was not able to isolate that product. It remained for Feodor Lynen of Munich to recognize what made coenzyme A tick. That knowledge provided him with the needed clue which enabled him to announce in 1951 success in isolating acetyl coenzyme A from yeast.

There was a striking parallel to the

case of the unknown active form of the fatty acids, but it was not immediately recognized as such. The first to draw the parallel were the microbiologists Horace A. Barker and Earl Stadtman at the University of California. They had been studying a microorganism which showed the remarkable capacity to synthesize fatty acids in the absence of oxygen in a medium containing ethyl alcohol as the sole source of carbon. In effect this organism was carrying out fatty acid oxidation in reverse. Barker and Stadtman discovered that the organism needed coenzyme A for this process, and they surmised that the active form of fatty acid for which investigators had been searching was a derivative of coenzyme A, just as the active form of acetic acid was acetyl coenzyme A. In short, the x in the fatty acid equation turned out to be coenzyme A.

Biochemists were now able to get on with working out the details of fatty acid oxidation. This called for a radical change in strategy. First ways and means had to be found for preparing the various fatty acid derivatives that were oxidized. Then the enzymes which catalyzed the successive reactions had to be isolated one by one. The investigation was blocked at the outset by the scarcity of purified coenzyme A; it was available only in milligram amounts. A group of investigators at the University of Wisconsin solved this difficulty by recognizing that yeast was a rich and convenient source of the coenzyme, that the substance could readily be concentrated in charcoal chromatographic columns and that the coenzyme could then be purified by precipitation of its copper salt with a copper salt of glutathione. This made it possible to prepare coenzyme A in gram quantities instead of milligrams.

My colleagues Henry Mahler and Saleh Wakil then found a way to carry out the next step: synthesis of the needed fatty acid derivatives. They isolated from beef liver an enzyme which in the presence of ATP could convert various fatty acids into their corresponding coenzyme A derivatives. The process was uncomfortably expensive, but it could supply all the derivatives required. Then came the problem of identifying the enzyme that catalyzed each reaction. Our group at Wisconsin, following up an earlier observation by George Drysdale and Henry Lardy, who had worked only with rats, developed a technique for preparing mitochondria, in which the enzymes are housed, from slaughterhouse animals. After isolating the en-

Oxidation

$$\overset{\beta}{RCH_2}\overset{\alpha}{CH_2}COOH \longrightarrow \overset{\beta}{RCH}=\overset{\alpha}{CHCOOH}$$

Addition of water

$$\overset{\beta}{RCH}=\overset{\alpha}{CHCOOH} \longrightarrow \overset{\beta}{RCHOH}\overset{\alpha}{CH_2}COOH$$

Oxidation

$$\overset{\beta}{RCHOH}\overset{\alpha}{CH_2}COOH \longrightarrow \overset{\beta}{RCO}\overset{\alpha}{CH_2}COOH$$

Addition of water and splitting

$$\overset{\beta}{RCO}\overset{\alpha}{CH_2}COOH \longrightarrow \overset{\beta}{RCOOH} + \overset{\alpha}{CH_2}COOH$$

CLASSICAL SCHEME of fatty-acid oxidation was called beta oxidation. The carbon atom next to the carboxyl group is labeled alpha; the next carbon atom to the left, beta. The remainder of the molecule is indicated by R. The double lines represent double chemical bonds.

Acyl CoA dehydrogenase

$$RCH_2CH_2COS\ CoA \longrightarrow RCH=CHCOS\ CoA$$

Hydrase

$$RCH=CHCOS\ CoA + H_2O \longrightarrow RCHOHCH_2COS\ CoA$$

Beta-hydroxy acyl CoA dehydrogenase

$$RCHOHCH_2COS\ CoA \longrightarrow RCOCH_2COS\ CoA$$

Cleavage enzyme

$$RCOCH_2COS\ CoA + CoA \longrightarrow RCOS\ CoA + CH_3COS\ CoA$$

MODERN SCHEME of fatty acid oxidation supposes much the same four steps as the classical scheme. The principal difference is due to the role of coenzyme A, denoted by the symbol CoA. Above each of the four reactions is the name of the enzyme known to catalyze it.

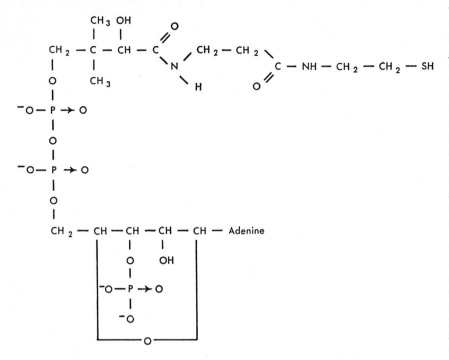

COENZYME A is essential to the oxidation of fatty acids. The upper part of its molecule consists of thioethanolamine (NH to SH) and pantothenic acid. The lower part, joined to the upper by a phosphate group (P), is adenylic acid. Another phosphate is near the bottom.

zymes from the mitochondria, the Wisconsin group systematically tested them and found, as might have been expected, that there was a separate enzyme for each of the four stages in the stepwise oxidation of fatty acids. The four enzymes and the reaction products have now been identified [*see illustration at bottom of preceding page*].

Lynen in Germany, collaborating with Severo Ochoa of New York University, reached the same objectives as the Wisconsin group by a completely different stratagem. Lacking their large-scale supplies of coenzyme A and the enzyme needed to prepare coenzyme A derivatives, he hit upon the ingenious expedient of offering synthetic derivatives for the oxidation-catalyzing enzymes to act upon. He used fatty acid derivatives of thioethanolamine, which is one of the building blocks of coenzyme A and which can be synthesized in the laboratory without too much difficulty. Some of the enzymes of the fatty acid oxidizing system did act upon these synthetic derivatives, and Lynen thus was able to purify those particular enzymes. It is not often that enzymes can be fooled in this way, but Lynen's bait did the trick.

In retrospect it is now easy to see why it was so difficult to isolate the intermediate products of fatty acid oxidation. The attachment of a fatty acid to coenzyme A is like the kiss of death. Once

attached, the fatty acid has no alternative but to go through the entire cycle of chemical change. Only at the end of the cycle is it possible for the end product (diacetic acid) to let go of the coenzyme. Nature has seen to it that release from the coenzyme takes place at the end of the ride and not before. This restriction makes sense from the standpoint of the cell. Since ATP has to foot the bill for making a coenzyme A derivative of the fatty acid, and since ATP is a most valuable asset which the cell can ill afford to squander, nature appears to have taken special precautions to prevent the breakdown of coenzyme A derivatives during fatty acid oxidation.

Perhaps you are wondering how the cell gets any energy profit from the oxidation of fatty acids if ATP has to be used to initiate the process. The answer is that the chain of oxidation reactions returns as many as 100 molecules of ATP for each one invested. For each penny on deposit the cell gets back a dollar.

Why all this fuss about finding out the enzymatic details of the steps in fatty acid oxidation? Biochemists are in no position at present to say what fruits may come from it, but the study of mechanisms has in general been one of the most rewarding pursuits of biochemistry. The knowledge of the mechanism of fatty acid oxidation will permit us to probe deeply into areas which hitherto have been impenetrable. Some of the nuggets

of information which it has uncovered thus far are that three B vitamins (flavin, niacin and pantothenic acid) are involved in the oxidation process, that ATP sparks it by energizing the conversion of a fatty acid to its coenzyme A derivative, that copper teams up with flavin to assist the enzyme which carries out the first oxidative step. By way of illustration of how one finding leads to another, this last discovery has led our group to the recognition that molybdenum and iron serve as functional groups in other flavin-containing enzymes not involved in fatty acid oxidation.

From the height the enzyme chemist has scaled in elucidating the oxidation of fatty acids he can see other eminences which may be approachable by similar tactics. The reverse of this oxidation process, *i.e.*, the synthesis of long-chain fatty acids, proceeds in somewhat the same way as the synthesis of cholesterol and other steroids, of plant carotenoids (*e.g.*, vitamin A) and of rubber. All these synthetic processes appear to depend upon the combination of the same fundamental units. They differ only in detail. In fatty acid synthesis carbon atoms join together in a linear arrangement like beads on a string. In carotenoid synthesis the only difference is that side spurs of carbon atoms are attached at regular intervals along the string. In cholesterol synthesis the string loops around and forms a series of rings. From what has been learned about the enzymes participating in fatty acid oxidation there is good reason to believe that it will be possible to carry out these synthetic processes artificially with isolated enzymes within the next five to 10 years.

Our new knowledge about fatty acid oxidation may also eventually help to explain some mysteries of diabetes. Many diabetics are unable to oxidize fats completely: their urine contains abnormal amounts of products of partial oxidation. Furthermore, the amount of fat in their tissues declines to a very low level. Injections of insulin enable these patients to carry the oxidation to completion and increase remarkably their capacity to synthesize and deposit fat. It seems altogether likely that a block in the enzyme systems involved in the synthesis of fat plays a substantial part in diabetes. In this connection it should be pointed out that the same enzymes which bring about fatty acid oxidation in animal tissues can be made to work backward and under appropriate conditions synthesize fatty acids.

27

Protein-digesting Enzymes

HANS NEURATH

December 1964

A problem that fascinates biochemists is how the living cell performs with such speed and precision a multitude of chemical reactions that otherwise occur with immeasurable slowness at the same temperature and pressure. It has long been known that the secret is to be found in the remarkable catalysts created by the living cell. A catalyst is defined as a substance that promotes a chemical reaction without itself being used up in the process. The biological catalysts that mediate all the chemical reactions necessary for life are called enzymes. All enzymes are proteins, although some work in concert with the simpler inorganic or organic compounds known as coenzymes. Each enzyme is tailored to accelerate one specific type of chemical reaction, and since the cell must carry out thousands of different reactions it must have the services of thousands of different enzymes.

One important class of enzymes has the task of degrading, or digesting, other proteins. Because the process is also termed lysis (from the Greek word for "loosing"), these enzymes are called proteolytic. Present in all living organisms, they degrade cellular proteins as part of the cell's metabolic cycle. They also take apart the protein molecules that the organism ingests as food and make the subunits available for constructing the new proteins the organism needs for its own sustenance.

The molecules of proteins are complex structures composed of hundreds or thousands of amino acid subunits of about 20 different kinds. These subunits are linked together in various proportions—exact for each protein—to form polypeptide chains. The term "peptide" refers to the bond that is formed when two amino acids link together and in the process release a molecule of water. The portion of the amino acid molecule that remains in the polypeptide chain after the loss of the atoms in water is termed an amino acid residue.

Proteolytic enzymes have the ability to restore the elements of water by a process of hydrolysis that involves only the protein, the proteolytic enzyme and the water in which both are dissolved. Protein hydrolysis occurs when the peptide bond, which links a carbon atom on one amino acid residue with a nitrogen atom on the next, is broken. Simultaneously the hydroxyl ion (OH^-) of a water molecule is added to the carbon end of the broken protein chain and the remaining hydrogen ion (H^+) is added to the nitrogen end [see top illustration on page 250].

Like all other chemical reactions, protein hydrolysis involves an exchange of electrons between certain atoms of the reacting molecules. In the absence of a catalyst this exchange occurs so slowly that it cannot be measured. It can be accelerated by the addition of acids, which increase the supply of hydrogen ions, or of bases, which provide hydroxyl ions. The acids and bases act as true catalysts: they are not consumed in the process. If a protein is boiled in a concentrated acid, it will decompose completely into free amino acids. Such conditions would obviously destroy a living cell. Proteolytic enzymes produce the same result even faster and with no harm to the organism. And whereas hydrogen ions act indiscriminately on all proteins and on all peptide linkages in any protein, proteolytic enzymes are specific, acting only on certain kinds of linkage.

Since proteolytic enzymes are themselves proteins, their action is directed toward the same compounds from which they are made. What, then, differentiates a protein that is a proteolytic enzyme from the protein the enzyme digests? How does a proteolytic enzyme exert its catalytic function without destroying itself or the cell in which it originates? An answer to these fundamental questions would do much to clarify how all enzymes perform their functions. In the 30 years since a proteolytic enzyme (trypsin) was first isolated and crystallized (by Moses Kunitz of the Rockefeller Institute) proteolytic enzymes have served as prototypes in studies relating protein structure to enzyme function.

Because of their role in one of man's most important functions, that of nourishing himself, the proteolytic enzymes of the digestive tract have a long history of investigation, surpassed perhaps only by the study of the enzymes involved in the fermentation of alcohol by yeast (from which the term "enzyme," meaning "in yeast," is derived). Among the digestive enzymes, those secreted by the pancreas—trypsin, chymotrypsin and the carboxypeptidases—are the most completely analyzed and best understood. Hence they will serve to illustrate what is now known about the specificity, structure and mode of action of all proteolytic enzymes.

The proteolytic enzymes of the pancreas are synthesized in the form of precursors called zymogens, and they are stored in the pancreas in intracellular bodies known as zymogen granules. In the zymogen form proteolytic enzymes are inactive and so are prevented from exerting their destructive action on the protein components of the tissue in which they originate. Activation takes place after the zymogens are secreted into the small intestine, where a certain enzyme makes small but important changes in the structure of the zymogen molecule. Such changes will be considered in more detail later in this article.

As I have indicated, proteolytic en-

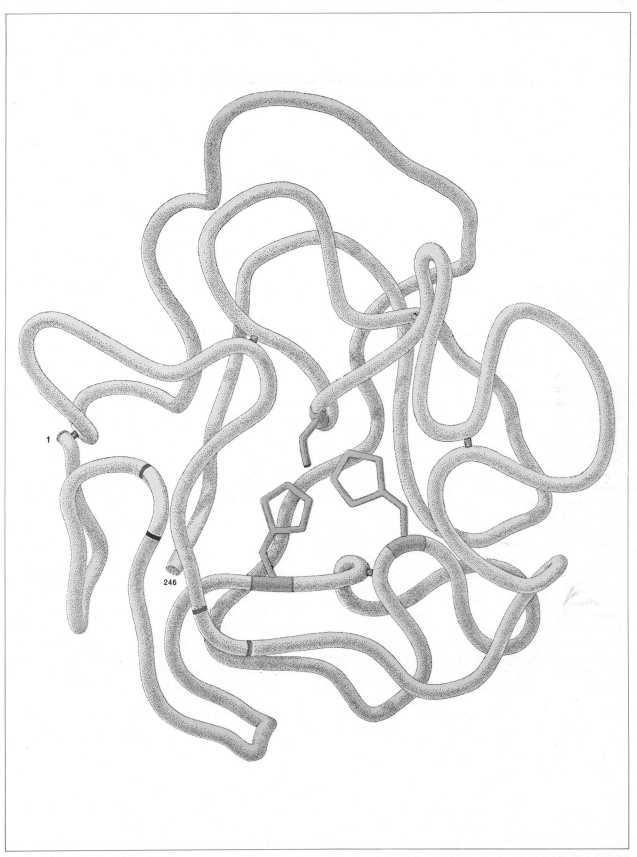

CHYMOTRYPSINOGEN MOLECULE, the inactive precursor of the protein-digesting enzyme chymotrypsin, may look something like this. This drawing, based on a model built by the author, shows the hypothetical route of the molecule's central chain composed of 246 amino acid subunits, often referred to as residues. The model takes into account many of the known chemical features of this enzyme secreted by the pancreas. The three-dimensional conformation is dictated, in part, by sulfur-sulfur linkages, or disulfide bridges, which tie the molecular chain together at five points. The molecule becomes an active enzyme when split by trypsin at the point indicated by the black ring. Three gray rings show secondary cleavage points. The active site of the molecule is believed to lie in a small region that includes two residues of histidine and a residue of serine, all three shown in dark color.

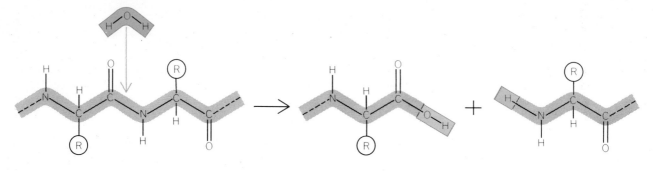

CLEAVAGE OF A "PEPTIDE" BOND is the fundamental step in the degradation, or digestion, of a protein molecule. A peptide bond is the carbon-nitrogen linkage formed when two amino acids are united with the simultaneous release of a molecule of water.

The reverse process, peptide hydrolysis, is shown here. Without a catalyst, hydrolysis is immeasurably slow. The letter "R" represents any of the various side groups found in the 20 common amino acids from which the polypeptide chains of proteins are assembled.

zymes are highly selective in their catalytic effect. An enzyme such as trypsin will hydrolyze certain bonds in a protein molecule but will have no measurable effect on certain others. The explanation is that, although all peptide bonds are chemically similar, their immediate environment is modified by the chemical nature of the amino acid residues on either side of a given bond. Each of the proteolytic enzymes requires a specific chemical environment in order to catalyze the hydrolysis of a peptide bond.

Trypsin, for example, hydrolyzes only peptide bonds whose carbonyl group (C=O) is contributed by an amino acid (e.g., arginine or lysine) that has a positively charged side group. Chymotrypsin acts preferentially on peptide bonds whose carbonyl group is adjacent to an amino acid (e.g., tyrosine or phenylalanine) that has a six-carbon ring in its side group. In contrast, carboxypeptidases exclusively hydrolyze the last peptide bond in a polypeptide chain. Carboxypeptidase A acts preferentially on peptide bonds adjacent to terminal amino acid residues with a six-carbon-ring side group, and carboxypeptidase B on those adjacent to terminal residues (e.g., lysine or arginine) whose side groups end in an amino group (NH₂). An illustration of the specificities of these enzymes toward a hypothetical polypeptide is shown at the bottom of these two pages.

Broadly speaking, trypsin and chymotrypsin cleave peptide bonds that occupy internal positions in the polypeptide chain, and hence they are referred to as "endopeptidases." Carboxypeptidases, which cleave the outermost peptide bonds, are called exopeptidases. As we shall see, it happens that the two endopeptidases, trypsin and chymotrypsin, operate by a common mechanism that is different from the one involved in the action of carboxypeptidases.

A typical protein molecule containing several hundred amino acid residues in a linear sequence will have many peptide bonds that can be attacked by an enzyme such as trypsin. The enzyme can hydrolyze the chain at every peptide bond adjacent to an arginine or a lysine residue, giving rise to polypeptide fragments with arginine or lysine residues at the ends. If the same protein is exposed to the action of a carboxypeptidase rather than trypsin, the terminal peptide bonds will be hydrolyzed sequentially, giving rise to free

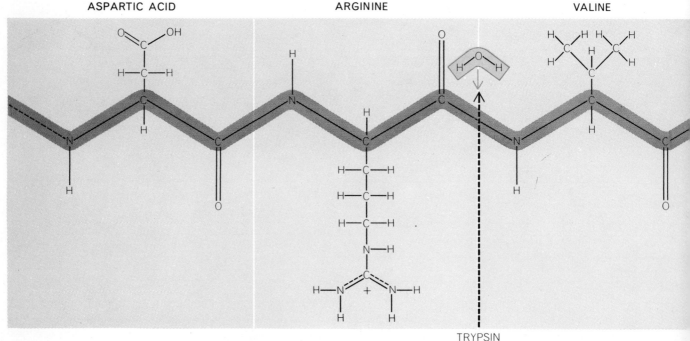

ASPARTIC ACID   ARGININE   VALINE

TRYPSIN

SPECIFICITY OF PEPTIDE BOND CLEAVAGE is an important characteristic of enzyme action. Three of the principal "proteo-

lytic," or protein-digesting, enzymes are trypsin, chymotrypsin and carboxypeptidase A. Each will split only peptide bonds that are in

amino acids one at a time until a peptide bond is reached that does not meet the specific requirements of the attacking enzyme. Through the combined action of endopeptidases and exopeptidases a protein can be digested into fragments of various lengths and ultimately degraded into free amino acids. This process is physiologically significant: it provides both free amino acids and larger fragments for absorption through the intestinal wall. The selective hydrolysis of proteins by proteolytic enzymes has also been an important experimental tool for the determination of the amino acid sequence of proteins [see "The Chemical Structure of Proteins," by William H. Stein and Stanford Moore, which begins on page 23 of this volume].

A major step toward understanding the specificity of proteolytic enzymes was taken some 25 years ago at the Rockefeller Institute, when Max Bergmann, Joseph S. Fruton (now at the Yale University School of Medicine) and their associates found that relatively simple synthetic compounds with only one or two peptide bonds were also susceptible to hydrolysis by proteolytic enzymes. They found, for instance, that trypsin rapidly hydrolyzes a compound designated N-acyl argininamide, whose molecular structure is derived from the amino acid arginine [see *upper illustration on next page*]. Molecules of this kind have an amide (a nitrogen-containing group) where arginine has a carboxyl group (COOH); at the other end they have an acyl group (a derivative of an organic acid, such as acetic acid) where arginine has its primary amino group. The hydrolysis of such molecules by trypsin yields N-acyl arginine and ammonia.

Several years later my associates George Schwert, Seymour Kaufman, John Snoke and I, then working at the Duke University School of Medicine, were able to narrow down still further the minimum structural elements required in a molecule that could be hydrolyzed by trypsin. We found that when the nitrogen of the amide group in N-acyl argininamide is replaced by oxygen, the resulting esters are hydrolyzed even more rapidly than the original amide compound. These synthetic compounds, like all other substances on which enzymes act, are commonly called substrates.

The recognition that substrates of such relatively simple and specified properties are attacked in the same way as complex proteins has helped considerably in clarifying how proteolytic enzymes work. It was immediately evident that the large size of the natural substrate molecule does not play a unique part in the action of proteolytic enzymes. Furthermore, synthetic substrate molecules with a limited number of reactive groups have provided a tool for testing the contribution of each structural element of the substrate to the specificity of the enzyme, just as a set of keys can be used to determine the precision and uniqueness of a lock. A great many investigations of this kind, extending the work of Bergmann and his associates, have been conducted in numerous laboratories, particularly those of Emil L. Smith at the University of Utah College of Medicine, of Carl Niemann at the California Institute of Technology and in our own laboratory at the University of Washington. These studies have provided a rich catalogue of information relating the structure of synthetic molecules to their interaction with proteolytic enzymes.

This catalogue contains a special section listing a group of compounds that react with both trypsin and chymotrypsin as if they had little regard for the different specificities of the two enzymes. These compounds are highly reactive esters, formed by the coupling of an "aromatic" alcohol (one having a six-carbon ring) with certain organic acids. Let us therefore consider at this point some basic principles of the mechanism of action of these enzymes.

Each atom has only a limited number of electrons that can be shared with surrounding atoms to form chemical bonds. When additional electrons are offered such an atom, it can accept them only by letting go of electrons already being used, causing that bond to rupture. In the hydrolysis of polypeptides, bond breakage is usually initiated by a nucleophile, a compound with electrons to spare [see *lower illus-*

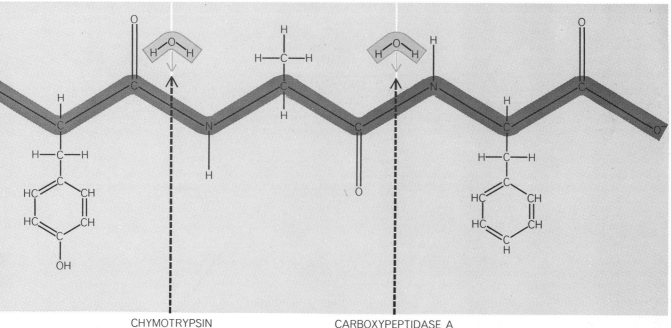

TYROSINE   ALANINE   PHENYLALANINE

CHYMOTRYPSIN   CARBOXYPEPTIDASE A

a particular chemical environment. Thus trypsin splits the peptide bond to the right of an arginine residue; chymotrypsin splits the bond to the right of a tyrosine residue; carboxypeptidase *A* splits a terminal peptide bond to the left of a phenylalanine residue.

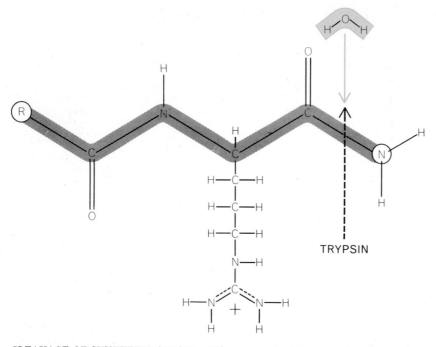

CLEAVAGE OF SYNTHETIC SUBSTRATES, compounds that are acted on by enzymes, can provide important information about enzyme mechanisms. The molecule shown here, *N*-acyl argininamide, is a derivative of the amino acid arginine and one of the simplest compounds cleaved by trypsin. The acyl group (R·CO) replaces a hydrogen atom normally present in arginine; the amino group (NH₂) at right replaces the hydroxyl group (OH).

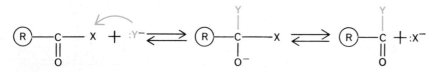

CLEAVAGE MECHANISM is believed to require a nucleophile, a reactive group with electrons to spare. The nucleophile represented here by :Y has two lone electrons in its outer shell. The nucleophile reacts with the substrate (R·CO·X) to form an unstable intermediate in which each of the carbon atom's four bonds is linked to another atom or group. When the C·X bond breaks, X is expelled. X is a nitrogen atom in polypeptides or an oxygen atom in esters. An ester is produced when an acid combines with an alcohol.

tration above]. As the electrons are accepted by the carbon atom of the peptide bond, the link between the carbon and the nitrogen is broken and the amide group is detached. An enzyme such as chymotrypsin is believed to promote this reaction because certain groups on the surface of its molecule are effective electron donors.

It is clear, however, that many other features of an enzyme are involved in the process. To begin with, the enzyme binds the substrate to itself and thereby brings the reacting groups of both substrate and enzyme in close contact with each other. The enzyme's reacting groups include effective nucleophiles, such as the five-atom imidazole ring of the amino acid histidine. Other enzyme groups tend to stabilize the intermediate products formed during hydrolysis. One of these is the short but reactive side group of the amino acid serine,

which can transiently capture the acid portion of the substrate, forming an ester [*see illustration on opposite page*].

The operation of these factors can be illustrated by the hydrolysis of the synthetic substrate *p*-nitrophenylacetate, which is the acetic acid ester of the aromatic alcohol nitrophenol. That this substrate can be hydrolyzed both by trypsin and by chymotrypsin was shown by B. S. Hartley and B. A. Kilby of the University of Cambridge. The hydrolysis begins when the enzyme encounters the substrate in solution and the two molecules form what is described as an enzyme-substrate complex. In the second step the ester is split into its acidic and basic constituents. The former, or acetyl portion, combines with the enzyme, giving rise to an intermediate called the acyl enzyme; the latter is released as the alcohol nitrophenol. In the third step the acyl enzyme is hydro-

lyzed by water, which regenerates free enzyme and liberates the acyl group as the corresponding acid (in this case acetic acid).

The first step happens so fast that it cannot be separated from the second; the third step, however, takes place more slowly. The initial burst of activity representing the first two steps can be followed by measuring the liberation of nitrophenol; the measurements are made easier by the fact that this alcohol is yellow. The third step can be followed by measuring the release of the acid. Since it is the slowest step, it governs the overall rate of the process. The mechanism of each of these steps has been studied intensively, notably by Thomas C. Bruice, first at Cornell University and more recently at the University of California at Santa Barbara, and by Myron L. Bender at Northwestern University. A particular effort has been made to identify the specific groups on the enzyme surface that participate in each of the postulated steps.

So far two kinds of group have been clearly implicated in the proteolytic activity of trypsin and chymotrypsin. The reaction with *p*-nitrophenylacetate can be stopped at the end of the second step, for instance, by carrying out the reaction in a mildly acidic solution. When the acyl enzyme is removed and analyzed, it is found that the acyl fraction is invariably bound to the hydroxyl group of a serine residue of the enzyme. Although trypsin and chymotrypsin each contain some 30 serine residues per molecule, only one of them is capable of capturing the acyl group during reaction with synthetic substrates. The location of this active serine has been identified within the structure of each of the two enzymes. Because serine is involved in their reactivity, trypsin, chymotrypsin and several other enzymes that function in the same way have been given the name "serine proteases."

The other group that has been definitely implicated as a participant in the enzymatic reaction is the imidazole ring of a histidine residue, which contains three carbon atoms and two nitrogen atoms. It is an effective nucleophile because it can donate two electrons from one of the two nitrogen atoms of the ring structure. Therefore it is believed that the histidine residue partakes in the second step of the reaction by initiating the attack on the peptide bond or the equivalent bond in an ester, and possibly also in the third step by initiating the hydrolysis of the acyl enzyme.

Chymotrypsin contains two histidine

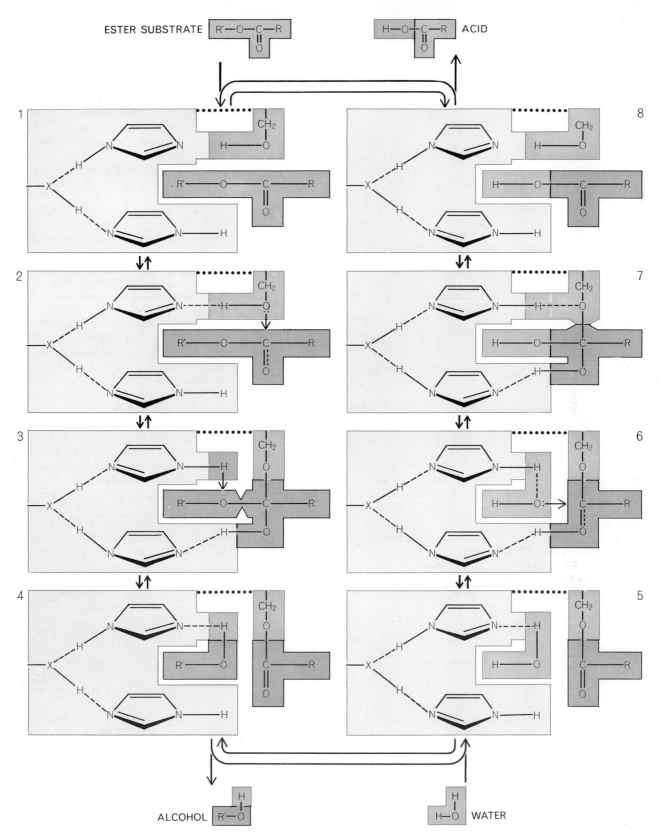

HYDROLYSIS OF ENZYME SUBSTRATE by the active site in chymotrypsin or trypsin may take place as shown here. The active site contains the functional groups of two histidine residues (*light colored area containing two imidazole rings*) and of a serine residue (*dark color*). The chemical nature of the group X is not established. In Step 1 the ester enters the active region. In Step 2 the OH group of the serine residue begins its nucleophilic attack. In Step 3 an unstable intermediate is formed. In Step 4 the ester is cleaved and an acyl enzyme is formed. The alcohol created by the cleavage of the ester is released and is replaced by a molecule of water (*Step 5*). In Step 6 a second nucleophilic attack is launched by the OH group of water. In Step 7 another unstable intermediate is formed. And in Step 8 the acid fraction of the ester is released and the free enzyme is restored to its original active condition. The scheme shown here is based in part on concepts proposed by Myron L. Bender and F. J. Kézdy of Northwestern University.

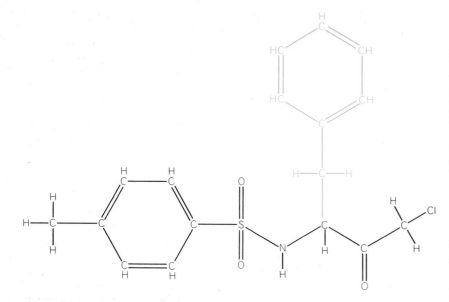

SYNTHETIC ENZYME INHIBITORS can abolish the activity of chymotrypsin and trypsin by reacting with one of the histidine residues in the active site of the enzyme. The compound shown here, *p*-toluenesulfonyl-phenylalanyl-chloromethylketone (TPCK), resembles chymotrypsin substrates and reacts only with chymotrypsin. If the side chain containing the six-carbon ring is replaced by the straight side chain found in lysine, the compound (then known as TLCK) resembles trypsin substrates and reacts only with trypsin.

the terms suggest that only a portion of the enzyme molecule is involved in enzyme action. The active region is only the relatively small area that comes in direct contact with the substrate. Considerable effort is currently being expended to identify the reactive groups in the active centers of enzymes. Much of the evidence for the existence of such centers has come from investigations of enzyme inhibition, a subject to which I shall now turn.

Enzyme Inhibition

It is to be expected that the functioning of an enzyme will be impaired if any of the groups required for binding or for catalysis are not available to interact with the substrate. Certain naturally occurring inhibitors of trypsin and chymotrypsin have a high affinity for these enzymes, and they have molecules so large that presumably they block off much if not all of the active center. Among these substances are the trypsin inhibitor found in the pancreas and the trypsin inhibitors isolated from the soybean. Other inhibitors structurally resemble a normal substrate but lack the reactive bond in the required position. These substrate analogues are believed to occupy the binding site on the enzyme, thus blocking the normal substrate.

One of the earliest observations implicating a serine residue as a component of the active center of trypsin and chymotrypsin was the discovery

residues and trypsin three of them. As we shall see, there is reason to believe that not one but two histidine residues are in fact cooperating in this process. One of them pushes the electrons toward the bond being attacked; the other pulls electrons from the opposite side. In this reaction scheme only the second and third steps involve the actual breaking of chemical bonds. The first step, on the other hand, does not necessarily

lead to a reaction. This step is dependent on the affinity of the enzyme for the substrate and hence is an expression of enzyme specificity, as distinguished from the catalytic function performed in the second and third steps. The groups on the enzyme that contribute either to specificity or to catalysis constitute what is often termed the active site, or active center. The existence of such a region is hypothetical;

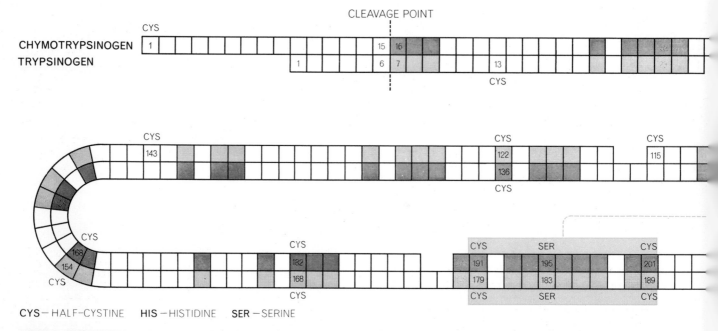

CYS — HALF-CYSTINE   HIS — HISTIDINE   SER — SERINE

LINEAR SEQUENCES of the amino acid residues of chymotrypsinogen and trypsinogen, the inactive precursor of trypsin, have been established except for one short stretch (84–87) in trypsin-

ogen. When the two sequences are aligned as shown here, it is found that about 40 percent of the positions in the two chains are occupied by the same amino acid residues. These regions of

by A. K. Balls of Purdue University and Eugene F. Jansen of the U.S. Department of Agriculture that the two enzymes are inhibited by a nerve gas, diisopropylfluorophosphate (DFP). Two years earlier Abraham Mazur and Oscar Bodansky of the Medical Division of the Chemical Warfare Service at Edgewood Arsenal had shown that DFP similarly inhibits acetylcholine esterase, an enzyme involved in the conduction of nerve impulses. When the inhibited chymotrypsin was subsequently broken down and analyzed, a phosphorus-containing fragment of DFP was invariably found to be attached to a specific serine residue—the same residue that later was found to be acylated during reaction with *p*-nitrophenylacetate. Thus the chemical modification of a single residue—serine—completely abolished enzyme function.

A clear demonstration that a histidine residue is another constituent of the active site has recently been provided by Elliott N. Shaw and his co-workers at Tulane University. These investigators synthesized compounds that in structure simulate specific substrates but contain, instead of the bond normally hydrolyzed, a group that reacts irreversibly with a histidine residue. For example, the compound *p*-toluene-sulfonyl - phenylalanyl - chloromethylketone (TPCK) resembles substrates for chymotrypsin [*see top illustration on opposite page*]. It reacts with a nucleophile in the active center, specifically a histidine residue, completely inhibiting

the enzyme. The compound known as TLCK is analogous, except that it simulates specific substrates for trypsin and therefore reacts with a histidine residue in the active center of trypsin only. In addition to serine and histidine, other specific residues seem to be important for the catalytic function of trypsin and chymotrypsin, but their role is still to be clarified.

Enzyme Structure

The relation between the structure of the entire enzyme molecule and its active site is not fully understood. In most cases, however, the maintenance of the three-dimensional structure of the entire molecule is necessary for maintaining the conformation of the active center. Hence many processes that change the conformation of the protein are accompanied by a loss of enzymatic activity. Trypsin, chymotrypsin and carboxypeptidases contain some 200 to 300 amino acid residues per molecule, equivalent to between 3,000 and 5,000 atoms. The active site involves only a small fraction of the residues, perhaps not more than 20. In order to appreciate the magnitude of the problem of characterizing the active site, let us consider what is now known about the chemical composition and structure of these enzymes.

The chemical composition of a compound is usually expressed by the number of atoms of which it is composed. On this basis glucose has the composi-

tion $C_6H_{12}O_6$. Chymotrypsinogen—the inactive precursor, or zymogen, of chymotrypsin—has the elemental composition $C_{1,130}H_{1,782}O_{356}N_{308}S_{12}$. This formula tells us virtually nothing, however, about the arrangement of the atoms in the molecule. For such giant protein molecules the composition is usually expressed in terms of the constituent amino acid residues rather than the atoms. Thus the composition of chymotrypsinogen, which contains 246 amino acid residues, can be written: alanine$_{22}$ arginine$_4$ aspartic acid$_9$ asparagine$_{14}$ half-cystine$_{10}$ glutamic acid$_5$ glutamine$_{10}$ glycine$_{23}$ histidine$_2$ isoleucine$_{10}$ leucine$_{19}$ lysine$_{14}$ methionine$_2$ phenylalanine$_6$ proline$_9$ serine$_{29}$ threonine$_{23}$ tryptophan$_8$ tyrosine$_4$ valine$_{23}$.

But even this representation is not adequate to describe the properties of a protein, any more than the formula $C_6H_{12}O_6$ genuinely describes the chemical properties of glucose. A more meaningful representation of the structure of proteins is given in terms of their amino acid sequence, that is, the linear arrangement of the amino acid residues. Such an analysis is a formidable undertaking; until recently it had been accomplished for only one enzyme—ribonuclease, a pancreatic enzyme whose molecule is made up of 124 amino acid residues.

The amino acid sequence of both trypsinogen (the precursor of trypsin) and chymotrypsinogen have been announced within the past year. The trypsinogen molecule is composed of a

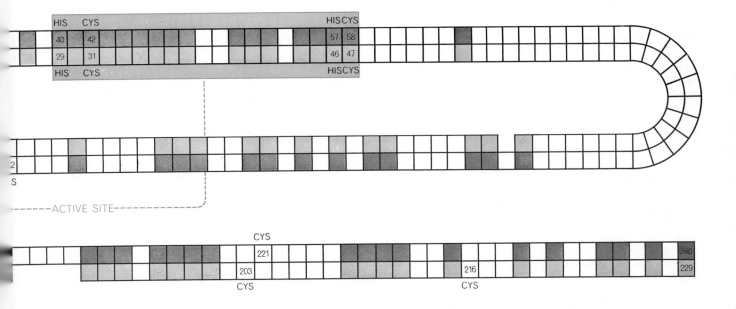

homology are indicated by filled squares. The longest homologous sequences involve areas believed to be part of the active sites of the two enzymes. The 10 half-cystine residues in chymotrypsinogen link up to form five disulfide bridges and the 12 half-cystines in trypsinogen form six disulfide bridges. The effect on the two-dimensional geometry of the two enzymes is shown on the next two pages.

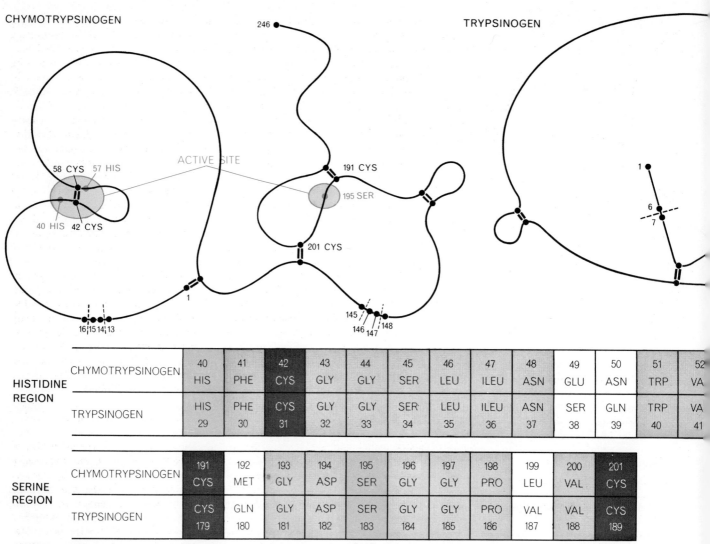

CHYMOTRYPSINOGEN

TRYPSINOGEN

		40	41	42	43	44	45	46	47	48	49	50	51	52
HISTIDINE REGION	CHYMOTRYPSINOGEN	HIS	PHE	CYS	GLY	GLY	SER	LEU	ILEU	ASN	GLU	ASN	TRP	VA
	TRYPSINOGEN	HIS	PHE	CYS	GLY	GLY	SER	LEU	ILEU	ASN	SER	GLN	TRP	VA
		29	30	31	32	33	34	35	36	37	38	39	40	41

		191	192	193	194	195	196	197	198	199	200	201
SERINE REGION	CHYMOTRYPSINOGEN	CYS	MET	GLY	ASP	SER	GLY	GLY	PRO	LEU	VAL	CYS
	TRYPSINOGEN	CYS	GLN	GLY	ASP	SER	GLY	GLY	PRO	VAL	VAL	CYS
		179	180	181	182	183	184	185	186	187	188	189

ACTIVE SITES in chymotrypsinogen and trypsinogen, labeled "histidine region" and "serine region," are almost identical. In each homologous region there are two half-cystine residues (*dark gray*) that form disulfide bridges in the actual molecule and serve to lock the active histidine and serine residues in a fixed position. The disulfide bridges are shown as short double bonds in the schematic two-dimensional representations of the two enzymes. In trypsinogen the heavy bonds indicate the three disulfide bridges whose location is known; the lighter bonds show possible bridge locations. When cleaved between residues 15 and 16, chymotrypsinogen

single polypeptide chain of 229 amino acid residues, or 17 fewer than chymotrypsinogen. The amino acid sequence of chymotrypsinogen was established by Hartley at Cambridge and independently by B. Keil and F. Šorm of the Czechoslovak Academy of Science in Prague. The amino acid sequence of trypsinogen was subsequently reported from our laboratory by K. A. Walsh and his co-workers, and a partial sequence was published by the Prague group. In each laboratory some 15 man-years of work have gone into the sequence analysis of each of these two proteins.

Although the amino acid sequence does not reveal the three-dimensional structure of a protein, it provides much information of value to the enzyme chemist. For example, it permits the identification of any residue that participates directly or indirectly in enzyme

catalysis. In the case of the zymogens chymotrypsinogen and trypsinogen it also discloses the location of the peptide bonds in the molecule that are cleaved during activation. Chymotrypsinogen is converted to chymotrypsin by cleavage of the bond between the 15th and 16th amino acid residues in the chymotrypsinogen chain. The activation of trypsinogen is accomplished by a cleavage between its sixth and seventh residues. Subsidiary cleavage points in chymotrypsinogen will be mentioned later.

An important feature of linear polypeptide chains is that they are often folded and cross-linked at one or more points. Such cross-links, or bridges, can have an important role in establishing a protein's three-dimensional structure. A cross-link is formed when two sulfur atoms protruding at different points on the polypeptide chain join in a disulfide

(—S—S—) bond. The individual sulfur atoms enter the chain appended to cysteine residues, but when two such residues are linked by a disulfide bond, the combination entity is called a cystine residue. The chymotrypsinogen molecule has five cystine (or 10 half-cystine) residues, which serve to tie the molecule together at five different points. The location of these disulfide bridges is shown at the upper left in the illustration above. The trypsinogen molecule has 12 half-cystine residues and therefore six bridges, but only three have been precisely located.

The Active Centers

When the amino acid sequences of chymotrypsinogen and trypsinogen were unraveled, biochemists immediately looked for the location of the histidine

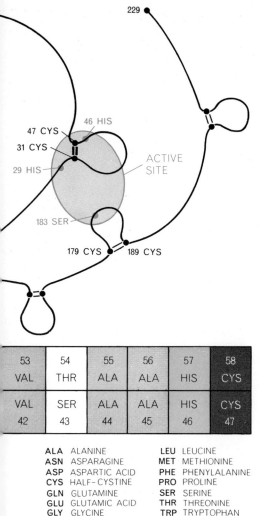

53	54	55	56	57	58
VAL	THR	ALA	ALA	HIS	CYS
VAL	SER	ALA	ALA	HIS	CYS
42	43	44	45	46	47

ALA	ALANINE	**LEU**	LEUCINE
ASN	ASPARAGINE	**MET**	METHIONINE
ASP	ASPARTIC ACID	**PHE**	PHENYLALANINE
CYS	HALF–CYSTINE	**PRO**	PROLINE
GLN	GLUTAMINE	**SER**	SERINE
GLU	GLUTAMIC ACID	**THR**	THREONINE
GLY	GLYCINE	**TRP**	TRYPTOPHAN
HIS	HISTIDINE	**VAL**	VALINE
ILEU	ISOLEUCINE		

is converted to the active enzyme chymotrypsin. Cleavage of trypsinogen between residues 6 and 7 yields active trypsin. (The lighter broken lines in chymotrypsinogen indicate secondary cleavage points.)

and serine residues that had been identified with the active centers of the two molecules. In chymotrypsinogen the active histidines are at positions 40 and 57; in trypsinogen, the shorter molecule, they are at positions 29 and 46. In both molecules the spacing between the two histidines is exactly the same. In both there are neighboring cystine residues that tie the polypeptide chain together in such a way that the two histidine residues are brought close together. Thus chymotrypsinogen has a cystine bridge between positions 42 and 58, which gives rise to a loop in the molecular chain. Similarly, trypsinogen has a cystine bridge between positions 31 and 47, forming another loop. Brought into proximity at the entrance to these loops, the two histidines can cooperate in acting as electron donors in protein hydrolysis.

Where in the two structures are the reactive serines? In chymotrypsinogen the reactive serine is at position 195 and in trypsinogen it is at position 183. Again note the similarity in location. And although in each molecule there is a large linear distance between the two histidines and the reactive serine, there is good reason to believe that the three residues actually lie close together in the active region of the three-dimensional molecule.

The resemblance in chemical structure between chymotrypsinogen and trypsinogen goes even further. When the amino acid sequences of the two molecules are compared side by side, after a common starting point has been chosen, it is found that about 40 percent of the amino acid residues are the same in both molecules [*see illustration on pages 254 and 255*]. Moreover, the most striking similarity in sequence occurs in the neighborhood of the histidine residues and the reactive serine [*see illustration at left*].

This marked similarity in structure of two enzymes that operate by the same mechanism but differ in specificity suggests that the two may have evolved from a common archetype. In the course of evolution those elements of the structure that are necessary for enzyme function would have remained unchanged. A similar conservation of chemical character, together with preservation of biological function, had previously been observed in the amino acid sequence of the cytochrome and hemoglobin molecules found in various species of animals [see "The Hemoglobin Molecule," by M. F. Perutz, which begins on page 40 of this volume].

The three-dimensional structure of chymotrypsinogen and trypsinogen is still unknown. The method of X-ray crystallography, which has been so successful in determining the three-dimensional structure of hemoglobin and its close relative myoglobin, has proved to be much more difficult to apply to the proteolytic enzymes. The data available so far for chymotrypsinogen and chymotrypsin reveal something that has been facetiously described as "complex but unintelligible." In the absence of direct evidence we have attempted to construct a hypothetical model of chymotrypsinogen that incorporates certain principles we believe to be correct [*see illustration on page 249*]. The model shows, for instance, the close juxtaposition of the two histidines and the active serine, the restrictions imposed by the disulfide bonds, the tendency of water-soluble amino acid residues to be on the outside of the molecule and water-insoluble residues to be on the inside, and the necessity for the peptide bonds cleaved during activation to be readily accessible. How many of the model's features are correct only future research will tell.

The zymogen precursors of proteolytic enzymes are manufactured within the cells of the digestive organs but are converted into active enzymes after they have been secreted by the cells. In all known cases the conversion involves the splitting of a specific peptide bond in the zymogen molecule. Representative examples of zymogen activation, in addition to the activation of chymotrypsinogen and trypsinogen, are the conversion of pepsinogen to pepsin and of procarboxypeptidase to carboxypeptidase. The phenomenon is not limited to proteolytic enzymes; for instance, many of the proteins involved in the process of blood clotting require similar activation, such as the conversion of prothrombin to thrombin, of plasminogen to plasmin and of fibrinogen to fibrin.

Zymogen Activation

The key enzyme in the activation of pancreatic zymogens is enterokinase, a proteolytic enzyme secreted by the mucous membranes of the intestine. Its prime function is to convert trypsinogen to trypsin; trypsin then becomes the key for the activation of all other pancreatic zymogens. Enterokinase is not, however, the only enzyme that can activate trypsinogen; the activation can be accomplished by trypsin itself and by several other enzymes, some of them found in bacteria. As far as is known, all these enzymes function in the same way: they cleave a specific peptide bond in the polypeptide chain of trypsinogen. In the trypsinogen obtained from cattle the cleavage occurs between the sixth and seventh amino acid residues of the chain. Since each molecule of trypsin released can activate another molecule of trypsinogen, it is apparent that the activation of trypsinogen is a self-accelerating process. Chymotrypsinogen similarly becomes an active enzyme when it is cleaved by trypsin. The cleavage takes place near one end of the chain (between residues 15 and 16) but no fragment is released because residue 1 is tied to the remainder of the molecule by a disulfide bond.

In these activation reactions the hydrolytic effect of trypsin comes to a halt after the first peptide bond has been cleaved. Presumably all other peptide bonds in the zymogen molecule that could have been cleaved are so located within the structure of the molecule as to remain completely resistant to the action of the enzyme. In the activation of chymotrypsinogen, hydrolysis can go a bit further because the chymotrypsin formed acts as a proteolytic enzyme on itself and can cleave three additional peptide bonds; they lie between positions 13 and 14, 145 and 146, and 147 and 148. All the resulting fragments are enzymatically active. But the bond between positions 15 and 16 must first be split by trypsin.

All known zymogens of the pancreas follow the same pattern of activation when they become converted to the active form. The activation requires the cleavage of a peptide bond adjacent to an arginine or a lysine residue near the beginning of the polypeptide chain of the zymogen. Some zymogens, however, must undergo additional transformations before they become activated. For example, the zymogen procarboxypeptidase A exists in the pancreatic juice as an aggregate of three large molecular subunits. Only one of these, subunit I, can be regarded as the immediate precursor of the enzyme carboxypeptidase A. Subunit II is the precursor of an enzyme that is similar in specificity to chymotrypsin but differs in composition from the chymotrypsin we have been discussing. The nature and role of subunit III is unknown. When trypsin is added to the three aggregated subunits, subunit I is converted to carboxypeptidase A only after subunit II has first become activated.

Why and how does the cleavage of a single and specific peptide bond in the zymogen give rise to an active enzyme? At present one can offer only a partial explanation, based largely on reasoning and only indirectly supported by experimental facts. I have mentioned previously that the action of an enzyme seems to involve two steps: the specific binding of the substrate and the subsequent bond-cleaving. Singly or in combination these steps require the proper configuration of groups on the enzyme molecule: the binding site and the catalytic site. The absence of either site or both in the zymogen would preclude enzyme function. Experiments have shown that chymotrypsinogen can bind substrates or inhibitors for chymotrypsin in much the same way that chymotrypsin itself does. These observations suggest that the binding site exists in the zymogen and hence that the catalytic site is not functional unless and until the specific peptide bond is cleaved during activation.

This cleavage is believed to change the conformation of the protein molecule so as to bring the groups involved in the bond-cleaving mechanism into the proper spatial relation. In the case of trypsin and chymotrypsin these groups are the reactive serine residue and the two histidine residues. Since the binding site and the catalytic site together form the active center, however, they must occupy adjacent or overlapping areas. Inasmuch as one of them is already present in the zymogen, it follows that the conformational changes involved in zymogen activation must be localized within a very small region of the molecule. The relation between these two sites is perhaps analogous to the relation of the back and the seat of a folding chair: the back can be regarded as determining the specificity and the seat the function. Obviously it is only after the chair is unfolded that it becomes functional.

Although this article has drawn almost exclusively on trypsin and chymotrypsin to illustrate the relation between chemical structure and enzymatic function, it would be wrong to conclude that all proteolytic enzymes utilize the same mechanism for the hydrolysis of peptide bonds. The range of structures essential for catalytic function is not limited to the cooperation of serine and histidine residues. For instance, the proteolytic enzymes of a group found in plants require a free thiol group (SH) for catalytic activity. These include papain, a proteolytic enzyme extracted from papaya juice, and ficin, an enzyme obtained from the fig tree. Papain, commercially used as a meat tenderizer, has a polypeptide chain of some 180 amino acid residues; the chain of ficin is probably somewhat longer.

Other proteolytic enzymes, such as pepsin and certain enzymes found in bacteria, are active only in slightly acid solution. Some aminopeptidases and the carboxypeptidases require the participation of specific metals for enzymatic function. (The former are exopeptidases that cleave only the first bond in a polypeptide chain; the latter are exopeptidases that cleave only the last bond.) The aminopeptidases usually require as coenzymes the ions of such metals as manganese and magnesium. The carboxypeptidases usually contain in their active center a firmly bound atom of a metal such as zinc.

Carboxypeptidase A exemplifies the behavior of these metal-containing enzymes. It has a single chain of some 300 amino acid residues; their complete sequence is still unknown. Yet the mode of action of this enzyme and the structure of its active site are remarkably well understood. Bert L. Vallee and his associates at the Harvard Medical School have shown that the natural enzyme contains an atom of zinc that is believed to be anchored to a thiol group somewhere in the chain and to an amino group of the first residue in the chain. When zinc is present, the enzyme will hydrolyze both polypeptides and their corresponding esters. When the zinc is removed, the protein completely loses its enzymatic activity.

If zinc is replaced by another metal, the specificity of the enzyme is altered. For example, when zinc is replaced by cadmium, the enzyme no longer hydrolyzes peptides but hydrolyzes esters even more effectively than the zinc enzyme does. When zinc is replaced by copper, the enzyme again becomes in-

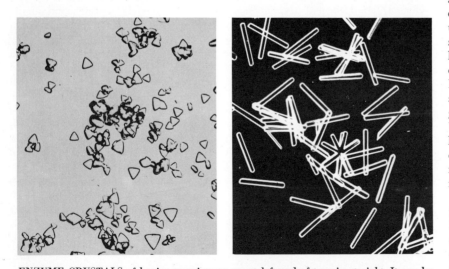

ENZYME CRYSTALS of bovine trypsinogen are at left and of trypsin at right. It can be seen that activation of the former produces a striking change in crystal structure. The two photomicrographs were made in 1935 by Moses Kunitz of the Rockefeller Institute.

active. Vallee and his associates have shown that it is possible not only to modify the activity of carboxypeptidase by replacement of the metal but also to manipulate the activity and specificity of the enzyme still further by chemical alteration of the active center. Their work has shown that at least five groups must participate in the enzyme's proteolytic activity: the metal, the two amino acid residues to which the metal is bound and two tyrosine residues that, when chemically modified, produce a change in the enzyme's specificity.

The Task Ahead

The foregoing examples were selected to illustrate the range and variety of structures encountered in the search for a chemical explanation of the function and mechanism of proteolytic enzymes.

We have only recently determined the linear structure of a few hydrolytic enzymes. We still do not know how they are folded into three-dimensional structures, but we are by no means sure that a three-dimensional model of the molecule will tell us how it functions as an enzyme. Scientific inquiries do not always proceed in an orderly and systematic manner, and perhaps we shall not have to wait until the last detail of the structure of these enzymes is known to understand their function.

The most exciting problem is the elucidation of the structure of the active center. One attempts to do this by "mapping" those groups on the enzyme molecule that are directly involved in enzyme function. The mapping process essentially consists of testing the effect of chemical modification of specific groups in abolishing or inducing en-

zyme activity. Yet there is no assurance that the notion of an active center is a physical reality and that an isolated structure that reproduced the groupings believed to constitute this site, in the proper spatial relations, would display full enzymatic function. Nature is seldom wasteful, and there is a real possibility that the entire enzyme molecule may be necessary for it to exhibit its full range of function.

Although much remains to be learned about proteolytic enzymes, enough is now known about them to enable investigators to use them to test various hypotheses of the way all enzymes function. It would be fitting if some of the earliest known enzymes, serving one of the most fundamental needs of man, should enable us to understand the mode of action of enzymes in general.

28

Molecular Isomers in Vision

RUTH HUBBARD AND ALLEN KROPF

June 1967

Molecular biology, which today is so often associated with very large molecules such as the nucleic acids and proteins, actually embraces the entire effort to describe the structure and function of living organisms in molecular terms. We are coming to see how the manifold activities of the living cell depend on interactions among molecules of thousands of different sizes and shapes, and we can speculate on how evolutionary processes have selected each molecule for its particular functional properties. The significance of precise molecular architecture has become a central theme of molecular biology.

One of the more recent observations is that biological molecules are not static structures but, in a number of well-established cases, change shape in response to outside influences. As an example, the molecule of hemoglobin has one shape when it is carrying oxygen from the lungs to cells elsewhere in the body and a slightly different shape when it is returning to the lungs without oxygen [see "The Hemoglobin Molecule," by M. F. Perutz, on page 40 of this volume]. A somewhat similar changeability in the molecule of lysozyme, which breaks down the walls of certain bacterial cells, was described in these pages last November by David C. Phillips of the University of Oxford. In this article we shall describe some of the simplest changes in shape that can take place in much smaller organic molecules and show how change of this type provides the basis of vision throughout the animal kingdom.

A "Childish Fantasy"

The notion that molecules of the same atomic composition might have different spatial arrangements is less than 100 years old. It dates back to a paper titled "*Sur les formules de structure dans l'espace,*" written in 1874 by Jacobus Henricus van't Hoff, then an obscure chemist at the Veterinary College of Utrecht. At that time it was still respectable to doubt the existence of atoms; to speak of the three-dimensional arrangement of atoms in molecules was a speculative leap of great audacity. Van't Hoff's paper provoked Hermann Kolbe, one of the most eminent organic chemists of his day, to publish a withering denunciation.

"Not long ago," Kolbe wrote in 1877, "I expressed the view that the lack of general education and of thorough training in chemistry of quite a few professors of chemistry was one of the causes of the deterioration of chemical research in Germany.... Will anyone to whom my worries may seem exaggerated please read, if he can, a recent memoir by a Herr van't Hoff on 'The Arrangements of Atoms in Space,' a document crammed to the hilt with the outpourings of a childish fantasy. This Dr. J. H. van't Hoff, employed by the Veterinary College at Utrecht, has, so it seems, no taste for accurate chemical research. He finds it more convenient to mount his Pegasus (evidently taken from the stables of the Veterinary College) and to announce how, on his daring flight to Mount Parnassus, he saw the atoms arranged in space."

Van't Hoff's "childish fantasy" was put forth independently by the French chemist Jules Achille le Bel and was soon championed by a number of leading chemists. In spite of Kolbe's opinion, evidence in support of the three-dimensional configuration of molecules rapidly accumulated. In 1900 van't Hoff was named the first recipient of the Nobel prize in chemistry.

Even before van't Hoff's paper of 1874 chemists had begun using the concept of the valence bond, commonly represented by a line connecting two atoms. It was not unnatural, therefore, to associate the valence bond concept with the idea that atoms were arranged precisely in space. The simplest hydrocarbon, methane (CH_4), would then be represented as a regular tetrahedron with a hydrogen atom at each vertex joined by a single valence bond to a carbon atom at the center of the structure [*see illustration on page 262*].

The valence bond remained an elusive concept, however, until G. N. Lewis postulated in 1916 that a common type of bond—the covalent bond—was formed when two atoms shared two electrons. "When two atoms of hydrogen join to form the diatomic molecule," he wrote, "each furnishes one electron of the pair which constitutes the bond. Representing each valence electron by a dot, we may therefore write as the graphical formula of hydrogen H : H." He visualized this bond to be "that 'hook and eye,' which is part of the creed of the organic chemist." To explain why electrons should tend to pair in this manner, Lewis could offer nothing beyond an intuitive principle that he called "the rule of two."

The rule of two entered the physicist's description of the atom when Wolfgang Pauli put forward the exclusion principle in 1923. This states that electrons in atoms and molecules are found in "orbitals" that can accommodate at most two electrons. Since electrons can be regarded as minuscule spinning negative charges, and thus as tiny electromagnets, the two electrons in each orbital must be spinning in opposite directions.

Let us return, however, to some of the chemical observations that gave rise to van't Hoff's ideas of stereochemistry late in the 19th century. Chemists were confronted by a series of puzzling observations best exemplified by two simple compounds: maleic acid and fumaric acid [*see illustrations on page 263*]. Here were two distinct, chemically pure substances, each with four atoms of carbon, four of hydrogen and four of oxygen ($C_4H_4O_4$). It was known, moreover, that the connections between atoms in the two molecules were exactly the same and that the two central carbon atoms in each molecule were connected by a double bond. Yet the two compounds were indisputably different. Whereas crystals of maleic acid melted at 128 degrees centigrade, crystals of fumaric acid did not melt until heated to about 290 degrees C. Furthermore, maleic acid was

about 100 times more soluble in water and 10 times stronger as an acid than fumaric acid. When maleic acid was heated in a vacuum, it gave off water vapor and became a new substance, maleic anhydride, which readily recombined with water and reverted to maleic acid. Fumaric acid underwent no such reaction. On the other hand, if either compound was heated in the presence of hydrogen, it was transformed into the identical compound, succinic acid ($C_4H_6O_4$), which contains two more hydrogen atoms per molecule than maleic or fumaric acid.

It was known that the four carbon atoms in maleic and fumaric acids form a chain. The only way to explain the differences between the compounds is to assume that the two halves of a molecule

that are connected by a double bond are not free to rotate with respect to each other. Thus the form of the $C_4H_4O_4$ molecule in which the two terminal COOH groups lie on the same side of the double bond (maleic acid) is not identical with the form in which the COOH groups lie on opposite sides (fumaric acid). Molecules that assume distinct shapes in this way are called geometrical or *cis-trans* isomers of one another. "*Cis*" is from the Latin meaning on the same side; "*trans*" means on opposite sides. Therefore maleic acid is the *cis* isomer of the $C_4H_4O_4$ molecule and fumaric acid is the *trans* isomer. When the double carbon-carbon bond of either isomer is reduced to a single bond by the addition of two more hydrogen atoms, the two halves of the molecule are free

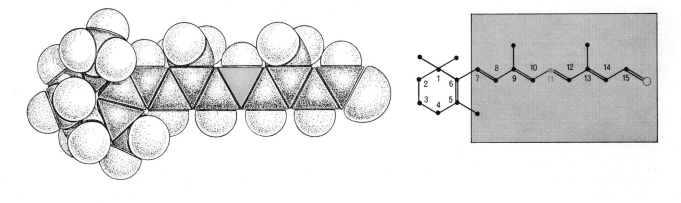

ALL-*TRANS* RETINAL

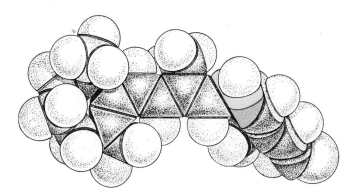

11-*CIS* RETINAL

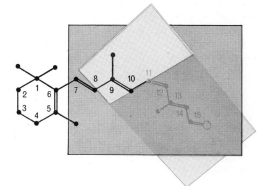

FUNDAMENTAL MOLECULE OF VISION is retinal ($C_{20}H_{28}O$), also known as retinene, which combines with proteins called opsins to form visual pigments. Because the nine-member carbon chain in retinal contains an alternating sequence of single and double bonds, it can assume a variety of bent forms. Each distinct form is termed an isomer. Two isomers of retinal are depicted here. In the models (*left*) carbon atoms are dark, except carbon No. 11, which is shown in color; hydrogen atoms are light. The large atom attached to carbon No. 15 is oxygen. In the structural formulas (*right*) hydrogen atoms are omitted. The parts of each isomer that lie in a plane are marked by background panels. When tightly bound to opsin, retinal is in the bent and twisted form known as 11-*cis*. When struck by light, it straightens out into the all-*trans* configuration. This simple photochemical event provides the basis for vision.

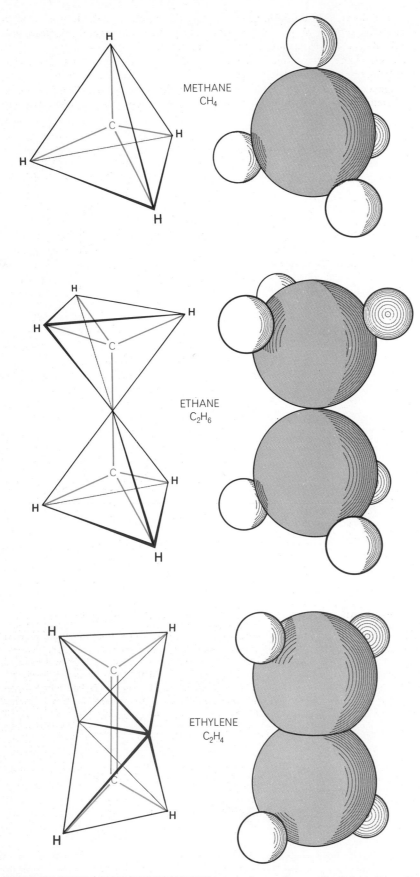

METHANE
CH₄

ETHANE
C₂H₆

ETHYLENE
C₂H₄

SIMPLEST HYDROCARBON MOLECULES are methane, ethane and ethylene. In methane the carbon atom lies at the center of a tetrahedron that has a hydrogen atom at each apex. The models at right show relative diameters of carbon and hydrogen. Ethane can be visualized as two tetrahedrons joined apex to apex. Ethylene, the simplest hydrocarbon that has a carbon-carbon double bond, can be visualized as two tetrahedrons joined edge to edge. The C≡C bond in ethylene is about 15 percent shorter than the C—C bond in ethane.

to rotate with respect to each other and a single compound results: succinic acid.

Van't Hoff proposed that when two carbon atoms are joined by a single bond they can be regarded as the centers of two tetrahedrons that meet apex to apex, thus allowing the two bodies to rotate freely. To represent a double bond, he visualized the two tetrahedrons as being joined edge to edge so that they were no longer free to rotate. Apart from minor modifications his proposals have stood up extremely well.

Electrons in Orbitals

Van't Hoff's explanation, of course, was a purely formal one and provided no real insight into *why* a double bond prevents the parts of a molecule it joins from rotating with respect to each other. This was not understood for another 50 years, when the development of wave mechanics by Erwin Schrödinger set the stage for one of the most productive periods in theoretical chemistry. With Schrödinger's wave equation to guide them, chemists and physicists could compute the orbitals around atoms where pairs of electrons could be found. The valence bonds, which chemists had been drawing as lines for almost a century, now took on physical reality in the form of pairs of electrons confined to orbitals that were generally located in the regions where the valence lines had been drawn.

The first molecule to be analyzed successfully by the new wave mechanics was hydrogen (H_2). Walter Heitler and Fritz London applied Schrödinger's prescription and obtained the first profound insight into the nature of chemical bonding. Their results define the region in space most likely to be frequented by the pair of electrons associated with the two hydrogen atoms in the hydrogen molecule. The region resembles a peanut, each end of which contains a proton, or hydrogen nucleus [*see top illustration on page 264*].

The phrase "most likely to be frequented" must be used because, as Max Born convincingly argued in the late 1920's, the best one can do in the new era of quantum mechanics is to calculate the probability of finding electrons in certain regions; all hope of placing them in fixed orbits must be abandoned. The new methods were quickly applied to many kinds of molecule, including some with double bonds.

One of the most fruitful methods for describing doubly bonded molecules—the molecular-orbital method—was devised by Robert S. Mulliken of the University of Chicago, who last year received the Nobel prize in chemistry. In Mulliken's concept a double bond can be visualized as three peanut-shaped regions [*see bottom illustration on next page*]. The central peanut, the "sigma" orbital, encloses the nuclei of the two

adjacent atoms, as in the hydrogen molecule. The other two peanuts, which jointly form the "pi" orbital, lie along each side of the sigma orbital. The implication of this model is that in forming the sigma orbital the two electrons occupy a common volume, whereas in form-

ing the pi orbital both electrons tend to occupy the two separate volumes simultaneously.

One can say that the sigma bond connects the atoms like an axle that joins two wheels but leaves them free to rotate separately. The pi bond ties the

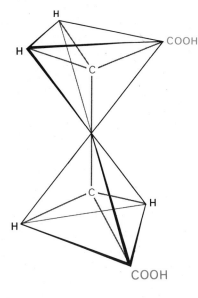
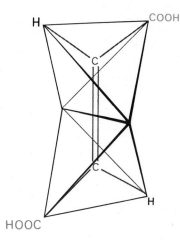
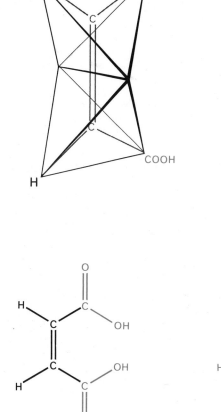

SUCCINIC ACID   MALEIC ACID   FUMARIC ACID

MOLECULAR PUZZLE was presented to chemists of the 19th century by maleic acid and fumaric acid, which have the same formula, C₄H₄O₄, and can be converted to succinic acid by the addition of two hydrogen atoms. Nevertheless, maleic and fumaric acids have very different properties. In 1874 Jacobus Henricus van't Hoff suggested that the central pair of carbon atoms in the three

acids could be visualized as occupying the center of tetrahedrons that were joined edge to edge in the case of maleic and fumaric acids and apex to apex in the case of succinic acid. Thus the spatial relations of the two carboxyl (COOH) groups would be rigidly fixed in maleic and fumaric acids but not in succinic acid, because in the latter molecule the tetrahedrons would be free to rotate.

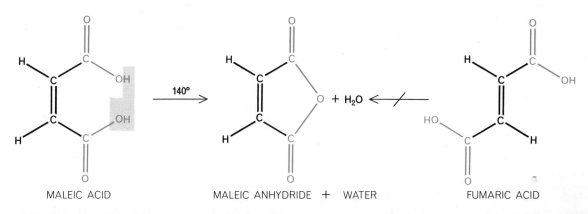

MALEIC ACID   MALEIC ANHYDRIDE + WATER   FUMARIC ACID

ONE CONSEQUENCE OF ISOMERISM is that maleic acid readily loses a molecule of water when heated, yielding maleic anhy-

dride. Fumaric acid does not undergo this reaction because its carboxyl groups are held apart at opposite ends of the molecule.

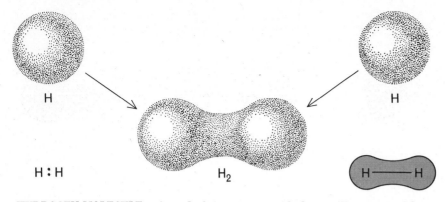

HYDROGEN MOLECULE is formed when two atoms of hydrogen (*H*) are joined by a chemical bond. The bond is created by the pairing of two electrons, one from each atom, which must have opposite magnetic properties if the atoms are to attract each other. The position of the electrons as they orbit around the hydrogen nuclei cannot be precisely known but can be represented by an "orbital," a fuzzy region in which the electrons spend most of their time. Known as a sigma orbital, it can be stylized as at lower right. The formula for the hydrogen molecule can be written as at lower left; the dots indicate electrons.

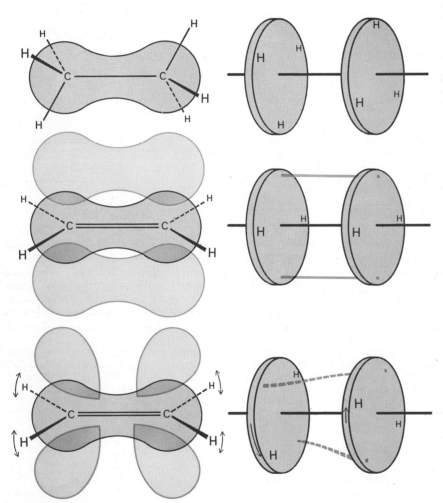

MOLECULAR ORBITALS help to explain why molecules held together by single bonds differ from molecules with double bonds. For example, the two carbon atoms in ethane are joined by two electrons in a sigma orbital, similar to the orbital in the hydrogen molecule. The two ends of the molecule, like wheels joined by a simple axle, are able to rotate. The two carbon atoms in ethylene (*middle*) are joined by two additional electrons in a "pi" orbital (*color*), as well as by two electrons in a sigma orbital. The four hydrogen atoms in ethylene are held in a plane perpendicular to the plane of the orbitals. The effect is as if two wheels were held together by two rigid rods in addition to an axle. When ethylene is in an "excited" state (*bottom*), one of the pi electrons occupies the four-lobed orbital. This lessens the rigidity of the double bond and gives it more of the character of a single bond.

two wheels together so that they must rotate as a unit. It also forces the two halves of the molecule to lie in the same plane, exactly as if two tetrahedrons were cemented edge to edge. In this way the molecular-orbital description of bonding provides a quantum-mechanical explanation of *cis-trans* isomerism.

The single bond joining two atoms, such as the carbon atoms of the two methyl groups in ethane (CH_3—CH_3), is a sigma bond, which leaves the groups attached to the two carbons free to rotate with respect to each other. Actually the two methyl groups in ethane are known to have a preferred configuration, so that they are not completely freewheeling. Nonetheless, at ordinary temperatures enough energy is available to make 360-degree rotations so frequent that derivatives of ethane (in which one hydrogen in each methyl group is replaced by a different kind of atom) do not form *cis-trans* isomers. There are exceptions, however, if the groups of atoms that replace hydrogen are so bulky that they collide and prevent rotation. In general, therefore, *cis-trans* isomerism is confined to molecules incorporating double bonds.

Electrons Delocalized

So much for molecules that have one double bond. What is the situation when a molecule has two or more double bonds? Specifically, what stereochemical behavior can be expected when single and double bonds alternate to form what is called a conjugated system?

The simplest conjugated system is found in 1,3-butadiene, a major ingredient in the manufacture of synthetic rubber, which can be written C_4H_6 or CH_2=CH—CH=CH_2. The designation "1,3" indicates that the double bonds originate at the first and third carbon atoms. Some of the properties of the biologically more interesting conjugated molecules are exhibited by butadiene. From the foregoing discussion one might expect that the second and third carbon atoms in the molecule would be free to rotate around the sigma bond connecting them. In actuality the rotation is not free: all the atoms in butadiene tend to lie in a plane.

It can also be shown that the energy content of each double bond in butadiene differs significantly from the energy content of the one double bond in the closely related compound 1-butene (CH_2=CH—CH_2—CH_3). The energy released in changing the two double bonds

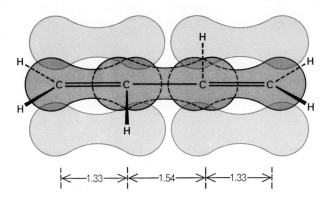
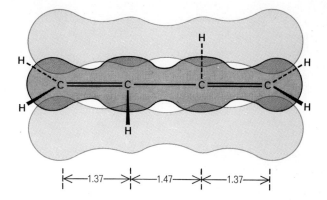

DELOCALIZED ORBITALS are found in "conjugated" systems: molecules in which single and double bonds alternate. The simplest conjugated molecule is 1,3-butadiene (C_4H_6). If its pi orbitals (*color*) were simply confined to the double bonds, as in ethylene, its orbital structure and carbon-carbon distances (in angstrom units) would be as shown at the left. Even in the lowest energy state, however, the pi electrons tend to spread across the entire molecule (*right*). As a result double bonds are lengthened and the single bond is shortened, making each type of bond more like the other. As a consequence the entire molecule is planar, or flat.

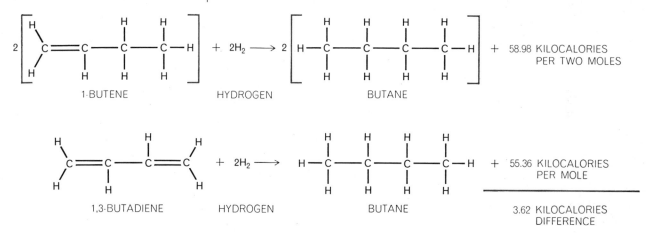

1-BUTENE   HYDROGEN   BUTANE   + 58.98 KILOCALORIES PER TWO MOLES

1,3-BUTADIENE   HYDROGEN   BUTANE   + 55.36 KILOCALORIES PER MOLE

3.62 KILOCALORIES DIFFERENCE

EVIDENCE FOR BOND MODIFICATION in a conjugated molecule can be obtained by measuring the energy released when double bonds are converted to single bonds by adding hydrogen. Hydrogenation of the double bond in 1-butene, which is not a conjugated molecule, yields 29.49 kilocalories for every mole of reactant. A mole is a weight in grams equal to the molecular weight of a substance: 56 for butene and 54 for butadiene. Hydrogenation of two moles of butene, hence the hydrogenation of twice as many double bonds, would therefore yield 58.98 kilocalories. Hydrogenation of the same number of double bonds in butadiene (present in a single mole) yields only 55.36 kilocalories. The difference is 3.62 kilocalories per mole for the two bonds, or 1.81 kilocalories for each double bond. The lesser energy in the butadiene double bonds indicates that they are more stable than the double bond in 1-butene.

of butadiene into the single bonds of butane ($CH_3-CH_2-CH_2-CH_3$) is about 55,400 calories per mole of butane formed. (A mole is a weight in grams equal to the molecular weight of the molecule: 58 for butane, 54 for butadiene.) The energy released in converting 1-butene, which has only one double bond, into butane is about 29,500 calories per mole. When expressed in terms of equivalent numbers of double bonds hydrogenated, the latter reaction yields some 1,800 calories more than the former [see *lower illustration above*]. The greater energy release means that the double bond in 1-butene is more reactive than either of those in 1,3-butadiene.

The added stability of the bonds in 1,3-butadiene was not unexpected; the same kind of result had been obtained for benzene, whose famous ring structure is formed by six carbon atoms connected alternately by single and double bonds. One can picture the extra energy of stabilization as arising from the tendency of electrons in the pi orbitals to leak out and become delocalized. Indeed, the phenomenon is called delocalization. The pi orbitals spread over larger portions of conjugated molecules than one might have thought, so that the properties of delocalized systems can no longer be described in terms of the properties of the double and single bonds as they are usually drawn. In order to represent the pi orbitals of 1,3-butadiene more accurately one must stretch them across all four carbon atoms of the molecule [see *upper illustration above*]. The stretching helps to explain why butadiene is not completely free to rotate around the central single bond: the bond has some of the characteristics of a double bond.

The altered character of butadiene's central carbon-carbon bond has been confirmed by X-ray-diffraction studies of butadiene. Whereas the usual carbon-carbon bond lengths are about 1.54 angstrom units for a single bond and 1.33 angstroms for a double bond, the length of the central single bond in 1,3-butadiene is only 1.47 angstroms. (An angstrom is 10^{-8} centimeter.) Linus Pauling, who did much to clarify the nature of the chemical bond, has estimated that the observed shortening of the central carbon-carbon bond of butadiene implies that it has about 15 percent of the double-bond character. One consequence of this is that the molecular configuration of butadiene tends to remain planar, or flat.

The tendency toward planarity in

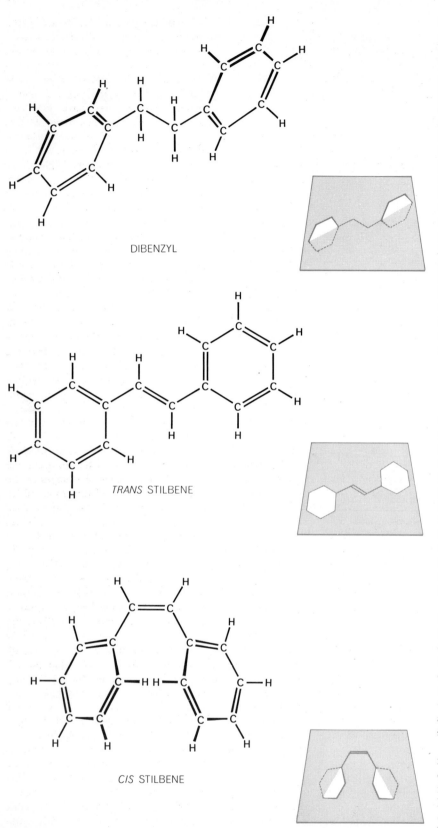

DIBENZYL

TRANS STILBENE

CIS STILBENE

PREFERENCE FOR FLATNESS in conjugated systems is exhibited by molecules of dibenzyl and two isomers of stilbene. The latter have a double bond in the carbon-carbon bridge linking the two benzene rings, whereas dibenzyl has a single bond. In dibenzyl the two rings are practically at right angles to the plane of the bridge. In *trans* stilbene all the atoms lie essentially in a plane. In *cis* stilbene, as can be demonstrated with molecular models, the two rings interfere with each other and thus cannot lie flat. The twisting of the rings has been established by X-ray studies of a related compound, *cis* azobenzene, in which the two rings are joined through a doubly bonded nitrogen (N=N) bridge.

conjugated systems was clearly demonstrated by the Scottish X-ray crystallographer J. M. Robertson and his colleagues in the mid-1930's. They compared the configurations of dibenzyl and *trans* stilbene, both of which contain two benzene rings joined by two carbon atoms [*see illustration at left*]. The difference between the two molecules is that in dibenzyl the two carbons are joined by a single bond, whereas in stilbene they are joined by a double bond. Robertson showed that the rings in dibenzyl are essentially at right angles to the connecting carbon-carbon bridge. In the *trans* form of stilbene the rings and the bridge lie in a plane, and the single bonds that join the rings to the two carbons in the bridge are foreshortened from the normal single-bond length to about 1.44 angstroms. In the *cis* form of stilbene the two rings cannot lie in a plane because they bump into each other.

Light-sensitive Molecules

We turn now to *cis-trans* isomerism in the family of molecules we have worked with most directly, the carotenoids and their near relatives, retinal (also known as retinene) and vitamin A. These molecules are built up from units of isoprene, which is like 1,3-butadiene in every respect but one: at the second carbon of isoprene a methyl group (CH_3) replaces the hydrogen atom present in butadiene. Natural rubber is polyisoprene, a long conjugated chain of carbon atoms with a methyl group attached to every fourth carbon.

The compound known as beta-carotene, which is responsible for the color of carrots, consists of an 18-carbon conjugated chain terminated at both ends by a six-member carbon ring, each of which adds another double bond to the conjugated system. The molecule has 40 carbon atoms in all and is presumably assembled from eight isoprene units [*see illustration on page 267*].

Until about 15 years ago the *cis-trans* isomers of the carotenoids entered biology in only one rather trivial way: in determining the color of tomatoes. Laszlo T. Zechmeister and his collaborators at the California Institute of Technology found in the early 1940's that normal red tomatoes contain the carotenoid lycopene in the all-*trans* configuration. (Lycopene differs from beta-carotene only in that the six carbon atoms at each end of the molecule do not close to form rings.) The yellow mutant known as the tangerine tomato contains

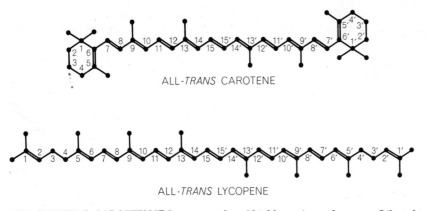

ALL-*TRANS* CAROTENE

ALL-*TRANS* LYCOPENE

TWO NATURAL CAROTENOIDS are examples of highly conjugated systems. Like other carotenoids, they are built up from units of isoprene (C_5H_8), also known as 2-methyl butadiene. In these diagrams hydrogen atoms are omitted so that the carbon skeletons can be seen more clearly. Both molecules contain 40 carbon atoms and are symmetrical around the central carbon-carbon double bond, numbered 15–15′. Beta-carotene gives carrots their characteristic orange color. *Trans* lycopene is responsible for the red color of tomatoes.

a yellow *cis* isomer of lycopene called prolycopene. Zechmeister, who contributed more than anyone else to our present understanding of carotenoid chemistry, liked to demonstrate how a yellow solution of prolycopene, extracted from tangerine tomatoes, could be converted into a brilliant orange solution of all-*trans* lycopene simply by adding a trace of iodine in the presence of a strong light.

The discovery that the *cis-trans* isomerism of a carotenoid plays a crucial role in biology was made in the laboratory of George Wald of Harvard University, where it was found that the *cis-trans* isomerism of retinal is intrinsic to the way in which visual pigments react to light. The discovery of these pigments is usually attributed to the German physiologist Franz Boll.

The Chemistry of Vision

In 1877, the same year that Kolbe was ridiculing van't Hoff's work on stereochemistry, Boll noted that a frog's retina, when removed from the eye, was initially bright red but bleached as he watched it, becoming first yellow and finally colorless. Subsequently Boll observed that in a live frog the red color of the retina could be bleached by a strong light and would slowly return if the animal was put in a dark chamber. Recognizing that the bleachable substance must somehow be connected with the frog's ability to perceive light, Boll named it "erythropsin" or "Sehrot" (visual red). Before long Willy Kühne of Heidelberg found the red pigment in the retinal rod cells of many animals and renamed it "rhodopsin" or "Sehpurpur" (visual purple), which it has been called

ever since. Kühne also named the yellow product of bleaching "Sehgelb" (visual yellow) and the white product "Sehweiss" (visual white).

The chemistry of the rhodopsin system remained largely descriptive until 1933, when Wald, then a postdoctoral fellow working in Otto Warburg's laboratory in Berlin and Paul Karrer's laboratory in Zurich, demonstrated that the eye contains vitamin A. Wald showed that the vitamin appears when rhodopsin is bleached by light—the physiological process known as light adaptation—and disappears when rhodopsin is resynthesized during dark adaptation [see "Night Blindness," by John E. Dowling; this is available as Offprint #1053]. He found that rhodopsin consists of a colorless protein (later named opsin) that carries as its chromophore, or color bearer, an unknown yellow carotenoid that he called retinene. Wald went on to show that the bleaching of rhodopsin to visual yellow corresponds to the liberation of retinene from its attachment to opsin, and that the fading of visual yellow to visual white represents the conversion of retinene to vitamin A. During dark adaptation rhodopsin is resynthesized from these precursors.

The chemical relation between retinene and vitamin A was elucidated in 1944 by R. A. Morton of the University of Liverpool. He showed that retinene is formed when vitamin A, an alcohol, is converted to an aldehyde, a change that involves the removal of two atoms of hydrogen from the terminal carbon atom of the molecule. As a result of Morton's finding the name retinene was recently changed to retinal.

In 1952 one of us (Hubbard), then a graduate student in Wald's laboratory, demonstrated that only the 11-*cis* isomer of retinal can serve as the chromophore of rhodopsin. This has since been confirmed for all the visual pigments whose chromophores have been examined. These pigments found in both the rod and cone cells of the eye contain various opsins, which combine either with retinal (strictly speaking retinal₁) or with a slightly modified form of retinal known as retinal₂. One other isomer of retinal, the 9-*cis* isomer, also combines with opsins to form light-sensitive pigments, but they are readily distinguishable from the visual pigments in their properties and have never been found to occur naturally. They have been called isopigments.

In 1959 we showed that the only thing light does in vision is to change the shape of the retinal chromophore by isomerizing it from the 11-*cis* to the all-*trans* configuration [*see illustration on page 261*]. Everything else—further chemical changes, nerve excitation, perception of light, behavioral responses—are consequences of this single photochemical act.

The change in the shape of the chromophore alters its relation to opsin and ushers in a sequence of changes in the mutual interactions of the chromophore and opsin, which is observed as a sequence of color changes. In vertebrates the all-*trans* isomer of retinal and opsin are incompatible and come apart. In some invertebrates, such as the squid, the octopus and the lobster, a metastable state is reached in which the all-*trans* chromophore remains bound to opsin.

Until the structure of opsin is established there is no way to know just how 11-*cis* retinal is bound to the opsin molecule. In the 1950's F. D. Collins, G. A. J. Pitt and others in Morton's laboratory showed that in cattle rhodopsin the aldehyde (C=O) group of 11-*cis* retinal forms what is called a Schiff's base with an amino (NH_2) group in the opsin molecule. Recently Deric Bownds in Wald's laboratory has found that the amino group belongs to lysine, one of the amino acid units in the opsin molecule, and has identified the amino acids in its immediate vicinity. There is little doubt that 11-*cis* retinal also has secondary points of attachment to opsin; otherwise it would be hard to explain why only the 11-*cis* isomer serves as the chromophore in visual pigments. Light changes the shape of the chromophore and thus alters its spatial relation to opsin. This leads, in turn, to changes in the shape of the

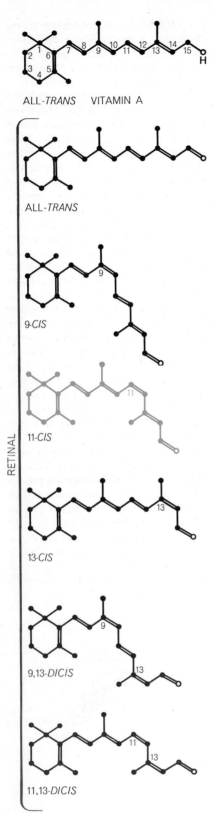

ALL-*TRANS*   VITAMIN A

ALL-*TRANS*

9-*CIS*

11-*CIS*

13-*CIS*

9,13-*DICIS*

11,13-*DICIS*

SIX ISOMERS OF RETINAL are represented in skeleton form below the structure of all-*trans* vitamin A. Hydrogen atoms are omitted, except for the H in the hydroxyl group of vitamin A. If that H and one other on the final carbon are removed, all-*trans* retinal results. This isomer and 11-*cis* retinal, which combines with opsin to form rhodopsin, are the isomers involved in vision.

opsin molecule [*see lower illustraion on page 269*]. The details of these changes, however, are still obscure.

How Molecules Twist

Let us examine somewhat more closely the various isomers of retinal. The six known isomers are illustrated at the left: the all-*trans* isomer and five *cis* isomers of one kind or another. Experiments with models, together with other evidence, show that four of the six isomers are essentially planar. The two that are not are the 11-*cis* isomer and the 11,13-*dicis* isomer. In these isomers there is considerable steric hindrance, or intramolecular crowding, between the hydrogen atom on carbon No. 10 (C_{10}) and the methyl group attached to C_{13}. Thus the double bond that joins C_{11} and C_{12} cannot be rotated by 180 degrees from the *trans* to a planar *cis* configuration. In the 11-*cis* isomers the tail of the molecule from C_{11} through C_{15} is therefore twisted out of the plane formed by the rest of the molecule.

This twisted geometry introduces two configurations, called enantiomers, that are mirror images of each other; if the molecule could be viewed from the ring end, one form would be twisted to the left and the other to the right. It is possible that opsin may combine selectively with only one enantiomer.

As Pauling had predicted in the 1930's, the steric hindrance that necessitates the twist in the 11-*cis* isomer makes it less stable than the all-*trans* or the 9-*cis* and 13-*cis* forms. We have recently found, for example, that the 11-*cis* form contains about 1,500 calories more "free energy" per mole than the *trans* form. One has to put in about 25,000 calories per mole, however, to rotate the molecule from one form to the other. This amount of energy, which is much more than a molecule is likely to acquire through chance collisions with its neighbors, is known as the activation energy: the energy required to surmount the barrier that separates the *cis* and *trans* states.

This raises an important point. How can two parts of a molecule be rotated around a double bond? The interconversion of *cis* and *trans* isomeric forms to another requires gross departures from flatness. How can this be accomplished?

Here we must introduce the concept of the excited state. One can think of molecules as existing in two kinds of state: a "ground," or stable, state of relatively low internal energy and various less stable states of higher energy—

the excited states. Molecules are raised from the ground state into one or another excited state by a sudden influx of energy, which can be in the form of heat or light. They return to the ground state by giving up their excess energy, usually as heat but occasionally as light, as in fluorescence or phosphorescence.

The orbital diagrams we have described apply to molecules in the ground state. When molecules are in an excited state, their electrons have more energy and therefore occupy different orbitals. Quantum-mechanical calculations show that an excited pi electron divides its time between the two ends of a double bond [*see bottom illustration on page 264*]. The net effect is to make the double bond in an excited molecule more like a single bond and less like a double bond. In a conjugated molecule, in which pi electrons are already delocalized, the changes in bond character are not uniform throughout the conjugated system but depend on the nature of the excitation and the structure of the molecule that is excited.

When one tries to isomerize carotenoids in the laboratory, it is usually helpful to add catalysts such as bromine or iodine. (The reader will recall that Zechmeister used iodine in his demonstrations.) Heat and light favor the existence of excited states. Bromine and iodine probably function by dissociating into atomic bromine and iodine, a process that is also favored by light. A bromine or iodine atom adds fleetingly to the double bond and converts it into a single bond, which is then momentarily free to rotate until the bromine or iodine atom has departed. The actual lifetime of the singly bonded form can be very brief indeed: the time required for one rotation around a carbon-carbon single bond is only about 10^{-12} second.

The Sensitivity of Eyes

It may seem remarkable that all animal visual systems so far studied depend on the photoisomerization of retinal for light detection. Three main branches of the animal kingdom—the mollusks, the arthropods and the vertebrates—have evolved types of eyes that differ profoundly in their anatomy. It seems that various anatomical (that is, optical) arrangements will do; apparently the photochemistry, once it had evolved, was universally accepted. Presumably the visual pigments of all animals must within narrow limits be equally sensitive to light, otherwise the more light-sensitive animals would eventually

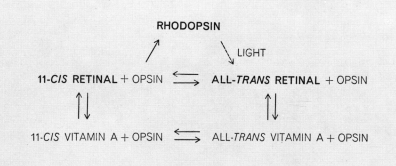

RHODOPSIN

11-*CIS* RETINAL + OPSIN ⇌ ALL-*TRANS* RETINAL + OPSIN

LIGHT

11-*CIS* VITAMIN A + OPSIN ⇌ ALL-*TRANS* VITAMIN A + OPSIN

PHOTOCHEMICAL EVENTS IN VISION involve the protein opsin and isomers of retinal and its derivative, vitamin A. Opsin joined to 11-*cis* retinal forms rhodopsin. When struck by light, the 11-*cis* chromophore is converted to an all-*trans* configuration and subsequently all-*trans* retinal becomes detached from opsin. With the addition of two hydrogen atoms, all-*trans* retinal is converted to all-*trans* vitamin A. Within the eye this isomer must be converted to 11-*cis* vitamin A, thence to 11-*cis* retinal, which recombines with opsin to form rhodopsin.

replace those whose eyes were less sensitive.

How sensitive to light is the animal retina? In a series of experiments conducted about 1940 Selig Hecht and his collaborators at Columbia University showed that the dark-adapted human eye will detect a very brief flash of light when only five quanta of light are absorbed by five rod cells. From this Hecht concluded that a single quantum is enough to trigger the discharge of a dark-adapted rod cell in the retina.

It is therefore essential that the quantum efficiency of the initial photochemical event be close to unity. In oth-

er words, virtually every quantum of light absorbed by a molecule of rhodopsin must isomerize the 11-*cis* chromophore to the all-*trans* configuration. It was shown many years ago by the British workers H. J. A. Dartnall, C. F. Goodeve and R. J. Lythgoe that an absorbed quantum has about a 60 percent chance of bleaching frog rhodopsin. One of us (Kropf) has found a similar quantum efficiency for the isomerization of the 11-*cis* retinal chromophore of cattle rhodopsin. Our work also shows that 11-*cis* retinal is more photosensitive than either the 9-*cis* or the all-*trans* isomers when they are attached as chromophores

to opsin, and this may be the reason why the geometrically hindered and therefore comparatively unstable 11-*cis* isomer has evolved into the chromophore of the visual pigments.

We have also recently measured the quantum efficiency of the photoisomerization of retinal and several closely related carotenoids in solution. Retinal turns out to be considerably more photosensitive than any of them and nearly as photosensitive as rhodopsin.

Although all animal eyes seem to employ 11-*cis* retinal as their light-sensitive agent, there are slight variations in the opsins that combine with retinal, just as there are variations in other proteins, such as hemoglobin, from species to species. Within the next few years we may learn the complete amino acid sequence of one of the opsins, and thereafter we should be able to compare such sequences for two or more species. It may be many years, however, before X-ray crystallographers have established the complete three-dimensional structure of an opsin molecule and are able to describe the site that binds it to retinal. One can conjecture that the binding site will be quite similar in the various opsins, even those from animals of different phyla, but there may be surprises in store. Whatever the precise details, it is clear that evolution has produced a remarkably efficient system for translating the absorption of light into the language of biochemistry—a language whose vocabulary and syntax are built on the various ways proteins interact with one another and with smaller molecules in their environment.

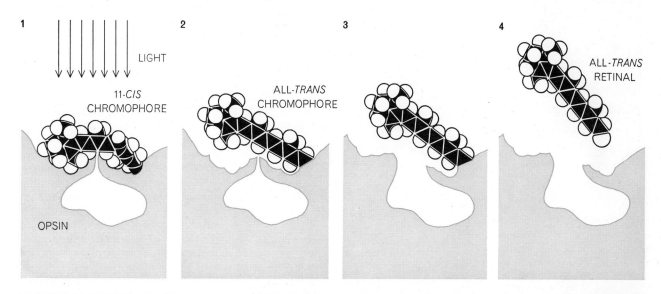

MOLECULAR EVENTS IN VISION can be inferred from the known changes in the configuration of 11-*cis* retinal after the absorption of light. In these schematic diagrams the twisted isomer is shown attached to its binding site in the much larger protein molecule of opsin (1). After absorbing light the 11-*cis* chromophore straightens into the all-*trans* isomer (2). Presumably a change in the shape of opsin (3) facilitates the release of all-*trans* retinal (4). The configuration of the binding site in opsin is not yet known.

29

The Genetic Code: II

MARSHALL W. NIRENBERG

March 1963

Just 10 years ago James D. Watson and Francis H. C. Crick proposed the now familiar model for the structure of DNA (deoxyribonucleic acid), for which they, together with Maurice H. F. Wilkins, received a Nobel prize last year. DNA is the giant helical molecule that embodies the genetic code of all living organisms. In the October 1962 issue of *Scientific American* F. H. C. Crick described this code (Offprint #123).

By ingenious experiments with bacterial viruses he and his colleagues established that the "letters" in the code are read off in simple sequence and that "words" in the code most probably consist of groups of three letters. The code letters in the DNA molecule are the four bases, or chemical subunits, adenine, guanine, cytosine and thymine, respectively denoted A, G, C and T.

This article describes how various combinations of these bases, or code letters, provide the specific biochemical information used by the cell in the construction of proteins: giant molecules assembled from 20 common kinds of amino acids. Each amino acid subunit is directed to its proper site in the protein chain by a sequence of code letters in the DNA molecule (or molecules) that each organism inherits from its ancestors. It is this DNA that is shaped by evolution. Organisms compete with each other for survival; occasional random changes in their information content, carried by DNA, are sometimes advantageous in this competition. In this way organisms slowly become enriched with instructions facilitating their survival.

The exact number of proteins required for the functioning of a typical living cell is not known, but it runs to many hundreds. The great majority, if not all, of the proteins act as enzymes, or biological catalysts, which direct the hundreds of different chemical reactions that go on simultaneously within each cell. A typical protein is a molecular chain containing about 200 amino acid subunits linked together in a specific sequence. Each protein usually contains all or most of the 20 different kinds of amino acids. The code for each protein is carried by a single gene, which in turn is a particular region on the linear DNA molecule. To describe a protein containing 200 amino acid subunits a gene must contain at least 200 code words, represented by a sequence of perhaps 600 bases. No one yet knows the complete base sequence for a single gene. Viruses, the smallest structures containing the blueprints for their own replication, may contain from a few to several hundred genes. Bacteria may contain 1,000 genes; a human cell may contain a million. The human genes are not strung together in

EXPERIMENT BEGINS when cells of the colon bacillus are ground in a mortar with finely divided aluminum oxide. "Sap" released from ruptured cells still synthesizes protein.

STEPS IN CODE BREAKING are shown in this sequence of photographs taken in the author's laboratory at the National Institutes of Health in Bethesda, Md. The open test tubes at upper left contain samples of the cell-free bacterial system capable of synthesizing protein when properly stimulated. The photograph shows stimulants being added. They include synthetic "messenger RNA" (ribonucleic acid) and amino acids, one of which is radioactive. The protein is produced when the samples are incubated 10 to 90 minutes. At upper right the protein is precipitated by the addition of trichloroacetic acid (TCA). At lower left the precipitate is transferred to filter-paper disks, which will be placed in carriers called planchettes. At lower right the planchettes are stacked in a radiation counting unit. Radiation measurement indicates how well a given sample of messenger RNA has directed amino acids into protein.

BASES

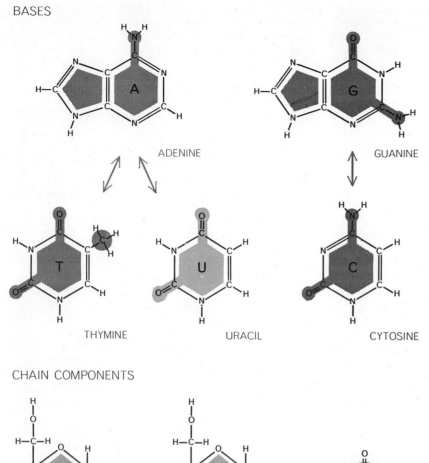

ADENINE

GUANINE

THYMINE

URACIL

CYTOSINE

CHAIN COMPONENTS

DEOXYRIBOSE

RIBOSE

PHOSPHORIC ACID

COMPONENTS OF DNA (deoxyribonucleic acid) are four bases adenine, guanine, thymine and cytosine (symbolized A, G, T, C), which act as code letters. Other components, deoxyribose and phosphoric acid, form chains to which bases attach (see below). In closely related RNA, uracil (U) replaces thymine and ribose replaces deoxyribose.

DNA STRUCTURE

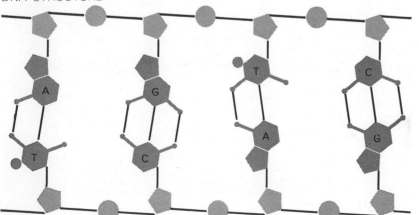

DNA MOLECULE resembles a chain ladder (actually twisted into a helix) in which pairs of bases join two linear chains constructed from deoxyribose and phosphate subunits. The bases invariably pair so that A links to T and G to C. The genetic code is the sequence of bases as read down one side of the ladder. The deoxyribose-phosphate linkages in the two linear chains run in opposite directions. DNA molecules contain thousands of base pairs.

one long chain but must be divided among at least 46 DNA molecules. The minimum number is set by the number of human chromosomes (46), which collectively carry the hereditary material. In fact, each chromosome apparently carries not one or two but several copies of the same genetic message. If it were possible to assemble the DNA in a single human cell into one continuous thread, it would be about a yard long. This three-foot set of instructions for each individual is produced by the fusion of egg and sperm at conception and must be precisely replicated billions of times as the embryo develops.

The bottom illustration at left shows how the bases in DNA form the cross links connecting two helical strands composed of alternating units of deoxyribose (a simple sugar) and phosphate. The bases are attached to the sugar units and always occur in complementary pairs: A joined to T, and G joined to C. As a result one strand of the DNA molecule, with its associated bases, can serve as the template for creating a second strand that has a complementary set of bases. The faithful replication of genes during cell division evidently depends on such a copying mechanism.

The coding problem centers around the question: How can a four-letter alphabet (the bases A, G, C and T) specify a 20-word dictionary corresponding to the 20 amino acids? In 1954 the theoretical physicist George Gamow, now at the University of Colorado, pointed out that the code words in such a dictionary would have to contain at least three bases. It is obvious that only four code words can be formed if the words are only one letter in length. With two letters 4×4, or 16, code words can be formed. And with three letters $4 \times 4 \times 4$, or 64, code words become available—more than enough to handle the 20-word amino acid dictionary [see top illustration on page 278]. Subsequently many suggestions were made as to the nature of the genetic code, but extensive experimental knowledge of the code has been obtained only within the past 18 months.

The Genetic Messenger

It was recognized soon after the formulation of the Watson-Crick model of DNA that DNA itself might not be directly involved in the synthesis of protein, and that a template of RNA (ribonucleic acid) might be an intermediate in the process. Protein synthesis is conducted by cellular particles called ribosomes, which are about half protein and half RNA (ribosomal RNA). Several years ago Jacques Monod and François Jacob of the Pasteur Institute in Paris coined the term "messenger RNA" to describe the template RNA that carried genetic messages from DNA to the ribosomes.

A few years ago evidence for the enzymatic synthesis of RNA complementary to DNA was found by Jerard Hurwitz of the New York University School of Medicine, by Samuel Weiss of the University of Chicago, by Audrey Stevens of St. Louis University and their respective collaborators [see "Messenger RNA," by Jerard Hurwitz and J. J. Furth; this is available as Offprint #119]. These groups, and others, showed that an enzyme, RNA polymerase, catalyzes the synthesis of strands of RNA on the pattern of strands of DNA.

RNA is similar to DNA except that RNA contains the sugar ribose instead of deoxyribose and the base uracil instead of thymine. When RNA is being formed on a DNA template, uracil appears in the RNA chain wherever adenine appears at the complementary site on the DNA chain. One fraction of the RNA formed by this process is messenger RNA; it directs the synthesis of protein. Messenger RNA leaves the nucleus of the cell and attaches to the ribosomes. The sequence of bases in the messenger

RNA specifies the amino acid sequence in the protein to be synthesized.

The amino acids are transported to the proper sites on the messenger RNA by still another form of RNA called transfer RNA. Each cell contains a specific activating enzyme that attaches a specific amino acid to its particular transfer RNA. Moreover, cells evidently contain more than one kind of transfer RNA capable of recognizing a given amino acid. The significance of this fact will become apparent later. Although direct recognition of messenger RNA code words by transfer RNA molecules has not been demonstrated, it is clear that these molecules perform at least part of the job of placing amino acids in the proper position in the protein chain. When the amino acids arrive at the proper site in the chain, they are linked to each other by enzymic processes that are only partly understood. The linking is accomplished by the formation of a peptide bond: a chemical bond created when a molecule of water is removed from two adjacent molecules of amino acid. The process requires a transfer enzyme, at least one other enzyme and a cofactor: guanosine triphosphate. It appears that amino acid subunits are bonded into the growing protein chain one at a time, starting at the end of the chain carrying an amino group (NH_2)

and proceeding toward the end that terminates with a carboxyl group (COOH).

The process of protein synthesis can be studied conveniently in cell-free extracts of the colon bacillus (*Escherichia coli*). The bacteria grow rapidly in suitable nutrients and are harvested by sedimenting them out of suspension with a centrifuge. The cells are gently broken open by grinding them with finely powdered alumina [*see illustration on page 2*]; this releases the cell sap, containing DNA, messenger RNA, ribosomes, enzymes and other components. Such extracts are called cell-free systems, and when they are fortified with energy-rich substances (chiefly adenosine triphosphate), they readily incorporate amino acids into protein. The incorporation process can be followed by using amino acids containing carbon 14, a radioactive isotope of carbon.

Optimal conditions for protein synthesis in bacterial cell-free systems were determined by workers in many laboratories, notably Alfred Tissières of Harvard University, Marvin Lamborg and Paul C. Zamecnik of the Massachusetts General Hospital, G. David Novelli of the Oak Ridge National Laboratory and Sol Spiegelman of the University of Illinois. When we began our work at the National Institutes of Health, our

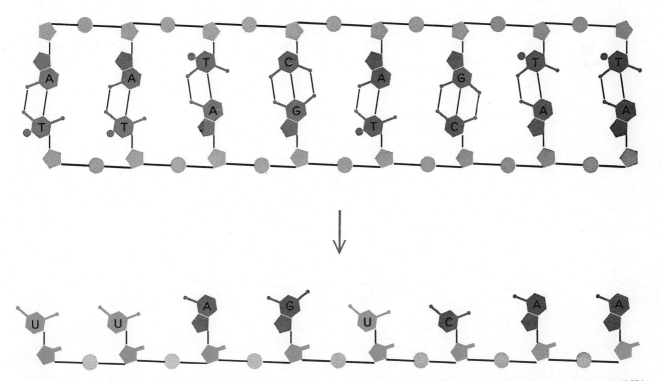

MESSENGER RNA is the molecular agent that transcribes the genetic code from DNA and carries it to the sites in the cell (the ribosomes) where protein synthesis takes place. The letters in messenger RNA are complementary to those in one strand of the DNA molecule. In this example UUAGUCAA is complementary to AATCAGTT. The exact mechanism of transcription is not known.

progress was slow because we had to prepare fresh enzyme extracts for each experiment. Later my colleague J. Heinrich Matthaei and I found a way to stabilize the extracts so that they could be stored for many weeks without appreciable loss of activity.

Normally the proteins produced in such extracts are those specified by the cell's own DNA. If one could establish the base sequence in one of the cell's genes—or part of a gene—and correlate it with the amino acid sequence in the protein coded by that gene, one would

be able to translate the genetic code. Although the amino acid sequence is known for a number of proteins, no one has yet determined the base sequence of a gene, hence the correlation cannot be performed.

The study of cell-free protein syn-

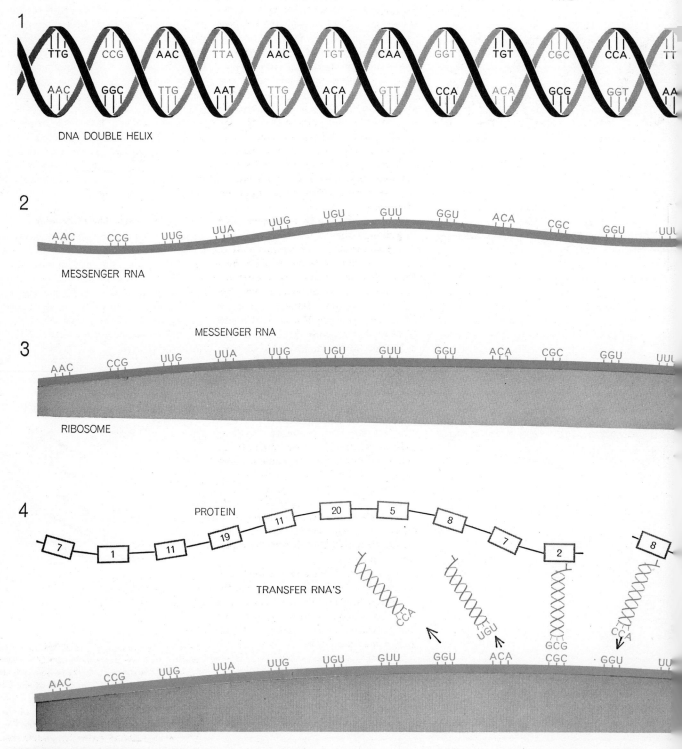

SYNTHESIS OF PROTEIN begins with the genetic code embodied in DNA (1). The code is transcribed into messenger RNA (2). In the diagram it is assumed that the message has been derived from the DNA strand bearing dark letters. The messenger RNA finds its way to a ribosome (3), the site of protein synthesis. Amino acids, indicated by numbered rectangles, are carried to proper sites on the messenger RNA by molecules of transfer RNA (see illustration on opposite page). Bases are actually equidistant, not

thesis provided an indirect approach to the coding problem. Tissières, Novelli and Bention Nisman, then at the Pasteur Institute, had reported that protein synthesis could be halted in cell-free extracts by adding deoxyribonuclease, or DNAase, an enzyme that specifically de-

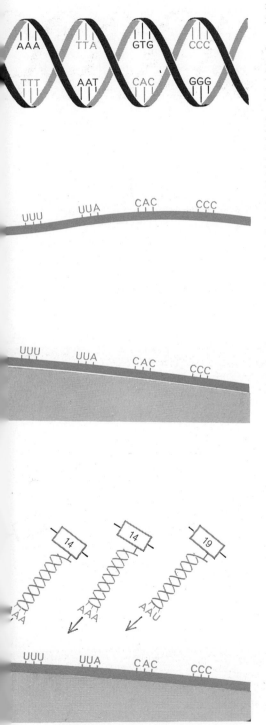

stroys DNA. Matthaei and I also observed this effect and studied its characteristics. It seemed probable that protein synthesis stopped after the messenger RNA had been depleted. When we added crude fractions of messenger RNA to such extracts, we found that they stimulated protein synthesis. The development of this cell-free assay for messenger RNA provided the rationale for all our subsequent work.

We obtained RNA fractions from various natural sources, including viruses, and found that many of them were highly active in directing protein synthesis in the cell-free system of the colon bacillus. The ribosomes of the colon bacillus were found to accept RNA "blueprints" obtained from foreign organisms, including viruses. It should be emphasized that only minute amounts of protein were synthesized in these experiments.

It occurred to us that synthetic RNA containing only one or two bases might direct the synthesis of simple proteins containing only a few amino acids. Synthetic RNA molecules can be prepared with the aid of an enzyme, polynucleotide phosphorylase, found in 1955 by Marianne Grunberg-Manago and Severo Ochoa of the New York University School of Medicine. Unlike RNA polymerase, this enzyme does not follow the pattern of DNA. Instead it forms RNA polymers by linking bases together in random order.

A synthetic RNA polymer containing only uracil (called polyuridylic acid, or poly-U) was prepared and added to the active cell-free system together with mixtures of the 20 amino acids. In each mixture one of the amino acids contained radioactive carbon 14; the other 19 amino acids were nonradioactive. In this way one could determine the particular amino acid directed into protein by poly-U.

It proved to be the amino acid phenylalanine. This provided evidence that the RNA code word for phenylalanine was a sequence of U's contained in poly-U. The code word for another amino acid, proline, was found to be a sequence of C's in polycytidylic acid, or poly-C. Thus a cell-free system capable of synthesizing protein under the direction of chemically defined preparations of RNA provided a simple means for translating the genetic code.

The Code-Word Dictionary

Ochoa and his collaborators and our group at the National Institutes of

grouped in triplets, and mechanism of recognition between transfer RNA and messenger RNA is hypothetical. Linkage of amino acid subunits creates a protein molecule.

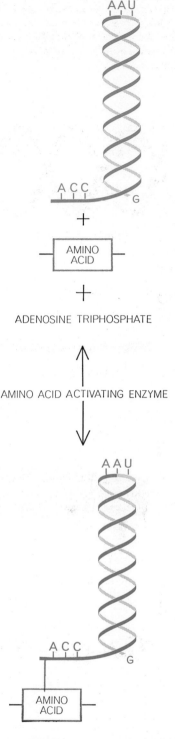

TRANSFER RNA is a special helical form of RNA that transports amino acids to their proper site in the protein chain. There is at least one transfer RNA for each of the 20 common amino acids. All, however, seem to carry the bases ACC where the amino acids attach and G at the opposite end. The attachment requires a specific enzyme and energy supplied by adenosine triphosphate. Unpaired bases in transfer RNA (AAU in the example) may provide the means by which the transfer RNA "recognizes" the place to deposit its amino acid package.

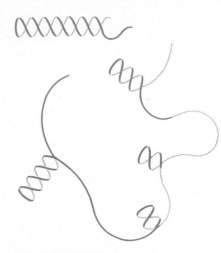

RNA STRUCTURE can take various forms. Transfer RNA (*top*) seems to be a fairly short double helix (probably less perfect than shown) that is closed at one end. Some RNA molecules contain a mixture of coiled and uncoiled regions (*bottom*).

Health, working independently, have now synthesized and tested polymers containing all possible combinations of the four RNA bases A, G, C and U. In the initial experiments only RNA polymers containing U were assayed, but recently many non-U polymers with high template activity have been found by M. Bretscher and Grunberg-Manago of the University of Cambridge, and also by Oliver W. Jones and me. All the results so far are summarized in the table at the bottom of pages 278 and 279. It lists the

RNA polymers containing the minimum number of bases capable of stimulating protein formation. The inclusion of another base in a polymer usually enables it to code for additional amino acids.

With only two kinds of base it is possible to make six varieties of RNA polymer: poly-AC, poly-AG, poly-AU, poly-CG, poly-CU and poly-GU. If the ratio of the bases is adjusted with care, each variety can be shown to code with great specificity for different sets of amino acids. The relative amount of one amino acid directed into protein compared with another depends on the ratio of bases in the RNA. Assuming a random sequence of bases in the RNA, the theoretical probabilities of finding particular sequences of two, three or more bases can be calculated easily if the base ratio is known. For example, if poly-UC contains 70 per cent U and 30 per cent C, the probability of the occurrence of the triplet sequence UUU is $.7 \times .7 \times .7$, or .34. That is, 34 per cent of the triplets in the polymer are expected to be UUU. The probability of obtaining the sequence UUC is $.7 \times .7 \times .3$, or .147. Thus 14.7 per cent of the triplets in such a polymer are probably UUC. This type of calculation, however, assumes randomness, and it is not certain that all the actual polymers are truly random.

It had been predicted by Gamow, Crick and others that for each amino acid there might be more than one code word, since there are 64 possible triplets and

only 20 amino acids. A code with multiple words for each object coded is termed degenerate. Our experiments show that the genetic code is indeed degenerate. Leucine, for example, is coded by RNA polymers containing U alone, or U and A, or U and C, or U and G.

It must be emphasized that degeneracy of this sort does not imply lack of specificity in the construction of proteins. It means, rather, that a specific amino acid can be directed to the proper site in a protein chain by more than one code word. Presumably this flexibility of coding is advantageous to the cell in ways not yet fully understood.

A molecular explanation of degeneracy has been provided recently in a striking manner. It has been known that some organisms contain more than one species of transfer RNA capable of recognizing a given amino acid. The colon bacillus, for example, contains two readily distinguishable species that transfer leucine. Bernard Weisblum and Seymour Benzer of Purdue University and Robert W. Holley of Cornell University separated the two leucine-transfer species and tested them in cell-free systems. They found that one of the species recognizes poly-UC but not poly-UG. The other species recognizes poly-UG but not poly-UC [*see top illustration on page 277*]. Although the number of transfer RNA species per cell is unknown, it is possible that each species corresponds to a different code word.

There is, however, the possibility of

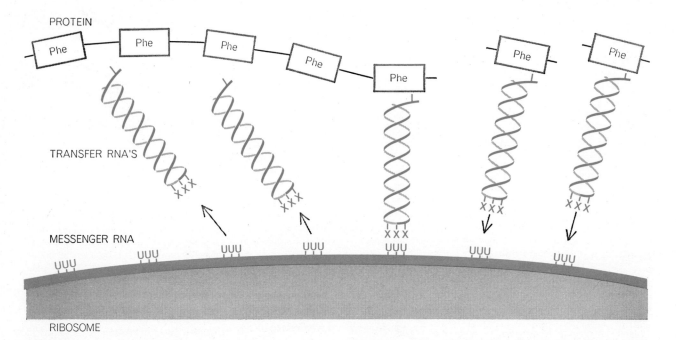

FIRST BREAK IN GENETIC CODE was the discovery that a synthetic messenger RNA containing only uracil (poly-U) directed the manufacture of a synthetic protein containing only one amino acid, phenylalanine (*Phe*). The finding was made by the author and J. Heinrich Matthaei. The X's in transfer RNA signify that the bases that respond to code words in messenger RNA are not known.

real ambiguity in protein synthesis. This would occur if one code word were to direct two or more kinds of amino acid into protein. So far only one such ambiguity has been found. Poly-U directs small amounts of leucine as well as phenylalanine into protein. The ratio of the two amino acids incorporated is about 20 or 30 molecules of phenylalanine to one of leucine. In the absence of phenylalanine, poly-U codes for leucine about half as well as it does for phenylalanine. The molecular basis of this ambiguity is not known. Nor is it known if the dual coding occurs in living systems as well as in cell-free systems.

Base sequences that do not encode for any amino acid are termed "nonsense words." This term may be misleading, for such sequences, if they exist, might have meaning to the cell. For example, they might indicate the beginning or end of a portion of the genetic message. An indirect estimate of the frequency of nonsense words can be obtained by comparing the efficiency of random RNA preparations with that of natural messenger RNA. We have found that many of the synthetic polymers containing four, three or two kinds of base are as efficient in stimulating protein synthesis as natural polymers are. This high efficiency, together with high coding specificity, suggests that relatively few base sequences are nonsense words.

In his article in *Scientific American* F. H. C. Crick presented the arguments for believing that the coding ratio is either three or a multiple of three. Recently we have determined the relative amounts of different amino acids directed into protein by synthetic RNA preparations of known base ratios, and the evidence suggests that some code words almost surely contain three bases. Yet, as the table at the bottom of the next two pages shows, 18 of the 20 amino acids can be coded by words containing only two different bases. The exceptions are aspartic acid and methionine, which seem to require some combination of U, G and A. (Some uncertainty still exists about the code words for these amino acids, because even poly-UGA directs very little aspartic acid or methionine into protein.) If the entire code indeed consists of triplets, it is possible that correct coding is achieved, in some instances, when only two out of the three bases read are recognized. Such imperfect recognition might occur more often with synthetic RNA polymers containing only one or two bases than it does with natural messenger RNA, which always contains a mixture of all four. The results obtained with synthetic RNA may dem-

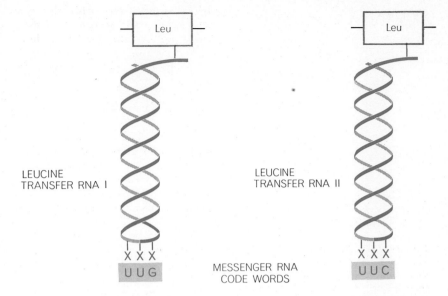

TWO KINDS OF TRANSFER RNA have been found, each capable of transporting leucine (*Leu*). One kind (*left*) recognizes the code word UUG; the other (*right*) recognizes UUC.

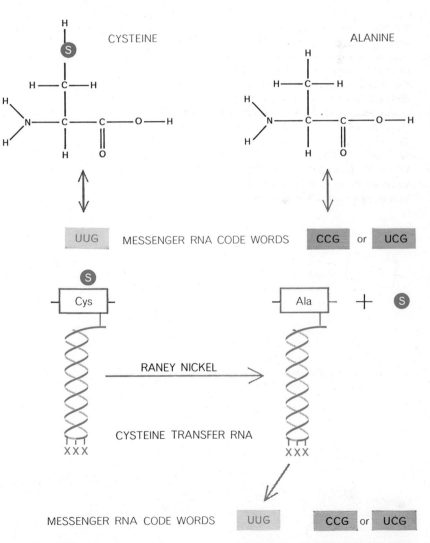

INGENIOUS EXPERIMENT showed that code-word recognition depends on the specificity of transfer RNA, not on the structure of the amino acid being transported. Cysteine is coded by UUG, alanine by CCG or UCG. Cysteine was hooked to its specific transfer RNA and sulfur was removed by a catalyst (Raney nickel). With sulfur removed from the molecule, cysteine became alanine. It was still directed into protein, however, as if it were cysteine.

SINGLET CODE (4 WORDS)	DOUBLET CODE (16 WORDS)				TRIPLET CODE (64 WORDS)			
					AAA	AAG	AAC	AAU
					AGA	AGG	AGC	AGU
					ACA	ACG	ACC	ACU
					AUA	AUG	AUC	AUU
					GAA	GAG	GAC	GAU
					GGA	GGG	GGC	GGU
A	AA	AG	AC	AU	GCA	GCG	GCC	GCU
G	GA	GG	GC	GU	GUA	GUG	GUC	GUU
C	CA	CG	CC	CU	CAA	CAG	CAC	CAU
U	UA	UG	UC	UU	CGA	CGG	CGC	CGU
					CCA	CCG	CCC	CCU
					CUA	CUG	CUC	CUU
					UAA	UAG	UAC	UAU
					UGA	UGG	UGC	UGU
					UCA	UCG	UCC	UCU
					UUA	UUG	UUC	UUU

CODE-LETTER COMBINATIONS increase sharply with the length of the code word. Since at least 20 code words are needed to identify the 20 common amino acids, the minimum code length is a sequence of three letters, assuming that all words are the same length.

onstrate the coding potential of the cell; that is, it may reveal code words that function routinely in the living cell and potential words that would be recognized if appropriate mutations were to occur in the cellular DNA. The table on page 12 summarizes the code-word dictionary on the assumption that all code words are triplets.

The Universality of the Code

Does each plant or animal species have its own genetic code, or is the same genetic language used by all species on this planet? Preliminary evidence suggests that the code is essentially universal and that even species at opposite ends of the evolutionary scale use much the same code. For instance, a number of laboratories in the U.S. and England have recently reported that synthetic RNA polymers code the same way in mammalian cell-free systems as they do in the bacterial system. The base compositions of mammalian code words corresponding to about six amino acids have been determined so far. It nevertheless seems probable that some differences may be found in the future. Since certain amino acids are coded by multiple words, it is not unlikely that one species may use one word and another species a different one.

An indirect check on the validity of code words obtained in cell-free systems can be made by studying natural proteins that differ in amino acid composition at only one point in the protein chain. For example, the hemoglobin of an individual suffering from "sickle cell" anemia differs from normal hemoglobin in that it has valine at one point in the chain instead of glutamic acid. Another abnormal hemoglobin has lysine at the same point. One might be able to show, by examining the code-word dictionary, that these three amino acids—glutamic acid, valine and lysine—have similar code words. One could then infer that the two

abnormal hemoglobins came into being as a result of a mutation that substituted a single base for another in the gene that controls the production of hemoglobin. As a matter of fact, the code-word dictionary shows that the code words are similar enough for this to have happened. One of the code groups for glutamic acid is AGU. Substitution of a U for A produces UGU, the code group for valine. Substitution of an A for a U yields AGA, one of the code groups for lysine. Similar analyses have been made for other proteins in which amino acid substitutions are known, and in most cases the substitutions can be explained by alteration of a single base in code-word triplets. Presumably more code words will be found in the future and the correlation between genetic base sequences and amino acid sequences can be made with greater assurance.

The Nature of Messenger RNA

Does each molecule of messenger RNA function only once or many times in directing the synthesis of protein? The question has proved difficult because most of the poly-U in the experimental system is degraded before it is able to function as a messenger. We have found, nevertheless, that only about 1.5 U's in poly-U are required to direct the incorporation of one molecule of phenylalanine into protein. And George Spyrides and Fritz A. Lipmann of the Rockefeller Institute have reported that only about .75 U's are required per molecule of amino acid in their studies. If the coding is done by triplets, three U's would be required if the messenger functioned only once. Evidently each poly-U molecule directs the synthesis of more than one long-chain molecule of polyphenylalanine. Similar results have been obtained in intact cells. Cyrus Levinthal and his associates at the Massachusetts Institute

	U	A	C	G
AMINO ACIDS CODED	PHENYLALANINE	LYSINE	PROLINE●	
	LEUCINE■			

■ POLY U CODES PREFERENTIALLY FOR PHENYLALANINE
● REPORTED BY ONLY ONE LABORATORY; STILL TO BE CONFIRMED
▲ REQUIRES ONLY FIRST OF TWO BASES LISTED
△ REQUIRES ONLY SECOND OF TWO BASES LISTED

SPECIFICITY OF CODING is shown in this table, which lists 18 amino acids that can be coded by synthetic RNA polymers containing no more than one or two kinds of base. The only amino acids that seem to require more than two bases for coding are aspartic acid and methionine, which need U, A and G. The relative amounts of amino acids directed into pro-

of Technology inhibited messenger RNA synthesis in living bacteria with the antibiotic actinomycin and found that each messenger RNA molecule present at the time messenger synthesis was turned off directed the synthesis of 10 to 20 molecules of protein.

We have observed that two factors in addition to base sequence have a profound effect on the activity of messenger RNA: the length of the RNA chain and its over-all structure. Poly-U molecules that contain more than 100 U's are much more active than molecules with fewer than 50. Robert G. Martin and Bruce Ames of the National Institutes of Health have found that chains of poly-U containing 450 to 700 U's are optimal for directing protein synthesis.

There is still much to be learned about the effect of structure on RNA function. Unlike DNA, RNA molecules are usually single-stranded. Frequently, however, one part of the RNA molecule loops back and forms hydrogen bonds with another portion of the same molecule. The extent of such internal pairing is influenced by the base sequence in the molecule. When poly-U is in solution, it usually has little secondary structure; that is, it consists of a simple chain with few, if any, loops or knots. Other types of RNA molecules display a considerable amount of secondary structure [see top illustration on page 276].

We have found that such a secondary structure interferes with the activity of messenger RNA. When solutions of poly-U and poly-A are mixed, they form double-strand (U-A) and triple-strand (U-A-U) helices, which are completely inactive in directing the synthesis of polyphenylalanine. In collaboration with Maxine F. Singer of the National Institutes of Health we have shown that poly-UG containing a high degree of ordered secondary structure (possibly due to G-G hydrogen-bonding) is unable to code for amino acids.

It is conceivable that natural messenger RNA contains at intervals short regions of secondary structure resembling knots in a rope. These regions might signify the beginning or the end of a protein. Alternative hypotheses suggest that the beginning and end are indicated by particular base sequences in the genetic message. In any case it seems probable that the secondary structure assumed by different types of RNA will be found to have great influence on their biological function.

The Reading Mechanism

Still not completely understood is the manner in which a given amino acid finds its way to the proper site in a protein chain. Although transfer RNA was found to be required for the synthesis of polyphenylalanine, the possibility remained that the amino acid rather than the transfer RNA recognized the code word embodied in the poly-U messenger RNA.

To distinguish between these alternative possibilities, a brilliant experiment was performed jointly by François Chapeville and Lipmann of the Rockefeller Institute, Günter von Ehrenstein of Johns Hopkins University and three Purdue workers: Benzer, Weisblum and William J. Ray, Jr. One amino acid, cysteine, is directed into protein by poly-UG. Alanine, which is identical with cysteine except that it lacks a sulfur atom, is directed into protein by poly-CG or poly-UCG. Cysteine is transported by one species of transfer RNA and alanine by another. Chapeville and his associates enzymatically attached cysteine, labeled with carbon 14, to its particular type of transfer RNA. They then exposed the molecular complex to a nickel catalyst, called Raney nickel, that removed the sulfur from cysteine and converted it

to alanine—without detaching it from cysteine-transfer RNA. Now they could ask: Will the labeled alanine be coded as if it were alanine or cysteine? They found it was coded by poly-UG, just as if it were cysteine [see bottom illustration on page 277]. This experiment shows that an amino acid loses its identity after combining with transfer RNA and is carried willy-nilly to the code word recognized by the transfer RNA.

The secondary structure of transfer RNA itself has been clarified further this past year by workers at King's College of the University of London. From X-ray evidence they have deduced that transfer RNA consists of a double helix very much like the secondary structure found in DNA. One difference is that the transfer RNA molecule is folded back on itself, like a hairpin that has been twisted around its long axis. The molecule seems to contain a number of unpaired bases; it is possible that these provide the means for recognizing specific code words in messenger RNA [see illustration at right on page 275].

There is still considerable mystery about the way messenger RNA attaches to ribosomes and the part that ribosomes play in protein synthesis. It has been known for some time that colon bacillus ribosomes are composed of at least two types of subunit and that under certain conditions they form aggregates consisting of two subunits (dimers) and four subunits (tetramers). In collaboration with Samuel Barondes, we found that the addition of poly-U to reaction mixtures initiated further ribosome aggregation. In early experiments only tetramers or still larger aggregates supported the synthesis of polyphenylalanine. Spyrides and Lipmann have shown that poly-U makes only certain "active" ribosomes aggregate and that the remaining monomers and dimers do not support polyphenylalanine syn-

BASES PRESENT IN SYNTHETIC RNA

UA	UC	UG	AC	AG	CG
PHENYLALANINE ▲	PHENYLALANINE ▲	PHENYLALANINE ▲	LYSINE ▲	LYSINE ▲	PROLINE ▲
LYSINE △	PROLINE △	LEUCINE	PROLINE △	GLUTAMIC ACID	ARGININE ●
TYROSINE	LEUCINE	VALINE	HISTIDINE	ARGININE ●	ALANINE ●
LEUCINE	SERINE	CYSTEINE	ASPARAGINE	GLUTAMINE ●	
ISOLEUCINE		TRYPTOPHAN	GLUTAMINE	GLYCINE ●	
ASPARAGINE ●		GLYCINE	THREONINE		

tein by RNA polymers containing two bases depend on the base ratios. When the polymers contain a third and fourth base, additional kinds of amino acids are incorporated into protein. Thus the activity of poly-UCG (an RNA polymer containing U, C and

G) resembles that of poly-UC plus poly-UG. Poly-G has not been found to code for any amino acid. Future work will undoubtedly yield data that will necessitate revisions in this table. An RNA-code-word dictionary derived from the table appears on page 280.

AMINO ACID	RNA CODE WORDS			
ALANINE	CCG	UCG ■		
ARGININE	CGC	AGA	UCG ■	
ASPARAGINE	ACA	AUA		
ASPARTIC ACID	GUA			
CYSTEINE	UUG △			
GLUTAMIC ACID	GAA	AGU ■		
GLUTAMINE	ACA	AGA	AGU ■	
GLYCINE	UGG	AGG		
HISTIDINE	ACC			
ISOLEUCINE	UAU	UAA		
LEUCINE	UUG	UUC	UUA	UUU ◻
LYSINE	AAA	AAG ●	AAU ●	
METHIONINE	UGA ■			
PHENYLALANINE	UUU			
PROLINE	CCC	CCU ▲	CCA ▲	CCG ▲
SERINE	UCU	UCC	UCG	
THREONINE	CAC	CAA		
TRYPTOPHAN	GGU			
TYROSINE	AUU			
VALINE	UGU			

△ UNCERTAIN WHETHER CODE IS UUG OR GGU

■ NEED FOR U UNCERTAIN

◻ CODES PREFERENTIALLY FOR PHENYLALANINE

● NEED FOR G AND U UNCERTAIN

▲ NEED FOR U A G UNCERTAIN

GENETIC-CODE DICTIONARY lists the code words that correspond to each of the 20 common amino acids, assuming that all the words are triplets. The sequences of the letters in the code words have not been established, hence the order shown is arbitrary. Although half of the amino acids have more than one code word, it is believed that each triplet codes uniquely for a particular amino acid. Thus various combinations of AAC presumably code for asparagine, glutamine and threonine. Only one exception has been found to this presumed rule. The triplet UUU codes for phenylalanine and, less effectively, for leucine.

thesis.

A possibly related phenomenon has been observed in living cells by Alexander Rich and his associates at the Massachusetts Institute of Technology. They find that in reticulocytes obtained from rabbit blood, protein synthesis seems to be carried out predominantly by aggregates of five ribosomes, which may be held together by a single thread of messenger RNA. They have named the aggregate a polysome.

Many compelling problems still lie ahead. One is to establish the actual sequence of bases in code words. At present the code resembles an anagram. We know the letters but not the order of most words.

Another intriguing question is whether in living cells the double strand of DNA serves as a template for the production of a single strand of messenger RNA, or whether each strand of DNA serves as a template for the production of two different, complementary strands of RNA. If the latter occurs—and available evidence suggests that it does—the function of each strand must be elucidated.

Ultimately one hopes that cell-free systems will shed light on genetic control mechanisms. Such mechanisms, still undiscovered, permit the selective retrieval of genetic information. Two cells may contain identical sets of genes, but certain genes may be turned on in one cell and off in another in highly specific fashion. With cell-free systems the powerful tools of enzymology can be brought to bear on these and other problems, with the promise that the molecular understanding of genetics will continue to advance rapidly in the near future.

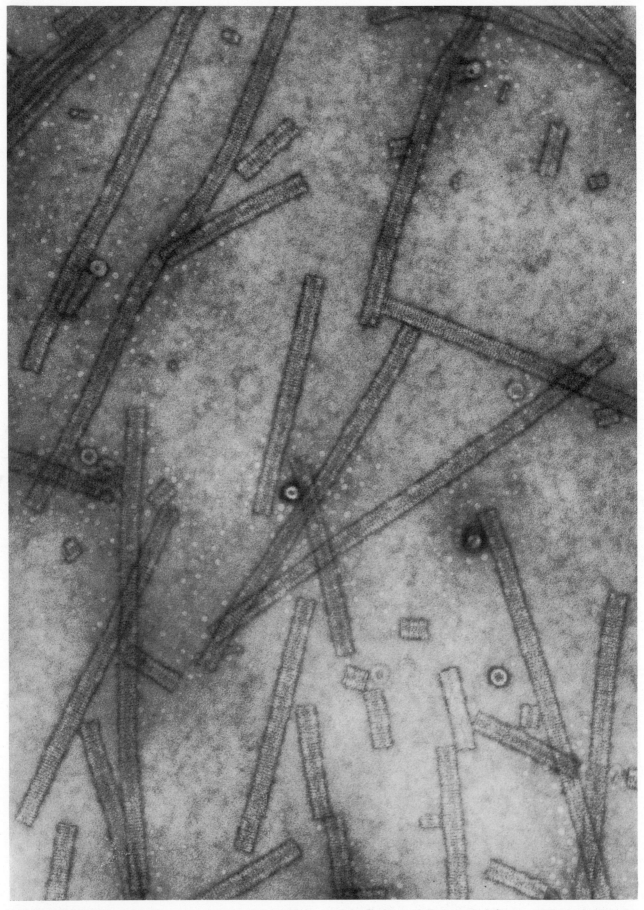

RODLIKE STRANDS of the tobacco mosaic virus are magnified 750,000 times in this electron micrograph made by H. L. Nixon of the Rothamsted Experimental Station in England. Only the larger particles are full-length viruses, capable of infecting cells.

30

The Genetic Code of a Virus

HEINZ FRAENKEL-CONRAT

October 1964

A few years ago it seemed that the virus that causes the mosaic disease of tobacco plants might serve as a Rosetta stone for deciphering the genetic code. The sequence of amino acid subunits in the protein that forms the coat of the tobacco mosaic virus was almost completely established. The ribonucleic acid (RNA) of the virus was believed to carry the coded information needed for the construction of this one protein. It was hoped that it would not be too difficult to work out the sequence of nucleotide subunits in the RNA; the code could then be deduced directly by matching up the sequence of amino acids in the protein with the sequence of groups of nucleotides, or "words," in the RNA molecule. Such a translation would go a long way toward disclosing how the chainlike molecules of RNA and deoxyribonucleic acid (DNA) are able to direct the construction of three-dimensional living cells.

Unhappily (or happily, as some prefer to look at it) nature does not make things easy by providing simple Rosetta stones. The RNA molecule of the tobacco mosaic virus turned out to be an enormously long chain composed of 6,400 nucleotide subunits. Furthermore, the molecule bears various messages: it carries directions for synthesizing not only the coat protein but also other proteins, that is, certain enzymes. Thus it has become apparent that decipherment of its language will be a complicated task. This article will describe some current attacks on the problem and the progress that has been made.

The recent advances in chemical genetics have been recounted in several articles in *Scientific American* [see "The Genetic Code," by F. F. C. Crick (Offprint #123), and "The Genetic Code: II," by Marshall Nirenberg (see page 270)]. I need review here only a few of the principal features of the chemical machinery for the reproduction of viruses. The tobacco mosaic virus consists of a long strand of RNA wrapped in a coat of protein [*see illustration on this page*]. The 6,400 nucleotide subunits of the RNA are of four kinds: guanine (G), cytosine (C), adenine (A) and uracil (U). After the viral RNA has invaded a tobacco leaf cell, it reproduces by acting as a template for the formation of complementary chains. Each guanine in the original chain combines with a cytosine from the intracellular environment and each cytosine with a guanine; similarly, each adenine combines with a uracil and each uracil with an adenine. Each of the subunits includes a ribose group and a phosphate group; the subunits are linked by bridges of phosphate. When a duplicate chain has been formed on the template, it peels off and is ready to combine with coat protein to form a new virus particle. The process requires the catalytic assistance of at least one enzyme—more probably two. It used to be supposed that the host cell supplied these enzymes ready-made, but it has now been established that the viral RNA directs the synthesis of the enzymes, using the cell's amino acids as the building material.

The coat protein of the tobacco mosaic virus has 158 amino acid subunits. If we suppose the RNA code word, or "codon," for each amino acid consists of three nucleotides, then a chain of 474 nucleotides would suffice to provide the information for synthesizing the coat protein. Adding the message required for synthesizing an enzyme (presumably a larger molecule than the coat protein) could raise the requirement to a chain of about 1,500 nucleotides. The fact that the RNA molecule of the virus is four times longer suggests that it probably directs the synthesis of more than one molecule of enzyme or other protein.

To decipher the code embodied in the virus's RNA we are confronted, then, with a molecule 6,400 nucleotides long carrying a series of different messages along its length. A beginning toward analysis of the structure of this molecule has been made by chopping off the nucleotides at the ends of the chain one by one with enzymes and alkalies [*see illustration on page 286*]. The RNA chain is so long, however, that this method is not likely to get us very far toward determining the full structure of the molecule or deciphering its code.

The specific topic of this article is

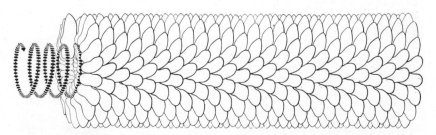

TOBACCO MOSAIC VIRUS has a coat of protein molecules (*the radially arranged white structures*) surrounding a strand of ribonucleic acid (RNA), represented by the black helix.

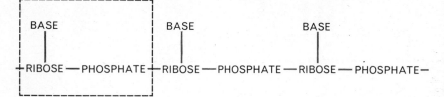

RIBONUCLEIC ACID is represented as a chain of repeating units of ribose sugar and phosphate. Extending from each ribose is a base: guanine, cytosine, adenine or uracil.

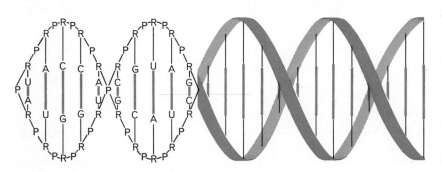

VIRAL RNA replicates by forming a double helix. The tobacco mosaic virus helix would consist of 6,400 subunits of guanine, cytosine, adenine and uracil (G, C, A and U).

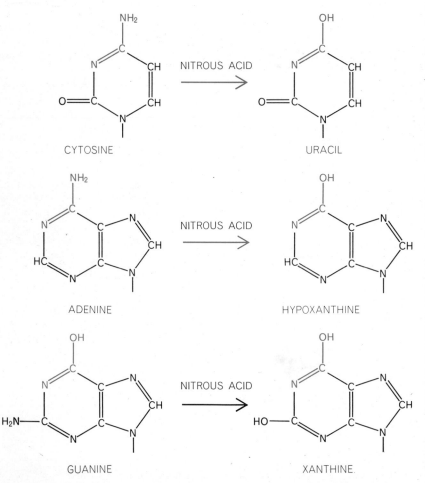

CHEMICAL MUTATION occurs when nitrous acid causes a replacement of the amino group (NH₂) in cytosine and adenine with the hydroxyl group (OH). The respective products of such mutation, uracil and hypoxanthine, appear at top and middle right. Guanine does not carry its amino group at a corresponding site on the molecule. Since the colored parts of the molecules are those interacting during replication or in double-strand molecules such as helical RNA, no mutant RNA results from the mutation of guanine to xanthine.

another approach to the problem, which, although more roundabout, has yielded some highly rewarding results. This method, pursued in our laboratory at the University of California at Berkeley and in several others, consists in making slight changes in the chemical structure of the RNA and then observing what effect these changes have on its genetic activity. Roughly speaking, the strategy is analogous to changing a letter or two in a verbal message to see how it changes the sense of the message.

Of the various reagents used to change the RNA, by far the most useful has proved to be nitrous acid. A particle of tobacco mosaic virus treated with this chemical is often so changed that it produces different disease symptoms in the tobacco plant it infects. Its new properties are transmitted to its progeny. Frequently the behavior of the altered strain of virus resembles that of a known natural strain—a known mutant—of the virus. Clearly in such cases the change in the treated virus represents a genuine mutation.

A study of the reaction between nitrous acid and the nucleotides of RNA shows how the mutation is brought about. Nitrous acid causes the replacement of the amino group (NH₂) in a nucleotide with a hydroxyl group (OH). In the case of cytosine this results in transformation of the cytosine to uracil [*see bottom illustration on this page*]. The conversion of one, two or three cytosines in the RNA chain into uracils may well convert the virus to a viable new strain that produces somewhat different disease symptoms. In the case of adenine the deamination by nitrous acid changes the adenine to hypoxanthine, a nucleotide that is not normally present in RNA but that is like guanine in part of its structure and therefore can combine with cytosine. Because adenine is thus converted to a base that resembles guanine (combining with cytosine instead of uracil), this change may sometimes result in a mutant virus. No mutation results, however, when guanine is deaminated to xanthine, because xanthine behaves like guanine itself; that is, it links up with cytosine as guanine does.

It has been established, then, that a localized change in the nucleotide composition of the viral RNA can produce a noticeable change in the activity of the virus. This circumstance does not provide a means for locating the changed nucleotides in the RNA's of different strains of tobacco mosaic virus. In a molecule with 6,400 nucleotides, comprising between 1,100 and 1,800 of

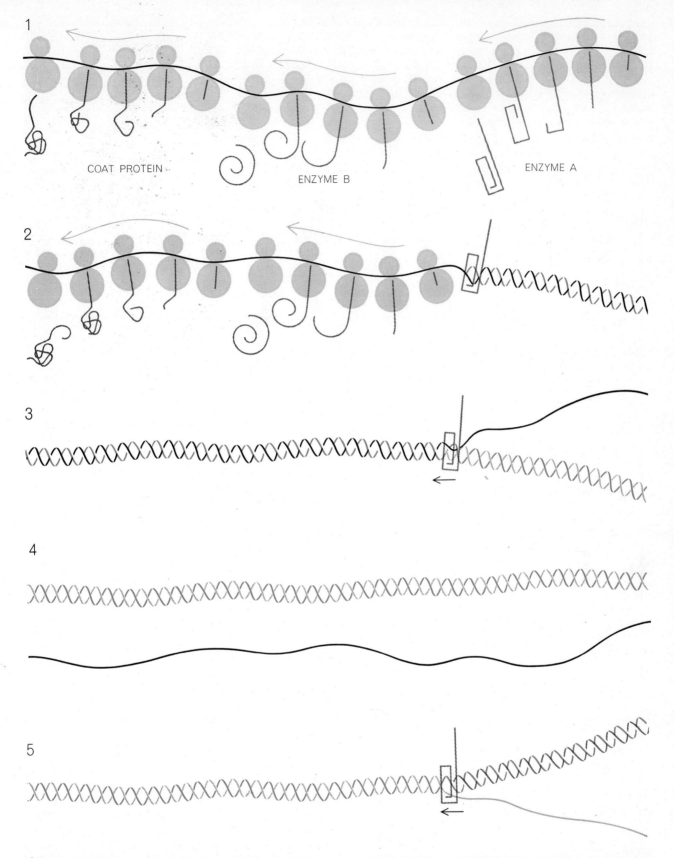

1

COAT PROTEIN   ENZYME B   ENZYME A

2

3

4

5

WITHIN THE CELL viral RNA (*black strand at top*) attaches to ribosomes (*double balls*) that travel along the strand synthesizing peptide chains of various proteins. Products of the process might include the material of the virus coat and two enzymes, represented by differently shaped structures emerging in the first step. In the second step the single RNA strand binds to an enzyme that catalyzes production of a complementary strand (*dark colored line*). This double strand RNA is shown uncurling (*step 3*), again under the influence of an enzyme. It makes a new strand (*light colored line in step 3*) and releases the original one. The first complementary strand then releases its progeny strand (*step 4*) and makes another (*gray curve in step 5*) under the influence of an enzyme. A released strand either can make protein as in step 1, or undergo a process of replication as in steps 2 through 4.

each of the four nucleotide types, the problem of detecting a difference of just a few nucleotides between one strain and another is beyond any present analytical technique. We therefore turned to studies of the proteins synthesized by artificially altered RNA.

The protein coat wrapped around the RNA core of the tobacco mosaic virus consists of nearly 2,200 molecules. Thus any change in the RNA that is reflected in the construction of the protein is amplified many times, and the change in the structure of the protein should be comparatively easy to detect. Moreover, a change in just one of the 16 different kinds of amino acid composing the protein amounts to a change of 5 percent or more in the total amino acid composition of the molecule. This composition was known to vary considerably even among natural strains of tobacco mosaic virus, and it could be assumed that such variations in the

SNAKE VENOM PHOSPHODIESTERASE
(37°, 24 HOURS)

SNAKE VENOM PHOSPHODIESTERASE
(0°, 10 MINUTES)

POLYNUCLEOTIDE PHOSPHORYLASE
(0°, 10 MINUTES)

T-1 RIBONUCLEASE
(37°, 24 HOURS)

PANCREATIC RIBONUCLEASE
(37°, 24 HOURS)

BACTERIUM SUBTILIS RIBONUCLEASE
(37°, 24 HOURS)

ALKALI
(25°, 24 HOURS,

END GROUPS removed from RNA provide clues to its structure. RNA appears at top right as a chain of bases (*B*), phosphates (*P*) and ribose (*symbolized by vertical lines*), the approximate length of which, 6,400 subunits, is denoted by *n* (for number of nucleotides). The method of removing an end group is given above the evidence thus gathered. The certain presence of guanine, cytosine, adenine or uracil at a given site is shown in dark color. If experiments only narrow the possibilities, light color is used. The effects of an enzyme from snake venom, phosphodiesterase, are shown in five stages, during which end groups are successively broken off. The effect of polynucleotide phosphorylase is similarly represented. In the RNA at bottom the identified nucleotides are dark-colored.

chemically modified strains would be easily and accurately measurable. Systematic programs of analysis of the proteins in mutant tobacco mosaic viruses were undertaken in our laboratory by two visiting Japanese workers, Akira Tsugita and Gunku Funatsu, and at the University of Tübingen by Hans Wittmann.

Most of the studies undertaken in our laboratory made use of virus mutants that produce unusual lesions in tobacco plants of the variety *Nicotiana sylvestris.* The common tobacco mosaic virus causes a discoloration and a distortion of leaves that spreads over the entire plant. A typical mutant we have investigated causes only local, walled-off lesions at the sites of inoculation. Altogether some 200 chemically induced mutants have been studied in the two laboratories. In general both laboratories agree in their findings concerning the changes in the amino acids of these mutants' coats, but they differ in some respects, on which I shall comment later.

Of the 200 mutants, about 120 apparently still had the same coat protein as they had had before mutation. At least the protein's overall amino acid composition was unchanged. Although it is possible that changes of the amino acids within the molecule might have been masked by alterations in one direction offsetting those in another, we can safely dismiss this explanation as highly unlikely, in view of the very tiny probability that such precisely balancing changes would take place in more than half of the mutants. Of the approximately 80 mutants that did show a change in the coat protein, nearly all were altered in only one, two or occasionally three amino acids. (There were a few that differed radically—in as many as 30 amino acids—from the common strain of the tobacco mosaic virus; possibly these were not artificial mutants but uncommon strains that happened to be present in the inoculated material.)

Certain patterns showed up in the mutations. All the changes were one-way; for example, there were many cases of conversion of the amino acid serine to the amino acid phenylalanine but not a single instance of transformation of phenylalanine to serine. Most interesting was the fact that of the 272 possible conversions of one amino acid to another (among the 16 present in the virus) only 21 actually occurred, and of these transformations only 14 showed up more than once [*see illustration on next two pages*]. Let us now consider

LEAVES from the tobacco plant *Nicotiana sylvestris* are compared. At top is a leaf free from infection. Below it is a leaf generally discolored by infection with tobacco mosaic virus. At bottom is a leaf with local lesions, an effect caused by some 200 mutant strains.

what interpretations we can extract from the results.

In their work on the genetic code Marshall W. Nirenberg and his associates at the National Institutes of Health had connected certain nucleotide combinations, or code words, with specific amino acids (as Nirenberg explained in the *Scientific American* article to which I have already referred). He had found that a synthetic RNA consisting only of uracils caused just the amino acid phenylalanine to form a chain, from which he concluded that the code word for incorporating phenylalanine into a protein was UUU. Similarly, an RNA-like molecule composed only of cytosine (thus constituting the codon CCC) carried specific instructions for polymerizing the amino acid proline. A combination of two parts of

uracil with one part of cytosine, forming a codon containing two U's and one C in some unknown order, directed the polymerization of leucine; a switch in the nucleotide proportions to one part of uracil and two parts of cytosine, that is, to a codon containing one U and two C's, favored the polymerization of serine.

Applying these findings to our virus mutants, we found that the two corresponded remarkably well. Let us say that the treatment of the virus with nitrous acid deaminated one of the cytosines in its RNA and thereby changed it to uracil. This might alter a CCC codon to one containing a U and two C's, which would result in the replacement of a proline by a leucine in the protein coat of the virus. In the same way a CUU sequence would be changed to UUU, which would lead to

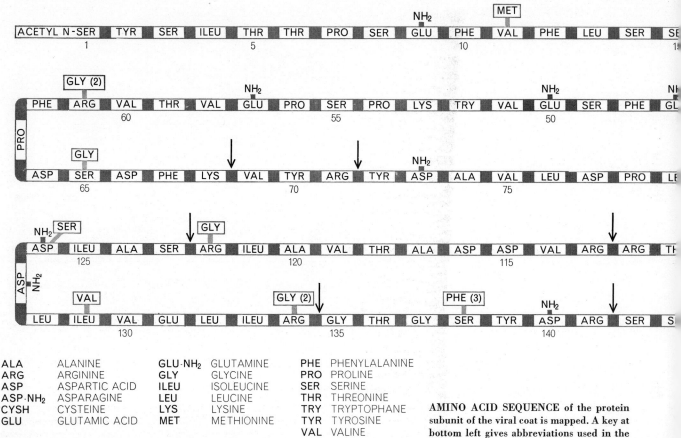

ALA	ALANINE	GLU-NH₂	GLUTAMINE	PHE	PHENYLALANINE
ARG	ARGININE	GLY	GLYCINE	PRO	PROLINE
ASP	ASPARTIC ACID	ILEU	ISOLEUCINE	SER	SERINE
ASP-NH₂	ASPARAGINE	LEU	LEUCINE	THR	THREONINE
CYSH	CYSTEINE	LYS	LYSINE	TRY	TRYPTOPHANE
GLU	GLUTAMIC ACID	MET	METHIONINE	TYR	TYROSINE
				VAL	VALINE

AMINO ACID SEQUENCE of the protein subunit of the viral coat is mapped. A key at bottom left gives abbreviations used in the

the replacement of a serine in the protein by a phenylalanine. As we have noted, in our mutants there was often a change from serine to phenylalanine or from proline to leucine, but it was never the other way around.

Studying the protein-building effects of various nucleotide combinations, Nirenberg and others have steadily enlarged the codon dictionary. Unfortunately the dictionary has grown in ambiguity as it has grown in size. Some amino acids apparently can be coded by as many as five different codons, or nucleotide triplets; leucine, for example, has been found to be represented by five codons and serine by four. This indicates that the code is highly ambiguous, or "degenerate." The reasons for this ambiguity in the genetic language remain obscure and certainly hide complexities still not understood. At all events, Wittmann has proposed a scheme of step-by-step transformations of the codons for four amino acids that illustrates the degeneracy of the code and may provide a way to determine the sequence of the nucleotides in each codon, which is not yet known [see top illustration on page 290].

The table at the bottom of page 10 summarizes all the amino acid changes in artificial mutants that have been observed in our laboratory and in Witt-

mann's at Tübingen. It includes cases in which the RNA nucleotides were altered by the attachment of a bromine atom or a methyl group instead of by deamination. The summary shows that all the amino acid transformations that occurred more than once in our laboratory can be accounted for either by a conversion of cytosine to uracil or by a change of adenine to guanine by way of hypoxanthine. But it also raises some puzzling questions. What about those cases, particularly some of the transformations obtained repeatedly by Wittmann, that cannot be explained by such conversions? By what chemical mechanism can methylation or bromination give rise to the same amino acid replacements, even though they do not affect the cytosine or adenine as deamination does? These questions are still unanswered.

Pursuing another line of investigation, Nirenberg initiated an intriguing experiment in collaboration with our laboratory. His system for exploring the coding effects of RNA uses a medium containing extracts from cells of the bacterium Escherichia coli. It contains ribosomes, enzymes, adenosine triphosphate (as the energy source) and amino acids attached to "transfer" RNA—in short, all the apparatus needed for the synthesis of proteins or polypeptides with the ex-

ception of the genetic material itself. The addition to this system of any type of RNA or DNA, even a synthetic RNA of the simplest kind, will bring about the linking of amino acids into chains in a sequence specified by the added RNA. Would the tobacco mosaic virus RNA induce the system to synthesize the tobacco mosaic virus coat protein?

The experiment was undertaken, and our first interpretation of the results was guardedly optimistic. This interpretation, however, was later corrected; there was no evidence that the system produced any identifiable tobacco mosaic virus protein. On the other hand, Daniel Nathans and his colleagues at the Rockefeller Institute found that the RNA of a virus that attacks E. coli would cause a cell-free extract of the bacterium to produce the coat protein of that virus. The most plausible explanation for this discrepancy seems to be that the code is too ambiguous, or degenerate, to carry over from a plant to a bacterial system. The tobacco plant cells and the E. coli system may preferentially use different codons to represent a given amino acid, and therefore a message may become garbled when it is transferred from one system to the other. It is as if the genetic code, although universal in principle, contained varying dialects, the cells of different species

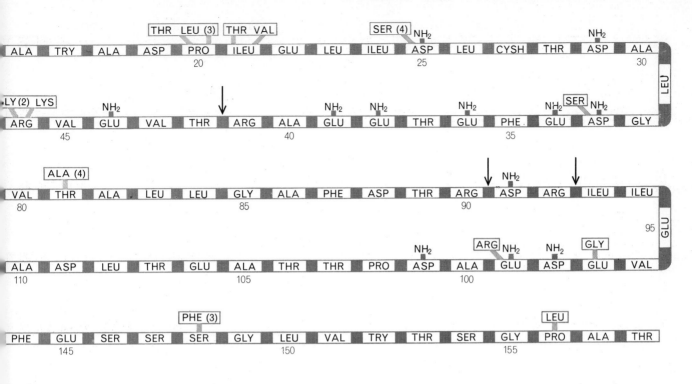

map. When the protein is decomposed by the enzyme trypsin, it fragments at sites marked by arrows. Replacements of amino acids occur in chemically induced mutants as shown in rectangles above sites at which they appear, with numbers indicating instances of observation. The protein coat of a virus particle has nearly 2,200 subunits. Its RNA, now under study, contains three times as many.

using different versions of the general language.

Apart from what our virus mutants may reveal about the genetic code, they interest us profoundly for another reason. The experiments in controlled alteration of their protein coats promise to help unravel the three-dimensional structure of the protein. The elucidation of protein structure is widely recognized as a central problem in biology. Next to the machinery of heredity, the three-dimensional structure of proteins holds perhaps the most important key to all the processes of life. Molecular structure determines the activities of enzymes in catalyzing biochemical reactions, of antibodies in precipitating foreign substances, of protein hormones and other specific proteins in regulating metabolism; in sum, it is a prime factor accounting for the properties and functions of all proteins from those in the coat of a virus to those in the cells of the brain. Each protein is characterized by specific internal bonds that maintain its three-dimensional form and by special surfaces that selectively bind to it certain ions, simple molecules or other proteins.

The spatial organization of a few proteins has been worked out by studying the patterns of X rays diffracted by crystals of the proteins in a dry state.

Such analyses do not necessarily show what form the proteins take in their natural condition in water solution, nor do they throw light on the nature of the internal bonds that maintain the protein molecule's shape. These questions are being investigated indirectly in many laboratories by gentle chemical methods probing the reactivity of specific protein molecules at various points in the molecular chain. Along this line our virus mutants have provided helpful information.

The protein coat of the tobacco mosaic virus performs certain definite functions in protecting the integrity and promoting the infectivity of the virus, and we have studied these functions in detail in our laboratory [see "Rebuilding a Virus," by Heinz Fraenkel-Conrat; this is available as Offprint #9]. One can assume that the protein coat of the common strain of the virus, as it has evolved by natural selection, is highly efficient, and that any mutation is likely to reduce the virus's viability. We were therefore interested in seeing just how and to what extent each chemically induced change in the amino acid sequence would affect the virus.

As I have mentioned, almost the entire sequence of the 158 amino acids in this protein was known. It was also

known that, when one attacked the protein coat of the common tobacco mosaic virus with an enzyme that removes amino acids from the carboxyl (COOH) end of a protein chain, it was able to chop off only a single amino acid, threonine, at the very end of the chain. Surprisingly, it turned out that this amputation (removing a total of 2,200 threonine units from the 2,200 protein molecules forming the coat of the virus) did not markedly affect the biological properties of the virus. Our very first mutant, however, showed a dramatic increase in vulnerability. As it happened, this mutation had replaced a proline near the end of the chain (No. 156 in the sequence) with leucine. The change made the protein much more susceptible to digestion by the enzyme. The enzyme was now able to clip three amino acids off the protein in the virus (and many more than three when it attacked the protein alone, stripped away from the virus). The three-amino-acid amputation made the virus distinctly less viable. This showed clearly that a single mutation, producing only an apparently minor change in the protein, could greatly reduce the virus's chances of survival.

Later studies have indicated that some RNA mutations render the RNA incapable even of forming the protein

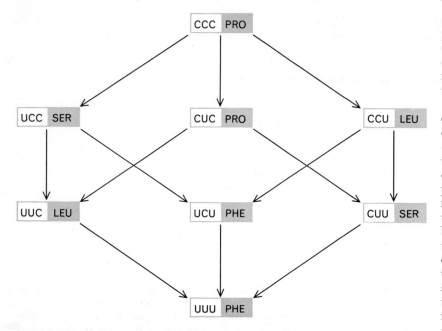

DEAMINATION that changes cytosine to uracil is represented by this octet arrangement of single steps from the triplet CCC to UUU. Amino acid equivalents given at right of the "codons" represent often-observed exchanges in mutants induced by deamination.

NATURE OF EXCHANGES		DEAMINATION	BROMINATION	METHYLATION	POSSIBLE CODON EXCHANGES	
ASP	GLY	(2)			AGC	GGC
	ALA	(4)				
ASP-NH₂ →	SER	4 (2)	3		ACA	GCA
THR	ALA	2			ACA	GCA
	ILEU	(8)			CAA	UAA
	MET	(3)				
SER	PHE	4 (4)	2	2	CUU	UUU
	GLY		1		ACG	GCG
	LEU	(2)				
GLU	GLY	1 (1)			AUG	GUG
GLU-NH₂	ARG	1				
	VAL	(2)				
PRO	LEU	3 (1)	4	4	CUC	UUC
	SER	(3)			CCU	UCU
VAL	MET	1				
ILEU	VAL	2 (3)			AUU	GUU
	THR		1			
	MET	(1)			AUA	GUA
LEU	PHE	(1)			CUU	UUU
ARG	GLY	3	3	1	AGA	GGA
	LYS	1	1			

REPLACEMENTS in chemically induced mutants of the tobacco mosaic virus are charted by frequency of observation. At left is the amino acid exchange taking place; in middle, the process that induced it; at right, possible codon exchanges for various mutants. The figures listed parenthetically were obtained by Hans Wittmann of the University of Tübingen.

coat. Most often, however, the mutant proteins that were examined showed exchanges of amino acids only near the ends of the chain, where the alteration might do the least damage to the functioning of the protein.

In contrast to the chain ends and certain inner parts around the middle of the chain, which also showed exchanges, there is a certain segment (between No. 108 and No. 122 in the sequence) that strongly resists attack. This part of the chain is the same in all natural strains of the virus and remains unchanged in all the mutants that have been investigated. Its stability suggests that it constitutes a portion of the molecule that is particularly important for the proper folding of the chain. In this segment there is a pair of arginines close to a pair of aspartic acid units, and it may be that these amino acid pairs play a role in the folding.

It should be recognized that the frequently recurring exchanges are probably not the result of mutations occurring preferentially at these sites, but are due to natural selection. It appears certain that these are sites where exchanges cause the least harm to the function of the protein of forming a protective shell for the RNA. Thus the exchanges greatly predominate among those mutants that are viable enough to be isolated in amounts sufficient for chemical study. A change of a serine to a phenylalanine elsewhere in the molecule than at positions No. 138 or No. 148 presumably renders the protein nonfunctional.

By means of chemical probing and genetic mutation the entire protein molecule is being explored for clues to its three-dimensional structure. Such clues include the distances between specific groups in the chain and the chemical reactivity of the various parts of the chain. It can be deduced, for instance, that units in the chain that resist reaction with applied reagents are likely to be inside folds where they are tied up in internal bonding. One such probe has shown that the tyrosine at position No. 72 in the sequence is remarkably recalcitrant to reaction with any chemical applied to the intact virus; the tyrosine at position No. 139, on the other hand, readily reacts with iodine.

Gradually, through genetic and chemical soundings of this kind, we hope to build up a complete picture of the protein bonding and structure that give the tobacco mosaic virus its extraordinary architectural perfection and stability.

31

Memory and Protein Synthesis

BERNARD W. AGRANOFF

June 1967

What is the mechanism of memory? The question has not yet been answered, but the kind of evidence needed to answer it has slowly been accumulating. One important fact that has emerged is that there are two types of memory: short-term and long-term. To put it another way, the process of learning is different from the process of memory-storage; what is learned must somehow be fixed or consolidated before it can be remembered. For example, people who have received shock treatment in the course of psychiatric care report that they cannot remember experiences they had immediately before the treatment. It is as though the shock treatment had disrupted the process of consolidating their memory of the experiences.

In our laboratory at the University of Michigan we have demonstrated that there is a connection between the consolidation of memory and the manufacture of protein in the brain. Our experimental animal is the common goldfish (*Carassius auratus*). Basically what we do is train a large number of goldfish to perform a simple task and at various times before, during and after the training inject into their skulls a substance that interferes with the synthesis of protein. Then we observe the effect of the injections on the goldfish's performance.

Why seek a connection between memory and protein synthesis? For one thing, enzymes are proteins, and enzymes catalyze all the chemical reactions of life. It would seem reasonable to expect that memory, like all other life processes, is dependent on enzyme-catalyzed reactions. What is perhaps more to the point, the manufacture of new enzymes is characteristic of long-term changes in living organisms, such as growth and the differentiation of cells in the embryo. And long-term memory is by definition a long-term change.

The investigation of a connection between memory and protein synthesis is made possible by the profound advances in knowledge of protein synthesis that have come in the past 10 years. A molecule of protein is made from 20 differ-

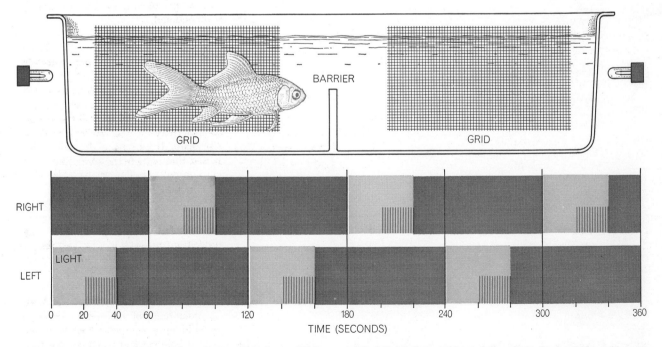

TRAINING TANK the author used was designed so that goldfish learned to swim from the light end to the dark end. A learning trial began with the illumination of the left end of the tank (*chart at bottom*), followed after a pause by mild electric shocks (*colored vertical lines*) from grids at that end. At first a fish would swim over the central barrier in response to shock; then increasingly the fish came to respond to light cue alone as sequence of light, shock and darkness was alternately repeated at each end of the tank.

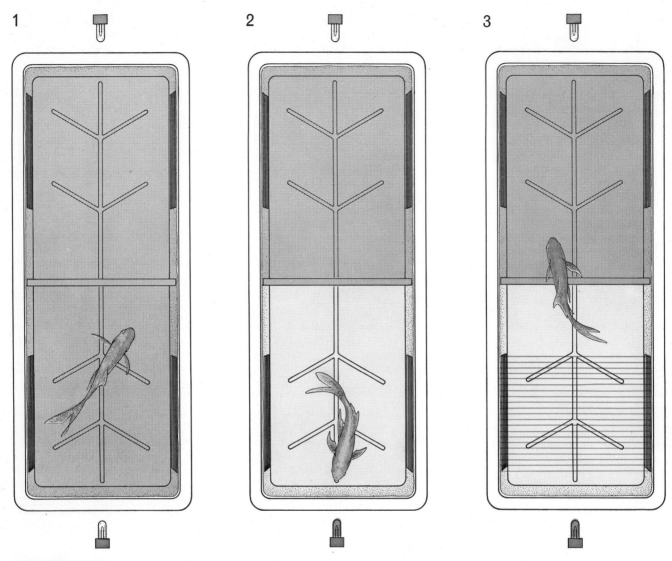

GOLDFISH LEARN in successive trials to solve the problem the shuttle box presents. Following 20 seconds of darkness (1) the end of the box where the fish is swimming is lighted for an equal period of time (2). The fish fails to respond, swimming over the barrier

ent kinds of amino acid molecule, strung together in a polypeptide chain. The stringing is done in the small bodies in the living cell called ribosomes. Each amino acid molecule is brought to the ribosome by a molecule of transfer RNA, a form of ribonucleic acid. The instructions according to which the amino acids are linked in a specific sequence are brought to the ribosome by another form of ribonucleic acid: messenger RNA. These instructions have been transcribed by the messenger RNA from deoxyribonucleic acid (DNA), the cell's central library of information.

With this much knowledge of protein synthesis one can begin to think of examining the process by interfering with it in selective ways. Such interference can be accomplished with antibiotics. Whereas some substances that interfere with the machinery of the cell, such as cyanide, are quite general in their ef-

fects, antibiotics can be highly selective. Indeed, some of them block only one step in cellular metabolism. As an example, the antibiotic puromycin simply stops the growth of the polypeptide chain in the ribosome. This it does by virtue of the fact that its molecule resembles one end of the transfer RNA molecule with an amino acid attached to it. Accordingly the puromycin molecule is joined to the growing end of the polypeptide chain and blocks its further growth. The truncated chain is released attached to the puromycin molecule.

Numerous workers have had the idea of using agents such as puromycin to block protein synthesis in animals and then observing the effects on the animals' behavior. Among them have been C. Wesley Dingman II and M. B. Sporn of the National Institutes of Health, who injected 8-azaguanine into rats; T. J. Chamberlain, G. H. Rothschild and

Ralph W. Gerard of the University of Michigan, who administered the same substance to rats, and Josefa B. Flexner, Louis B. Flexner and Eliot Stellar of the University of Pennsylvania, who injected puromycin into mice. Such experiments encouraged us to try our hand with the goldfish.

We chose the goldfish for our experiments because it is readily available and can be accommodated in the laboratory in large numbers. Moreover, a simple and automatically controlled training task for goldfish had already been developed by M. E. Bitterman of Bryn Mawr College. One might wonder if a fish has such a thing as long-term memory; in the opinion of numerous psychologists and anglers there can be no doubt of it.

Our training apparatus is called a shuttle box. It is an oblong plastic tank

4

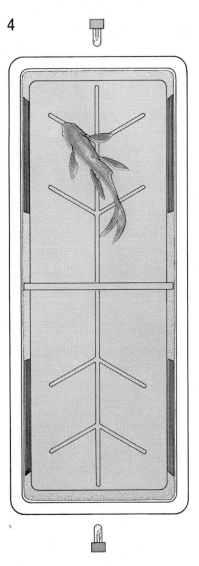

5

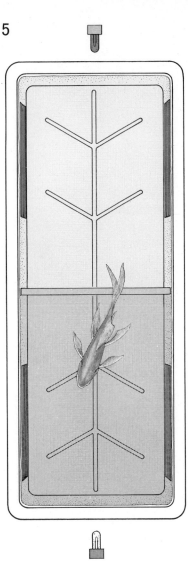

6

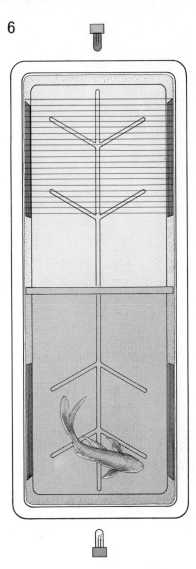

only after the shock period heralded by light has begun (3). When the same events are repeated at the other end of the box (4, 5 and 6), the fish shown here succeeds in crossing the barrier during the 20 seconds of light that precede the period of intermittent shock.

divided into two compartments by a barrier that comes to within an inch of the water surface [*see illustration on page 291*]. At each end of the box is a light that can be turned on and off. On opposite sides of each compartment are grids by means of which the fish can be given a mild electric shock through the water.

The task to be learned by the fish is that when it is in one compartment and the light goes on at that end of the box, it should swim over the barrier into the other compartment. In our initial experiments we left the fish in the dark for five minutes and then gave it five one-minute trials. Each trial consisted in (1) turning on the light at the fish's end of the box, (2) 20 seconds later intermittently turning on the shocking grids and (3) 20 seconds after that turning off both the shocking grids and the light. If the fish crossed the barrier into the other

compartment during the first 20 seconds, it *avoided* the shock; if it crossed the barrier during the second 20 seconds, it *escaped* the shock.

An untrained goldfish almost always escaped the shock, that is, it swam across the barrier only when the shock began. Whether the fish escaped the shock or avoided it, it crossed the barrier into the other compartment. Then, after 20 seconds of darkness, the light at that end was turned on to start the second trial. Thus the fish shuttled back and forth with each trial. If a fish failed to either avoid or escape, it missed the next trial. Such missed trials were rare and generally came only at the beginning of training.

In these experiments the goldfish went through five consecutive cycles of five minutes of darkness followed by five training trials; accordingly they received a total of 20 trials in 40 minutes. They

were then placed in individual "home" tanks—plastic tanks that are slightly smaller than the shuttle boxes—and kept there for three days. On the third day they were returned to the shuttle box, where they were given 10 more trials in 20 minutes.

The fish readily learned to move from one compartment to the other when the light went on, thereby avoiding the shock. Untrained fish avoided the shock in about 20 percent of the first 10 trials and continued to improve with further trials. If they were allowed to perform the task day after day, the curve of learning flattened out at about 80 percent correct responses.

What was even more significant for our experiments was what happened when we changed the interval between the first cycle of trials and the second, that is, between the 20th and the 21st of the 30 trials. If the second cycle was

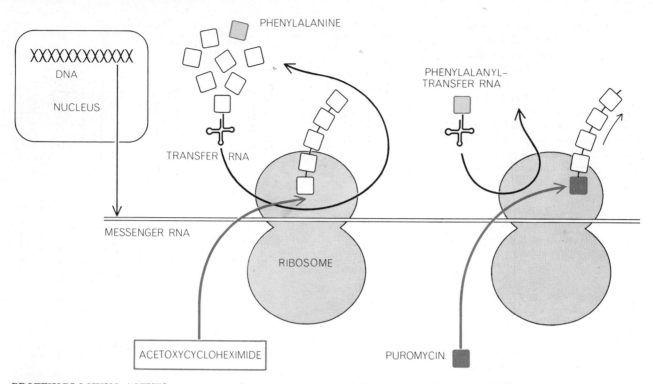

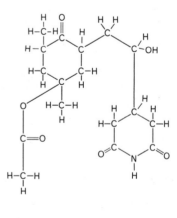

PROTEIN-BLOCKING AGENTS can interrupt the formation of molecules at the ribosome, where the amino acid units of protein are linked according to instructions embodied in messenger ribonucleic acid (mRNA). One agent, acetoxycycloheximide, interferes with the bonding mechanism that links amino acids brought to the ribosome by transfer RNA (tRNA). Puromycin, another agent, resembles the combination of tRNA and the amino acid phenylalanine. Thus it is taken into chain and prematurely halts its growth.

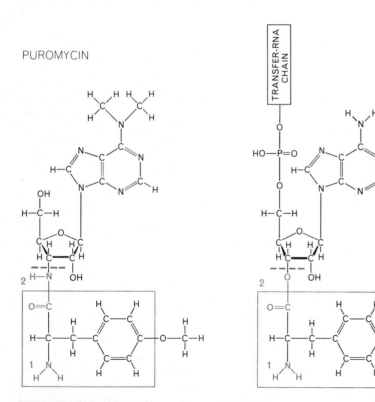

MOLECULAR DIAGRAMS show the resemblance between puromycin and the combination phenylalanyl-tRNA. In both cases the portion of the molecule below the broken line is incorporated into a growing protein molecule, joining at the free amino group (*1*). But in puromycin the CONH group (*2*), unlike the corresponding group (COO) of phenylalanyl, will not accept another amino acid and the chain is broken. Acetoxycycloheximide does not resemble amino acid but slows rate at which the chain forms.

begun a full month after the first, the fish performed as well as they did on the third day. If the second cycle was begun on the day after the first, the fish performed equally well, as one would expect. In short, the fish had perfect memory of their training.

We found that we could predict the training scores of groups of fish on the third day on the basis of their scores on the first day. This made it easier for us to determine the effect of antibiotics on the fish's memory: we could compare the training scores of fish receiving antibiotics with the predicted scores. Since we conducted these initial experiments we have made several improvements in our procedure. We now record the escapes and avoidances automatically with photodetectors, and we have arranged matters so that a fish does not miss a trial if it fails to escape. We have altered the trial sequence and the time interval between the turning on of the light and the turning on of the shocking grid. The results obtained with these improved procedures are essentially the same as our earlier ones.

The principal antibiotic we use in our experiments is puromycin, whose effect on protein synthesis was described earlier. We inject the drug directly into the skull of the goldfish with a hypodermic syringe. A thin needle easily penetrates the skull; 10 microliters of solution is then injected over the fish's brain (not into it). In an early series of experiments we injected 170 micrograms of puromycin in that amount of solution at various stages in our training procedures.

We found that if the puromycin was injected immediately after training, memory of the training was obliterated. If the same amount of the drug was injected an hour after training, on the other hand, memory was unaffected. Injection 30 minutes after training produced an intermediate effect. Reducing the amount of puromycin caused a smaller loss of memory.

After the injection the fish seemed to swim normally. We were therefore encouraged to test whether or not puromycin interferes with the changes that occur in the brain as the fish is being trained. This we did by injecting the fish before their initial training. We found that they learned the task at a normal rate, that is, their improvement during the first 20 trials was normal. Fish tested three days later, however, showed a profound loss of memory. This indicated to us that puromycin did not block the short-term memory demonstrated during

TRACE FROM RECORDER shows the performances of 10 goldfish in 30 trials. Each horizontal row represents a trial, beginning at the bottom with trial 1. A blip (*left side*) indicates that a fish either escaped or avoided the shock; a dash in the same row (*right*) signifies an avoidance, that is, a correct response for the trial. These fish learned at the normal rate.

learning but did interfere with the consolidation of long-term memory. And since an injection an hour after training has no effect on long-term memory, whereas an injection immediately after training obliterates it, it appears that consolidation can take place within an hour.

One observation puzzled us. The animals had received their initial training during a 40-minute period, 20 minutes of which was spent in the dark. Puromycin could erase all memory of this training; none of the memory was consolidated. Yet the experiment in which we injected puromycin 30 minutes after training had shown that more than half of the memory was consolidated during that period. How was it that no memory at all was consolidated at least toward the end of the 40-minute training period? To be sure, the fish that had been injected 30 minutes after the training period had been removed from the shuttle boxes and placed in their home tanks. But what was different about the time spent in the shuttle box and the time spent in the home tank that memory could be consolidated in the home tank

but could not be in the shuttle box?

Roger E. Davis of our laboratory undertook further experiments to clarify the phenomenon. He found that fish that were allowed to remain in the shuttle box for several hours after training and were then returned to their home tank showed no loss of memory when they were tested four days later. On the other hand, fish that were allowed to remain in the shuttle box for the same length of time and were then injected with puromycin and returned to their home tank had a marked memory loss! In other words, the fish in the first group did not consolidate memory of their training until after they had been placed in their home tank. It appears that simply being in the shuttle box prevents the fixation of memory. Subsequent studies have led us to the idea that memory fixation is blocked when the organism is in an environment associated with a high level of stimulation. This effect indicates that the formation of memory is environment-dependent, just as the consolidation of memory is time-dependent.

We conclude from all these experiments that long-term memory of training in the goldfish is formed by a puromycin-sensitive step that begins after training and requires that the animal be removed from the training environment. The initial acquisition of information by the fish is puromycin-insensitive and is a qualitatively different process. But what does the action of puromycin on memory formation have to do with its known biochemical effect: the inhibition of protein synthesis?

We undertook to establish that puromycin blocks protein synthesis in the goldfish brain under the conditions of our experiments. This we did in the following manner. First we injected puromycin into the skull of the fish. Next we injected into the abdominal cavity of the fish leucine that had been labeled with tritium, or radioactive hydrogen. Now, leucine is an amino acid, and if labeled leucine is injected into a goldfish's abdominal cavity, it will be incorporated into whatever protein is being synthesized throughout the goldfish's body. By measuring the amount of labeled leucine incorporated into protein after, say, 30 minutes, one can determine the rate of protein synthesis during that time.

We compared the amount of labeled leucine incorporated into protein in goldfish that had received an injection of puromycin with the amount incorporated in fish that had received either no

injection or an injection of inactive salt solution. We found that protein synthesis in the brain of fish that had been injected with puromycin was deeply inhibited. The effects of different doses of puromycin and the length of time it took the drug to act did not, however, closely correspond to what we had observed in our experiments involving the behavioral performance of the goldfish. In retrospect this result is not surprising. Various experiments, including our own, had shown that the rate of memory consolidation can be altered by changes in the conditions of training. Moreover, the rate of leucine incorporation can be affected by complex physiological factors.

Another way to check whether or not puromycin exerts its effects on memory by inhibiting protein synthesis would be to perform the memory experiments with a second drug known to inhibit such synthesis. Then if puromycin blocks long-term memory by some other mechanism, the second drug would have no effect on memory. It would be even better if the second drug did not resemble puromycin in molecular structure, so that its effect on protein synthesis would not be the same as puromycin's. Such a drug exists in acetoxycycloheximide. Where puromycin blocks the growth of the polypeptide chain by taking the place of an amino acid, acetoxycycloheximide simply slows down the rate at

which the amino acids are linked together. We found that a small amount of this drug (.1 microgram, or one 1,700th the weight of the amount of puromycin we had been using) produced a measurable memory deficit in goldfish. Moreover, it commensurately inhibited the synthesis of protein in the goldfish brain.

These experiments suggest that protein synthesis is required for the consolidation of memory, but they are not conclusive. Louis Flexner and his colleagues have found that puromycin can interfere with memory in mice. On the other hand, they find that acetoxycycloheximide has no such effect. They conclude that protein is required for the expression of memory but that experience acts not on protein synthesis directly but on messenger RNA. The conditions of their experiments and the fact that they are working with a different animal do not allow any ready comparison with our experiments.

Our studies of the goldfish have led us to view learning and memory as a form of biological development. One may think of the brain of an animal as being completely "wired" by heredity; all possible pathways are present, but not all are "soldered." It may be that in short-term memory, pathways are selected rapidly but impermanently. In that case protein synthesis would not be required, which may explain why puromycin has no effect on short-term memory. If the consolidation of memory calls for more permanent connections among pathways, it seems reasonable that protein synthesis would be involved. The formation of such connections, of course, would be blocked by puromycin and acetoxycycloheximide.

Another possibility is that the drugs block not the formation of permanent pathways but the transmission of a signal to fix what has just been learned. There is some evidence for this notion in what happens to people who suffer damage to certain parts of the brain (the mammillary bodies and the hippocampus). They retain older memories and are capable of new learning, but they cannot form new long-term memories. Experiments with animals also provide some evidence for a "fix" signal. We are currently doing experiments in the hope of determining which of these hypotheses best fits the effects of puromycin and acetoxycycloheximide on memory in the goldfish.

Quite apart from our own work, it has been suggested by others that it is possible to transfer patterns of behavior

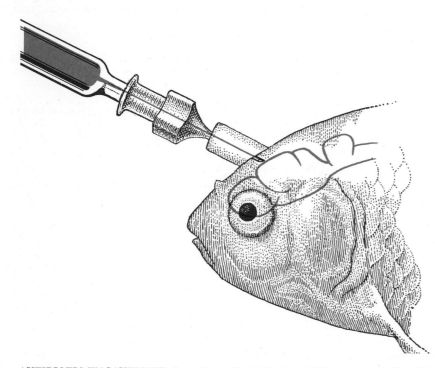

ANTIBIOTIC WAS INJECTED through the thin skull of a goldfish and over rather than into the brain. The antibiotic was puromycin, which inhibits protein synthesis. Following its injection the fish were able to swim normally. They could then be tested for memory loss.

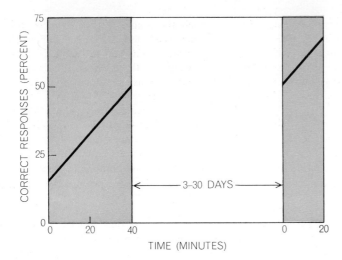

NORMAL LEARNING RATE of goldfish in 30 shuttle-box trials is shown by the black curve. Whether the last 10 trials were given three days after the first 20 (the regular procedure) or as much as a month later, fish demonstrated the same rate of improvement.

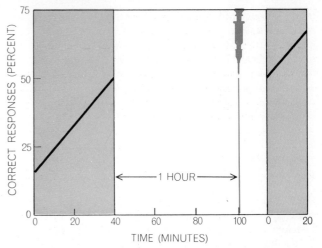

INJECTION WITH PUROMYCIN one hour after completion of 20 learning trials did not disrupt memory. Goldfish given the antibiotic at this point scored as well as those in the control group in the sequence of 10 trials that followed three days afterward.

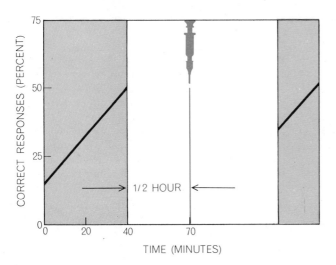

INJECTION HALF AN HOUR AFTER the first 20 trials cut the level of correct responses to half the level without such injection.

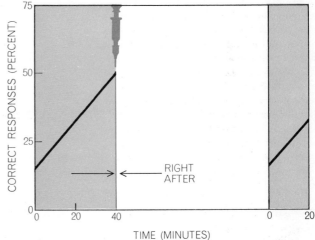

INJECTION IMMEDIATELY AFTER the first 20 trials erased all memory of training. The fish scored at the untrained level.

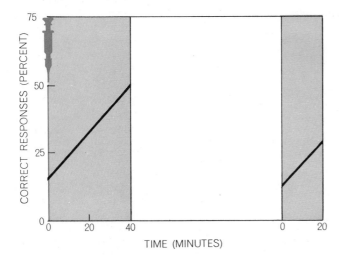

INJECTION PRIOR TO TRAINING did not affect the rate at which goldfish learned to solve the shuttle-box problem. But puromycin given at this point did suppress the formation of long-term memory, as shown by the drop in the scores three days afterward.

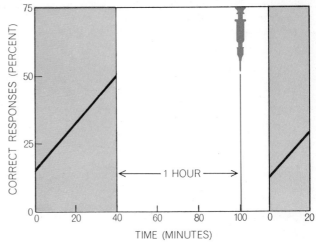

ENVIRONMENTAL FACTOR in the formation of lasting memory was seen when fish remained in training (instead of "home") tanks during the fixation period. Under these conditions fixation did not occur. Puromycin given at end of period still erased memory.

from one animal to another (even to an animal of a different species) by inject- ing RNA or protein from the brain of a trained animal into the brain (or even the abdominal cavity) of an untrained one. If such transfers of behavior pat- terns can actually be accomplished, they imply that memory resides in molecules of RNA or protein. Nothing we have learned with the goldfish argues for or against the possibility that a behavior pattern is stored in such a molecule.

It can be observed, however, that there is no precedent in biology for such storage. What could be required would be a kind of somatic mutation: a change in the cell's store of information that would give rise to a protein with a new sequence of amino acids. It seems un- likely that such a process could operate at the speed required for learning.

It might also be that learning and memory involve the formation of short segments of RNA or protein that some- how label an individual brain cell. Rich- ard Santen of our laboratory has calcu- lated (on the basis of DNA content) the number of cells in the brain of a rat: it comes to 500 million. With this figure one can calculate further that a poly- peptide chain of seven amino acids, ar- ranged in every possible sequence, could provide each cell in the rat's brain with two unique markers.

The concept that each nerve cell has its own chemical marker is supported by experiments on the regeneration of the optic nerve performed by Roger W. Sperry of the California Institute of Technology. If the optic nerve of a frog is cut and the two ends of the nerve are put back together rotated 180 degrees with respect to each other, the severed fibers of the nerve link up with the same

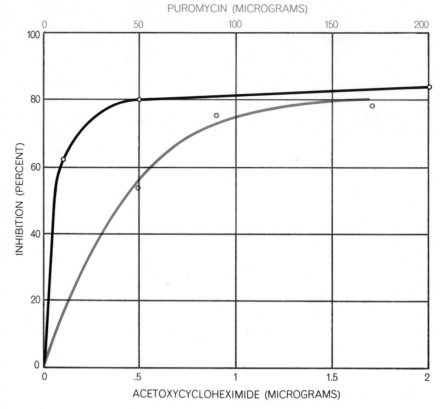

SLOWED PROTEIN SYNTHESIS in the brain of goldfish is induced both by acetoxycyclo- heximide (*black line*) and the antibiotic puromycin (*colored line*), agents that block the fixation of memory. The author tested the effect on goldfish of various quantities of the two drugs; acetoxycycloheximide was found several hundred times more potent than puromycin.

fiber as before. This of course suggests that each fiber has a unique marker that in the course of regeneration enables it to recognize its mate.

Is it possible, then, that a cell "turned on" by the learning process manufac- tures a chemical marker? And could such a process give rise to a substance that, when it is injected into another animal, finds its way to the exact location where

it can effectuate memory? Thus far the evidence put forward in support of such ideas has not been impressive. In this exciting period of discovery in brain re- search clear-cut experiments are more important than theories. Certain long- term memories held by investigators in this area may be more of a hindrance than a help in exploring all its possibili- ties.

32

Ultraviolet Radiation and Nucleic Acid

R. A. DEERING

December 1962

Ever since the discovery in 1877 that ultraviolet radiation can kill bacteria, workers in several disciplines have been studying the effects of the radiation on living things. Its actions have turned out to be many and varied. Ultraviolet can temporarily delay cell division and can also delay the synthesis of certain substances by cells; it can change the way in which substances pass across the membranes of the cell; it can cause abnormalities in chromosomes; it can produce mutations. Obviously it is a potent tool for the study of living cells, and it has been extensively employed by experimenters. If its exact modes of action at the molecular level were fully understood, the tool would be even sharper and more useful. This article reports the considerable progress that has been made in the past few years toward understanding the biophysical and biochemical role of ultraviolet.

Most of the recent work has concentrated on the interaction of ultraviolet radiation and the molecule of the genetic material deoxyribonucleic acid (DNA), and that is what I shall discuss. There is no doubt that many of the effects of ultraviolet are exerted solely or chiefly by means of changes in DNA. The fact that DNA strongly absorbs ultraviolet,

and that its absorption spectrum resembles the ultraviolet "action spectrum" for many biological changes (that is, the biological effectiveness of various wavelengths), show that this must be true. Therefore DNA is the logical starting point in the investigation of the biological activity of ultraviolet radiation.

This radiation falls between visible light and X rays in the spectrum of electromagnetic waves, ranging in wavelength from about 4,000 to a few hundred angstrom units. (An angstrom unit is one hundred-millionth of a centimeter.) The important wavelengths for the biologist are those between 2,000 and 3,000 angstroms. The sun is a powerful emitter of ultraviolet, but a layer of ozone in the upper atmosphere absorbs most of the radiation below 2,900 angstroms. Were it not for the ozone, sunlight would damage or kill every exposed cell on earth.

In the laboratory, working with monochromatic ultraviolet radiation at various wavelengths, investigators have established that the region most potent in its effects on living things is near 2,600 angstroms. When DNA was isolated, it was found to absorb most strongly at just these wavelengths. In the past five years workers in several laboratories

have begun to discover what happens to the DNA molecule when it absorbs ultraviolet energy.

Natural DNA, as the readers of this magazine are well aware, normally consists of a double-strand helix. The helices proper—the twin "backbones" of the molecule—consist of an alternation of sugar (deoxyribose) and phosphate groups. Attached to each of the sugars is one of four nitrogenous "bases," generally adenine, guanine, thymine and cytosine. The bases on the two backbones are joined in pairs by hydrogen bonds, the adenine on one chain always being paired with thymine on the other, and the guanine with cytosine. The hydrogen bonds that join the base pairs are weaker than ordinary chemical bonds. Simply heating double-strand DNA breaks the bonds and partially or completely separates the two backbones into two strands of "denatured" DNA.

Ultraviolet radiation falling on DNA is absorbed primarily by the bases, which exhibit about the same absorption peak at 2,600 angstroms as the whole DNA molecule does. This being the case, the first approach was to study the effects of ultraviolet radiation on the isolated bases. It soon turned out that thymine and cytosine, which belong to the class

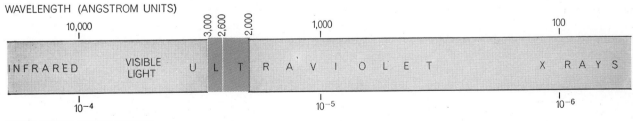

ULTRAVIOLET portion of the electromagnetic spectrum lies between visible light and X rays. The wavelengths between 2,000 and 3,000 angstrom units are of primary biological importance. DNA, the genetic material, absorbs most strongly at 2,600 angstroms.

of substances called pyrimidines, are far more sensitive to ultraviolet than are adenine and guanine, which are purines. About one in every 100 quanta of ultraviolet energy absorbed by pyrimidines alters the molecules; for purines the ratio is one in 10,000. (In general only a few of the quanta absorbed by a molecule will be effective in producing permanent changes.) The search was therefore narrowed to the pyrimidines.

The first effect to be discovered was that ultraviolet acts on cytosine molecules or the cytosine units of DNA in water solution, adding a water molecule across a double bond [*see middle illustration on page 302*]. Heating the altered cytosine, even to the temperatures required for biological growth, or acidifying it, partly reverses the reaction. Therefore the hydration of cytosine did not seem likely to be of major biological importance.

For some years, however, this hydration was the only sensitive, ultraviolet-induced change in the bases that could be detected. Heavy doses of radiation did produce complex rearrangements, but these doses were far in excess of the smallest ones known to have biological effects. About three years ago a breakthrough in the photochemistry of DNA came when R. Beukers, J. Ijlstra and W. Berends of the Technological

University of Delft in Holland and Shih Yi Wang, now of Johns Hopkins University, discovered that although in a liquid solution thymine is not particularly sensitive to ultraviolet, in a concentrated, frozen aqueous solution it is extremely sensitive. It developed that irradiation of the frozen solution causes thymine molecules to combine and form two-molecule chains, or dimers. As in the case of the cytosine conversion, a double bond changes to a single, and new bonds between carbon atoms link the two thymines [*see bottom illustration on page 302*]. Unlike the altered cytosine, the thymine dimer is stable to heat and acid. But when the solution is melted, irradiation can convert the dimer back into the two original thymine molecules. What the freezing does is to hold the thymines close together in a crystalline or semicrystalline configuration, making it possible for the dimer bonds to form between two neighboring thymines when they absorb ultraviolet. It seemed likely that such a conversion would also occur in DNA, where thymine units are sometimes adjacent to each other on a helical strand and are held in relatively fixed positions. In 1960 Adolf Wacker and his associates at the University of Frankfort found thymine dimers in DNA extracted from irradiated bacteria.

In order to get more complete information on the formation and splitting

of thymine dimers in polymer chains such as DNA, Richard B. Setlow and I carried out experiments on some model polymers at the Oak Ridge National Laboratory. Similar experiments were performed independently at the California Institute of Technology by Harold Johns and his collaborators. The compounds we used were short polymers—in effect short single strands of DNA in which all the bases were thymine. Some of our test molecules contained only two backbone units and two thymines; others had 12 or more. Since the sugar-phosphate backbone holds the thymines in fairly close proximity, we anticipated that ultraviolet radiation should form dimers between adjacent thymines in a chain even in a liquid solution. And we expected that once the dimers had formed they would be subject to breakage by ultraviolet, as were the isolated thymine dimers. When thymine loses a double bond in changing to a dimer, it also loses its ability to absorb light at 2,600 angstroms. Therefore measuring the change in 2,600-angstrom absorption gives an indication of the ratio between thymine monomers and thymine dimers in the solution.

When we irradiated our polymers, dimers were in fact produced. Since the rate of formation did not vary with thymine concentration, we concluded

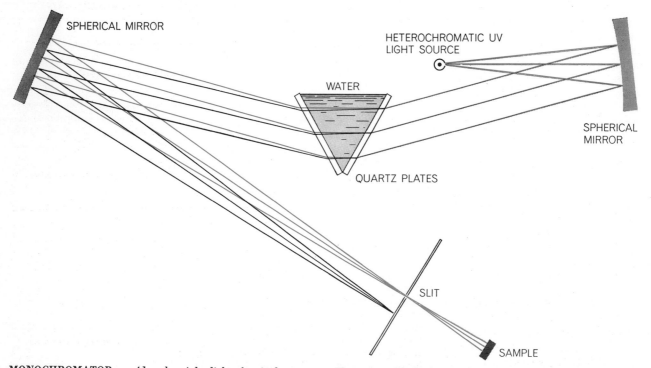

MONOCHROMATOR provides ultraviolet light of a single wavelength for experiments. Light of mixed wavelengths is rendered parallel by a spherical mirror and passes through a quartz-and-water prism. (Glass would not transmit the desired wavelengths.)

The prism splits the light into many components of different wavelengths, only two of which are indicated here, and the beams are refocused by a second mirror. The sample to be irradiated is positioned behind a slit that excludes all but the desired wavelength.

that they were formed within, rather than between, individual polymers. Dimers also broke up into monomers, but not at the same rate at which they formed. The process is analogous to a reversible chemical reaction in which forward and backward reactions proceed at different rates, with an equilibrium eventually being reached between the reactants and the products. We found that for every wavelength of ultraviolet there is at high doses an equilibrium between the number of dimers being formed and the number being broken [see bottom left illustration page 303]. At each wavelength and intensity there is a certain rate for dimer formation and a different one for breakage; the equilibrium level is determined by the relative rates of the forward and backward reactions. At 2,800 angstroms the equilibrium state is on the dimer side: most of the thymines are dimerized. At 2,400 angstroms the opposite is true: most of the thymines are monomers. The relative number of monomers and dimers in the polymer solutions can be controlled by changing the wavelength of the incident ultraviolet.

When the data from a number of experiments are plotted [see bottom right illustration page 303], the resulting curves show the ability of each wavelength to make and break dimers in these model polymers. The curves approximately parallel the absorption spectra of the monomer and dimer respectively, indicating that it is difference in absorption capacity that accounts for the different action of various wavelengths. The "quantum yield," or number of molecules altered by each quantum, does not change greatly with wavelength; for dimer formation in the polymers containing only thymine it is of the order of .01 and for breakage it is near 1.

The next step was to relate molecular changes to changes in the properties of DNA and in its biological activity. Julius Marmur and Lawrence Grossman of Brandeis University have shown recently that when double-strand DNA is exposed to ultraviolet, the two strands become more strongly linked, apparently by chemical bonds rather than by the original weak hydrogen bonds. Marmur and Grossman believe the strong link is the result of interchain dimerization, that is, the formation of dimers between thymine units on opposite strands of the double helix.

At Oak Ridge, Frederick J. Bollum and Setlow found that ultraviolet can induce dimer linkages between adjacent thymine units in single-strand DNA.

They suspect that the same thing can happen between adjacent thymines in natural DNA, but in this case some of the hydrogen bonds in a local region may have to be broken before dimerization is possible. Marmur and Grossman have shown that irradiation does indeed disrupt hydrogen bonding between strands of natural DNA.

Another effect of ultraviolet on isolated DNA that has been clearly identified is a breaking of the sugar-phosphate backbone, but this occurs only at uninterestingly high doses. Among the sensitive reactions only the cytosine and thymine conversions are understood well enough for their biological implications to be assessed. There are surely other important effects, but they remain to be discovered.

Although the biological significance of the cytosine hydration has generally been discounted because it reverses at body temperature or lower, the reversal may be slower in intact DNA than in the isolated base. There is no direct evidence that the hydration product would be detrimental to the biological activity of DNA, but it might affect the hydrogen bonding in a segment of the helix and thereby give rise to the broken bonds observed by Marmur and Grossman.

The formation of thymine dimers should in theory be of great biological significance. When DNA makes a replica of itself, according to the widely accepted hypothesis, the hydrogen bonds break and a new complementary chain forms along each of the old strands. A dimer cross link between strands would interrupt the separation, blocking replication. Dimers between adjacent thymines on the same strand would interfere with proper pairing of the bases. Normally an adenine should come into position opposite each thymine on the parent strand. The joining of two adjacent thymines would probably change matters enough to impair the proper incorporation of adenine; replication might stop short at

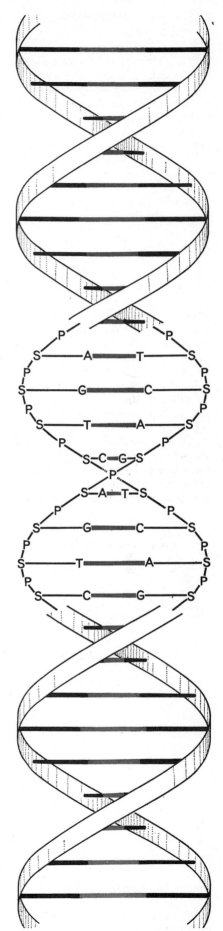

DNA MOLECULE is a double helix, diagramed here schematically. (One strand is actually displaced along the axis of the helix with regard to the other.) The backbone strands are composed of alternating sugar (S) and phosphate (P) groups. Attached to each sugar is one of four bases, usually adenine (A), guanine (G), thymine (T) and cytosine (C). Hydrogen bonds (gray) between bases link the strands. Adenine is always paired with thymine, guanine with cytosine. Genetic information is provided by the sequence of bases along a strand.

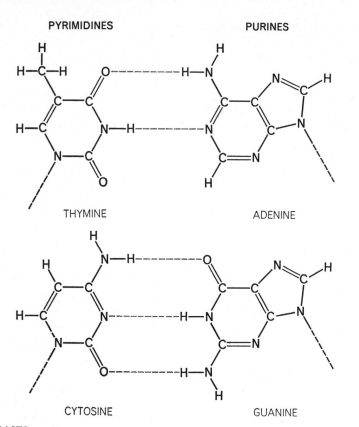

PYRIMIDINES   PURINES

THYMINE   ADENINE

CYTOSINE   GUANINE

FOUR BASES are diagramed as they are paired in DNA. Adenine and guanine, the larger molecules, are purines; thymine and cytosine are pyrimidines. The broken black lines show points of attachment to sugar groups; the broken gray lines are interchain hydrogen bonds.

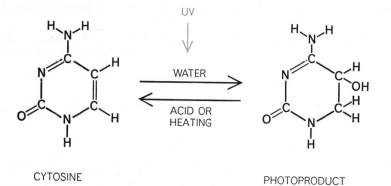

CYTOSINE   PHOTOPRODUCT

CYTOSINE in a water solution is altered by irradiation with ultraviolet. A water molecule is added across the double bond between two carbon atoms, the double bond changing to a single bond. When the cytosine solution is heated or acidified, the process is reversed.

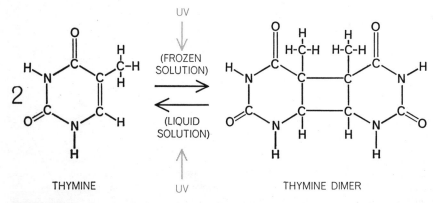

THYMINE   THYMINE DIMER

THYMINE in a frozen solution undergoes the reaction shown here when it is irradiated. The double bond between carbon atoms changes to single and two thymines are linked in a double molecule. or dimer. When the solution is melted, irradiation breaks the dimer.

that point or might proceed incorrectly, with an altered base sequence on the newly formed chain. On subsequent replication this altered strand would replicate itself, producing a molecule with the wrong base sequence in both strands —in other words, a mutated gene.

Recent work at Oak Ridge has provided direct experimental proof that thymine dimerization is one of the important ways in which the biological activity of DNA is altered by ultraviolet. Setlow and Bollum studied the ability of irradiated single strands of DNA to serve as a template in the manufacture of new DNA in a variety of cell-free test-tube preparations. Irradiation at 2,800 angstroms cut down the priming ability of DNA, the reduction being proportional to the adenine-thymine content of the various preparations. Subsequent irradiation at 2,400 angstroms partially restored template activity. Presumably irradiation at 2,800 angstroms formed dimers between adjacent thymines on the template DNA, blocking or slowing down the normal synthesis of new DNA strands. Irradiation at 2,400 angstroms evidently broke some of the dimers, partially restoring template activity.

In another series of experiments Setlow and his wife Jane K. Setlow worked with a form of DNA called "transforming principle," studying its ability to carry specific bits of genetic information from one cell to another. The measure of the biological activity of the DNA in this case was its effectiveness in transforming a given trait in the new cell. The Setlows found that irradiation at 2,800 angstroms destroyed the transforming ability of a portion of the DNA molecules. Again, when the irradiated DNA was exposed to 2,400-angstrom radiation, some of its molecules regained their transforming ability. The experimenters could account quantitatively for their results by assuming that about 50 per cent of the inactivation of the transforming DNA was due to thymine dimerization. They do not know what changes account for the rest.

When some types of cells that have been damaged by ultraviolet are exposed to ordinary blue light, a great deal of the damage is reversed; even bacteria that appear to have been killed are revived [see "Revival by Light," by Albert Kelner; SCIENTIFIC AMERICAN, May, 1951]. Claud S. Rupert and his associates at Johns Hopkins University had shown that this photoreactivation takes place through light-mediated enzyme reactions, but the details were not known. Recently Daniel L. Wulff and

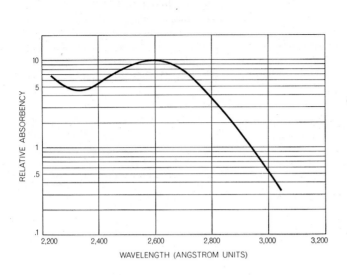

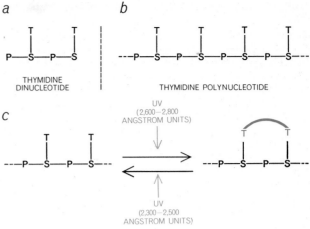

ABSORPTION SPECTRUM of DNA shows its ability to absorb ultraviolet radiation of various wavelengths. The peak is at 2,600 angstrom units, the wavelength known to be most harmful to cells.

MODEL POLYMERS exposed to ultraviolet were synthetic all-thymine DNA strands composed of either two nucleotide (phosphate-sugar-base) units (a) or 12 or more units (b). Irradiation both formed and broke dimers between adjacent thymines (c). Irradiation with high doses of the longer wavelengths led to an equilibrium condition in which most of the thymines were dimerized; exposure to shorter wavelengths tended to break the dimers.

Rupert have identified one mechanism of reactivation: a particular enzyme preparation, in the presence of blue light, can break up to 90 per cent of the thymine dimers in irradiated DNA. Marmur and Grossman have also shown that the enzyme system can break the ultraviolet-induced cross links between two DNA strands, thereby strengthening the idea that these links result from interchain thymine dimers.

Some bacteria apparently can produce enzymes that repair ultraviolet-damaged DNA without the need for visible light. The extreme resistance to ultraviolet displayed by certain bacteria may come from an ability to produce large amounts of these repair enzymes.

To sum up, it is clear that ultraviolet can change DNA in specific ways and can partially reverse those changes. Moreover, both the forward and backward alterations are reflected in DNA function. There is considerable evidence that much of the damage that ultraviolet radiation inflicts on cells and viruses is caused directly by its effects on DNA.

In the case of viruses this may be the whole story. When they infect a cell to

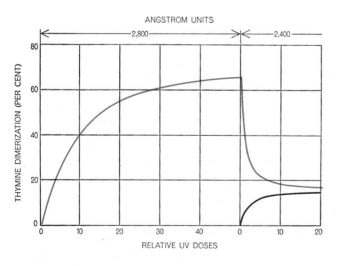

DEGREE OF DIMERIZATION varies with wavelength and dose. Increasing the exposure at 2,800 angstrom units increases the proportion of thymine units that are dimerized until an equilibrium state is attained with 65 per cent of the thymine units as dimers (*colored curve*). Irradiation at 2,400 angstrom units of the same sample, or of a different sample (*black curve*), results in a new equilibrium level with about 17 per cent of the thymines dimerized.

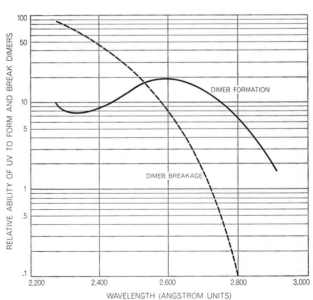

VARIOUS WAVELENGTHS differ in their ability to form and break dimers. Those over 2,540 angstrom units are more able to form dimers; the reverse is true of the shorter wavelengths.

replicate themselves, only their nucleic acid is injected into the cell. Therefore damage to DNA must be directly reflected in the ability of the virus to take over the cell's metabolism and multiply. In cells, however, one cannot assume that the only important effects of ultraviolet are those involving DNA. The radiation is absorbed by proteins, by ribonucleic acid (RNA) outside the nucleus and by other substances that play a part in cell metabolism, and it presumably changes their structures too. The task of identifying all the ultraviolet reactions in living organisms has been well begun, but there is much to learn.

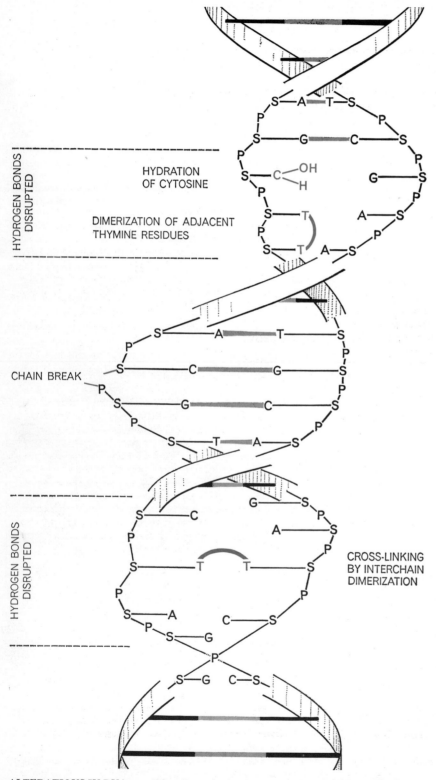

ALTERATIONS IN DNA caused by ultraviolet irradiation are diagramed here. The formation of thymine dimers is the change most likely to do damage to living cells and viruses.

Biographical Notes
and Bibliographies

The biographical and bibliographical data are those that were available
at the time the articles appeared in *Scientific American*.

SECTION I: MACROMOLECULAR ARCHITECTURE

1. Giant Molecules

The Author

HERMAN F. MARK is himself one of the giants of the exciting
new field of polymer chemistry. Born in 1895 in Vienna, the
son of a prominent physician, Mark early distinguished himself in athletics as well as scholarship: he played in the
Austrian national soccer league at 17. An excellent skier, he
joined an Austro-Hungarian mountain regiment during World
War I, fought on two fronts, rose from private to captain and
was captured by the Italians, from whom he eventually escaped disguised as a British officer: (His knowledge of the
physical properties of snow later made him an invaluable
member of the team that developed the snow-traversing
"weasel" in 180 days during World War II.) In 1921 he received a Ph.D. *summa cum laude* from the University of
Vienna. He taught for a year at the University of Berlin, then
moved on to the Kaiser Wilhelm Institute for Fiber Chemistry, where the first X-ray studies of polymers were made.
In 1926 he joined the research laboratories of I. G. Farben-
industrie, where he collaborated on classic studies of cellulose
and other polymer structures. When the Nazis came to power,
Mark resigned from I. G. Farben and became director of the
First Chemical Institute of the University of Vienna. The
German invasion of Austria caused his dismissal from the
University and from the city's board of education, of which
he had been an active member. For two years he worked for
a Canadian pulp company; then he accepted a teaching post
at the Polytechnic Institute of Brooklyn. There he gathered
together a group of American and refugee scholars which in
five years grew under his leadership into the Polymer Research
Institute.

Bibliography

CONFERENCE ON TISSUE FINE STRUCTURE. *The Journal of Bio-
physical and Biochemical Cytology*, Vol. 2, No. 4, Part 2
(Supplement), pages 1–454; July 25, 1956.
MACROMOLECULAR INTERACTION PATTERNS IN BIOLOGICAL SYS-
TEMS. Francis O. Schmitt in *Proceedings of the American
Philosophical Society*. Vol. 100, No. 5, pages 476–486;
October 15, 1956.
DIE SUBMIKROSKOPISCHE STRUCKTUR DES CYTOPLASMAS. A. Frey-
Wyssling in *Protoplasmatologia*, Band 2^2. Springer-Ver-
lag, 1955.
SYMPOSIA OF THE SOCIETY FOR EXPERIMENTAL BIOLOGY, NO. IX:
FIBROUS PROTEINS AND THEIR BIOLOGICAL SIGNIFICANCE.
Cambridge University Press, 1955.
SYMPOSIUM ON BIOMOLECULAR ORGANIZATION AND LIFE-PROC-
ESSES. Francis O. Schmitt, Paul Doty, Cecil E. Hall, Rob-
ley C. Williams and Paul A. Weiss in *Proceedings of the
National Academy of Sciences*, Vol. 42, No. 11, pages
789–830; November 15, 1956.

2. Proteins

The Author

PAUL DOTY, editor of the *Journal of Polymer Science*, is a Harvard University physical chemist who was once an assistant
professor of chemistry at the Polytechnic Institute of Brooklyn.
Born in Charleston, W. Va., in 1920, Doty studied at Pennsylvania State College and at Columbia University, where he
took his Ph.D. under J. E. Mayer. At that time he had already
begun his association with Brooklyn Poly; during his three
years there he directed a research project for the U. S. Army
Quartermaster Corps. In 1946 Doty went to the University of
Cambridge as a Rockefeller Foundation Fellow. In 1947 he
taught at Notre Dame, and in 1948 joined the Harvard faculty,
soon rising to full professorship. He has an active concern for
the social implications of science and has served as chairman
of the Federation of American Scientists.

Bibliography

THE NATIVE AND DENATURED STATES OF SOLUBLE COLLAGEN.
Helga Boedtker and Paul Doty in *Journal of the Amer-
ican Chemical Society*, Vol. 78, No. 17, pages 4,267–4,280;
September 5, 1956.
THE OPTICAL ROTATORY DISPERSION OF POLYPEPTIDES AND PRO-
TEINS IN RELATION TO CONFIGURATION. Jen Tsi Yang and
Paul Doty in *Journal of the American Chemical Society*,
Vol. 79, No. 4, pages 761–775; February 27, 1957.
POLYPEPTIDES, VIII: MOLECULAR CONFIGURATIONS OF POLY-L-
GLUTAMIC ACID IN WATER-DIOXANE SOLUTION. Paul Doty,
A. Wada, Jen Tsi Yang and E. R. Blout in *Journal of
Polymer Science*, Vol. 23, No. 104, pages 851–861; Feb-
ruary, 1957.
SYNTHETIC POLYPEPTIDES: PREPARATION, STRUCTURE, AND PROP-
ERTIES. C. H. Bamford, A. Elliott and W. E. Hanby.
Academic Press Inc., 1956.

3. The Chemical Structure of Proteins

The Authors

WILLIAM H. STEIN and STANFORD MOORE are both professors of biochemistry on the faculty of the Rockefeller Institute, where they began to collaborate on the chemistry of proteins more than two decades ago. Stein, who took his B.S. at Harvard University in 1933, did graduate work in biochemistry under the direction of Edgar G. Miller and Hans T. Clarke at Columbia University, receiving his Ph.D. in 1937. He went to the Rockefeller Institute in 1939 to work in the laboratory of the noted biochemist Max Bergmann. Moore joined Bergmann's laboratory that year, having acquired a B.A. at Vanderbilt University in 1935 and a Ph.D. in organic chemistry at the University of Wisconsin in 1938. During World War II Stein remained at the Institute to work on problems connected with chemical warfare, while Moore served with the Office of Scientific Research and Development in Washington. They resumed their joint research in 1945.

Bibliography

AUTOMATIC RECORDING APPARATUS FOR USE IN THE CHROMATOGRAPHY OF AMINO ACIDS. Stanford Moore, Daniel H. Spackman and William H. Stein in *Federation Proceedings*, Vol. 17, No. 4, pages 1107–1115; December, 1958.

THE DISULFIDE BONDS OF RIBONUCLEASE. D. H. Spackman, William H. Stein and Stanford Moore in *The Journal of Biological Chemistry*, Vol. 235, No. 3, pages 633–647; March, 1960.

GENERAL PROPERTIES OF PROTEINS. Joseph S. Fruton and Sofia Simmonds in *General Biochemistry*, pages 14–44. John Wiley & Sons, Inc., 1958.

MOLECULAR COMPLEMENTARITY AND ANTIDOTES FOR ALKYLPHOSPHATE POISONING. Irwin B. Wilson in *Federation Proceedings*, Vol. 18, No. 2, Part I, pages 752–758; July, 1959.

THE SEQUENCE OF THE AMINO ACID RESIDUES IN PERFORMIC ACID OXIDIZED RIBONUCLEASE. C. H. W. Hirs, Stanford Moore and William H. Stein in *The Journal of Biological Chemistry*, Vol. 235, No. 3, pages 648–659; March, 1960.

4. The Insulin Molecule

The Author

E. O. P. THOMPSON is a biochemist with the Commonwealth Scientific and Industrial Research Organization of Australia. Born in Sydney, he was graduated with first-class honors in organic chemistry from Sydney University in 1945 and after five years of teaching and research there obtained a fellowship which enabled him to go to England to work on insulin under Frederick Sanger at Cambridge University. Thompson carried out further studies on proteins during 1953 at the College of Medicine of the University of Utah at Salt Lake City. He is now investigating the chemistry of wool, "a complex protein material," in the Wool Textile Research Laboratories in Australia.

Bibliography

THE AMINO-ACID SEQUENCE IN THE GLYCYL CHAIN OF INSULIN. F. Sanger and E. O. P. Thompson in *The Biochemical Journal*, Vol. 53, No. 3, pages 353–374; February, 1953.

THE CHEMISTRY OF INSULIN. F. Sanger in *Annual Reports on the Chemical Society*, Vol. 45, pages 283–292; 1949.

THE PRINCIPLES OF CHROMATOGRAPHY. A. J. P. Martin in *Endeavor*, Vol. 6, No. 21, pages 21–28; January, 1947.

5. The Hemoglobin Molecule

The Author

M. F. PERUTZ is chairman of the Laboratory of Molecular Biology in Cambridge, England. Perutz was born in Vienna in 1914 and did his undergraduate work in chemistry at the University of Vienna. In 1936 he went to England to do research under J. D. Bernal at the Cavendish Laboratory of the University of Cambridge. He received a Ph.D. in X-ray crystallography from Cambridge in 1940. From 1939 to 1945 he worked as a research assistant to W. L. Bragg at the Cavendish Laboratory. In 1947 Perutz was made director of the newly constituted Medical Research Council Unit for Molecular Biology, a post he held until 1962, when the Medical Research Council built the Laboratory of Molecular Biology for him and his colleagues. Perutz' work on the structure of hemoglobin, he writes, "started as a result of a conversation with F. Haurowitz in Prague in September, 1937. G. A. Adair made me the first crystals of horse haemoglobin and Bernal and I. Fankuchen showed me how to take X-ray pictures and how to interpret them. Early in 1938 Bernal, Fankuchen and I published a joint paper on X-ray diffraction from crystals of haemoglobin and chymotrypsin. The chymotrypsin crystals were twinned and therefore difficult to work with, and so I continued with haemoglobin." It was not until 15 years later, in 1953, that Perutz finally discovered a method for solving the structure of the protein molecules. His method led to the solution of the structure of myoglobin by John C. Kendrew and of the structure of hemoglobin by Perutz himself. For these discoveries Perutz and Kendrew were awarded the Nobel prize in chemistry in 1962. On that occasion Perutz remarked: "I have had the good fortune of being joined by colleagues of great ability, several of whom have now been honored with the Nobel prize at the same time as myself. Kendrew came in 1946, [F. H. C.] Crick in 1948, and [J. D.] Watson arrived as a visitor in 1948. Recently F. Sanger, who received the Nobel prize in 1958, also joined forces with us. I am extremely happy at the generous recognition given by the Royal Caroline Institute to our great common adventures and hope that it will spur us to new endeavours."

Bibliography

THE CHEMISTRY AND FUNCTION OF PROTEINS. Felix Haurowitz. Academic Press, 1963.

RELATION BETWEEN STRUCTURE AND SEQUENCE OF HAEMOGLOBIN. M. F. Perutz in *Nature*, Vol. 194, No. 4832, pages 914–918; June, 1962.

STRUCTURE OF HAEMOGLOBIN: A THREE-DIMENSIONAL FOURIER SYNTHESIS OF REDUCED HUMAN HAEMOGLOBIN AT 5.5 Å RESOLUTION. Hilary Muirhead and M. F. Perutz in *Nature*, Vol. 199, No. 4894, pages 633–639; August, 1963.

6. The Evolution of Hemoglobin

The Author

EMILE ZUCKERKANDL is an investigator with the French National Center for Scientific Research, working at the Physico-Chemical Colloidal Laboratory in Montpellier. A native of Vienna, he became a French citizen in 1938. After he was graduated from the Sorbonne, he obtained a master's degree at the University of Illinois and then returned to the Sorbonne for his doctorate. For several years he served at a marine biological station in Brittany, investigating proteins. From 1959 to 1964 he worked with Linus Pauling at the California Institute of Technology, investigating hemoglobin.

He is now at work in "the new field of chemical paleogenics," attempting "to elucidate questions related to the evolutionary succession of major and minor components of a polypeptide chain and to the correlation, in hemoglobins, between structure and function."

Bibliography

EVOLUTIONARY DIVERGENCE AND CONVERGENCE IN PROTEINS. Emile Zuckerkandl and Linus Pauling in *Evolving Genes and Proteins*, edited by Henry J. Vogel. Academic Press, in press.

GENE EVOLUTION AND THE HAEMOGLOBINS. Vernon M. Ingram in *Nature*, Vol. 189, No. 4766, pages 704–708; March 4, 1961.

THE HEMOGLOBINS. G. Braunitzer, K. Hilse, V. Rudloff and N. Hilschmann in *Advances in Protein Chemistry: Vol. XIX*, edited by C. B. Anfinsen, Jr., John T. Edsall, M. L. Anson and Frederic M. Richards. Academic Press, 1964.

MOLECULAR DISEASE, EVOLUTION, AND GENIC HETEROGENEITY. Emile Zuckerkandl and Linus Pauling in *Horizons in Biochemistry*, edited by Michael Kasha and Bernard Pullman. Academic Press, 1962.

7. The Three-dimensional Structure of an Enzyme Molecule

The Author

DAVID C. PHILLIPS is professor of molecular biophysics at the University of Oxford. After taking bachelor's and doctor's degrees at the University of Wales, he worked at the National Research Laboratories in Ottawa for four years, investigating with X-rays the structure of small organic molecules. From 1956 until this year he was at the Royal Institution in London, working with Sir Lawrence Bragg, J. C. Kendrew, M. F. Perutz and others on X-ray analysis of protein structures. Phillips writes that his nonprofessional interests include "reading (mainly history), growing vegetables and talking with children."

Bibliography

BIOSYNTHESIS OF MACROMOLECULES. Vernon M. Ingram. W. A. Benjamin, Inc., 1965.

INTRODUCTION TO MOLECULAR BIOLOGY. G. H. Haggis, D. Michie, A. R. Muir, K. B. Roberts and P. M. B. Walker. John Wiley & Sons, Inc., 1964.

THE MOLECULAR BIOLOGY OF THE GENE. J. D. Watson. W. A. Benjamin, Inc., 1965.

PROTEIN AND NUCLEIC ACIDS: STRUCTURE AND FUNCTION. M. F. Perutz. American Elsevier Publishing Company, Inc., 1962.

STRUCTURE OF HEN EGG-WHITE LYSOZYME: A THREE-DIMENSIONAL FOURIER SYNTHESIS AT 2 A. RESOLUTION. C. C. F. Blake, D. F. Koenig, G. A. Mair, A. C. T. North, D. C. Phillips and V. R. Sarma in *Nature*, Vol. 206, No. 4986, pages 757–763; May 22, 1965.

8. The Structure of the Hereditary Material

The Author

F. H. C. CRICK originally set out to be a physicist, but decided to go into molecular biology after spending the war years designing mines for the British Admiralty. Awarded a fellowship by the Medical Research Council, he took further training at the Strangeways Laboratories in Cambridge, where he worked on the viscosity of the cytoplasm of chick fibroblasts. Recently, he has been in the U. S., at the Polytechnic Institute of Brooklyn, working on X-ray diffraction of crystals of ribonucleic acid, the subject of this chapter. Crick is carrying on his work at the University of Cambridge.

Bibliography

THE BIOCHEMISTRY OF THE NUCLEIC ACIDS. J. N. Davidson. Methuen & Co., Ltd., 1954.

HELICAL STRUCTURE OF DEOXYPENTOSE NUCLEIC ACID. M. H. F. Wilkins and others in *Nature*, Vol. 172, No. 4382, pages 759–762; October 24, 1953.

SYMPOSIUM PAPERS ON THE NUCLEIC ACIDS. Proceedings of the National Academy of Sciences (*in press*).

9. The Nucleotide Sequence of a Nucleic Acid

The Author

ROBERT W. HOLLEY is professor of biochemistry and chairman of the section of biochemistry and molecular biology of the division of biological sciences at Cornell University. He was graduated from the University of Illinois in 1942 and obtained a Ph.D. at Cornell in 1947. He joined the Cornell faculty in 1948, and during his years there he has also worked with the U. S. Plant, Soil and Nutrition Laboratory at the university. Holley and his colleagues spent four years isolating one gram of pure transfer ribonucleic acid and three more years ascertaining its chemical structure. Holley received the 1965 Albert D. Lasker award for basic medical research for the work described in his article.

Bibliography

ISOLATION OF LARGE OLIGONUCLEOTIDE FRAGMENTS FROM THE ALANINE RNA. Jean Apgar, George A. Everett and Robert W. Holley in *Proceedings of the National Academy of Sciences*, Vol. 53, No. 3, pages 546–548; March, 1965.

LABORATORY EXTRACTION AND COUNTERCURRENT DISTRIBUTION. Lyman C. Craig and David Craig in *Technique of Organic Chemistry, Volume III, Part I: Separation and Purification*, edited by Arnold Weissberger. Interscience Publishers, Inc., 1956. See pages 149–332.

SPECIFIC CLEAVAGE OF THE YEAST ALANINE RNA INTO TWO LARGE FRAGMENTS. John Robert Penswick and Robert W. Holley in *Proceedings of the National Academy of Sciences*, Vol. 53, No. 3, pages 543–546; March, 1965.

STRUCTURE OF A RIBONUCLEIC ACID. Robert W. Holley, Jean Apgar, George A. Everett, James T. Madison, Mark Marquisee, Susan H. Merrill, John Robert Penswick and Ada Zamir in *Science*, Vol. 147, No. 3664, pages 1462–1465; March 19, 1965.

10. Precisely Constructed Polymers

The Author

GIULIO NATTA is director of the Institute of Industrial Chemistry at the Politecnico di Milano. Born at Imperia on the Italian Riviera in 1903, Natta studied chemical engineering at the Politecnico di Milano, where he received a degree in 1924. From 1926 to 1933 he taught at the University of Pavia, and from 1933 to 1939 he was professor of physical chemistry at the University of Rome. He joined the Institute of Industrial Chemistry in 1939. A fellow of Italy's famous Society of Lynxes (to which Galileo belonged), Natta was the first chemist to synthesize wood alcohol. His development of a method for converting alcohol to butadiene became the basis of the Italian synthetic-rubber industry. Natta was the author of "How Giant Molecules Are Made," which appeared in the September 1957 issue of SCIENTIFIC AMERICAN.

Bibliography

CONFORMATION OF LINEAR CHAINS AND THEIR MODE OF PACKING IN THE CRYSTAL STATE. Giulio Natta and Paolo Corradini in *Journal of Polymer Science*, Vol. 39, No. 135, pages 29–46; September, 1959.

THE KINETICS OF THE STEREOSPECIFIC POLYMERIZATION OF α-OLEFINS. G. Natta and I. Pasquon in *Advances in Catalysis*, Vol. 11, pages 1–66; 1959.

ORGANOMETALLIC COMPLEXES AS CATALYSTS IN IONIC POLYMERIZATIONS. G. Natta and G. Mazzanti in *Tetrahedron*, Vol. 8, pages 86–100; 1960.

PROGRESS IN FIVE YEARS OF RESEARCH IN STEREOSPECIFIC POLYMERIZATION. Giulio Natta in *The Society of Plastics Engineers Journal*, Vol. 15, No. 5, pages 373–382; May, 1959.

RESEARCH ON CRYSTALLINE SYNTHETIC HIGH POLYMERS WITH A STERICALLY REGULAR STRUCTURE. *Nuovo Cimento* (Supplement), Vol. 15, Series 10, No. 1; 1960.

SECTION II: BIOLOGICAL REGULATORS

11. Kinins

The Author

H. O. J. COLLIER is director of pharmacological research at the London branch of Parke, Davis & Co. At Trinity Hall, Cambridge, his teachers included the Nobel Laureate Sir Edgar Adrian. From 1937 to 1941 Collier taught physiology at the University of Manchester and then went into the pharmaceutical industry, "partly to support a growing family and partly because I was interested in applying science to human welfare." He worked first for Imperial Chemical Industries and for Allen and Hanburys Ltd. before joining Parke, Davis. Collier has participated in the development of several drugs, some of which are widely used as anesthetics and disinfectants. Along the way he became interested in the cause and relief of pain, which introduced him to kinins, substances suspected of participating in pain and inflammation. For the British Broadcasting Company he has written dramatizations covering the history and uses of drugs such as curare and quinine. He also appears occasionally on a B.B.C. science-question program.

Bibliography

ACTIVE POLYPEPTIDES DERIVED FROM PLASMA PROTEINS. G. P. Lewis in *Physiological Reviews*, Vol. 40, No. 4, pages 647–676; October, 1960.

BRADYKININ. G. P. Lewis in *Nature*, Vol. 192, No. 4803, pages 596–599; November 18, 1961.

POLYPEPTIDES WHICH AFFECT SMOOTH MUSCLES AND BLOOD VESSELS. Edited by M. Schachter. Pergamon Press, 1960. See pages 199–271.

POLYPEPTIDES WHICH STIMULATE PLAIN MUSCLE. Edited by J. H. Gaddum. E. & S. Livingstone Ltd. See chapters 1, 2, 4, 7 and 8.

12. The Control of Growth in Plant Cells

The Author

F. C. STEWARD is professor of botany and director of the Laboratory for Cell Physiology, Growth and Development at Cornell University. A native of London, Steward was graduated with first-class honors in chemistry from the University of Leeds in 1924. He received a Ph.D. in botany from Leeds in 1926 and was a member of that university's faculty from 1926 to 1933. As a Rockefeller Fellow, Steward came to this country in 1927 and again in 1933 to study at Cornell, the University of California at Berkeley and the Carnegie Institution of Washington. He joined the faculty of the University of London in 1934 and obtained a D.Sc. in botany there in 1936. During World War II Steward served as director of aircraft equipment in the British Ministry of Aircraft Production. Following the war he spent a year doing research at the University of Chicago before becoming visiting professor and chairman of the department of botany at the University of Rochester in 1946. He joined the Cornell faculty in 1950 and was elected a Fellow of the Royal Society of London in 1957.

Bibliography

THE CHEMICAL REGULATION OF GROWTH: SOME SUBSTANCES AND EXTRACTS WHICH INDUCE GROWTH AND MORPHOGENESIS. F. C. Steward and E. M. Shantz in *Annual Review of Plant Physiology*, Vol. 10, pages 379–404; 1959.

DETERMINING FACTORS IN CELL GROWTH: SOME IMPLICATIONS FOR MORPHOGENESIS IN PLANTS. F. C. Steward and H. Y. Mohan Ram in *Advances in Morphogenesis: Volume I*. Academic Press, 1961.

SYNTHESIS OF MOLECULAR AND CELLULAR STRUCTURE: NINETEENTH SYMPOSIUM OF THE SOCIETY FOR THE STUDY OF DEVELOPMENT AND GROWTH. Edited by Dorothea Rudnick. The Ronald Press Company, 1961.

13. Pheromones

The Author

EDWARD O. WILSON is associate professor of zoology at Harvard University. As a native of Alabama, Wilson fairly early in life became acquainted with the Southern agricultural pest known as the fire ant, which he discussed in an article for SCIENTIFIC AMERICAN ("The Fire Ant," March, 1958). Wilson received B.S. and M.S. degrees from the University of Alabama in 1949 and 1950. He took a Ph.D. in biology at Harvard, where he held a National Science Foundation fellowship and a junior fellowship in the Society of Fellows. He joined the Harvard faculty in 1956.

Bibliography

OLFACTORY STIMULI IN MAMMALIAN REPRODUCTION. A. S. Parkes and H. M. Bruce in *Science*, Vol. 134, No. 3485, pages 1049–1054; October, 1961.

PHEROMONES (ECTOHORMONES) IN INSECTS. Peter Karlson and Adolf Butenandt in *Annual Review of Entomology*, Vol. 4, pages 39–58; 1959.

THE SOCIAL BIOLOGY OF ANTS. Edward O. Wilson in *Annual Review of Entomology*, Vol. 8, pages 345–368; 1963.

14. Insect Attractants

The Authors

MARTIN JACOBSON and MORTON BEROZA are research chemists in the Pesticide Chemicals Research Branch of the U.S. Department of Agriculture's Entomology Research Division in Beltsville, Md. Jacobson, who is in charge of natural-product research, was graduated from the City College of the City of New York in 1940 and did graduate work at George Washington University before joining the staff of the National Institutes of Health in 1941. He began his research on the chemistry of insect-control agents for the Department of Agriculture in 1942. Beroza, who directs synthesis investigations, received a B.S. from George Washington University in 1943 and an M.A. and a Ph.D. from Georgetown University in 1946 and 1950 respectively. He joined the Department of Agriculture in 1948. Jacobson and Beroza were joint recipients of the Hillebrand Prize for 1963, awarded by the Washington Section of the American Chemical Society for elucidating the chemistry of sex attractants isolated from insects and for synthesizing new compounds useful in attracting harmful insects.

Bibliography

CHEMICAL INSECT ATTRACTANTS. Martin Jacobson and Morton Beroza in *Science,* Vol. 140, No. 3574, pages 1367–1373; June, 1963.

CHEMICAL INSECT ATTRACTANTS AND REPELLENTS. Vincent G. Dethier. The Blakiston Company, 1947.

NEW APPROACHES TO PEST CONTROL AND ERADICATION. *Advances in Chemistry Series 41.* American Chemical Society, 1963.

15. Flower Pigments

The Author

SARAH CLEVENGER is assistant professor of botany at Indiana State College. A graduate of Miami University in Ohio, she received a Ph.D. from Indiana University in 1957. Her interest in flower pigments stems from graduate work done under the direction of Charles W. Hagen, Jr., at Indiana University. Before joining the faculty of Indiana State she taught at Berea College in Kentucky.

Bibliography

THE CHEMISTRY OF FLAVONOID COMPOUNDS. Edited by T. A. Geissman. The Macmillan Company, 1962.

THE STORY OF POLLINATION. B. J. D. Meeuse. The Ronald Press Company, 1961.

16. The Stereochemical Theory of Odor

The Authors

JOHN E. AMOORE, JAMES W. JOHNSTON, JR., and MARTIN RUBIN collaborated in the writing of this article by means of an extensive cross-country correspondence. Amoore does his share of the research at the Western Regional Research Laboratory of the U.S. Department of Agriculture in Albany, Calif. A native of England, he has an M.A. and a D.Phil. in biochemistry from the University of Oxford. Since 1952 he has done research in the chemistry department of the California Institute of Technology, in the botany department of the University of Edinburgh and in the zoology department of the University of California at Berkeley. Amoore worked out the theoretical basis of the stereochemical theory of odor in 1952 while still an undergraduate at Oxford. He began his long correspondence and collaboration with Johnston and Rubin in 1954 but did not meet them until 1962. Both Johnston and Rubin are members of the faculty of Georgetown University. Johnston is associate professor of physiology in the School of Medicine. A graduate of Syracuse University, he obtained a Ph.D. in physiology and ecology from Harvard University in 1936. Since joining the Georgetown faculty in 1950 he has worked mainly on the problem of measuring olfaction in humans, rabbits, dogs and insects. Rubin is associate professor of chemistry both in the Georgetown School of Medicine and the Georgetown Graduate School. He received a B.S. from the City College of the City of New York in 1936 and a Ph.D. in organic chemistry from Columbia University in 1942. His original synthesis of the pimelates and lactones was a major contribution to this joint research effort.

Bibliography

THE CHEMICAL SENSES. R. W. Moncrieff. Leonard Hill, Limited, 1951.

THE NATURE OF THE UNIVERSE. Lucretius. Translated by R. E. Latham. Penguin Books, 1951.

THE SENSES OF ANIMALS AND MEN. Lorus and Marjory Milne. Atheneum, 1962.

THE STEREOCHEMICAL THEORY OF OLFACTION. John E. Amoore, Martin Rubin and James W. Johnston, Jr., in *Proceedings of the Scientific Section of the Toilet Goods Association,* Special Supplement to No. 37, pages 1–47; October, 1962.

17. Steroids

The Author

LOUIS F. FIESER is Sheldon Emery Professor of Organic Chemistry at Harvard University. He was born in Columbus, Ohio, did his undergraduate work at Williams College and his graduate work at Harvard and in Europe in the 1920s. The author of a notable output of research (284 research papers and four books), he has honorary degrees from Williams College and the University of Paris and in 1941 received the Katherine Berkhan Judd Prize for Cancer Research. He lives in Belmont, Mass., with his wife and collaborator, Mary Fieser, and a bevy of Siamese cats. The cats, in fact, are also collaborators of a sort; a portrait of one of them, J. G. Pooh (named after the jellied gasoline bombs Fieser conceived) graces the third edition of the well-known Fieser book on *Phenanthrene.* An unauthorized translation of the book is now circulating among Russian chemists; the cat was not appreciated by the Soviet publishers and was omitted. Fieser writes: "The other day we submitted the final chapter of the 3rd edition of *Experiments in Organic Chemistry.* That night in celebration we went to the cat show and put down $75 for a beautiful little Burmese kitten. He looks pretty good; maybe he will have a book."

Bibliography

CIBA FOUNDATION COLLOQUIA ON ENDOCRINOLOGY. VOL. I: STEROID HORMONES AND TUMOR GROWTH AND STEROID HORMONES AND ENZYMES. VOL. II: STEROID METABOLISM AND ESTIMATION. The Blakiston Co., 1952.

CIBA FOUNDATION SYMPOSIA ON ENDOCRINOLOGY. VOL. VII: SYNTHESIS AND METABOLISM OF ADRENOCORTICAL STEROIDS. Little, Brown and Company, 1953.

NATURAL PRODUCTS RELATED TO PHENANTHRENE. Louis F. Fieser and Mary Fieser. Reinhold Publishing Corporation, 1949.

18. Alkaloids

The Author

TREVOR ROBINSON teaches in the department of bacteriology and botany at Syracuse University. "I received my A.B. at Harvard in 1950," he says, "majoring in a hodge-podge field called 'biochemical sciences'—a smattering of courses on a number of subjects. As I intended to be a high-school teacher, I stayed on at Harvard for an A.M. in science education. Despite the supposed need for science teachers nobody wanted to hire me, so I took some more advanced courses at the University of Massachusetts. There I became so interested in biochemical research that I gave up the idea of high-school teaching and took an M.S. in chemistry. Next I went to the department of biochemistry at Cornell University, taking my Ph.D. in 1956. While at Cornell I became entranced by the fantastic array of peculiar compounds found in plants. In addition to alkaloids I have studied plant tannins, another peculiar class of materials. In quite a different vein, I have been carrying on research on the inactivation of dilute enzyme solutions by ionizing radiation."

Bibliography

THE ALKALOIDS. K. W. Bentley. Interscience Publishers, Inc., 1957.
THE PLANT ALKALOIDS. Thomas Anderson Henry. P. Blakiston's Son & Co. Inc., 1939.
THE STRUCTURAL RELATIONS OF NATURAL PRODUCTS. Robert Robinson. Oxford University Press, 1955.

19. Analgesic Drugs

The Author

MARSHALL GATES is professor of chemistry at the University of Rochester. After obtaining bachelor's and master's degrees at Rice Institute in 1936 and 1938 respectively he received a doctorate from Harvard University in 1941 and began teaching chemistry at Bryn Mawr College. He has been at the University of Rochester since 1949. Since 1963 he has served as editor of the *Journal of the American Chemical Society*. Gates, whose interests are synthetic organic chemistry and the chemistry of natural products and organic medicinals, achieved the first synthesis of morphine in 1952. He writes that aside from his professional interests he is "a keen sailor in the summer and skier in the winter, not very proficient at either."

Bibliography

ANALGESIA AND ADDICTION. L. B. Mellett and L. A. Woods in *Progress in Drug Research*, Vol. 5, pages 155–267; 1963.
THE CHEMISTRY OF THE MORPHINE ALKALOIDS. K. W. Bentley. Oxford University Press, 1954.
NARCOTIC ANTAGONISTS. Sydney Archer and L. S. Harris in *Progress in Drug Research*, Vol. 8, pages 261–320; 1965.
THE OPIUM ALKALOIDS. David Ginsburg. Interscience Publishers, 1962.

20. The Hallucinogenic Drugs

The Authors

FRANK BARRON, MURRAY E. JARVIK and STERLING BUNNELL, JR. do research on this subject in New York and California. Barron is a research psychologist at the University of California's Institute of Personality Assessment and Research in Berkeley. A graduate of La Salle College in Philadelphia, he received an M.A. from the University of Minnesota in 1948 and a Ph.D. from the University of California at Berkeley in 1950. He has taught at Bryn Mawr College, Harvard University, Wesleyan University and the University of California. Jarvik is associate professor of pharmacology at the Albert Einstein College of Medicine and attending physician at Bellevue Hospital in New York. He was graduated from the City College of the City of New York in 1944 and subse-

quently acquired an M.A. in psychology from the University of California at Los Angeles in 1945, an M.D. from the University of California School of Medicine in 1951 and a Ph.D. in psychology from the University of California at Berkeley in 1952. He has taught and done research in the fields of pharmacology, psychology and neurophysiology at various institutions. Bunnell is a resident in psychiatry at the Mount Zion Medical Center in San Francisco. He received an M.D. from the University of California School of Medicine in 1958 and is currently working on a Ph.D. in neurophysiology at the University of California at Berkeley.

Bibliography

THE CLINICAL PHARMACOLOGY OF THE HALLUCINOGENS. Erik Jacobsen in *Clinical Pharmacology and Therapeutics*, Vol. 4, No. 4, pages 480–504; July–August, 1963.
LYSERGIC ACID DIETHYLAMIDE (LSD-25) AND EGO FUNCTIONS. G. D. Klee in *Archives of General Psychiatry*, Vol. 8, No. 5, pages 461–474; May, 1963.
PROLONGED ADVERSE REACTIONS TO LYSERGIC ACID DIETHYL-AMIDE. S. Cohen and K. S. Ditman in *Archives of General Psychiatry*, Vol. 8, No. 5, pages 475–480; May, 1963.
THE PSYCHOTOMIMETIC DRUGS: AN OVERVIEW. Jonathan O. Cole and Martin M. Katz in *The Journal of the American Medical Association*, Vol. 187, No. 10, pages 758–761; March, 1964.

21. Barbiturates

The Author

ELIJAH ADAMS was recently appointed professor and director of the pharmacology department of the Saint Louis University School of Medicine. A graduate of the Johns Hopkins University, he took his M.D. at the University of Rochester in 1942. He served as an Army physician during World War II, but on return to civilian life left medicine for research in enzyme biochemistry. Adams, who has been teaching pharmacology at the New York University College of Medicine, still finds biochemistry his main interest, but believes that the fields are merging "as biochemistry tends to become more physiologic and pharmacology more biochemical."

Bibliography

THE DISTRIBUTION IN THE BODY AND METABOLIC FATE OF BARBITURATES. J. Raventós in *The Journal of Pharmacy and Pharmacology*, Vol. 6, No. 4, pages 217–235; April, 1954.
REPORT ON BARBITURATES. The New York Academy of Medicine Committee on Public Health, Subcommittee on Barbiturates, in *Bulletin of the New York Academy of Medicine*, Vol. 32, No. 6, pages 456–481; June, 1956.
SYMPOSIUM ON SEDATIVE & HYPNOTIC DRUGS. The Williams & Wilkins Company, 1954.

22. Aspirin

The Author

H. O. J. COLLIER is director of pharmacological research at Parke, Davis & Company in Hounslow, England. Born of English parents in Brazil in 1912, Collier holds a B.A. and a Ph.D. in comparative physiology from the University of Cambridge. He taught physiology at the University of Manchester from 1937 to 1941, when he joined the staff of Imperial Chemical Industries. He spent the next four years at the School of Tropical Medicine in Liverpool, doing research on the treatment of spirochaetal diseases with penicillin. In 1945 he set up a pharmacology laboratory for Allen & Hanbury's, Limited, which he directed until 1958, when he joined Parke,

Davis. Collier has participated in the development of several drugs, some of which are widely used as neuromuscular blocking and antimicrobial agents. In August of this year he took part in the international pharmacological meeting held in Prague. He is the author of the article "Kinins," which appeared in the August 1962 issue of SCIENTIFIC AMERICAN.

Bibliography

ANTI-ANAPHYLACTIC ACTION OF ACETYLSALICYLATE IN GUINEA PIG LUNG. H. O. J. Collier, A. R. Hammond and Barbara Whitely in *Nature*, Vol. 200, No. 4902, pages 176–178; October 12, 1963.

CELLULAR MECHANISMS IN ANAPHYLAXIS. J. L. Mongar and H. O. Schild in *Physiological Reviews*, Vol. 42, No. 2, pages 226–270; April, 1962.

HISTAMINE. Edited by G. E. W. Wolstenholme and Cecilia M. O'Connor. Little, Brown and Company, 1956.

NON-NARCOTIC ANALGESICS. Lowell O. Randall in *Physiological Pharmacology, Volume I: The Nervous System, Part A*, edited by Walter S. Root and Frederick G. Hofmann. Academic Press, 1963.

THE SALICYLATES: A CRITICAL BIBLIOGRAPHIC REVIEW. Martin Gross and Leon A. Greenberg. Hillhouse Press, 1948.

SLOW REACTING SUBSTANCE AND RELATED COMPOUNDS. W. E. Brocklehurst in *Progress in Allergy*, Vol. 6, pages 539–558; 1962.

SECTION III: CHEMICAL BIODYNAMICS

23. Chemical Fossils

The Authors

GEOFFREY EGLINTON and MELVIN CALVIN are respectively senior lecturer in chemistry at the University of Glasgow and professor of chemistry at the University of California at Berkeley. Eglinton obtained a Ph.D. from the University of Manchester in 1951. He writes: "I once mountaineered in the Alps and the Rockies but now feel nervous peering through the protective glass at the top of the Empire State Building." Calvin, winner of the Nobel prize for chemistry in 1961 for his work in elucidating the chemical pathways of carbon in photosynthesis, is a member of the President's Science Advisory Committee and a foreign member of the Royal Society. He was graduated from the Michigan College of Mining and Technology in 1931 and received a Ph.D. from the University of Minnesota in 1935. From 1935 to 1937 he was a research fellow at the University of Manchester; he joined the faculty of the University of California at Berkeley as an instructor in chemistry in 1937.

Bibliography

CHEMICAL EVOLUTION. M. Calvin in *Proceedings of the Royal Society*, Series A, Vol. 288, No. 1415, pages 441–466; November 30, 1965.

OCCURRENCE OF ISOPRENOID FATTY ACIDS IN THE GREEN RIVER SHALE. J. N. Ramsay, James R. Maxwell, A. G. Douglas and Geoffrey Eglinton in *Science*, Vol. 153, No. 3740, pages 1133–1134; September 2, 1966.

ORGANIC PIGMENTS: THEIR LONG-TERM FATE. Max Blumer in *Science*, Vol. 149, No. 3685, pages 722–726; August 13, 1965.

24. The Path of Carbon in Photosynthesis

The Author

J. A. BASSHAM is research chemist and lecturer in chemistry at the University of California, where he received his B.S. in 1945. Bassham did his doctoral research at the University of California under Melvin Calvin on the path of carbon in photosynthesis and received his Ph.D. in 1949. Since then he has been in Calvin's Bio-Organic Chemistry Group at the Lawrence Radiation Laboratory, except for a two-year tour of duty in the Navy and a year in H. A. Krebs's laboratory at the University of Oxford.

Bibliography

NEW ASPECTS OF PHOTOSYNTHESIS. J. A. Bassham in *Journal of Chemical Education*, Vol. 38, No. 3, pages 151–155; March, 1961.

THE NURTURE OF CREATIVE SCIENCE AND THE MEN WHO MAKE IT. THE PHOTOSYNTHESIS STORY: A CASE HISTORY. Melvin Calvin in *Journal of Chemical Education*, Vol. 35, No. 9, pages 428–432; September, 1958.

THE PATH OF CARBON IN PHOTOSYNTHESIS. Melvin Calvin and James A. Bassham. Prentice-Hall, Inc., 1957.

THE PATH OF CARBON IN PHOTOSYNTHESIS. XXI: THE CYCLIC REGENERATION OF CARBON DIOXIDE ACCEPTOR. J. A. Bassham, A. A. Benson, Lorel D. Kay, Anne Z. Harris, A. T. Wilson and M. Calvin in *Journal of the American Chemical Society*, Vol. 76, No. 7, pages 1760–1770; April 5, 1954.

PHOTOSYNTHESIS. J. A. Bassham in *Journal of Chemical Education*, Vol. 36, No. 11, pages 548–554; November, 1959.

THE PHOTOSYNTHESIS OF CARBON COMPOUNDS. Melvin Calvin and James A. Bassham. W. A. Benjamin, Inc., 1962.

25. Energy Transformation in the Cell

The Author

ALBERT L. LEHNINGER has since 1952 been DeLamar Professor of Physiological Chemistry and director of the department of physiological chemistry at the Johns Hopkins School of Medicine. He received his B.A. from Wesleyan University in 1939 and his M.S. and Ph.D. from the University of Wisconsin respectively in 1940 and 1942. After teaching at Wisconsin until 1945, Lehninger joined the faculty of the University of Chicago. In 1951 he went to the University of Frankfurt as an exchange professor, and in 1951 and 1952 he was a Guggenheim fellow and Fulbright research professor at the University of Cambridge. In 1948 Lehninger discovered that the enzymes involved in the citric acid and respiratory cycles of energy transformation in the cell are located in the mitochondria.

Bibliography

GENERAL BIOCHEMISTRY. Joseph S. Fruton and Sofia Simmonds, pages 284–386; 520–524. John Wiley & Sons, Inc., 1958.

OXIDATIVE PHOSPHORYLATION. Albert L. Lehninger in *The Harvey Lectures*, Series XLIX, pages 176–215; 1955.

THE RESPIRATORY CHAIN AND OXIDATIVE PHOSPHORYLATION. Britton Chance and G. R. Williams in *Advances in Enzymology*, Vol. XVII, pages 65–130; 1956.

REVERSAL OF VARIOUS TYPES OF MITOCHONDRIAL SWELLING BY ADENOSINE TRIPHOSPHATE. Albert L. Lehninger in *The Journal of Biological Chemistry*, Vol. 234, No. 9, pages 2,465–2,471; September, 1959.

26. The Metabolism of Fats

The Author

DAVID E. GREEN is one of the pioneers in the field of enzyme chemistry. He first became interested in the subject in 1930, just after his graduation from New York University. As a summer student at the Marine Biological Laboratory in Woods Hole, Mass., he heard about the work being done on enzymes in England and decided to go to the University of Cambridge. After taking his Ph.D. there he remained as a research fellow for seven years, returning to the U.S. in 1941 to take charge of the enzyme laboratory of the College of Physicians and Surgeons at Columbia University. In 1948 he left Columbia to become professor of enzyme chemistry in the Institute for Enzyme Research at the University of Wisconsin; he is now co-director of the Institute and editor of *Currents in Biochemical Research*. A native New Yorker, Green acquired his hobby of figure skating on the rink at Radio City; he now practices it on Wisconsin and Minnesota lakes.

Bibliography

ENZYMES AND ENZYME SYSTEMS—THEIR STATE IN NATURE. Edited by John T. Edsall. Harvard University Press, 1951.
ENZYMES OF FATTY ACID METABOLISM. F. Lynen and S. Ochoa in *Biochimica et Biophysica Acta*, Vol. 12, page 299; 1953.
LIPID METABOLISM. Cambridge University Press, 1952.
ROLE OF COENZYME A IN FATTY ACID METABOLISM. H. R. Mahler. *Federation Proceedings*, Vol. 12, page 694; 1953.
THE BIOLOGICAL OXIDATION OF FATTY ACIDS. S. Gurin. *Cold Spring Harbor Symposia on Quantitative Biology*, Vol. 13, page 118; 1948.

27. Protein-digesting Enzymes

The Author

HANS NEURATH is professor and chairman of the department of biochemistry at the University of Washington. A native of Austria, Neurath received a Ph.D. in colloid chemistry from the University of Vienna in 1933. After a year of postdoctoral work at the University of London, he came to this country in 1935 to do research in biochemistry at the University of Minnesota. Neurath taught and did research at Cornell University and the Duke University School of Medicine until 1950, when he was appointed to his present posts.

Bibliography

ACTIVE CENTER OF CARBOXYPEPTIDASE A. Bert L. Vallee in *Federation Proceedings of American Societies for Experimental Biology*, Vol. 23, No. 1, Part 1, pages 8–17; January–February, 1964.
CORRELATION OF STRUCTURE AND FUNCTION IN ENZYME ACTION. D. E. Koshland, Jr., in *Science*, Vol. 142, No. 3599, pages 1533–1541; December, 1963.
MECHANISM OF ZYMOGEN ACTIVATION. Hans Neurath in *Federation Proceedings of American Societies for Experimental Biology*, Vol. 23, No. 1, Part 1, pages 1–7; January–February, 1964.
TRYPSINOGEN AND CHYMOTRYPSINOGEN AS HOMOLOGOUS PROTEINS. Kenneth A. Walsh and Hans Neurath in *Proceedings of the National Academy of Sciences*, Vol. 52, No. 4, pages 884–889; October, 1964.

28. Molecular Isomers in Vision

The Authors

RUTH HUBBARD and ALLEN KROPF are respectively resident associate in biology at Harvard University and associate professor of chemistry at Amherst College. Miss Hubbard, who was born in Vienna, took a Ph.D. in biology at Radcliffe College in 1950 and since then, except for a year as a Guggenheim fellow in Copenhagen, has worked with George Wald (to whom she was married in 1958) in his laboratory at Harvard. Kropf, who was graduated from Queens College in 1951 and obtained a Ph.D. at the University of Utah in 1954, became interested in the chemistry of vision after hearing Wald lecture on the subject at the University of Utah. From 1956 to 1958 Kropf worked with Wald at Harvard, going to Amherst in 1958.

Bibliography

THE CHEMISTRY OF VISUAL PHOTORECEPTION. Ruth Hubbard, Deric Bownds and Tôru Yoshizawa in *Cold Spring Harbor Symposia on Quantitative Biology: Vol. XXX*, Cold Spring Harbor Biological Laboratory, 1965.
CIS-TRANS ISOMERS OF RETINENE IN VISUAL PROCESSES. G. A. J. Pitt and R. A. Morton in *Steric Aspects of the Chemistry and Biochemistry of Natural Products*, edited by J. K. Grant and W. Klyne. Cambridge University Press, 1960.
MOLECULAR ASPECTS OF VISUAL EXCITATION. Ruth Hubbard and Allen Kropf in *Annals of the New York Academy of Sciences*, Vol. 81, Art. 2, pages 388–398; August 28, 1959.
VALENCE. Charles A. Coulson. Oxford University Press, 1961.

29. The Genetic Code: II

The Author

MARSHALL W. NIRENBERG is head of the Section of Biochemical Genetics at the National Heart Institute, one of the nine National Institutes of Health. Nirenberg took a B.S. at the University of Florida in 1948. After receiving an M.S. in biology from the University of Florida in 1952, Nirenberg went to the department of biological chemistry at the University of Michigan, where he acquired a Ph.D. in 1957. A two-year postdoctoral fellowship from the American Cancer Society brought him to the National Institute of Arthritis and Metabolic Diseases later the same year, where he remained until he took his present post in June of last year.

Bibliography

THE DEPENDENCE OF CELL-FREE PROTEIN SYNTHESIS IN E. COLI UPON NATURALLY OCCURRING OR SYNTHETIC POLYRIBONUCLEOTIDES. M. W. Nirenberg and J. H. Matthaei in *Proceedings of the National Academy of Sciences of the U.S.A.*, Vol. 47, No. 10, pages 1588–1602; October, 1961.
A PHYSICAL BASIS FOR DEGENERACY IN THE AMINO ACID CODE. Bernard Weisblum, Seymour Benzer and Robert W. Holley in *Proceedings of the National Academy of Sciences of the U.S.A.*, Vol. 48, No. 8, pages 1449–1453; August, 1962.
POLYRIBONUCLEOTIDE-DIRECTED PROTEIN SYNTHESIS USING AN E. COLI CELL-FREE SYSTEM. M. S. Bretscher and M. Grunberg-Manago in *Nature*, Vol. 195, No. 4838, pages 283–284; July 21, 1962.
QUALITATIVE SURVEY OF RNA CODE-WORDS. Oliver W. Jones, Jr., and Marshall W. Nirenberg in *Proceedings of the National Academy of Sciences of the U.S.A.*, Vol. 48, No. 12, pages 2115–2123; December, 1962.
SYNTHETIC POLYNUCLEOTIDES AND THE AMINO ACID CODE, IV. J. F. Speyer, P. Lengyel, C. Basilio and S. Ochoa in *Proceedings of the National Academy of Sciences of the U.S.A.*, Vol. 48, No. 3, pages 441–448; March, 1962.

30. The Genetic Code of a Virus

The Author

HEINZ FRAENKEL-CONRAT is professor of molecular biology at the University of California at Berkeley. Born in Breslau, Germany, he obtained an M.D. there in 1933 and a Ph.D. in biochemistry at the University of Edinburgh in 1936. He then came to the U.S., working at the Rockefeller Institute for Medical Research. He also did research at the Institute Butantan in São Paulo before going to Berkeley in 1938. After four years there he spent eight years at the Western Regional Laboratory of the U.S. Department of Agriculture and a year abroad. He joined the Virus Laboratory at Berkeley in 1952. His investigations have been concerned with enzymes, snake venoms, hormones, egg proteins and viruses.

Bibliography

THE AMINO ACID COMPOSITION AND C-TERMINAL SEQUENCE OF A CHEMICALLY EVOKED MUTANT OF TMV. A. Tsugita and H. Fraenkel-Conrat in *Proceedings of the National Academy of Sciences*, Vol. 46, No. 5, pages 636–642; May, 1960.

BIOSYNTHESIS OF THE COAT PROTEIN OF COLIPHAGE *f2* BY E. COLI EXTRACTS. D. Nathans, G. Notani, J. H. Schwartz and N. D. Zinder in *Proceedings of the National Academy of Sciences*, Vol. 48, No. 8, pages 1424–1431; August, 1962.

THE COMPLETE AMINO ACID SEQUENCE OF THE PROTEIN OF TOBACCO MOSAIC VIRUS. A. Tsugita, D. T. Gish, J. Young, H. Fraenkel-Conrat, C. A. Knight and W. M. Stanley in *Proceedings of the National Academy of Sciences*, Vol. 46, No. 11, pages 1463–1469; November, 1960.

THE DEPENDENCE OF CELL-FREE PROTEIN SYNTHESIS IN E. COLI UPON NATURALLY OCCURRING OR SYNTHETIC POLYRIBONUCLEOTIDES. Marshall W. Nirenberg and J. Heinrich Matthaei in *Proceedings of the National Academy of Sciences*, Vol. 47, No. 10, pages 1588–1602; October, 1961.

31. Memory and Protein Synthesis

The Author

BERNARD W. AGRANOFF is coordinator of biological science in the Mental Health Research Institute at the University of Michigan. He holds a medical degree, which he received at Wayne State University in 1950, but he has worked mainly as a research biochemist. From 1954 to 1960 he was a research biochemist at the National Institute of Neurological Diseases and Blindness; he went to Michigan in 1960. For the past three years he has been engaged in research on biochemical aspects of the formation of memory in the goldfish.

Bibliography

ANTIMETABOLITES AFFECTING PROTEINS OR NUCLEIC ACID SYNTHESIS: PHLEOMYCIN, AN INHIBITOR OF DNA POLYMERASE. Arturo Falaschi and Arthur Kornberg in *Federation Proceedings*, Vol. 23, No. 5, Part I, pages 940–989; September–October, 1964.

CHEMICAL STUDIES ON MEMORY FIXATION IN GOLDFISH. Bernard W. Agranoff, Roger E. Davis and John J. Brink in *Brain Research*, Vol. 1, No. 3, pages 303–309; March–April, 1966.

MEMORY IN MICE AS AFFECTED BY INTRACEREBRAL PUROMYCIN. Josefa B. Flexner, Louis B. Flexner and Eliot Stellar in *Science*, Vol. 141, No. 3575, pages 57–59; July 5, 1963.

32. Ultraviolet Radiation and Nucleic Acid

The Author

R. A. DEERING is assistant professor of physics at the New Mexico Highlands University. Deering took a B.S. in engineering physics at the University of Maine in 1954 and a Ph.D. in biophysics at Yale University in 1958. After a year of teaching physics at Southern Illinois University, a year at the University of Oslo as a Fulbright research grantee and two years at Yale as a research associate in biophysics, Deering took his present job in 1961.

Bibliography

DISAPPEARANCE OF THYMINE PHOTODIMER IN ULTRAVIOLET IRRADIATED DNA UPON TREATMENT WITH A PHOTOREACTIVATING ENZYME FROM BAKER'S YEAST. Daniel L. Wulff and Claud S. Rupert in *Biochemical and Biophysical Research Communications*, Vol. 7, No. 3, pages 237–240; April, 1962.

THE EFFECTS OF U.V.-IRRADIATION ON NUCLEIC ACIDS AND THEIR COMPONENTS. R. Beukers and W. Berends in *Biochimica et Biophysica Acta*, Vol. 49, No. 1, pages 181–189; April, 1961.

EVIDENCE THAT ULTRAVIOLET-INDUCED THYMINE DIMERS IN DNA CAUSE BIOLOGICAL DAMAGE. Richard B. Setlow and Jane K. Setlow in *Proceedings of the National Academy of Sciences of the U.S.A.*, Vol. 48, No. 7, pages 1250–1257; July, 1962.

PHOTOCHEMISTRY OF NUCLEIC ACIDS AND THEIR CONSTITUENTS. D. Shugar in *The Nucleic Acids*, Vol. III, edited by E. Chargaff and J. N. Davidson. Academic Press, Inc., 1960.

Index